Edexcel BTEC National

Public Services

Textbook

Nick Cullingworth

Stanley Thornes (Publishers) Ltd

For Barry Spir

First published 2000 by

Stanley Thornes Publishers Ltd
Ellenborough House
Wellington Street
Cheltenham
GL50 1YW
UK

ISBN 0 7487 3032 X

00 01 02 03 04/ 10 9 8 7 6 5 4 3 2 1

A catalogue record for this book is available from The British Library.

Typeset by GreenGate Publishing Services, Tonbridge, Kent
Printed and bound in Great Britain by Redwood Books, Trowbridge, Wiltshire

The author and publishers wish to make it clear that this resource has been produced to support the delivery of the BTEC National Public Services course but has not been developed in conjunction with the Edexcel Foundation.

Contents

Unit 13: Traffic and Transport

Unit 14: Fires and Accidents

Unit 15: Leadership

Unit 16: Community and Culture

Unit 17: Contemporary Issues

Introduction

This book is written for students on BTEC National programmes in Public Services. It contains information and ideas which will help them to complete their assignments and give them a wider understanding of issues which are important in public service work.

Though BTEC Nationals in Public Services have existed for about ten years now, the syllabus followed before 1998 was a draft syllabus. This was completely rewritten by Edexcel BTEC, producing a new and much improved syllabus. The new syllabus is a broad and demanding one, and this book has been written to satisfy the need for a textbook which will cover the subject content, outcomes and assessment criteria of the syllabus in an accessible and helpful way.

The book follows the syllabus structure, as given in the *BTEC Nationals in Public Services – Guidance and Units* – Issue 2, which was published by the Edexcel Foundation in June 1998. After a brief introduction, and a section for students on 'How to Use this Book', the book covers each of the core and option units. For each unit there is a lead-in, followed by information and ideas on each of the outcomes. As in the syllabus, each outcome is divided into assessment criteria, which state what the student has to do in order to pass the unit. For each assessment criterion, this book gives information and explanation which should enable to the student to fulfil all course requirements.

The 'content' given in the syllabus is also covered. This is to ensure that the 'spirit' of the syllabus as a whole is covered, as well as the 'letter' of the assessment criteria. The overall aim of the BTEC Nationals in Public Services is to produce students who would have the right knowledge and attitudes to enable them to apply – with a realistic chance of success – for public service work at an officer level. This means firefighters, police officers, prison officers and army officers – among others.

BTEC National programmes grade students using assignments, and it is expected that this book will be used in conjunction with assignments. Since assignments consist of tasks which put students' knowledge into a practical context, and require them to display a range of skills, it is not expected that students will copy sections wholesale out of this book! Instead, they will be able to select information which is useful to them in completing their tasks, and present it in an appropriate form. In addition, students will be able to use this book as a starting point for further research, particularly as short lists of helpful books are given at the end of each unit.

Staff may also find this book useful as a teaching aid. It aims to give clear explanations and descriptions which place information and ideas in a meaningful context. This 'meaningful context' is very often a public service one. But the book also takes a broader view of society, and the roles which students might eventually fulfil in it. This is because, in practice, only a minority of BTEC National Public Service students eventually find work in the public services. Others go on to university, usually to study programmes related to the social sciences or human behaviour, while some go into such fields as nursing, management, sales or the Civil Service.

The public services are a challenging, exciting and vitally important career – a career which is constantly changing, and which demands both strength and adaptability. In addition, people who work in the public services need to have lively and inquiring minds, and must be interested – at a practical level – in both people and ideas. As well as satisfying the needs of a syllabus, this book also aims to stimulate a deeper interest in public service work, and in the key subjects which have a bearing on public service work, such as human behaviour, culture, politics, sociology and sport. In this sense this book can be seen as a broader introduction to many of the living issues in society at the beginning of the 21st century.

How to use this book

This book is for you, the student, to use during your BTEC National programme in public services.

It is divided into units, outcomes and assessment criteria, just like the syllabus. This should help you to find your way about it, and extract the information you need for your assignments with the minimum of effort.

In this book you will find:

- information relating to all the units except Languages
- explanations and analysis of all the key ideas you need to know
- tips on how to use the information in assignments, so that you get good grades
- guidance on how to improve your skills
- useful general knowledge for people interested in the public services.

As a BTEC National student in Public Services you have three main aims. These are:

- to pass your BTEC National, by getting as high a grade as possible in each unit
- to enjoy your course
- to improve your chances of getting into the career you want.

This book should help you achieve all these aims. Even if you decide not to go into the public services, it will help your job prospects by giving you a greater understanding of the wider world. And if you apply for university or some other form of higher education, it will give you a useful foundation for your studies there.

Other sources of information and ideas

Books

This should not be the only book you read. At the end of each unit there are brief suggestions for further reading, which you might well decide to follow up if you want to go into a subject in more detail. In addition you can always go to your college or local library to look up subjects connected with your BTEC National in Public Services. Different libraries have different ways of classifying or shelving their books. If you can't find the kind of book you are looking for, ask. People who work in libraries are only too happy to give help and advice. If the worst comes to the worst, show them your assignment brief and see if they can suggest the books you will need.

Magazines

In addition you should aim to keep up to date by reading some of the magazines listed opposite.

The Internet

The Internet is a major source of information about the public services (and, for that matter, everything else!). Many police forces have informative sites on it, and so has the Home Office. It is packed with information about fire service work – especially in relation to major disasters and disaster management. It tells you as much as you want to know about how the public services work together in major incidents. Most of this information is both up to date and reliable.

The Internet is also choc-a-block with information about psychology, sociology, politics, health and safety, crime and the law. Unfortunately information about these subjects is less reliable than information about disaster management. In the case of psychology, sociology and politics this is because opinions on these subjects vary wildly, and some of the material on the Internet is biased, to say the least. But not all of it. There are plenty of reasonable people out there, as well as screwballs. When in doubt about information you have downloaded from the Internet, check with your tutor who will tell you whether you should use it or bin it.

Journals and magazines of interest to Public Services students

Journal Title	Publisher	Frequency
Safety Management	British Safety Council	Monthly
Journal of Social Policy	Cambridge University Press	Four times a year
Psychology Review	Phillip Allen Publishers	Four times a year
Critical Social Policy	Sage	Four times a year
Health and Safety at Work	Tolley	Four times a year
NATO Review	NATO, Brussels, 1100 Brussels	Bi-monthly
New Statesman & Society	Foundation House	Weekly
New Internationalist	New Internationalist Publications	Monthly
Spectrum	Phillip Allen Publishers	Four times a year
The Magistrate	ITC	Ten per year
Police Review	Magistrates Association	Weekly
Police	Police Review Publications	Monthly
Civil Protection	Police Federation	Four times a year
Fire	Home Office	Monthly
Fire Prevention	FMJ International Publications	Ten per year
Fire Safety Journal	Fire Protection Association	Eight per year
In Attendance	Elsevier Science Publishers	Four times a year
Customs & Excise Group	Gateacre Press Ltd	Monthly
Prison Service News	Nat Union of Civil & Public Servants	Monthly
Forces News	Home Office	Bi-monthly
Naval Review	Mandrake Associates Ltd	Four times a year
RAF News	Cornhill House	Fortnightly
Royal Military Police	TG Scott & Sons	Four times a year
The Great Outdoors	Combined Services Publications	Monthly
Climber and Hillwalker	Holmes McDougall	Monthly

(Source: Edexcel BTEC)

People

The very best source of information is real people. Employees of public services, if approached politely and with consideration, are a mine of useful, fascinating and real-life information. And never forget to ask your tutors for help and advice if you need it!

Acknowledgements

The authors and publishers are grateful to the following for permission to reproduce material:

Amnesty International, Butterworth Heinemann, Chadwyck-Healey Ltd, The Crowood Press, *Fire* magazine, Greater Manchester Police, *The Huddersfield Daily Examiner*, Human Kinetics, *The Knutsford Guardian*, Lancashire Constabulary, The McGraw Hill Companies, Zig Layton-Henry, Ministry of Agriculture, Fisheries and Food, the Office for National Statistics, Ordnance Survey, Routledge, Surrey Police, Touchline Insurance Services, the Vehicle Inspectorate, West Yorkshire Police. Crown copyright is reproduced with the permission of the Controller of Her Majesty's Stationery Office.

Every effort has been made to contact copyright holders and we apologise if any have been overlooked.

I have received a great deal of valuable help in the preparation of this book. I am particularly grateful to Rachel Warner for her unflagging encouragement and support, and for all the useful and tactful advice she gave me. I am also most grateful to Rick Jackman, for guiding and motivating me with such skill, and to all the editorial team at Stanley Thornes (Publishers) and at GreenGate Publishing Services. In addition, I was fortunate to receive detailed and very discerning criticism and comment from Sarah Lockyer BSc, MSc, Course Tutor in Public Services at Bradford College, and Barry Spir, Edexcel External Verifier, Public Services. This book has benefited enormously from their input. Finally, I would like to reserve my deepest thanks for Loretta Cullingworth – for everything.

Nick Cullingworth
November 1999

UNIT 1 Working in Public Service

Unit outcome 1
Examine the roles of a range of public services

Assessment criteria
- Identify and explain the primary role of at least three public services.
- Describe in detail how these roles are fulfilled.

For our purposes the public services are:
- *the police*
- *the fire service*
- *the ambulance service*
- *the armed forces (the British Army, RAF, Royal Navy)*
- *the prison service*
- *Her Majesty's Customs and Excise*
- *the coastguards.*

In addition to these there are some voluntary organisations, such as mountain rescue. And then there are people whose work resembles these, such as security officers or traffic wardens, or prison officers who work not directly for the government but for privatised prisons.

The primary role of public services

Identify and explain the primary role of at least three public services.

'Primary role' means the main function or job that the services do for the public. The role is sometimes called the 'philosophy' or the 'purpose'.

1 Role of the police

> **FOCUS**
>
> Here is a statement by the Greater Manchester Police outlining their role and how they aim to fulfil it. (The role itself is in bold.)
>
> **Philosophy of the Greater Manchester Police**
>
> Our purpose is **to uphold the law fairly and firmly by preventing crime, bringing law breakers to justice and keeping the peace – protecting, helping and reassuring the community.**
>
> Reproduced by permission of the Chief Constable, Greater Manchester Police

ANALYSIS

1 'To uphold the law fairly and firmly': this means – making sure that people do not break the law, and doing this by treating everybody in the same way. Police actions which support this part of their role include:

- patrolling streets, roads and motorways
- interviewing and questioning possible offenders or witnesses
- recording information in writing or on the computer.

2 'By preventing crime': this means discouraging people from breaking the law. Police actions which support this part of their role include:

- being visible on the streets so that people will think twice before breaking the law
- giving advice to all members of the public (either in person or through leaflets) on how to avoid being victims of crime
- educating children and young people in good citizenship, and encouraging them to avoid criminal behaviour.

3 'Bringing law breakers to justice': this means arresting and charging people suspected of criminal offences. Police actions which support this part of their role include:

- gathering information about offences and offenders through interviewing people
- investigation at scenes of crime, and other detective work
- preparing files on offences and offenders to be sent to the Crown Prosecution Service, so that offenders can be tried in court.

4 'Keeping the peace': this means making sure that people behave in a reasonably orderly and non-threatening way at all times (while at the same time being free to enjoy themselves without disturbing, frightening or offending others). Police actions which support this part of their role include:

- being present at football matches and other large public gatherings
- protecting peaceful marches and demonstrations from onlookers who may not be so peaceful
- ensuring the free and orderly flow of both pedestrian and motor traffic.

5 'Protecting, helping and reassuring the community': this means providing an environment for 'good' people to live and work in which is safe from other 'bad' people. If the police are fulfilling their role successfully, people should be able to go about their business in all public places, at any hour of the day or night, without fear of being threatened, robbed or attacked.

THINK ABOUT IT ...

Ask any police officer what he or she does in an average day's work – and note down the answers.

2 Role of the fire service

The focus box opposite contains a statement from the Home Office explaining the fire service role.

ANALYSIS

The role of the fire service is expressed in the three headings of this extract. It is:

- to deal with emergencies
- to promote fire safety
- to carry out research into equipment and methods.

Each paragraph clearly explains part of that role.

THINK ABOUT IT ...

Visit a fire station and ask a firefighter what his or her job involves. And take notes!

3 Role of the army

FOCUS

The army describes itself 'in brief' as:

'An organisation of 100,000 men and women tasked with providing a defence force for the UK and ready for deployment in international crises throughout the world.'

FOCUS

The work of the fire service

Dealing with emergencies

Technology obviously plays a major role in helping firefighters to tackle emergencies as efficiently as possible. For example, at brigade headquarters control room computers store street plans, details of high risk buildings and the latest information on hazardous materials. This ensures that as soon as an emergency call is received – whether a fire, chemical spillage or road traffic accident – controllers can immediately access what appliances are required.

On attending at a fire, the firefighters have to make a very quick assessment of the situation – as materials used in homes and factories change, so does the way a fire is tackled. A house fire may require two appliances, whereas a commercial or factory fire may involve several appliances as well as requiring thousands of litres of water and foam, plus the use of specialist equipment.

There is also the hazard of toxic fumes and heavy smoke which can be generated from the modern materials – for example foam-filled furniture. This makes tackling a fire that much more difficult and firefighters always go fully protected with equipment such as breathing apparatus as well as personal radio sets to keep them in contact with their colleagues at the scene, or back at brigade headquarters.

Firefighters will also have a range of other equipment at their disposal depending on the incident to which they have been called: cutting and lifting gear to deal with traffic accidents; protective suits for use at chemical spills and thermal imaging cameras to help locate victims in smoke filled rooms.

Fire safety: a key area of work

Specialist training for officers involved in fire safety is provided at the national Fire Safety College in Gloucestershire and within individual brigades. Many fire officers also undertake professional qualifications in Fire Engineering, and there is the opportunity to study for other relevant academic qualifications, such as the membership of the Institution of Fire Engineers.

Training in fire safety is critical to much of the day to day work of a firefighter. Factories, offices, shops, hotels, boarding houses and railway premises are all required to comply with certain fire precaution measures, which include providing adequate means of escape. It is the job of the fire brigade to ensure on behalf of the Fire Authority that these requirements are being followed and effectively maintained.

Research and development

Brigades also provide specialist fire prevention advice to local authorities who are responsible for licensing buildings such as: theatres, cinemas, clubs, and sports grounds. Hospitals, schools, nursing homes and many other institutions also need professional advice regarding fire safety.

Another important area of work is promoting fire safety through education and publicity to the general public. Local brigades are often renowned for the enthusiasm and ingenuity they devote to these education and publicity initiatives.

Larger brigades have their own research and development departments which are involved with testing existing equipment and designing equipment for the future. These departments work closely with the Fire Experimental Unit in Gloucestershire to improve the equipment and clothing used by brigades.

ANALYSIS

The army's role, then, is to:

- provide a defence force for the UK and
- be deployed in international crises throughout the world.

1 The army, like the other armed forces, is designed to serve the British public mainly outside Britain. Exceptions include guard duty of places and VIPs within Britain, officiating at certain ceremonies and dealing with large-scale emergencies such as floods. And of course the army has been kept busy in Northern Ireland – which is part of the UK – for

many years. But only if Britain were invaded by an enemy would the army's main active work be done inside Britain.

The words 'defence force for the UK' have been carefully chosen. Note the use of 'defence' and not 'war'. We are living at peace, more or less, with other countries, and it is not the job of the British Army to go out and start a war. For over a century now, the British Army has only fought because some other country attacked Britain or its interests first, in a way which could not be ignored. So the message here is that we are not a country of warmongers, and we will only fight if there is no alternative. We prefer to get round the table and talk about it.

As Churchill said, 'Jaw jaw is better than war war.'

2 The word 'force', though, is as significant as the word 'defence'. The army is trained to fight: fighting is its greatest skill. And the word 'force' is there as a deterrent. For the role of the army is also to deter. It lets all the world know that Britain will stand and fight if it has to. Many potential enemies look at the British Army and its fighting capability, and either put their guns away, or decide to go and fight someone else instead. Deterrence is rather like crime prevention or fire prevention. It stops the problem before it has started. And it isn't costly in lives and money, as fighting is.

'For the UK' means for England, Wales, Scotland and Northern Ireland, and for any territories anywhere in the world (such as the Falkland Islands) which still belong to Britain. The army will fight if anybody tries to invade any of these places.

But more importantly, if we look at recent history, the army will also be expected to fight if British interests are threatened. In 1991, in the Gulf War, there was a situation in which our oil supplies, and those of America and Europe, could have been cut off. This situation was a threat, not to the land-mass of our country, but to the wealth and well-being of the people. So we went to war. We didn't start the problem, but it was in our interests – that is, to our advantage – to finish it.

3 The deployment in international crises takes two forms:

- peacekeeping, usually as part of a larger organisation, such as the United Nations in Bosnia or NATO, the North Atlantic Treaty Organisation, in Kosovo
- disaster relief, for example units from the Duke of Wellington's Regiment helped out in Central America after the devastation caused by Hurricane Mitch in 1998.

> **THINK ABOUT IT ...**
>
> Ask a soldier or army officer what his or her work is like – and take notes.

We have explained the roles of three public services. But since the work of the public services is increasingly interconnected, you ought to look at the roles of some of the others. So find out what you can about the roles of the ambulance service, the prison service, Customs and Excise, and a voluntary service such as mountain rescue. Contact them directly, or check out the Internet under these headings – and see how much information you can get!

Fulfilling public service roles

Describe in detail how these roles are fulfilled.

The police

The work of the police is too varied and complicated to be described in detail here. There is no substitute for visiting the police and finding out for yourself!

But the following points can be made. The police:

- deter people from crime by keeping a uniformed, easily recognised presence on the street – they also reassure the public by doing this
- patrol the streets on foot and in vehicles, ready to investigate any crime which is reported to them
- prevent crime by educating the public about security and personal safety, and by giving advice about security to whoever asks for it
- gather information about crime, either by talking to informers, interviewing suspects or recording crime reports and feeding the details into their computers
- stop, search and arrest suspects
- enforce all the laws connected with safe driving
- liaise with community groups, probation workers and social workers, so that they can reach out to the disaffected or criminal elements in society, or give a positive example to young people who might otherwise turn to crime
- collect and process crime statistics so that they can monitor their own success
- guide victim support and neighbourhood watch schemes, in order to deter crime, gather information, and improve their public image
- work with civilian police employees at scenes of crime, protecting and investigating the scene
- analyse criminal intelligence using computers and statistics, as well as forensic departments and police psychologists
- operate a control room where information about crime and traffic offences is collected, and where CCTV monitors can be watched
- respond to 999 calls, often in liaison with other services such as the fire service and the ambulance service
- liaise with the police authority – a committee of civilians who make sure that the work of a police force fits in with the needs and wishes of local people
- organise and plan their own work, by studying the crime trends and trying to tackle types of crime which are becoming more common or dangerous (e.g. drug-related crime)
- train and use dogs to detect drugs and explosives, find evidence, tackle armed criminals and search for bodies
- guard protesters, demonstrators and VIPs
- keep public order at football matches, disasters and other places where crowds might gather
- set targets for themselves about crime detection and recruitment, so that they can monitor their service to the public – and improve on it
- are organised into units and ranks (see p 49) so that they can operate more efficiently and effectively – they are inspected by Her Majesty's Inspectors, who check on their performance and give advice or criticism if it is needed; the inspectors also pass on 'good practice' from one police force to another, and publish useful and informative reports, which are available on the Internet
- are financed by central government (51 per cent of the money) and local taxation (49 per cent)
- are independent (on the whole) from the government – ultimately it is the chief constable of each force who decides policy.

Here is an example of how the police would work if a burglary was reported to them.

1. The telephone message (perhaps from a neighbour who sees the burglary) is recorded.
2. The nearest patrol car is radioed and sent to the scene of the crime.
3. The house is searched for the burglar – who is arrested if found.
4. Police speak to the neighbour who saw – or reported – the incident.
5. A description is obtained of the burglar if possible.
6. The police radio to all nearby patrolling officers – in case they may have seen the burglar.
7. Other neighbours may be interviewed – in case they saw something.

8 Police secure the building that has been broken into.
9 They examine the house for clues such as fingerprints or tool-marks. Civilian scenes-of-crime officers may be brought in to do this.
10 A computer crime report is made out, which includes details of the stolen property.

The police may not catch the burglar – but by doing these things they have maximised the chance of doing so.

THINK ABOUT IT ...

If you are 18½ or over, have you considered joining the Special Constabulary?

The 'Specials' are volunteer police who work in uniform, and get their expenses paid. Joining them is better than any work placement and may help you to get into the police!

The fire service

The fire service also leads a varied life, and again it is well worth visiting, or inviting to your college so that you can interrogate them about their work.

Though we call them the fire service, most of their work nowadays tends to involve road traffic accidents. Their role includes:

- responding to 999 calls and rescuing people whose lives are at risk – often these are people trapped in crashed cars, but the fire service is equally skilled at getting people out of burning buildings, saving people from the effects of chemical spills, rescuing people from floods or digging them out of old mineshafts
- putting out fires of every description – if they aren't safely contained in a fireplace
- salvaging property from fire and flood damage
- carrying out emergency first aid – especially if they arrive at the scene of a serious accident before the ambulance service does
- investigating the causes of serious fires and accidents – every fire service has a fire investigation team
- liaising with other public services in the event of a serious fire, accident or disaster – and especially with the police over malicious false alarms, and arson which makes up over 40 per cent of all fires
- collecting and processing data on fires and their causes
- educating the public about the dangers of fire, and other hazards
- inspecting buildings and giving out fire certificates to show that they are (reasonably) safe from fire
- advising the public and industry on all matters to do with fire prevention and safety
- educating the public – and especially young people – about fire dangers and prevention.

Like the police, the fire service is organised regionally, and each regional service has a public committee called a fire authority which ensures that their work reflects the public's needs. Also like the police, the fire service is funded partly by central government and partly by local government. The way they spend their money is looked at by both the local fire authority and the Audit Commission, a government committee. They have efficiency targets and inspections designed to improve their performance year on year. Like other public services they wear a uniform, which makes them easily recognisable to the public and gives them a sense of team spirit. They also have a rank structure, to encourage and reward effort:

- leading firefighter
- sub-officer
- station officer
- assistant divisional officer
- divisional officer grade III
- divisional officer grade II
- divisional officer grade I
- senior divisional officer
- assistant chief officer/assistant firemaster
- chief officer/firemaster.

Not all firefighters are full time. Many are 'retained firefighters': skilled volunteers who turn out when necessary. These people are to the fire service what the Special Constabulary are to the police.

There are also some civilian employees in the fire service, who do secretarial work or maintain vehicles – but far fewer than there are in the police.

The army

The army is one of the biggest employers in the country, and has perhaps the widest range of jobs. The full list can be found by looking in the British Army website at army.mod.uk. Taken almost at random they include: aircraft technicians, bricklayers, chefs, mechanics of all kinds, armourers, electricians, dog trainers, dental technicians, infantry soldiers, gunners, drivers, musicians, military engineers, Royal Military Police, student nurses and veterinary technicians. And that's just among the ordinary soldiers. There is also a wide range of specialities available for officers.

The reason why the army has such a wide range of jobs is that it must be self-sufficient. If it is operating in a hostile country soldiers aren't going to be able to say, 'I've got toothache, sarge – better just nip out to the dentist!' Everybody they need has to travel with them.

The modern army is a major job training organisation. Gone are the days when old soldiers were slung out of the army without having a clue what they were going to do next. The army has adapted to peacetime and to modern conditions by using civilian qualifications, partly to ensure consistent standards and partly to provide a future for people who wish to leave the army after a number of years.

Like other public services the modern army is expected to save money where possible, and demonstrate that it has spent its money wisely. On the other hand, unlike the police or the fire service, it is not accountable to any local bodies such as the police authority or the fire authority. Instead it inspects itself – rigorously and frequently, at all levels. But it doesn't have to publish priorities and targets as civilian public services do.

Besides, there has always been a tradition of secrecy in the army. Why give information away to the enemy?

To know whether it is fulfilling its role successfully – whether in Kosovo or anywhere else – the army monitors its own performance. Officers write reports and submit them to their commanding officers. The key information ends up with the Ministry of Defence and with the top army command. In addition reports have to be made to other organisations such as NATO and the United Nations, which have a degree of control over some British forces.

Britain is (on the whole) at peace. So when the army isn't fighting it is training to fight. To maintain its fighting capability the army goes on exercises, not just on Salisbury Plain or round Catterick Camp, but in places like Canada, Belize and Kenya, so that they can have first-hand experience of every possible kind of fighting environment. It is only by maintaining its standards by constant training, exercising and updating equipment and weapons that the army can continue to command respect, fulfil its deterrent role, and work effectively for British interests in the 21st century.

The army – like other armed forces – is less civilianised than the police or the fire service. Most of the routine work is done by soldiers themselves – and this includes jobs such as cooking and cleaning. The army has its own police service, the Royal Military Police, which is run by the Adjutant Generals Corps.

Army ranks are shown in the table on the following page.

You can see there is a very full career structure. The purpose of the career structure is to increase army loyalty and efficiency by:
- rewarding ability and effort
- giving incentives (encouragement) for effort and commitment.

The career structure also keeps people in the army, so that the expense of training recruits is not wasted.

The territorial army (TA)

These are part-time soldiers. In some ways the TA resembles the Special Constabulary and retained firefighters – but there is a difference: the territorials get paid. If there were to be a full scale war the territorials would be expected to be

Army ranks

Soldiers	Officers
Young soldiers	Short Service Limited Commission
Private over 17½ on entry	Officer Cadet
Private Class III	Graduate Officer Cadet
Private Class II	Second Lieutenant
Private Class I	Lieutenant
Lance Corporal Class I	Captain
Corporal Class I	Major
Sergeant	Lieutenant Colonel
Staff Sergeant	Colonel
Warrant Officer Class II	Brigadier
Warrant Officer Class I	

available for full-time fighting, though (touch wood) this is less likely to happen than at any time in the past. They sometimes help the regular army out on exercises and other activities.

! THINK ABOUT IT ...

The TA offers excellent training for people who want to join the army, or simply want to improve their fitness, self-discipline, and see another side of life.

They also give free driving lessons! If you are interested, why not apply?

Unit outcome 2
Describe initial training programmes within the public services

Assessment criteria

- Identify the essential requirements of initial training programmes in at least two public services.
- Describe at least five skills and abilities which are developed in initial training programmes.

The essential requirements of initial training

There are many jobs where you walk in and start work in the first day or so. But these are just jobs. They're not careers. And the public services are careers. This means they take training seriously.

The police

The first thing to note about it is that the structure of the police training programme varies from force to force. Each has their own training centre, though there are national centres as well which can be used by all forces. But despite the small variations the

FOCUS

Police initial training

Probationary training – foundation course

Initial training is generally the same throughout the country and is a combination of 'hands-on' training and college based courses throughout the two-year cycle. Probationer training starts with a foundation course split into seven modules.

Module 1

Takes place in force and is an introduction to the many different aspects of policing. Acting as an observer, you'll gain a basic understanding of how shifts work and get used to people seeing you in uniform.

Module 2

Is a ten-week residential course at the District Training Centre. You'll study law and procedure, gain professional skills and undergo physical training. The emphasis here will be on interactive and discussion-based learning.

Module 3

Structured street experience in the company of a 'tutor constable' who will guide you through incidents, procedures and paperwork.

Module 4

A further five weeks at the District Training Centre will allow you to develop your knowledge and begin to match theory with your experiences and those of your colleagues.

Module 5

A week's holiday.

Module 6

Back in your force you will be working on your own, albeit under your tutor constable's guidance, but also consolidating what you have learnt.

Module 7

Is a critical week: your performance will be assessed and a decision made on whether you are ready for independent patrol. If so, your future training and development needs will be discussed and you will move on to the post foundation phase.

Source: © Crown Copyright 1997

essential requirements are the same for all forces. They have to be, in order to ensure that officers in each force have the same professional skills and standards.

The training is done in modules, or sections. Some of these are done at the police station where recruits are based.

It takes two years to complete all the initial training outlined here. At the end of that time you have finished your probationary period and you have (if you want it, and continue to show the right attitude) a job for life.

The essential elements of police training are as follows.

Personal development

This includes: confidence, loyalty and dependability, the ability to relate to people, decision-making, good attitudes, moral values, a sense of purpose and a positive underlying approach to life.

Fitness training

Police officers don't need to be as fit as the Royal Marines – but it helps. There are occasions (not too often) when the job can get physical, and the rest of the time it needs excellent health and stamina.

Professional skills

There is a vast range of these, and many of them are related to personal skills which we use in our everyday life. They include an ability to work in teams, yet also an ability to plan your own work and do it on your own, without help or encouragement. Other skills are: how to patrol, how to interview people, how to write clear, relevant statements, how to defend yourself both verbally and physically, how to make efficient use of computers when necessary, how to conduct a search, how to be observant, how to break bad news, how to drive fast yet safely – and so on.

Professional knowledge

Much of this is knowledge of the law, and of the police powers (of arrest, search, etc.) outlined in the Police and Criminal Evidence Act Code of Practice. Then you need to know about the district in which you will be working. Next there is the knowledge of procedures, paperwork and form-filling. And a working knowledge of the basics of criminology, psychology, sociology, race relations and many other aspects of human behaviour is essential. On top of all these a keen awareness of health and safety issues is very important.

THINK ABOUT IT ...

Note that this outline is simply the essential requirements.

If you use your initiative you will be able to get much more detailed information from:
- your tutors
- an approach to your local force
- the community and youth liaison officer (or equivalent) of your local police force
- individual (young!) police officers who have recently been through the training themselves, and are willing to give you the low-down.

The army

Many of you will have friends who have joined the army as ordinary soldiers. You may even intend to do this yourself. But since you are taking a BTEC National in Public Services, it makes more sense to apply as an officer.

The army gives detailed information about officer training at the Royal Military Academy at Sandhurst on the army website.

The essential elements of army officer training are as follows.

Personal development

This includes: confidence, loyalty and dependability, the ability to relate to people, decision-making, good attitudes, moral values, a sense of purpose and a positive underlying approach to life. The personal development of the officer as a mature and purposeful individual cannot be separated from the professional qualities needed for the army. 'Initiative, resourcefulness and courage' are examples of personal qualities developed by Sandhurst training.

Fitness training

'Top physical condition' is expected of army officers on leaving Sandhurst. Both strength and stamina are required, to an even greater degree than in the police.

Professional skills

There are a vast range of these, and many of them are related to personal skills which we use in our everyday life. They include: an ability to work in teams, yet also an ability to plan your own work and do it on your own, without help or encouragement. Leadership skills are vitally important for army officers because, much more than police constables, their role is one of command and leadership, both of a formal kind and of leadership by example (police constables also lead by example but in a less obvious way). Other professional skills include survival methods, weapons training, techniques of discipline and self-assessment, and the ability to make good decisions under difficult circumstances. As with the police, many of these professional qualities are closely allied to personal qualities.

Professional knowledge

The professional knowledge of officers is on the whole different from that of the police. It includes techniques of warfare, military strategy (large-scale planning), logistics and support, the structure and administration of the army and a basic understanding of military hardware. There is also the need for a knowledge of world politics, and the situations in which there is potential conflict – and why that potential conflict is there. Like the police, officers need a working knowledge of the basics of criminology, psychology, sociology, race relations, culture and many other aspects of human behaviour – particularly in relation to likely peacekeeping and disaster relief duties. And a keen

A keen awareness of health and safety issues in a military context is vitally important

awareness of health and safety issues in a military context is vitally important.

Developing skills and abilities

Describe at least five skills and abilities which are developed in initial training programmes.

There are many of these and they vary from public service to public service. Here are five examples:

1 Self-reliance

Self-reliance is the ability to make decisions without having to ask other people for help and advice. It is also the ability to work without needing reassurance and encouragement from others.

The requirements for self-reliance are:
- strength of character: that is, the ability to take on responsibility and the emotional strength not to be discouraged by difficulties
- perseverance: the ability to stick at a task until it is finished to a high standard
- self-confidence: the belief that you have the ability and qualities to succeed
- experience: the knowledge that you have been successful on previous occasions
- resilience: the ability to stand up to criticism
- professional knowledge and expertise: so that you don't have to keep running to others for information and advice
- the intellectual ability and thinking skills to solve difficult practical problems
- good health and stamina.

These qualities are developed through simulations and other forms of training. Because the training is often done in groups, recruits can measure their performance against that of their peers, and so develop confidence in their own abilities and a realistic sense of what they are capable of.

2 Assertiveness

Assertiveness means sticking up for yourself in a straightforward way, which enables you to get what you want from a situation, without provoking anger or aggression from other people. Suppose a public service student misses a deadline for an assignment. The teacher then refuses to accept the work. There are three ways of dealing with this situation from the student's point of view.

1 Aggressive: being rude to the teacher and shouting at him or her for being unreasonable. Threatening to 'set the lads onto you'.

2 Passive: bursting into tears, apologising too much, explaining at great length, grovelling, making unrealistic promises (such as that you will never be late with an assignment again).

3 Assertive: giving a single reason why the assignment is late. Saying what you want from the situation (an extension of the deadline). Suggesting a new deadline of your own which will be feasible. These statements and requests are made in a calm, polite and reasonable way.

The police are also taught to deal with aggression, for example using a checklist like the one below:
- Does the individual have a history of violence?
- Does the individual have a history of mental illness?
- Am I a serious threat to the individual? (For example, am I going to be seen as taking their children, or their freedom, away from them?)
- Is the individual showing signs of strong emotion (such as sweating, changes in complexion, staring, or absence of eye contact, clenched fists etc.)?
- Does the individual appear to be under the influence of alcohol or drugs?
- In the event of an attack, do I have (or need) an escape route?
- Does the individual I am talking to need an escape route? Am I boxing them in too much?
- Is the individual armed (or likely to be armed)?
- Is the individual physically stronger than me?
- Are there any objects lying about which might be used as weapons?
- What means of defence do I have?
- Does anybody know where I am?
- Do I need help?
- Is there anything I can do or say which will defuse the situation?

Training in the ability to be assertive is a twin track approach. On the one hand it develops emotional control in situations where tempers may be frayed. On the other hand it develops intellectual control by focusing your mind on the intended outcome of the interaction.

3 Form-filling and report writing

The single biggest problem faced by BTEC National students applying for the police is lack of skill and confidence in written English. The police place considerable emphasis on these skills because they are necessary for effective police work.

The police don't expect their trainees to be faultless at written English, but they do expect them to be able to write confidently and reasonably fast, and to produce something which is clear and competent. They value good spelling, even though there are very effective and skilful police officers who cannot spell the word 'college'. A person who writes 'thing' when he means to write 'night' would not be able to get into the police or succeed in training.

4 A basic understanding of war

Trainee army officers, like most of the rest of us, have no personal experience of war, or even of being in a war zone. But they have to learn about war and be prepared for it. For if war does break out, it is the full-time officer and soldier who will be the first to be personally involved.

War is not an easy subject to understand. Much of what is written about it is propaganda, and most of the rest is top secret. But from the mishmash of information, and with the help of their instructors, trainee officers have to understand the following:

- the causes of war
- the strategies (the overall plans and the major troop movements)
- tactics (small scale planning)
- weapons and vehicles and their capabilities
- morale
- external factors like terrain, weather and climate and their influence on the techniques of war
- how the different armed forces work together (because the army would rarely operate outside the British Isles without backup from the Royal Navy and the RAF – not to mention the forces of other countries or groups of countries)
- support services, transport, communications, supplies and logistics (moving weapons, vehicles, supplies and troops around)
- relationships with civilian populations.

5 A working knowledge of the Police and Criminal Evidence Act

One of the vital skills in public service work is that of making practical use of theoretical knowledge: in other words, putting what you learn in the classroom to use on the street. Here is an example.

The Police and Criminal Evidence Act 1984 (the so-called PACE Act) is the most important law that the police have to learn, since it governs the way they interact with the public. If they stop, search, arrest or question suspects, everything they do is governed by this Act. And since it is fairly complicated, and parts of it are altered or updated from time to time, police officers have to carry round with them a Code of Practice booklet, to remind them of the details.

If officers don't deal with suspects in the way set out in the Act, any evidence they get from them, any information, statements or confessions, will be worthless – at least if the Crown Prosecution Service, defence lawyers, magistrates or judges find out about it! The Act was brought in because police officers in the early 1980s were abusing their power – and that is something a police officer should never do.

The basic provisions of the Act include the following.

If somebody is stopped and/or searched on the street there must be:

- grounds for stopping them (for example an informant says the person is carrying a flick-knife)
- a reason for stopping them (in this case, to see if they really are carrying an offensive weapon and, if so, to find out why – and then charge them if necessary).

There are also:

- strict rules for searching people in public (officers

can only search their outer pockets, or ask them to remove a jacket and gloves)
- regulations about issuing a caution before questioning suspects (see p 149)
- strict rules about taking the suspect to the police station, and what happens when he gets there
- strict rules about interviews – they must be taped or videoed, and recorded in such a way that there is no doubt about when they took place, and no risk of falsifying the evidence
- rules about vulnerable people
- rules about keeping suspects in custody, and how they should be treated
- rules about access for the accused person to solicitors and others.

Because the Act is both necessary and complicated, learning to work within its guidelines is a series of skills in itself. But if officers don't work within these guidelines they will do more harm than good. So until trainee constables can understand the Police and Criminal Evidence Act and use it correctly and with confidence, they might as well go on patrol wearing a gag, and with both hands tied behind their backs.

Unit outcome 3
Examine jobs within the public services

Assessment criteria

- Describe the type of work done by at least three different personnel from within a public service.
- Explain in detail the conditions of service and typical work routine of a given job within a public service.
- Analyse the effects of a life-saving or threatening situation on a member of the public services.

Type of work

Describe the type of work done by at least three different personnel from within a public service.

Public service work varies more than other kinds of work. One of the main things which attracts people to work in the public services is that no two days are alike, and the unexpected can be expected. Nevertheless, there is a basic range of duties for each job.

Here are some examples:

Example 1: infantry soldier

INFANTRY SOLDIER ARMY CORPS: combat arms, the infantry
STATUS: soldier
GENDER: male
JOB DESCRIPTION: after completing your training, you will become a rifleman in your battalion. You will be in a team with seven others, as part of a larger team of 28. Your time will be divided between operations, perfecting your military skills, and improving your fitness and confidence through sport and adventurous training. These activities

take place in the UK and abroad. Your main job during wartime will be to close with and defeat the enemy – you will be in the thick of the action.

ANALYSIS

1 The infantry are trained to do the front-line fighting in a war. In many ways theirs is potentially the most difficult and dangerous of all army jobs. They receive orders, but they do not give them; they are trained to kill, and they run the risk, in war, of being killed themselves. Their job demands courage and practical intelligence, and also the ability to work as a team. In addition they have to withstand hardship, and sometimes, as in the famous 'yomps' of the Falklands Conflict in 1982, when they had to march 50 miles in a day carrying heavy loads, they are expected to display great strength and stamina.

2 In peacetime the job of the infantry is to train and then go on operations in various parts of the world. Their training consists of fitness training, survival skills, weapons training, basic theory of war, tactics and so on. Much of the training is practical, taking part in military exercises. While in camp they carry out guard duties and a range of routine tasks.

3 The 'operations' they are sent on consist mainly of peacekeeping duties. The duties may be in Northern Ireland, Kosovo, or any other place where the government has decided that Britain or British interests are being put at risk. While doing these duties, the job of the infantry is to go on patrol and provide the threat of force if the army's authority is challenged. They also protect teams of international observers from the United Nations or any other organisation which is working in cooperation with the British or allied governments. And again, they act as guards, of airports, ammunition stores or other strategic sites. If anybody attacks these sites, it is the infantry's job to defend them, by force if necessary.

Example 2: REME platoon commander

REME PLATOON COMMANDER ARMY CORPS: services Royal Electrical and Mechanical Engineers (REME)

STATUS: officer

GENDER: male/female

JOB DESCRIPTION: the role of the REME is to recover, repair and maintain army equipment including helicopters, tanks, road vehicles and weapon systems. REME officers command the units and assets which achieve this aim. They manage production, set priorities and solve technical problems both in barracks and on operations. They are also responsible for providing career management, military and adventure training and welfare sport for soldiers, as well as fostering 'esprit de corps'. Above all, they command REME soldiers.

ANALYSIS

Army officers are trained to command, and their primary job is to maintain discipline, motivation and skills in the units under their responsibility. They maintain discipline by the use of their personal leadership qualities and the special skills they have developed, together with the authority which comes with their higher rank in the army organisation. In peacetime they maintain motivation by developing and organising useful, interesting and rewarding activities for the soldiers under their command. They develop their units' general fighting skills through weapons training, exercises and other activities.

Since they are, in a sense 'middle management'; they also carry out orders and directives from higher up. These are things which are done by all officers, whatever corps (section) they happen to be in. It is their 'generic' role.

But officers also have a specialised role connected with the kind of units they command. Officers in the Royal Electrical and Mechanical Engineers must have enough technical ability and know-how to organise the technical and maintenance work of the people under their command. They are responsible for ordering and organising the testing of new equipment or weapons, and for training people in their correct use and maintenance. Their responsibility is not only for the safety and effectiveness of the people they are training: they also have responsibility for large amounts of highly complex, sophisticated and expensive equipment. This technical work, connected with engineering, is their specialised role.

Example 3: police inspector

Here is a job description for a police inspector.

The role of the inspector

Promotion to inspector is a reminder of the accelerated nature of the APSG (accelerated promotion scheme for graduates), in that you may be much younger in service than most other inspectors in your district and it may seem strange at first to be on first name terms with people who, only a short while ago, were your supervisors.

Inspector rank brings you to middle management and ensuring the most effective use of resources. Quite apart from the obvious fact of managing more officers – a team of sergeants and constables – you will have additional, wider responsibilities. For example, you could be deciding the location of the division's 'response' vehicles according to where problems are occurring on your patch. You will be expected to be the think-tank of the shift, and to run budgets or take on projects.

Above all, it means leadership: evaluating levels of performance, anticipating difficulties and moving people and equipment around to the right place at the right time. Quite often that means transforming imprecise information about a set of circumstances into a series of clear commands for your team.

ANALYSIS

The work of police inspectors has something in common with that of army officers. Like the REME officer we have just looked at, police inspectors have responsibility for the teams working under them. So police inspectors must be able to lead, motivate, organise, discipline and, sometimes, counsel. The way they do this is to some extent left up to them, and depends on their own management styles. Their authority comes from their character, skills and position in the police hierarchy. As well as using their human skills to manage effectively, their seniority and ability means that they are often consulted for opinions, guidance or advice.

They have generic police skills and knowledge which will serve them well whichever department they may happen to be working in. But they will also have skills and knowledge of a more specialised nature. For example an inspector on traffic will be an expert in traffic laws and traffic policing.

Like army officers, police inspectors have an administrative role: their knowledge needs to be theoretical as well as practical, so that they can devise plans of their own, as well as carry out the plans of others. Also like army officers, they have to satisfy their superiors as well as those people who are below them in the police command structure. For example, if their teams want new equipment and their superiors tell them to save money, they will have to make a decision which will satisfy, as far as possible, both groups of people.

Conditions of service

Explain in detail the conditions of service and typical work routine of a given job within a public service.

Conditions of service are the statutory rights of an employee. They include pay, holidays, working conditions and so on. All jobs have conditions of service, and in the public sector these are, in effect, laid down by law, because they are decided by the government. Public service jobs are almost always in the public sector (the main exception being Group 4 and the privatised prisons), and they have fixed conditions of service which do not vary from place to place (except for London, where there are certain differences in pay and other entitlements).

Let's look at conditions of service in the fire service.

The fire service

FOCUS

Conditions of service

Members of the fire service work a 42-hour week. Duties are divided into day and night shifts, with an average of at least two days off a week.

Paid leave when you join the service is 28 days a year in addition to public holidays, but if you are required to work on these days you are paid in double time and given time off in lieu.

If you choose to retire with 25 years of service at the age of 50 or more you will receive a pension of roughly the rate of half pay; if you complete 30 years' service the rate is two-thirds. Special pension provision is made for retirement due to ill-health or injury on duty and for dependants.

Salary scales

The table below shows salaries in the fire service with effect from 7 November 1999.

Salaries in the fire service	
Firefighter	on entry – £15,831 per annum rising to (5th year) £20,121
Leading firefighter	£21,546 – £22,434
Sub-officer	£22,092 – £23,832
Station officer	£25,629 – £27,639
Assistant divisional officer	£27,012 – £29,535
Divisional officer grade III	£28,932 – £31,023
Divisional officer grade II	£30,720 – £34,056
Divisional officer grade I	£33,933 – £36,375
Senior divisional officer	£36,528 – £39,402
Assistant chief officer chief officer/ firemaster	receive varying rates of pay

ANALYSIS

Conditions of service include:

- pay
- working hours
- shift system
- holidays
- promotion
- training
- equal opportunities
- retirement
- pension.

Other things which would come under the heading of conditions of service include trade union rights and grievance procedures.

Pay

Fire service pay as a whole rises from time to time, roughly in line with the rate of pay inflation – that is, the average rates of pay rise in the public sector. This means that after every two or three years there will be an increase of about five per cent. As with all public service work, pay for individual firefighters rises by increments – small yearly increases until the pay reaches a 'ceiling' beyond which there are no more incremental increases.

The pay for each rank is higher than the one below it. This encourages firefighters to stay in the service, work to a high standard, and apply for promotion. Rates of pay are roughly in line with those for the police. Pay is fixed by a royal commission, so it is not negotiated as it is in some of the larger private industries. But if firefighters are not happy about it, their trade union will complain.

There is extra pay for public holidays, but not for 'unsocial hours'. This is because the shift system ensures that every firefighter works the same number of unsocial hours.

The work

Each fire station has three shifts, called 'watches', and each watch lasts eight hours. Firefighters are actually on the premises for longer than this, to ensure a smooth changeover. This system provides full 24-hour cover for call-outs to fires and accidents. The watches are named after colours, and each firefighter stays with the same watch, so that they can 'bond' as a team.

Fire officers follow a busy training schedule when they are not out on operational duty. They practise routine activities such as hose-rolling and ladder climbing, and maintain equipment. They spend a good deal of time learning about new equipment and new rescue techniques, and in learning about liaison with other public services. Sometimes this involves going away on residential courses, especially to the Fire Service Training College at Moreton-in-Marsh, Gloucestershire. They also spend time in fitness training. When they are on call they may relax in the station, but they are always ready to go out at a moment's notice. Large fire stations have dormitories where firefighters stay overnight when they are on duty.

THINK ABOUT IT ...

This is a rough outline. Contact your local fire service for more details!

Holidays

Firefighters' holidays are average for the public services. But because of the shift system firefighters often have two days off a week and this, together with the weekends, can mean that they have four days off work at a stretch. This will not give them a holiday in the Seychelles, but it works wonders for their golf!

Promotion

As with most public services, promotion is on merit, not length of service as it is in some jobs. Promotion is never based on 'Buggins' turn'!

Life-saving or threatening situations

Analyse the effects of a life-saving or threatening situation on a member of the public services.

'Life-saving and threatening situations' means occasions when you might save a life, or occasions when you – or others – are clearly at risk from something or somebody. Many sensational things which happen to public service employees are threatening. An example is shown at the top of the next page.

ANALYSIS

This incident was potentially very serious, and many members of the public services were involved in the following ways:

(a) they were working to save lives which were threatened by the collision of the two ships
(b) they were working to prevent the ships from sinking
(c) they were physically threatened because they were in some danger themselves
(d) they were mentally and emotionally threatened by the possibility that they might fail to save lives.

It is clear enough what life-saving situations are. But the same cannot be said of threatening situations.

Dover Coastguard Called to Assist in Passenger Ship Collision

At 1.15 a.m. on 23 August 1999, Dover Coastguard were called to coordinate an incident off Falls Bank, 20 miles north east of Margate, involving a passenger ship, the *Norwegian Dream* and a container ship *Ever Decent*. Forty people were on board the *Ever Decent*, which is Panamanian registered. It is currently at a 40 degree list. The *Norwegian Dream* is a Bahamian registered cruise liner. It has 2,400 people on board.

The following are assisting:

- lifeboats from Dover, Ramsgate, Margate
- rescue helicopters 125 and 128 from Watisham
- five other merchant vessels in the area
- Kent Fire Brigade assembling at Manston
- an RAF Nimrod overhead.

There are three casualties with minor injuries on board *Norwegian Dream*. They are being evacuated by helicopter. District controller Rod Johnson said: 'The *Ever Decent* is taking water and on fire. It is being assisted by a helicopter and lifeboat. A tug is on its way.' The container ship is heading towards low water and preparing to beach. The *Norwegian Dream* is heading the 40 miles towards Dover. Winds are light and north easterly. There is a slight sea and good visibility.

There are basically four kinds of threat:

(a) the physical threat of pain, sickness, injury or death
(b) the material threat of the loss or destruction of property
(c) the mental threat of being unable to think clearly, sensibly or logically
(d) the emotional threat which comes from fear of failure, or of losing self-respect.

In the situation of the ships colliding, threat (a) was the danger of drowning or burning faced by the passengers on one ship, and the merchant seamen on the other. Threat (b) was the threat of the ships sinking. This was faced by the owners of the ships. Threat (c) was faced by the rescue workers who found themselves confronted by a problem they might not be able to solve. It was closely linked to threat (d), which was also suffered by the rescue workers. Public service workers pride themselves on their ability to help people and to save lives. Like many professionals, if they fail they have a tendency to blame themselves even if the failure is not their fault.

A public service student once asked a fire officer what his personal experience of life-saving and threatening situations was. The fire officer was happier to talk about the subject in a general way, rather than dredge up particular horrific incidents which he had experienced. But he noted certain experiences which he thought were shared by many rescue workers.

1 The most distressing situations involved the death or suffering of children.

2 The most difficult thing to live with was the idea that you might – if you had done something differently – have been able to save a child who actually died.

3 Many public service workers became quite 'thick skinned' about dealing with death and other forms of horrific experience. For example a friend of his had once cracked a joke about 'the brain now waiting at platform two', when they were looking for the body parts of a suicide who had been run over by an express train. The joke was not funny, but it had been that officer's way of distancing himself from something that would otherwise have been too horrible to think about.

4 Part of the challenge of being a professional was to continue to function normally even in the face of death and horror. But there were risks in this. If officers suppressed their feelings too much, it could lead to various kinds of emotional and mental illness. This is why all public services are now employing counsellors who help officers to get over the effects of a horrific incident. For example after the Hillsborough disaster, when a wrong decision by the police was said to be responsible for the deaths of nearly 100 football fans, many of the officers who had been present went for counselling in order to overcome feelings of horror, shock, failure and guilt.

Immediate effects

Flight and fight

The natural immediate reaction to danger is either to run away from it, or to stay and fight. These two responses have been called 'flight' and 'fight' by psychologists. They cause a rise in heart rate, blood pressure, blood sugar levels and adrenalin levels. Either fear or aggression takes over, and people (or animals) react accordingly.

Public service workers do not have the option either of running away or fighting. They are expected to work calmly and coolly to save lives and property, even when part of them would rather go berserk – or just bottle out.

Long-term effects

Post traumatic stress disorder

The long-term effects are called 'post traumatic stress disorder'. The police have special arrangements for helping officers who suffer from PTSD. They are (a) occupational therapy, where counselling is given for work, family and money worries; (b) the force surgeon, who diagnoses problems, refers the sufferer to specialists or gives the officer sick leave or early retirement and (c) the force psychiatrist, who gives in-depth counselling and psychotherapy. (b) and (c) are shared by the fire service. PTSD can also be treated using drugs.

On a more positive note, saving a life is a wonderful achievement, and the fact that it is part of somebody's duties as a firefighter or soldier does not make it any less wonderful. If heroism is seen and recognised it may, however, impose its own kind of stress. Firefighters who have saved lives are sometimes asked to talk about it on television: usually they protect themselves from the emotion of the situation by displaying great modesty, claiming that they didn't really do anything special. Sometimes great happiness and a sense of achievement may cause its own psychological difficulties. A public service worker who saves a life may later feel a sense of anticlimax or 'let down', when things return to dull normality. As the rush of adrenalin which follows a great achievement dies away, a feeling of depression may set in. In this sense, public service work, especially involving rescues, can be something of an emotional roller-coaster ride, and if it becomes too much for the officer, he may need counselling or some other form of sympathetic treatment.

FOCUS

Post traumatic stress disorder, also known as PTSD, is a mental condition that follows a psychologically distressing event outside the range of usual human experience. It includes:

- recurring nightmares about the event, including possibly intrusive memory flashbacks
- difficulty sleeping or changes in appetite
- feelings of anxiety and fear, especially when exposed to events or situations reminiscent of the trauma
- jumpiness, edginess, exaggerated startle reflex, or becoming overly alert
- depression, sadness, and lack of energy
- spontaneous crying
- sense of despair and hopelessness
- memory problems, including difficulty in remembering aspects of the trauma
- feeling 'scattered' or 'off centre', and unable to focus on work or daily activities
- difficulty making decisions or carrying out plans
- irritability, agitation, or feelings of anger and resentment
- feeling emotionally 'numb', withdrawn, disconnected, or different from others
- overprotectiveness of loved ones, or fear for the safety of loved ones
- not being able to face certain aspects of the trauma, and avoiding activities, places, or even people that remind you of the event
- panic attacks, racing heart, breathlessness.

Unit outcome 4
Explain how public service organisations deal with complaints

Assessment criteria

- Describe a range of complaints which arise in a public service organisation.
- Compare the complaints procedures of at least two public service organisations.
- Describe the characteristics of at least two grievance procedures available to public service employees.

What is a complaint?

As sure as day follows night, if you work in the public services someone will complain about you. Indeed, in some public services, such as the police, if nobody complains about you, then you are not doing your job properly.

A complaint is an official statement by a member of the public, or an organisation, making it clear (either in speech or writing) that they are not happy with the work of the police as a whole, or of an individual officer. For the purposes of the Police and Criminal Evidence Act 1984 it is 'any complaint about the conduct of a police officer which is submitted by the public, or on behalf of a member of the public and with his written consent. Complaints may be received directly from a member of the public or from some person or organisation which takes up his cause provided that such a person gives his written consent.' (*Police Training Manual*, Jack English, 1996 McGraw Hill p 9)

In this section we are looking at official complaints, not the unofficial whinges, grouses and moans which everybody makes to their friends or family about the police at one time or another.

THINK ABOUT IT ...

Why will a good police officer always get complaints?

Complaints which arise against the police

At the most basic level there are only two complaints ever made about the police. These are:

- incompetence
- malpractice.

Incompetence includes things like being slow, stupid, inefficient, unreliable, forgetful, ignorant and lazy. In other words, the officer has not done something which is wrong. He has failed to do something which is right. Incompetence is not deliberate. People (including police officers) are incompetent only because they can't help it.

Malpractice means deliberate wrongdoing. So dishonesty, theft, discrimination and brutality come under this heading. Malpractice is not just a matter of failing to do that which is right. It means actively doing that which is wrong. All crimes (apart perhaps from criminal negligence) can be seen as malpractice, so police malpractice is, in effect, criminal behaviour by the police.

In reality, if a police officer does something which attracts a complaint, it may not always be clear whether the complaint is about incompetence or malpractice. For example, if an officer fails to record an interview properly, that may be incompetence because he forgot to turn on the tape recorder, or malpractice because he said things he shouldn't have done, and deliberately erased the tape.

Types of complaint

The complaints which are made against the police always come under the same headings as those points of the police discipline code which relate to the public. They include the following.

Discreditable conduct

Here the member of the public complains because the police officer is behaving in a way which makes the police force look unprofessional. It could be bad language, or uncontrolled, inappropriate or undignified behaviour.

Neglect of duty

Officers fail to do what they are expected to do. For example if a member of the public thought there was a riot or a breach of the peace, and the officers present seemed to be doing nothing about it, there could be a complaint of neglect of duty.

Falsehood

Any form of lying is falsehood. For example a judge, magistrate, lawyer, suspect or member of the public could complain if an officer had made records of an incident – perhaps in a notebook – which were deliberately untrue.

Improper disclosure of information

If police officers started gossiping about people's private business, this would be good grounds for a complaint from a member of the public.

Improper practice

This means taking bribes or gifts. The officer who did this would be breaking the law, and it is likely that the public would complain about it.

Abuse of authority

A few years ago a police officer slapped a child who had been cheeky. A parent could have done this (within reason) without breaking the law. But the police have no right to carry out corporal punishment, and there were therefore complaints from the public that the officer was abusing his authority.

Racially discriminatory behaviour

There are many complaints from the public about racially discriminatory behaviour by the police – and these now have to be properly investigated. Usually these complaints involve racially abusive language such as 'nigger' or 'Paki', picking on non-white members of the public (for example a black driver with a distinctive car), or treating black suspects differently from white suspects.

Improper dress or untidiness

People complain if male police officers wear their hair too long, or if women police officers wear inappropriate jewellery.

Drink or drugs

Police officers must never be under the influence of drink or drugs when on duty.

Criminal conduct

There have been cases where police officers, encouraged or pressured by the criminals they work with, have taken to crime themselves.

Complaints which arise against the prison service

Different public services attract different types of complaint. These complaints reflect:

(a) the main types of work that public service does
(b) the types of people who come in contact with the public service.

The main type of work the prison service does is to keep people in prison. And the main group of people who come in contact with the prison service are prisoners. This means that – unlike the police – the prison service do not receive complaints from the public as a whole. Instead they receive complaints mainly from that section of the public with which they work – in other words, prisoners.

The following complaints were collected by inspectors who went to Shrewsbury Prison.

We met a group of prisoners who told us that:

- wages were very low: £5.50 – £7; there was no in-cell electricity; most of the wages were spent on batteries (the governor later advised that earnings averaged £9)
- enhanced regime prisoners were allowed to spend £15 each week but four £4 phone cards cost £16; 'if phone cards were purchased there was no money for anything else; if you smoke that's that'. If money was not spent in any week the allowance was not carried over to the following week; pay was inadequate and other prisons paid £40 – £50 wages
- there was no work for those on the Basic level of the Incentives Scheme; although they were allowed to spend £2.50, they couldn't buy anything
- transfers to other prisons happened with very little notice
- there was an induction programme but no local information hand-outs; new receptions got very confused, especially about the Incentives and Earned Privileges Scheme and spending arrangements; there was no fire evacuation training, doors were unlocked independently, staff were the fire parties. There had been no evacuation exercises. There had been some small fires but none had been serious [...]
- the prison was safe to be in; there were some bullies but they were identified and were shifted
- cell thefts occurred regularly when the cell doors were left open; there were no locker keys
- red squares had been painted on the cell walls where pictures, posters, etc. were to be placed; nothing was allowed on the back wall
- there were no instructions about what you could put up on the walls
- the cells had not been decorated for ages; some of the walls were awful. There was no self-decoration programme, yet lots of prisoners were unemployed and could paint the cells [...]
- there was a video orderly who selected the films for association: there was too much 'blood and guts'; he appeased the youngsters
- the dentist only pulled teeth and did no fillings, he got paid by the number of prisoners he treated [...]
- paracetamol was issued for all illnesses.

Source: Home Office Website

These complaints are all about small things which are big in the eyes of the prisoners. They tend to be about incompetence rather than malpractice – since the prison as a whole got a good report from the inspectors and relations between staff and prisoners were said to be – in general – good.

Complaints procedures

Compare the complaints procedures of at least two public service organisations

Every public service has a complaints procedure. Complaints can come from either inside or outside the service. The ones that come from inside are dealt with in the section on grievance procedures (see pages 26–27).

Police complaints procedure

'Minor' complaints

If the complaint is a minor one, it can be investigated internally. The following box gives the procedure for the Greater Manchester Police.

> **FOCUS**
>
> The branch investigates complaints against the police and internal discipline enquiries. The Police Complaints Authority supervises the more serious complaints.
>
> The branch is divided into teams working from Force Headquarters, Sedgley Park, and Mottram Police Station. The teams are led by senior officers who have assistants to help them.
>
> The branch also produces management information on complaints which helps divisional commanders to measure levels of satisfaction with our service, and produce better service as a result.
>
> Reproduced by permission of the Greater Manchester Police

The more serious the complaint, the more formal the investigation. If it is a complaint of rudeness, requiring only an apology, it will be dealt with by less senior officers working in one of the branch teams. But it is still a proper investigation, because all complaints are recorded in writing and signed by the complainant. A copy of the report into every complaint is sent to the Police Complaints Authority (see below). And all the complaints, their investigation and the outcome are eventually recorded in official Home Office statistics.

Many complaints are followed by disciplinary procedures. The table below shows some examples of these.

Since the passing of the Police Act in 1996, the police authority (see p 5) attached to each force has had a role in investigating and monitoring complaints. Each police authority has a complaints committee which meets several times a year to review complaints against the local police force. The police authority can study the reports and make recommendations.

'Major' complaints

Serious complaints are not dealt with by the police force to which they have been made. The reason for this is to avoid all suspicion of a cover-up. Instead they are dealt with by an independent organisation called the Police Complaints Authority.

The Police Complaints Authority was set up in 1985 under the provisions of the Police and Criminal Evidence Act 1984. Though it was set up by the Home Office, which is responsible for the police, it is entirely independent of the police. No police officers or retired police officers can be members of it.

The Authority is basically a committee of people appointed for their skill at understanding and resolving complaints.

The role of the Police Complaints Authority is:

- 'to supervise the investigation of the most serious complaints against the police
- to supervise the investigation into matters not resulting from complaints, but which have been referred to the Authority by police services because of their potential gravity
- to review the outcome of investigations and decide whether disciplinary action should be taken against any police officer'.

Source: Police Complaints Authority

The Police Complaints Authority has wide powers of investigation into serious complaints – for example involving death, serious injury or corruption. They visit scenes of incidents, sit in on police interviews, interview witnesses and meet senior police officers, community leaders, bereaved relatives and journalists.

Overleaf is an example of a complaint dealt with by the Police Complaints Authority.

Discipline hearings 1998/1999

No	Offence	Finding	Punishment
1	Criminal conduct	Guilty	Reprimand
2	Neglect of duty	Guilty	Fined three days' pay
3	Falsehood	Not guilty	
4	Criminal conduct	Guilty	Dismissed
5	Misconduct towards a member of a police force	Guilty	Reduction in pay by two increments for one year
6	Disobedience to orders	Guilty	Reprimand
7	Neglect of duty	Guilty	Reprimand

Source: West Midlands Police

POLICE COMPLAINTS AUTHORITY 20 June 1998

Police Complaints Authority supervising investigation into West Yorkshire death

The independent Police Complaints Authority have started supervision of the investigation into the death of a 29-year-old Leeds man in a police cell today. The man had been taken to Holbeck Police Station for an alleged public order offence just after midnight this morning. Four hours later he was found collapsed in his cell. He was pronounced dead later. A post mortem examination was being held this morning. West Yorkshire Police voluntarily referred the matter to the PCA this morning. Authority member Mr Tony Williams has agreed to the appointment of Superintendent Phil Read of West Yorkshire Police Discipline and Complaints Department as the investigating officer. Mr Williams said: 'We do not yet know the cause of this tragic death. We will of course ensure that the investigation is fair and thorough. The results will go to HM Coroner who will hold the inquest in public.'

Other channels for complaints against the police

The courts

A famous example of use of the courts occurred when the parents of Stephen Lawrence took the young men who were alleged to have killed their son to court in a private prosecution. This was because they felt the police had failed to deal with the case properly.

The media

Major complaints against the police are news, and will often be reported in newspapers or on television. In the case of Stephen Lawrence the media played a major part in bringing the complaint to the notice of the public and the government – even though they had no official role in the complaints procedure.

The ombudsman

The first ombudsman was in Denmark, and this Danish word is now used in Britain as well. The ombudsman is an independent government officer who has special responsibility for dealing with complaints against the public services.

The kinds of complaints the ombudsman deals with are:

- avoidable delay
- faulty procedures or failing to follow correct procedures
- not telling you about any rights of appeal you have
- unfairness, bias or prejudice
- giving advice which is misleading or inadequate
- refusing to answer reasonable questions
- discourtesy, and failure to apologise properly for errors
- mistakes in handling your claims
- not offering an adequate remedy where one is due.

It is usually necessary to complain in writing to an MP before the complaint can be referred to the office of the ombudsman.

A public inquiry

After the Brixton riots in 1981, Lord Scarman carried out his famous inquiry into its causes. Much of the evidence he received was of malpractice by the police, both before and during the riots. The main complaints he heard were included in his report on the riots, published in the same year. A public inquiry was also carried out into the Stephen Lawrence case.

Parliament

Both the House of Lords and the House of Commons can consider complaints against the police. These are usually complaints against the way the police as a whole are being run, rather than complaints about individual officers in particular cases. Following the Scarman Report on the Brixton riots, Parliament produced a new law to control the activities of the police. This new law was the Police and Criminal Evidence Act 1984, and it had to go through both the House of Commons and the House of Lords before it could be passed.

Her Majesty's Inspectors

Her Majesty's Inspectors (HMIs) visit police stations, and make complaints which are not directly from the public – though they are on behalf of the public, who want a good, efficient police service. These complaints are recorded in the inspectors' reports, and most police forces act on the inspectors' recommendations as quickly and fully as possible.

Prison service complaints procedure

Procedures for complaints in the prison service are less formal than in the police. Here is a brief outline from the Home Office.

'If a person detained in a prison or young offenders institution (YOI) wishes to make a complaint he/she can take it up with a member of staff, ask to see the governor, use the written requests and complaints system and then, if necessary, go to prison service headquarters. Complaints may also be raised at any time with a member of the independent board of visitors, a member of Parliament, or the person's legal advisor.

If a person remains dissatisfied after pursuing a complaint with the prison service then a request for an independent investigation can be made to the prisons ombudsman.'

The Prisoners' Information Book, 1996, published by the Prison Reform Trust, gives the following outline of complaints procedures from the prisoner's point of view.

In the prison system

Stage 1

1 Talk to a member of staff – if this doesn't sort out the problem you should then continue with (2).

2 Make a written application to your landing officer or wing manager (a senior prison officer) – the officer will discuss your complaint on the same day.

3 Make a governor's application – this means you can discuss your complaint either with the governor, a senior member of staff, the medical officer, the chaplain, or a member of the board of visitors.

If the complaint is against a member of the prison staff it should include:

- what the member of staff did wrong
- what was said and done at the time
- names of witnesses
- any evidence to support the complaint.

You can ask members of staff to help you with the complaint. The complaint may also be sent in confidentially, in a sealed envelope, if you wish.

If the problem still isn't sorted out, a written request can be made to the governor. There should be a full reply within seven days. If nothing is going to be done about the complaint, there should be an explanation why.

Stage 2

1 If you are not satisfied with the result of the complaint, you can appeal to the prison service Headquarters using an appeal form. The appeal will be considered by the prison casework unit. There should be a reply within six weeks. If you are still not happy then you should continue with (2).

2 Write to the prisons ombudsman – an independent person appointed by the government to investigate complaints from prisoners. If you are not happy with the response to your complaint from the governor you can send your complaint to him. You must write to him yourself, giving as much detail as you can about your complaint.

After this he or one of his staff may visit you. When he has all the information he will write his report about your complaint, and if he agrees with it, he will write to the prison service recommending how they can put the problem right.

The prisons ombudsman deals with many complaints in an average year.

Complaints can also be made by prisoners to:

- boards of visitors – prison visitors are an association of civilians who visit prisoners and help their rehabilitation, and eventual re-entry into society when they are released
- MPs – usually the MP whose constituency includes the prisoner's home address
- a solicitor

- the police – usually by writing to the chief constable or, in London, the commissioner of the Metropolitan Police
- the Queen or Parliament. Writing to the Queen or to Parliament might be useful in a case of wrongful imprisonment
- the European Parliament
- the European Commission for Human Rights
- The Criminal Injuries Compensation Board – this would be useful for a prisoner who had been assaulted in prison
- The Commission for Racial Equality – racial incidents can sometimes be a serious problem in prisons.

A comparison of complaints procedures

The table below compares the police complaints procedure and the prison complaints procedure.

Grievance procedures

Describe the characteristics of two grievance procedures available to public service employees.

Grievances are complaints from within a public service. Usually they concern:

- pay
- conditions of service
- the behaviour of other officers.

Police and prison complaints procedures

Similarities	Differences
• Both deal with vast numbers of complaints. • Both originated as a result of serious riots, one in Brixton, London, the other in Strangeways Prison, Manchester. • Many of the complaints come from criminals which means that: (a) they may not be true; (b) they may be associated with criminal activities, such as assaults; (c) if the complaints are not acted upon, violence could result. • Both procedures are detailed and complicated. • Many of the complaints can result in legal action. • Police officers and prison officers have a duty to attend to every complaint. • Both services have different systems to deal with minor and serious complaints. • Both services have an in-house procedure, and other procedures which are independent. • In each case, people who complain have a choice of methods, including the legal and political channels which are their statutory rights. • Both services can use an ombudsman to sort out difficult cases. • There is a confidential system of complaints in prison, because of the risk of victimisation by other prisoners or by (unprofessional) prison officers.	• Many prisoner complaints are about 'domestic issues' to do with the conditions of their imprisonment. • Almost all police complaints are against the police themselves. But many prisoner complaints are against other prison inmates (for example bullies). • It is easier to complain in prison, and prisoners are actively encouraged to complain if they are unhappy. (This is to reduce the risk of prison riots.) • 20 per cent of prisoners are regarded as mentally ill. Their level of literacy is often very low. All prison officers are expected to assist prisoners in their complaints if necessary – for example by writing the complaint down for them. • Complaints to the police are divided into complaints of incompetence and complaints of malpractice, and are more likely to be directed at individual actions by individual officers. • The general public are more likely to criticise the police than the prison service, because they have more contact with them. The police are in the public eye more than the prison service are. • Complaints about the police are more likely to become major political issues than complaints about prisons. Many people don't mind if prisoners are treated badly – they think they deserve it. But bad treatment of someone by a police officer is seen as a human rights abuse.

Grievances about pay and conditions of service can be seen as collective grievances, since they would be shared by many officers. Grievances about other officers are individual grievances.

Pay and conditions of service: the police

Unlike most other employees the police are not allowed to go on strike if they have a grievance about pay or conditions of service. So they do not have a trade union. Instead they have a professional association called the Police Federation which looks after the interests of ordinary police officers. If the police are not happy about their pay it is the Police Federation who will complain to the government and ask for something to be done about it. Another body called the Association of Chief Police Officers (ACPO) looks after the interests of the highest ranks. These organisations help to keep an eye on pensions, conditions of service and other issues which affect the well-being of police officers. They also deal with grievances, as we will see below. However, they have no official role with regard to pay, and they certainly cannot negotiate for higher pay in the way that some trade unions, such as UNISON (which represents civilian police employees) can.

The behaviour of other officers: the police

Teamwork is not always easy, and police officers often have grievances about other officers they work with. If a senior officer dislikes the actions of a junior officer, it usually becomes a disciplinary matter. But if a junior officer dislikes the actions or behaviour of an equal colleague or a senior officer, it is a grievance.

Such grievances are usually based on some form of discrimination or harassment. They are dealt with as follows.

1 The officer with the grievance complains (informally) to his or her superior officer – unless that superior officer is the cause of the grievance. If this is the case, the complaint goes to the officer above the one who causes the grievance. So normally a constable would complain to a sergeant, but if the sergeant was the cause of the problem, the complaint would go to the inspector who is above the sergeant. It is most likely that the grievance is no more than a 'personality clash', which can be settled by discussion with the supervisory officer or line manager.

2 If the first informal complaint does no good, it can be put in writing. Again, an attempt will be made to solve the problem through discussion within the team.

3 If that still doesn't work, the local branch of the Police Federation will be asked to do something about the problem. It will involve meetings, the taking of statements, persuasion, and an investigation to find out whether the grievance is a reasonable one or not.

4 If this doesn't work the officer with the grievance can go to an industrial tribunal. This was what happened in 1990 with Alison Holford, the Assistant Chief Constable of Merseyside Police, who felt that she had been passed over for promotion because she was a woman.

5 In extreme cases, grievances can be taken to the European Court of Human Rights, if the complainant feels that justice has not been done in Britain.

6 If the grievance is about race discrimination, the officer can go to the Commission for Racial Equality (CRE), who will conduct an investigation and make a decision. If the grievance is upheld by an industrial tribunal (which is a kind of civil court) or the CRE, compensation may be paid to the officer with the grievance.

> **!** **THINK ABOUT IT ...**
>
> What is the grievance procedure at your college, your workplace, or the public service in which you are most interested?
>
> What are the arguments for and against public services having trade unions and being allowed to go on strike?

UNIT 2

Entry to Public Services

Unit outcome 1
Investigate the entry and selection stages for a given public service

Assessment criteria

- Accurately describe the current entry and selection stages for a given public service.
- Explain the reasons for the different selection tests for a given public service.
- Complete an application form, letter of application and CV for a job in a given public service.

You probably joined your Edexcel BTEC National course in Public Services because you are interested in working in a public service. In this unit we are going to look at entry procedures, tests, interviews and career development within the public services. In other words, this is a run-down on how you get in – and get on!

Joining a public service

> **THINK ABOUT IT ...**
>
> All public services recruit in different ways and at different times.
>
> If you want to know more about these telephone the headquarters or recruitment officers of your local public services and ask for information about recruiting. Many public services – including individual police forces – also have lots of recruitment information on the Internet. Check out their websites.

Joining a public service is not as easy as falling off a log. And it certainly isn't as easy as getting 'a normal job'. There are a number of reasons for this.

- Public service work is a career, not a job. The public services want to recruit people who will stay with them for years, and progress up the career ladder.
- Public service work is demanding, and it is important that public services recruit people of the right character and ability so that the job is done to the highest standards.
- Public service work is teamwork. So the recruiters are just as interested in your character and personality as they are in your intelligence or your physical fitness.
- Public service training is expensive. If they recruit the wrong people they have wasted a lot of money.
- Everybody wants to join the public services. Recently a fire service had 60 vacancies. With one advertisement they got 4,000 applications – most of them of high quality. Competition is hot! They could afford to pick and choose.

- Many public services do not have entry requirements in terms of GCSE passes or A levels (or even BTEC Nationals!). Their detailed recruitment procedures replace the information they might otherwise have gained from examination results.

Current entry and selection stages: the police

Accurately describe the current entry and selection stages for a given public service (and) explain the reason for the different selection tests in a given public service.

Police forces in England and Wales recruit to a standard pattern – but with slight variations from force to force. A good example of the standard pattern is the following one from Cheshire Constabulary.

FOCUS

Probationer Recruitment Process

Stage 1 Receipt of application
Stage 2 Paper sift selection of best candidates based upon eligibility and evidence provided on application forms
Stage 3 Written entrance examination and physical fitness test
Stage 4 One-day assessment
Stage 5 Background enquiries and checking of references
Stage 6 Two-day extended assessment at Dovey
Stage 7 Medical examination and uniform fitting
Stage 8 Formal acceptance (issuing of joining instructions)

You will be informed at each stage whether your application is to be progressed further. From stage 3 onwards, we will give you a specific time period within which you will be notified of your results. Due to the high volume of applications, we are unable to deal with general telephone enquiries about the progress of your application except in exceptional circumstances. Due to the high level of interest in joining the police service and the selection procedures employed, it may be several months before some candidates complete the selection process. The Constabulary only recruits during specific campaigns. Please check the vacancy section for latest details.

ANALYSIS

Stage 1: application

From the point of view of the applicant, the entry procedure begins with the first contact. This is when you telephone the police force of your choice and ask them to send you an application form, and any other information about the job.

THINK ABOUT IT ...

It may be a good idea to have an informal chat with somebody in recruitment at this stage, especially if there is anything about applying to the police which you feel unsure about.

What questions would you ask – before you even start?

Letter

It is possible that the force will ask you to write in for your form. If so, your letter should be like this:

13 Kennel Road
Dogley
West Yorkshire
PK9 9OK

12 October 2001

Recruitment
Essex Police
PO Box 2
Springfield
Chelmsford
Essex CM2 6DA

Dear Sir or Madam

Request for application form (police constable)

Could you please send me an application form and any other information relating to the vacancies for police constables which you advertised in the Chelmsford Echo on 11 October 2001.

Yours faithfully

B Eagle

There is no need to give any more information at this stage.

Preliminary application form

Some forces ask you to send in a preliminary application form before you get the full one. A typical preliminary form asks for the following information:

- what post you are applying for
- surname
- forename
- address
- telephone number(s)
- date and place of birth
- occupation
- convictions/cautions
- summons/court action for debt
- illness/disability/injury
- previous application to this or any other force
- ethnic origin 'for purposes of monitoring only'.

Full application form

Whether you write a letter or fill in a preliminary application form, you should get your full form within the week. It is of the utmost importance that you fill in this form to the very highest standard. If it isn't good enough, the police will reject you at this stage.

The form must be fully completed and sent off to the police before the date given on the covering letter. A late application is not an application at all. It is a piece of waste paper with a stamp on it.

There is more information about application forms and how to fill them in on pages 33–37 below.

Reasons for stage 1

The full application form will tell the police a great deal about you. If your literacy is not at the level they want, they will know. The form is filled in in your own handwriting, and handwriting is very revealing of a person's character and ability. In addition, when they get all the forms together, they will have a general impression of the quality of applicants. Police entry requirements are not fixed, so if they have many high quality applicants and only a few vacancies, they will be able to be more choosy, and make their requirements higher.

Stage 2: 'paper sift'

This means that police recruitment study your application form closely, to see if there is anything which they don't like. If the form is scruffy and badly written, or if it appears to have been written by someone else, such as your tutor, or the local vicar, they will not waste any more time on it. Equally, if it contains weird gaps in your life history, when you might have been fighting as a mercenary in East Timor, or cooling your heels in 'Doncatraz', it will take a one-way trip into the waste-bin. And if the autobiography section is boring, showing that you have never done anything except collect fossils, they will suggest that you apply to the museums service instead of the police service.

In particular they will check their national records to see if you have any criminal convictions. Such convictions will not necessarily disqualify you – but you must be honest about them. If you have a skeleton in the cupboard the police will find it! Where nationality is concerned, you have to be 'a British citizen, a Commonwealth citizen with unrestricted right of residence in the UK, or a citizen of the Irish Republic': this is for 'reasons of security'. If you live in licensed premises, which usually means a pub, you have to move out before you apply, otherwise they will turn you down because – in their words – there is 'a conflict of interest'. And if you are disabled, or have a history of serious illness, such as epilepsy, you will also be unable to join the police as a constable, however brilliant you are on paper. On the other hand, they may suggest that you apply for a civilian job with the police instead. Bad eyesight or hearing would stop you from being a copper, but you might still be able to be a forensic scientist!

Sifting means sorting, and if they have sorted through your form and are happy with it, you will go on to the next stage.

Reasons for stage 2

Recruiting is expensive, and training is even more expensive. The police save money and time by 'weeding out' unsuitable applicants at the earliest possible stage.

Stage 3: written entrance examination

The written entrance examination is often called the PIRT (Police Initial Recruitment Test). It is a paper and pencil test, where you sit down under examination conditions in a room of their choice, and work like stink for about an hour and a half. The style of this test is exactly the same whichever police force you apply for.

It consists of five sections, as shown in the following table.

Sections of the PIRT

Section	Time allowed
1 Verbal usage	12 mins
2 Checking test	8 mins
3 Working with numbers	12 mins
4 Verbal reasoning	25 mins
5 Observation test	20 mins

The Police Initial Recruitment Test is not publicly available, but police forces do put out a sheet of samples so that applicants know roughly what to expect. These are obtainable on demand from all recruiting police forces.

The PIRT has remained much the same since 1991. A new millennium may mean a new PIRT – nothing lasts for ever! It is wise to keep your ear to the ground and – perhaps by questioning recently appointed police constables, or your tutor – find out if there are any major changes.

The verbal usage test contains 30 questions like this one, in which you are required to circle the most appropriate letter:

4 Drink-driving campaigns . . . . a significant . . . . on the way people drive around Christmas.

A	B	C	D	E
is	make	have	play	None of these
	affect	affect	effect	effect

Such questions are designed to show a good working knowledge of grammar and spelling.

The checking test contains questions like this:

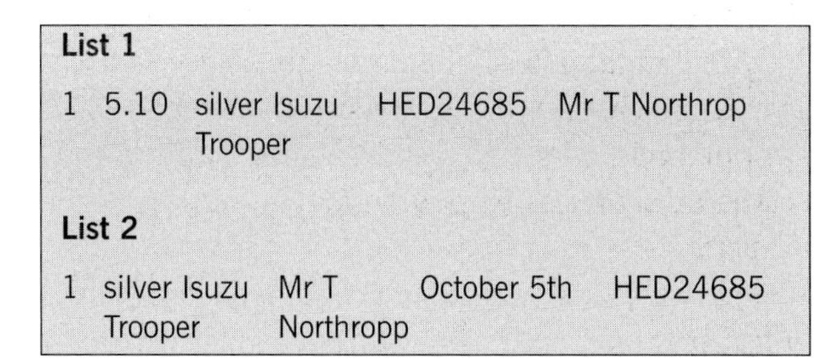

List 1

1 5.10 silver Isuzu Trooper HED24685 Mr T Northrop

List 2

1 silver Isuzu Trooper Mr T Northropp October 5th HED24685

You are expected to note the differences between list 1 and 2 on an answer sheet. The aim of the test is to show whether you can check information accurately and at speed. There are 30 questions to be done in eight minutes.

Here is a question of the type you will find in the working with numbers test:

6 If, in your local area, there is an average of 15 arrests for drinking and driving per week, how many would you expect in 4 weeks?

A	B	C	D	E
15	30	65	60	50

In this test there are 30 questions to be done in 12 minutes.

The questions in the verbal reasoning test are longer, and are based on information given. From the information you have to decide whether certain other statements are true or false – or whether it is impossible to say.

Finally there is an observation test in which you look at a number of short video clips. You are then asked to remember details from those clips. For example the clip might show a number of youths getting into a car. You might be asked afterwards what the youths were wearing.

Stage 3: physical fitness test

The physical fitness test is carried out in a gym, using standard equipment. The items in the test are as follows.

- Test 1 – estimation of body fat percentage (using callipers to measure the thickness of the fat under the skin and then, by using tables, getting an idea of the percentage of the applicant's body weight which is made up of fat).
- Test 2 – measure of grip strength using a dynamometer to measure how strong the applicant's hands are. Applicants squeeze the dynamometer as hard as they can, and it gives a reading.
- Test 3 – flexibility (can you touch your toes, or scratch that spot on your back?)
- Test 4 – press ups (maximum in one minute). (Tests arm and shoulder strength in relation to body weight.)
- Test 5 – sit ups (maximum in one minute). (Tests thigh and stomach muscles.)
- Test 6 – standing long jump (tests leg strength in relation to body weight).
- Test 7 – endurance test.

The endurance test consists of a 'bleep test', where you run backwards and forwards at increasing speed between two lines on the floor. These tests are described more fully on page 43.

Reasons for stage 3

The PIRT gives a basic indication of whether the applicant has the kind of active intelligence which is needed in the police force. It does not test what you already know, so much as whether or not you are capable of learning.

Many of the questions have a police slant, so indirectly it also tests your interest in the police as a career.

The fitness test is used because police officers need to be physically strong and fit. In the old days it was said that a 'policeman' should be able to overpower two ordinary men in a 'fair fight'. And it is still true that police officers should be able to defend themselves against hostile members of the public. Equally important is the ability to run to safety if necessary – police officers don't always have to be heroes! Perhaps more important than both these points is the fact that police officers have a demanding and tiring job, and they need the strength and stamina simply to keep going, and to function effectively even at the end of a long shift.

Stage 4: assessment

This is a one-day assessment carried out at a centre used by the police. These assessments vary from force to force, and may include:

- spelling tests
- tests involving the processing of information: for example you may be asked to look at three differing accounts of a road accident, and, using them, write your own account of what probably happened
- 'carousel' type tests.

Carousel tests are role-plays in which you are confronted with a situation. For example, in one scenario you might see somebody lying down on the floor of the bus station. What would you do – not as a police officer, but as a sensible and concerned member of the public? You are observed and assessed on the way in which you role-play these situations.

Reasons for stage 4

These tests are a practical extension of the PIRT. They look at how you might function in a real-life situation, rather than in an examination room. This is because different people have different types of intelligence, and the police take a 'holistic', all-round, view of intelligence – they are not just looking for one kind. Thus it might be that an applicant who is borderline on the verbal usage test is brilliant when faced with a practical, human challenge. Someone else who is slow on the checking test might be excellent when it comes to comparing more complex information of the kind found in differing witness statements. Spelling tests may be included because the multiple choice format of the PIRT does not allow this skill to be assessed properly. In any event, these tests give a clearer and fuller indication of how the applicant's mind works in solving a range of realistic problems.

Stage 5: checking

Background enquiries are now made and your references checked.This stage involves a detailed, and sometimes slow, investigation of your family, personal and educational background. Claims that you have made on your application forms are checked if they haven't been checked already. If you have relatives with criminal records, or who are in prison, your closeness to them is investigated, and if it seems your links are too close, your application may fail at this point.

Reasons for stage 5

Criminals or people with close criminal connections could have a real career boost if they infiltrated the police. It is of vital importance that the police only recruit people whose first loyalty is to preventing and fighting crime, and who they can always trust to put the police first. Both the police and criminals make their living out of crime – but not in the same way!

Stage 6: two-day extended assessment

This is a residential assessment, where you will be kept under lengthy observation. You may do some tests like those described under stage 4 above, and others which look more closely at your attitudes, relationships with others, beliefs and temperament. You will be with other recruits, and your reactions to them will be studied and assessed. The police will want to know, for example, whether you are a 'leader' or a 'follower', whether you relate easily to people from different backgrounds, whether you are a good listener, whether you are calm or easily rattled – and so on.

You will also have a thorough interview at this stage, in which your views and approach to the police will be probed in detail. In particular your motivation and interest in policing will be examined – both through your feelings about the job, and the knowledge you have already gathered about it.

Reasons for stage 6

Police officers work closely together in teams, on long shifts. There is no point in having someone brilliant on the team, if everyone hates their guts. A nice chatty person may turn out to be a 'motormouth' once they get in the force, while an applicant who seems open and honest may be too open, and unable to keep secrets once they are policing the community. A born leader may turn out to be a born bully, and a good listener may be a lazy daydreamer who pretends to listen and doesn't take any of it in. In addition, the police need to find out if any of their new recruits are likely to be racist, sexist or homophobic – for prejudiced officers have no place in a modern police force. To avoid recruiting the wrong people, the police try to get an in-depth understanding of their applicants at this stage.

Stage 7: medical examination

The police, like other public services, give candidates a thorough medical examination once the time for acceptance comes near. Health factors they will be particularly interested in include: asthma, epilepsy, any history of mental illness or phobias, allergies, any serious injuries or operations, colour-blindness, eyesight and hearing. (The police are happy to discuss their health requirements at the outset of the application procedure, so most candidates who reach the medical examination will already be confident that their health is up to police standards.)

If you pass the medical, having passed every other stage, the Cheshire Constabulary will accept you and fit you for your uniform.

Reasons for stage 7

Police officers need good health. If they keep taking sick leave their work and their colleagues suffer. Public service requires people who are dependable, and nobody can be dependable if their health is poor. Furthermore, officers themselves may be at risk if they have asthma, epilepsy or some other serious condition.

Completing an application: the police

Complete an application form, letter of application and CV for a job in a given public service.

The police application form is long and complex. At the time of writing it comes in two parts: the preliminary form and the supplementary form.

The preliminary form

The sections in the preliminary form are:

1 Details of candidate – name, address, phone numbers, age, nationality.
2 Education – (a) name and address of school, college, university; (b) all examination results.
3 Particulars of any application to or service in a police force (this includes constables, cadets, specials and civilian staff – and refers both to current applications and previous police employment. The police do not allow multiple applications.)
4 Employment history – (a) past jobs: addresses, nature of job, dates starting and leaving and reason for leaving; (b) present employer.
5 Voluntary/community work.
6 Achievements – anything you feel proud of which you think could help you in your application.
7 Why you wish to join the police service and, in particular, the force to which you are applying. (This is an important question, and you are given two and a half pages in the form to answer it. Deep thought needs to be given to this – though an outline of possible reasons is given on page 35.)
8 Health – (a) medical conditions which might affect your performance as a police officer; (b) eyesight (standards vary from force to force).
9 Convictions/cautions – (a) in the past; (b) at present. (There is a warning in this section: 'If you have been convicted or cautioned you may still be eligible for appointment depending on the nature and circumstances of the offence. However, failure to disclose details could count against you.')
10 Continuation – spaces for longer answers to earlier questions where required.
11 Equal opportunity statement – the statement is followed by gender and ethnic monitoring questions.

12 Declaration – 'that all the statements I have made in this application are true to the best of my knowledge and belief'. You sign this.

At the end of the form it says, 'The Chief Officer retains the right to reject any application without giving a reason.'

The supplementary form

The sections in the supplementary form are:

1 Previous addresses of applicant.
2 Referees (two people – not police officers and not related to you).
3 Additional skills – (a) driving licence; (b) other languages; (c) swimming; (d) first aid certificates.
4 Financial position – (a) Are you in arrears of any loan or account? (b) Is there now, or has there previously been, any court action taken against you for any debt or has a court/tribunal judgement been made against you?
5 Family details – (a) parents' names at birth, date of birth, place of birth, nationality at birth, nationality now, address, occupation. Similar questions are asked for brothers, sisters, husbands, wives, cohabitee, spouse's/partner's parents, children and stepchildren.
6 Continuation – space for longer answers.
7 Declaration.

Checklist

Here is a checklist of the things you need to remember when you are filling in police preliminary application forms.

- Make sure you understand what each question is getting at.
- Follow the instructions about handwriting, black ink and capital letters, and make sure that everything you write is neat and easily readable.
- Don't leave any gaps, and make sure that all dates, names and addresses are correct.
- In section 2 be accurate about your examination results.
- In section 4 be accurate about your employment. Include work placements if appropriate. Remember to put in your main duties – especially those which show that you can deal effectively with the public, or that you can be trusted.
- In section 5, any voluntary or community work will show that you are a responsible and caring person – so put it in!
- When you are writing about your achievements in section 6, focus on those which show your strength of character, ability to overcome difficulties, courage, quickness of thought and desire to help other people. Ideally you should have three or four achievements of different kinds.

Section 7

For section 7 possible answers might include:

- You want an interesting and varied job (career) which makes the most of your abilities.
- You wish to do something useful with your life, and preventing and fighting crime are very useful.
- You enjoy working with people and feel you can be a good influence on them.
- You feel you are a good team player.
- You also enjoy working on your own and using your initiative.
- You are interested in people and how they behave.
- You want an active job which is not tied to a desk.
- You enjoy solving problems.
- You want to do a job which will help to make the world a better place.
- You have always wanted to be a police officer (even when you were young, and were not sure why you liked the idea of the police).
- You want a career which has prospects and which offers adequate pay.
- You have friends or relatives whom you admire, and who are in the police.

THINK ABOUT IT ...

Are there any more?

Still on section 7, you need to say why you wish to join 'the force to which you are applying'.

Possible answers here include:

- You believe the force is a good, progressive one, which will give you an excellent grounding in the skills and knowledge of policing.
- The area covered by the force is diverse socially and ethnically, and will be an interesting area in which to work.
- You have read something about the force in *Police Review* (or any other appropriate place).
- You wish to move away from home, and would value the challenge of policing in (say) London or the West Midlands.
- If you have personal reasons such as 'it's not too far from my family', these should not be stated as the main reasons (even though, in your own mind, they might be).

Section 8

Be honest about your health. Remember you can always ask the advice of the recruiting section before you fill in your form.

Sections 9 and 10

- Be honest about convictions and cautions in section 9. You may not be rejected if you have done something wrong in the past. But you will certainly be rejected if you try to hide the fact.
- The continuation, section 10, is there to be used. You may have a good deal to say in Section 7, for instance, so don't be afraid to use this extra space.
- Write each section in rough, or on a photocopy of the form, before you write it out in the real form.

- Don't be too modest, and don't be big-headed.
- Give reasons, explanations or evidence for what you say or think.
- Put in things which show your interest in a police career, and your suitability for it. Remember that the police are looking for qualities such as reliability, maturity, honesty, intelligence, an interest in people and society, an open mind, initiative, teamwork ability, thoughtfulness, unselfishness, independence and a spirit of adventure.
- Get someone to look at your rough answers and check spelling, grammar and other points.

Points to be aware of for the supplementary form include:

- Section 1 – leave no gaps
- Section 2 – try to choose referees who have known you for at least two years, and ask their permission before you use their names
- Section 3 – all these are useful skills!
- Section 4 – be accurate

FOCUS

Some police forces also use a self-appraisal form. This asks questions similar to those you might be asked in the interview. The questions include:

1 What do you think will be the most interesting and challenging aspects of police work?

2 What personal qualities do you possess which will make you a successful police officer?

3 What difficulties do you think you will have to overcome in adjusting to life in the police service?

4 What characteristics in yourself do you think other people find unattractive?

5 What qualities in yourself do you think are admired by people you know?

6 What, so far, has been the high spot or low spot in your life?

7 List any qualifications or awards you hold relating to spare time activities, including details of any voluntary work carried out. Please give some details of not just 'reading' but the kind of books you read; not just 'sport' but the actual games you play and the extent of your involvement.

8 A police officer needs to be sensitive to the needs of others, being unselfish and willing to help any member of the general public. Give examples of where you have shown understanding and helped others.

9 A police officer needs to be punctual, reliable and to have high standards of honesty and integrity. Give an example of how you have displayed each of the above, in either a work situation, or a position of responsibility.

10 The majority of police officers work a rota of ten-hour shifts. (This obviously disrupts normal social activities.) How do you think this will affect you?

11 If you have a partner, have you discussed this application with them considering the possible effects? How will you deal with this?

12 Once accepted to be a police officer you can be posted anywhere in the area, and this may mean moving house or leaving home. Do you have any experience of this?

13 In the course of your work you will be called upon to talk to an extremely wide range of individuals. Obviously some situations will be easier to deal with than others. Below we have 12 types of individual you may come across. Rate them in a scale of 1–10, 1 being easy to deal with and 10 being hard.

prostitutes	physically abused	drug addicts	sex offenders
the mentally ill	juveniles	flea-ridden tramps	the elderly
bereaved families	civilian staff	sexually abused	superior ranks

14 During your service how often do you think you will be assaulted each year? Twice; three times; more; no idea.

15 What are your long-term career plans? Do you want promotion? If you were still a constable at the end of your service would you feel that your career had been a success?

- Section 5 – again, be accurate: the police will be able to check most of what you write.

Covering letter

Together with your completed forms you should enclose a covering letter. It ought to be something like the one on the right.

13 Kennel Road
Dogley
West Yorkshire
PK9 9OK

19 October 2001

Mr A Iredale
Recruitment
Essex Police
PO Box 2
Springfield
Chelmsford
Essex CM2 6DA

Dear Mr Iredale

Thank you very much for the application forms you sent me for the post of police constable.

I am now returning these, completed, together with a stamped, addressed postcard for your acknowledgement.

I look forward to hearing from you.

Yours sincerely

Brenda Eagle (Miss)

THINK ABOUT IT ...

Why do the police ask you to fill in their application forms in your own handwriting?

Make sure you have a good CV on disk – in case you need one!

Unit outcome 2
Investigate interview and related selection procedures for a given public service

Assessment criteria

- Practise interview techniques and selection tests for a given public service.
- Evaluate personal strengths and weaknesses in relation to the different stages of the selection procedures.
- Produce a detailed plan in order to improve own performance in selection tests.

Interviews and selection tests

Some people say, 'I can't do interviews. I never do well in them: I'm just no good at them.'

They have got it wrong. There is no such thing as a bad interviewee – there are only bad interviews. If you want to join the public services you should never label yourself as a 'bad interviewee'. If you do, you are just shooting yourself in the foot. Far better to study this unit – and become good at interviews!

We are going to look in detail at police interviews and selection in this section. But if you are not interested in the police, don't be put off. When it comes to interviews and selection, all the public services are looking for much the same things. And all public service interviews and selection processes have many more similarities than differences.

An interview is a kind of examination. So there is no escape: you have to prepare for it! But if you are well prepared, you can hardly go wrong.

You should start preparing for an interview as soon as you know you are going to have one. And if you really want to succeed your preparations should be very thorough, and should come under three headings: mental, emotional and physical. Each of these is extremely important, and we will now look at them separately.

Mental preparation

You must prepare yourself mentally for the interview.

1 Learn as much as you can about the organisation you are applying for. If, say, you are applying for the Cumbria police, get hold of the chief constable's annual report, and the policing plan for this year – or next. These are booklets, each about 50 pages long, and packed with useful facts and ideas about policing in Cumbria. A good applicant will swot up these booklets to find out such things as, who the chief constable is, what the main types of crime are, crime trends, who sits on the police authority, what the police think of as their priorities and why – and so on. If you don't come from Cumbria get a map of the place so that you know where the main towns are. As it is a mainly rural area, think about the special challenges of rural policing, and learn something about the problems of rural society. Why do farmers have such a high suicide rate? What kinds of crime are connected with tourism? What do young people do when it appears to you that there is nothing for them to do except look at sheep? What links do Cumbria police have with the mountain rescue services?

2 Think about yourself and the special qualities you have to offer. If you're keen on driving – good. Cumbria is a big area compared with that covered by most police forces. You have some experience of living in the country? Excellent! The tradition of Cumbria is a tradition of rural life, and if you can relate to that tradition it will help you to fit in and see the community with clear eyes. You like rock climbing? Good again, but the panel will hope that that is not the only reason why you're applying for a job in Cumbria. You're adaptable? That's very good, because the area is varied: there are some industrial towns as well as wide open spaces, and some places which are very poor, while others are very affluent. If you're adaptable then you can cope with variety – and you'll get plenty of that.

These qualities that you've got: driving skills, honesty, adaptability, a good understanding of different types of people, an interest in rock climbing – they're all positive qualities. But it's not enough to sit down at an interview and say, 'Well, I'm the person you want because I'm very adaptable!' You need to have evidence that you are adaptable. If you're being interviewed by police officers they won't just take your word for it. How are you going to be able to prove to them that you are adaptable?

3 Prepare evidence of your qualities. Evidence at an interview can take many forms. These include certificates, reports and records of achievement. Also useful are testimonials from people who know you (though these are not as good as the evidence that the employers get from a confidential reference, from the referees you have named on your application form). (Note: Testimonials are written statements beginning 'To Whom it may Concern' which you see. Confidential references are filled in secretly by your referee and sent off in the post.)

Newspaper cuttings are a good form of evidence if you have them: 'Public Service student saves tutor from mad dog attack'. You could also have ready some stories or examples that you can tell the interviewers to prove that you are the kind of person you say you are. If you are claiming to be adaptable, you could say, for example, that when you were on work placement you were once asked to translate, at short notice, for someone who could speak no English. Or perhaps you organised an outing for a youth club where everything went wrong but, thanks to your resourcefulness, everybody still had a great time.

4 Think about the questions you might be asked and think about the answers you will give. Then write down both the expected questions and the answers you will give.

Below is an example of expected questions and answers prepared in writing.

These are not meant to be perfect answers, but they illustrate two important points:

- the good qualities are genuinely relevant to the career (police work) being applied for
- the bad qualities are not very bad, and, looked at a little differently, they could be good qualities – being 'a soft touch' is almost the same thing as being generous (which is a good quality), and is related to the interviewee's interest in people.

THINK ABOUT IT ...

Invent some more likely interview questions for the public service of your choice. Then jot down, as fully as you can, what your answers would be. Having done this, show them to a friend or teacher to get their comments.

Sample interview questions and answers

Expected question	Possible answer
What do you think your strengths would be as a police officer?	I think I'm inquisitive about people and I tend to notice what they do – especially if they do something which is a bit out of the ordinary. In fact I got into the newspaper because of this. I was at Southwaite Services once, on the motorway, and I saw a dog jump out of the cab of a Spanish lorry. So I went to the checkout and asked them to ring the police, because I thought that dog might have come into the country illegally – without quarantine. It turned out that I was right, and I was mentioned in the paper as 'a vigilant member of the public'. I'm also fairly persistent. Last summer, with a few friends, I did a sponsored walk of the Pennine Way. Only three of us finished out of eight, but we raised £350 for cancer research, and had a good cheap holiday into the bargain.
What do you think your weaknesses would be as a police officer?	Because I'm interested in people I have a bad habit of chatting with anybody and everybody. The other week I went past my stop on the bus because I was talking to an old lady about her son who was in the Antarctic studying meteorites. And sometimes I'm a bit of a soft touch for a hard luck story. Somebody borrowed £10 from me the other week and I still haven't got it back!

Emotional preparation

This is a matter of getting yourself into the right emotional state for your interview. The way to do this is as follows.

1 Analyse what kind of emotional state you are in when you do something very well. Are you the kind of person who does best when they feel calm and relaxed, or do you do better when you feel excited and 'geed up'? If you do best when you are calm, practise relaxation and breathing exercises. If you do better when you feel excited, it is still a good idea to relax before the interview. Then, when the interview comes, the contrast will get your adrenalin flowing and you will make a better job of it, because you will be more alert and in a higher state of arousal.

2 Write yourself a list of everything you need to take with you to the interview.

3 Check that you know exactly when and where the interview is. If you are in any doubt, ring the interviewers to confirm everything.

4 Make sure your transport is arranged so that you get to the interview venue with at least half an hour to spare.

5 Make sure that your clothes are clean and ready, and that you have enough money with you!

FOCUS

Relaxation exercises

- Sit comfortably, close your eyes and breathe deeply and slowly for one minute – in through your nose and out through your mouth.
- Practise relaxing each muscle in your body in turn, starting with the feet and working your way up to the muscles of the face. Once you have relaxed a muscle-group, do not tense them up again until after you have relaxed all your muscles.
- Rotate your head and shoulders (as athletes sometimes do before a race), and practise other gentle stretching exercises.
- Practise meditation exercises. For example, close your eyes, clear your mind of all words, and imagine a peaceful scene, such as moonlight on a calm sea.
- Listen to music which you find calm and liberating, and think about a time when you were very happy.

Physical preparation

1 Have no late nights for a full week before the interview. And try to sleep eight hours a night. This will establish your body rhythms and ensure maximum alertness throughout the interview and selection period.

2 Eat regularly, with good balanced meals. There should be no binges and no starvation.

3 It is best to avoid alcohol, and you should on no account get drunk.

4 If you wish to join a public service you should never take any banned drug. Some of these – including cannabis – remain in the body for long periods of time, and can be detected in a drugs test or medical examination.

5 Avoid rows, quarrels and emotional outbursts. You need to focus your mind, and you don't want problems and distractions. If your friends are the type that try to use up your emotional energy, keep away from them.

Techniques for the interview itself

1 You need to be properly dressed, and presented to best advantage. So – be clean! Hair, nails, etc. should be in good condition and of an appropriate length and style. A man should wear a suit and tie, and a woman too should be dressed in a formal and businesslike way. Most public services will not accept people with visible tattoos. Any jewellery should be very restrained. Men should not wear earrings or any form of body piercing; women should not have more than one earring in each ear. You should not wear a strong scent. Men should beware of beards and moustaches. They are not banned in the public services, but there is firm psychological evidence that they rub other bearded and moustached men up the wrong way!

2 Greet your interviewers with a handshake and a smile. Handshakes are worth practising. You don't want to hold out a wet fish (many young people do this and it suggests immaturity to an interviewer). But at the same time you don't want to put the interviewer's hand in plaster.

3 Make eye contact with your interviewers. Follow the guidelines in the next paragraph if you feel uneasy about it.

Because it is a problem area in many relationships, psychologists have studied eye contact in some detail. They have discovered that, in Western society, in a one-to-one conversation, it is normal for the listener to make more eye contact than the speaker. On average the listener looks at the speaker's eyes 39 per cent of the time. But the speaker only looks at the listener's eyes for 17 per cent of the time.

4 Sit up straight and, in general, keep your hands clasped in your lap – and away from your face. This way you will look alert without seeming over-anxious. Avoid facial mannerisms such as biting your lips or frowning unnecessarily.

5 Speak clearly and avoid using slang. Have confidence in yourself – the fact that you have been invited to the interview means that the interviewers have some faith in you. Make sure you speak up – a surprising number of older people are slightly deaf! Feel free to smile, but don't smile for no reason, and resist the temptation to laugh uncontrollably. Generally, be yourself and have confidence in your own ability.

6 All being well you will have predicted the questions and prepared your answers for them. If you are not sure of an answer, say something like, 'I'm not sure about this, but what I would probably do ... ' If you are quite certain you don't know the answer, admit it honestly by saying, 'I'm sorry; I don't know the answer to that.'

7 If you have said all you have to say on a question, stop talking. It is the interviewer's job to fill any awkward silences – not yours. Besides, some people don't like working with chatterboxes.

8 The interviewers want to know about your knowledge and your ideas. But they need to know about your personality as well. If they ask you a difficult question in a formal interview, they may want to know whether you will get rattled by the question, or lose your temper. In an interview you should always keep calm and in control of yourself.

9 At the end of the interview you may be asked if you have any questions of your own. It is a good thing to have one up your sleeve – but preferably one which is not about money, holidays or working hours. When the interview is over, say something like, 'Thank you very much,' and leave. You can ask when you will hear the result of the interview, but don't make any comments about the interview itself!

What happens if you are asked a really annoying question – perhaps one which is racist or sexist? There is no easy answer. But the following might be helpful:

(a) Make a mental note of what the question was, and why it annoyed you.
(b) If you still want the job, answer it calmly and hope that it was just a mistake on the interviewer's part.
(c) If, perhaps, the aim of the question was to test your own attitudes on race or sex, give an answer which makes it clear that you are not racist or sexist.
(d) You may be tempted to walk out of the interview. But remember that, whatever happens, you have done nothing wrong. In any event, keep your dignity.
(e) **Never make jokes about race or sex during any part of the assessment process.**

Selection tests

For many people interviews are the most frightening part of getting into the police or any other public service. But remember that public service selection is more than just an interview, and you are kept under observation by your prospective employers all the time! In these circumstances they will be making judgements about your character, personality, ability and general fitness for the job, whatever you are doing. So, for example, if, at some part of the fitness test, you say, 'I can't be arsed to do this!' it may stand against you in the overall assessment of your suitability. And it is no use doing brilliantly in the 'carousel' role-plays, if you are then rude or off-hand to the real-life tea lady. Remember that if you are spending two days at a centre for your police selection, such lapses will certainly be noticed.

The same comments apply in your relationship to your fellow recruits. Some applicants think they will impress the selectors if they conduct a kind of psychological warfare against the other applicants, in order to look better than them. These tactics will backfire. If you try to make yourself look good, by making someone else look a fool, you will be the fool in the eyes of the selectors. Selectors and interviewers will study the way you and the other potential recruits interact, because that points the way to how you – and they – will interact if you are accepted into the service.

Your strengths and weaknesses

Evaluate personal strengths and weaknesses in relation to the different stages of the selection procedures.

Evaluate means:
- identify, then
- assess the importance of.

Here is a specimen evaluation of personal strengths and weaknesses for Jo, an imaginary applicant.

- Stage 1: Receipt of application
- Stage 2: Paper sift – the selection of the best candidates is based upon eligibility and evidence provided on application forms (see above)
- Stage 3: Written examination and physical fitness test
- Stage 4: One-day assessment
- Stage 5: Background enquiries and checking of references
- Stage 6: Two-day extended assessment
- Stage 7: Medical examination and uniform fitting
- Stage 8: Formal acceptance – at this stage you will be issued with joining instructions.

Jo's evaluation of stages 1, 3, 4, 5, 6 and 7 are given in the following tables.

Stage 1: Receipt of application

Strengths	Weaknesses
1 **Neat handwriting** Easy to read. Shows an orderly mind. Shows commitment to the application and a serious interest in the job.	1 **Poor handwriting** Illegible. May show an ill-organised mind, or lack of real interest in the application and the job. May give the impression that I do not have the ability needed.
2 **Good spelling** Shows a perfectionist approach. Suggests academic ability; shows that I can learn effectively. Implies a general accuracy and carefulness in what I do.	2 **Poor spelling** This will be a problem, since there is a spelling test at a later stage. It gives a bad impression; they will think I am careless or not clever.

Cont'd

3 Good grammar Sentences well organised and punctuated. This means I can express myself clearly and convey complex ideas without confusing the reader. Useful in taking statements and writing reports.	**3 Poor grammar** This may give the impression that I can't think straight. I have never understood commas and full stops. I wish I'd paid more attention at school!
4 Accurate, relevant information Shows a well-organised person who has a respect for the truth (essential for police work!). Shows that I can distinguish between important and unimportant facts.	**4 Lack of accurate information** Police work consists of gathering information, and if I can't do it for the application form, how am I going to be able to do it as part of the job?
5 Knowledge about the force This shows my research skills, my enthusiasm and my commitment to joining the Loamshire Constabulary.	**5 Lack of knowledge about the force** Again, I should have spent more time doing research. I should have written to Loamshire Police Authority, or asked my tutor for help!

Stage 3: Written examination and physical fitness test

Strengths	Weaknesses
1 PIRT verbal usage Good grammar and spelling. Suggests I can produce good paperwork – a useful ability in the police. Of course what you write is important, as well as how you write it.	**1 PIRT verbal usage** Poor grammar and spelling will give a poor impression to the public and to other police officers. They suggest lack of ability.
2 PIRT checking test Accurate checking at speed shows that I will be efficient at some key police tasks. I will not be the 'Mr Plod' type of officer who is always making simple mistakes.	**2 PIRT checking test** Slow or inaccurate checking means I will have difficulty in spotting errors or discrepancies in statements, computer printouts, etc. This will make me less effective as a police officer.
3 PIRT working with number Good performance means I can do calculations in my head. An understanding of figures will help me handle theft cases – and official statistics.	**3 PIRT working with number** Poor performance means I will give an impression of stupidity, if other officers can work sums out in their heads and I can't. The police may not even trust me to handle money!
4 PIRT verbal reasoning A good score means I can think logically and see how one fact relates to another. I can also tell the difference between fact and opinion – which is essential when I am assessing evidence.	**4 PIRT verbal reasoning** A poor score means I am a muddled thinker. I cannot argue my way out of a paper bag. Either that, or I panicked in the test.
5 PIRT observation test A good performance means I have a keen eye and a good memory for the kind of details which count in police work.	**5 PIRT observation test** A poor performance suggests that I may miss important details at a crime scene, and that I will be a poor witness in court.

Cont'd

Strengths	Weaknesses
6 Physical test Good score on bleep test = good stamina. Good score on press-ups = good upper body strength. Good score on sit-ups = strength and flexibility. Optimum body fat percentage = I am the right weight for my height, and in good physical shape. Strong grip = useful in arresting people! I will be effective in the physical side of policing.	**6 Physical test** Poor scores in some or all of these abilities mean that I will be less effective in an emergency – for example, chasing a suspect or rescuing somebody. I may also lack the stamina for long, gruelling shifts.

Stage 4: One-day assessment

Strengths	Weaknesses
1 Carousel role-plays A good performance shows I can think quickly and clearly in an emergency and that I have good powers of reasoning and common sense. Even if I do not know exactly what the police would do in these situations, I have shown that I could easily learn, because I have a good foundation: that I care for other people and have a responsible attitude towards their problems and concerns. I don't just 'walk on by'.	**1 Carousel role-plays** A poor performance may show: a tendency to panic; possible lack of common sense; that I haven't thought enough about my responsibilities in relation to other people and their problems; I am naive and lack experience of life.
2 A good self-evaluation after the Carousel role-plays shows that I am capable of thinking about my actions and analysing them without bias. I do not try to pretend that I am better than I am, nor do I suffer from false modesty. It also shows that I am capable of learning from my mistakes, and building on the things I am good at. Finally, it shows that I can put my thoughts into a logical sequence, and tell the difference between fact and opinion.	**2** A poor self-evaluation after the Carousel role-plays shows that: I lack insight into my own behaviour, and may therefore not be mature enough to be a police officer; I lack the courage to confront what I am really like; I may have difficulty in expressing abstract ideas – for example, about social conscience or initiative.
3 My ability to read conflicting witness-type statements and make some sort of sense of them shows that: I can think clearly; I can solve problems; I notice discrepancies or lies in people's statements; I can 'see the wood for the trees'; in other words I can tell the difference between what is important and what is not; I can write a clear statement myself, using the mixed-up information I have been given.	**3** My inability to read conflicting witness-type statements and make good sense of them shows that: my own thinking could be muddled; I lack problem-solving skills; I dislike doing exercises that remind me of school 'comprehensions' in English; I have difficulty in deciding what is important and what is trivial; I am not good at expressing myself clearly and confidently on paper.

Cont'd

4 My ability to recognise wrong spellings means: I will be able to check my own written work for errors; I am a perfectionist who likes to get things right, and am able to do so; I have an interest in language (this suggests an awareness of the underlying meanings of words, which is often important in police work).	**4** My inability to recognise wrong spellings may mean that I do not do enough reading; I am poor at spelling and/or I have difficulty in concentrating on activities which I find boring or pointless.

Stage 5: Background enquiries and checking of references

Strengths	**Weaknesses**[1]
My background is suitable for police work. I have no close criminal connections; I have never been bankrupt; I have no criminal record; I do not live in licensed premises (i.e. in a pub). All these factors will help me to resist bribery, corruption and law-breaking if I join the police. I have never taken part in extremist political activity, such as National Front marches.	**1** I am worried that my parents run a hotel – which means I live in licensed premises. **2** I have taken part in two animal rights marches in the past year.[2] I didn't throw anything, but I was carrying a banner and have probably been photographed.

1 Other weaknesses could be: that a family member or close friend is a convicted criminal, that Jo has been bankrupt or is in debt or that she has a criminal record herself (and the crime is recent, serious or 'premeditated').
2 Political extremism may count against her if it shows that she is prepared to break the law for her beliefs.
Political activities will also count against her if they show that she does not have an open-minded view on such issues as race, gender, sexual orientation or poverty.

Stage 6: Two-day extended assessment

Strengths[1]	**Weaknesses**[2]
1 I show that I can relate well to a variety of people.	**1** I find that I have difficulties relating to people.
2 People trust and respect me, and listen to what I have to say.	**2** People seem not to trust and respect me, and ignore or reject what I have to say.
3 I am polite, but I also know how to be honest and assert myself.	**3** I was not always polite, and I had difficulty being honest and asserting myself.
4 I have the courage to speak to groups and individuals I have never met before, on a range of subjects, both familiar and unfamiliar.	**4** I was unable to talk well to groups or individuals. I felt silly talking about certain subjects.
5 I am clean, well-organised and moderate in my behaviour.	**5** After one night my bedroom was a pigsty.

Cont'd

6 I am enthusiastic and will have a go at things I have not done before.	**6** I didn't like having to do all those 'stupid things'.
7 I did well in the formal interview. I was well prepared and I made a good impression.	**7** I messed up in the formal interview. I was not well prepared and I made a poor impression.

1 Statements in this column show a mature, confident approach to people, and an ability to make the best of unfamiliar situations – both qualities needed in the police.

2 Statements in this column show that I probably lack the social skills (at the moment) for joining the police, and that even if they accepted me, I would not be happy in the job.

Stage 7: Medical examination and uniform fitting

Strengths	**Weaknesses**
Near perfect health – which is needed for police work as it is difficult and demanding.	Failed medical (fallen arches; damaged left elbow).
Uniform fits.	I don't know if the uniform fits or not, because I have failed the medical.

Action planning

Produce a detailed plan in order to improve own performance in selection tests.

You have probably done action planning before. It is the sort of thing we are always doing in our heads anyway, but for something as important as a career you should write your action plan down. It will probably look something like Jo's, given in the table below.

Assume that Jo, who was assessing herself in the tables above, wishes to join the police two years from now. This means that she has plenty of time to improve her performance in various selection tests. Here is her 'detailed plan'.

Stage, selection test or activity	Weakness identified	Action needed	By what time
Stage 1: Receipt of application Stage 2: Paper sift	(a) Scruffy handwriting.	(a) Get book on handwriting. Practise handwriting. Am I doing it too fast or slow? Get rid of time-wasting mannerisms, like circles to dot i's. Learn to join letters correctly and get my writing upright.	(a) Stick at it till I get it right.

Cont'd

	(b) Unsure of dates when I got my qualifications.	(b) Get these sorted out and write a proper CV. Put CV on disk so I can always refer to it.	(b) Discuss with Mum today! Write it down!
	(c) Had difficulty explaining in writing why I want to join the police.	(c) Think about this, and discuss it with my most helpful teacher.	(c) Try again in 1 month.
Stage 3: Written entrance examination and physical fitness test	(a) Poor performance on 'working with number'.	(a) Get a part-time job working in a checkout or newsagent's, where I have to make quick money calculations and give change. Start doing mathematical puzzles.	(a) Start looking for job tomorrow.
	(b) Low score on standing long jump.	(b) Start going to gym and work on legs. Eat less chocolate but more rice.	(b) Join gym; go 3x a week; review situation after 3 months.
Stage 4: One-day assessment	(a) 'Froze' in carousel when dealing with 'drunk'.	(a) Ask police (again!) for work shadowing; talk with Brenda – ambulance worker who lives 2 doors away.	(a) Get it done within the month.
Stage 5: Background enquiries and checking of references	(a) Jack (boyfriend) has criminal conviction for joyriding.	(a) Do I 'chuck' Jack – or what?	(a) You must be joking!
Stage 6: Two-day extended assessment at Dovey	(a) Tried to show off by using too many long words.	(a) At least I know some long words. Or should I join a youth club, and get some less 'studentish' friends?	(a) Get that job in a checkout – for at least 6 months. Kill 2 birds with 1 stone.
	(b) Got into an argument about whether HIV+ mothers should be allowed to breast-feed their babies.	(b) I was right. Frederica was just being narrow-minded, and Matt didn't know what he was talking about.	(b) Train myself not to argue with fools – no time limit.
Stage 7: Medical examination and uniform fitting	(a) My left elbow has been wonky ever since I fell off my bike at 13 and broke my arm. Seems to me it's getting more double-jointed than ever.	(a) Ask Dr Harris to check with the police whether it would be a problem.	(a) Do it next week.

Notice that Jo has set herself targets, and that they are realistic and achievable. In your own case, you should set definite dates (in the 'by what time' column) for achieving your targets.

THINK ABOUT IT ...

Think of as many reasons as you can why it is better to do this kind of planning in writing, rather than just in your head.

Write your own career action plan – and keep updating it, as you achieve each aim.

Unit outcome 3
Examine the qualities which are needed for career development within a given public service

Assessment criteria

- Briefly describe the promotional structure for a given public service.
- Evaluate in detail the qualities needed for promotion in a given public service.
- Produce a realistic action plan for career development.

Promotional structures

The promotional structure for a public service is based on the rank system. So, for example, in the police, promotion starts at constable and goes through sergeant, inspector, chief inspector, superintendent, chief superintendent (where these exist), assistant chief constable and chief constable.

All police officers, without exception, start their careers at the rank of constable.

All professional public services have a clear promotion structure. The reasons for this are as follows:

- To give the junior ranks something to aim for. In other words the promotion structure provides an incentive for good employees to stay in the service and work hard.
- To save money by reducing staff turnover. Able and ambitious young officers will leave a public service if they feel that their careers are not going anywhere. This means that the money spent on their training has been wasted.
- To reward ability and hard work.
- To ensure that those in command have first hand experience of being in a junior rank, and a deep understanding of the ethos and purpose of that public service.
- To create discipline by making it clear who leads or manages whom, and who should take responsibility for each area or type of activity.
- To provide a system for communicating information both 'up' and 'down' the organisation, so that directives can be given from above, and feedback received from below. This has the effect of unifying the service and strengthening its common purpose. At the same time (in the army for example) feedback or directives can be cut off at certain points in the structure, enabling the spread of information to

be controlled on what is called a 'need to know' basis. This allows information to be kept confidential where necessary, and helps to prevent the leaking of operational secrets to the enemy, or to criminals.

A promotion structure is a structure of rewards. The rewards take the form of money (higher salaries and pensions for those higher up the rank structure), and power (or status), which can be described as the right to tell other people what to do, and to command respect and loyalty from them. In addition, the type of work changes with promotion, becoming less 'hands-on', and involving more administration, planning and decision-making. Conditions of service are also better for those higher up the promotion structure. The chief constable, for example, gets longer holidays and does not have to work nights.

The structure is triangular. In the police there is a single person – the chief constable – at the top of the structure for any given force. Moving down the ranks there are increasing numbers of officers in each rank, with the largest number being constables, who are at the bottom of the triangle. Members of each rank are responsible to a line manager who is immediately above them, and for a number of officers in the rank immediately below them. Each team or section reflects, therefore, in its triangular promotional structure, the triangular promotional structure of the organisation as a whole.

The qualities needed for promotion

Evaluate in detail the qualities needed for promotion in a given public service.

This is a complex subject. For one thing it is difficult to define 'qualities'. But they can be described as personal or professional attributes, characteristics or styles of behaviour. They include such things as personality and the way people's minds appear to work. And they can be divided up into different types (see the table below).

The police

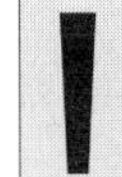

THINK ABOUT IT ...

Promotion is always one step at a time.

It is not possible to 'leapfrog' over the rank of sergeant or inspector on your way up the promotion ladder. Why is this so?

Examples of qualities

Mental	Moral	Emotional or social	Physical
Intelligence	Honesty	Calmness	Strength
Ability at problem solving	Fair-mindedness	Self-control	Beauty
Ability to think quickly	Unselfishness	Good temper	Neatness
Good with numbers	Generosity	Ability to relax	'Image'
Good command of detail	Courage	Sociability	Clothes worn
Ability to plan ahead	Determination	Friendliness	Age
Imagination	Perseverance	Moodiness	Sex
Stupidity	Tolerance	Violence	Race
Lack of subtlety	Dishonesty	Sarcasm	Height
	Deviousness	Need for respect	Weight
	Reliability	Humour	Any other aspect of
	Loyalty	Cruelty	physical appearance

1 Promotion from constable to sergeant

Here is a statement about this from a police website.

'In the police service promotion is strictly on merit and every man or woman starts at the same level with the same basic training and the same opportunities. The first step – to the rank of sergeant – is the most important one. You learn basic management principles and the proper deployment of officers and equipment. You help to make your officers efficient, weld them into an effective team, bring out their special abilities and encourage confidence and good morale. There are two stages in the promotion process. You must pass an examination in police subjects and you must be selected by your senior officers as suitable.'

This statement indicates the qualities needed for promotion from constable to sergeant.

ANALYSIS

1 Promotion is 'strictly on merit' – so you have to be good at your job. But of course it may – to some extent – be a matter of opinion what 'merit' is. People can rarely agree entirely about their colleagues – or even their classmates!

2 Sergeants need to understand 'management principles' and the 'proper deployment of officers and equipment'. They must therefore have a good understanding of how the police are organised, and must be able to make good decisions.

3 A sergeant has to lead an 'efficient', 'effective' team. Efficiency means getting the maximum result from the minimum effort or expense – in other words avoiding waste of effort or money. It requires clear, focused thinking, determination and a good sense of priorities to be efficient. 'Effective' means getting the desired result or outcome. If crime prevention is effective, then crime stops (or decreases). An effective team succeeds in what it sets out to do. So effectiveness – in other words a track record of success – is important for a constable who wishes to be promoted to sergeant. The success must not only be in the officer's mind. There must be evidence for it. Evidence is very often on paper, in the form of good reports, so a would-be sergeant must be better than average at paperwork.

4 Constables who wish to be promoted to sergeant need to have good skills with people, and be able to use a range of leadership styles. This is shown in the statement: 'bring out their [the team's] special abilities and encourage confidence and good morale'. Sergeants have to be skilled at discipline in its wider sense, which is as much a positive, motivational thing as a negative 'you do as you're told' quality.

5 These qualities in 1–4 will be mainly assessed by senior officers who, of course, appraise constables at regular intervals, checking on their progress and the development of their skills and knowledge. But in addition there is the sergeants' examination – the Objective Structured Performance-Related Examination (OSPRE) – in 'police subjects'. The applicants are tested rigorously on their knowledge of laws, procedures and police powers. The tests take the form of situations where the candidates state what they would do in that situation and why. The examination therefore tests not only their knowledge – but, more importantly, how they would apply that knowledge practically. Candidates for sergeant therefore need an excellent memory and a good practical understanding of some of the more complex aspects of police law. So these intellectual qualities are needed for constables who wish to be promoted to sergeant.

2 Promotion from sergeant to inspector

There are fewer inspectors than there are sergeants, so promotion from sergeant to inspector is much rarer than promotion from constable to sergeant.

The Lancashire Police therefore have less to say on the subject:

'The next stage is promotion to inspector. Again there are two stages of examination and selection. There are no qualifying examinations above the rank of inspector.'

ANALYSIS

The qualities needed to be promoted from sergeant to inspector include the following.

1 A successful track record as a sergeant. A person who is perceived as having done the job badly, or only to an average standard, will not be promoted.

2 High levels of efficiency and effectiveness. An inspector needs to be a good organiser, capable of making important tactical decisions.

3 An ability to relate well with 'superior' officers – which is not surprising since they play a major role in selecting new inspectors.

4 Excellent communication skills, not only with sergeants, constables, support staff and specials, but with the higher ranks too, since the inspector is a vital link between the decision-making levels of the police force, and those who carry out the decisions. In addition, inspectors have to be coherent and clear communicators with the public – and this may well include the police authority and the media who will take an interest in major cases – such as murders or large-scale frauds – for which inspectors often have responsibility. In the final analysis, this means excellent communication with the public at large. An inspector who can speak clearly on radio or television, and who can give good interviews to the press, is communicating to the wider public – the taxpayers who fund the police and trust them to look after the well-being of society.

5 The examination taken by a sergeant wishing to be promoted to inspector is more difficult and demanding than that taken by constables who wish to become sergeants. And instead of concentrating on law and policing, the inspectors' examination concentrates on management and training skills. This is because the inspector's role is largely a management role, with very little routine policing.

Promotion to chief inspector

At this level, and higher up, promotion is by appointment only. There are no exams. Chief inspectors' posts are sometimes advertised. The job is complex and the advertisements are long. Here is an extract to show you some of the abilities the job requires.

'It is essential that all post holders will have well-developed skills to motivate, question, listen, influence, negotiate, counsel and coach the divisional workforce. It is essential that all post holders will have well-developed abilities in all forms of written communication and a sound knowledge of Force administrative procedures. The ability to analyse and evaluate existing systems within the division to ensure that they are appropriate, or to recommend change where necessary to increase the level of service provided, both internally and externally. The ability to recognise the direction in which the organisation is moving and to generate supportive attitudes amongst staff by assisting the divisional commander in the identification of factors that will encourage revitalisation and in the design of appropriate objectives. Post holders should have an understanding of how annual budgets are derived and amended and should be able to develop a working knowledge of the difference between revenue and capital expenditures as well as the external influences that could restrict the scope of decisions on spending. The ability to manage all personnel irrespective of their individual conditions of service so as to engender harmony and an effective team spirit in the division.'

This is very much a job of management and coordination. It carries considerable power and influence, and the person promoted to it must have a wide range of thinking and communication skills, together with a good deal of successful policing experience in the lower ranks.

The police have an accelerated promotion scheme for graduates (APSG), but this does not mean that graduates automatically progress faster up the promotion ladder than non-graduates. They have to prove that they are suitable for promotion by doing excellent police work. At all levels promotion is strictly on merit.

The higher ranks of the police used to consist mainly of white, middle-aged males. This was because, in the past, far more men than women made policing their career, and very few people from ethnic minorities either applied or were accepted. In addition, there may well have been discrimination (perhaps unintentional) against women and people from ethnic minorities where promotion was concerned. All this has changed and there are now excellent promotion prospects, to the highest level, for women and ethnic minority officers in the police.

There is probably a political factor involved in promotion, especially where chief constables and assistant chief constables are concerned. A political extremist would have difficulties becoming chief constable (though this has not always been the case in the past). Life will be easier for high ranking police officers if they are politically in tune with the police authority for their force.

The higher the rank, the more important it is to present an acceptable face to the media. The success of Keith Hellawell, former Chief Constable of West Yorkshire, who became the 'drugs czar', owed a good deal to his skills in dealing with the media, where he showed both moderation and determination on the issue of drugs.

Planning career development

Produce a realistic action plan for career development.

Let us imagine a 16-year-old BTEC Public Service student. Her name is Emma Bovary. She has left school and is in the first term of her course at a further education college. She is sure that she wants to join the police when she is about 20, and to be promoted to at least the rank of inspector. What sort of plan should Emma make? Here is a suggestion.

She should start off by considering her present position, using a SWOT analysis. This means looking closely at her Strengths, Weaknesses, Opportunities and Threats. The following table gives a sample analysis.

Strengths	Weaknesses
• Determined to join police. • Am studying a police-orientated public service course. • Am physically healthy and fit and like sport. • Quite good at English, medium at maths, interested in psychology. • Like playing football; belong to team. • I can make friends, and people like telling me their secrets. • Have never actually set foot in a police station! (No criminal record.)	• Have never actually set foot in a police station! • Shy with strangers. • Too keen on dancing, raving, etc. • Smoking. • I get impatient with teachers who go on a lot. • I only got a D in GCSE maths. • I'm a bit overweight, despite being so active. • Spend too much time worrying about Charles, or going out with him.
Opportunities	**Threats**
• It's the right time of year to contact the police for a work placement. • They're looking for a part-time youth leader down at the club. • I could volunteer to train a girls' football team at Brierley Middle School (my cousin teaches there). • There's a new gym opened at Oldthorpe: I could go there and get properly fit. • I could go and share a flat with Charles – but aren't I too young?	• I might get like my friend Mandy and start going out with too many boys. • I might want to take a year out and travel round the world as soon as I've finished my BTEC. • I could start getting slack about assignments and deadlines: they seem to be piling them on at the moment, and people who hand them in late are still getting graded. • Dad is always running me down, for some reason.

Emma can use her SWOT analysis as a starting point for her action plan for career development. She then needs to write herself a timetable.

To be realistic, her timetable should not stretch too far into the future, nor should she pretend that she can do things which she cannot. A realistic action plan is one which the planner believes in.

On the other hand, being realistic needn't mean being limited and unambitious. If you want something, you should believe that it is possible – and then work for it. It is always better to try, rather than just lie down and admit defeat.

A possible action plan for Emma is shown below. Of course, you could make this plan longer. But then there would be more options ....

The main thing to note is that, on the whole, Emma chooses activities which will help her to get into the police. They will either help her to pass the entrance procedures, or they will look good on her CV. Her personal life is a bit vague, and though it may be relevant to the choices she makes, she (and you) may not want to put such details down on an action plan which is going to be seen by other people. Obviously, the decision is yours.

By age	Action/target	Outcome
17	(a) Apply for work placement with police. (b) Stop smoking. (c) Start fitness training at gym. (d) Start training football team. (e) Aim for distinctions on my course. Should I consider going to university? (f) Start learning to drive.	(a) If successful, make good use of placement. If not, reapply, or try another public service. (b) Good for health and pocket. (c) Good for health. (d) Will look good on CV. (e) Good for CV – but not sure about university. (f) Has to be done.
18	(a) Consider leaving home, but only if it won't affect my college work. (b) Apply to work in special constabulary. (c) Retake GCSE maths. (d) Join amateur dramatics club to help overcome shyness. (e) Will complete BTEC National in Public Service. Keep working for distinctions. (f) Pass driving test.	(a) But not with Charles; he might be boring to live with. (b) Increase chances of getting in police. (c) Pass – I hope! (d) Should improve confidence. (e) University? I don't think I'll want to go, but would it help me to get into the police? (f) Or retake? I mustn't give up, whatever happens.
19	(a) Apply for the police. There are some people who get in at 19. (b) If I don't apply, I'll get a full-time job. I feel I need more experience of life. What kind of job? Retail? Something working with people, and which will improve my mental arithmetic. (c) Should I go round the world instead?	(a) This is what I would like – but will I be too young? They might think I'm not mature enough. (b) This idea is a poor second best. Needs more thought. (c) NO – seems like running away. I shouldn't do this, and I probably won't want to when the time comes.

THINK ABOUT IT ...

Note down your own action plan for career development – then discuss it with a friend and/or your tutor.

UNIT 3

Understanding Discipline

Unit outcome 1
Examine the role of discipline in the public services

Assessment criteria

- Explain the role of discipline in public services.
- Explain the need for discipline in an least two public services.

Discipline means obedience, order, control and self-control.

The public services value discipline greatly, and expect their employees and officers to be highly disciplined. One of the purposes of this unit is to help you to understand discipline fully – so that you don't become unstuck at a later date!

What does discipline mean?

In the public services discipline can mean any or all of the following:

- following orders
- efficiency
- self-respect
- respect for others
- hard work
- giving a good impression to the public
- teamwork
- a sense of duty
- punctuality and promptness
- patience
- putting other people's needs before your own
- keeping fit
- organising your work
- good manners
- professionalism
- working to improve your understanding of the job
- developing skills
- evaluating your own performance
- always giving of your best
- doing what you can to ensure that others give of their best
- knowing what to do in a life-threatening situation – and doing it.

What is the role of discipline?

Explain the role of discipline in public services.

The role of discipline is to:

- create trust, both inside and outside the service
- enable people to work successfully in teams
- maximise efficiency
- save public money
- help people to work under stress without cracking up
- allow people to work with each other without quarrelling
- increase job satisfaction
- limit accidents
- save lives both inside and outside the service
- enable a public service to be good
- enable a public service to show that it is good.

These roles are explained below.

ANALYSIS

Discipline and trust

The most important aspect of unified, effective teamwork is trust. In the public services people work hard: there is a lot of work to get through. So team members have to trust each other to pull their weight. There is no room for slackers. Nothing is more annoying and disruptive for a team if, in their daily work, the members feel that one of them is 'a passenger'. So team members have to be able to trust each other to do the work – and to do it when they say they are going to do it.

Trust is also vital when people are being put to the test. In the army, soldiers are put in danger, by the very nature of their job. They have to trust their fellows to keep their nerve, and not to bottle out. There is no shame in feeling fear: the shame is in giving way to it. A disciplined army knows the meaning of fear, and if it has to take a risk it is a calculated risk. But without discipline you do not have the coolness of mind to calculate those risks – and minimise them. So the army controls its fear through discipline – and self-discipline – because uncontrolled fear leads to panic, which leads to mistakes and costs lives.

Trust is knowing that someone is batting for you. A disciplined team has high morale and people back each other up. They do not go round nit-picking or dishing the dirt. If the team feels that one of its members is going wrong, it will talk to that member and try to sort the problem out before going to higher authority. But of course where a serious issue is concerned a disciplined officer will not try to cover up.

There is another side to trust. All public service workers – but perhaps especially the police – have to deal with vast amounts of confidential information. Gossip, tittle-tattle, and spilling the beans is not part of public service work. A disciplined officer is a safe pair of hands where information is concerned. Someone who leaks even innocent-seeming information is likely to be breaking the new Data Protection Act 1999. Confidentiality is a vital aspect of trust and must be respected by a disciplined officer.

Discipline and teamwork

Teams have leaders. The leaders must exercise appropriate discipline over the team, and they must also demonstrate discipline themselves, and set a good example. A disciplined team is one that works hard and in which the members respect each other and their work. The purpose of the discipline is to enable teams to work hard and efficiently, but also sustainably – so that they don't overstress themselves and burn themselves out.

Discipline and efficiency

Efficiency means getting the maximum output from work with the minimum input. It means not cutting a lawn with a pair of scissors when you have a lawnmower to do the job. There is too much work to be done in the public services for it to be done in an inefficient way. So discipline means looking analytically at the tasks which have to be done, and finding the most cost-effective way of doing them.

Discipline and saving money

Modern public services are run on a tight budget, and disciplined officers can no longer spend money as if there was no tomorrow. This means taking the trouble to understand how much money is available and how and when it can be spent. It also means recording transactions in the appropriate way, not only for convenience, but also because you have to be accountable to others: after all, in a public service it is public money that is being spent!

Discipline and stress

A well organised and disciplined workplace is less stressful, because people know what they should do, who is doing it, and when it should be done by.

Discipline and conflict-avoidance

People who choose to work in the public services are often positive, forceful and ambitious people. They have natural leadership qualities and tend not to like it if they don't get their own way. If two ambitious people meet they can be like dogs snarling. Disciplined people find ways of avoiding conflict without backing down on matters of principle (i.e. where it really matters). They are able to control their feelings, and not to respond to every challenge with aggression. The secret is to be assertive, not aggressive: to have the discipline to say what you want calmly, positively and honestly, without either exaggerating or under-playing your own feelings. And remember that disciplined people prefer to use their brains to their fists!

Discipline and job satisfaction

The feeling of 'a job well done' is a very satisfying one. But without discipline – which means planning and targets – there is no way of knowing whether a job has been well done or not. A disorganised worker is one who wastes his or her own and other people's time – undermining job satisfaction for all concerned.

Discipline, accidents, health and safety

Bad discipline costs lives. Even dropping a file on the floor might make someone trip up, fall down a flight of stairs, and break their neck. In any workplace accidents happen, and most of them are down to failures of discipline.

In recent years most deaths in the army have taken place not in combat, but in accidents. The accidents might be on the firing range, or they might involve vehicles. Armies are full of high-spirited, even aggressive, young men; a recipe for disaster if they do not have the discipline to channel their energies into safe and productive activities.

Discipline and saving lives

Again this is a matter of following procedures, which may be difficult, complex and dangerous. Officers have also to make split-second decisions when saving lives. These decisions are likely to be wrong, unless there has been training and practice. Discipline and self-discipline are vital ingredients in any successful training programme to deal with life-saving or threatening situations. It takes discipline to learn how to act in an emergency – no one is born with the knowledge of how to save a life.

Discipline and good public services

Discipline is a moral as well as a practical thing. It is the knowledge of right and wrong which each of us carries round inside us. Have you ever asked yourself why no one with a criminal record, however slight, is ever accepted into the fire service?

Well, firefighters can have the run of a burning house. The occupants are in shock. What is to stop them from rummaging through the drawers and taking the jewellery while people's backs are turned?

It comes down to trust again, doesn't it?

Discipline to show that a public service is good

Much public service work consists of public relations. Good public relations means looking good as well as being good. This is where uniforms come in. But uniforms are not just fancy dress. They remind the officers themselves that they are:

- professional
- trained
- unbiased
- disciplined.

The need for discipline in public services

Explain the need for discipline in at least two public services.

1 The police

The police have a disciplinary code which contains the following types of offence.

ANALYSIS

1 Discreditable conduct. An example of this occurred where police officers went to a pub to check on after-hours drinking. In the course of their investigation they became incapable of doing their duty, and eventually had to be removed by their colleagues! In another case an officer allowed himself to be handcuffed to some railings for a prank.

These are cases where poor discipline has made the police into a laughing stock. The police are as human as anyone else, but their special role in society means that they have to be more disciplined than other people. They provide discipline to society itself – therefore they must have the highest standards of discipline and self-discipline.

2 Misconduct towards a member of a police force. This includes harassment, victimisation or assault of another officer.

Where there is good discipline people work together harmoniously and productively. They enjoy their work and they get on with it. But where there is any form of harassment discipline is bound to break down. The person who is harassing is not doing his or her job properly, and the person who is being harassed will be unable to feel loyalty to the team or to the person who is doing the harassing. Furthermore, if the police themselves are not able to control harassment within their ranks, it shows that discipline is breaking down on a larger scale, and morale and efficiency could be affected.

3 Disobedience to orders. The orders can be either spoken or written. They may be issued at a particular time, or they may be permanently in force.

At the very least, disobedience to orders wastes time. But it could also mean that operations such as raids could be bungled, and criminals will escape justice. If criminals do escape justice they will continue to carry out crimes and the public will suffer. So the cost of disobeying an order could be very high. However, it ought to be borne in mind that obeying orders in the police does not mean blind, unthinking obedience to an order, regardless of whether it is good or bad. In a disciplined organisation orders must be well thought through and given by people who know what they are doing – otherwise the people giving orders cannot really expect them to be obeyed.

4 Neglect of duty. This includes things like being absent without leave, unpunctuality, carelessness with possessions or money, and general laxness.

Without being neurotic about it, police officers have to try to be perfectionists. Their job demands high standards, often in difficult conditions. Carelessness, sloppiness and poor timekeeping undermine other people's efforts to do their best, and therefore undermine discipline as a whole. There is a knock-on effect of such neglect so, being a disciplined service, the police rightly clamp down on breaches of discipline under this heading.

5 Falsehood or prevarication. In the past police officers have sometimes got themselves into trouble by altering records in their pocket books or telling lies and half-truths in court. This is a serious disciplinary offence, since the most valuable single quality of a police officer is honesty.

Dishonesty and crime are very close to each other. We talk of fighting fire with fire, or that 'it takes a thief to catch a thief' – but these old sayings are not relevant to modern public services. It may seem unfair but the police have to be better than the rest of us, using 'the simple sword of truth'. In the past many court cases were thrown out because police evidence was thought to be fabricated. It is unfortunately true that the police often know that someone is a criminal, but they can't legally prove it. Here the police have to be disciplined enough to resist the temptation to tamper with evidence, since in the long run this will do more harm than good in the fight against crime.

6 Improper disclosure of information. As we have said before, the police have access to any amount of confidential information. They are not allowed to leak it.

Honesty is not the same thing as blabbing to every Tom, Dick or Harry about all the juicy bits of information which happen to be in police files. The job of the police is to collect information, not to give it out. If they do start giving out information in a thoughtless and ill-disciplined way, and get a reputation for it, their sources of information will soon dry up. And without sources of information there is very little that the police can do in the never-ending fight against crime.

7 Corrupt or improper practice. Police officers should not accept bribes – or even presents – from members of the public. If they do they may be seen as placing themselves under an obligation to that member of the public rather than to the public as a whole – which it is their duty as public service officers to serve.

In many countries the police, badly paid, demoralised and undisciplined, are happy to take bribes. But they pay for it through the nose, because they are not respected by the people, and organised crime, often on a vast scale, flourishes everywhere. Taking bribes is illegal, and encourages lawbreaking. Even accepting presents is dangerous for a police officer, unless it is absolutely certain that it has nothing whatsoever to do with their work.

> **!** THINK ABOUT IT ...
>
> Former American president, George Bush, once said, 'There is no such thing as a free lunch.' Do you agree?

8 Abuse of authority. In effect this means being rude to or bullying members of the public, or generally being 'out of order'. Unnecessary searches, or violence, would also come under this heading.

More than almost any other job, police work involves public relations. A piece of rudeness by a police officer gets talked about in pubs and clubs by the victim, and at the end of a week several hundred people may have heard about it. And they may all be people who are inclined to dislike the police anyway. So a single act of indiscipline can make the police several hundred enemies within a week. This may carry a heavy cost, in the long run, in terms of lost information, uncooperative behaviour, or even assaults on police officers.

9 Racially discriminatory behaviour. The British police are less racist than police in other 'white' countries. But unfortunately for them, this only means that cases of racism are all the more noticeable when they occur. Some of them involve assaults, uninvestigated deaths, or deaths in police custody – and because of various high profile cases the police are always put under the microscope where racism is suspected. Only through disciplining themselves to eliminate 'institutionalised racism' (the hidden unconscious racism which is a feature of British society) can the police root out the racism that is left in their organisation. This is difficult, because it involves using self-assessment and self-examination to find something which – being unconscious – is difficult to identify anyway. But the effort needs to be made to prevent miscarriages of justice and to build up support for the police in a multicultural Britain.

10 Improper dress or untidiness. Police officers can wear what they like when they are off duty, on holiday or in bed. But (unless on undercover operations) they must not be scruffy on duty, or carry out impersonations of Rab C. Nesbitt during working hours. If they do, people will assume that they are not well disciplined.

11 Neglect of health. This includes reckless behaviour on duty, or trying to extend sick leave by unhealthy practices.

This is probably directed at officers who drink too much in their own time. In Britain we have not yet reached the stage of disciplining officers for putting on weight, as they are said to do in America. But a well-disciplined person can do much to ensure that they remain in good health, by taking exercise, eating the right kind of food, and avoiding overwork and other stress-inducing activities. Since police officers cost a lot to train, and are (reasonably) well paid, they represent an investment of public money – and are therefore encouraged, by disciplinary procedures, to look after their health.

12 Damage to police property. This aspect of discipline has two parts to it. One is wilful damage

– such as through reckless driving of a police vehicle; the other is failure to report such damage.

It is obviously unacceptable for police officers wilfully or recklessly to damage police property. Officers who do this may have some psychological problem (in which case it may not be a disciplinary offence) or they may have a grudge against some individual – in which case it is a disciplinary offence because the officer should be able to do something about it by complaining through the proper channels. If the damage is as a result of a grudge against the police as an organisation, the officer concerned would need to have a long, hard think about whether he or she should stay in the police at all.

13 Drunkenness. Being under the influence of drugs would come under this heading as well.

A person who is under the influence of alcohol cannot behave in a disciplined manner. Police officers addicted to alcohol and other drugs would not be able to put the police first. They would be open to blackmail or other pressures from outside the police, and might be a bad influence on their fellow-officers.

14 Drinking on duty or soliciting drink. Again, this type of indiscipline would present the police in a bad light, and leave them open to various outside pressures.

15 Entering licensed premises 'without good and sufficient cause'. The dangers of 'the demon drink' are taken seriously in the police force. There is a long tradition in some sections of British society, dating from Victorian times, of thinking that alcohol is the root of all evil. Some passers-by would assume that if an officer went into a pub it might be to get a drink. Such officers could then be targeted as unreliable, and it might affect the way people regarded them or their work.

16 Criminal conduct. This is one of the few disciplinary offences which can lead – fairly quickly – to dismissal from the force. It is particularly relevant to cases of corruption or where (as has been known to happen) police officers commit crimes such as rape or armed robbery.

17 Being an accessory to a discipline offence. What this means is that police officers must on no account cover up for their colleagues who have done something wrong. In a disciplined force police officers have to be loyal to each other. But the greatest loyalty must always be to the force itself, not to individuals within that force. Covering up indiscipline is in some ways worse than the original offence, because it shows that the force is becoming corrupt. This attitude stems from the old idea that one or two rotten apples can make all the other apples bad as well.

2 The army

In the army the main disciplinary procedures are set out in the Queen's Regulations. These must be followed if disciplinary action – in other words punishment – is being taken.

More is explained about discipline in the army on pages 54–55. Here is a summary of the army's attitude towards discipline.

ANALYSIS

1 Discipline creates trust between group members. This trust is essential if people are going to be able to give that 110 per cent which is expected of them in the army. In difficult or dangerous situations you must be able to rely on your comrades.

2 Discipline ensures that everybody does their fair share of the work – no one is given an easy ride but no one is exploited either.

3 It is natural for soldiers to feel fear at certain times. They are only human. But discipline gives them a framework in which to control that fear and continue to work safely and efficiently when undisciplined and untrained people would panic.

4 Morale – a feeling that things are going well (even if they aren't!) – is important in an army. Discipline creates a feeling of normality and control which is good for morale. It gives a reassuring feeling of certainty and authority to decisions which are taken.

5 Discipline is linked to loyalty – putting your comrades first, and being unselfish at all times.

6 Discipline makes teamwork organised and efficient. Jobs get done quickly and without hassle if there is good discipline. And discipline unifies a team, and makes it tougher.

7 Good discipline eliminates favouritism, scapegoating (blaming somebody for everything) and bullying. These can be problems in the army – and other institutions as well.

8 Discipline makes for efficiency, which is obtaining the maximum result from the minimum of resources. Discipline saves time, money and effort – without lowering the quality of the end result.

9 Because everybody knows who is supposed to make the decisions (even though others may be consulted) discipline takes some of the stress out of decision-making. It is also less stressful for those who are taking the orders, partly because, as disciplined soldiers, they have been trained to take orders, and partly because they have confidence in the orders and the people who are giving them.

10 In a well-disciplined organisation everybody knows who is supposed to be doing what. This avoids conflicts and demarcation disputes within the army. It also prevents people from saying or doing things which are 'out of order' and would cause bad feeling.

11 In the army, as elsewhere, there is more job satisfaction if there is an effective system of discipline (firm yet fair) which suits people's needs. People feel happy and secure in their roles.

12 Good discipline is an essential requirement for health and safety. Many accidents are caused by negligence, or by lax systems of discipline which do not place a clear responsibility on people for carrying out risk assessments and maintaining safe practices.

13 Discipline really comes into its own in an emergency. Since it is a habit, and has been practised effectively, soldiers in a life-threatening situation are able to use their discipline, and the instructions of a disciplined commanding officer, to help them think clearly, keep cool, and give of their best while minimising the risks.

14 People sometimes forget that discipline is a moral value. A soldier who is well disciplined is a force for good – someone who, in any situation, will always try to do what is right. Disciplined soldiers are therefore honest – and this is important when people are living together in barracks. Soldiers who tell lies, or who steal from their comrades, are undisciplined themselves, undermine the discipline of others and do more harm than good in an army.

15 Well-disciplined soldiers are smart, and this reflects on their discipline in their lives and work. And if they have a night off, or are on leave, because they are disciplined they know how to enjoy themselves and relax without bringing the army into disrepute. Large army camps such as Catterick have a huge effect on the social life of the surrounding area. If the soldiers are well disciplined this will be a good effect, bringing prosperity and well-being – and the army will be appreciated for what it does. But if soldiers are undisciplined there will be bad relations with the public, and frequent complaints and court cases which will reflect badly on the army and its soldiers.

THINK ABOUT IT ...

Why is discipline needed in other public services, such as the prison service, the fire service or customs and excise?

Write yourself notes along the lines of the ones above.

Unit outcome 2
Examine conformity and obedience

Assessment criteria

- Briefly describe the main features of conformity and obedience.
- Isolate three factors which influence conformity and three factors which influence obedience.

Features of conformity and obedience

Conformity means changing your behaviour and ideas so that they are the same as the group of people you are with. Obedience means doing as you are told.

For many years now there has been great interest in what makes people conform, and what makes them obey. The reasons for this interest are as follows:

1 Governments, businesses, public services and schools all try to control people so that they act in certain ways. It would make their job so much easier if they could find a sure-fire way of doing it.

2 If someone could find a magic formula to make people conform and obey they would be able to rule the world, end crime, and probably walk on water as well.

3 Perhaps someone did find this formula – Adolf Hitler – and he did anything but end crime. So now people want to find out why so many people obeyed him, when he was so obviously evil.

Conformity

The first person to study conformity was Jenness, in 1932. He had people estimating the number of beans in a bottle – first one at a time, then in a group. After the group had agreed on an estimate, he then got the individuals to make a second estimate – and found that this time they were closer to the group estimate.

The next experiment was done by someone called Sherif, in 1935. He sat a human guinea pig in a dark room, asked him to stare at a tiny point of light projected on the wall, and then asked him to estimate how far it had moved. In fact it hadn't moved at all, but Sherif knew his participants' eyes would play tricks on them, and the participants, one at a time, gave wildly differing guesses as to how far the point of light had moved. Once they had guessed individually, Sherif let his subjects hear each others' guesses, and then asked them to guess again. Their guesses became more and more alike as time went on. In the end a group agreement was reached which was close to the average of all the original individual estimates.

Then in 1951 Asch did an even better experiment. He started off with some individuals and gave them two cards with straight lines on, like the cards in figure 3.1 below:

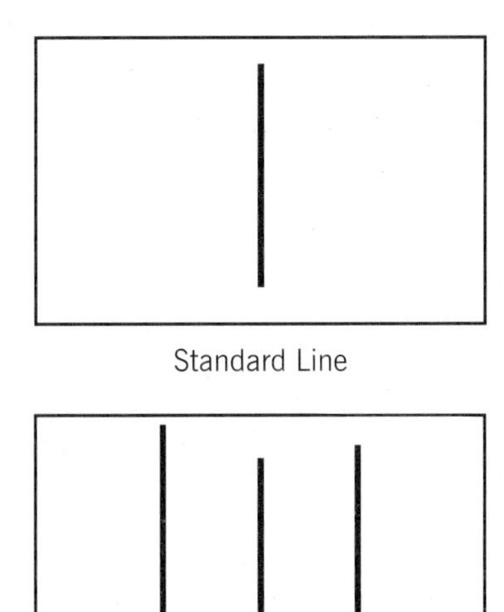

Figure 3.1 *Stimulus cards used in Asch's conformity experiments (1951, 1952, 1956)*

The individuals simply had to match the standard line with the comparison line of the same length.

Then he had them doing the same thing but with a group.

Easy. In both cases they got the right answer. But then Asch put each individual in with a group which (secretly) he had instructed to agree on the wrong answer. He arranged it so that his chosen individual had to make a decision only after all the others had already given the wrong answer. He found that 32 per cent of his subjects started giving the wrong answers as well! And this was true whenever there was a group of three or more.

FOCUS

Asch, followed by Deutsch and Gerard (1955), discovered that people conform:

- if they can see the faces of the people they are expected to conform with
- when they are not sure of something, but the rest of the group is
- when they are afraid of being mocked or rejected by a group
- when they have low self-esteem (confidence) – a confident person doesn't mind being different from the group, but a person who is unsure of themselves will conform in order to fit in with the group
- when they are the kind of person who needs the approval of others – a person who doesn't care what other people think of them is less likely to conform
- more over simple things like dress or hairstyle than complicated things such as religion.

Obedience

The difference between conformity and obedience is that conformity results from a decision by the person who conforms to 'go along with the group', while obedience is imposed from outside. Nobody has to tell a person to conform: they just do it. But where obedience is concerned, someone else tells them to do it.

Suppose a student with long hair joins a class where everybody else has short hair. If he thinks: 'I feel an idiot with hair down to my shoulders while everyone else has crew-cuts', and goes to the barber, he is conforming.

But if the same student is told by his teacher, 'Get your hair cut!' – and does so – then he is obeying.

Obedience was not studied seriously by psychologists until after World War II – when they wanted to find out why the Germans had 'obeyed orders' and killed six million Jews.

THINK ABOUT IT ...

Look at your class or group on any given day.

Jot down the conformity rate on such matters as:

(a) Clothing. How many class members are wearing (i) jeans and (ii) trainers?
(b) Breakfast. How many of you ate breakfast this morning?
(c) Ownership of mobile phones. How many of you have one with you?
(d) How many of you are learning to drive or have already done so?
(e) How many of you (i) belong to a religion or church and (ii) go regularly?

Do you find that your class conforms more about some things than others – and if so, why do you think this is?

The key experiment which demonstrated how obedient people will be – if the right conditions are met – was carried out by Stanley Milgram in 1963. The basic scenario of the experiment was that volunteers took part in a carefully staged 'learning experiment'. It was not really a learning experiment at all, but an experiment to find out how obedient people would be if they were told to give a 'learner' – who was just an actor – electric shocks (which were not real electric shocks). Milgram discovered that 65 per cent of his volunteers gave electric shocks up to 450 volts, which is enough to kill a horse, never mind a human being. They did this even though the actor produced cries of pain which they could hear, and begged them not to go on.

This was the first of a series of experiments in which the scenario was changed in various ways, to find out what factors, if any, would influence or alter this high level of obedience.

Milgram found out that factors which influenced obedience included the following.

1 How obviously cruel or unreasonable the order was. Volunteers were more obedient if they did not see the 'learner' they were giving electric shocks to. They would do something cruel if they could not see the effects of it.

2 Whether anybody present disobeyed the order. Volunteers stopped obeying if they had a 'colleague' (actually trained by Milgram) who stopped obeying first. People are more obedient if they feel isolated and unsupported.

3 Whether the order had to be carried out in person, or whether it could be carried out by someone else. Volunteers were more obedient if the trained 'colleague' gave the shocks. In other words they were even happier to stand by and watch other people give the shocks than to give them themselves. People will accept a 'bad' order if they do not have to carry it out in person.

4 Whether the person giving the order was standing close to the person receiving it. If the researcher was standing over the volunteer, the volunteer was much more obedient than if the researcher kept his distance. And if the researcher left the room the obedience rate dropped to only 20 per cent. People will obey if they think someone is breathing down their neck.

Other people have tried Milgram's experiments in different countries and found that

- in some countries such as Australia and (to a lesser extent) the UK, the obedience rate was lower than in the US, but in most European countries the obedience rate was higher
- women had the same obedience rate as men
- people who volunteer for experiments are less authoritarian than the population as a whole, so Milgram's results may actually underestimate the level of obedience in society.

Milgram's experiment is very famous, and there have been television programmes about it. Perhaps because it is so well known, the obedience rates have tended to drop in recent years. But it has been possible to carry out similar experiments using different scenarios. In 1966 Hofling carried out an obedience experiment on nurses. A supposedly new drug, which was actually glucose tablets, was introduced in various American hospitals. The maximum dose was clearly labelled on the box. In the experiment a 'Dr Smith' – who was not known to the nurses – instructed them by phone to give a dose higher than the dose stated on the box to a 'patient' who was 'in urgent need of the drug'. In effect 'Dr Smith' was asking the nurses to break three basic rules of nursing. This was because:

- the dose was above the maximum allowed
- 'Dr Smith' had not given written authorisation – he said he would 'come round in ten minutes' and do this
- the nurses had no way of knowing that 'Dr Smith' was a genuine doctor – after all, anybody can ring up and say they are 'Dr Smith'.

In the experiment the nurses were observed following the phone call from 'Dr Smith', and 21 out of 22 nurses followed 'Dr Smith's' instructions.

In Hofling's experiment the scenario was far more realistic than it had been in Milgram's, so the obedience rate was higher. It was also carried out in an environment where the nurses worked, and where they were used to obeying orders.

THINK ABOUT IT ...

Are these experiments immoral, and if so why?

Factors which influence conformity

1 A single person who feels that they are on their own is much more likely to conform than two or more people who can back each other up against the group. So a girl who was the only person in a new class wearing a nose-stud might feel like taking it out. But if another girl was also wearing a nose-stud she would not feel under nearly so much pressure to conform.

2 A person will feel pressure to conform to a group if there are three or more people in the group. But the pressure will be no greater if there are 10, or 20, people in the group than if there are three. So where conformity is concerned, there is a lot of truth in the saying: 'Two's company, three's a crowd.'

3 Where ideas, questions or behaviour are involved, the pressure to conform is stronger when the ideas, questions or behaviour at issue are simple rather than complex. This is an interesting finding, but we can see its relevance to real life and, if it comes to that, to public service work. Wearing uniform is a simple matter, and someone who joins the police would want to wear the uniform because of the pressure to conform. But religion (for example) is a complex matter, and a Muslim who joined the police would not feel under pressure to conform and become Christian just because all the other officers at that station were Christians. In other words, in modern society, we are put under pressure to conform over simple things, like what we wear or what time we come to work, but complex things are much less of an issue.

Factors which influence obedience

Status

If the person giving orders is older, more experienced, richer, more successful, or physically stronger, the person receiving the orders is more likely to obey them. That is because all these qualities are linked with status (that is, a person's importance in the eyes of other people). And in an organisation like the army, the soldier of lower rank will obey the soldier of higher rank. The greater the difference in status between the person giving the command and the person receiving it, the greater the likelihood that the command will be obeyed. On the other hand, a person of higher status will hardly ever obey an order given by a person of lower status. If they do, it might mean that – for the moment – the status of the 'lower' person is raised. Thus a judge will obey a firefighter who tells him to leave a burning building.

Power to reward or punish

Teachers are obeyed in school because there is, in the background, a possibility or threat of punishment. Sometimes an order linked to a threat: 'Stop messing about with the lift or I'll call security!', may cause swifter obedience than an order without a threat. On the other hand using a threat may diminish the speaker's authority, since it suggests the possibility that, without the threat, he will not be obeyed.

Conditioning

Obedience is learnt, at an early age. This kind of early learning is sometimes called 'conditioning'. A child who has been trained to obey (as most of us are) at an early age, may be more likely to obey orders in later life. Equally, such a child may also give orders more effectively in later life, because they have learnt what obedience and discipline are.

Learning is too complex a subject to be discussed at any length in this unit. But much learning, both in animals and humans, takes the form of linking cause and effect or, as psychologists call it, stimulus and response. In its most basic form, this type of learning is called conditioning.

There are two types of conditioning:

- classical conditioning
- operant conditioning.

The famous experiments in classical conditioning were carried out by Ivan Pavlov in the 1920s. He discovered that dogs salivated when they saw food. Nothing is surprising in this, but then he found out that if he sounded a buzzer before the food appeared, on a regular basis, the dogs salivated at the sound of the buzzer. He called this conditioning – but in fact it was a type of learning based on a frequent repetition of the same actions, or stimuli. In this classical conditioning, learning takes place because of what happens before the stimulus (which is the appearance of the food). In other words, the learning comes about by association – closeness in time – but not by cause and effect.

Pavlov's research was followed up in 1938 by BF Skinner. Skinner taught rats to press levers and obtain food. At first the hungry rat only touched the lever and got the food by accident, as it was scuttling about inside its cage. But it wasn't long before the rat learned that pressing the lever would cause a food pellet to appear. This type of conditioning, where an animal is trained to do something which is followed by a reward, is called operant conditioning. In 'operant' conditioning the learning comes about through cause and effect.

These researchers investigated learning by using rewards, but others used punishments, such as loud noises and electric shocks. Watson, for example, in 1924, managed to make a young boy frightened of rats by hitting a four foot metal bar and making a loud unpleasant noise every time he showed him a rat. It wasn't long before the boy was terrified of anything that was hairy – even a model of Father Christmas.

The essential feature about conditioning is that if the stimulus and response are repeated often enough, learning will take place, even in fairly unteachable animals, such as cats.

Children learn much faster than animals, and they learn much more, but the method is similar: frequent repetition, and the use of rewards or punishments. With children the rewards and punishments may simply be words, such as 'Well done,' or 'No – that's not right. Try again.' In the family, and later in school and in the peer group, children learn what is acceptable and what is not by constant 'reinforcement' – rewards and punishments which act like those used by the early psychologists in their experiments. Potty training is one example – but there are hundreds of others. Every experience carries with it memories of rewards and punishments, and that is why we learn, as the rats in their cages did, by trial and error.

So personal experience of rejection or mockery that comes through failing or refusing to conform acts as a 'negative reinforcement' – in the sense that the unpleasant experience of being rejected or mocked can be ended by conforming. Similarly, years of obeying parents and teachers, connected with negative reinforcement (such as the end of a punishment) or positive reinforcement (some kind of reward) conditions us (trains us) to be more obedient.

If experience is the most important basis of our need to conform, training or conditioning may be the most important of all factors bringing about obedience. Thus the army and other public services lay great stress on basic training, where recruits receive huge numbers of instructions, time and again, and are expected to obey them promptly and without question. The aim is to be sure that recruits can be trusted to obey whenever necessary after the training period is over.

Unit outcome 3
Examine self-discipline

Assessment criteria

- Specify four qualities needed for self-discipline in a given public service.
- Describe in detail how these qualities are necessary for the effective operation of a given public service.

What is self-discipline?

Discipline is a habit, and in that sense it is a form of conditioning. If you tell a dog to sit, before you take it across the road, it won't sit first time round. But if you train it to sit, time and again, eventually it will sit down when you come to a road whether you tell it to or not. People, as we have already seen, are much the same. They receive a good deal of discipline – training and conditioning – from others before the discipline gets inside them and it becomes self-discipline.

Though children can display self-discipline on occasion, self-discipline is really a characteristic of adults, and a sign of maturity. Self-discipline is knowing what has to be done and doing it – without having to be told.

Self discipline is connected to the idea of rewards, but in a different way from discipline imposed by someone else. Take this example. You are a student and you get an assignment. The assignment has to be done by a certain deadline. There are three ways of approaching it:

(a) get it done as soon as possible
(b) leave it as long as possible but make sure it is completed by the deadline
(c) not get it done by the deadline.

In case (a) getting the assignment off your back is the reward. Then there is the secondary reward of swanning about seeing everybody else getting into a flat spin because they haven't finished it, while you have. OK, you missed a night out because you stayed in and did it while your friends went off for a rave somewhere. But at least you got it done, and you feel good about yourself for handing it in on time.

In case (b) you get the best of both worlds. You have your night out, then you get down to your research. Unlike case (a) you didn't dash the assignment off, just to get it out of the way. Maybe you wrote a few letters or made a few phone calls, in order to pick up some snippets of information from the Home Office, or from your cousin in the police. If they are slow in replying, that gives you a pretty sound excuse if your assignment isn't done on time, and the letters you get back from the Home Office will prove that you did your research. Also you might pick up some nifty ideas in the last few days before you actually write your notes up. Sometimes it's a good idea not to rush at something, because it gives your brain time to mull the questions over. On the other hand you have to wait a while before you have the satisfaction of getting the thing done and out of the way.

In case (c) the assignment ... er ... well ... it doesn't get done. Bit of a problem, that. You had some great nights out but ... er. Your mates (call themselves mates!) won't lend you their assignments. One of them's handed his in, and the other's still working on hers. Yeah, well, it's time for the excuses. Sir, the dog ate my assignment ... Trouble is, the dog's already eaten three other assignments. Had to have an operation to get the last one out of its stomach. Er ... my grandma's died. There's been a high mortality rate among my grandmas in the last six months. Four of them kicked the bucket. Is that possible? Maybe I ought to pull a sickie ...

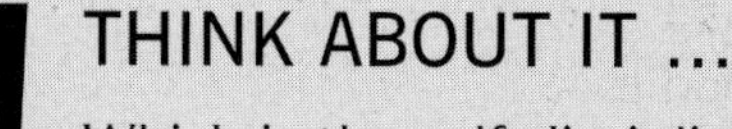

THINK ABOUT IT ...

Which is the self-disciplined student?

People who get on in life go for deferred gratification. At least, this is what the sociologists think. According to David Lockwood it is the mark of the 'middle class subculture' to which the police belong. See *Sociology: Themes and Perspectives*, Haralambos & Holborn, p74, 4th ed, 1995, Collins Educational.

FOCUS

Gratification

Immediate gratification = getting pleasure right now

Deferred gratification = getting pleasure sometime in the future

Immediate gratification is: 'I'm off out with the lads'.

Deferred gratification is: 'I'm off out with the lads but I'm going to finish this assignment first'.

Immediate gratification is: 'I'm eighteen and a half so I'm applying for the police right now!'

Deferred gratification is: 'I'm eighteen and a half, and I want to join the police. But I know they won't accept me, (a) because they don't usually accept people at eighteen and a half, (b) because I'm not fit enough and anyway (c) I haven't finished my course. But if I start fitness training now, and do some research on which forces are recruiting, and get my driving test passed, then I can apply next year and I reckon that by then I'll stand a pretty good chance'.

Qualities needed for self-discipline in the public services

The qualities needed for self-discipline are much the same in any public service. They are as follows.

1 Good personal presentation – for example the smartness required by soldiers on parade.
2 Punctuality – accident and emergency ambulances must get to their destination as quickly as possible since lives are at stake.
3 Good time management – the patient transport service has to collect outpatients (for example for kidney dialysis) from rural areas, and must not keep them waiting more than necessary, which means planning the best collection route and keeping good time.
4 Reliability – in army teamwork everybody must be able to trust everybody else.
5 Good attendance – ambulance workers must be punctual, good attenders, since the service is stretched and people will suffer if someone is absent without notice.
6 Composure – army officers must keep calm under attack.
7 Good attitude – ambulance workers must not get 'stroppy' with sick members of the public, and must never discriminate.
8 Good performance – paramedics must be efficient, skilled and knowledgeable, even if they are working in the middle of the night.
9 Suitable personality – soldiers must be brave, uncomplaining, adaptable and loyal.

Why is self-discipline important?

Describe in detail how these qualities are necessary for the effective operation of the police.

1 Personal presentation

Not everybody is handsome or beautiful, even in the police. After all, a police station is not a catwalk. No recruiting panel is going to say, 'Mr Gump is a good candidate but we'll have to turn him down because of his jug-handle ears'.

A police station is not a catwalk

Good personal presentation, though, is a different matter. Police officers have a uniform and they are expected to wear it. There are rules about how it should be worn, and these must be followed. The police tailor will make sure that it fits.

Being clean is the most vital aspect of good presentation. During army basic training new recruits are taught to wash themselves, from head to foot (just in case they were never taught when they lived at home). A clean face by itself is not enough. Clean hands are very important, and so is having nails of an appropriate length and colour. Women should have short nails so that they don't get broken or cause injury. Men who have a tendency to play rugby or rummage around the insides of oily machines in their spare time have to pay special attention to their fingernails. The public expects its police officers to look like police officers, not mechanics or dry-stone wallers.

Hair too must be clean. It should not be too obviously dyed, and it should be worn in an appropriate style – one which can take a hat without causing physical injury. If it is hanging loose it may be a health and safety risk. Some police officers wear beards, but these should be neat and well-cared for.

Bodily cleanliness is also important because of ... phew! BO. And oral hygiene matters. Visit your dentist regularly, to stop your teeth from dropping out and to avoid halitosis.

Jewellery is a problem area, and the police discourage it, partly for safety reasons, and partly because the general public has mixed feelings about body-piercing. People over 50 seem to be allergic to it. As for tattoos, the public services look on them as a form of graffiti, and as you read this someone, somewhere, will be having tattoos removed by laser treatment so they can apply to the fire service or the police.

Because the police represent society and its tradition of law and order they feel strongly about being smart, and giving a good impression through good personal presentation.

2 Reliability

Doing what you say you are going to do, when you say you are going to do it – and giving help and support when help and support are needed: these are what is meant by reliability. But reliability goes deeper than this.

People turn to the police when they need help. They might not even think about the police for years – and then something goes wrong: they are robbed or beaten up or threatened – and they need help. People turn to the police when, for whatever reason, they have reached the end of the line and have nowhere else to turn.

This means that the police have a special duty to be reliable, because the public is relying on them. Here is an example.

> A man heard a knock on his front door at 8 p.m. on a dark winter's night. He was surprised because his front path is overgrown with bushes and nobody ever uses that door. He therefore opened the door on the chain. Two men in leather jackets stood outside and threatened to beat him up if he didn't keep his mouth shut. The man had no idea what it was all about, said so, and the leather-jacketed men went away. But the man was left feeling rather anxious. He was not used to complete strangers threatening to beat him up. So he called the police.
>
> They said they would come in ten minutes – and they did. They took a careful, detailed statement. Their manner was calm and reassuring, and they thought the man had done exactly the right thing in calling the police. They said that oddly enough there had already been a complaint of something similar in the area that night. They then went away, leaving the man and his wife feeling considerably safer than they had been doing half an hour before.

The story has no ending, because nothing else happened. But the moral of the story is that the man relied on the police, and the police were reliable. They gave exactly the right impression to a member of the public, and inspired complete confidence.

So reliability is vital for the police when dealing with the public. It builds up a feeling of cooperation and confidence which ensures that relations between the police and public are good. And, as we've noted before, where there are good relations between the public and the police, a solid foundation is laid for combatting crime – because criminals have nowhere to hide.

Reliability is also crucial within the police station, and in teamwork. Statements such as, 'Oh well – he said he'd be here but he must have got lost', or 'Well, you know what he's like – he's always half an hour late or half an hour early', or 'He couldn't organise his way out of a paper bag', show how people feel about unreliable team-mates.

Everybody can slip up once in a while, but the keys to reliability are:

- checking what you are supposed to be doing – not obsessively, but often enough to keep on top of things
- forward planning and imagination – for example if you have to go and see someone at Newtown Youth Club at 4.30 p.m. do you know where the youth club is, and what the traffic will be like at that time?
- realising that other people's time is as valuable to them as yours is to you
- caring about doing the job well, and the impression you give
- caring about the reputation of your employers – the police.

3 Attitude

Attitude is a rather vague word connected with how emotions, viewpoints, beliefs or stereotypes are shown. Attitude can be either good or bad. Bad attitude involves stereotyping people in a negative way, and then showing those negative stereotypes through body language, tone of voice or choice of words which are unacceptable to colleagues or to the public. For example sexist attitudes would be shown in the use of slang words such as 'bitch' or 'slag', which are not acceptable because of the prejudice they show, and the bad viewpoint towards women. Homophobic attitudes may be shown in 'limp-wristed' mimes, or the use of words such as 'puff', 'poofter' and 'queer'. (There are plenty of others which are even worse.) Racist attitudes are shown in the use of unacceptable words such as 'nigger' or 'wog', or 'jokes' about racial attributes such as flat noses or thick lips. The word 'coloured' is also associated with race prejudice. And remarks about religious practices, such as purdah, and even about food and clothing, can indicate unacceptable racist attitudes.

Attitude can be either conscious or unconscious. A conscious racist would not be employed in the police. Unconscious racism is a much more difficult thing to deal with. Some people believe that everybody is unconsciously racist in one way or another. Others feel that only white people are unconsciously racist. Still others see racism, sexism and other kinds of prejudice as connected with the distribution of power or wealth in society. They say that it is absurd to think of sexism or racism being practised by the poor or the weak against the rich or the powerful. And they may be right. But the police, of course, have power – and this puts them in the position of being more likely to be accused of having a wrong attitude. So attitude is important in the police.

> **THINK ABOUT IT ...**
> Is it possible for people to change their attitudes?
> Is it possible for people to hide their attitudes?
> What harm can a wrong attitude have for an individual police officer?

4 Personality

Personality describes the way in which individuals relate to other individuals or to situations. There have been many attempts to understand the differences in people's personalities, and there is no general agreement. The most famous approach to personality is that of the psychologist HJ Eysenck. The diagram in figure 3.2 shows his way of looking at personality.

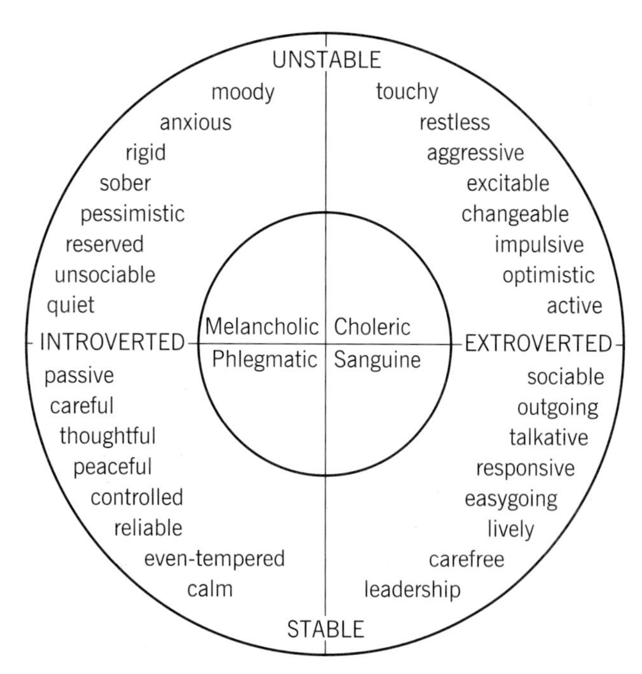

Figure 3.2 *Dimensions of personality (Source: HJ Eysenck, 1965 from* Psychology – the Science of Mind and Behaviour *R Gross (3rd ed.), Hodder & Stoughton, 1996, p 752)*

Eysenck suggests there are two main dimensions to personality. One runs from stable to unstable, the other from extroverted to introverted.

A stable personality is a strong, fixed personality which is not greatly affected by moods or passing emotion. An unstable personality is dominated by passing emotions and may therefore appear to change from day to day, or even from minute to minute.

An extroverted personality is warm, outgoing, and relates easily to other people. An extrovert can be the life and soul of the party – or, equally, someone who never stops talking! Extroverted means something like 'turned outwards', in the sense that an extrovert is open and doesn't hide his feelings.

By contrast an introvert is quiet, often the kind of person who is said to have 'hidden depths'. Introverts don't need to be with other people – in fact they often prefer being by themselves. At a party they might either say practically nothing, or sneak off at the earliest possible opportunity!

If we look at these personality features, or 'traits', we can see that some would be useful in the public services, and others would not. Since police officers have to be dependable, and a source of strength to those around them, it is better if they have stable personalities rather than unstable ones. People with unstable personalities, who are dominated by their moods, can be difficult and tiring to work with, because they act and think so differently at different times. They may be brilliant, but not all the time. Paul Gascoigne, the footballer, might be a good example of an unstable personality.

Police work is working with people. If you want to work with fingerprints, blood and semen stains you need a scientific background and you can work for the police as a civilian employee in a forensic team. As a scientist working for the police you could be as introverted as you like, but a true introvert would find it hard to be a police officer. Police officers are 'people people' and like being with others. They relate to people and can always think of something to say. So it helps if they are extroverts. Introverts find it hard to relate to people in general, and would therefore find police work more difficult and stressful than an extrovert. It may be that some introverts can force themselves to appear like extroverts, but after a while the strain will begin to show. An introvert who joins the police and then spends all his time trying to be an extrovert might find the job very stressful indeed. Introverts are better at jobs where they can concentrate on single tasks for long periods of time, rather than juggling several tasks at once, as police officers have to do.

Having said all this, most of us are partly extrovert and partly introvert. A person who is only extrovert can be a pain in the neck, while a person who is wholly introvert would be happiest being a trappist monk. Whatever the case for an individual officer, he has to use his personality to relate effectively to the people he works with, whether they are colleagues, criminals, or members of the public, in order to get the best out of police work.

THINK ABOUT IT ...

Choose any four of the nine qualities listed above on page 67, and show how they are needed for a public service other than the police.

Unit outcome 4
Investigate the nature of authority

Assessment criteria
- Briefly define authority.
- Identify and explain four types of authority.
- Analyse the problems involved in blind obedience to authority.

What is authority?

Authority can be described as the acceptable control of
- one person by another person
- one group of people by another group of people
- one person by a group of people
- a group of people by one person.

Another similar definition is 'legitimate power'. (Here the word 'legitimate' means agreed or accepted in some way. A mad axe-man has the power to chop down all the trees in a park – but he has no authority to do so!)

A further definition of authority would be 'the right to do something'.

Four types of authority

Identify and explain four types of authority.

Human history is the study of authority and how to overthrow it, so people have thought deeply about authority over the centuries. But they didn't start to classify it in a way that was relevant to modern life until Max Weber (1864–1920) had a go. You can read more about his ideas in Unit 15 page 367.

Weber decided that there were three kinds of authority.

1 Charismatic authority. This is the authority an individual has from his strength of character and his ability to charm, bully, persuade or otherwise influence people. Note that this is strength of character – not physical strength.

2 Traditional authority. This kind of authority comes not from the person himself so much as the traditional organisation that he represents. If we consider someone like the pope, his authority comes partly from his character (after all, he would never have been appointed as pope if his character and ability hadn't been suitable) – but also from his position as the representative of God on earth, and head of the largest Christian church. So for people who belong to the Catholic church (which a sociologist would see as the Catholic tradition), he has great authority. But for non-Catholics, who do not belong to that tradition, his authority is very limited indeed. This is shown by the fact that many Catholics will not use contraception, because he has forbidden it. But how many non-Catholics refuse to use contraception because the pope has forbidden it?

3 Rational-legal authority. This is an updated form of traditional authority. But it is based on people's skills and knowledge, and their position in a modern institution such as a company or a public service. So, for example, the authority of a High Court judge is based on (a) knowledge of the law, (b) skill in practising it, and (c) the status of being a High Court judge, one of the top lawyers in the country. It is rational because – with his or her ability – he or she is one of the best people for the job. It is legal, not only because the judge is a lawyer, but because he or she fits into an organised and officially recognised system which carries out a complex and necessary job.

This kind of authority is sometimes called expert authority. It is rational because it makes sense. If a prime minister wanted to learn how to build a dry-stone wall, he would go to a dry-stone waller. In the world as a whole a prime minister would have much more authority than the dry-stone waller. But on the subject of building good walls without cement, the dry-stone waller would have the authority because of his expertise and experience.

Weber's thoughts on authority are very interesting, but people have found them difficult to understand, and society has changed since he made his classification. Nevertheless, later classifications have been similar to his. The only real difference is that they include more types of authority.

A helpful classification of five types of authority was produced in 1959 by French and Raven. They add a fourth type of authority to Weber's three.

4 Coercive authority. Coercive authority comes through the power to punish rather than reward. It is a very old idea. An example is given in this story from an ancient Greek play, *Lysistrata*. The plot is about as simple as it gets: Athenian women, fed up with the Peloponnesian War, barricade themselves in the Acropolis and go on a sex strike to force their husbands to vote for peace with Sparta.

In a modern setting, a good deal of authority is reinforced with coercion. For example the British army has a ban on drugs. They have random drug tests and if someone tests positive they are out of the army. The authority of the drug ban is strengthened by the seriousness of the punishment. The authority is legitimate because recruits to the army know that they are not allowed to take drugs, and sign that – as recruits – they will accept all the army's rulings. They also know that the punishment is legal, so they accept the authority based on it.

THINK ABOUT IT ...

The opposite of coercive authority is 'reward authority'.

Can you think of any examples?

The problem of blind obedience

Analyse the problems involved in blind obedience to authority.

Discipline is a good thing. There is no doubt about that. Self-discipline is even better. And in the public services, both are essential – not only for the effectiveness of the public service as a whole, but also for the well-being and happiness of each individual working in that public service.

But you can have too much of a good thing, and this is true of discipline. Too much discipline can lead to blind obedience.

As blind obedience can cause extremely serious problems in the world, and has led to the deaths of millions, it is analysed in detail below.

What does blind obedience mean?

Blind obedience to authority means obeying without thinking. The idea seems simple, but it needs some disentangling, because there are different types of blind obedience.

1 Automatism. This is the blindest form of blind obedience, and it is generally regarded as a kind of mental illness. It is like sleepwalking or hypnotism – where a person does things without knowing that they have done them. It is rare but might interest the police, because it can be a defence against a murder charge.

2 The obedience of young children. When very young children are being trained, they learn, but they do not remember learning. For this reason their obedience to the instructions of the parents may be a kind of blind obedience. Being taught to hold a spoon would come under this category.

At a slightly older age, the involvement of children in acts of sex abuse may be the result of blind obedience. The child obeys the abusing adult, but it does not understand the implications of what it is doing (or the effects the abuse may have in later life).

3 Blind obedience in normal adults. Normal – or apparently normal – adults will show blind obedience when put under abnormal pressure. This is in contrast to automatism, where the person rather than the pressure is abnormal. There have been many cases of blind obedience in normal adults in the past – usually linked to war.

Blind obedience in religion

In rare cases members of religious cults get together and either kill each other, or commit mass suicide. Often it is difficult for the police or the emergency services to tell what has happened afterwards, because of the scale of destruction and because everybody who would have known about it is dead.

It is likely that this kind of event has happened throughout history, and we associate it with the religious fanaticism and extremism of the Middle Ages. But it can still happen today.

In 1994 *Time* magazine carried this report.

The leaders of the Solar Temple are among the dead in the mass murder-suicide, but many mysteries linger

Allegations of gunrunning in Australia and money laundering in Canada and Europe. A suicide note addressed to the French Interior Minister. Two more booby-trapped houses, primed to erupt in flames at a telephone call.

Those were some of the mysteries that tantalized investigators on three continents last week as they continued to probe the deaths of 53 members of the Order of the Solar Temple, an apocalyptic religious cult, in Switzerland and Canada two weeks ago.

Source: *Time Domestic*, 24 October 1994, **144** (17), by Michael S Serrill

As the extract suggests, this cult posed a major problem for the police and other public services. The cult was active in several countries, and the organisers were cunning and devious. The crime was carefully planned. But it was hard to tell whether the motivation was greed, religion, or some bizarre mixture of the two.

The problems posed to public services by this kind of blind obedience are:

- cult deaths are illegal because they are either murder disguised to look like suicide, or suicide pacts
- it is hard to tell whether the victims or perpetrators are sane or not – this means that the authorities cannot tell whether they are crimes, or signs of mental disorder
- the psychological and criminological aspects of cult deaths are mysterious because few people live to tell the tale – and those who do live may be unable or unwilling to explain what happened
- in a world of telecommunications and the Internet, cult members are able to coordinate their activities in a way which makes them hard to track down.

THINK ABOUT IT ...

Research the Waco Massacre, the killings of the Aum cult in Japan and the Jonestown Massacre.

Blind obedience in warfare

Soldiers have always been expected to obey orders, and in warfare they often get killed as a result of following these orders. For many reasons the collective emotion of warfare overcomes the natural fear that people would feel in life-threatening situations. The state of war increases the authority of the generals and officers, so that soldiers will often go to their deaths uncomplainingly. A famous example of this was at Gallipoli, in what is now Turkey, in World War I, where thousands of Australian and New Zealand soldiers were sent to their deaths by incompetent generals. Another possible example was in the Iran–Iraq war of the 1980s. Here, young Shia Muslims from Iran were told by their leaders that it was a *Jihad*, or Holy War, even though it was being fought against another Islamic nation. Their blind obedience was encouraged by the belief that they would go to paradise, having died as martyrs.

Problems with this kind of blind obedience:

- it seems morally wrong that young people are being sent to their deaths while the generals who are sending them are well back from the battle front, and are not risking their own safety
- fanatical soldiers make a difficult and unpredictable enemy, and pose a risk to peacekeeping forces in places like Kosovo.

The Holocaust

This is the name given to the deliberate killing of six million Jews by the Germans during the course of World War II. Most of the killing was done by gassing the victims. After the war, at the Nuremberg trials, the officials who organised this genocide tried to excuse or explain themselves by saying that they were 'only obeying orders'. As this did not seem a satisfactory explanation, many historians, psychologists and others have assumed either that they were lying, or that they were acting under 'blind obedience'.

This kind of blind obedience poses the following very serious problems.

1. Are all human beings capable of terrible crimes, if they are put under terrible pressures?
2. Why were so many of the systematic killings of the Holocaust carried out by officials who were, in effect, public service workers?
3. What can a person do (either in the public services or in civilian life) if they are given an order which they feel is morally wrong?
4. What can the countries of the world (and their armies) do to ensure that nothing like the Holocaust ever happens again?
5. Should the public services in Britain and elsewhere clamp down on 'neo-Nazi' groups such as the National Front and the British National Party?
6. Should people who support Nazism or genocide be allowed freedom of speech?

THINK ABOUT IT ...

Read more about the history of a war or of the Holocaust, and identify examples of blind obedience.

Watch the film *Schindler's List*.

Imagine the government brings in a law with which you strongly disagree (e.g. that nobody under 25 will be allowed to drive). List as many ways as you can – under two columns: 'legal' and 'illegal' – in which you could oppose this law.

What answers would you give to questions 1 to 6 above?

UNIT 4

Public Service and Society

Unit outcome 1
Examine the main theories of how society operates

Assessment criteria
- Describe three different theories of society.
- Briefly describe how two different theories interpret the functioning of society.

The public services work with people. So if you hope to join the police, the fire service, the ambulance service, the armed forces, the prison service – or any of the others – you need a good understanding of how people behave, both as individuals and as groups. In this unit we are going to look at how people behave as groups, and how this group behaviour affects public service work. While we are doing this we should never forget that the public services are themselves groups. The relationships between the public services and society are the relationships between one set of groups and another.

Theories of society

1 Functionalism

This theory of society is strongly related to capitalism, which is mentioned under 'content' for Outcome 1, Public Service and Society, in the *Edexcel BTEC National in Public Services Guidance and Units*. You will see more about capitalism, socialism and communism from a slightly different viewpoint, on page 130 of Unit 6: Political Awareness.

There is a famous passage in the Bible, and another in Shakespeare, which compares society to the human body. The hands are people who do all the hard work; the brain is people like philosophers and sociologists who spend all their time thinking; greedy people are the mouth or stomach ... and so on.

Functionalism is rather like this idea. It says that every aspect of society has some sort of purpose in keeping the whole shooting match together. Farming exists to provide food; education trains us to be useful members of society; the family provides all the informal care that children, and adults, need; politics and politicians organise us and regulate power in society so that we know who's boss; religions show us how to act morally towards each other so that we aren't always stabbing people in the back, or stealing things, and so on. Functionalism is really saying that society is divided up into parts which all have a purpose, or function, in keeping the whole working reasonably well. In other words, every part of society is useful to the other parts.

Institutions

These 'parts', such as the family, schools, governments or teams (and there are many more) are called institutions. According to functionalism these institutions are all useful to each other and are connected up into an overall structure, or pattern. The usefulness of each institution is described as its role: in other words, this is what it does. And within each institution each person has a role. Thus, in the family, the role of the father might be to go out to work, while the mother's role might be to stay inside and look after the childen. The fact that the roles can just as easily be reversed does not worry the functionalists. They think that any roles are in some way helpful to society as a whole, whoever does them. According to functionalists even criminals may have a useful role in society by giving a warning to the rest of us that crime doesn't pay, or that we will be rejected by most of society if we break the law.

Norms and values

Functionalists believe that we should describe institutions by describing their norms and values. Norms are the usual (or 'normal') ways of behaving for a particular group of people. Values are what a group of people think or believe is right.

So norms in the fire service include wearing a certain type of uniform, and rushing out to deal with fires and accidents. But in a given fire station the norms might also be to play volleyball while waiting for a call-out, or to swear at somebody who puts boots on the furniture. The only difference between the norms given here are that some are formal (official) and others are informal.

The formal values of the fire service are a belief in saving life and property, and in serving the public. But a given group of firefighters might have some less formal (and less desirable) values, such as a belief that a woman could never do the job as well as a man.

> **THINK ABOUT IT ...**
>
> If you were a functionalist, how would you explain the usefulness to society of
> (a) poverty (b) skinheads
> (c) hospices for the terminally ill?

2 Marxism

Marxism is a set of beliefs based on the writings of Karl Marx, who lived from 1818 to 1883. Marx spent most of his life in a dusty attic writing heavy books on economics and politics. His writings – especially *Das Kapital* (1867) – have had a vast effect on the whole of 20th century history.

There are many subjects in the world which people don't give two hoots about. But Marxism is different. Mention Marxism to one person, and it will be like setting off a firework; mention it to someone else and they will try to scrape you off their shoe. People feel strongly about Marxism.

Marx says that to understand society we must understand that the most important thing people do for their survival is to produce food and material objects. Modern society is based on the creation of wealth – 'capital' – through the production of food and goods. Marx was the person who first described modern society as capitalist, and his description of capitalist society is agreed on by many (but not all) experts.

He divides production into three aspects:

1. The forces of production – these include technology, science and raw materials.
2. The means of production – these are all of the forces of production that can be bought and sold. So machines, buildings, raw materials, transport and so on are all means of production.
3. The relations of production – these are the relationship between the employers, who own the means of production, and the workers, who own nothing but their labour, which they sell to the employer in return for their wages.

In a sense labour is one of the forces of production, but it is the only one owned by the workers. The pay they get for selling their labour is always less than the value of the products they make. So for example if people are making cars, the total value of the payment they receive is always much less than the total value of the cars they make. Marx calls this difference 'surplus value': other people call it profit.

Marx sees the relations of production – the relationship between bosses and workers – as one of exploitation. The bosses are exploiting the workers because they are buying their labour, their work, from them at much less than it is really worth. This is why the bosses get rich and the workers remain poor.

Where functionalists see society as a kind of agreement, Marxists see it as a battleground. What is good for the bosses is bad for the workers, and what is good for the workers is bad for the bosses. Functionalists say that if a firm makes a good profit some of this money will inevitably benefit the workers. Marx says that if a firm makes big profits the workers have merely been taken for a ride, and their bosses will become even richer 'fat cats'.

Marx says that everything else in society follows the same pattern that we see in the relations of production. This is because the bosses are the ruling class, and they design society to increase their own power and make the power of the workers less. According to Marxists, laws exist to 'maintain the *status quo*' which means to keep society as it is, with the rich exploiting the poor. Marx saw capitalist society as a kind of con-trick, with the rich persuading the poor that everything was alright, and that capitalism worked. As a result of the con-trick, many people who *were* workers, such as teachers and police officers, did not see themselves as workers, but as something else – the 'middle classes', perhaps. Marx said that this was an illusion, and he called it 'false consciousness'. He saw his work as an attempt to make people see the world as it really was: a conflict between the rich and the poor, between those who have power and those who do not.

A Marxist would see education as follows. The classroom is a conflict situation. The aim of the teacher is to get as much work as possible out of the students, while doing as little work as possible himself. The aim of the student is to cause the teacher as much work as possible, while doing as little work as possible himself. But functionalists would say that both teacher and students are working together for the same ends, and that if students cooperate then both they and the teacher will benefit.

Marx believed that in the long run capitalist society would destroy itself, because the oppressed, exploited workers would rise up and destroy the capitalists in a class war. After all, the workers were the people who provided labour, an essential ingredient in the creation of wealth, and they were getting paid peanuts.This prediction has not come true. It seemed to be coming true in Russia in 1917 with the Communist revolution, but in 1989 Communism in the USSR finally broke down. And though China is still officially Communist it is taking on many aspects of capitalism.

3 Interactionism

Interactionism is different from the two theories we have already looked at. While functionalism and Marxism look at society as a whole, interactionism looks at society by examining the relationships between small groups of people within it.

Furthermore, instead of setting out with abstract statements, such as 'all people and institutions have fixed roles in society', or 'everybody is either a boss or a worker', interactionists try to approach society with an open mind, observe what is happening, and then draw conclusions. They take the view that because people are not machines, they do not always behave in the same way, and they are not easy to classify.

Interactionists see social life as a series of encounters which they describe as interactions. The importance of these interactions is first and foremost the meaning they have for the people involved. This is because the meaning of a situation doesn't exist outside the heads of the people who are involved in it, or watching it.

In fact, it's like the riddle: 'Does a tree falling in a forest make a noise if there is nobody around to hear it?' Functionalists and Marxists would both say the falling tree made a noise whether anyone was there or not. (They would just disagree about what kind of noise it was.) Interactionists would say that the question is pointless; what matters is the noise that people hear if they do happen to be there.

The meaning that interactions have is decided by the people involved. Suppose a pretty girl is walking along the street. A man rushes up to her and jumps on top of her. She might shout 'Rape!' But if a bomb goes off at that moment the man might have done it to save her life. So the meaning of the interaction is decided by the circumstances. A real-life example of this occurred once when a student fell asleep in a teacher's class. The head of department, who was very strict, called the teacher out and told him off for allowing the student to go to sleep. 'Besides,' he said, 'the student might have been ill, in which case you should have sent him to the nurse.' The teacher said afterwards to a colleague, 'I was quite happy for the student to go to sleep in my class. It showed he had a good, relaxed relationship with the teacher.' The student may well have said to his mates, 'That was such a boring lesson I just had to go to sleep!' Here again the meaning of an interaction is decided by the participants.

Of course interactionism wouldn't be much use if all it said was that everything that happens is a matter of opinion. Instead of helping us to understand society it would dodge the problem by saying that there was no point in even bothering to try.

But interactionists then go on to say that the meaning we give to interactions is based on our self-concept, our view of ourselves, which itself is based on previous interactions. Suppose I – a public service lecturer – lose a student's assignment. An interaction will follow during which the student will accuse me of losing his assignment. If I am well organised and have never lost a student's assignment I might say, 'No I didn't lose it. You never handed it in!' If, on the other hand, my desk is hidden under a heap of disorganised papers, and I know very well that I lost six assignments last year, my self-concept will force me to say, 'Er – yes – I may have lost it. I'll have a look.' In this case the self-concept will be reinforced, because yet another assignment has been lost, and it is more than ever clear, both to myself and the student, that I am the type of tutor who loses assignments. This is rather like labelling theory, in pyschology, and stereotyping. You can read about these in Unit 5: Human Behaviour, pages 106–129.

Interactionists see human relationships and interactions as a series of 'negotiations' where, as in the above example, roles exist, but they are not fixed. They are determined by the situation and its context.

Interactionism is more useful to the public services than functionalism and Marxism, because it enables people to study what happens when people meet or quarrel or, for that matter, commit crimes. It might not explain much about society as a whole, but it explains a great deal at the level at which we have to deal with it.

Summary

Functionalism

- Society is made up of parts, called institutions, which all work together reasonably successfully most of the time.
- Each institution is related to others and has some 'usefulness'.
- People and institutions have fixed roles.
- Capitalist society sees itself in a functionalist way.
- Functionalism is associated with the political thinking of centre and centre-right parties (such as the Conservatives).

Marxism

- Society is at war with itself, rich versus poor.
- The rich own the means of production (factories, machines, etc.).
- The poor sell their labour in return for wages.
- The value of these wages is much less than the value of what they make.
- The rich therefore make a profit, which Marxists call 'surplus value'.
- Capitalist society will destroy itself when workers learn how they are being exploited, and rise up to defeat the rich.
- Socialism is Marxism in a society where the rich have not yet been completely defeated.
- Communism is a society of collective ownership and equality: a kind of perfect world in the future where there will be peace and plenty.
- Marxism is associated with the political left wing.

Interactionism

- Looks at society from close up, and examines the details of encounters called interactions – these can be seen as actions between individuals or small groups.
- The importance of interactions lies in the meanings people attach to them.
- Each person has a self-concept – a 'character' which decides the way they look at interactions, and respond to them.
- Roles are not fixed but decided (often on the spur of the moment) by people during interactions.
- The process of altering or developing new roles in an interaction is called negotiation. (But it is usually not like the kind of negotiation in politics where people discuss matters openly.)
- Interactionism is useful for understanding the kinds of things that happen in public service work (for example interviewing crime suspects).

Interpretations of society

Briefly explain how two different theories interpret the functioning of society.

ANALYSIS

Functionalist interpretation

Functionalism looks at society in a traditional way. It sees people as belonging to groupings called institutions, each of which has a role in society as a whole. There is nothing particularly mysterious about these roles – most of them are those which common sense would lead us to expect, for example that the role of the police is to uphold the law.

Functionalism says that there is a 'consensus' or agreement about who does what in society. Roles are clearly defined for most people, and fit in with the roles, norms and value systems of others. Individuals are all different, but there are so many roles available in society that there is something for everyone.

One of the good things about functionalism is that it recognises our individual differences, and sees these as useful for society as a whole. This idea makes sense. If we were all the same, with the same norms, values and skills, we would have nothing to offer other people that they did not already possess themselves. There would be no point, for example, in somebody getting a job as a mechanic, because everybody else would be equally skilled at being a mechanic. But functionalism fits in with the idea that some of us are good at some things, and others at others, and yet we can all 'serve' society in some way, because we are all better than most people at something.

Education allows us to specialise, and so discover the roles that we will later take up in society. It prepares us for institutions (such as the police or the army) in which we will be able to work and take our place. Functionalism encourages this diversity and individualism, by stressing that all the thousands of institutions have some value. It doesn't try to lump us all together under the single crude category of 'workers' as Marxism does.

For this reason, as noted above, functionalism fits in well with capitalism. In a sense we are all cogs in a machine for making wealth. Even if we don't get equal wealth we all get something out of it.

Marxist interpretation

More than functionalism or interactionism, Marxism looks at society from the point of view of the distribution of wealth and power. And when Marxists look at capitalist society – of the type, for example, that we have in Britain – they do not like what they see.

The essential idea in Marxism is conflict, and it looks at society as a form of civil war instead of an exercise in cooperation. Workers are always exploited by their employers, and according to Marxism they will continue to be exploited unless they get together and struggle for their freedom. Since capitalists will not willingly give up their wealth, Marxists expect that eventually there will be a revolution in which the capitalists will be forced to give up their wealth by the workers (whom Marx called the 'proletariat').

The functionalist idea of everybody being in different institutions doesn't impress Marxists. They see this idea as part of the 'false consciousness' put about by capitalists, who try to persuade us that we are not being exploited. Marxists say that all these institutions amount to one thing: exploitation. For this reason workers have to get together in trade unions or revolutionary movements (see 'Liberation movements' in Unit 8: International Perspectives, pages 181–210). They need to educate themselves about how they are being exploited, then 'organise, organise, organise' (as Mao Tse-tung, the Chinese communist leader put it) to overthrow the rich oppressors.

To everybody except Marxists it seems that Marxism was tried, and failed, in the USSR between 1917 (the date of the Russian revolution) and 1989, when Mikhail Gorbachov allowed democratic elections and Boris Yeltsin became the first non-Communist leader of Russia since the Tsar. This is because capitalism has changed in ways which Marx didn't predict. These changes include the following:

1 Some acceptance of trade unions, which allowed workers to bargain for better pay and conditions through much of the 20th century. Unions, which are based on particular industries, have done much to raise the living standards for employees. They reached the height of their power in Britain in the 1950s and 60s. After the 1970s they declined under the Conservative government of Margaret Thatcher, partly because laws were passed to make striking more difficult, and partly because increased unemployment and changes in manufacturing industry cut their membership.

2 Keynesian (pronounced 'caynzian') economics. John Maynard Keynes, a government economist who was active in the 1930s, put forward the idea that if workers were made wealthier, they would spend their money on luxuries and so increase the productivity and profitability of manufacturing industry. He also said it was a good idea if the government put money into industry to encourage investment, employment and productivity. He was not a socialist, but his ideas had the effect of making working people better off.

3 Changes in the organisation of factories, and the abolition of assembly lines, has blurred the difference between workers and bosses. The computer revolution has also changed the nature of work. Furthermore much of industry now provides services (e.g. banking and tourism) rather than goods. All this has weakened traditional socialism, but strengthened the position of many working people.

4 Compulsory education has changed the nature of working people, who no longer see themselves as 'workers' in the way they did. This has weakened socialism in Britain, and undermined the influence of Marx. Modern-day Marxists have had to follow other thinkers such as Trotsky and Gramsci in an effort to put new life into the Marxist interpretation of society.

Unit outcome 2
Examine the effects of the inequalities of income and wealth distribution in society

Assessment criteria
- Describe patterns of income and wealth distribution in contemporary Britain.
- Briefly analyse the effects on the individual of inequalities of income and wealth.
- Identify the consequences of income and wealth inequality for a given public service.

Patterns of income and wealth distribution in contemporary Britain

Here are two definitions:
- income: money that comes to us from somewhere else – earnings, benefits, pensions, interest from investments and so on
- wealth: money or property that we already own – money in the bank, investments, cars, houses, land.

It would be pleasant if everybody in the world was well off – but they aren't. The 'average' American has an income 112 times higher than the average inhabitant of Madagascar. And even in Britain there are big variations in wealth.

Many factors influence the income and wealth that people in Britain have. Here are some of the main ones.

The job you do

Look at the table in figure 4.1.

This tells you, among other things, that solicitors get twice as much as nurses and four times as much as waiters and waitresses. And solicitors are not the best paid people in the country. But they are paid better than average.

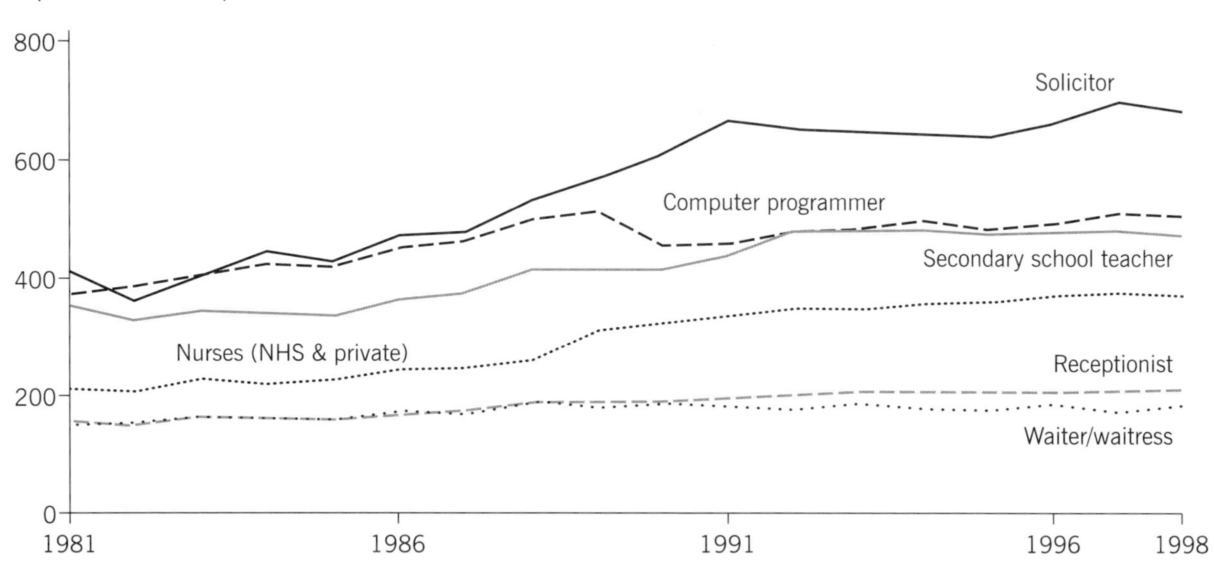

Figure 4.1 *Real gross weekly earnings: by selected occupation (Source:* Social Trends *1999, p. 89)*

Why do solicitors get paid more than most of us? This is not an easy question to answer. But possible answers include:

- they are well educated, and have to train longer than teachers or police officers (six years at least after leaving school at the age of 18)
- their job is highly skilled, and many people wouldn't have the ability to do it well however long they trained
- there are not enough high quality solicitors to satisfy society's demand for them, so up to a point they can name their fees
- the companies and individuals who employ them are often wealthy, and can afford to pay well.

On the other hand, waiters and waitresses are near the bottom of the heap. They work hard; their hours are unsocial, and it requires some skill to do the job well, but they still get paid peanuts. Why? Possible answers include:

- many of them are young, and young people do not get paid as much as older ones
- the job does not require a great deal of training
- plenty of people are capable of doing the job, so they are easily replaced
- many work for small restaurants or family businesses which cannot afford to pay them well
- often it is only a part-time or temporary job.

FOCUS

THE CLASS SYSTEM

This is the official British class system as defined by the Registrar General's office (a branch of the civil service).

Class I Professional etc. occupations
company directors, lawyers, doctors, bank managers, police inspectors and above

Class II Managerial and technical occupations
teachers, administrators, police constables and sergeants, fire officers

Class III Skilled occupations
(N) non-manual – office workers, secretaries
(M) manual – electricians, plumbers, builders, engineering workers

Class IV Partly-skilled occupations
drivers, postal workers

Class V Unskilled occupations
labourers, shop assistants, unemployed

Not all sociologists agree with this categorisation, and not all jobs are easy to classify, but nevertheless this system is generally accepted by public service workers and others. It has the advantage of being simple to understand, since it is based entirely on the jobs people do. The top jobs are those in Class I. They are the best paid and have the highest status (respect from society) – hence they represent the highest social class. Unskilled occupations have the lowest pay and status, and people doing these are in Class V. The fact is that in Britain the job you do has a big influence on your income and wealth.

The unemployed

Unemployed people have the lowest average income of all, since they survive on benefits. It may be that some of them work on the side – but this does not show up in the official figures.

The underclass

Some experts describe the people who live below the poverty line, who are long-term unemployed or who are homeless as the 'underclass'. They seem to be cut off from the rest of society, and have great difficulty in 'climbing back' into the rest of the class system. They are also stereotyped by many people as 'dossers', 'low-lifes' and 'scum'. And the police and prison service are sometimes seen as guilty of this kind of labelling themselves.

Where you live

The map in figure 4.2 has a few gaps in it where information is not available. Evidently people in Wales and Cheshire don't like to talk about how much they earn! Nevertheless it shows clearly that the highest average earnings (pay) are found in the south east of England, and that generally people get paid less the further they live from London.

Reasons for this include:

- many of the top jobs are in London, because it is the capital city
- many jobs – teaching for example – have a London allowance or 'weighting' which means that teachers in London get paid more than

teachers doing the same job in other parts of the country: this is because it is harder to recruit teachers to work in London, and the cost of living and accommodation is higher
- some parts of the country (for instance Wales and Scotland) have industries such as tourism and hill-farming where people are traditionally less well paid.

Male or female

Although the Sex Discrimination Act 1975 made it illegal to pay a man more than a woman for doing the same job, the average earnings of men are significantly higher than the average earnings of women. In many age groups the average difference can be as much as 25 per cent, as shown in figure 4.3 below.

It is only among young people that males and females get almost the same average pay – even for full-time jobs. Reasons for this inequality are:
- men are more likely to get promoted than women, and most of the well-paid jobs are still done by men: except in a few professions such as nursing and teaching the culture (atmosphere) of the workplace is dominated by men

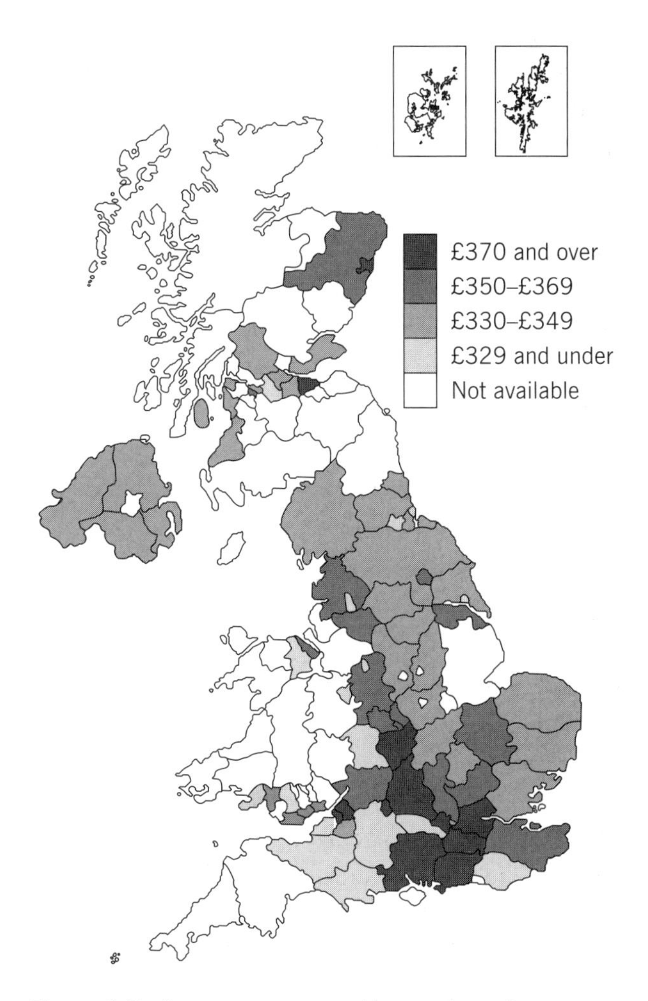

Figure 4.2 *Average gross weekly earnings: by area, April 1998 (Source:* Social Trends *29, 1999, p. 89)*

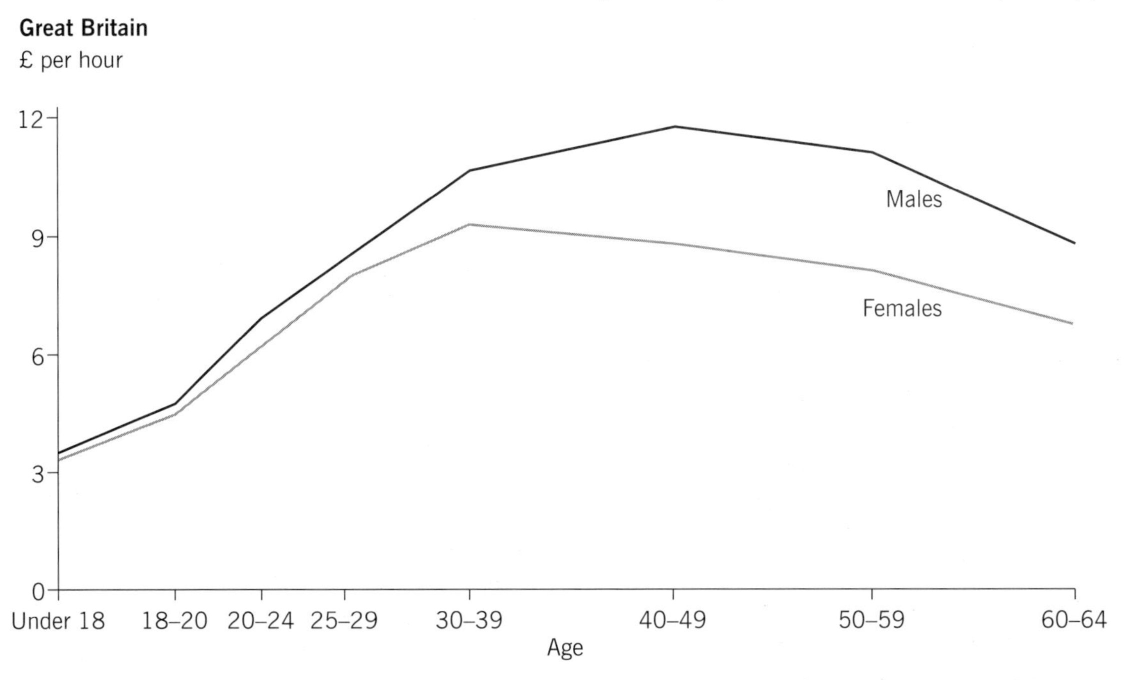

Figure 4.3 *Hourly earnings from full-time employment: by gender and age, April 1998 (Source:* Social Trends *29, 1999, p. 92)*

- women are still subject to family commitments, so that maternity leave and other factors are likely to hold back their careers
- in the past more attention was paid to the education of boys than girls, so that (until about 15 years ago) boys did better than girls in most exams: among older people, men are therefore likely to be better qualified than women, and this means that they tend to have better paid jobs.

How old you are

The diagram shown in figure 4.3 above doesn't simply show the difference in average earnings between men and women. It also shows how earnings vary with age.

The National Minimum Wage, introduced in April 1999, is £3.00 for people under 22 and £3.60 an hour for people over 22. This reflects the normal practice in British society, which is to pay young people less. The figure dates from before the introduction of the minimum wage, but if the same diagram was drawn for today's figures it would still look much the same.

People's wages (weekly pay) and salaries (monthly pay) rise until they reach a certain age, then tail off again. The reasons for this vary.

- For manual workers such as bricklayers, who get paid by the amount of bricks they lay, earnings are highest when they are under 30, because their fitness and health are at a peak then, and they can work faster.
- For public service workers and others who work for the government promotion is most rapid before the age of forty.
- People with very high salaries often retire around the age of 50 so they can spend more time on the yacht. They are therefore taken out of the figures for older people, so the average earnings drop.
- In their high earning years, many employees work abroad, on oil rigs or in other places where they get many extra allowances, expenses and 'perks'. This puts their earnings up. As they get older, they return to base and get less income as a result.
- Another factor may simply be ageism. If a person changes their job in their fifties, or returns to work after a period of unemployment, they often have to accept a lower salary.
- New technology is creating jobs which require quick understanding and up-to-date knowledge of the kind that young people are more likely to have. Computer development work and trading in the new computerised stock markets require flexibility, intelligence, alertness and stamina. The young score better on all these counts. In a meritocracy – a society where there is payment by results – they deserve to be well paid.

Your ethnic background

In Britain people from ethnic minorities have lower average incomes and wealth than the white population. For example, 89 per cent of white people have some form of savings – which is a measure of wealth. But only 57 per cent of people from Pakistani or Bangladeshi backgrounds have savings.

It is a similar story where income is concerned, for workers from ethnic minorities are – as they always have been – concentrated in the worst-paid jobs, and in part-time work. And there are higher rates of unemployment among the (non-white) ethnic minorities than among the white population.

Disability

Disabled people are much worse off than most of the rest of society. If they have learning difficulties, or are mentally ill, they may not be capable of well-paid work. And if they are physically disabled – or blind, or deaf – this places huge barriers to their progress in the workplace. However, campaigns are having an effect and a few disabled people have very good jobs. Through equal opportunities policies organisations are now employing disabled people when, at one time, they would not have done. But it seems likely that disabled people will always be disadvantaged, on average, where income and wealth are concerned.

One-parent families

Here are some statistics.

- Five out of six lone parents claim a means-tested benefit.
- 60 per cent of lone parent families live on or below the poverty line.
- 33 per cent of those on Income Support and 21 per cent of those on Family Credit experience severe hardship.
- The average disposable income of lone parents is only approximately 39 per cent of that of couples with two children.
- Children of lone parents on average have 10 per cent less spent on them than in two-parent families, even though the lone parent makes more sacrifices.
- Over 30 per cent of children of lone parents not in paid work are poor and 15 per cent severely poor.
- Poor children are six times more likely and severely poor children ten times more likely to go without than children as a whole – especially on food and clothing items.

Source: Gingerbread website

These facts, from a charity for lone parents, show how they are disadvantaged in income and wealth. This situation may be made worse, as the government has recently cut lone-parent benefit. Since lone parents are more likely to be female than male, this is a factor affecting the relative poverty of women in this country.

The inequalities of income and wealth

Briefly analyse the effects on the individual of inequalities of income and wealth.

The amount of money and wealth people have affects them in many ways.

Health

Poor people have poor health. On average people in social class I live seven years longer than in social class V (see page 82). And for every known illness except skin cancer, sickness levels and death rates are higher for poor people than for the rich. Many reasons have been put forward for these disturbing facts:

- poor people eat lower quality food
- they spend too much of their money on drink and cigarettes
- they live in worse housing, in areas where there is more noise and pollution
- their lives are more stressful because they have no power over others, and everyone else has power over them
- there are high crime levels in poor areas, also leading to stress
- poor people are less active, do less sport, take less exercise and have fewer holidays
- they are poorly educated and therefore do not know how to keep themselves healthy
- their standards of hygiene are lower
- they are afraid to go to the doctor, and cannot afford prescription charges
- doctors in poor areas are overworked, and perhaps not as good at their job as they should be
- unemployment is bad for your health
- poor people are genetically less able to withstand illness, and include the disabled and the chronically ill.

THINK ABOUT IT ...

Which of the above statements do you think might be untrue?

Class, culture and lifestyle

The class system, which divides people into social classes on the basis of their occupations, is also a good guide as to whether an individual is well off or not. As a rule, those in the higher social classes have higher incomes and wealth than those in the lower social classes.

Wealth, or the lack of it, shows itself in all sorts of ways connected with who we are, and the way we act. Here are some examples.

- The way people speak: people who speak with strong regional accents are likely to be worse off than those who speak with slight accents or none

at all. Standard English is the English of the middle classes; regional English is the English of the working classes. The difference is not as clear as it used to be, but it is still there.
- The way people dress: expensive clothes look different from cheap ones, and enable wealthier people to show off their relative wealth without really trying. For poorer people this can be humiliating – for example when their children ask for expensive trainers because other children at school are wearing them.
- Other possessions: cars, houses and many other possessions all reflect the wealth or poverty of the owner. Wealthy people can afford to buy luxuries which will give them pleasure. A person driving a new Porsche will gain a different experience from it than the person who drives an old Y-registered 'banger', or who jolts along in a slow and smelly bus. Now that there are more things to buy than ever before, what we drive, what we wear, what we eat and what we drink have become important indicators of lifestyle. This stress on the importance of what we buy is called 'consumerism'. The good side of consumerism is that we have the choice to buy – and therefore to be – whatever we want. The bad side is that it makes us materialistic and shallow in our thinking, putting possessions before people. And consumerism tends to humiliate and degrade everybody who cannot afford to buy.
- Holidays: according to *Social Trends* 1999, 40 per cent of British people feel they cannot afford to take a week's holiday each year. The rich may still find their holidays expensive, but they do have them, and they last longer than one week.

Education

In the British education system the great majority of children – 85 per cent – are educated in the state system. At secondary level they go mainly to comprehensive schools. But if their parents are rich they can go to other kinds of school, such as independent, grant-maintained or even 'public' schools (which are strictly speaking private). On average these schools have higher academic standards than those in the state sector – but they cost parents thousands of pounds a year.

Crime

Rates of recorded crime are higher in poor areas than rich ones (see figure 4.4). Poor people are more likely to be convicted of crime than rich people. They are also more likely to be the victims of crime.

The following points can be made:
- Crime figures are unreliable for a number of reasons (see Unit 11, Law and Criminology, pages 256–276).
- It is more logical that poor people should steal from the rich than that rich people should steal from the poor.
- Peer groups are stronger in poor areas because the family influence is often weaker. Peer groups are more likely to encourage young people to commit crimes than the family are.
- Crimes by poor people are more likely to be detected and reported than crimes by the rich. This because they often involve theft against individuals, or crimes of violence in public.
- The police may stereotype the poor, or target poor areas, which will tend to increase the number of poor people convicted of offences.
- Poor people do not have the money to protect their homes as the rich do.

England & Wales						Percentage
	Council estates and low income	Affluent urban	Affluent family	New home-owning	Mature home-owning	Affluent suburban and rural
Vehicle crime (owners)						
All thefts	23	19	18	18	17	14
Vandalism	10	12	6	9	7	6
Bicycle thefts (owners)	10	8	3	7	5	3
Burglary	9	8	4	6	5	4
Home vandalism	5	4	4	4	4	3
Other household theft	9	7	6	8	7	5
Any household offence	34	32	31	29	25	

Figure 4.4 *Risk of being a victim of crime: by type of area, 1995–1997 (Source:* Social Trends *29, 9.8, p.155)*

- Because poor people suffer from stress and have low self-esteem they may turn more easily to crime.
- There is a subculture of criminality on some poor estates which makes crime seem exciting and glamorous to the young people who live there.

The consequences of inequality

Identify the consequences of income and wealth inequality for the prison service.

Juvenile crime

FOCUS

The following figures, from the Annual Report of HM Inspector of Prisons for England and Wales, 1996/97, clearly show the relationship of juvenile crime to poverty and other social problems:

- 73% left school before the statutory age
- 55% had been expelled of whom – 35% for fighting – 15% for being disruptive and not working – 11% for drugs offences or glue sniffing – 11% for assaulting a teacher
- 42% truanted regularly: eight out of ten failed to attain formal educational qualifications of any kind. Over eight out of ten had no experience of trade training
- Almost six out of ten had never been employed in any capacity
- 55% reported significant experience (two years or more) of being in care
- 49% had experienced divorce or separation of their parents before they were 15
- 19% had been disowned by their parents before the age of 15
- 18% only were living with both natural parents
- 34% reported living on their own or with friends
- 24% living with a single parent – mother
- 11% living with 2 parents – one a step-parent
- 14% are, or soon will be, a parent themselves
- 34% of all girls under 18 admitted to prison are already, or are about to become, mothers
- 36% gave the effects of drugs as the reason for their offence
- 25% gave alcohol as the reason for their offence
- 25% gave peer influence
- 25% that they needed money
- 11% that they were seeking excitement or relief from boredom
- 46% had been referred for psychiatric examination
- 17% reported a history of self-harm.

Most prisoners come from the poorer sections of society and, as the profile of young prisoners above shows, they suffer from a wide range of social problems. Among the points listed there is evidence of deprivation and disadvantage of the type found in large council estates and inner cities. Poverty, and the fact that the government cannot afford or does not know how to reduce it, may have pushed many of these young prisoners into crime.

Inside the prison service

Inequalities of wealth have important effects within the prison service as well. These are as follows.

Prison officers are recruited from all social backgrounds. Some of them come from poor homes, some from rich. Yet however different their backgrounds, they have to work together closely and willingly, and with a good team spirit. So the divisions which come from having rich or poor backgrounds have to be healed if prison officers are to do their work properly. Prison officers are therefore:

- trained to have an esprit de corps (team spirit) which makes them loyal to their colleagues, not their own social background
- dressed in uniform which conceals their differences in background (just as a school uniform would with children)
- trained not to discriminate against each other for any reason whatsoever – including relative wealth or poverty.

The other aspect of inequality of wealth and income within the prison service is its salary and rank structure. Wealth from outside the service is not supposed to influence prison officers' behaviour, but the salary structure is. Here are the reasons for having a salary and rank structure:

1 To encourage officers to stay in the prison service. This is partly because it costs a lot to train them, and the money is wasted if they leave. But it is also bad for morale if there is a high turnover of staff. And since good prison officers are learning all their lives, it makes sense if they can be encouraged to stay in the job as long as possible. For this reason a system of increments is used so that officers automatically get a salary rise after each year.

2 To produce a system of seniority and rank, which helps to maintain firm discipline, and gives a career structure. This shows new recruits that the prison service is more than a job – it is a career with good long-term prospects and rewards for people who work hard and show the right qualities.

3 To motivate officers to take on extra responsibility, and to fulfil their ambition and potential by applying for promotion. This helps to keep skilled and able officers in the service – otherwise they might leave and go into some other career.

4 Promotion can be seen as a reward as well as an encouragement; a way of showing officers that their efforts are appreciated.

THINK ABOUT IT ...

Normally we talk about inequalities of income and wealth as if they were bad things. Yet these inequalities are a necessary part of the organisation and motivation of the prison and other public services.

So could it be that inequalities of wealth and income are just as necessary for society as a whole as they are for the public services? What do you think?

Unit outcome 3
Investigate the consequences for a given public service operating in a multicultural society

Assessment criteria

- Briefly describe how cultural diversity has emerged in contemporary Britain.
- Briefly examine the effectiveness of legislative approaches to four issues of equality.
- Examine in detail two consequences of operating in a multicultural society for a given public service.

Cultural diversity

Culture can be defined, perhaps not very helpfully, as 'the sum total of everything we learn after birth'. It includes our norms – that is the way we behave, both in our everyday life and on special occasions – and our values, which are all the things we believe in. Because our culture affects the way we see and understand the world we are not aware of it, any more than a person who wears spectacles is aware of having them on. But we do notice our own cultural expectations if we meet someone from a different culture who behaves and thinks differently from the way we do.

The word 'culture' has become mixed up in people's mind with the word 'race', and in this unit we are certainly going to look at culture in connection with racial issues. But it is worth stressing that culture does not necessarily have anything to do with race. For example, the culture of sheep farmers in the Lake District has always been different from the culture of Yorkshire coal miners, or of office workers who live in the London suburbs. In other words the way these different groups of people behave and see life is different. But they speak (roughly) the same language, have similar religious backgrounds, wear clothes which are not totally different, and traditionally live in 'nuclear' families. And they all think of themselves as English. So though their cultures are different, they do not differ as widely as the cultures of people who come from different countries and continents do.

From the point of view of the public services, it is cultures which have come from other parts of the world which have had the greatest recent effect on the way they work and the way they look at society. So this is what we are going to focus on first.

How cultural diversity has emerged in modern Britain

The history of Britain is partly the history of people coming in to the country from outside and changing it, usually gradually. The Celts arrived in ancient times followed by Romans, Saxons, Vikings and Normans. Each of these arrivals were invasions, but since 1066 the pattern has changed, and people have been coming in peacefully in groups of various sizes. In the Middle Ages, for example, many Jewish people came, and in the 18th century Huguenots, who were protestant refugees from France. In the 19th century large numbers of Irish people came, partly because of the great disaster of the potato famine in 1845, and partly to work in building the canals, railways and towns that sprang up in Victorian times. In the 20th century the main influx of people started after World War II in 1945. They came from the countries now classified as 'Pakistan and the New Commonwealth'; in other words, countries that used to be colonised by Britain but which achieved freedom in the years following World War II.

Immigration

People moving permanently into a country are called immigrants. Immigrants from India, Pakistan and the West Indies were invited into Britain by the government and by various private industries during the late 1940s and the 1950s. They were invited because Britain was reconstructing itself after the war, and there were not enough British workers available. Furthermore, workers from southern Asia and the West Indies were willing to work for lower wages than British workers.

The main phase of immigration was between 1953 and 1962. The numbers, and the main countries they came from, are shown in figure 4.5.

Many British people, especially those in the working classes who felt that their jobs and way of life were being threatened by the new arrivals, became worried about the numbers of people coming in. Various inner city disturbances, which some people called 'race riots' (normally associated with America), didn't help, and in 1962 the Commonwealth Immigrants Act was brought in, to control the number of people entering the country.

The Act was racist in that it only controlled the numbers coming in from 'non-white' countries. There was, for example, no control in the numbers of people coming in from Ireland.

Further controls were introduced in 1965, and in 1968 the next Commonwealth Immigrants Act restricted entry by East African Asians even though they held full British passports. This caused an outcry at the time, because the immigrants were fleeing persecution in East African countries – especially Uganda. But at the same time racist politicians such as Enoch Powell were making dangerous speeches about 'rivers of blood', which were seen as encouraging race riots in British cities. So a further Immigration Act was passed in 1971, restricting entry except to people who had a parent or grandparent born in Britain. Effectively, this discriminated againt anybody who wasn't white. Nevertheless, in 1972 Britain did accept 27,000 Ugandan Asians as refugees.

In 1981 the British Nationality Act made it even more difficult to get British citizenship. It also tried to limit 'marriages of convenience' which enabled people to get British citizenship by marrying someone who was already a British citizen. From this time on they had to live in Britain for three years before applying for citizenship.

Over the 1980s immigration declined because:

- the laws got much stricter and
- there were high levels of unemployment – not much work was available.

People who wished to leave 'Pakistan and the New Commonwealth' went to Canada instead, where they had a higher standard of living than they could have obtained in Britain. But the numbers of people coming into Britain were still large: 59,000 in 1981, 48,000 in 1986, 54,000 in 1991 and 53,000 in 1992.

	West Indies	India	Pakistan	Others	Total
1953	2,000				2,000
1954	11,000				11,000
1955	27,500	5,800	1,850	7,500	42,650
1956	29,800	5,600	2,050	9,350	46,800
1957	23,000	6,600	5,200	7,600	42,400
1958	15,000	6,200	4,700	3,950	29,850
1959	16,400	2,950	850	1,400	21,600
1960	49,650	5,900	2,500	–350	57,700
1961	66,300	23,750	25,100	21,250	136,400
1962[1]	31,800	19,050	25,080	18,970	94,900

[1] First six months up to introduction of controls.

Figure 4.5 *Estimated net immigration from the New Commonweath, 1953–1962 (Source: Zig Layton-Henry (1992)* The Politics of Immigration, *Blackwell, Oxford, p13)*

Other aspects of cultural diversity

Feminism

Feminism is the idea that women have been unfairly discriminated against in the past, and that women are entitled to full equality in all legal rights, and in their treatment in private life. The main aims of feminism are:

- to give women and men the promise of equal power and influence
- to give women and men equal pay for equal work
- to release the abilities of women, who used to be kept at home but can now contribute fully to all aspects of life – to the great benefit of society as a whole
- to enrich women's lives in the process, by giving them a full choice of employment and lifestyles
- to free women from the humiliation of being discriminated against
- to free women from sexual and other kinds of harassment
- to change the power relations in the family, by giving women more status
- to enable men to see themselves in a different way, for example by sharing childrearing
- to make other forms of prejudice and intolerance less acceptable.

The gay movement

Homosexuality used to be the sin that 'dare not speak its name', or 'the English disease', and most people understood very little about it. It is still a subject that people tend to know all or nothing about, but as a result of the gay movement it is no longer a taboo subject, or 'the great unmentionable'.

The increased toleration of homosexuality, which has now led to government ministers such as Chris Smith and Nick Brown openly stating that they are gay, has been happening, very gradually, throughout the 20th century. But it is only since the 1960s that gay people have made their voice heard, first in America, later in Britain. The movement can be seen as part of a general tendency to be more liberal and open-minded on the subject of sex.

The influence of the gay movement has probably been increased by the challenge (to put it no more strongly than that) of AIDS, which appeared in the early 1980s and has led to the deaths of many thousands of male homosexuals as well as heterosexuals. People have been made aware of the great dignity with which sufferers from the disease face the unfolding tragedy and the old idea that male homosexuals were somehow 'cissie', or 'soft' has been increasingly replaced by acceptance and even admiration. This has given all homosexuals a respect and status in society which they have never had before.

To summarise, the main effects of the gay movement have been:

- a great improvement in the quality of life of the five per cent or so of people who are homosexual – in particular they don't need to be as secretive about it as they once were
- a reduction of the harassment of homosexuals – though there is still a problem in this area: the nail bomb which killed two people in a gay pub in 1999 is a reminder of the dangers that homosexuals have to face
- the inclusion of 'sexual orientation' as a part of equal opportunities – so that gay people are less discriminated against in their careers
- increased acceptance for lesbians – and a more mature attitude towards them in society
- less tolerance towards brutal behaviour and 'homophobia' in general.

Among ethnic minorities gay behaviour is still, on the whole, unacceptable, but even here there is probably more tolerance.

Equality and the law

Briefly examine the effectiveness of legislative approaches to four issues of equality.

1 The Race Relations Act 1976

The Race Relations Act 1976 makes racial discrimination unlawful in employment, vocational training and related areas. It defines racial discrimination as discrimination on the grounds of colour, race, nationality, or ethnic or national origins.

There are two types of racial discrimination:
- direct
- indirect.

Direct discrimination
This arises where one person treats another less favourably, on racial grounds, than he or she treats (or would treat) someone else. For example if a black waiter was sacked because customers in a restaurant had said they didn't want a black waiter, that would be direct discrimination. It is not necessary to show that unfavourable treatment on racial grounds was openly intended.

Indirect discrimination
This is treatment that may be equal in the sense that it applies to employees of different racial groups, but may be indirectly discriminatory by means of its effect on one particular racial group. A ruling such as 'all women working here must wear skirts' would be discriminatory against women of Asian background who wear trousers.

It is also unlawful to:
- segregate a person from others on racial grounds
- victimise anyone on racial grounds, or because they have tried to help someone else of a different race
- advertise a job in a racially discriminatory way.

The Criminal Justice and Public Order Act 1994 created a new offence of:
- intentionally causing harassment, alarm or distress through the use of threatening, abusive or insulting behaviour, words or displays.

The new offence can apply where the harassment is racially motivated. Convictions may result in imprisonment, a heavy fine or both.

It is unlawful for an employer to discriminate:
- in recruitment: including arrangements for deciding who should be offered employment in the terms offered or by refusing or deliberately omitting to offer a person employment
- in terms and conditions: during employment
- in access to, or by denial of, opportunities: for promotion, transfer, training or any other benefits, schemes, facilities or services
- by dismissing an employee or causing him or her any other detriment.

Exceptions to the Race Relations Act
1 Genuine occupational qualification – for example: where a person of a particular racial group is needed in a dramatic performance or as a photographic model – or to work in a Chinese restaurant.

2 Positive action – to help members of under-represented racial groups compete on equal terms with others in the labour market. This refers to training courses for members of ethnic minorities.

Advice on the Act is given by The Commission for Racial Equality (CRE).

The role of employment tribunals
Anyone who considers that they have been discriminated against in employment on grounds of race can complain to an employment tribunal. If the tribunal agrees that discrimination has taken place it can order compensation to be paid.

Is the Race Relations Act effective?
The Race Relations Act has generally been effective in tackling racial discrimination. Advertisers and others take care to follow the guidelines. And where racial discrimination by an employer has been proved, industrial tribunals have awarded large sums of money in compensation: e.g. a £28,500 award in *Johnson* v. *HM Prison Service* in 1996.

It has been less successful:
- in dealing with racial harassment outside the workplace – such cases, if they seem like a threat to public order, can be taken to the police, but there is always the suspicion that the police are not as keen as they should be to take them up (see the Macpherson Report published by the Stationery Office in 1999, following the Stephen Lawrence case) although this may change in the future

- in dealing with racial harassment in schools and colleges, where it is the responsibility of the college and the lecturers there to ensure that such harassment does not take place: if the harassment comes from other students or pupils it can be hard to get anything done about it, because of the difficulty of persuading teachers or lecturers that anything has happened
- in ensuring that members of ethnic minorities get employment in the public services – ethnic minorities are seriously under-represented in all public services
- in sorting out religious discrimination which is often linked to racial discrimination: Jews and Sikhs are defined as races under the Act; Muslims are not, so the Jewish and Sikh religions therefore have more protection under British law than the Muslim religion
- in tackling the problem of institutionalised racism (again, see the Macpherson Report 1999) – this applies especially to the police; up to the year 2000 they were exempt from prosecution for indirect discrimination, but this is likely to change.

2 Ageism

People over the age of 40 – and even more over the age of 50 – often feel that they are being discriminated against in employment, and 'passed over for a younger person'. But governments have been reluctant to introduce laws on this subject. The reasons for this reluctance include:

- a dislike of interfering in the running of private businesses
- high levels of youth unemployment (the government doesn't want to persuade firms not to employ young people)
- the fact that employers want the best person for the job – and often the best person happens to be young: young people tend to learn faster, they are more energetic and quick-thinking, and have greater stamina than older people
- the fact that young people are commonly seen as more attractive and responsive.

There seems little doubt that there is discrimination against older people in the workplace. But for the reasons given above, and because old people are a problem which will go away with time, it seems unlikely that many new laws will be brought in to help them.

On the other hand there is a general public feeling that people should not be thrown on the scrap heap just because they are over 50, and equal opportunities employers (often in the public sector) are beginning to have a more positive attitude towards older people.

This more positive attitude is reflected in the public services. The police and the fire service no longer have a fixed upper age limit for applicants. There are also provisions in the civilian public services for officers to move to less physically strenuous work as they get older, without losing pay or status. In the armed forces there is less flexibility: the maximum age for ordinary soldiers to join the army is 26, and for officers it is 25. This may reflect the more physically demanding nature of the work, and the fact that, on the whole, the armed forces prefer applicants without family ties.

FOCUS

Age Concern, an organisation which campaigns for older people, has this to say on the subject:

'Age discrimination affects all areas of life often with devastating consequences. Perhaps one of the most distressing aspects of age discrimination is where people are turned down for a job because of their age. Unfortunately, it is still perfectly legal to discriminate against someone because they are perceived as being too young or too old. Age Concern's policy is that there is a real need for comprehensive legislation to outlaw age discrimination in all its forms and to establish a commission to enforce that legislation. However, we welcome the Government's recent initiative in developing a voluntary *Code of Practice for Age Diversity in Employment* as an important first step. The draft *Code of Practice for Age Diversity in Employment*, published in November 1998, aimed to explain the benefits of an age diverse workforce in order to reduce age discrimination in employment. The draft code covered the following areas: recruitment; selection; promotion; training and development; redundancy and retirement.'

Source: Age Concern website

3 Sex discrimination

There are two main laws dealing with this issue:
- The Equal Pay Act 1970
- The Sex Discrimination Act 1975.

FOCUS

The Equal Pay Act

This Act said that 'women were entitled to equal pay to men if they were doing the same or broadly similar work, or if their work was shown through a job evaluation scheme to be of the same value as that carried out by men' (Haralambos 1995)

The Sex Discrimination Act

This Act says it is against the law to:
- discriminate against you because of your sex, marital status, or pregnancy
- sexually harass you
- dismiss you from your job because of your family responsibilities.

You can complain to the Human Rights and Equal Opportunity Commission if you experience treatment that you think may be unlawful under the Act.

It is against the law for anyone to victimise you because you have complained to the Commission.

Investigation by the Commission can result in:
- financial compensation
- reinstatement
- promotion
- an apology
- changes in policies or practices
- the promise that the behaviour will cease
- the introduction of training and education programmes.

The Equal Pay and Sex Discrimination Acts have been effective in removing most cases of sex discrimination. Though long overdue, they have done a great deal to ensure that in law women have roughly equal status with men. They have been of vital importance in:
- ensuring that there is justice in our society in this most important issue
- protecting women against exploitation by man both at work and at home.

Sex discrimination is a serious social evil, and these Acts have not totally succeeded in giving women equal wealth and status to men in practical terms. As we saw on page 83, the average pay of women in full-time employment is still about 25 per cent less than that of men in full-time employment.

In the public services, especially the fire service, women are badly under-represented, and in the last two years there have been cases where female fire officers have complained of sexual harassment. There are also problems in the police. According to *Socialist Review*, 'The testimony of black people and women police officers who have been driven out of the police force shows how deep seated racist and sexist ideas are within it.' The public services are working hard to get rid of sex discrimination and harassment of women officers – but there is still some way to go.

FOCUS

'The West Yorkshire Police force is committed to serving the whole community regardless of sexual orientation or racial origin and we are keen that this is reflected in the makeup of the force.'

Source: Spokesman after a court case in March 1999 in which the West Yorkshire Police were told they had contravened the Sex Discrimination Actand should accept a transsexual applicant, who had changed from being a man to a woman.

4 Disability issues

Disability is another serious issue of equality. The main law dealing with this problem is the Disability Discrimination Act 1995.

Thanks to this Act, and changes in public opinion, employers are making greater efforts than ever before to employ disabled people, and to make arrangements for them so that they can get safely in and out of the workplace.

But there is still a long way to go. People seem to be unsure of the extent to which allowances should be made for disabled people, and what is meant by 'reasonable adjustments to the workplace'. And there are serious health and safety problems about evacuating disabled people from buildings in the case of a fire.

Since the health and safety of the public depend on the ability of the public services to carry out rescues and other activities, the public services will only employ disabled people as civilians – not as constables, firefighters, paramedics or soldiers. In fact the fitness requirements in the entry tests ensure that many people who are not disabled are also excluded from serving except as civilians – on such grounds as poor eyesight or inability to jump their own height in a standing long jump.

FOCUS

Disability Discrimination Act 1995

This Act applies to people who have a physical or mental impairment which has a substantial and long-term adverse effect on the person's ability to carry out normal day-to-day activities. It also applies to people who have had a disability. It provides new rights for disabled people in the areas of: employment; education; public transport; access to goods, facilities and services; and the sale and letting of land or property. The Act also applies in Northern Ireland.

The employment provisions of the Act make it unlawful for an employer to treat a disabled person – for a reason related to the disability – less favourably than other people unless there are justifiable reasons for doing so. The Act also requires employers to make a reasonable adjustment to the workplace and to employment arrangements where that would help overcome the practical effects of an individual's disability. The employment provisions do not apply to employers with fewer than 20 employees.

If disabled people think they have been discriminated against in employment, there is a right of redress through the industrial tribunal system, with the possibility of unlimited compensation.

The government published – on 25 July 1996 – a statutory Code of Practice for the elimination of discrimination in the field of employment against disabled persons.

Public services in a multicultural society

Examine in detail two consequences of operating in a multicultural society for a given public service.

Within the police service

The police are more closely linked with society as a whole than the other public services. Unless they reflect society and do what society wants, they cannot count on public support, and without public support they cannot be effective in preventing, fighting and detecting crime.

Recruitment

The first consequence of operating in a multicultural society for the police is that recruitment must reflect the society the police force are trying to serve.

FOCUS

The proportion of ethnic minority officers in the police forces of England and Wales is 2.0 per cent. The proportion of ethnic minority people in England and Wales is 5.6 per cent.

ANALYSIS

If 6 per cent of the population of the area policed by a given force come from ethnic minorities, then that police force itself must aim to consist of 6 per cent ethnic minorities. Equally, 50 per cent of its officers should be women, since this will be (roughly) the proportion of women in the area it serves. And as the quotation from the West Yorkshire police (page 94) shows, police forces should also include members of other minorities such as gays and even transsexuals.

Some people feel that the police should not have to do all this, and that it is merely playing the 'numbers game'. However, research and experience show that if people cannot identify with their police force, they will regard the police as the enemy, and crime rates will rise. In particular there is a risk of inner-city rioting. In America, for example, they have long experience of serious rioting in which many people have died, and these riots have often been the result of black people protesting against a mainly white police force. The most famous of the recent riots was in Los Angeles in 1992, when white police officers were videoed beating up a black motorist, Rodney King.

FOCUS

Place: USA
Year: 1992

In the wake of the Rodney King verdict, South-Central Los Angeles went up in flames and Kansas City was on guard.

In Kansas City, the fear was that the fire this time would spread like the riots that had engulfed the nation's cities 24 years earlier in the aftermath of Martin Luther King Jr's assassination. Police watched intently for trouble as African-Americans, whites, Hispanics and Asians crowded the Westport nightlife district.

Internal ethos

The second consequence of operating in a multi-cultural society is that the so-called 'canteen culture' must go.

Many people who study the police have described the 'canteen culture'. A book called *The Force*, by Robert Chesshyre (Macmillan General Books, 1989) considers it to be one of the worst features of police life. The 'canteen culture' is the sexist, racist, jokey way in which some white men, usually middle aged, talk, act and think when they have been working together for too long and feel they know it all. It is attacked as a cause of racism (and incompetence) in the Macpherson Report.

Outside the police service

The changes which the police are bringing about in their recruitment and ethos (general way of thinking) need to be reflected in the way they deal with the public.

In the matter of race relations, the police have been very seriously criticised. The main facts in the Michael Menson case, given opposite, illustrate this.

The police investigation of the murder of Stephen Lawrence in 1993 was an even worse example of their approach to people from ethnic minorities. The facts are stated by the mother of the murdered black teenager – and were confirmed in the Macpherson Report 1999.

FOCUS

Doreen Lawrence: 'They are just playing around with words by using the word unwittingly, and I think that's the only term Sir Paul Condon reckons that he'll accept because the terminology has changed ... racism is still rife within the institution. There is racism within the police, but they found individual police officers not being racists, and that is where I find that I just don't believe any of that, because I want to know why, if those individuals weren't racists, they allowed my son to bleed to death. They never touched him. They didn't do any of those things.'

Source: BBC interview with Jonathan Dimbleby

A report by Her Majesty's Inspectors of Police – the *Thematic Inspection on Police, Community and Race Relations*, October 1997 (Stationery Office) – was

Two years ago on 28 January 1997 Michael Tachie Menson, a 39-year-old black man, was brutally murdered by racists. He was set on fire by four white youths in Edmonton, north London.

Passers-by contacted the emergency services who took him to hospital. Michael suffered 30 per cent third degree burns on his back. He remained conscious for almost one week – and then suffered a massive heart attack from which he never recovered. Michael died on 13 February 1997.

On the night of the assault police were contacted immediately. But during the first week while Michael was still conscious in hospital, they failed, despite constant reminders from the family, to take a statement from him. It has taken sustained campaigning over these long months by his family and friends to force the police to begin to admit even some of the truth about the circumstances of his murder.

Only in recent weeks have the police acknowledged for the first time what supporters have argued from the beginning: that Michael's death was a racist murder.

Source: *Socialist Review*

critical of the police response to operating in a multicultural society.

The main recommendations of the report were that forces should:

- publicly re-affirm their commitment to investing in good community and race relations as a core function of policing
- give a higher priority to dealing with neighbourhood incidents and anti-social behaviour
- clearly state that they regard the behaviour of officers who show racial or other prejudice in their behaviour and language as completely unacceptable
- continue to attract minority ethnic recruits and retain them
- consider a community and race relations audit to identify areas needing improvement. The report also recommended that training in community and race relations should be given greater emphasis, and priority should initially be targeted towards first line supervision.

The main point here is that the police need to put more thought and effort into their policing of racial incidents, or incidents which might be racial incidents. They need to be able to convince the public that they take racially motivated crime seriously – even if the crime seems to be at a low level. And they need to convince the public that they will not just 'close ranks' and claim that nothing is wrong, if they are accused of making mistakes in cases involving race issues.

Unit outcome 4
Examine how social control operates in society

Assessment criterion

- Examine in detail the influence of four agencies of social control on individual behaviour.

THINK ABOUT IT ...

What makes us the kind of people we are?

This is one of the most difficult questions to answer.

- If someone has blue eyes, is it because their parents have blue eyes, or is it something to do with the way they are brought up and what they eat?
- If someone is tall, is it because their parents are tall, or is it because of what they eat or the exercise they take?
- If someone is clever, is it because their parents are clever, or is it because of the way they have been brought up and taught at school?
- If someone is honest, are they born honest or is it in their upbringing?
- If someone is a criminal, is the criminality there from birth, in their genes, or is it in their upbringing and the experiences they have in their early lives?

What is your answer to each of these questions?

Social control

Social control is the process of growing up and becoming what we are when we are mature adults. Through it we learn how to fit in with other people and become part of society. Sometimes it is called socialisation: the process of becoming social beings. Social control is carried out by institutions or forces in society which act as agencies.

The main agencies of social control are:
- the family
- the peer group
- education
- the media
- religion
- the law.

These are arranged roughly in order of importance (for most people), and we will now look at the first four in more detail.

1 The family

A child has a closer link with its mother than it will ever have with anyone else in later life. This is because it comes out of its mother's body and is fed and kept alive by its mother in the early years. The mother is therefore the most important single factor in the socialisation (or social control) of the child. All research suggests that the relationship between a child and its mother is of the utmost importance in the process of socialisation. Having said this, it doesn't mean that if the mother dies, or abandons the child, the child will not 'grow up right'. But someone has to take the place of the mother, and in effect become its mother, for the child's social development to continue successfully.

Social control from the family, and especially the mother, is more difficult to understand than social control which happens later in life. This is because a baby is – in a sense – not fully conscious, and a young child is not able to explain or describe its feelings. Some psychologists used to carry out experiments on young children – and they found out that alterations in their relationship with their mother had a big (often harmful) effect on their later development. Since these experiments are themselves harmful, they have been discontinued. Now, if people want to find out the effects of disturbing the relationship between mother and child, they have to go to war zones or famines, and study what happens to orphans who have lost their mothers.

Maternal deprivation

Bowlby (1951) studied the effects on children of maternal deprivation – which means separation from their mother, or 'lack of good mothering'. His main findings were:
- 'mother love in infancy and childhood is as important for mental health as are vitamins and proteins for physical health'
- many mental illnesses result from 'disturbed bonding' between mother and child
- a secure relationship with the mother is needed if a child is to have secure relationships with other people later on in life.

Others such as Ainsworth (1973), whose work follows on from Bowlby, said
- children who have a secure relationship with their mothers are less distressed if they are separated from them, than those who have insecure relationships
- young children whose mothers do not relate to them well form more intense, but short-lived, relationships with other 'carers' who temporarily take the place of the mother: such children may attempt to bond with almost anybody.

Ainsworth distinguished betweeen 'sensitive' and 'insensitive' mothers. Sensitive mothers seemed to be aware of their child's needs and tried to satisfy the child. Insensitive mothers were more aware of their own needs, wishes and moods, and tried to use the child to satisfy those needs. He found that:
- 'sensitive' mothers had secure children who explored their surroundings confidently, knowing that they had somewhere (and someone) safe to go back to.
- 'insensitive' mothers had babies who either got very angry when they were ignored, or remained almost indifferent.

These researches suggest that maternal deprivation can be very harmful to a child's emotional development. Furthermore they show that deprivation is not just the physical absence of the mother. It can also be an absence of the mother's love or care – even though the mother is physically present. If the mother 'takes against' the child, labelling it as 'bad', this would be another form of maternal deprivation.

Intellectual deprivation

The mother, and the family in general, are also very important for a child's intellectual development – the development of its powers of observation, thinking, problem-solving and so on. For there is such a thing as intellectual deprivation as well as emotional deprivation. A mother who ignores her child's discoveries and interests, who provides no toys or playmates and (for example) just sits the child in front of the television for long periods of time, is slowing down the development of that child's mind. The long-term effects of this lack of stimulus and interest will be a lower intelligence, as measured by IQ tests (problem solving, etc.) and slower progress when the child goes to school.

In August 1999 the American Academy of Paediatricians, who study child development, stressed the importance of children being active even at a very young age. Miriam Baron, their chairperson, said, 'Children under two should be interacting with a puzzle or digging in the dirt – anything which is active.' This finding follows on from earlier research. Goldfarb, in 1943, compared two sets of children of equal intelligence. One group was kept in an orphanage which was clean and well run according to the standards of the time, but where there was very little for the children to do. The other group was sent to foster homes where they had foster brothers and sisters and plenty of toys. At the age of three, after two years in these environments, the children's intelligence was tested. In 'abstract thinking', 'social maturity', and 'their ability to follow rules and make friends', the group which had been sent to foster homes did far better, and Goldfarb concluded that this was because they had been living in much richer and more interactive environments. In addition they received much more 'mothering' and 'love' than children who had remained in the orphanage.

Fathers matter too, though there has been less research done on their influence on children's intellectual and emotional development. In recent years, due to changing employment patterns and gender roles, fathers have played a much more active part in bringing up their children.

FOCUS

Types of family

It ought to be stressed that families differ very much in different parts of the world and in different cultures. Here is a summary of the types.

Mother-child

This is the basic bond for young children, and the smallest possible family group. Such 'one-parent families' are effective provided they have the necessary support, both economic and personal, from friends, social services and other sources. But the difficulty of rearing a child and earning a living at the same time can cause problems, as can the loneliness of a mother who does not have support from friends or the wider family.

Nuclear family

This is the mother, the father and their children. In British culture this is often what is meant by 'the family'. In recent years it has seemed less like the norm, since over one third of marriages end in divorce while unemployment and other factors have changed the roles of mother and father considerably.

Extended family

This definition of the family includes uncles, cousins, aunts, grandparents and grandchildren, and is the type of family characteristic of many countries outside the West. In Pakistan, for example, or Africa, this type of family is an important unit of society.

All these types of family are alike in that they are the first and most important agency of social control for the children who are brought up in them.

ANALYSIS

The family is like a laboratory in which young children can carry out experiments to find out who they are and what they are really like. In the family children learn how to communicate, not only by speech but by gesture and other forms of non-verbal communication. They learn about ownership through toys and clothes and about territory – for example, whose bedroom is whose. They learn bodily functions – eating and excretion – and the socially acceptable way to perform these functions. They learn to express likes and dislikes, and in doing so build up a clearer idea of their own identity and differentness from others. At a later age they learn basic rules of human interaction – politeness, for example, and the need to think of others. They learn discipline, and they learn how to quarrel – and how to make it up afterwards. They learn gender roles, perhaps by playing with certain toys or in the allocation of small household jobs. Whether what they learn is 'good' or 'bad' is a matter of opinion: the main point is that they learn, through the family, much of what they need to know to fit into society and get through life.

To summarise, the family as an agency of social control:

- gives us the ability to have relationships with other people
- gives us the ability to think and learn
- teaches us how to speak and communicate
- gives us self-esteem – in other words self-respect and the feeling that what we do and think matters
- gives us security and the ability to face difficulties with confidence
- teaches us to see beyond our immediate needs
- gives us a moral sense of right and wrong
- teaches us gender roles
- teaches us many basic truths about society as a whole.

Dysfunctional family

If the family is 'dysfunctional' it means that the relationships within it are not working properly. This can lead to insecurity, low self-esteem, deviance, criminal behaviour, emotional inadequacy and mental illness in later life.

Family sanctions

These are punishments or deterrents. All agencies of social control exercise their power by sanctions and the family is no exception. For example a parent might smack a child who misbehaves. This is a sanction because smacking is a form of punishment, designed to stop the child from doing whatever it did again. But equally a parent might use other sanctions – such as a telling-off, or a 'grounding'. Some sanctions are so slight that they may hardly be noticed by the outsider – a raised eyebrow, for example. But they may still have a strong effect on the child. Sanctions in the family are informal. This means they do not take a fixed form and are not written down in any rule-book.

A formal sanction is like detention in school, or imprisonment for a rapist; it is an 'official' punishment which would be the same for anyone who had broken the norms of the agency of social control. Formal sanctions are often written down in the form of laws or rules.

Rewards

Rewards are the opposite of sanctions, but they have the same purpose in that they manipulate behaviour and exercise social control. They do this by giving pleasure rather than pain to the person who is being socialised.

Role model

A role model is a person that a child admires and tries to imitate. In a family it might be the mother, father, or an older sister or brother. This process of imitation is another way in which social control is carried out.

2 The peer group

'Peers' are equals. So our peer group is our friends, our classmates, our gang, our team, people of the same age as ourselves and work colleagues of roughly equal rank.

At the age of about two children start to have friends – and from this time onwards they are developing a peer group. For the rest of their lives the peer group will be an important influence on their feelings, ideas, values, behaviour and norms. In other words it will be an agency of social control.

As children grow older and become more independent from their parents, the peer group becomes more and more important to them. But the social control offered by the peer group often conflicts with that of the parents. The norms and values of the peer group differ from those of the family. This is why children and adolescents are often told by their parents things like: 'I don't want you to go around with ... , he's a bad influence.' A public service student once told his tutor, 'Whenever I spend a night away from home I always tell my mother I'm staying with X. He's the only one of my friends my mother likes.' Needless to say, X was a very well-behaved and polite young man, exactly the type that the average mother would approve of. But all the student's other friends had norms and values that his mother would not have accepted.

Peer groups are a necessary form of social control. They are the bridge from the family to the rest of society. Through peer groups we learn the following ideas about society and ourselves:

- **Norms and values acceptable to the peer group** – these may well be unacceptable to our family or to other institutions which act as agencies of social control, such as school or church. If the peer group is deviant (unacceptable to society as a whole) or criminal (involved in illegal activities such as, say, joyriding or drug-taking) it may give its members norms and values which are wholly unacceptable to the rest of society. But this is still social control, even if it is seen by other people as antisocial.
- **The idea of who we are and what we are really like** – we do this through trial and error, by finding the kind of people we like and the kind we don't like. People in our peer group are like landmarks that we use to orientate ourselves in the unfamiliar terrain of growing up. They give us feedback on the things we do and say. If the feedback is encouraging we develop our character and interests in that direction. If it is discouraging it acts as an informal sanction, showing us that we have said or done something which is against the norms and values of the peer group.
- **How to make relationships outside the family** – these include friends and, perhaps, lovers.

Much of the information that young people learn about sex in modern British society comes through the peer group. Again, these norms and values may well be different from those taught by the family.

ANALYSIS

Peer groups are often blamed for crime and regarded as a bad thing. But in fact they are not bad in themselves at all. It is only their norms and values which are sometimes bad – and that can be said of any agency of social control, including the family. For example a family in which children were sexually abused would have norms which were very harmful indeed, worse than almost any peer group.

Without a peer group a person would be friendless, and would have the greatest difficulty in making relationships or developing to full emotional maturity. In a sense a peer group is like an extension of the family, offering emotional guidance and support which carries on where the family leaves off.

In poor areas where families are not effective agencies of social control, peer groups have a more powerful influence than in more affluent areas or where families are more effective. In poor areas the peer group can take the form of teenage gangs which carry out deviant and criminal activities. Reasons for this may include the following.

- **Alienation** – this means the peer group feel cut off from mainstream society or from any hope of success at work or school, so they live 'for the moment' or for crime. Alienation is linked to the Marxist idea of class war and this kind of peer group may be seen as an 'underclass' 'at war' with the rest of oppressive society. This could be why so much youth crime seems malicious, designed to hurt others.
- **Low self-esteem** – due to poor parenting or other reasons.
- **Contrasuggestibility** – the natural adolescent desire to do and think the opposite of what adults (especially parents and teachers) tell them.

- **Fear** – because teenage gangs can be violent and impose harsh sanctions (beatings, etc.) on members who 'grass' on them.
- **The need for excitement** – because mainstream life is boring and offers no immediate gratification (pleasure).
- **The need to display qualities that echo those shown by the most successful members of mainstream society** – (a) toughness, (b) smartness (c) loyalty and (d) bravery. All these are good qualities if they are put to good use, but when used by delinquent teenage gangs they lead to crime.

Peer groups of the kind leading to delinquency (criminal behaviour among the young) have been described by researchers such as Becker, Lemert (1967), Hepburn (1989) and Agnew (1993). Agnew in particular noticed that delinquency was greatest among angry or frustrated young people who associated with delinquent peers. Becker said that if young delinquents joined an organised group such as a gang they in effect labelled themselves, and saw themselves as society saw them. Lemert said this could increase the destructive effect of the peer group because members of the gang were then reacting against society's reaction to them.

Negative labelling by society ('yobs', 'louts' or 'hooligans') can itself, as described by HS Becker in 1963, lead to delinquency. Other researchers, such as Hepburn, and Agnew in 1993, confirmed this idea.

Peer group sanctions

Peer group sanctions are usually informal, but some gangs may have their own rules about punishments and deterrents. For example, in Northern Ireland paramilitary gangs have carried out kneecappings and other sanctions. The most extreme form of sanction carried out by criminal peer groups is the execution, the so-called 'gangland killing'.

Rewards in the peer group may include small things, such as the peer group laughing at a joke or approving what is done by a more junior member. A bigger reward is to be allowed, by the peer group, to move up the 'pecking order'.

The pecking order (named after hens, some of which peck, while others get pecked) is a status ranking within a peer group. Members who are seen as 'hard' or 'cool' may be higher up the pecking order than those who are seen as 'soft' or 'thick'. This informal system mirrors the pecking orders of mainstream society – for example the way that older children in a family have more rights and responsibilities than younger ones, or the rank structure of an organisation such as the army.

Peer groups make use of role models even more, perhaps, than the family does, as a means of social control. The role models, whether they know it or not, can have a significant effect on the norms and values of the 'junior' members of the peer group who imitate them. If the role models have criminal norms and values they will be seen as a bad influence on their peers by people outside the peer group, such as families, social workers or the police.

FOCUS

Values of an American peer group – girls

'Beating my 15-year-old [boy] cousin in Jetskiing.' (Age 12)

'Boys. Going out, TV, Nintendo, family, friends. Dressing cool, like me.' (Age 13)

'Music, body piercing.' (Age 14)

'Dying your hair purple, bell bottoms ... the 60s were cool.' (Age 14)

'I live in the projects [housing estate], everybody dresses a certain way [baggy jeans]. For me, that's cool, being totally different from everybody else.' (Age 14)

'Being yourself. Staying on a straight line, not getting pregnant at 14, using drugs, smoking cigarettes, thinking it's cool. It's NOT cool. If people would stop looking for approval, they'd be happy being themselves.' (Age 18)

3 Education

Education is an important agency of social control, but it is not as universal as the family or the peer group. The family and peer group were up and running in prehistoric times, long before education in the formal sense was ever thought of.

The origins of education are linked to the idea of apprenticeship, where young people were taught skills – initially hunting and farming, but later other things as well – by their elders. Education also came out of religion, which sociologists regard as a part of culture.

The part of education which came out of apprenticeships is now the part which deals with skills training – in other words subjects like English and Maths, and practical ones such as Craft, Design and Technology. The work that you do on your BTEC National in Public Services which is linked to public service work also comes under this heading. All this learning is concerned with survival, which includes having a career and earning money. This type of education is sometimes called 'vocational', or 'training'.

The part of education which originates from religion or the passing down of culture includes subjects such as Geography, History, Sociology, Languages and Science. These subjects are not directly concerned with survival unless they are studied at a higher level and the student plans to use them directly in teaching or research. The purpose of studying these subjects is to fit the learner more fully into the culture and society he or she belongs to, and to ensure that the culture and society, with its norms and values, survives into the future.

In practice many of the subjects in schools and colleges combine the vocational and the personal elements. Education also has a 'hidden curriculum'; training pupils to obey authority in almost all the interactions which take place between teacher and pupil, even when 'obedience' is not mentioned.

ANALYSIS

Where it works well, and fits the learner's intellectual and emotional needs, school is a valuable experience and a successful agency of social control. But school doesn't always work well and sometimes, like a 'bad' family or 'bad' friends, it can do more harm than good. It is still an agency of social control, but it can have the following negative effects.

- By allowing pupils to fail it can make them believe that they will always be failures. As a result of this their self-esteem drops and they see no reason why they shouldn't resort to deviance or crime, since mainstream society can do nothing for them
- It sets up conflict situations between the learner and authority. This teaches the learner that society, as represented by the school, is 'the enemy' – and again this can encourage deviance and crime. Because young people are contrasuggestible, a school which is too authoritarian (strict) may also alienate the children and so encourage first truancy, then crime.
- It can stifle creativity by suggesting that everything in life can be taught, and that nothing is of any value unless it follows the rules. This can limit the learner's intellectual and emotional development.
- It can fail to prevent bullying, which has a very harmful effect on the self-esteem of the bullied person – leading in extreme cases to suicide. By a different mechanism the self-esteem of the bullies is also reduced, so that they too may suffer problems in later life.
- The 'hidden curriculum' of 'you do as you're told' which operates in many educational institutions may encourage learners not to take their moral responsibilities seriously, and go in for 'blind obedience' instead (see Unit 3: Understanding Discipline page 54).

Summary

This agency of social control is more formal than the two we have looked at so far. Its functions are as follows.

- To develop ways of thinking and of expressing and communicating our thoughts.
- To educate us so that we can find out about our real interests and needs and so fulfil our potential as individuals.

- To teach us the traditions of our society and culture.
- To give us the knowledge and skills to adapt to changes in that culture, and even to add to that culture if we get the opportunity.
- To make us understand and obey formal rules in human groups and institutions.
- To develop professional skills which will be useful to us later in supporting ourselves and the society we work in.
- To teach us theories which enable us to interpret the world around us.
- To enable us to become what we would like to be.
- To enable us to become what other people would like us to be.
- To extend our understanding of morality, and of right and wrong.
- To enable us to respond more fully to other agencies of control such as the media and the law.

When education doesn't work it can encourage crime and anti-social attitudes – the exact opposite of what society expects.

Sanctions in education

Education provides children with their first real experience of formal sanctions – for example detention – and formal rewards, such as gold stars or good examination grades. Good teachers provide successful role models – but perhaps not for every student. Some students will prefer to find their role models outside school, in the peer group or the media, and for them school will probably be a less satisfying experience.

Academic success is important in turning young people away from crime. Paternoster and Mazerolle, in 1994, found that 'good school grades inhibit delinquency'.

4 The media

Like all agencies of social control the media are of interest to the police, because of the strong effect they have on people's behaviour.

The media include television, radio, books, magazines, newspapers, music, films, videos, art, photography, dance, advertising and the Internet. The mass media are those which are easily available and which affect vast numbers of people all over the world.

The media are agencies of social control because they present powerful images and stories which people find romantic and exciting and which they want to be influenced by. Because the people they show us are not people we know personally, they cannot give us sanctions and rewards in the way that our family, peer group or school can. But they can still affect our behaviour by being role models which we like to imitate. Thus girls will perhaps act and think differently after watching the Spice Girls, and boys who see films of Arnold Schwartzenegger may then want to take up bodybuilding.

ANALYSIS

The media are in many ways an excellent thing. Much of what we know about the world comes through them, and living without the media would be rather like living with your head in a bucket. Thanks to the media we experience the best of what the world has to offer in sport, music, entertainment and film, and we know what interests people in America, Australia, Japan, India or Africa. In other words, the media make us citizens of the world.

To a certain extent the media support the work of the public services. They glamorise the police in programmes like *The Bill* and (in a more subtle way) *NYPD Blues*, and sometimes encourage us to uphold the law. But not always.

The norms and values put across by the media often go against the norms and values followed by the family, the school or the police. Pop singers take drugs, and their songs sometimes advertise drugs and the pleasure they can give. Rap has been accused of encouraging crime, violence and sexual attacks on women. The films of Quentin Tarantino have been criticised as immoral and a bad influence on the young. As for the Internet, it is full of pornography if you look for it, and paedophiles use it to get in touch with each other and to download pictures of child abuse. No wonder there is a stand-off between 'respectable society' and parts of the media! The media can be used to present a world of freedom where anything goes. The average family and school, not to mention the police and government, don't like that.

What particularly concerns society is the effect the media can have on young children. The media are a powerful agency of social control which can have destructive effects. According to the American Academy of Paediatrics, young children are 'vulnerable to the insidious build-up of the wrong messages from television. Cigarettes and alcohol are shown as cool and attractive, but carry no health warning [in the US]. Fighting is often used as a way to handle conflict successfully.'

In a free society it is difficult and probably undesirable to try to control the media – other than by stopping things which are illegal such as libel, harassment and open racism and obscenity. And while most people believe that the media encourage violence and crime, it is almost impossible to prove it.

THINK ABOUT IT ...

If you had the power, would you try to control the media more? And if so, how – and why?

Summary

The media

- Allow us to develop our interests and characters beyond the limits set by the local community.
- Offer signposts and role models for self-development, like peer groups.
- Show us (for example in sport or the arts) the best the world has to offer.
- Tend to 'glamorise' crime, and make it appear more attractive and less harmful than it really is.
- Make violence seem painless – and more like fun.
- Sometimes encourage drug-taking.
- Suggest that people can live happily and successfully without conventional morality.
- Can communicate destructive political propaganda and antisocial ideas such as racism and fascism.
- Both support and undermine the work of the police.

Sanctions in the media

The media are not able to give sanctions or rewards (except possibly through the pleasure or pain they give us).

UNIT 5 Human Behaviour

Unit outcome 1
Examine the three main approaches to psychology

Assessment criteria

- Explain in detail the main features of the three main approaches to psychology.
- Evaluate each approach in its usefulness for explaining human nature.

The word 'psychology' comes from an ancient Greek term meaning 'the study of the mind'. It may sound straightforward to study the mind, but it isn't. It is the only subject in the universe where something studies itself!

What is 'the mind'? The mind could be defined as 'the way we think', 'our thinking' or even 'the total of all our thoughts'. It does not exist in the same way as a jam sandwich or a wellington boot exists. You cannot touch, taste, smell, see or hear it. Even if you cut somebody's head up you will never find it, because the mind is a collection of ideas. It doesn't even have a fixed position inside the head. In fact it doesn't have a position at all.

Psychologists and philosophers (who study ideas) have been struggling with the idea of 'mind' ever since the word was invented. They still can't agree on what it is.

The 'brain' is a different matter. It seems to have something to do with the mind, because if you don't have any brain, you don't have any thoughts (so they say). The brain, however, unlike the mind, is an organ. The brain has a shape, a size, a weight and a colour. It may look like a giant grey walnut but it controls and records everything we do.

You might wonder what the mind and the brain have to do with behaviour.

Plenty of other people have done. But like a lot of questions in psychology, there's no simple answer. It all depends on your approach. When studying human behaviour we try to describe people's actions, and explain the reasons for them. Since public service work is, above all, working with people, it is most important to develop your understanding of what people do and why they do it.

Three approaches to psychology

Explain in detail the main features of the three main approaches to psychology.

1 Behaviourism

Behaviourism takes the view that there's no point in trying to find out how the mind works because the mind is basically unknowable. We might be able to look into our own minds (but we can't prove it). And we definitely can't look into anybody else's minds – since we aren't telepathic. So instead of studying the mind we have to do the next best thing, which is to study behaviour.

So behaviourists carry out experiments, on people and on animals, to find out what they can actually do. They have rats running through mazes and pushing at levers. They make dogs salivate by ringing bells at them instead of throwing bones for them. And they try to make people do things by changing their environment because they believe – or want to believe – that all human actions are caused by things outside ourselves.

At first this might sound a bit like a joke. Imagine a thief who appears in court charged with stealing a cement mixer. The lawyer says to him: 'Why did you steal that cement mixer?' 'It made me steal it,' is the reply. Then the lawyer says, 'Come on, you must have a better reason than that.' 'Why should I?' says the thief. 'I'm a behaviourist.'

A behaviourist would tend to agree with the thief's approach. Not that the behaviourist would put the cement mixer in prison for causing the crime, but he could well claim that the crime was in some way a reaction to the cement mixer.

Joking apart, a behaviourist would say that it is much easier to see a connection between a person's actions and the surrounding world, than between the actions and the person's thoughts, which are a closed book except to himself.

Behaviourists therefore believe that the best thing psychologists can do, in order to understand human behaviour, is to study how external events affect us. They call these external events 'stimuli', and our behaviour 'responses'. Strictly speaking we cannot say the stimulus causes the response (because that brings in the idea of mind, which behaviourists don't like). Instead, behaviourists talk of an 'association' between stimulus and response, but do not try to explain what that association is.

Behaviourists often experiment with animals, because animal behaviour is easier to understand than human behaviour. Also, animals are more honest than humans, and do not fake their responses. However, many of the behaviourists' animal experiments work with humans as well.

Examples of the ideas and experiments associated with behaviourism are shown opposite.

2 Humanism

Many people don't like behaviourism because it seems to treat people as animals. They also don't like the animal experiments which behaviourists carry out. In addition they think that people are so different from animals that a different psychological approach is needed to understand them.

In 1961 Carl Rogers started a backlash against behaviourism. He argued that whereas animals were all the same, people were all different, and that each person was unique. He looked at the work of Abraham Maslow (see Unit 15: Leadership) and decided that the two most important ideas in psychology were:

- **self-actualisation** (the opportunity for a person to be themselves and fulfil their unique potential)
- **positive regard** (the need to be liked, loved or respected by others).

Rogers was interested in personality: those qualities that make us different from each other and able to form meaningful relationships. If we were 'just' animals we wouldn't have all the different, complex needs that we have, nor would we be able to offer anything to other people in the form of love, help or understanding, because the other person would be just like us anyway.

The word 'humanist' means 'putting the individual first', or seeing people as people and not collections of stimuli and responses, like animals or little robots (as behaviourists have tended to do). Rogers

FOCUS

Conditioning

Conditioning is another type of learning. An animal is able to detect a stimulus and then to predict what is likely to happen, simply because it has happened several times before. The animal associates two events which occur together. For example, cattle respond to the farmer entering the field in his tractor, but ignore other people with other vehicles. They associate the farmer and his tractor with food.

In his original experiments on conditioning, the Russian physiologist, Ivan Pavlov (1849–1936) recorded saliva produced by hungry dogs which were given food. Pavlov delivered a neutral stimulus, the sound of a bell, at the same time as the food. The dogs began to connect the neutral stimulus with food and, after a short time, the animals would salivate at the sound of the bell, whether food appeared or not. We now call this type of learning classical conditioning and the response it produces a conditioned reflex. It is found in all complex animals.

Source: Collins Educational website. Main experimenters: JB Watson 1924; BF Skinner 1972 believed that all of us were capable of growing and developing throughout our lives, and this was why he considered the idea of self-actualisation so important. Instead of acting in an automatic way, as behaviourists thought, we are able to control our behaviour. And though he agreed with behaviourists that we can be influenced by our surroundings (whether people or places), he believed that we could in turn influence them, and that our feelings, ideas and minds were important, as well as our actions.

FOCUS

Other words used by Rogers:

Unconditional positive regard: this is like the attitude of a loving parent or partner. It is a case of loving or respecting the person whatever they do, and continuing to show that love or respect even if they do or say something which we do not like.

Encounter groups: these were groups of people set up in the 1960s, originally by Rogers, then by his followers. The members of the groups tried to cure the bad effects of a difficult upbringing or a cruel and heartless society by showing positive regard and real interest towards each other.

3 The psychoanalytic approach to psychology

By far the most famous psychologist is Sigmund Freud, whose main work was done at the end of the 19th century. He invented psychoanalysis, which means 'analysing people's minds'.

Freud was one of the great geniuses of his age, which means that a lot of his ideas appeared ridiculous or incomprehensible when they first came out. Like other great ideas which came out around the same time, such as Darwin's theory of evolution, Marx's ideas on economics and politics, or Einstein's theory of relativity, Freud's ideas still do seem ridiculous and incomprehensible to many people.

Freud made enemies. He quarrelled with his followers, and some people claim that he faked his results. As a family man he was less than perfect, and all sorts of weird things have been said about

Sigmund Freud

his sex life. But this isn't the place to go into them ... Freud's ideas could fill a book. In fact they have already filled hundreds of books. People just can't stop writing about the man.

He wasn't a scientist in any normal sense. He worked mainly with people who were mentally ill, and he listened to what they had to say about themselves. He didn't care if they told a pack of lies, because he thought their lies were just as revealing as the things they thought were true. Anyway, who were they to say what was true and what wasn't? That was his job.

Free association

He, like other psychoanalysts since, worked with free association. This is rather like games where someone says a word and you are supposed to say the first thing that comes into your mind. A says 'green' and B immediately says 'cabbage' or 'slime' – without thinking first. In the case of Freud, it appears that if he said 'green', most of his patients immediately said, 'sex', rather like Father Jack, in the TV programme *Father Ted*. The jury is still out on whether this is a reflection on him or his patients.

Freud's psychoanalysis often consisted of putting his patients on a couch and getting them to talk about their dreams. He interpreted these dreams in order to get at the cause of their mental illness. He believed these dreams were full of hidden memories, usually about sex, breast-feeding or potty training, and that if these problems could be talked about and brought out into the open, the patient would feel a lot better.

As a result of his researches Freud came to the conclusion that our minds were like icebergs. One fifth was conscious – in other words, we had some idea what was going on in it – and the rest, under the water, was unconscious. We could only get at our unconscious mind through dreams, mistakes in our speech called 'Freudian slips', and psychoanalysis. But our unconscious mind could get at us by making us forget things we didn't want to remember, or giving us delusions, fantasies, obsessions and mental illnesses.

Freud used some Latin names for different parts of the unconscious mind. The *id* was the desire for pleasure, which was very strong in Freud's patients. The *ego* was the self, and the *super-ego* was what we (or society) wanted us to be. The *ego* had a number of defence-mechanisms, listed in the table below.

Defence mechanisms of the ego

Defence mechanism	Explanation
Denial:	refusing to accept that something is true, when it obviously is.
Repression:	not remembering things which are too horrible to remember (e.g. a rape).
Regression:	trying to escape a problem by reacting to it like a child.
Projection:	imagining that other people have the same qualities as yourself.
Reaction-formation:	hating someone because you think they have a quality which you fear (and hide) in yourself, e.g. homosexuality.
Identification with oppressor	e.g. becoming a bully because you have been bullied yourself.

These defence mechanisms are all ways of coping with problems caused by the unconscious mind.

Freud believed, as a result of listening to his patients, that everyone passed through various erotic (sexual) stages as they grew up: oral, anal, phallic and genital. He also believed that boys, at a certain stage of their development, fell in love with their mothers: he called this the 'Oedipus Complex', after a character in an ancient Greek play who had the same problem. A further Freudian idea is the death wish, which he called thanatos.

Evaluation of these approaches

Evaluate each approach in its usefulness for explaining human nature.

Each of these approaches to psychology makes some attempt to tell us 'what people are really like' or 'what makes people tick'. But none of them has all the answers to this most difficult of questions. Still, it is useful to try and assess the strengths and weakness of each approach in clarifying and explaining human nature.

ANALYSIS

1 Behaviourism

This is the most scientific of the three main approaches to psychology. It uses hypotheses (clearly stated theories), experiments and careful, numerical observation. The experiments can be done by other researchers in order to make sure that they show what they are supposed to show. They are intended to be valid, reliable and verifiable, and are done under carefully controlled conditions.

These factors mean that the information that comes from behaviourism is more widely accepted as true than the information that comes from humanism or psychoanalysis. But much of the research is done with animals which show few of the complexities of human behaviour. Even if our responses are similar to animal responses, we can override them and behave in ways which are different from what our 'instincts' tell us. And though rats and rabbits are social creatures, they are nothing like as social as we are, nor do they have language. So behaviourism is in some ways more limited than the other two approaches.

Behaviourism has important implications for education, and for public service work. It suggests that the way we bring up and educate children is of enormous importance in ensuring that they end up as good and useful people. It tells us that schooling ought to be made more interesting and enjoyable. But behaviourism also tells us that we must carefully control our children at all times if we are to get the best out of them. If this approach was carried to its logical conclusion it might deprive children of a good deal of freedom, and also lead to their being treated as if they were all the same, whereas in fact each child is a unique and different individual. And in society as a whole, behaviourism could lead to a 'Big Brother is watching you' attitude from governments or the police, with everybody being controlled, manipulated and conditioned by the media.

As we saw earlier on, behaviourism is not entirely helpful in explaining or dealing with crime. It is true that people who live in poor areas, who come from broken homes, and have poor education, are more likely to be convicted of crimes. But on the other hand, if all our actions are caused by things outside ourselves, how can anybody take personal blame for what they do? According to behaviourism criminals would never be to blame for their crimes, because people can never have free will. Everything they do is triggered off by something else. They could be locked away because they were 'bad influences', but never because they were guilty. There can be no such thing as guilt if people do not have freedom of action.

Finally, whether we like it or not, the vast majority of people believe in the importance of the mind, even though we cannot point to it or look at it under the microscope as we can with the brain. We believe we have free will because life would seem dull or meaningless without it. Things like culture, spirituality, happiness or humour seem to have no place in the world of behaviourism, unless behaviourism is extended to include some humanism as well.

2 Humanism

Humanism is not scientific, and therefore it cannot really enable us to 'prove' things about human nature in the way that the experiments of behaviourism can. It has only two main beliefs, which again would seem to limit its usefulness in explaining something as vast and complicated as human nature.

'Self-actualisation' and 'positive regard' are phrases which look and sound like jargon. They are the kind of long-winded, high-sounding expressions which give psychology a bad name among ordinary people. They beg the question of what is meant by the word 'self'. This is a word rather like 'mind' which behaviourists would avoid like the plague. 'Positive regard', too, could mean almost anything you want it to mean, rather like 'love'.

In a sense, humanism is like a religion without a god. It tells us that we should be nice to each other, without telling us why, except that it seems to work. Perhaps this is a good enough reason for being nice to each other, but it still doesn't go far towards 'explaining human nature'.

If self-actualisation is so important, it means that humanism is telling us that we exist not just to have children and continue the species, but to fulfil ourselves as unique individuals. But humanism does not tell us why we should bother to try to 'actualise' ourselves: it seems to take it for granted that we know.

At the same time there is no doubt that the ideas of Carl Rogers, the main humanist, have been very influential in areas like counselling and some kinds of psychotherapy. These are both ways of listening to people, but not really in the way that Freud did. Humanism encourages people with problems to sort them out themselves (with sympathetic help and a good listener). In Freudian psychoanalysis, it is the analyst, or psychiatrist, who does most of the sorting out.

Counselling has become popular in many areas of society, including the public services, where stress counselling is widely used. Public service work is stressful, partly because teams are working together closely under demanding conditions, partly because it is shift work, and partly because public service workers come into contact with death and extreme suffering. The stress is not only suffered by the officers themselves, but also their families. Counselling, usually based on humanistic principles of raising the sufferer's self-esteem, is effective when it is skilfully carried out. But providing a useful tool for helping individuals to solve their personal problems is not the same thing as 'explaining human nature' as a whole.

3 The psychoanalytic approach

The psychoanalytic approach was the first psychological approach, and in many ways it was much the best. For one thing, Freud was a man who seemed to know no fear where his ideas were concerned. He was brave enough to dig deep into the unknown parts of the human mind. And this means that, unlike the others, he made a full attempt to explain human nature, from top to bottom – all of it.

The writings of Freud and his followers had an enormous effect on writers, film-makers, philosophers, religious thinkers – in fact many of the great intellectuals of the 20th century. He gave us a completely new view of human nature, and though it is hard to prove that the psychoanalytic approach is right, it is even harder to prove that it's wrong.

And the psychoanalytic approach has turned out useful, judging by the number of people who have tried to follow it. Jung, Adler, and many other famous psychologists took most of Freud's ideas on board. Even behaviourists and humanists often accept that there is likely to be an unconscious mind, and that people repress things in their minds that they don't like.

We have all heard about people going to their 'shrink' or 'therapist'. Rock stars and film stars are forever going off to lie on a couch and get themselves straightened out by a psychiatrist. Poor people may have to make do with humanistic counselling, but it seems as though many of the rich are not happy unless they have a regular dose of psychoanalysis. In fact America is full of psychoanalysts, all earning a good living. For some reason we don't have as many of them in Britain. But it doesn't meant to say that we wouldn't, if we could afford them. Certainly psychoanalysts are seen as being very useful for explaining the (individual) human nature of those people who visit them.

However, the psychoanalytic approach does have problems. The main one is that it is not very scientific. It is all very well somebody saying that your marriage has broken up because of something that your mother did to you when you were four – but how can they prove it? Psychoanalysis assumes that most of the important things happen in our lives when we are young children, and we cannot remember them unless something brings them back to the surface of our minds. But often it is only an assumption. A few psychoanalytic ideas have been supported by experiments carried out by behaviourists, but many of the things which Freud said could never really be proved by any experiment (otherwise somebody would have done it by now).

Another problem of the psychoanalytic approach (which it shares with the other two) is that it was invented by a man and is very male orientated. It is true that Freud and his followers were interested in women and their problems, but they saw them through men's eyes. Freud, for example, thought that women suffered from 'penis envy' (because they hadn't got penises), and that this gave them a sense of inferiority at an early age from which they never really recovered. Ideas like this have tended to put at least half the population off the psychoanalytic approach.

A third problem with this approach is that it is very complicated. Psychoanalysts are expensive to train and to employ, and the understanding they develop of individuals is not always useful. This means that the ideas of human nature which they have given us are very complex and difficult, and not particularly helpful for the average person. The ordinary humanistic counselling now common in Britain actually has more success in dealing with the everyday problems of ordinary people than the clever, complicated and expensive methods of psychoanalysis. It doesn't really give us more understanding of human nature, but it seems to be more practical and efficient.

> **THINK ABOUT IT ...**
>
> A young man rapes a woman. How might a behaviourist, a humanist and a believer in the psychoanalytical approach try to explain this crime?

Further reading

- *Foundations of Psychology: An Introductory Text* Nicky Hayes, Routledge 1998.
- *Psychology: The Science of Mind and Behaviour*, R Gross, 3rd ed., Hodder & Stoughton 1996.
- *Psychology for You*, Dolan and Groves, Stanley Thornes (Publishers) 1999.

Unit outcome 2
Explain atypical behaviour in relation to public service

Assessment criteria

- Describe four ways of classifying behaviour as atypical.
- Produce a diagram of a recognised classification system.
- Describe in detail one type of behaviour relevant to public service that is classified as atypical.

Classifying behaviour as atypical

What is 'atypical behaviour'?

The word 'atypical' is not heard much in everyday conversation. You will not hear your mother ask, 'Your bedroom's looking atypical today. Have you been tidying it?' Nor will your best friend say, 'Your girlfriend has atypically large feet.' In fact we could say it's quite an atypical word. Worst of all, if you look it up in the contents or index of a psychology textbook, 'atypical' might not even be there. And that might make you think there is no such thing as 'atypical behaviour'.

What you ought to be looking for is 'abnormal behaviour'. Atypical means abnormal, unusual, strange, bizarre, off-the-wall or crazy.

Then why use the word 'atypical', when we could say 'abnormal'? You could say it's all down to 'political correctness'. 'Abnormal' is a word with a spin on it. It sounds bad, as if you were criticising the person. 'Atypical' means the same thing, but it doesn't sound as though you're trying to slag someone off. In other words, you are just describing the person; you're not being biased, you're not stereotyping them, and you're not trying to use a value-judgement.

THINK ABOUT IT ...

- What types of atypical behaviour do you see in your teachers?
- What types of atypical behaviour do you see in your friends?

Which are acceptable, and which are not?

Ground-rules

There are certain useful words you need to remind yourself of. 'Norms' are ways of behaving which are generally accepted. It doesn't matter whether they are good or bad.

Different groups of people have different norms. For example a group of young men might go out and drink eight pints of lager a night. That would be their 'norm'. But it would not be a norm for a group of bingo-playing grannies.

'Atypical' does not mean 'bad'; it just means different. If somebody was to dress entirely in yellow, day in and day out, it would be atypical, but they wouldn't be doing anybody any harm.

'Behaviour' means actions. We're not talking thoughts. Someone who thinks that we're all green jellies from the Planet Barf has atypical thoughts, but they may not lead to any atypical behaviour at all. Outwardly the person might be just as typical (normal) as you or me.

But some atypical behaviour is no joke. When it takes the form of mental illness it causes serious problems. These problems may be:

- to the sufferers themselves
- to other people
- to the public services who have to pick up the pieces.

A recent newspaper report suggested that 20 per cent of all inmates in British prisons were mentally ill. The underlying point that the report was trying to make was that these people should not be in prison at all, but in mental hospitals.

It was also made clear that instead of being treated by qualified doctors, nurses and psychiatrists, these mentally ill people had been punished for their illness (which was surely not their fault) and were being looked after by public service officers (prison warders) who had no real in-depth training in looking after the mentally ill.

Mental illness is not always obvious, or easy to diagnose. It isn't something simple, like an ingrowing toenail or an impacted wisdom tooth. And in its early stages it might be so slight that people can't decide whether it's illness or just oddness.

In any case, different psychologists look at mental health in different ways. One psychologist will think that the act of checking twice whether you've locked the door is an example of obsessive compulsive disorder and a sign of mental illness. Another will say that even someone who appears barking mad is actually quite sane. Some people believe that mental illness is invented by society to make us all conform, or to give psychiatrists something to do, or that it's all a political plot. In this book we're going to take a normal, average, middle-of-the-road approach to the question. We're going to be as typical as possible ...

1 Anxiety disorders

These mental illnesses include phobias, serious panic attacks, obsessive compulsive disorder, post traumatic stress disorders and shell shock. Sometimes the word 'neurosis' is used for these illnesses.

As the name suggests, all these mental illnesses cause feelings of intense, unreasoning fear. The word 'unreasoning' is important here. If somebody ties you down to a railway track and you hear a train coming, you will feel intense fear. But that is not unreasoning. You have every reason to be afraid when you are in real danger, and your fear is a sign of normality.

On the other hand, if somebody is so terrified of open spaces that they dare not leave the house, this is an unreasoning fear. A healthy person knows that it is far better to go out and about and live a normal life than stay locked up at home all the time, even though there is a chance in a billion that you might be run over by a bus, or hit by lightning.

Phobias are intense fears. They include:
- agoraphobia – fear of being out in the open
- claustrophobia – fear of being stuck in a small space
- acrophobia – fear of heights
- herpetophobia – fear of snakes
- arachnophobia – fear of spiders
- siderodromophobia – fear of railways.

Many people have these phobias, and unless they cause serious problems they are not usually regarded as mental illnesses. Obviously people with agoraphobia, claustrophobia or acrophobia would have problems working for the fire service, and herpetophobes should not work in zoos. People with siderodromophobia should learn how to drive.

A more serious phobia is social phobia, which is fear of meeting other people. Those who suffer from social phobia are extremely shy, and would be quite unsuited to public service work.

These phobias develop in young people or adolescents, and can last through life. Their causes may lie in the behaviour of parents. In some cases they can be treated.

Post traumatic stress disorder

This is a serious mental illness, and there are various forms of it. What they all have in common is that the fear is the result of some shocking or very painful event, such as a fire, crash or war. For more about this, see page 19.

2 Dissociative and somatoform illnesses

These consist of:
- amnesia (loss of memory)
- multiple personality
- hypochondria
- psychosomatic illnesses.

The above are mental illnesses which produce the symptoms of physical illnesses, yet have no obvious physical or 'organic' cause. 'Dissociative' means being separated from reality or from your 'real' self; 'somatoform' means that the mental illness has physical symptoms, usually pain or numbness.

The difficulty of diagnosing and treating them is that they may look like ordinary illnesses, or seem to have a physical cause. Amnesia, for example, can have a physical cause such as a stroke, or a bang on the head. But sometimes amnesia can be caused by emotional shocks, and then it becomes a mental illness rather than a physical one.

Amnesia is related to fugue – when someone runs away, and starts a new life as a new person. These people often completely forget their old life. But eventually they flip back into their old selves – and then they completely forget their second life when they were in their fugue, or 'flight from reality', state.

Multiple personality is a very rare illness, but a serious one. Occasionally murders have been committed by people who claim to have been taken over by an evil personality for a short time, then changed back to (one of) their normal selves. A multiple personality might be a murderer, an artist and an unemployed teacher all in the same body! One day they could be one of these people, and the next, another – or they might change in mid-sentence. It is hard to diagnose this kind of illness, because sometimes people pretend to have it, especially when accused of a serious crime. But in a real case of the illness, the sufferer changes personality completely, and may be deeply distressed by it. Sometimes one of the personalities takes overall control – in which case the illness clears up.

Hypochondria and psychosomatic illnesses are where sufferers believe themselves to be physically ill, but 'it's all in the mind'. Examples are people who are sure they have cancer, yet the doctors can find no trace of it.

3 Mood disorders

The main ones are depression and mania. A person who swings between the two is sometimes said to be manic-depressive.

Depression is a serious illness which can ruin people's lives and make them commit crimes or kill themselves. It's quite different from that gloomy feeling we all have on a Monday morning.

The symptoms of clinical (severe) depression are an inability to do anything or to go out and meet people, a feeling of continuous deep sadness, failure and helplessness. Even food, drink or sex don't give any pleasure. Depressive people either do not eat enough, or eat too much ('comfort eating'). They may have eating disorders, and they may sleep up to 15 hours a day.

Manic people rise out of their depression and become unnaturally active, cheerful or aggressive – but only for a short time. Manic behaviour can seriously disrupt someone's personal or working life. It does not necessarily lead to crime, but it can lead to drinking binges, or excessive spending and even bankruptcy.

4 Schizophrenia and paranoia

When people think of mental illness or madness, it is usually schizophrenia that they are thinking of. The word 'schizophrenia' means 'split mind', and it leads to disturbed and confused thinking and behaviour.

Since the introduction of 'care in the community', where mentally ill people are not locked up, we have become far more likely to see schizophrenics wandering the streets, and the police and other public service workers often have to deal with them. In general schizophrenics are not dangerous – but a few are, and there have been some famous random killings carried out by schizophrenics.

It is hard to generalise about schizophrenics, because every schizophrenic is different. But usually their behaviour is bizarre and strange, and if the illness is severe they cannot hold down jobs or relate to people normally. Their speech is confused, full of odd words and expressions. One schizophrenic described himself as 'like an agitated hamburger distributed infinitely throughout the universe'; others talk what seems like complete nonsense. Schizophrenics also suffer distortions. Things don't look, smell or taste normal, and they often claim to hear voices in their heads.

In a third of all cases the schizophrenia is severe, and the patient remains more or less schizophrenic for life. In another third, the illness can be treated with therapy and medication, but the patient is still ill from time to time. In the last third the patient recovers completely.

Schizophrenia is a mysterious and frightening disease, and there is still some doubt about its causes. It does not usually appear until adolescence or young adulthood. It may appear suddenly or gradually, and its symptoms may be extreme, or only slightly different from normal behaviour. It has a slight tendency to run in families, but that does not prove that it is a hereditary illness, carried in the genes. However, there is evidence to suggest that it is caused, or partly caused, by chemical imbalances in the brain, or even by some differences in the structure of the brain: there are spaces in the back of the brain called vesicles which seem to be bigger in the brains of schizophrenics.

But there are other possible causes besides medical ones. It may be that problems of personal relationships, study or work have a part to play in triggering the actual symptoms of the illness, which up till then may have been lying hidden. There may be some genetic factors involved, because schizophrenia is more common in people of African descent than in other racial groups. But on the other hand, this may reflect prejudice among Western doctors, or the poverty and cultural stress which people of African descent often suffer in American and British society – or, for that matter, the poverty and hardship in Africa itself.

The treatment of schizophrenia is often a long and difficult business. Because the illness can affect young, intelligent people it is especially distressing to family and friends, even though the actual victim may not seem to be suffering much. Nowadays medication is the most important single treatment, and some sufferers can remain in reasonable health provided they continue taking prescribed medication. Unfortunately, schizophrenics can be very unreliable and it is hard to ensure that they look after themselves properly. Many of the people who sleep on the streets in London and elsewhere have a history of this kind of illness, or may actually be suffering from it.

As well as drugs, schizophrenics can be treated with various kinds of therapy and counselling. Because schizophrenia can be made much worse by problems in the sufferer's life, such as family break-up or tension, any treatment which provides them with a stable and supportive environment is likely to do them good. There are many support groups in Britain which help schizophrenics and their families.

Paranoia is a mental illness which is sometimes linked to schizophrenia. It results in the sufferers feeling that everybody is out to get them in some way. They feel that even their closest friends and family are just waiting for a chance to stab them in the back, or do them some harm. Where it is linked with schizophrenia it can be responsible for murders or violent attacks. Peter Sutcliffe, the Yorkshire Ripper, who killed 13 young women around 1980, claimed to be a paranoid schizophrenic, though the courts decided that he was probably pretending and he was judged guilty of murder.

Paranoid schizophrenia may have some connection with psychopathy. A psychopath is a person who is unable to feel guilt, and can therefore commit a crime without feeling sorry afterwards. The murderer Denis Nilson, who cut up his victims on the kitchen floor without feeling any emotion at all, is an example. But though psychopaths may be dangerous criminals, they are not classified as mentally ill, because the condition is thought to be totally incurable. In any case (despite what Nilson says about his feelings) there is no proof that psychopaths behave any differently than anyone else – unless they happen to be killers as well.

Classification systems for mental illness

Classification systems for mental illness are very complex and keep changing. Public service workers would not normally need to know them. Most of them come from America. A well-known one is the *Diagnostic and Statistical Manual for Mental Disorders*, a large American book which keeps being updated. It is usually abbreviated to DSM-V (with V being the number of the edition – five).

DSM publish full lists of mental illnesses, and diagrams which show the probable connections between them.

DSM categories of mental illness

A simplified list of main DSM categories (types) of mental illness is shown in the table on the next page.

Drug dependence and abuse

Describe in detail one type of behaviour relevant to public service that is classified as atypical.

In Britain at least five million people 'do' cannabis on a regular basis, and many people are dependent on alcohol. In addition there is increasing dependence on so-called hard drugs, such as heroin and cocaine. There are other widely-used illegal drugs too, such as amphetamines – ecstasy and speed. It is hard to find reliable statistics on the extent of drug abuse in the country, but it is likely that well over a third of the British population use drugs which can affect their behaviour in one way or another. (This is ignoring drugs like nicotine and caffeine which have only a minor effect on people's behaviour, but which may nevertheless be medically harmful.)

Although so many people take drugs, drug abuse can still be classified as atypical behaviour. Many drugs are recreational, taken for pleasure and 'the

Categories of mental illness

Listed in DSM-V	Explanation
1 Delirium, dementia, amnesia	Affect sufferer's ability to think, remember or understand – e.g. Alzheimer's
2 Schizophrenic and other psychotic disorders	'Madness', with confused thinking
3 Substance related disorders	Mental illness linked with alcohol and drug misuse
4 Mood disorders	Illnesses like depression which seriously affect the emotions
5 Anxiety disorders	Extreme fear, terror and phobia
6 Somatoform disorders	Mental illness having physical signs – e.g. false pregnancy, 'imaginary' cancer
7 Dissociative disorders	Feelings of unreality, or not being human
8 Adjustment disorders	Shell-shock, post traumatic stress
9 Disorders first noticed in infancy or adolescence	Learning difficulties, autism (child cannot relate to others), etc.
10 Personality disorders	Paranoid or schizoid, but not fully developed into true paranoia or schizophrenia; emotional strangeness or instability
11 Sexual identity and gender disorders	'Perversions'; abnormal sexual desires
12 Impulse control disorders not otherwise classified	Gambling, stealing, arson, etc. where they are caused by mental illness
13 Factitious disorders	Deceiving other people in order to get attention; sufferers make themselves or others ill
14 Sleep disorders	Serious insomnia which causes distress to sufferer or others
15 Eating disorders	Bingeing, anorexia, bulimia – eating too much or too little; deliberate vomiting
16 Other conditions that may be a focus of medical attention	Brain damage, tumours and infection

buzz'. They are of deep concern to the public services, especially the police, because:

- they are illegal (except for alcohol)
- they affect behaviour and can result in violence and death
- they are a powerful cause of crime, because drug users need to finance their habit, and drug dealers are often members of large criminal gangs.

Taking drugs is not in itself a sign of mental illness, but it is likely to cause an abnormal mental state. And for people with a tendency to mental illness, drug use is likely to 'push them over the edge'. While under the influence of drugs and alcohol, people show abnormal behaviour patterns which are not unlike the behaviour shown in some mental illnesses.

Except for alcohol and cocaine, drugs do not appear to cause violent behaviour directly – and even alcohol and cocaine only cause violence sometimes. Heroin, for example, does not cause violence, but the user's need to obtain more heroin may well cause violence. Cannabis (spliffs, draw, etc.) does not seem to cause violence, but if it leads people into using other behaviour-changing drugs, then it might be seen as indirectly leading people towards violence.

Some people take alcohol and drugs and 'control' them, so that other people outside their immediate circle do not know that they are using them. But many other people suffer from their habit in much the same ways as schizophrenics and other mentally ill people suffer. These effects include:

- preoccupation or obsession with the drug (and getting hold of it)
- increasing dosage to get the same effect
- withdrawal symptoms: when alcoholics are 'on the wagon' or heroin addicts are 'rattling' they suffer symptoms like those of the mentally ill with anxiety disorders
- physical injury and accidents, due to falls, crashes or fights
- damage to their family, study and working life: many relationships break up because of drugs or alcohol
- total dependence and inability to stop the habit – the chances of people recovering from alcoholism are no better than their chances of recovering from schizophrenia (i.e. 33 per cent).

Effects on the public services

About 40 per cent of traffic accidents are alcohol related. There may also be many which are cannabis related, since cannabis is thought to affect the user's ability to judge speed, space and distance. Violence, both public and domestic, is often linked to drugs, especially alcohol. A large amount of theft is carried out to support drug habits. Because drugs are illegal, their supply is controlled by criminal gangs, who themselves carry out criminal trading with the drug, and have 'turf wars' with other gangs. Drugs are a cause of large-scale international crime which reaches to all parts of the world. In some countries, drug-trading even finances wars.

If everybody gave up taking drugs tomorrow, the public services, especially the police and the prison service, could be halved. The place would be full of unemployed coppers, screws and ambulance workers. Social workers could be sacked as well, and taxes would fall with a bump. People could stop locking their front doors when they nip down to the shops, security firms would go out of business, and the casualty wards of some hospitals could be shut down. Little old ladies could start walking about at dead of night again without fear of being mugged. There would be no more babies born addicted to alcohol or heroin.

But since that isn't going to happen, the police are going to continue to spend half their time working on cases related to drink or drugs. The fire service will go on scraping people off the tarmac and disentangling them from crashed vehicles. Hospitals will keep on buying life support machines and prisons will still be bursting at the seams. And the army will continue to have their random drug tests.

It's a problem that will keep the public services busy in the 21st century. The police are already too stretched to enforce the law against cannabis and alcohol. Public education about the dangers of drugs is a possible answer, but every young person knows someone who uses drugs who doesn't seem to be harmed by them – so one version of reality contradicts the other. Legalising all drugs is another possible answer: it might put the drug barons out of business and allow drugs to be taxed – which might pay for the cost of clearing up the mess they cause. It may even be that fashions will change and people will become addicted to cyberspace or jogging instead. But it seems unlikely.

! THINK ABOUT IT ...

What do you see as the future for drugs?

- Is the picture given above an exaggeration?
- What are the arguments for and against legalising all recreational drugs?
- Is there a racist element in the drug laws?

Unit outcome 3
Explore communication in relation to public service

Assessment criteria

- Describe in detail three methods of communication.
- Explain the relevance of each method of communication to a given public service.

Methods of communication

Communication takes the following forms: listening, speaking, reading, writing and non-verbal communication. It must not be confused with communications (with the 's' at the end), which involves transmitting and receiving radio waves, bouncing them off satellites, producing television pictures and so on.

As a matter of fact, both are vital for the public services. But here we are considering the human behaviour unit, not the radar unit.

1 Spoken (verbal) communication

Churchill said, 'Words are given us to conceal our thoughts', but whatever we use them for they are a vital means of communication. Spoken words, in particular, are the most powerful tool we have for giving and receiving ideas, information and emotions. They are of vital importance in all public service work.

In any communication there is a sender and a receiver. In this case the speaker is the sender and the listener is the receiver. For the communication to be effective there has to be an awareness of its form, its content, its purpose and its audience.

In speech the form of the communication depends on its purpose or function. If the purpose is to discover information, then the form is a question. If the purpose is to amuse, the form is a joke. If the purpose is to inform, the form may be a long lecture, or it may be a brief piece of advice. If the purpose is to warn, it may be a single shout, such as 'Stop!'

The content is information, but information can take many forms. If someone is smoking on a bus, and someone else says, 'Excuse me – could you please put that cigarette out?' it may not appear at first sight that information is being given. But in fact it is. The speaker is informing the listener that he doesn't like smoking. But he is also showing that he is prepared to be polite about it, and doesn't want any hassle. The fact that he says anything at all also indicates that it is a no smoking zone. And as the purpose of the sentence is to ask someone to do something, it takes the form of a request. Despite the tone of voice, it is not a question. If it was, it would merely be asking the smoker if it was theoretically possible for him to put out his cigarette, which of course it would be, unless it was really a firework, or had been soaked in paraffin.

The key to successful speaking is to know the purpose of what you are saying, and to know your audience. This applies whether you are speaking to one person or a hundred. It also applies whether you are close friends, or a lover, of the receiver, or whether you are talking to a total stranger.

Register

The audience, or listener(s) determine the register in which you speak. Register is, to put it simply, a measure of the 'formality' with which we speak. Often, with our friends, we speak in a regional accent, use slang, and don't bother whether our sentences are grammatical or not. And why should we? We can do what we like with our friends. But strangers are a different matter, and with them we sometimes have to use a 'higher' register. For example, if you were lucky enough to meet your local chief constable, you would not speak to him in the same way as you would speak to your best mate. You would probably pronounce your words differently, check that your words were put together properly, and avoid slang as much as possible. That is not to say that you would try and speak like the Queen, but you would take some care over what you said and how you said it.

Ideas about register come from a sociologist called Bernstein, who wrote about 'restricted' and 'elaborated' code. Restricted code was a 'low' register, slangy, informal, and with fewer words; elaborated code was the speech of educated people, with more long words and less slang. Now some other words have come in to describe the same thing:

FOCUS

Here are some words for your jargon bank.

Acrolect – elaborated code (posh)

Mesolect – in between (normal)

Basilect – restricted code (slang)

Some people are snobs about language, but if someone talked in posh acrolect all the time, they would never be able to tell a joke in a pub, or shout support at a football match, or tell a platoon of soldiers how to get round an assault course. They would have to spend their whole time sitting around in a university, or answering questions on the kind of Radio 4 programme that uses words like 'coprolite' or 'eructation'.

The key to successful spoken communication is: be appropriate. Adapt your speech to your audience, and speak to them in a way that will get through to them. A communication is no good unless you can get people to listen to it. You might as well talk to a brick wall. But if you choose the right words, and say them in the right way, it is 100 per cent certain that you will be listened to.

It is not just whether you know your listener that determines how you speak to him or her. If you are talking about a technical subject you may need to use technical language. For example, in a police station you would talk about a control centre, not a computer room, even though the control centre is a room full of computers.

You also need to be aware that certain words carry strong emotional overtones. The word f**k, for example, will offend some people even when the speaker has no intention of offending anybody. If you tell a joke in which a woman is described as a 'bitch', it will cause offence even among many men. And there are racial words too, such as 'nigger', which should never be spoken in public. It will help you in both your personal and your working life to be aware of the overtones that words carry, as well as their dictionary meanings.

And, talking of dictionaries, how do you 'increase your word power'? Not by reading dictionaries, but just by reading. Anything you read will increase your confidence and knowledge of the language. If you enjoy stories, then read fiction books or magazines; if you have hobbies, then read about your hobbies. When it comes to speaking, many public service officers are extremely skilled, and they have achieved this skill by listening, reading and practising – to develop their confidence and expertise at every kind of speaking.

2 Written communication

In many ways written communication is like spoken communication. It has a purpose and an audience, and the form it takes, and the words used, must reflect the purpose and the audience. For example the layout, content, words, sentences and paragraphs must be suitable for the situation.

A famous American horror writer, HP Lovecraft, once applied for a job. Though he had never worked in his life, his CV was ten pages long. He didn't get the job. In fact he never got any job, and eventually died a horrible death, like the characters in his books. As a policeman he would have been about as much use as a broken leg, even though he was a brilliant writer. Everything might have been different for him if he had thought about the purpose and audience of his CV before writing it.

Most people who work in the public services need to be able to write reasonably quickly and efficiently. It's no use if they have to chew a pencil for ten minutes before putting down the first word. Police officers, for instance, have to be able to write memos, reports, notes, notices and so on. It doesn't matter if they make the odd spelling mistake, but if their spelling is so bad that people lose confidence in them, then it will be a problem. Anyway, the public services won't even employ you if your spelling is terrible.

A written communication is made of words put in the right order. The words are called 'lexis' or 'vocabulary', the order of the words is 'grammar' or 'syntax'. The grammatical pattern of a normal sentence is either:

Subject + verb + object. The cat caught a mouse.

or

Subject + verb + adverbial. The cat sat on the mat.

If a sentence doesn't have a verb in it, it isn't a sentence. The subject is the person or thing doing an action; the verb is the action, and the object is the thing which has the action done to it. The adverbial tells us about things like time and place.

Anyway, that's enough of grammar. You will find dozens of books on it in your college library, and some of them are good fun, so check them out!

Writing has to have punctuation. This is to organise the sentences and split up the different ideas. Punctuation, like driving, is well worth learning if you intend to work in a public service.

Writing also has paragraphs. When you move from one main idea to the next, you should start a new paragraph, so that your readers know you're going somewhere. Notice that the newspapers which have the most readers, like the *Sun* or the *Daily Mirror*, are also those which use the shortest paragraphs.

And remember that writing, like speech, has register. You avoid slang when you're writing assignments, business letters, reports and so on. You can use as much slang as you like when you're sending letters or e-mails to your close friends.

3 Non-verbal communication

Non-verbal communication includes:

- the way we dress
- the way we move
- how, and where, we stand and sit
- how we gesture (with arms, etc.)
- face expressions
- eye contact
- tone of voice.

Non-verbal communication is like a secret weapon. How do so many ugly blokes get beautiful girlfriends? Is it because their girlfriends have bad eyesight? It's more likely to be because of their non-verbal communication (NVC).

Sadly, it is not the purpose of this book to tell you how to 'pull'. And some body language is beyond our control. For example, did you know that if you see someone you like the look of, the pupils of your eyes enlarge, giving a secret signal to that person?

But there are some things that can be controlled. They include the following.

1 Dress. With your friends, dress as you like. Clothes can show your character, or the character of the group you go around with. Ordinary or dull clothes hide your character. For public service interviews wear smart clothes which fit you well, and which you feel comfortable in. When in doubt, ask advice from someone who knows.

2 The way people move. Everybody walks differently. Slouching may show rebellion, an artistic nature, a lack of self-respect or a low opinion of yourself. Whatever the reason, people in the public services do not slouch. Strutting (short quick steps) may indicate anger, aggression or bossiness. You can't go too far wrong if you walk in the way that comes naturally to you.

3 Standing and sitting. Moving freely around a room shows power and confidence. Remaining in a corner shows shyness and submission. Standing close to someone shows either intimacy or aggression. If you stand too close to a stranger they may well back off. Teachers say that pupils who stand too close have behavioural problems. If you stand too far from people it may show dislike or snobbery. People from some cultures stand closer than others. If you are working with people such as Arabs who prefer to be close, it may suggest racism or (literally) stand-offishness, if a British person keeps his distance. In the case of sitting, if you face someone directly it shows aggression and confrontation. If you sit sideways the effect may be friendlier.

4 Gestures. Too many gestures give an effect of nervousness, or over-excitement. Too few, and you seem formal and cold-blooded. Folding your arms suggests you are not prepared to listen. Touching your face suggests dishonesty. Plucking at your ear suggests you would rather be with someone else than the person you are talking to. Touching your cheeks may be a sign of flirting. Stroking your hair is a sign of vanity or conceit (big-headedness). Scratching suggests anxiety (or fleas).

5 Facial expressions. These are very complicated. Raised eyebrows express surprise, or disbelief, but can be a friendly gesture of recognition if you are about to greet someone. Twisting your mouth can suggest nerves or aggression. Exaggerated expressions suggesting thoughts often mean that the person is not really thinking – but just pretending.

6 Eye contact. For speakers, eye contact lasts on average for only 17 per cent of the time. Listeners make more eye contact – for about 39 per cent of the time. (This is when two people are talking to each other.) Prolonged eye contact means love, attraction, aggression or bad manners. Lack of eye contact means excessive shyness, and can be a serious problem. Sometimes avoiding eye contact can be a way of showing that you dislike or despise somebody.

7 Tone of voice is really an aspect of speech. A varied, animated tone suggests interest, and an informal, chatty conversation. Serious conversations, or long speeches, use less variety of tone. In general, the higher the register, the less varied the tone. (This may be why professors are often said to sound 'boring'.)

Further reading

If you are interested in non-verbal communication, sometimes called NVC or body-language, have a look at *Social Skills in Interpersonal Communication* (3rd ed.) by Hargie, Saunders and Dickson, published in 1994 by Routledge.

Using communcation

Explain the relevance of each method of communication to a given public service.

1 Verbal (spoken) communication

Where people work with each other, and with the public, spoken communication is bound to be very important. In the case of the police, for example, the functions of speech within the station are likely to include:

- '**bonding**' with colleagues: jokes and various kinds of supportive comment help to form a good team spirit
- giving **instructions** to team-mates or subordinates
- giving **information** to other officers
- making **suggestions**, formally or informally, in meetings and elsewhere
- **requesting** help
- asking **questions**
- **discussing** problems or plans in pairs or groups
- **reprimanding** (telling off) a subordinate on a disciplinary issue
- **calming** a difficult situation between two colleagues
- **negotiating** with officers from other units or services
- **lecturing** colleagues as part of an in-service training programme
- telephone and radio **conversations**
- **interviewing** applicants.

With the public, spoken communication may have the following functions:

- **eliciting** (gathering) information from informers and the public
- **encouraging** a group of young men to disperse or go home
- **mediating** between quarrelling neighbours
- **advising** security guards on crime risks
- **counselling** (perhaps informally) people with problems
- **comforting** the victims of crime
- **explaining** the role of the police to students or children
- **chairing** a meeting of community groups and the police
- **calling for** assistance (perhaps by radio)
- **confirming** information received with another informant
- **demanding** a driver's documents

and last but not least

- **listening** to all the people who want to talk to you.

THINK ABOUT IT ...

What other functions might speech have for the police?

Choose another public service and think of all the functions of spoken communication for that service.

2 Written communication

Within the station the police use written communications to:

- **make notes** before questioning suspects
- **take notes** on what suspects or others may say and from tape recordings
- **transcribe** tape recordings
- **plan agendas** of meetings
- **take minutes** of meetings
- **record** telephone messages
- **complete** forms
- **write memos**
- **write reports**
- **plan** operations
- **write letters** and **e-mails**
- **draw up notices** and **signs**
- **write instructions** and **leaflets**.

When working with the public, police will:

- **take notes** on what is said to them by victims or witnesses of crimes
- **make notes** to plan what they are going to say to individuals or groups of people
- **write teaching notes** for presentations to students and schoolchildren
- **fill in** forms.

Finally, the police have to do a lot of reading of reports, statements, internal memos and circulars, transcripts of interviews, letters from the public and other services and so on.

3 Non-verbal communication

1 Dress. The police are the visible face of the law. They have to be in tidy and correct uniforms. The uniforms show that they are an official public service, with full organisation and the backing of the government. However, the uniforms are different from army uniforms because the police are more of a service than a force, and there has always been a tradition in Britain that they should not be seen as a military organisation.

2 Movement. Police officers should move around in a dignified and serious manner, without seeming unfriendly or threatening. When on the beat they traditionally walk at two and a half miles (four kilometres) an hour. This is fast enough to look as though they are going somewhere, but slowly enough to keep an eye on their surroundings. A member of the public can stop them without having to break into a run.

3 Standing and sitting. Standing too close to members of the public might seem threatening, or over-familiar, to the public. It might also expose the officer to the risk of being stabbed or thumped. In seated interviews a face-to-face positioning would indicate confrontation; a sideways positioning would be less threatening and more collaborative. Police officers can choose their positioning to fit in with the demands of the interview. If they are putting pressure on someone they can show it (if they wish) in the way they sit.

4 Gestures. These must not be openly threatening (clenched fists, etc.) or abusive (fingers!). This would tend to make the officer seem childish, and undermine authority. Police can manipulate an interview with the appropriate head-tilt, folding arms to show disbelief or doubt, leaning forwards to raise the intensity, leaning back to show lack of interest, linking or separating hands to show concentration of thought, or the possibility of some kind of agreement. Obviously the gestures used when warning a hostile suspect or witness would be quite different from those used when liaising with a friendly colleague.

5 Facial expression. Rather like gestures, facial expressions can be used to influence the progress of an interview. Raised eyebrows may indicate doubt, frowns may suggest thought; twisting the lips can signal anger or underlying feelings of aggression without any threat being made. (You do not have to be angry to do this: there is an element of play-acting in interviewing.) Too many smiles in a man may be seen as a sign of weakness, or low status, but this is not necessarily the case with women. It is the job of the police to play these 'status games' and – in general – to appear of a (slightly) higher status than the person they are dealing with.

6 Eye contact. When dealing with the public it is useful to learn to control your eye contact. Some staring may increase your authority, but too much may be seen as a challenge, and cause aggression. As police work is a profession, officers try not to show personal feelings in their eye contact with

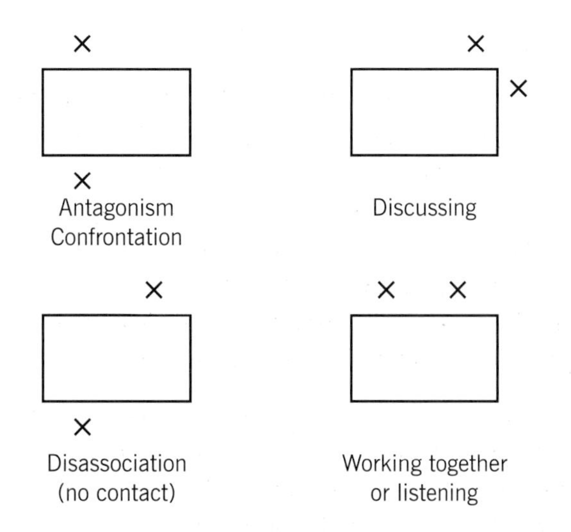

Seating positions at a table

members of the public. Officers will come across people they may hate, such as child-abusers, but their eye contact and body language should not show their personal feelings. Eye contact is sometimes an effective way of inviting people to speak.

7 Tone of voice. The experts call this 'paralanguage', because it gives extra meaning and emotional weight to your words. The police should modify their tone of voice to invite people to speak to them, to give warnings, advice, suggestions and so on. Each of the different functions (given in bold in the lists above) has an appropriate tone of voice. That is why you can often tell roughly what people are talking about even when you cannot hear the words.

Above all, the police must be aware of the body language of other people. Through it they can tell whether someone is friendly or hostile, sober or drunk, lying or telling the truth – or if they are about to pull a gun!

THINK ABOUT IT ...

With a friend, discuss what body language suggests that somebody:

- doesn't like you
- is looking for a fight
- 'fancies' you?

Together, make a brief guide for public service workers on the body language connected with these three situations.

Unit outcome 4
Examine group behaviour, demonstrating its relevance within public service

Assessment criteria

- Discuss in detail how individuals may behave in a group.
- Suggest how individual behaviour in groups may be used to benefit the operation of a given public service.

Group behaviour

Group behaviour is obviously of interest to people working in public services. Each public service is itself a very large group of people, broken down into smaller groups such as 'forces', 'ranks', 'regiments' and 'watches'. At a personal level all individuals are part of a team, in which they work closely. In a medium-sized police station there may be only seven or eight full-time officers, who all know each other well and make up a group. How does the fact that they form a group affect their behaviour and efficiency, and the behaviour of the people they deal with?

In addition, public service workers deal with groups of the public. This is especially true of the police. If the police raid a pub, they are raiding a group of people. If they arrest armed robbers, they are arresting a group. If they are working during a football match, the supporters are groups of people. What is the best way of dealing with these groups and influencing their behaviour?

You may find that you yourself behave differently when you are with your friends, or your classmates, than when you are by yourself. Teachers notice that some students are noisy and attention-seeking in class, yet quiet and polite when spoken to on a one-to-one basis. Students sometimes say: 'I'd rather do this work at home: I can't concentrate in college.' Parents of children who have got into trouble with the police often say, 'Oh – he's been led astray by his friends.' Why do we sometimes change into different people when we are with others?

Social facilitation

Part of the reason for this difference is 'social facilitation', which is the name given to the idea that, 'we do certain things better when we are in a group'. The group does not have to be our own friends or colleagues: it may be simply that we are being watched by a group of people, rather than just doing things by ourselves.

It is an interesting fact that athletes never set world records when they are by themselves, alone in a stadium except for an official with a stopwatch. Athletes tend to set records in front of a large, supportive crowd. This is an example of social facilitation.

As long ago as 1898 Triplett noticed that cyclists recorded faster times if they raced against each other than if they were racing against the clock. In 1920 Allport discovered that students did simple multiplication sums faster if they were with other students than if they were alone. Dashiell (1930) confirmed this, except that he also found that the students were more likely to make mistakes if they were together than if they were alone. Then Dashiell found that if the sums were complicated, people did worse in groups than if they were by themselves.

At the time these results didn't make much sense, but in 1965 Robert Zajonc worked out a theory showing that the social facilitation depended on the nature of the task. If the task was what he called 'dominant', in other words, well known or easy, people did it better and faster in groups. If the task was unfamiliar or difficult, people did it better when they were alone.

Football teams always prefer to play at home, and though this may have something to do with the inconvenience of travelling, research shows that they are more likely to win at home (you only need to look at the paper to see this). Carron, researching on soccer in the USA (a strange thing to do!), found that in 37,202 matches, 69 per cent were won by the home team.

Experimenters have found that social facilitation works best with people who you feel can (or might) judge your performance. But it works with complete strangers as well. Joggers speed up if they pass someone who is watching them. If the same person turns her back and reads a book, they do not speed up.

Social loafing

This is the opposite of social facilitation. In 1979 Latane, Williams and Harkins asked their students to shout as loud as they could. When they shouted by themselves, the volume of each student was higher than if they were shouting in a group.

The reason for this had probably already been suggested by Zajonc. Shouting loudly, for no reason, is an unfamiliar task, not a dominant one. There is no particular reward for it, as there would be for playing better in a football match (when you would gain the appreciation of your fans). Therefore there is no benefit in doing it better in a group, or with an audience.

Conformity

This is the idea that when people are in a group, they try to behave in the same way as the other members of the group. Read all about it in Unit 3: Discipline, page 61.

The bystander effect

We have all read stories of people who were attacked or raped in the city, yet the people who were walking past and saw what was happening did nothing about it. Experiments have shown that, in an incident of this sort, a single person walking past is more likely to get involved and try to stop the attack than a group of people. This seems illogical, because one bystander who gets involved is much more likely to get hurt than a group.

Latane and Darley investigated this in 1968. They carried out experiments which showed that groups were more likely to stand by and do nothing in an emergency than individuals. They suggested that the reasons for this non-involvement might be:

- failing to notice that anything was happening, because people in pairs or groups are less observant than individuals on their own
- embarrassment at acting independently of the group (fear of looking a fool, or being 'shown up')
- group reasoning followed by an agreement not to do anything (e.g. 'It isn't really a rape or an attack; it's just a quarrel between a man and his girlfriend'): this giving of reasons which may well be false is sometimes called rationalising.

However, experiments by Bryan and Test in 1967 did show that if one person in a group said they should help someone in distress, the rest of the group would be much more likely to follow.

Deindividuation and groupthink

In 1991 a video was made of a group of Los Angeles policemen beating up a black man called Rodney King. This led to riots in which over 40 people were killed. Psychologists have shown that because the policemen were acting in a group, they were able to do something which (probably) their consciences would not have allowed them to do individually. The group of policemen lost their individual identity and were 'deindividuated' by group pressure. Instead of thinking for themselves, they used 'groupthink'. This same herd instinct is seen in football hooligans, and in rioters, such as those who killed PC Blakelock in the Broadwater Farm riots in London in 1985.

Experiments have been carried out which support this common-sense view. Zimbardo (1970) arranged for abandoned cars to be left in two different places. The one which was left in a big city was vandalised much faster than the one that was left in a small town; therefore living in big cities also causes deindividuation, and a loss of the individual's moral responsibility, or sense of right and wrong.

Deindividuation is not necessarily a bad thing. The use of uniforms among the public services is also a form of deindividuation, which helps to ensure that officers in these services act as professionals, for the organisation and not for themselves.

Formation of groups

This is a very complex subject, and you might say, 'Well, it all depends on the group.' However, the following points could be made.

1 Groups are always composed of people who have something in common, even if it is only that they live in or near the same place. As groups they have, to some extent, a shared identity and a shared purpose.

2 Sometimes the purpose of a group is the only thing they have in common. For example motorway protesters may include hippies, unemployed people, middle-class local people, environmental activists from universities and members of extreme political parties. They come together as a group because, for different reasons, they share the same purpose of wishing to protest against the building of a new motorway.

3 Other groups share similarities of background or outlook – for example new age travellers, who have decided to give up city life and take to the road in caravans and old buses. This kind of group is often called a subculture.

4 Many groups are recreational: for example football supporters, ice hockey teams, or evening classes studying car maintenance or tai chi.

5 Professional groups are workers in a particular firm, institution or service. Firefighters are an example.

Other group characteristics

Roles

Where a group has a purpose, that purpose is called a role. Thus the role of the police (a rather complex one!) is to make sure that life is safe, peaceful and orderly, and to prevent and fight crime.

Norms

The norms of a group are its accepted ways of behaving. For example, the norms of skinheads include shaving their heads and listening to certain types of music which only they can stand.

Values

The values of a group are the things they believe. New age travellers believe in freedom and the value of a wandering life: Manchester United supporters believe (at the moment) in the perfection of Alex Ferguson, who can walk anywhere without getting his feet wet.

Group decisions

Stoner (1961) found that groups were more likely to make risky decisions than individuals, who tended to play safe.

Polarisation

This is the idea that the characteristics of groups become more extreme the longer the group exists. This may be why the extremists in the French Revolution became more extreme and bloodthirsty as time went on. Research has shown that if you have two groups of students, and one likes academic work and the other likes sport, the difference between the groups will be more marked at the end of two years than it was at the beginning. That is to say the academic students will be even more bookish and the sporty students will be even more sporty.

Group behaviour in public services

Suggest how individual behaviour in groups may be used to benefit the operation of a given public service.

The army has a long tradition of teamwork and groupwork, which has helped to make it one of the most respected armies in the world. This group identity is strengthened in a number of ways.

1. Recruitment of the right kind of people: people who will fit in. Army recruitment is searching and 'in-depth', and includes personality assessment which looks for the team player as well as the outstanding individual.
2. The use of a tough training system which creates close ties between recruits. If a group of people go through hardship together it creates a sense of team spirit (*esprit de corps*) between them.
3. The use of uniforms beneath which differences of wealth and background are hidden.
4. The use of propaganda – such as recruitment posters which say: 'The Army. Be the Best.'
5. The existence of long regimental traditions and history which is taught to recruits.
6. The movement of soldiers from one place to another so that they form bonds with each other, but not with local people.
7. The imposition of strict army discipline, which focuses attention on team duties and roles.
8. The fostering of a certain shared contempt for the 'softness' of civilian life and values (i.e. the way people live and think outside the army).
9. The use of slang words, expressions and a style of humour which is not met with much outside the army.
10. The fact that members of teams spend long hours, day and night, in each others' company, and with very little privacy.

The advantages of these and similar measures is that soldiers:

- know each other very well, and know that they can trust each other
- will, if their lives are threatened, put the lives of others, and the well-being of the army, before their own lives
- are able to work together efficiently in complex operations, with everybody doing something all the time
- are able to make quick decisions because they all share the same views about the things that matter
- are able to withstand hardship because the team spirit keeps them cheerful and optimistic
- can push themselves to the limit and beyond because of the social facilitation effect, which makes each of them stronger together than they would be as individuals – in other words 'the whole is more than the sum of its parts'

- are able to make risky decisions if necessary
- are able to share or spread responsibility for actions which they might not be able to do separately (such as killing the enemy) because of deindividuation
- have higher standards of conformity and obedience than they would have as individuals in civilian life
- have shared norms and values, so they don't waste time and energy quarrelling about things which don't matter
- become better at their work through polarisation – the strengthening of the qualities that they already have
- are physically and mentally stronger because they work in teams, and there is a sense of 'safety in numbers'.

THINK ABOUT IT ...

Try a similar analysis of the police, or any other public service, showing how they benefit from working in groups rather than individually.

UNIT 6 Political Awareness

Unit outcome 1
Examine major political ideologies

Assessment criteria

- Describe three major political ideologies.
- Explain how at least two British political parties reflect ideological positions.

Strange as it may seem, public service students have been known to ask questions like, 'Why do we have to study politics?' and 'What's this got to do with the public services?'

A public service tutor was once talking to a police officer about a student on work placement. The question he asked the officer was: 'What can this student do to improve his chances of getting into the police when he is old enough to apply?' Quick as a flash the officer said, 'Read the newspapers.'

A public service student finished his BTEC National Diploma in Public Services and applied to a fire brigade. At his interview he was cross-questioned about the political situation in Rwanda for half an hour. As he admitted afterwards to his former tutor, 'I just waffled. I know [nothing] about the situation in Rwanda.' He was accepted.

You should consider this question: why is Political Awareness one of the most important units for people who are studying for their BTEC National in Public Services and want to work in these public services? Clue: there is more than one answer. This unit will give you some ideas.

Types of political ideology

Describe three major political ideologies.

For our purposes an ideology is simply a system of political beliefs. There are plenty of ideologies: here are three of them.

1 Capitalism

This is any political system where land, factories, businesses and wealth are owned by individuals and not the government. 'Capital' means money or possessions belonging to a person or business, and under a capitalist system people are allowed to use this wealth to make more wealth by any legal means available. So under a capitalist system it is easy to start businesses and the purpose of those businesses is to make a profit. When the profit is made it belongs to the person or people who own 'the means of production' – that is a factory, farm or a service provider such as a bank or restaurant. The owners are individuals if the business is small, and shareholders if the business is large and has become a 'public limited company' or plc.

A capitalist is either:

(a) a person who believes in the system of capitalism as the best way to run society
(b) a self-employed person
(c) a person who employs others in a private business (i.e. one which is not run by the government).

Modern capitalism started around 1750 with the Industrial Revolution. Before that the basic system was feudalism, which consisted of powerful landowners – and labourers who were little better than slaves and did all the work. Except possibly in parts of the Scottish Highlands the feudal system has completely died out in Britain, but capitalism grew out of it, in the sense that power remained concentrated in the hands of a few rich individuals.

Advantages of capitalism:
- it is the main system in all Western countries, and in most other rich countries such as Japan
- it makes people rich
- it produces high quality goods
- it gives (some) people a lot of choice
- it encourages competition and brings prices down
- it is linked to low taxes
- it tends to let people do what they like (provided they can afford it)
- it allows people to keep their money and re-invest it, once they've made it
- it rewards people for hard work by making them rich, and punishes the lazy by making them poor: it therefore has a kind of built-in justice
- it gives rich or clever people the chance to control their own lives and fulfil their potential.

Disadvantages of capitalism:
- while it makes some people rich, it keeps others – employees and unemployed people – relatively poor
- for this reason it leads to the development of a rigid class system which discriminates against the poor: in the past it has led to serious exploitation of 'the working classes', and very severe poverty – and in some countries this is still the case
- it concentrates power in the hands of the rich: poor people have little or no say in how the country or society are run
- capitalism is bad news for the poor and the ill; because taxes are low there are few facilities for helping poor people – rich people can buy good education and health care, but the poor have to make do with low quality, cheap education and health care – or none at all
- it gives rich people choices, but the poor have no choice except to work hard at boring jobs for which they receive little money

- it tends to tolerate discrimination (by suggesting that people are free to discriminate)
- capitalism has no time for people who cannot or will not pay their way – it leads to a materialistic society where people are judged not by what they are, but by how much money they possess
- in its pure form capitalism leads to revolutions and social unrest, because poor people will not put up with being exploited for ever
- because it concentrates on individualism and free enterprise, it discourages people from working together for the good of society, and suggests that it is better to be selfish than generous – for this reason many people think that capitalism is immoral.

2 Socialism

Socialism is a very different political system from capitalism – but like capitalism it has its origins in the Industrial Revolution.

As we have seen, capitalism has a number of weaknesses, the most serious one being that it keeps many people poor. In the 19th century workers had such low wages that they could scarcely afford to feed, clothe or house themselves. Because of this poverty they grew up stunted and small, suffered from disease and died young. Capitalists made them go to church so they could learn to be obedient not only to God but also to the capitalists. The Bible's teaching: 'Blessed are the meek for they shall inherit the earth' came to mean, 'Do as you're told otherwise you'll get nothing.'

Because capitalism was based on competition between different employers, it was best for the employers if they kept wages low. They made more profit that way, because they paid people less. This punished working people and, if it was carried to its logical conclusion, led to starvation and death.

So in the 19th century (1800–1900) various employers realised that pure capitalism wouldn't work. It caused so much poverty and made the workers so hungry, weak and stupid that eventually it would backfire and make the rich less rich. So some of these employers, mill-owners like Richard Oastler and Titus Salt, began to look after their workers in the hope of raising productivity and satisfying their Christian consciences. Their 'paternalistic' thinking was the origin of conservatism (see page 135), but it also opened the door to socialism.

Modern socialism started with Karl Marx (1818–1883) (see pages 76–77), one of the most important of all political thinkers. He said that under capitalism the only way workers could improve their situation was to get together and change the system, or overthrow it completely.

Socialists believe that the world is divided into capitalists and workers. What is good for the capitalists is bad for the workers, and vice versa. This means there can never be any real agreement between them – and for this reason capitalism will not work. It may seem to work now, up to a point, but it 'contains the seeds of its own destruction', and will break down in the future.

Socialists stress the disadvantages of capitalism mentioned above. They say capitalism is bad because it exploits the workers, makes society unequal, limits the freedom of the poor and wastes resources.

Socialism therefore stresses:

- the importance of society rather than the individual
- the possibility of cooperation between social classes, instead of the capitalist 'class war' between rich and poor
- that people need to live and grow up in a good environment in order to bring out the best in them (for example, we should fight crime by improving people's living conditions and attacking poverty, rather than just banging offenders up in prison)
- the need to be unselfish in our relations with other people, and with other classes of people
- the value of collective rather than individual work
- collaboration (working together) rather than competition (working against each other)
- peace rather than conflict
- public rather than private ownership of wealth
- the need to tax the rich in order to help the poor.

Its advantages are:

- it emphasises the need to get rid of poverty
- it provides ways and ideas for reducing poverty
- it can create a culture of cooperation instead of aggression
- it is against discrimination
- it is in favour of increased democracy, and spreading power evenly through society, instead of concentrating power in the hands of the rich
- it enables the development of things like the National Health Service and free education
- it is an international movement which tends to look for peace
- it is in favour of equality of opportunity
- it is in favour of equal wealth – or at least reducing the differences between rich and poor
- it can work with capitalism, and lessen its bad effects
- it encourages education at all levels
- it provides a range of imaginative ways of dealing with social evils such as crime
- it inspires creative thinking about ways of making society better and fairer.

The disadvantages of socialism:

- it undermines the freedom of the individual, which is the most basic human right
- it is hard to put into practice, partly because it is theoretical and complex, and partly because capitalists try to fight it every inch of the way
- socialism raises taxes

- socialism attacks individuality and acts as a deterrent to people who want to work hard and get rich
- socialism creates a timewasting culture of meetings, working parties, committees and bureaucracy: it is a machine for making red tape
- it is immoral because it discourages hard work and rewards laziness by giving benefits to idle, workshy people and welfare scroungers – it leads to the creation of what has been called 'a dependency culture'
- because of high taxation it drives away the cleverest and most ambitious business people
- high taxation encourages fraud, and the flow of money out of the country to tax havens such as Switzerland and the Cayman Islands
- it creates a society where competitive sport is attacked, and 'political correctness' rules OK.

Political Health Warning

All ideologies are complex, and none more so than socialism. Some forms of socialism are much more 'extreme' and anti-capitalist than others.

- **Reformist socialism** believes that it can work with capitalists and slowly change society for the better by educating people and changing institutions – such as the education system – by degrees. Most socialism in Britain is of this type.
- **Revolutionary socialism** seeks to overthrow the government and our political system, and replace it with one based more closely on the ideas of Karl Marx.

3 Communism

This is a type of Marxism, since, like socialism, it originated from the ideas of Karl Marx. Communism is seen as an extreme ideology which, so far, has never been put into practice. In theory it involves:

- workers owning the means of production using a system of cooperative or joint ownership
- sharing everything; there is no such thing as private property
- the abolition of government as we know it
- an international system of communes (small, village-sized groups).

The Soviet Union, China, Cuba, North Korea, Albania and other countries have experimented with communism at various times between 1917 and about 1990. These communist governments have been variously known as Maoist, Leninist, Marxist-Leninist and Stalinist. They have had communes in the form of collective farms, which were collectively owned by the people who worked on them. In these countries all industry was owned by the regional or central government. There was no competition: instead, to encourage workers, the governments set production targets often known as 'five-year plans'. The value of money was artificially controlled by the government rather than by the Western system of money markets and national banks. These countries were always one-party states, where the only party was the communist party. Elections, if they occurred, were a sham in which the only candidate got 99 per cent of the vote. All these countries were very hostile to the West (though the USSR helped the West to win the war against Hitler's Germany). In an attempt to overthrow capitalism they flooded the world with cheap goods and built up huge armies. In the USSR technology advanced very fast and the Soviets were the first to put a satellite in space in 1959 – much to the horror of the Americans! But in the end this type of state communism broke down because:

- the countries were bankrupted by the West in the economic 'cold war'
- people living under these systems could see how much better life was in the West, and many of them got out if they could
- there was a lack of freedom and little respect for human rights in these countries: some people say that 60 million people were brutally murdered by Stalin and his supporters in the Soviet Union – which means that Stalin was responsible for more deaths than Hitler.

British political parties

Explain how at least two British political parties reflect ideological positions.

A political party is a large group of people who share similar political beliefs, and seek to gain power in national and local government. The main political parties in England are the Labour Party, the Conservative Party and the Liberal Democrats. The

Labour and Conservative parties are discussed on the following pages.

1 The Labour Party

What the table below means is that the present day Labour Party, which often calls itself 'New Labour', has moved away from its traditional socialism. This has made many 'traditional' and 'socialist' Labour supporters unhappy, because the party is giving up the ideology they like. To them, 'New Labour' sounds more like 'New Conservatives'. But the general public seems to support the removal of 'socialism' (a 'dirty word') from the Labour agenda. They seem to approve of the fact that the Labour party is moving politically to the right.

Ideological Socialist position	Actual position in 1999
• Society matters more than the individual.	New Labour is accused of being the 'party of the middle classes'. It is committed to not raising income tax, even though doing so would greatly improve the quality of social support for the poor and disadvantaged.
• Different social classes should cooperate, not fight.	This is the view of New Labour – though the long-term aim is a classless society. The classless society was first put forward by John Major, the last Conservative prime minister. Yet according to traditional socialism there can be no such thing as a classless society. So there's a clear shift from traditional socialist thinking.
• People need to live and grow up in a good environment in order to bring out the best in them. (For example, we should fight crime by improving people's living conditions and attacking poverty, rather than just locking offenders up in prison.)	General agreement on this in New Labour, but Jack Straw, the present home secretary, is keen to be seen as tough on crime. Traditionally it is the Conservatives who make a point of being tough on crime.
• The need to be unselfish in our relations with other people, and with other classes of people.	New Labour agrees with this, so here it is being true to traditional socialist thinking.
• The value of collective rather than individual work.	New Labour is keen to encourage small businesses, just as the Conservatives were. So it seems to have shifted from traditional socialism towards a more Conservative point of view.
• Collaboration (working together) rather than competition (working against each other).	In the 1970s, when there was the last Labour government, trade unions were very powerful, and brought the country to its knees in a series of strikes in the 'winter of discontent' in 1979. They were punished for their 'softness' towards trade unions by the voters, who put the Conservatives in power for the next 18 years. New Labour has learnt that the British public doesn't like too much collaboration, and dislikes trade unions. They have said they will keep the anti-trade union laws passed by the Conservatives. This means they have shifted away from the socialist view towards a Conservative one so they can stay in power. *Cont'd*

• Peace rather than conflict.	Maybe – but it didn't stop Tony Blair wading into the war in Kosovo. He was more 'hawkish' (keen on fighting) even than the Americans – and sounded more like a Conservative than a traditional socialist. So there was a big ideological shift here.
• Public rather than private ownership of wealth.	People like their wealth to be in their own bank accounts, not in the 'public purse'. They hate paying taxes, whatever they might say about wanting to help the poor (and paying taxes is the best way of helping the poor in the short-term). New Labour has promised not to increase income tax (this is a policy taken from the Conservatives). But they have tried to satisfy the socialists in their party by taxing petrol and other commodities at a very high rate. So they have watered down their socialist beliefs and are trying to please everybody at once – to raise their chances of getting elected next time round.
• The need to tax the rich in order to help the poor.	At the moment Labour are not even increasing taxes for the very rich. Instead they are trying to persuade rich people to take lower pay rises so as to reduce the difference between the very rich and the very poor. Old fashioned socialists would tax the rich until the pips squeak.

2 The Conservative Party

In 1997 the Conservative Party suffered their worst ever election defeat. John Major stepped down, William Hague was elected as the new leader, and the party shows signs of setting off in a new direction. But as yet it is not entirely clear how it stands on many of the ideological issues it used to believe in so strongly.

Ideological Conservative position	Actual position in 1999
• Changing society slowly – if at all.	In fact the Conservative government of 1979–1997 was a period of great change in British society – and much of that change was brought about by the government. It changed the tax system, though not always successfully. It attacked the trade unions and greatly reduced their power and influence. In doing so it lowered the level of strikes and of pay rises. Many government-owned businesses, such as the railways and British steel, were privatised – made into private companies. Council houses were sold, the National Health Service and education were reformed. What used to be called 'one-nation Toryism' (the old type of slow-changing conservatism) was replaced by an active right-wing government. Now William Hague is talking of more deep-rooted changes in party organisation and policy. So the ideology of slow change has certainly been put to one side.

Cont'd

• Capitalism is much better than socialism, and wherever possible society should be run on capitalist lines.	Margaret Thatcher stated that her aim was to destroy socialism. She did not succeed, but she managed to make it politically suicidal for the Labour party to talk about socialism. Traditional socialism has largely been kicked into touch, following two Conservative governments. Therefore Conservatism has stayed true to this part of its ideology.
• Taxes should be as low as possible, but there should be a 'safety net' of welfare provision. In other words nobody should have to live on the streets, and there should be medical care for the very poor – as there is in the USA.	Conservatives claimed – while in government – to be reducing taxes, but most experts thought this was not true. They reduced income tax but raised other, less obvious, types of tax. So in this sense they shifted from their traditional ideology. On the other hand they did, relatively speaking, reduce spending on the welfare state, and privatised some medical care by setting up doctors' practices as 'fundholding' (in other words, they were run more like private businesses). Medical care did not improve as much as it might have done while it was under their control, and the NHS was more like a safety net than a full 'cradle to grave' system of medical care – which was what it was first proposed to be in 1944.
• Conservatives believe their own country is better than any foreign country. They are therefore nationalistic. However, they are not so extremely nationalistic that they regard other nations as a lower form of life.	The Conservative Party has had split attitudes towards Europe for many years. Edward Heath, a 'left-wing' Conservative leader, took us into Europe in 1973, and was much less nationalistic than most Conservatives. Mrs Thatcher, though, was very nationalistic, and used to mock European union by calling it 'socialism by the back Delors'. (Jacques Delors was the French socialist leader of the European Community as it was then called. He got his own back on the Conservatives by devising the Maastricht Treaty, a masterpiece of European doublethink which split the Conservative Party right down the middle. Over Europe they fought themselves to a standstill and, as a result, lost power in 1997.) Despite all their problems over Europe the Conservatives remain true to their ideology as a nationalist party.
• Conservatives believe in 'small government' (less government interference in people's lives).	Mrs Thatcher often talked about 'small government' and wanted to 'roll back the frontiers of the state'. She succeeded in doing this in her programme of privatisation of the coal mines, the railways, the gas industry and water supplies. Her government even privatised further education – but there was still plenty of government interference. So the Conservatives have not followed this part of their ideology.

Cont'd

• They traditionally stress the importance of 'law and order' and of having a strong army.	When Michael Howard was home secretary the Conservatives tried to reorganise the police through the report of Sir William Sheehy (1993), and make them save money and explain what they did with the money they spent. He thus made enemies of the police. The prison service was partly privatised. He had a running battle with the courts, because most judges didn't like his ideas. The Conservatives put more people in prison than ever before. They also made heavy defence cuts. They lost the support of the public services in the 1990s by giving off conflicting signals about what they wanted, and by interfering too much in public service work. So in this area they were not true to their ideology.
• Conservatives do not see themselves as racists, but other political groups think that Conservatives are not as anti-racist as they should be.	In the past the Conservatives have been criticised for their attitude towards race, especially in the late 1960s when Enoch Powell, who was seen by many people as racist, made speeches saying that 'immigration' would cause 'rivers of blood'. In recent years they have cleaned up their act, but few non-white people join the Conservative Party, or vote for them.
• They are traditionally in favour of America and American concepts of freedom.	Mrs Thatcher was a great friend and supporter of the American President Ronald Reagan in the 1980s. She said there was a 'special relationship' between the British and American governments and this was probably true because the Americans helped us (reluctantly) in the Falklands Conflict. This relationship broke down later when Conservatives tried to advise the Republicans in the USA at the time of Bill Clinton's election in 1992 – in other words, they backed the wrong horse! They have not forgiven Clinton for winning, but they still like American freedoms and attitudes, and the fact that William Hague has been seen wearing a baseball cap is said to be a sign of this!
• Conservatives view gender roles in a traditional way, so they tend to be against feminism, and hard on gays.	Despite the fact that the Conservative Party was successfully led by a woman – Mrs Thatcher – between 1975 and 1990 – the Conservatives have for many years had a much lower percentage of women MPs than Labour. This is surprising since until recently women were more likely to vote Conservative than men. Conservative MPs have been less willing than Labour to 'come out' as gay, perhaps fearing that they will lose votes. This suggests that they see their followers as homophobic. However, they are trying to get rid of their old anti-feminist and homophobic image.

Cont'd

- They are not keen on the idea of everybody being equal, and think that the concept of 'choice' is more important. For this reason they are against the closing of private schools and the creation of a unified system of education. They also believe that there should be private as well as public hospitals.

Conservatives have always been consistent in these views. Recently in April 1999 Peter Lilley, the shadow home secretary said: 'Unless and until we are prepared to accept that there is more to life and more to Conservatism than defending and extending the free market we will always be on the intellectual back foot where the public services are concerned.' This was his way of saying that the Conservatives should try to learn from Labour and be more interested in the idea of equality. But this is only a slight ideological shift, and Peter Lilley may be sidelined because of these views.

From these explanations you can see that both the Labour Party and the Conservative Party have moved away from their ideological roots. If the Labour Party ever was a socialist party, it is generally agreed to be not very socialist at the moment. And the Conservative Party, which got its name from its desire to resist change, is at present very eager to change society. Compared with the people of some other countries, the British are not very keen on ideology. We prefer to make up our politics as we go along, rather than listen to the experts.

THINK ABOUT IT ...

Different political parties have different attitudes towards the public services.

If you were working in the public service of your choice, which political party would you like to have running the country – and why?

Unit outcome 2
Examine the machinery of government

Assessment criteria

- Describe the relationship between the prime minister, the cabinet, the House of Commons and the House of Lords.
- Outline the checks and balances operating within government.

Roles and relationships in government

We will first look at the roles of each of these, then describe the relationship.

The role of the prime minister

The work of the prime minister is a kind of public service, and therefore it includes many roles, such as:

- to appoint ministers and members of the cabinet

- to set the agenda for cabinet meetings
- to chair cabinet meetings
- to take part in prime minister's question time in the House of Commons (once a week)
- to represent Britain and British interests at the highest level overseas
- to appoint archbishops and some other people such as privy councillors
- to declare war, or involve Britain in a war
- to make policy decisions
- to consult special advisers
- to veto 'bad' ideas
- to liaise with the media (sometimes through a press secretary)
- to travel about the country visiting people and making speeches
- to decide when the next general election is going to be
- to discuss matters with the Queen about once a month (or less).

Exactly what the prime minister does depends enormously on his or her character and style of leadership. It also depends on how much they want to get involved in details.

The role of the cabinet

The cabinet is a committee which discusses major political issues and proposed new laws, and takes decisions on them. It meets about once a week in a special office in the prime minister's house at 10 Downing Street. The prime minister chairs the discussion and is responsible for the running of the meetings.

The exact role of the cabinet depends on:
(a) the issues being discussed
(b) the way the prime minister runs the meetings
(c) the characters and personalities of the cabinet members.

If the prime minister is forceful and the cabinet is less so it can come to act almost like a rubber stamp. But since in general the cabinet consists of able and ambitious people the meetings tend to be lively and argumentative affairs with everybody jockeying for position.

Collective responsibility

However much disagreement there is during cabinet meetings, cabinet members rarely mention their differences in public. If the cabinet decides something it is assumed that, in public, everybody agrees. If cabinet members don't like a decision they can always resign.

The present cabinet

The members of the cabinet are given in the table below.

Cabinet posts	Members of the cabinet formed by the Rt Hon Tony Blair MP, July 1998
Prime Minister, First Lord of the Treasury and Minister for the Civil Service	Rt Hon Tony Blair MP
Deputy Prime Minister and Secretary of State for the Environment, Transport and the Regions	Rt Hon John Prescott MP
Chancellor of the Exchequer	Rt Hon Gordon Brown MP
Secretary of State for Foreign and Commonwealth Affairs	Rt Hon Robin Cook MP
Lord Chancellor	Rt Hon Lord Irvine of Lairg QC
Secretary of State for the Home Department	Rt Hon Jack Straw MP
Secretary of State for Education & Employment	Rt Hon David Blunkett MP

Cont'd

President of the Council and Leader of the House of Commons	Rt Hon Margaret Beckett MP
Minister for the Cabinet Office and Chancellor of the Duchy Of Lancaster	Rt Hon Mo Mowlam MP
Secretary of State for Scotland	Rt Hon Dr John Reid MP
Secretary of State for Defence	Rt Hon George Robertson MP
Secretary of State for Health	Rt Hon Alan Milburn MP
Parliamentary Secretary to the Treasury (Chief Whip)	Rt Hon Ann Taylor MP
Secretary of State for Culture, Media and Sport	Rt Hon Chris Smith MP
Secretary of State for Northern Ireland	Rt Hon Peter Mandelson MP
Secretary of State for Wales	Rt Hon Alun Michael MP
Secretary of State for International Development	Rt Hon Clare Short MP
Secretary of State for Social Security	Rt Hon Alistair Darling MP
Minister of Agriculture, Fisheries and Food	Rt Hon Nick Brown MP
Lord Privy Seal, Leader of the House of Lords and Minister for Women	Rt Hon Baroness Jay of Paddington
Secretary of State for Trade and Industry	Rt Hon Stephen Byers MP
Chief Secretary to the Treasury	Rt Hon Keith Vaz MP

THINK ABOUT IT ...

Some of these post-holders may have changed by the time you study the table above.

Find out who holds these cabinet posts now.

The House of Commons

There are two 'houses' in Parliament: the House of Commons and the House of Lords. Of the two the House of Commons is much the more important.

Members of Parliament

The people who sit in the House of Commons are called members of Parliament, or MPs for short (not to be confused with military police!). They are ordinary people who join political parties and stand as candidates for a city or an area ('constituency') at general elections. General elections are held roughly every four years (see page 147). If a candidate gets more votes than any other party's candidate standing for that constituency at the same election they become its MP and take their seats in the House of Commons for the life of the government. Their job is to represent the constituency – in other words put forward the views of the people in their voting area (whether they voted for them or not) – and to debate, promote or oppose new laws that are being brought in all the time.

The role of the House of Commons

The role of the MPs in the House of Commons is to debate (discuss) new laws and decide whether they should be 'passed' (made official) or not. The MPs decide by voting. The votes are not secret because they have to walk out through an 'aye' or 'no' door to register their vote. From time to time the House also discusses a range of other major political problems. Most of its work is not done during the main debates but in the committees of MPs which they set up. You will find more about these committees on page 143.

The current political split

In the House of Commons there are MPs from all the main political parties – including political parties in Scotland and Northern Ireland. This is true even though Scotland already has a Parliament of its own, and Northern Ireland may soon have one as well. Here is a breakdown showing the numbers for each political party:

Party	MPs
Labour	418
Conservative	165
Liberal Democrats	46
Ulster Unionists	10
Scottish National Party	6
Plaid Cymru	4
Social Democratic & Labour Party	3
Ulster Democratic Unionist Party	2
Sinn Fein	2
United Kingdom Unionist	1
Independent	1
The Speaker (Stands as 'Speaker seeking re-election')	1
TOTAL	659*

*Government majority – 177
The 659 MPs included 120 women

The Labour Party is at present (1999) the party in government. As you can see, it has a huge majority. The Conservative Party's job is to attempt to show where the Labour Party's ideas and policies are going wrong. Then come the Liberal Democrats – a much smaller party who at present are closer to Labour than the Conservatives in their thinking. The Ulster Unionists represent the Protestants in Northern Ireland and traditionally support the Conservatives. The Scottish National Party wants independence for Scotland 'within Europe'. It is closer to Labour than the Conservatives in the English Parliament, though they fight tooth and nail in the Scottish Parliament. Plaid Cymru is the Welsh National Party and wants some form of independence or devolution (separation) for Wales. It is a fairly left-wing party and would normally support Labour. The other parties are small and mainly connected with Northern Ireland, and though they are important in their own communities they are beyond the scope of this discussion.

The job of opposition MPs

It is the job of the non-governing parties in the House of Commons to challenge the policies of the governing party. The non-governing parties are said to be 'in opposition'. This is because we have what is called an 'adversarial system of government'. People argue from opposite sides of the fence, testing new ideas by being as rude and destructive about them as possible. If the new laws and other ideas stand up to this bombardment of criticism, it is assumed that they are quite good ideas and that – having been put to the test – they can become law.

To make their opposition more effective, the non-governing party have a 'shadow cabinet' of MPs who each specialise in the work of a particular minister. Their aim is to give the government minister a hard time and make them look as though they are not up to the job.

THINK ABOUT IT ...

Can you name the Conservative shadow cabinet?

The job of government MPs

It is the job of governing party MPs to argue in favour of their own party, and to vote in favour of their prime minister and cabinet ministers whenever there is a division (vote) in the House. If you read MPs' speeches it will often seem as though they are grovelling and bootlicking – but again this is their job. If their MPs stop bootlicking, however, the prime minister and cabinet know that they do not have the support of their own party – let alone anybody else – and they will then have to alter their policies or risk their positions by appealing to the country through a general election.

Prime minister's question time

Once a week (it used to be twice but Tony Blair has changed it) there is prime minister's question time. The opposition asks the prime minister the most difficult and sarcastic questions they can think of, in the hope of exposing weaknesses in his policies. Sometimes they succeed – and sometimes they don't.

The speaker

People from other countries whose parliaments are orderly and polite are often surprised at the frankness of debate in our own House of Commons. In order to direct and, at times, control the pace and nature of these debates the House of Commons has a 'speaker'. It is the speaker's job to ensure that debates are as constructive as possible and do not degenerate into slanging matches.

The House of Lords

The job of the House of Lords is to go through the laws produced by the House of Commons. In effect they try to produce constructive criticism of the way laws have been drafted (written) by pointing out possible weaknesses and problems. Although this function can sometimes be a 'nit-picking' one, it also relieves the House of Commons of the time-consuming task of going through the workability of new laws in detail. Laws that are at the stage of being debated by the House of Lords are known as 'bills'. The Lords are able to send a bill back to the Commons for re-writing if they feel it necessary. Bills can sometimes be abandoned if the Lords and the Commons cannot agree on them.

Occasionally the Lords takes time out from scanning laws, and acts as a kind of law court, with senior judges settling some important political case or appeal. This is why it is sometimes described as 'the highest court in the land'.

The House of Lords is in the process of being reformed by the Labour government. Most of the hereditary peers (the lords whose fathers and grandfathers sat in the House before them) will be retired, and new members of the House of Lords will be either elected or appointed by special committee. It is likely that there will be 550 members of the reformed House. Eighty-seven of these will be regional members, so that every part of the country can feel represented. These regional members will be elected by the public or in some cases drawn from among the most active of the present hereditary peers. Twenty per cent of members should be politically independent. It should contain 26 Christian representatives (bishops etc.) and five members from other religions. Thirty per cent should be women. Many members will continue to be former MPs, but the new House of Lords should not be as political or adversarial (argumentative) as the House of Commons. Special committees, such as a new one on human rights, should be set up. The aim of the proposed changes is to make the new House of Lords more relevant and representative of 21st century Britain.

However much the House of Lords is changed, it will still be less important than the House of Commons.

Summary

The prime minister chooses the cabinet and chairs cabinet meetings. The cabinet discusses government policy, and cabinet ministers tell their departments what to do and think. The House of Commons debates new laws or other major issues and then votes on them. The people who sit in the House of Commons are called MPs. Most MPs either support or oppose the prime minister and the government to which he (or she) belongs. More MPs support the government than oppose it. At prime minister's question time the prime minister answers friendly questions from his own MPs, and hostile ones from the opposition. The House of Lords studies the new laws debated by the House of Commons, and either agrees or disagrees with them.

The role of the monarchy

Britain is a monarchy, which means the official head of state is the Queen. But she has no real political power. The Queen's Speech, which she gives at the opening of Parliament, outlining the new laws which are going to be brought in, is written by the government. The Queen has trained herself to read this speech in such a way that nobody, not even a Freudian psychologist, can tell whether she agrees with it or not. The Royal Assent – the approval she gives to new bills (laws) – is a formality: she has no choice in the matter. About once a month she meets the prime minister to be briefed on what is going on in the government, and in the world of politics generally. Rumour has it that the Queen understands politics very well, and gives good advice, but whether the prime minister pays any attention to this advice is a secret between him and the Queen.

Checks and balances

Outline the checks and balances operating within government.

We know by looking at some other countries that if the governments can do whatever they like, power goes to their heads like a bottle of vodka and they do all sorts of bad things. For example they lock people up without trial, or put them in mental hospital, just because they dare to criticise the head of state. Worse, they might have them shot – and have their families shot – or their whole community gassed. In these countries where the government has total power, newspapers dare not print their criticisms, and if they do their editors are tortured or killed. Meanwhile such governments, as if knowing they will not be in power for very long, steal as much public money as they can and stash it away in a Swiss bank.

It isn't like this in Britain. We have what are called 'checks and balances' to prevent the government gaining too much power. In Britain there are people and organisations simply queuing up to criticise the government the moment it makes an ill-considered move.

Our system is not foolproof. But there certainly are checks and balances. Here are some of them.

1 Parliament

Many government MPs are able to feel free to criticise their own party; Tony Benn acts as if New Labour are a load of fascists; Tam Dalyell says that we're a nation of war criminals because of the sinking of the Belgrano in 1982 during the Falklands Crisis. They get their views put out in the papers and on television. And this is tolerated to a certain extent in spite of the fact that they are supposed to be supporters of the government! As for the opposition MPs, as we have seen, it is their job to criticise the government at every opportunity.

In addition the Commons regulates itself, partly through its complex procedural rules which prevent time being wasted, partly through the speaker, who makes sure that people can have their say in debates, and partly through the Register of Members' Interests. This Register is a list in which MPs have to put down all their sources of income besides their parliamentary salary (which for an ordinary MP is £47,000 per year). The purpose of this, following various scandals, is to make sure that MPs are independent and cannot be bribed by foreign governments or rich business people.

2 The committee system

Parliament is full of committees, and the purpose of all of them is to check some aspect of its work and make sure that it is being done properly. There are different types of committee, which include the following.

Select Committees

These meet once a week to check or oversee the work of each government department. Even though they are made up of MPs from different parties they have to reach agreement, and if they find out that anything is wrong the government has to do something about it.

One of these committees – the Select Committee on Privileges – looks at cases where MPs are thought to have been dishonest. If they have been dishonest they can be

(a) punished by the House – for example by exclusion
(b) taken to court
(c) dismissed in rare cases, and a by-election held to select a new MP, as happened at Tatton in 1997 – see below.

FOCUS

'Neil Hamilton, testifying under oath and probably on television as well, will appear before the House of Commons Standards and Privileges Committee. He will challenge the conclusion of the Parliamentary Commissioner, Sir Gordon Downey, that there was 'compelling evidence' that he took Mr Al Fayed's cash for asking questions in the House.

In all this business, there are only three verdicts that matter:

- The people delivered theirs on election day.
- Sir Gordon added his at the beginning of July.
- Now it will be the turn of the committee, sitting in judgement on one of their former colleagues.'

Source: Martin Bell, *Knutsford Guardian* 1997

Standing Committees

These look at proposed new laws, called bills as we have seen, and make changes if they think it is necessary. The members are taken from different parties roughly in proportion to their numbers in the House of Commons. That means that at present most committee members will be Labour, because most MPs are Labour.

Joint Committees

These Committees have members both from the House of Commons and the House of Lords. They make recommendations on procedures of government, rather than laws which might directly affect the country as a whole.

3 The House of Lords

As we have already noted on page 142, the House of Lords studies all the major new bills that the House of Commons produces. It specialises in 'nit-picking'. As it says on the Parliament website: 'Normally, the consent of the Lords is required before Acts of Parliament can be passed, and the Lords can amend all legislation, with the exception of bills to raise taxation, long seen as the responsibility of the Commons. Amendments have to be agreed to by both Houses. The Lords are as active as the Commons in amending bills.' Amending bills means getting rid of all the extreme and impractical provisions which the government might have put into their first draft. So this procedure is therefore an important way of controlling and moderating the government's power.

4 The courts

There are times when a member of the public complains that he or she has been treated unjustly by new laws passed by the governmment – and takes the government to court. This has sometimes led to the law being changed – as in the case of the Child Support Agency in 1993, when the Conservative government expected fathers to start paying maintenance money for children by former wives or girlfriends. A number of alterations were made to the procedures of the CSA following court action at that time. More recently, in 1999, over the proposed deportation of Augusto Pinochet to Spain (see Unit 8: International Perspectives, page 187), Pinochet was able to argue through the courts that the decision was unsound because one of the original judges was linked with the human rights organisation Amnesty International.

5 Civil servants

Vast numbers of civil servants, who are supposed to be politically unbiased, work in the Houses of Parliament and in Whitehall, in London, advising politicians and helping them draft their bills and do all the other paperwork they have to do. Our idea of them is affected by TV comedies such as *Yes Minister* – and there is some truth in this view of the relationship between top civil servants and MPs. Top civil servants are often much cleverer than the MPs they serve. Normally this is a good thing, because, apart from anything else, it makes sure that the new laws are written in good English. On the other hand they are sometimes seen as a collection of snobs, biased towards the Conservatives. What is certain is that there are large numbers of them: 1,500, for example, work with the cabinet alone. As well as advising MPs they collect and process much of the information that the government needs to decide or put into practice its social and economic policies.

6 Pressure groups

These, and the groups discussed under the headings that follow, are not exactly 'in government', but they certainly act as 'checks and balances'. Pressure groups are organisations such as the League Against Cruel Sports, LIFE (the anti-abortion group), Greenpeace and so on. They are composed of people who feel strongly about an individual political, social or environmental issue and want to put pressure on the government to change the law. They influence the government by lobbying (hassling) MPs, writing to the papers, holding demonstrations, legal action – in fact anything and everything which will get their ideas noticed. Very often the government takes the first step by consulting pressure groups before they make a change in the law. For example, now that the government has said they will ban foxhunting in the next two years they will start consulting hunting and countryside pressure groups to see how it should be done.

7 The media

The government originally consisted of 'three estates' – the monarchy, the church and Parliament. The press (newspapers and the media) sometimes call themselves the 'fourth estate'. The Royal Charter which governs the behaviour of the BBC compels them to be unbiased in their reporting of news. This means they are allowed to criticise the government sometimes, as long as they support it at others. Obviously it is hard to judge the 'amount' of support or criticism they give, since it is not only the length of time but also the quality of support or criticism that matters. So in practice the BBC is quite free to criticise the government. The Conservative minister Norman Tebbit once bitterly attacked the BBC for bias against the government, and the Labour leader Neil Kinnock famously complained of being 'kebabbed' by James Naughtie, a BBC journalist supposedly sympathetic to Labour.

Newspapers are even more free to attack the government than the television companies are. But some newspapers support the government. At present the political support line-up looks a bit like this.

For The Labour Party:
- the *Daily Mirror*
- the *Guardian*
- the *Observer*
- the *Daily Express*
- the *Sun* (up to a point).

For The Conservative Party:
- the *Daily Mail*
- *The Times*
- the *Sunday Times*
- the *Daily Telegraph*.

Until shortly before the 1997 election the *Daily Express* and the *Sun* were Conservative ('Tory') papers, but they changed because they were impressed by the way Tony Blair had stamped his authority on the Labour Party and moved it towards the political right.

8 Quangos

A quango is not a South African antelope, nor is it the latest fizzy drink. It is a Quasi-Autonomous Non-Governmental Organisation. There are hundreds of these bodies about, affecting what the government thinks and does. A well-known one is the Commission for Racial Equality, which does what it can to ensure that the government follows anti-racist policies (for example in working to change the attitude and 'culture' of the police after the Stephen Lawrence inquiry reported in 1998). Another is the Health and Safety Executive, which makes sure that the government always has workers' health and safety near the top of its agenda.

9 Trade unions

These are groups of workers or employees who have got together to protect their interests against employers. Examples are the TGWU (Transport and General Workers Union) and NATFHE (National Association for Teachers in Further and Higher Education). These comment on government policy at their annual conferences or when it seems that laws are likely to be changed in their own work area. Sometimes they 'sponsor' MPs, which means that a particular MP tries to support them in the House of Commons (though without doing anything which might be seen as corrupt, of course).

10 Europe

Whether we like it or not we are part of the European Union, and as time goes on this relationship will get closer. Many of the laws passed in Europe now affect Britain – especially laws to do with things like trade, human rights and the environment. Even if we are not bound directly by laws passed in Brussels, they still influence the UK government's way of looking at things.

The government of the European Union (EU) is in three parts.

The European Commission

This is the most powerful part of the EU which consists of 22 commissioners chosen (not elected) by the 15 governments. The biggest countries choose two commissioners; the rest appoint one. So France, Germany, Italy, Spain and the UK all appoint two commissioners, while Austria, Belgium, Denmark, Finland, Greece, Ireland, Luxembourg, the Netherlands, Portugal and Sweden appoint one each. The job of the Commission is to put forward new laws.

The Council of Ministers

Below the European Commission comes the Council of Ministers. These are all heads of government departments. If there is a meeting of European home secretaries (or their equivalent) then Jack Straw would attend for the UK. Their job is to decide whether to accept or reject the laws which the Commission puts forward.

The European Parliament

The third part is the European Parliament. It is made up of the only directly elected officials in the European Union at present, though there are moves afoot to try to make the whole system more democratic. The European Parliament is much less powerful than the UK Parliament since it cannot put forward any new laws. Its job is only to 'supervise and scrutinise' new European laws.

11 Opinion polls

Opinion polls are rather like market research. Organisations such as MORI or NOP which specialise in this kind of work choose a sample of one or two thousand people up and down the country. They ask these people lots of questions – usually over the telephone, but sometimes face to face. Some of the questions are political ones, e.g. 'Do you think the following members of the government are doing a good job...?' And then they reel off a list of names in case you have forgotten who the members of the government are. Other questions are about the respondents' view of commercial products such as Coca Cola, Mars Bars, or timeshares in Lanzarote. When they get everybody's answers they separate off the commercial questions and process those answers for the companies which have paid MORI or NOP to ask the questions. The other, political answers are processed for the organisation (usually a newspaper or the government itself) which paid for them. By juggling and 'weighting' the statistics the opinion pollsters can get an accurate picture of how the country would vote if a general election was to be held on a particular date. These polls also give feedback on whether the government's policies are popular. If the government sees that it is annoying the electorate with its policies, it can start changing them. In this way the opinion polls can influence the way the government behaves.

12 General elections and the electorate

The electorate is you and me – people who can vote at elections. We are the last and most powerful of all the checks and balances. Because if we don't like a government we can just vote them out of office on election day, and start afresh with a new one. And if they don't do the job properly we can get rid of them as well.

General elections are held roughly every four years (but must be held within five). The country is divided into 659 constituencies, each of which elects a member of Parliament (MP). An average constituency has about 80,000 people of voting age living in it. In a general election between 60 and 70 per cent of these people will turn out to vote. But in a by-election (perhaps caused by the death of an MP, or the promotion of that MP to a new job in NATO or some other international organisation), sometimes only 30 or 40 per cent vote.

Voting behaviour

At least 60 per cent of people who bother to vote always vote for the same party. Other people change their vote from time to time. These people are called 'floating voters'. If they didn't keep changing their votes at each election, we would always have the same government.

Unit outcome 3
Examine political decisions and consequences

Assessment criteria

- Identify a political decision and evaluate the consequences for a given public service.
- Identify a political decision and evaluate the consequences for an individual.

Identifying political decisions and consequences

Imagine a world where there was no population growth, no new technology, no changing fashions and no new ideas. In this world there is always the same number of cars and the same number of mobile phones. People listen to the same records year in and year out, and always go to the same place for their holidays, where they read the same books in the same deckchairs swilling the same kind of plonk until, mercifully, they drop dead. In that planet, which we could call 'Zombie', nothing ever changes any more than if we were hedgehogs or snails, and there is no need for politics or political decisions.

On earth, they do things differently. Life is always changing; there are new hopes and new pressures – and no two years could possibly be alike. People make new machines, take new drugs, commit new crimes and dream new dreams. To deal with these challenges, which might sweep us all away, politicians pass new laws and make decisions – in the hope that with a bit of control life will go on in the new millennium.

The word 'identify' means to recognise and name something that is already there. But what is a political decision? It suggests a choice between two or more options. And the word 'political' makes us think that the choice is made by politicians. Yet it might not be as simple as that. Suppose, for example, the government decided to legalise cannabis. Obviously it doesn't mean that the home secretary wakes up one morning and thinks, 'I could do with a spliff so I'd better legalise it.' So he certainly doesn't choose to legalise it; it isn't only his decision. Perhaps he looks round and thinks: 'Everybody's doing it anyway – so I might as well make it legal. It will save the police some work.' But then some civil servant might say, 'Well, actually, Jack, there's only five million people taking the stuff on a regular basis, so you don't need to do anything. And besides, the police don't want to be put out of a job.' Next a chief constable might say to him, 'It's all very well legalising it, sir, but it's the thin end of the wedge, and the next thing we know we'll be legalising smack and crack. Besides, if people drive under the influence of pot they can't judge distances and that will mean another thousand people being killed in road accidents each year.' So we can imagine Jack Straw going to Keith Hellawell, the 'drugs czar' and saying, 'What do you make of this idea of legalising dope, Keith?' 'Not much,' Keith would probably say. 'It's the job of government to give a lead.' 'Yeah, yeah. But in what direction?' says Jack. 'That's the problem.'

You can see that the more someone thinks about an issue like the legalisation of cannabis, the more complicated it gets. And yet compared with most political issues it's very simple, because it's unimportant to most people compared with going to war or raising taxes. And after all, why should we in Britain make it legal when no other country is going to, and when the only people who are really going to benefit will be the cigarette manufacturers?

Let's look at some other decisions and try to evaluate them – in other words, not only say what the decision is, but examine what it means and whether its effects are good or bad.

The Police and Criminal Evidence Act 1984

The consequences for the police

The political decision to pass this far-reaching law affecting the powers of the police originated in the Brixton Riots in April 1981. During these riots hundreds of police officers were injured and for several hours parts of Brixton, in London, were no-go areas for the police. In other words it was a serious and frightening situation in which parts of the capital city were beyond the reach of the law. More by good luck than good management, nobody was killed, but as well as the many injuries millions of pounds' worth of damage was done.

The government – and most people in Britain – had no clear idea what had caused these riots. Many people had an opinion; for example it was widely said at the time that they were 'race riots'. To try to get to the root of the problem the government appointed a liberal-minded high court judge, Lord Justice Scarman, to investigate the riots and write a report on them.

Scarman did not have an easy job. Feelings ran high after the riots and not everybody wanted to cooperate with him. But it became clear to people that he was not 'your average high court judge'. He wasn't the kind of judge who had never heard of the Beatles or Gazza. His approach was unprejudiced and he was prepared to get out of his office and listen to anyone and everyone. He got people who hated the police to trust him and talk to him. Furthermore, if he couldn't visit people he got his wife to visit them instead. Later on in the same year he produced his report, which is about 250 pages long and was published by the government. Unlike many government reports it is written in straightforward language and makes a fascinating read.

Scarman had a lot to say about the police, and most of it was critical. He accused them of behaving in a racist manner, and more or less said that they were to blame for the riots in the first place. Even the government, which was strongly inclined to stick up for the police, realised that something had to be done. They couldn't do it quickly, because the problems ran too deep for that, but they did it in the end and in 1984 brought out the Police and Criminal Evidence Act.

Up till that time the police had been able to do what they liked on Britain's streets. Of course they had done a lot of excellent work, and their intentions were usually good. But there had been nothing to prevent them arresting people for no reason, or just because they didn't like the colour of their skin or the length of their hair. Under the old 'sus' laws they could stop and search people on 'suspicion', and it didn't really matter what they were suspicious of. In Brixton (and other places) they had got it into their heads that if a black man was walking down the streeet he was probably about to mug some sweet little old lady. They therefore hassled black people at every turn and made them empty their pockets so often that in the end it was the black people who felt they were being mugged. In Brixton they carried out a street-crime campaign called 'Operation Swamp', which went down like a lead balloon in the area, since even the name was racist. The Police and Criminal Evidence Act said all this had got to stop.

The Act also has a lot to say about interview procedures and the rights of the person being interviewed. No longer could the police shove a suspect in a cell and try to 'sweat' the information out of him.

The consequences for a police officer

1 Many police officers were not happy when the PACE Act was introduced. It seemed to limit their powers and make it harder for them to fight crime. They felt as though they had been forced into a position of knowing that someone had done something wrong, but being unable to do anything about it. Some felt this was frustrating, and a blow to their professional pride.

FOCUS

Some main provisions of the Police and Criminal Evidence (PACE) Act:

- police must have grounds (e.g. 'information received' from a 'grass', or a witness description) for stopping and searching someone
- they must have a reason for searching (e.g. to look for burglary equipment, such as a 'jemmy', an offensive weapon, or drugs)
- any searches must be covered by strict rules, and done in private
- arrests must only be done with a warrant, unless there is likely to be a breach of the peace
- people must always be given the 'caution' as follows before questioning a suspect: 'You do not have to say anything. But it may harm your defence if you do not mention when questioned something which you later rely on in court. Anything you do say may be given in evidence.'

2 Other police officers, especially the younger ones, could see that the new Act strengthened their position because it made their duties clearer and protected them from accusations of racism and brutality.

3 Police officers had a lot of new law to learn, which was hard work – considering that they were always, by the nature of their job, overworked. But the government brought out the Act in the form of a Code of Practice – a book they could carry round in their pocket and use to guide them whenever they felt like questioning or arresting somebody.

4 Most importantly it gave the police a way of building bridges with ethnic minorities. It presented the police as a 'service' rather than a 'force', and showed that the government was serious in ensuring that the police would serve black people as well as white. Community groups and others who had not wanted to work with the police because of their high-handed methods were now prepared to sit down and talk to them again.

5 Improved, more constructive, communication with the communities they policed helped the police to get more cooperation, and more information about crimes.

6 The fact that the police produced better evidence of crimes in following the new Code of Practice tended to increase the success rate of their prosecutions (though this remained a problem and eventually the paperwork for prosecutions was taken away from the police and given to the Crown Prosecution Service in 1986).

7 Having said all this, the PACE Act did not eliminate all the problems the police have had with multi-ethnic policing. The Macpherson Report in 1999 on the inadequate police response to the killing of the black teenager Stephen Lawrence in April 1993 indicated that the Metropolitan Police (and by implication all police forces) suffered from 'institutionalised racism'. Perhaps this means that the PACE Act did not solve the problem of police racism, but merely hid it.

8 The PACE Act strengthened the human rights of suspects and allowed them to be treated with more dignity. So from a human rights point of view it was basically a good political decision. It also made the police as individuals and as an organisation more aware of the importance of human rights.

9 However, the Act also meant that the police could not 'cut corners'. Morally this was a good thing, but it might also be said to have wasted police time, and no doubt some criminals got off as a result of it. On the other hand, if each conviction took longer to secure because the police had to work more slowly and carefully on each case, more police officers would be needed to achieve the same workload as they had achieved before the Act was brought in. This would mean that more police officers were recruited (and perhaps civilian police employees as well). But it would also mean that policing would become more costly, since salaries are by far the highest single item in the police budget. In the long run the added costs brought about by introducing the PACE Act would be reflected in higher taxes.

The consequences for a crime suspect

The PACE Act has led to better, fairer treatment for crime suspects in Britain. They have the right to contact a solicitor if they are arrested, to have all their statements recorded, and to be looked after properly while they are in custody. There is therefore much less risk of brutality. Some people also feel that the PACE Act has made it more difficult for the police to gather and prepare evidence against criminals. So there is the possibility that the PACE Act has made life easier for the criminals, and made it less likely that they will be prosecuted.

THINK ABOUT IT ...

Choose a political decision which you have heard about, and note down how it could affect you or your family financially and how it affects you emotionally.

Unit outcome 4
Investigate current political issues

Assessment criteria

- Conduct research into two current political issues, one national and one local.
- Evaluate the importance of the issues for a given public service and the individual.

Researching a political issue

First, make sure you know what your tutor wants you to do to cover this outcome. Almost certainly you will have been given an assignment brief which asks you to research a current national political issue. Find out when your deadline is, and then plan your research.

Your plan should be an 'action plan'. It should show:
(a) what you need to do to research your assignment
(b) who needs to do what (if it is a group assignment)
(c) When each bit of research needs to be completed (so that you have all your information in time to do your other tasks).

It should be set out in a table like this:

Person	Research	Deadline

Sources of information

1 Tutors, people you know. You can question them on the main points you want to know, and even if they are a bit hazy on the exact facts, they should be able to explain the general situation clearly.

2 Members of the public services if the issue involves them directly.

3 Newspapers. You will get most information from newspapers like *The Times*, *Guardian* and *Independent*. You will get more concise information from papers such as the *Daily Mail* and *Daily Express*. The information in the *Sun* and the *Daily Mirror* will be snappily written but rather brief. These papers will not normally give you enough detail or depth for a BTEC assignment. Some Sunday papers, such as the *Observer* and the *Sunday Times* or *Sunday Telegraph* may be useful. Remember that each of these papers has its own political bias (see page 145), so you may need to read more than one of them to get a balanced view.

4 CD-ROM. The *Guardian*, *The Times* and other newspapers, magazines and encylopaedias put out their information in an easy-to-get form on compact disc. Your college library should have these and you should get into the habit of using them. They will save you many hours of hard work!

5 Magazines. There are magazines such as the *New Statesman*, *The Economist* or *Time* which deal with political issues. *Time* is better for international political issues. These magazines may seem a bit dry – but you should look at them and make up your own mind.

6 Radio and television. Many political issues are covered in radio and TV news. When watching these you ought to have a pen and paper ready to note down facts you want to remember.

7 Books may give good background information on an issue, but they are unlikely to be bang up to date.

8 The Internet. This is the fullest and most user-friendly source of information on politics. The information is up to date and often very clearly expressed. You can print extracts and include them in your assignments – but always say which website you got them from.

9 MPs and local councillors. They will give you information from the horse's mouth! But approach them well before your deadline.

Using your information

- Never be afraid to write notes. Especially if you are questioning someone face-to-face you should take notes so that you do not forget what they have said.
- Learn to make notes from newspaper articles and other sources. This ensures that your work is in your own words, and that you have picked out the main points. When you are writing notes just put down the key words – full sentences are a waste of time and energy.
- Use only information which is relevant to the task(s) you have been given in your assignment brief.
- Practise expressing yourself clearly and accurately – whether it is in speech or writing.
- Follow all instructions given on your assignment brief or by your tutor.

Researching a national political issue: genetically modified foods

Introduction

For two years now there has been wide discussion in the media and by politicians about this subject.

It is a political issue because people are worried about it, and because it may require some action by the government.

Genetically modified (GM) foods are crops such as potatoes, tomatoes and soya beans whose DNA has been altered in order to change their characteristics. In particular they have had genes added to them from other species to make them resistant to insect pests, or to produce bigger yields. People are worried about them because:

(a) they may be dangerous to the health of people who eat them or products made from them
(b) their pollen may be taken to related plants so that new strains of plants grow, and the environment is permanently affected
(c) they may affect so-called organic crops that grow nearby
(d) they have not been sufficiently tested, and they may have other unforeseen bad effects, for example on wildlife
(e) they may put farmers or food manufacturers who refuse to use them out of business
(f) they may make various multinational corporations, such as Monsanto, now Pharmacia, very rich at everybody else's expense.

The Ministry of Agriculture, Fisheries and Foods (MAFF) gives out information about GM foods to the public, but how far are they to be trusted? Some of their information does not inspire confidence, for instance the following:

> 'Terminator technology' – the development and use of genes which prevent seed from germinating – has been patented in the USA but is unlikely to be developed further or introduced into any crops. Therefore this modification is not present in any crops growing in the UK or any other country. ACRE would have to fully consider the implications of this trait if a consent to grow such a crop were to be requested at some point in the future.'
>
> Source: MAFF © Crown copyright; reproduced by permission

It is hardly surprising if people are worried when they read things like this in a government document.

The government is clearer on the subject of what is being sold in the country at the moment.

What GM foods are for sale in the UK?

Three genetically modified foods and ingredients are currently on sale or used in foods in the UK.

(a) GM tomatoes sold only as tomato puree
(b) GM soya
(c) GM maize.

Under EC Regulation (1139/98) food is required to be labelled if GM material (DNA or protein) is present in the final product. This approach which was agreed unanimously by EU member states and endorsed by the European Parliament is seen as setting a precedent for the labelling of all GM foods approved under the novel foods regulations. The Food Labelling (Amendment) Regulations 1999 took effect from 19 March 1999. These enforce EC regulation 1139/98 in Great Britain so that local authorities can take action if products are not labelled correctly.

The number of regulations covering GM foods shows that the public is worried about them, and that they have become a political issue. But the MAFF extract also shows that most of them are being grown in America. This suggests that there may be great advantages in developing GM crops and foods. If we do not try and develop them, and they turn out to be a good thing, America will gain all the benefit. Can Britain and Europe afford to be left behind?

Public and expert opinion on GM foods

There have been news items about the political issue of GM foods all over the world. The following example copied from *Pesticide & Toxic Chemical News*, 29 October 1998, page 5, is about Britain but was published in America.

UK Genetic Crops Banned For A Year

UK Environment Minister Michael Meacher and Food Safety Minister Jeff Rooker announced tighter controls over the first commercial plantings of genetically modified crops in the UK, and then recently announced a year-long ban on the introduction of GM crops, according to an October 22 BBC report.

Some GM crops would be allowed for experimental purposes. The ban stops the introduction of an herbicide-resistant oil rapeseed that would have been the first commercially grown GM crop to be approved in Britain. A new ministerial group will be set up to look at the whole issue of GM crops, and a committee of experts will also consider the ethical consequences of GM crops.

Following growing consumer fears about food safety in the wake of the BSE crisis, the proposed measures aim to provide more information on GM produce. Environment Minister Meacher said the gap between public opinion and what many of the experts in the industry are saying regarding GM crops is very large and has got to be closed.

This extract shows that because of BSE, the British public do not trust the food industry or farmers. And also, because the government was evasive and misleading at the time of the BSE crisis, can we trust them any more now that there are these worries about GM foods?

Politicians do not know whether to accept public fears and ban GM foods, or take the risk of developing them. This may be because they – and we – do not understand the scientific background to the problem. But even if we understood the science, would we necessarily trust the scientists? For one thing it was scientists who developed the atomic bomb and nerve gases; for another they often contradict themselves and each other on the same subject. For every scientist who thinks GM foods are dangerous, there are others who think they are an excellent idea.

Protests about GM foods

There have been strong, even violent protests about GM foods. An example, from an article by Stuart Millar, in the *Guardian*, Tuesday 1 June 1999, is reported at the top of the following page.

The large number of organisations attacking GM foods, and the fact that the opinion polls are against GM foods, means that the government has to tread carefully from now on in this difficult political field.

Evaluation of the effects of the GM food issue

Evaluate the importance of the issue for a given public service and the individual.

On the police

The public service most likely to be immediately affected by this issue is the police. This is because there have been a number of cases of disorder and vandalism in and around farms where genetically modified crops have been grown (or thought to be grown). If the government strictly limits the number of experimental sites where GM crops are being tested, it is likely that protests will decline.

But there is also a possibility that secret experiments will be carried out. Genetically modified crops look no different to normal ones, to the untrained eye. This may lead to ordinary

First Blood to Anti-GM-Activists

Britain's rapidly expanding army of direct action campaigners against genetically modified crops have claimed their first major victory with the announcement by a leading seed company that it has been forced out of the field by sabotage of its trial crops.

Accusing protesters of destroying both GM an non-GM crops, CPB Twyford, based at Thriplow, Cambridgeshire, said that attacks on a number of its sites across the country in recent months had cost thousands of pounds.

Jack Blackman, the firm's technical director said: 'The risks involved in continuing were not worth taking while the threat of indiscriminate vandalism still exists.'

A Mori poll last year showed 77 per cent wanted GM crops banned and more than 60 per cent said they would not eat products with GM ingredients.

The alliance of groups calling for a halt on GM crops includes:

Action Aid
British Society of Nature Conservation
Catholic Institute for International Relations
Christian Aid
Council for the Protection of Rural England
Earth First!
Food Commission
Friends of the Earth
Genetic Engineering Network
Genetix Snowball
Genewatch
Greenpeace
Guild of Food Writers
Iceland Foods
Islamic Foundation for Ecology and Environment
National Trust
Natural Law Party
Soil Association
Super Heroes Against Genetix (SHAG)
The Wildlife Trust

farmers and commercial growers being put at risk from vandal attacks, or hoax announcements that they are test sites for GM crops.

Furthermore companies which have already been 'fingered', such as Monsanto, may have a security problem because of the strength of public feeling against their research work. The fact that Monsanto has now changed its name to Pharmacia may reflect this security risk. Like laboratories where animal experiments are carried out, these companies could suffer arson attacks on property, thefts of records, criminal damage and so on.

In addition it is likely that the organisations listed opposite will carry out mass demonstrations in London and other big cities, if the government or private companies decide to carry out more work on GM foods. (It is quite possible that they will, because many scientists consider GM foods safe and of great potential benefit.)

If the government allows large-scale tests of GM crops, and even commercial production, the police may become more heavily involved – unless the government can persuade people that GM crops are safe. If people accept them, then the issue will die down and cease to be a problem.

If supermarkets start selling large quantities of GM foods imported from other countries, at a time when they are not grown here, then the supermarkets will become targets for demonstrators. There will also be a need for increased security and surveillance because of the possibility of food being deliberately contaminated by activists wishing to draw attention to their opposition to GM foods. The police may then become involved in various kinds of safety and crime-prevention training for staff in these supermarkets – or even a programme of raising public awareness of the dangers of 'terrorist' food contamination.

On the individual

Many individuals will not be affected in any way by the GM food or crops controversy – because they know little about the issue and care less. They will eat tinned tomatoes wherever they come from, so long as they are reddish and sloppy. Other individuals will start reading food labels (because it is now compulsory to mention GM additives in food) and avoiding GM products like the plague. If GM foods turn out to be harmful to human health, there will be more work for the medical professions – doctors and nurses, and perhaps even undertakers – but GM foods may turn out to be cheaper and even more nutritious than unmodified foods. Activists will demonstrate and campaign against them. Governments may begin trade wars, refusing to import each others' goods as a protest against countries producing GM foods. But if GM foods turn out to be a good idea the Americans, who have dared to experiment with them, will get rich, while Europe will become a little poorer by comparison.

Socialists and left-wing people will be glad that the government has restricted development of GM crops, which they will see as an example of big business spoiling the environment for everybody in order to gain a fat profit for themselves.

Conservatives and right-wing people will – in general – be in favour of the developing of GM crops, and their patenting. This is because they believe that the people who do the work and experimentation deserve a reward for their efforts. And they also believe that only business people are hard-working and clever enough to make the most of the opportunities GM crops and foods offer.

Researching local political issues

Local political issues affect a particular town or area of the country. Like national ones they are political because they affect people's security, happiness, wealth, justice or freedom. And they involve government – in this case local government: the 'council'.

Such local political issues may be connected with local industry either closing down or starting up, and its effects on employment or the environment. Or they may be about developments such as new roads, or the pedestrianisation of a shopping centre. Local political issues can also involve pollution or the risk of it – especially if that pollution is the result of criminal negligence, or is potentially life-threatening. In some parts of the country, relationships with ethnic minorities or other disadvantaged groups can become a political issue. So can crime, if it is concentrated in a certain area and seems to be the result of bad planning decisions or inadequate policing. Even something like the housing of asylum seekers, or paedophiles released from prison, can become a major local political issue.

Local issues do not usually last as long as national ones. If you research them you will find yourself concentrating on local people, the council, the local paper, and local radio and television. You may find that your own parents and other people close to you know all about them and have strong feelings on the subject. From your point of view this is a good thing: it will make your research more interesting and meaningful.

You should use the same planning techniques that you used for the national political issue – as given on page 151 above.

On the following page is a brief example of a local political issue and the kinds of comments you could make when evaluating its importance for 'a given public service and the individual'.

Importance for a public service

The political issue described in this extract will probably be of more significance to the ambulance service than any other public service. The income will not matter, since it is only expected to be £26,000 a year, and will not go anywhere near an ambulance. It will mostly go to pay a local government officer to ensure that the scheme is carried out.

However, the real motivation for the scheme seems to be to increase safety for road users, whether they are pedestrians or drivers.

If there have been injuries caused by carelessly placed signs, with people bumping into them or tripping over them, these should stop if the signs are removed. This means there will be fewer casualties for the ambulances to take off to hospital. More importantly, if the signs have obstructed the streets, emergency ambulances will be able to reach people who have been taken suddenly ill, or hurt in accidents, more quickly and safely. The change will not have a great effect on the ambulance service – but they may notice it.

Importance for individuals

As usual, this depends on the individuals. Possible effects are:

- shopkeepers will object to being charged for their signs: it will cut their profits, and may mean that fewer people visit their shop
- people who regard the signs as ugly will be happy: they will be able to enjoy looking at the buildings instead, without having ugly advertisements blocking their view

- right-wing people will see the new regulations as a typical socialistic attack on people who are trying to make an honest living by business
- socialists and left-wing people will be rather glad that shopkeepers are being 'caned' by the local council, and will only be sorry that the charges aren't higher than they are.

THINK ABOUT IT ...

Find a local political issue, then note down who feels strongly about it – and why.

Clampdown on Street Displays

By Hazel Ettienne and Brigid Walsh

Shopkeepers will now have to pay a yearly fee to have advertising boards and displays on the pavement outside their shops.

The extra income it brings in will pay the £26,000-a-year wages of a Kirklees officer to enforce the new scheme.

And shops are warned that if they have advertising boards and displays they will need to take out public liability insurance for a whopping £21m.

Shopkeepers will have to pay £50 a year for an advertising sandwich board – also known as an A-board – and £50 per square metre for merchandise displayed on pavements. And an enforcement officer – yet to be appointed – will give the council power to get tough with traders who advertise illegally or obstruct pavements.

Fees are already charged for signs attached to lampposts and other objects in the streets by developers, businesses and charities. These cost £55 plus VAT per ten signs for commercial events and £26 plus VAT per ten signs for charity functions.

The plans have already been approved by Kirklees Highways and Transportation Committee, but no date has yet been set for the scheme to start. The report claims: 'Proper management of signs and A-boards will reduce the risk of injury to all highway users, particularly the disabled and visually impaired, and improve control over the appearance of town centres.'

A local shopkeeper said: 'If this policy is designed to make the place safer and more attractive then fine, but if prices are unreasonable then we would simply not display on the pavement. I would not consider £50 per annum plus VAT fair. Is this aimed at tidying up untidy shops and dangerous displays or merely a way of earning extra revenue?'

Courtesy of the *Huddersfield Daily Examiner*

UNIT 7 Expedition Skills

Unit outcome 1
Examine the essentials of effective navigation skills

Assessment criteria

- Demonstrate the use of a compass and Ordnance Survey maps in navigation.
- Plan a minimum ten-mile route using Ordnance Survey maps and route cards.

Expedition Skills introduces you to the great outdoors, and enables you to go walking, camping, backpacking, canoeing and so on. The activity that everyone has to carry out is camping, though this does not necessarily have to be in a tent! The other activities you carry out will depend on what is available. Pony-trekking, for example, or skiing, would be ideal if you are out in the right area during a season when these activities are possible. As you go on your expeditions you will learn more about yourself and your friends, and start to develop the initiative and teamwork skills which are so valuable in public service work.

Using a compass and maps

Demonstrate the use of a compass and OS maps in navigation.

There are dozens of different kinds of maps, and most of them are useless for expeditions. Road maps will get you to the expedition area, but are no use when you get there. Street maps will show you round town centres, but they don't cover the open countryside. Geological maps will tell you more than you want to know about what there is under the ground, but are about as much use as a broken leg for ordinary purposes. Weather maps will show you where the rain is now, but it will have moved by tonight. Star maps have their uses if you are travelling by balloon, or crossing the Atlantic on a raft. But what you need for Expedition Skills is an Ordnance Survey (OS) map.

Figure 7.1a (opposite) *Scale of 1:50 000. Reproduced from the Ordnance Survey map with the permission of The Controller of Her Majesty's Stationery Office, © Crown Copyright*

Types of OS map

Ordnance Survey maps come in many shapes and sizes – and there are two types you need to know about. One is called the Landranger Series, and is of a scale 1:50 000 (see figure 7.1a).

The other series goes under various names: Outdoor Leisure, Explorer and Pathfinder, and has a scale of 1:25 000 (see figure 7.1b).

Figure 7.1b *Scale of 1:25 000. Reproduced from the Ordnance Survey map with the permission of The Controller of Her Majesty's Stationery Office, © Crown Copyright*

Small scale map

1:50 000 is a small scale map: one metre on the map equals fifty thousand metres on the ground. More to the point, two centimetres equals one kilometre on a 1:50 000 scale map.

You will notice that these maps are covered with blue squares – each two centimetres across. One side of each of these squares is one kilometre exactly.

Large scale map

1:25 000 is a large scale map. It is called 'large' because everything looks bigger on it than it does on a small scale map. One metre on this map would be the same as 25 000 metres on the ground. Four centimetres equals one kilometre on a 1:25 000 scale map.

These maps are also covered in blue squares – but the squares are bigger. Each square is four centimetres across. But again, the side of each square is, on the map, one kilometre long.

Which scale should you use?

For most walking purposes, you will find the 1:25 000 is the most useful. The larger the scale of the map, the more detail it has on it. 1:25 000 maps are packed with information for the walker. If you can read them properly, it is almost impossible to get lost.

Mind you, it isn't easy to get lost with a 1:50 000 map either. This contains all the information a serious walker needs, and you get more land area for your money. You are less likely to have the annoyance of walking off the edge of the map.

Map symbols

If a map was like a photograph taken from an aeroplane it would just be a greenish blur, with about as much definition as a plateful of pea soup. So maps are drawn, and symbols are used to represent each feature clearly. These symbols are all shown at the edge of the map, and labelled (see figure 7.2).

General symbols are the main ones you need to know: others are given for special tourist features,

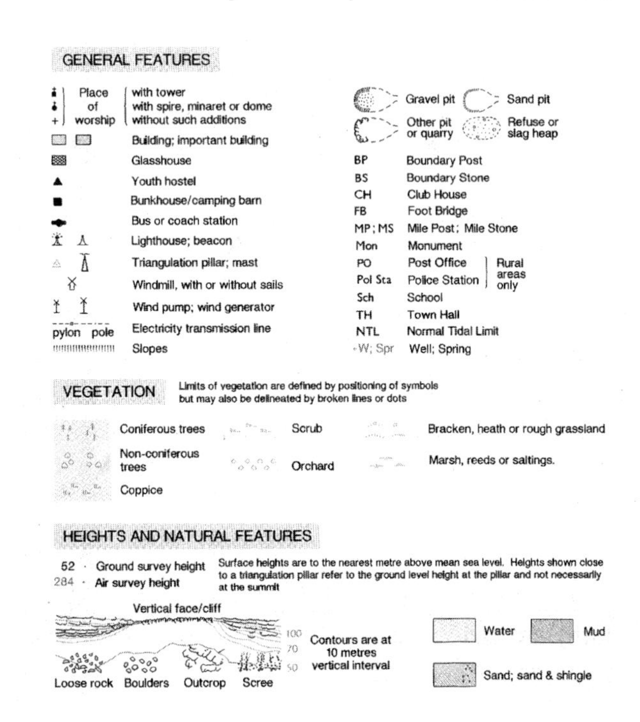

Figure 7.2 *Some OS 1:25 000 map symbols. Reproduced from the Ordnance Survey map with the permission of The Controller of Her Majesty's Stationery Office, © Crown Copyright*

or ancient monuments. When you examine your map, you will notice that buildings, roads, rivers, woods and other major features are all clearly marked. On the 1:25 000 you also get fences and walls in the form of thin black lines – useful information for walkers who don't want to get their trousers torn! Paths are clearly marked as well, and so are dangerous features such as cliffs. The 1:25 000 maps will even tell you whether the ground underfoot is rough and swampy, and whether the trees in the woods are coniferous or deciduous.

Contours

For a walker in a hilly area the contours, which are thin brown lines joining places of equal height above sea level, are a very useful guide. Where lots of these brown lines are packed together, there is a steep slope; where they are wide apart or absent, there is little or no slope. On both the 1:25 000 and the 1:50 000 map each contour is ten metres apart (in height, that is). This means that if you walk from one contour to the next you have risen or fallen ten metres.

The heights on the contours are marked in brown, with the numbers facing uphill. Heights are often given on hilltops as well. They are all in metres.

Grid references

As we have said, the 1:25 000 and the 1:50 000 maps are covered with blue squares. The lines that make up these squares all have numbers, which you can read on the edge of the map and, in places, in the middle of the map as well. These lines are called 'gridlines', and cover the whole country.

Eastings

The lines which go up and down (i.e. from north to south) are called eastings. Their numbers get higher as you go further east.

Northings

The lines which go across are called northings. Their numbers get higher as you go further north.

Using eastings and northings

Using these lines and their numbers you can pinpoint your position anywhere on one of these maps to within 100 metres. That is about as far as you can see in an average fog.

The number which you use to pinpoint your position, or the position of a feature on the map, is called a grid reference. Normally it only needs to have six figures. Figure 7.3 gives an example.

Figure 7.3 *How to give a grid reference*

The rule for making grid references is to put the eastings before the northings. The easting that matters is the one on the left, and the northing that matters is the one below the feature you want to pinpoint. So Well Farm is in the square 20 07.

This only pinpoints the farm to within a kilometre or so. To get more accurate you have to estimate tenths of the distance across the square, then up the square. If you do this you end up with a grid reference for Well Farm of 208 076.

The compass

In mountains, in foggy weather or in the dark, a compass can save your life. Therefore, for safe walking on unfamiliar ground you must take a compass.

A compass is basically a magnetised needle balanced on a point so that it can spin round easily. Sometimes these needles spin round too easily on a cheap compass, but a steady hand will normally make them settle down. Once the needle has settled down, one end of it should point north and the other end should point south.

When the compass needle points north it is also pointing towards the top of your map.

FOCUS

There are actually three kinds of north – though as they are all very similar the difference doesn't matter much. Magnetic North, the north the compass points to, is about seven degrees west of True North, which is the direction of the North Pole. Grid North is simply upwards on your map: in other words, the direction each of the eastings points towards.

A compass will work in all parts of Britain except the Cuillin Mountains in Skye, which contain so much iron that they disturb the Earth's magnetic field. But if you go to some other parts of the world the compass may not point north. If you go on an expedition outside Britain, and especially in the Arctic, you must check this.

THINK ABOUT IT ...

If you are lost in fog without a compass, there are other ways of finding out the direction. What do you think they are?

Planning a route

Plan a minimum ten-mile route using OS maps and route cards.

The first thing to notice is that ten miles is roughly the same as 16 kilometres. As the maps are now metric it is surely only a matter of time before signposts become metric, and the mile is 'consigned to the dustbin of history' – just as the ounce and the gallon have been. So for this unit you should teach yourself to think in kilometres as well as miles.

The next thing to ask yourself about is the word 'route'. The route is the way you go. It doesn't have to be on land, so you could certainly plan a route for canoes on a river or lake. The sea might be more difficult. Ordnance Survey maps don't give much information about it, so don't even think about going on the sea unless you have reliable, expert advice.

Normally the route would be a walking route, but a route for cycles or horses might also be appropriate. Let your tutor decide. Motor vehicles however, such as cars, motor-cycles, barges, paddle-steamers and tanks are off-limits for this unit.

Measuring distances

We have already said that the OS map you use will be either 1:25 000 or 1:50 000. In any case it will have the national grid of blue squares on it, and the side of each square is exactly one kilometre. If you take a row of 16 squares, that row will be ten miles long.

But people don't walk in straight lines. If you planned a straight-line walk, it would go over houses, trees and walls, and you might well find yourself wading through the odd river. You would not find it enjoyable unless you were doing it for a bet. The aim of a walk or any expedition is to be:

- achievable, and
- enjoyable.

If you are planning a walk you should try to make it as interesting and enjoyable as possible. Why walk through the middle of a plantation when you can walk along a ridge and have a good view? Why walk through a swamp when you can keep your feet dry? Why walk past a sewage works when you could be walking along the beach? If you want to go through a village to get breakfast, plan your walk through the village.

Using footpaths

Most walkers stick to footpaths. This saves them the trouble of climbing gates, walls and barbed wire fences, and reduces the likelihood of them being charged by a bull. It also makes life easier for farmers, who prefer not to have walkers trampling their wheat and dogs looking for lamb chops. So when you plan your route, try to stick to footpaths when on farmland. This will be easier and safer for you and everyone else.

Using roads

Roads are bad news for walkers. You can walk on roads in the town: you don't have to go out into the country to do it. And country roads don't have pavements, or spaces at the side, where walkers can go. Walking on a country road is dicing with death, and you can end up as flat as a hedgehog if you're not careful. So plan your route to avoid roads – especially main roads.

Going back to measuring distances, the 16 kilometres you walk will not be a straight line. So how do you measure it? There are various different ways. Here is a list of them, starting with the most accurate.

1 Use a piece of string and a ruler. Roughly plan your route without making any pencil marks on the map. (Only incompetent map-readers ever draw on a map.) Then lay your piece of string along the route you have chosen. When you have done this, place your string against a ruler. It should be 32 centimetres (the full length of the ruler and two centimetres more) long. You will then have a ten-mile route.

The only problem is that it might not get you to where you want to go. If you need to get back to where you started, or meet at a pre-arranged finishing point, you need to plan accordingly. If you find that the walk you want to do is less than 16 kilometres, you will have to lengthen it by adding on a bit. Equally, if you find that your planned walk is too long, you will need to shorten it.

2 Use a pair of dividers or compasses. By following your route with dividers which are, say, one centimetre apart (half a kilometre on the 1:50 000 map) you can reach an accurate measure of the total walk – provided you take into account all the wiggly bits. But make sure you don't dig holes in the map!

3 Use part of your finger or thumb. This depends on the size of your hand, but if you know that the end of your finger is, say, three centimetres long, then you know that 'two finger-ends' will equal three kilometres on the ground. Why bother with string or dividers when you're carrying your own measuring equipment round with you?

4 'Guesstimate' it using the blue grid squares and jotting down the length of each section on a piece of paper. The full distance can then be added up at the end. This is the lazy way of measuring your route, but it's better than nothing.

Safety

Is it safe? This is the first, middle and last question you should ask when planning an expedition, even if it is only ten miles long. A surprising number of people have died when they are out on a walk, just because they didn't plan it properly. A lot of other people have spent cold nights out, and scared their families and the emergency services, simply because they couldn't be bothered to plan in advance.

If things can go wrong they will do. British weather has a habit of starting hot and sunny, with hailstorms at lunchtime. The sight of walkers wandering about on a moor attracts cloud and rain like a magnet. And Britain can seem like the windiest country in the world outside Antarctica.

Fortunately, we have excellent weather forecasts in Britain. As they are not covered by the Official Secrets Act you can watch them on television, or, failing that, ask a local person what the day is going to be like. If the forecast is dire, you should (a) pack more clothes, (b) shorten your walk or (c) find a nice warm place and put your feet up for the day.

When planning an expedition you need to know about your party. How many of them are going? Do you know them well? Are they strong walkers? Are they all in good health at the present time? Do you all get on well together? Do you all like to walk at roughly the same speed, or are there some hares and tortoises? Check them out.

Contingency plan

If you are planning a walk, even a ten-mile walk, you must have a contingency plan. In other words, you must have a safe get-out if something goes wrong. When you are planning a walk, look for the roads which will lead you off the hill if the weather goes pear-shaped. If conditions get nasty, you can walk off down the road to the nearest safe place and phone for help. Make notes of escape routes from a mountain, and put them on your route card (see page 164).

Clothing

What do you wear? On the hills it is more important to be comfortable than smart. The chances are that nobody will see you except a few sheep, and it is well known that they have no dress sense.

You should wear:
- loose trousers, such as tracksuit bottoms
- walking boots (and make sure they fit you first! They should be one size bigger than your normal shoes)
- two pairs of woolly socks
- waterproof trousers, if it is already raining
- waterproof cagoule or jacket
- woolly or fleecy hat (depending on the feedback your ears are giving you)
- gloves if needed.

You should avoid:
- jeans, especially if they are tight: they do not keep out wind, wet or cold
- shoes which are only suitable for town wear, especially if they have raised heels
- boots with worn-down soles which would slip on steep grass.

Equipment

What do you carry? The easy answer is that you carry a rucksack, but that isn't much use unless you have the right things in it. Here is a suggested list.

You should carry:
- sandwiches
- chocolate and emergency rations
- bottle of water (or soft drink)
- spare warm pullover or other garment
- gloves
- woolly or fleecy hat
- plasters (for blisters)
- any personal medication
- map
- compass
- whistle (or mobile phone)
- waterproof top and trousers (if it isn't already raining when you set out)
- a torch.

You should leave at home:
- drugs
- alcohol
- valuables
- ghettoblasters
- hunting knives
- kitchen sinks.

Route cards

A properly planned expedition will have a route card, so that you and everyone else knows where you are going. The simplest form of route card is a few jottings giving the names of the main places you are going to. This is better than nothing, and may save your life if they have to send out search parties, but it might not get you through your BTEC National. In the BTEC National we do these things properly.

Figure 7.4 shows a 1:50 000 map of the area north of Pateley Bridge in Yorkshire. And following it, on page 164, is a specimen route card for a party of 17-year-olds doing a ten-mile (16 kilometre) expedition. We will assume that the time of year is mid-March.

> **THINK ABOUT IT ...**
>
> Continue the expedition back to Pateley Bridge, putting in appropriate grid references and other details.
>
> Where could the walk go on to if the weather was fine and you were all feeling fit?

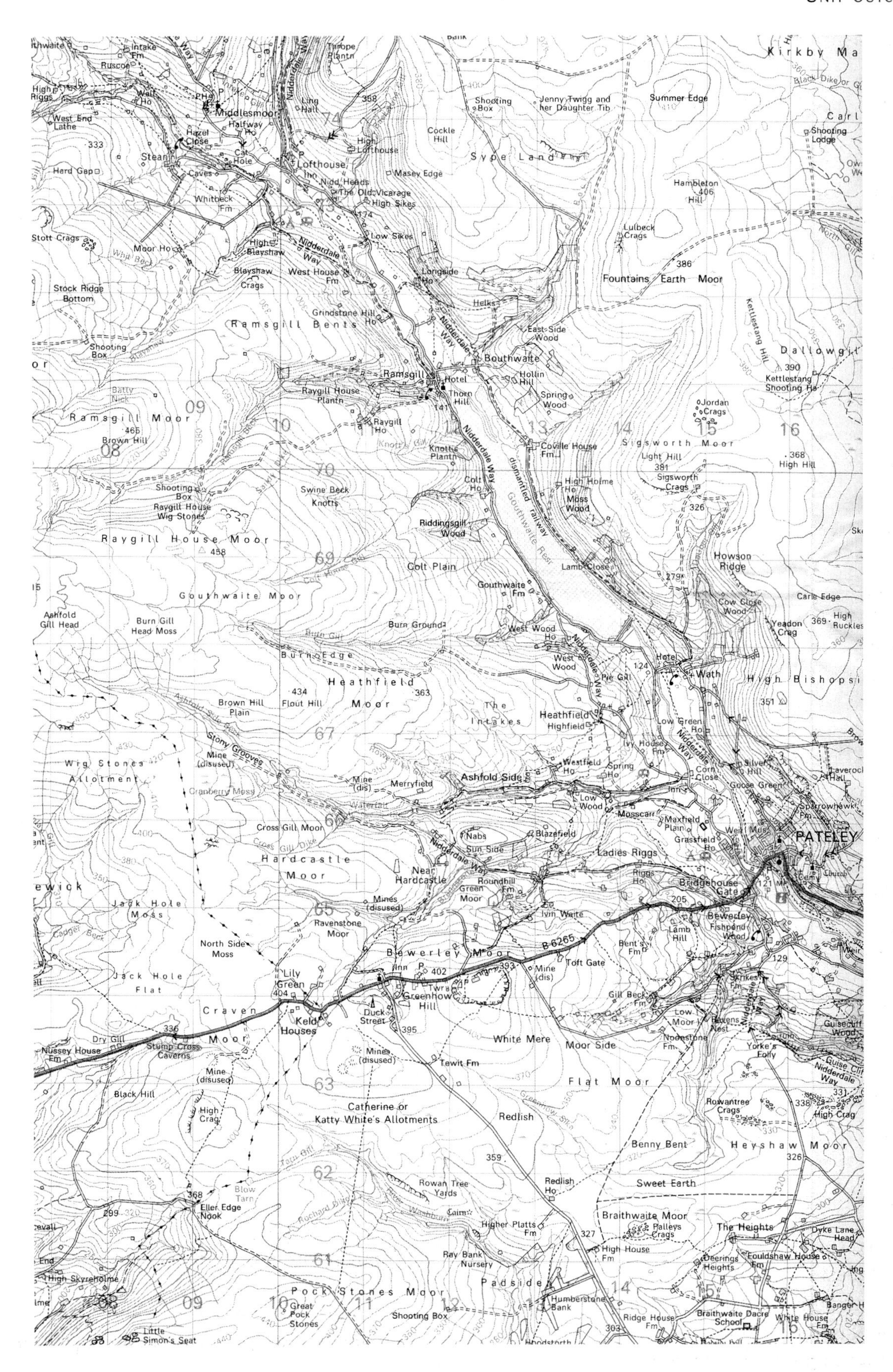

Figure 7.4 *Map of the Nidderdale area. Reproduced from the Ordnance Survey map with the permission of The Controller of Her Majesty's Stationery Office, © Crown Copyright*

Specimen route card

Name(s)..

Date...................... Expedition.. Starting time 10 a.m.

Stage	*From (name and grid ref)*	*To (name and grid ref)*	*Distance (km)*	*Direction*	*Height difference (m) + or –*	*Terrain and main features*	*Estimated time of arrival*
1	Information Office, Pateley Bridge 158656	Bridgehouse Gate 153651	0.5	SW	+40	B road, partly built-up (traffic danger)	1012 (+ 3 mins rest) = 1015
2	Bridgehouse Gate 153651	Near Hardcastle 118655	4	W	+150	Walled lane (good views to north)	1100 (+ 10 mins rest) = 1110
3	Near Hardcastle 118655	Mine (disused) 093667	3	WNW	+50	Unwalled cart track (be careful at the mine!) Eat here if weather cold.	1146 (+ 14 mins rest) = 1200
4	Mine (disused) 093667	Spot height 515 070685	3	NW	+115	No track; may be boggy & heavy going. Windy?	1245 (slower progress on rough ground)
5	Spot height 515 070685	Shooting Box 078714	3	NNE	–105	No track. Compass needed in cloud. Shooting box (a hut) will give some shelter, though it won't be open.	1320 (+ 10 mins rest) = 1330
6	Shooting Box 078714	Lofthouse 101734	3	mainly NE	–300	Unfenced track 2 km; walled track and lane. All downhill into valley. Walk straight back to Pateley Bridge if tired, or if weather too bad.	1406 (+ 9 mins rest or shopping?) = 1415

Unit outcome 2
Examine and demonstrate the benefits of outdoor pursuits and residentials

Assessment criteria
- Participate actively in at least two outdoor pursuits.
- Justify the use of outdoor pursuits and residentials for individual achievement and team building.

Appropriate outdoor pursuits

Any activity which has to be done outdoors is an outdoor pursuit. Thus road-mending, gardening or playing football are outdoor pursuits – but not where this unit is concerned. Here we're talking about:

- rock climbing
- abseiling
- walking
- mountaineering
- orienteering
- sailing
- caving
- potholing
- cycling
- pony-trekking
- kayaking
- canoeing
- rafting
- bungee jumping
- ghyll-scrambling
- scuba-diving
- sand-yachting
- skiing
- ice climbing
- surfing
- bog-snorkelling
- and other activities of this type

What these activites share in common is that they are all tests of character, endurance, teamwork, initiative and athleticism, and that they tend to be carried out in a wild, natural environment.

That's enough of the definitions. Now for the warnings.

The element of risk

All outdoor activities carry an element of risk. If they were as safe as sitting in an armchair, no one would bother to do them. Nevertheless, it must be the aim of you, your team-mates and your instructors to make every outdoor activity as safe as possible.

On Edexcel BTEC Nationals in Public Services you must have skilled, qualified instructors and the correct equipment for any outdoor activity that you undertake. **It is vitally important** that you carry out instructions exactly and to the letter. If you are unsure about any safety aspect – don't be shy – get clarification from your instructor. If you are not sure that you have the right equipment, or if you think a knot has been tied wrongly, tell your instructor and make sure he or she listens. From time to time people die in outdoor activities. You don't want to be one of them.

THINK ABOUT IT ...
What are the dangers of taking alcohol or drugs before outdoor activities?

When should you not do outdoor activities?

1. When under the influence of alcohol or drugs.
2. When you are ill (or feeling ill).
3. When you have recently recovered from an illness.
4. If you have been injured and are not fully recovered.
5. If you have a phobia about what you are expected to do.

If you are in any doubt about 2, 3 and 4, ask a doctor. Doctors know more about medicine than your tutors, and it's your body.

If you have a phobia such as acrophobia (extreme fear of heights) or claustrophobia (fear of being trapped in small spaces), it is possible that you might not be able to climb rocks or go into caves. If you are quite certain you can't do these things, it is best to face facts and say so. Reputable instructors will not force you to do something which you have a phobia about.

But encouragement is a different thing. It is your instructors' job to encourage you to try things you have never tried before. And nearly everyone is a bit afraid of heights, or getting stuck in a hole. So if you can overcome your fears, you should do. After all, people who work in the public services have to overcome these fears. How often have you seen police officers coaxing suicides off scaffolding or high bridges on the TV? And how often do firefighters have to crawl round in confined spaces to put out fires? Unless you are 100 per cent certain you have a phobia, try it first. You might find that your 'fear' turns into a buzz, and you enjoy it!

FOCUS

All the public services have training and character-building which use outdoor activities. If you can do it on your National then you'll be able to do it after you've joined the public services.

More on outdoor pursuits

What follows is a brief outline of some of the outdoor pursuits listed above on page 165. Unless you are already an expert, do not try to carry them out unless you have qualified help.

Rock climbing

Many parts of Britain, especially in the north and west, have natural cliffs and rocks which are suitable for rock climbing. There is even some limited rock climbing in Kent. But in some other places you may have to use indoor walls to get your first taste of this exciting sport.

It may seem an obvious point, but rock climbers always start from the bottom. They usually climb with a rope, which they can 'belay' (fasten) on to sticking-out rocks or metal pegs, so that if they fall they will not hit the ground. On a short cliff they can use a top rope, and have a helper at the top who, using the right methods and equipment, can hold them if they fall.

Rock-climbing equipment is specialised and expensive, and you are unlikely to be able to afford it yourself. If you enjoy rock climbing you should seriously consider joining a club, where you will meet other people who share your interest, and have access to the right equipment. Rock climbing is an excellent way of increasing your fitness and strength – but beware! It can become an obsession, and you may end up thinking about nothing else.

Abseiling

Abseiling is a way of getting down cliffs or mountains once you have climbed them. It is highly dangerous if you don't know how to do it or you haven't got the right equipment. You use ropes and harnesses to lower yourselves down cliffs, bridges or the sides of buildings, and get a pleasant sensation of being a human spider while you are doing it. With a qualified instructor abseiling is safe, and will give you a confidence with heights which you didn't know you had!

Walking

According to the statistics walking is the most popular pastime in Britain – even more popular than fishing. Perhaps walking offers people a chance to get away from themselves.

Walking gives people a chance to get away from themselves

Long distance walking, or walking up mountains, can be a good test of fitness and endurance, and it can enable you to see places you would never see otherwise. Many of the best expeditions are on foot, and involve backpacking – when you carry everything you need, including tents or survival bags, on your back.

Walking is cheap, even cheaper than taking the bus. There is specialised equipment available – fancy boots and waterproofs made of high-tech fabrics which 'breathe' whenever you start to sweat. But if the worst comes to the worst you can wear trainers (or even wellies) and your normal coat or jacket, and not come to too much harm unless the ground is extremely steep or the weather is very wet. At the end of a day's walking you normally feel good about yourself, and have an excellent appetite. It won't build your muscles up like lifting weights does, but it will keep you fit.

There are dangers in walking, so if you go for a walk on the hills you should always make sure that someone knows where you are going. Look at the weather forecast in advance, and prepare for the worst. Don't try and do more than you can manage, and make sure you are off the hills before dark. Some hills and mountains have dangerous holes and cliffs on them – so keep your wits about you and don't take unnecessary risks. And take the equipment listed above on page 162.

Mountaineering

Mountaineering is like walking only more so. There is no clear definition of what is a mountain, but you can't go too far wrong if you think of a mountain as a big hill. In Britain, 600 metres is a good dividing line between the height of a hill and a mountain.

In Britain there are only a handful of mountains that you cannot walk up safely. Most of these are in the Cuillins in Skye, where nearly every mountain involves some rock climbing to get to the top. But in other mountains, such as the Cairngorms, or Snowdonia, people die every year because they fall over cliffs. You need to take care. Falling is bad for your health, unless you are attached to a rope or a parachute.

The weather can be an enemy on any hill above, say, 300 metres. It can be a killer in winter, especially in Scotland. Every winter about 15 people die in the Scottish Highlands, either from falls, hypothermia or both. If you get lost on a mountain in heavy snow there are various things you should do, but the most important is to get out of the wind and wait for help. If you can dig yourself into a drift, so much the better. And whatever you do, don't get separated from the rest of your party.

Orienteering

Orienteering involves reading a map and running. Normally you take part on an individual basis, punching a card at various 'controls' that are indicated on a map. It will certainly help your map-reading skills and train you to be observant about your surroundings. For beginners, the only special equipment you need is a compass and an emergency whistle. The combination of the mental skill used to navigate and make route choices at speed with the physical fitness required to run over different sorts of ground is what makes this such a satisfying activity.

Sailing and rafting

Sailing is a complex and technical activity which many people find very enjoyable. Like rock climbing it can become an obsession and rule your life. Its main disadvantage is that the equipment (i.e. a boat) is extremely expensive.

Rafting is normally carried out on rivers, in inflatable plastic rafts or dinghies. The aim is to float down the river without mishap. It is more exciting if there is some white water or fast-flowing sections in the river. It is very popular in countries like France, where the rivers are long and the weather is warm.

Other pursuits

1 Bungee jumping. This experience is unlikely to be encountered on an Expedition Skills residential, but it is outdoor and it is an activity.

2 Ghyll-scrambling. An activity associated with places like the Lake District where there are fast-flowing, rocky streams coming down the hillsides. The aim is to climb up or down the stream itself! There is a fair chance of getting hurt and an excellent chance of getting wet. But it should be safe enough with a good instructor, and is an amusing way of developing teamwork skills.

3 Scuba-diving might not be considered an outdoor activity, as it is done under water. You need to do a full training course before you attempt it. Useful preparation for visiting a coral reef.

4 Sand-yachting. Yachting for people who don't like to get wet.

5 Caving is a major outdoor activity in certain parts of Britain. The bad news is that you can only do it where there are caves – that is, in South and North Wales, the Peak District, the Yorkshire Dales and parts of Northern Ireland. Caving is done on a bigger scale in France and in the Picos de Europa in Spain.

A cave is a natural hole, usually in limestone, and worn out by a stream or river. If the stream or river is still there you get wet, but many caves now are dry(ish), with most of the water running at a lower level. Caves are dark, so you take electric lighting with you. They are also hard hat areas, and you must wear a proper caving helmet. Caving is dangerous, so you must stick with your instructor and obey her or his instructions at all times.

6 Potholing. A pothole is a vertical cave. It's formed in the same way as a cave, found in limestone, only you cannot walk into it. You have to climb down a rope ladder, or perhaps several rope ladders. This is hard work, and you need to be secured by ropes and harnesses so you don't fall. You must on no account go into a pothole without a qualified, experienced instructor. If you do you might not get out again.

7 Cycling and mountain biking are popular outdoor activities on BTEC National programmes. As with all other outdoor activities you must wear the right protective clothing, and follow your instructor's wishes. The same goes for **pony-trekking**.

8 Kayaking is done on lakes and rivers. Like cycling it requires a certain amount of training and practice before you become proficient at it. People have been drowned in canoeing accidents – whether in kayaks or Canadian canoes – because they haven't looked at the weather forecast before setting out. A few years ago several canoeists were drowned off the south coast, and regulations have since become much stricter for this enjoyable sport.

9 Skiing is the most dangerous outdoor pursuit; we know this because of the cost of insurance. It is strenuous and testing, and vastly enjoyable, judging by its popularity. The equipment is expensive, and you need instruction if you are to be any good at it. It also helps to start young.

There are two types of skiing – downhill and cross-country. Both are very popular and require high levels of fitness. Skiing trips are expensive, and few Public Service courses undertake them – unfortunately.

10 Surfing resembles skiing in that you need instruction and specialised equipment. You will probably try it at some time anyway. As for bog-snorkelling ...

Why do outdoor pursuits?

Justify the use of outdoor pursuits and residentials for individual achievement and team building.

Forget about Edexcel BTEC; the public services themselves are hooked on outdoor activities. So, for that matter, are a lot of other organisations – such as private firms. Dozens of businesses providing outdoor pursuits have sprung up wherever there are rivers and mountains. Everywhere management trainees of all shapes and sizes are taking to the woods. Why?

It's because outdoor pursuits:

- develop fitness
- improve confidence
- encourage self-reliance
- develop initiative
- encourage teamwork
- develop character (whatever that may be)
- show you things about yourself you never knew
- show other people things about yourself you never knew
- show you things about other people you never knew
- get you out into the country
- are fun (believe it or not).

FOCUS

All public service training includes residentials: periods when you are away from home, in a special centre, with other trainees. This is so that your new employers can find out what you are really like.

You can justify outdoor pursuits by explaining why they are so popular with training organisations. They develop fitness because you are being active, out of doors, for long periods of time. This is the same fitness and stamina you would need for working long shifts in the police.

Your confidence is improved because you cope successfully with unfamiliar challenges, like abseiling down a 50-metre cliff, or going in a canoe for the first time. You'll be less afraid of heights, and if you apply for the army or the fire service, you'll be more ready for whatever they throw at you!

You become self-reliant because you have to read a map for yourself, or choose where to put your hand – with no one to guide you – on a rock climb. You make decisions, just as you might in the prison service, if an inmate decides to become violent at 2 a.m.

You show initiative because you find you can solve a problem that no one else could solve: you are the person who thinks of how to build the rope bridge across the river. The same kind of initiative – developed to a higher level – would serve you well if you were in the Royal Navy and had to rescue someone at sea.

On a foggy mountain you become part of a team, sharing with others the responsibility for finding your way to the next checkpoint. And you are sharing responsibilities if you are a firefighter in the first emergency tender to reach a motorway pile-up.

Your character develops because you talk to people you have never really talked to, about things you have never really talked about – and because you are finding out about other people's characters, you are also finding out about your own. Later, this character development could help you work better with your colleagues and the public – in any public service.

THINK ABOUT IT ...

Find the nearest places to where you live where you can do some of the activities mentioned.

Unit outcome 3
Plan and carry out a camping expedition

Assessment criteria

- Prepare for a camping expedition of at least two days, using appropriate clothing and a range of specialist equipment.
- Describe in detail the safety precautions necessary for such a camping expedition.

An overview of camping

What is camping?

For most people camping means spending a night out in a tent. For the public services camping also means spending a night out in a tent. But you don't have to bother with a tent if you don't want to. Just as long as you don't have a roof over your head, you are camping as far as the BTEC Nationals in Public Services are concerned. That said, nine times out of ten you will be in a tent.

What is a tent?

A tent is a portable shelter made of cloth. In the old days this cloth was cotton, and tents were very heavy. Now tents are made of lightweight nylon and other fabrics, and often weigh no more than two kilos. This is just as well, because on an expedition you have to carry your tent on your back. This is what is meant by a camping expedition.

Tents have been going since the year dot. They had tents in the Bible, and they were old in those days. You might think they would have gone out of fashion. But in the last 50 years they have come back in to fashion – in a big way.

Tents used to be primitive things. You could get wet in a tent even if it wasn't raining outside. You only had to look at the tent, or better still touch it, if you were inside, in order to get wet. But the modern tent is not like that. If you look after it, it will look after you. In a modern tent it can rain all night and the only thing that will keep you awake is the noise. In a modern tent you can camp in a blizzard and be as snug as a bug in a rug, provided you know how to do it.

Modern tents are state of the art. Millions of pounds goes into designing and marketing them because millions of people buy them for their holidays. They are the cheapest holiday accommodation – and for many people, the best.

From our point of view there are three kinds of tent:

- ridge tents
- dome tents
- motorists' tents.

Ridge tent

The ridge tent shown in figure 7.5 has two A-poles for the ends connected by a ridge pole made of lengths of aluminium tubing which slide into one another.

Provided the tent is not more than 30 years old it will also have a sewn-in groundsheet.

A ridge tent has an outer tent, or flysheet. The purpose of the flysheet is to protect the inner tent from rain or dew. The flysheet is also supported by the two poles. When the tent is pitched (erected), there must be a space of at least ten centimetres between the flysheet and the inner tent. That is, if you don't want to get wet.

Figure 7.5 *A ridge tent*

A ridge tent has to be fastened to the ground with pegs, otherwise the first gust of wind will wrap it round the nearest fence. This will amuse other people more than it amuses you. Ridge tents also have guy ropes attached to them. These are long pieces of nylon cord which need to be pegged down some way from the tent, so that it doesn't blow away in a gale.

Dome tent

Dome tents (see figure 7.6) were invented about 30 years ago, and they are now more popular than ridge tents. They come in a wide variety of designs – domes, hemispheres, half-cylinders, tunnels: the only thing they really have in common is that they are round-topped.

Figure 7.6 *A dome tent*

They don't have straight poles. In fact the poles aren't even stiff. They are made of the type of flexible plastic and graphite which is also used in fishing rods and tennis rackets. These slide into tubes of lightweight fabric in the inner tent, and are then further secured by plastic hooks. They then support an outer tent, which is just as dome-shaped as the inner tent.

Dome tents are lighter than ridge tents and more roomy for their size. But they don't always stand up quite as well to a Force 8 gale on a November night.

Like ridge tents, dome tents have sewn in groundsheets, and most of them have guy ropes as well, for added security.

Motorists' tents

These are for motorists; and since they are too heavy to carry, they have no place on an expedition. If you have been asked to bring your own tents, don't even think of bringing one of these.

Putting up a tent

When you go camping on a BTEC National residential, the chances are that you will have tents provided, and that you will be taught how to put them up. It isn't possible to give general instructions on how to pitch tents, because every make of tent is different.

But there are certain rules you must follow.

1. Pitch your tent on dry ground. This means ground that will remain dry even if it rains hard (as it probably will).
2. Have the door of the tent facing away from the wind. This will give you shelter for cooking, and reduce the chances of your tent blowing away in the night.
3. Do not pitch your tent under trees unless you have to.
4. Choose a site which is not covered with sticks and stones. They may not break your bones, but they could give you a lumpy night, and make holes in your groundsheet.
5. Put your pegs in at an angle of 45 degrees, with the head pointing away from the tent (see figure 7.7).

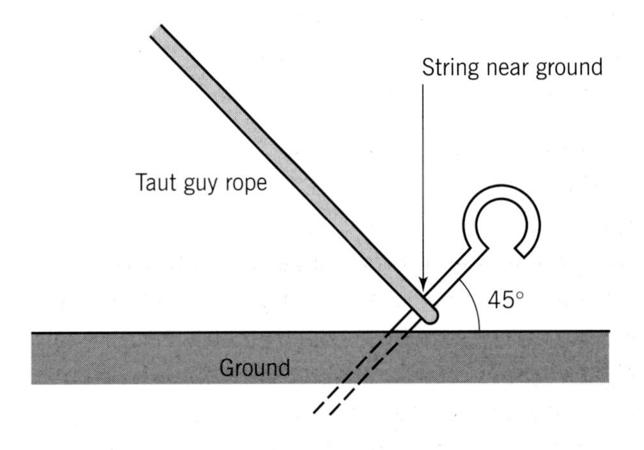

Figure 7.7 *The correct way to put in a tent peg*

6 Don't pitch your tent sideways across a slope. If there is a slope, pitch it up and down, so that you don't roll in the night.
7 Beware of riversides and places that might flood. Every year campers are killed by floods in their sleep.
8 Never smoke or cook inside a tent. Tents are firetraps.
9 Pitch your tent at least two metres – and preferably further – from the next tent. This is so that clowns don't trip over your guy-ropes in the middle of the night, just when you're trying to get to sleep.
10 Consider pitching your tents in a line, with their backs to a wall or hedge for shelter, and all facing the same way. This will be convenient for the whole group, and minimise the risk of people falling over your tent in the night as in 9 above.

Preparing for a camping expedition

1 Find out from your instructors when and where the expedition is taking place. The preparations you make will depend on where you are going, and what time of year it is. You will also need to take into account how long the expedition is going to last, and how far you will be expected to walk, carrying your things. Almost certainly you will have to carry everything on your back.

2 Decide who you will be sharing your tent with. Choose somebody with similar habits to yourself. If you are tidy, choose a companion (or companions) who are tidy. If you are a scruff, better make do with another scruff. On a BTEC camping expedition, don't try and share your tent with someone you don't get on with – or a person of the opposite sex.

3 Make lists – four of these lists are given below.

A list of things to borrow or hire from the organisers:

- tent
- sleeping bag
- rucksack
- walking boots (state size – preferably one size bigger than your normal shoes)
- waterproof leggings and top (state small, medium, large, extra large)
- wellies (for muddy situations or potholing).

A list of clothes (include what you are wearing as well as what you will carry):

- two spare pullovers
- change of underwear
- warm leggings
- woolly or fleecy hat
- gloves
- spare T-shirts (for added warmth on cold nights).

Other items:

- money
- whistle
- compass
- first aid (especially plasters for blisters)
- torch
- sleeping bag if you have one
- tin-opener
- spoon
- plastic cup
- plastic bowl
- stove
- meths (or other fuel)
- water bottle
- any medication you normally take.

Food:

- cereal or other dried foods
- dried soups, noodles etc.
- raisins, dried milk
- cheese
- bread
- chocolate and other 'iron rations'.

The kind of food you take will depend on the kind of expedition you are planning. Tins of food are heavy, since their contents are mainly water. Beanz meanz weight, among other things. Sardines in oil are good, if you can stand the taste. But it might be worth not taking any tins, and then you don't have to carry a tin-opener either.

If you are buying food as a group you will have to agree to buy food which (a) you all like, (b) which is not too expensive, (c) will give you energy and (d) which is not too heavy to carry. If you are camping for four days or less, your diet does not have to be perfectly balanced, but it must provide you with enough energy for strenuous outdoor activities. Plan carefully – and check with your tutor!

Cooking

Strictly speaking it is not necessary to cook if you are out camping and backpacking for a few days. You can remain perfectly fit, healthy and comfortable by eating cold food – and you save yourself the hassle and effort of carrying a stove, fuel and cooking equipment.

The *BTEC Nationals in Public Services Guidance and Units* says nothing about cooking, either in its contents, units or assessment criteria. But it does mention 'campcraft', and most people like to cook when they're camping.

Things take a long time to cook if you don't heat them up. So you need one of the following:

- a fire
- a meths stove
- a butane stove.

Fires

Fires are banned on most British campsites. They won't light unless the weather is dry, and they leave unsightly holes in the grass. They aren't much use for cooking anything except baked potatoes.

Meths stoves

Meths stoves, often called trangias, are the in thing at the moment. The army use them, and if you do your residentials with an army youth team, it's likely that you will use them as well.

They consist of a brass burner with a lid attached, and then several containers which fit round the burner when the stove is not in use (see figure 7.8). One of these containers is a kettle, and the lid of the whole arrangement can act as a frying pan. There is also a handle so that you can grip the pans without burning your fingers.

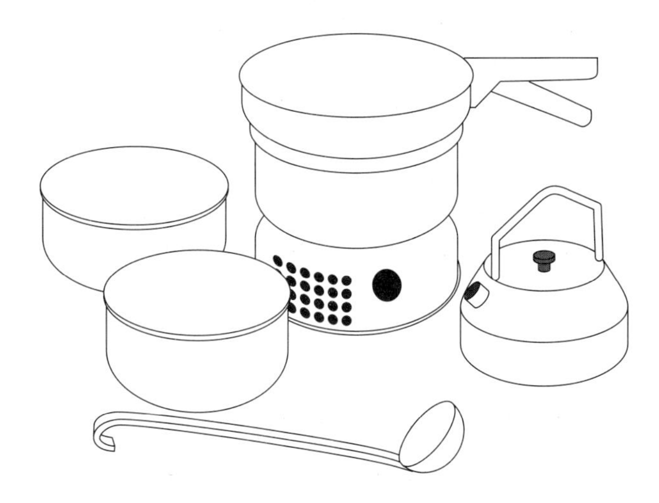

Figure 7.8 *Trangia or meths stove and equipment*

When the stove is in use the burner fits inside the biggest container, which shields it from the wind. Inside this big container are three metal brackets which flick up to support your pans.

The burner is simply a small brass pot with a lid in it. You pour meths into this pot, taking care not to spill the meths round the lip of the pot if you can help it. You then light the meths with a match and put your pan over the burner, resting it on the three metal supports.

Meths is very easy to light, but unfortunately it burns with a nearly invisible flame. This means you must be careful not to burn your fingers when lighting a trangia stove. If you do burn your fingers, pour plenty of cold water over them, or run them under a tap. This will prevent the burn from becoming painful later on.

If the stove goes out, it is almost certainly because all the meths in the burner has been used up. **Making sure that there is no flame left**, pour more meths into the burner and re-light it. **On no account must you pour meths into the burner while it is still alight.**

If you have finished cooking and the meths is still burning, use a stick, knife, spoon or tent peg (or similar metal object) to close the brass lid of the burner. This will smother the flame. Remember that the burner will stay hot for some minutes after you have put out the flame.

Meths stoves are easy to carry (though bulky) and give you a lot of cooking equipment without much weight. They work well even in wind, but there is a risk of burning yourself if you don't understand them, or if you are careless. When in doubt, consult your instructor – or somebody who understands them.

Safety first! Make sure you understand how your meths stove works before you start cooking – otherwise you might be the one who ends up being cooked!

When you have finished using your trangia, clean all the pans and make sure you haven't left any bits out of it. Then fit all the pans together and fasten it up, using the strap provided.

Butane stoves

Butane stoves come in a range of sizes and have been popular for some years (see figure 7.9). The burner screws into a blue gas canister and, as it seals itself, makes a hole in the canister, allowing the gas to come out into the burner. There is a black handle at the side of the burner which you turn anticlockwise, to allow the gas to escape. As the gas comes out you light the stove with a match, just as if you were lighting a gas cooker at home.

This kind of stove has four flat plastic feet which splay out if you twist them into the right position. Because the canister underneath is lighter than the burner on top there is a danger of them tipping over on soft or uneven ground. This risks a fire and, worse still, spoils your meal.

The gas comes out under pressure so you get a roaring flame which, under good conditions, cooks fast and efficiently. However, there is no windshield

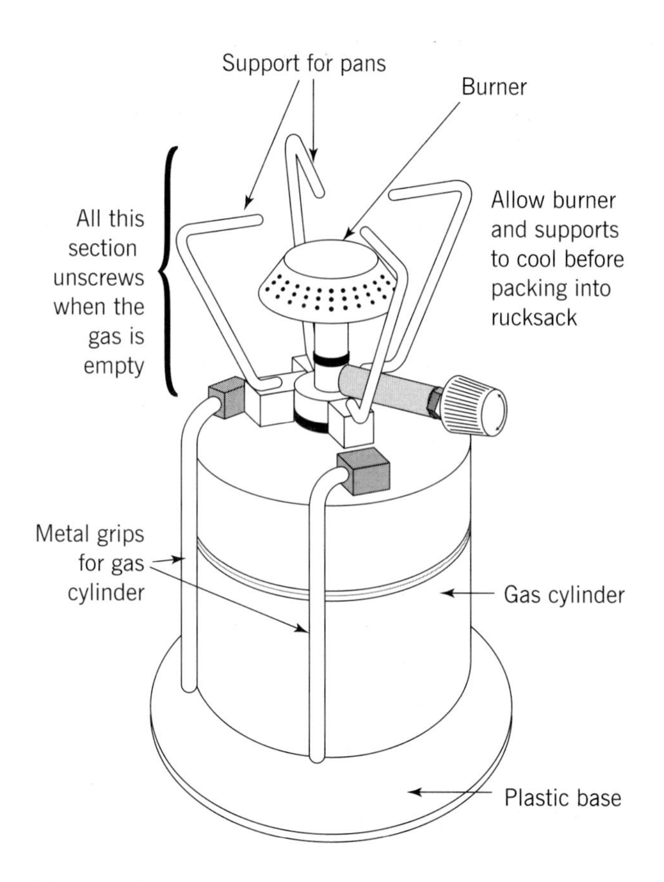

Figure 7.9 *A butane stove*

(unlike a trangia), so you need to be out of the wind to get the best out of this sort of stove.

Getting out of the wind does not mean getting into your tent. Butane stoves, if they have been carried in a rucksack, sometimes flare up like an oilwell when they are first lit. So when you light them, try not to bend over them, otherwise you will lose your eyebrows. If you try to light them inside the tent, you risk setting fire to the tent. Some tents burn very fiercely, and over the years plenty of campers have died in tent fires. Others have died because their tent went up in flames and they died of exposure. **You have been warned!**

After you have finished with your butane stove, turn off the gas and then **allow it to cool**. Don't pack it away while it is still hot, or it will burn a hole in your rucksack. It will also burn a hole in your hand if you touch it too soon. As long as you have turned the stove off properly, the gas should not leak during the day.

If you have any other kind of stove, check with your instructor that it is safe before using it.

Other aspects of campcraft

1 **Be organised.** Make sure you know where things are packed in your rucksack. Wrap your clothes in plastic dustbin liners (you can't have too many of these) so that they don't get wet if it rains hard.
2 **Think about the time of year.** Camping in Britain is always colder and wetter than you expect. Have an all-season sleeping bag unless you are sure the weather is going to be hot.
3 If you are taking your own tent on a camping expedition, **check that there is nothing missing** before you start. It is most embarrassing arriving at a campsite only to find that you have forgotten your poles or pegs.
4 **Don't take valuables.** Murphy's Law (Part 2) says that all valuables get lost on a camping expedition. Even a walkman can walk.
5 **Keep your tent firmly fastened** when you are not in it, otherwise mice, rats and foxes might take an interest in your food.
6 **Never play practical jokes** on other campers, unless you want them to play practical jokes on you.
7 **Don't try and carry too much weight** in your rucksack. Carrying heavy weights is for donkeys.
8 **Remember that some people go to the countryside for peace and quiet.** Don't shout and race about the campsite in the middle of the night, even if there is a full moon.
9 **Sheep and cows can choke to death on plastic bags.** Bin your litter, and if there are no bins take it home with you.
10 **Don't even think about taking drugs, alcohol, hunting knives or ghettoblasters.**

General safety precautions

Describe in detail the safety precautions necessary for such a camping expedition.

1 Check out the weather forecast before you go. If it's going to be cold, wet or snowy, take extra warm clothing, waterproofs and binbags. And don't go on any high hills or mountains if you are not fully equipped. If it's going to be hot and dry the risks are sunburn and dehydration. Now that we've got rid of our ozone layer, sunburn is more dangerous than ever before. If your skin is sensitive use sunblock and wear a suitable hat. Dehydration can cause collapse. Always drink enough in hot weather.

2 Horseplay is for asses. Camping can be good fun, but playing about near tents and stoves can lead to injuries and fires, not to mention damage to the equipment.

3 If you are ill, or have recently been ill, **you must tell your instructor.** Go and see your doctor if you have any doubts as to whether you are fit enough to go on a camping expedition. You will only spoil it for yourself and everyone else if you are taken ill on an expedition. And if you have any injuries that might prevent you carrying a rucksack, tell your instructor or organiser in advance.

Allergies, panic attacks, asthma, eating disorders or just plain homesickness can, in rare cases, cause difficulties on a camping trips. Make sure you take the medication you need with you, and share your problems with a member of staff before you go.

4 Many campsites are near pubs. But remember you are not allowed to drink in Britain in a public house if you are under 18, and if you are just over 18, it will be as well to take an ID. **If you are allowed to drink, drink responsibly and in moderation.**

Spirits, such as vodka, are dangerous on a camping expedition and should on no account be taken. They dilate your capillaries and, while producing a feeling of warmth at first, can later lead to hypothermia. If people stagger about in the night they will suffer, or cause, accidents, and if they go into a coma it takes a long time to get an ambulance to a remote campsite.

Drugs are also dangerous, and can impair your judgement the following day. Steer clear!

5 There is always a danger of burns and cuts when cooking or otherwise carrying out camp duties. So check that you know how to use all stoves and cooking equipment safely. Be careful with knives, tin-openers and tent pegs, and make sure you get first aid if you need it. Make sure you don't eat food which has 'gone off', or drink water which may have sewage or farm slurry in it. If you feel ill, tell somebody.

6 If you go off somewhere, tell people where you are going: don't just vanish because you feel like having some time by yourself. If you're on the mountains, make sure you are properly equipped, and that you can get help if you need it.

7 In case of emergency, make sure that your consent form, which you should fill in before you go on **any** residential, whether camping or not, has your home address and phone number, and your doctor's name and phone number on it.

THINK ABOUT IT ...

Make a full list of the things you would take on a camping expedition which is to last three days and two nights in May.

Show the list to your tutor or an experienced camper.
How would you persuade a reluctant camper that camping can be fun?

Unit outcome 4
Display environmentally friendly and safe practice during residentials

Assessment criteria

- Describe in detail and justify the need for an effective country code.
- Demonstrate the use of environmentally friendly and safe practice regarding the countryside during expeditions.

Why have a countryside code?

More than ever before, people are escaping from the towns and heading for the countryside for fresh air, exercise and adventure. The dales, mountains and moorlands of Britain are criss-crossed with tracks and bridleways, many of them now specially strengthened against the erosion of thousands of feet, hooves or mountain bike tyres. The countryside was a place of work but is now increasingly being treated as a leisure park. And there is worse to come, with more cars, more tourists, and more Public Service students doing their Expedition Skills unit ...

So this is why we have to look after the countryside. If we don't, there soon won't be any countryside left.

True? Maybe not, but it could be. That is why we have the Countryside Code. The wording is not always exactly the same, but this is a typical example:

FOCUS

The Country Code

- Enjoy the countryside and respect its life and work.
- Guard against all risk of fire.
- Fasten all gates.
- Keep your dogs under close control.
- Keep to public paths across farmland.
- Use gates and stiles to cross fences, hedges and walls.
- Leave livestock, crops and machinery alone.
- Take your litter home.
- Help to keep all water clean.
- Protect wildlife, plants and trees.
- Take special care on country roads.
- Make no unnecessary noise.

The Country Code was introduced about 40 years ago, though people have been worried about the effect of tourism on the countryside since the 1930s. The Code does not have the force of law, but if any of its instructions (except for the first one) are deliberately broken, the people or organisations concerned could be prosecuted for criminal damage.

The elements of the Country Code

Demonstrate the use of environmentally friendly and safe practice regarding the countryside during expeditions.

There are good reasons for each of the points in the code, and we will now look at them in more detail.

Respect

Respect the life and work of the countryside is a summary of all the points that follow.

Fire

Guard against all risk of fire. In many parts of Britain it appears to rain all the time, and you may think it is impossible even to light a fire, let alone cause one that could spread. But in fact fire is a serious risk in many country areas. It only needs a couple of weeks of fine weather to make the vegetation tinder dry, and with strong winds fires can spread very quickly. The following are special fire hazards in some country areas.

- **Dry hay, corn, straw and stubble.** At harvest time in particular these can burn fiercely, and fires can spread. Stubble burning is now illegal because of the smoke it causes.
- **Barns and outbuildings.** Many of these contain flammable materials such as wood, straw and petrol, and can burn violently. Fire brigades are not based in rural areas, and there are no fire hydrants. This means that where these fires occur they are very difficult to put out, even if firefighters can get to them in time.
- **Plantations.** The Forestry Commission has planted large areas of upland Britain with coniferous trees such as spruce, larch and fir. The wood and needles of these trees contain resins which burn fiercely, and dangerous and destructive fires can be caused by careless people (or arsonists) in these forests. Wildlife and even people can be put at risk.
- **Moorland.** In dry weather moorland covered with heather or certain species of grass will burn well, and moorland fires can spread over wide areas. Some controlled burning is done by gamekeepers to encourage the growth of young heather shoots, which are eaten by grouse, a game bird. But in August and September large fires can be started by careless walkers, campers and motorists. These fires can burn down into the peat, and smoulder underground right through until November or December, causing serious environmental damage.

The main causes of rural fires are carelessly dropped matches and cigarette ends, and broken bottles which can focus sunlight on dry grass and start fires. Other causes are camp fires which get out of control, and arson.

Gates

Fasten all gates. Until the 18th century much of Britain was common land. There were few walls, hedges, fences and gates, and sheep and cattle could wander about at will. This meant that they could not be bred in a controlled fashion, and it was difficult to improve the quality of grassland. Equally, it was difficult to protect crops from wandering animals. If we had this system in the UK nowadays, there would be little British food on the supermarket shelves.

Walls, hedges and fences divide fields so that animals can be controlled and crops protected. If animals get into fields where crops are growing, they can do considerable damage. Furthermore, animals have no road sense and if they escape on to the road they can cause fatal accidents, as well as getting killed themselves. Some animals such as bulls and rams are dangerous. They charge people first, and ask questions later. Each year in this country several people are killed by domestic animals.

In addition, some animals are valuable. Farmers are not going to welcome visitors who cross their private land on official footpaths, and then leave gates open so that cows or horses worth hundreds of pounds can wander off into the night. So if you do use a gate always make sure you shut it and fasten it after you.

Dogs

Keep your dogs under close control. Even the tamest and most lovable dog can turn into a hunter if it finds itself in a field of sheep. If the sheep happen to be pregnant they can miscarry and die themselves if they are chased by a dog. This is why farmers in Britain have a legal right to shoot a dog on sight if it is seen harassing sheep. Many of them have guns, and would not hesitate to use them in these circumstances.

And then again, there are some animals that would turn on the dog ...

Footpaths

Keep to public paths across farmland. In some countries, for example France, there are few paths across farmland, and walkers soon find themselves climbing fences and crawling through hedges backwards. But in Britain we are lucky. The Ramblers Association, other pressure groups, and the general popularity of recreational walking, have maintained and developed our vast network of footpaths. This means that walkers have plenty of choice, and less excuse to trespass. Most footpaths are now legal rights of way in any case, and walkers have a perfect right to be on them. By sticking to footpaths walkers avoid damaging crops, hedges, fences and walls, and get to their destination faster, and in greater comfort.

Farmers are also prohibited from putting dangerous animals, such as bulls, on public rights of way. If you keep to the footpaths you will avoid close encounters with horny beasts.

Fences, hedges and walls

Use gates and stiles to cross fences, hedges and walls. You can't break a leg or tear your trousers walking through a gate (provided the gate is open). A stile, which is a narrow gap in a wall, big enough for a human being, but a tight squeeze for a cow, is also painless (though some people do better if they go through sideways).

Walls in upland Britain are dry-stone walls. That means they aren't stuck together with cement. Many of them are hundreds of years old – and may have been built by prisoners of war from Napoleon's armies (around 1815). So they are a historical monument, and part of our heritage. Climbing over them is a special skill, and if you haven't got it, either you or the wall will suffer. If

the wall falls down it's vandalism, and if you fall down it serves you right.

As for barbed wire fences, and hedges, if you get on the wrong side of them, guess who's going to come off worse?

Livestock, crops and machinery

Leave livestock, crops and machinery alone. We have already talked about the dangers of livestock – animals – and the damage that can be done to crops. Messing about with a farmer's machinery is rather like having a stranger tampering with your car or bike in the college car park. It's a recipe for aggro. Furthermore, some farm machinery is perfectly designed for amputating limbs without anaesthetic, or changing somebody into a human kebab.

Litter

Take your litter home. In the country they don't usually have council workers sweeping the footpaths and going round with handcarts. If you drop litter it will stay there, and everybody who sees it will curse you and everyone associated with you. Litter is ugly, and can choke animals, or lodge in their bowels, condemning them to a cruel and lingering death. It weighs nothing, and costs nothing to take home.

Help to keep all water clean. This means not dropping litter in streams or lakes, and not using them as an outdoor toilet. If you go swimming in a stream or lake, don't do anything that you wouldn't do in a swimming bath. And keep out of reservoirs which contain drinking water, unless you like drinking other people's bathwater.

If you must go to the toilet in the open air, bury the result under a clod of earth or grass.

In country areas people sometimes get their domestic water from springs. If you see any black pipes snaking across the fields, the chances are it's somebody's water supply, so don't mess with it.

Wildlife, plants and trees

Protect wildlife, plants and trees. This is an important point, even though it doesn't directly involve money or safety, like some other features of the Country Code.

You may know that many wild animals, plants and trees are becoming rare as the environment is altered and damaged. Insecticides and fertilisers poison hedgerows and other places where rare birds, animals and plants live. Pastures are ploughed up and re-seeded with new types of grass – and all the wild flowers get killed off in the process. Machines cut hedges to exactly one metre in height, or dig them up altogether. For wildlife the countryside is becoming a bit of a disaster area, and it isn't simply walkers who are to blame. Some farmers are just as bad – not to mention the policies of the government, and the European Union's Common Agricultural Policy.

But walkers can do their bit to conserve wildlife. If we stick to the paths we are less likely to disturb nesting birds, and small animals. We are also less likely to trample the saplings of trees. And if we don't pick flowers we are protecting those too.

All over the world species are becoming extinct through human activity. We don't want to be part of this destructive process.

Country roads

Take special care on country roads. If you have ever walked in the country you will notice that they don't bother to build pavements on the road sides. That's because, usually, nobody walks along them.

And this means that if you are walking along a country road, the chances are that drivers won't expect you to be there. There are plenty of blind corners and no room to jump when cars rush round them. The best rule in Britain is to walk along the right-hand side of the road so that you face the oncoming traffic. That means you have a fighting chance of seeing them, even if they don't see you.

Noise

Make no unnecessary noise. The countryside used to be quiet. Now, sometimes, you can't hear yourself think. Apart from the animals mooing and bleating to each other, you have the quads rushing all over the moor, chainsaws massacring the forests, and muckspreaders in every field. But it might not always be like this – if you're lucky. When there is a break in the traffic, and the local quarry has stopped working, and they've given up training tornado fighter pilots for the day, you might just be able to stop, and breathe deep, and listen to … silence.

Provided, that is, you take your walkman plugs out first.

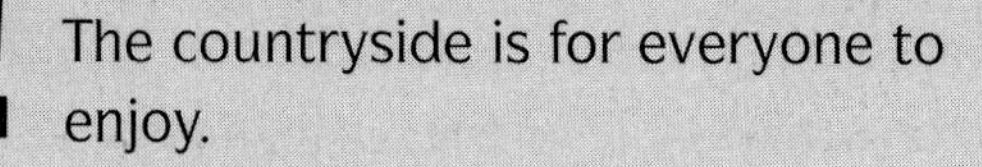

THINK ABOUT IT …

The countryside is for everyone to enjoy.

What can – or should – be done to reduce the pressure on it?

UNIT 8 International Perspectives

Unit outcome 1
Examine human rights and their violation

Assessment criteria

- Describe the key features of the United Nations Universal Declaration of Human Rights.
- Describe how human rights are violated in at least three countries.
- Summarise the work and influence of Amnesty International.

World War II, which ran from 1939 to 1945, was by far the most important human event in living memory. Much of western political and international thinking has come about as a result of it. The scale of the fighting, and the fact that Hitler was able to organise the killing of six million Jews almost under our noses, completely changed our thinking about human rights.

The United Nations Organisation was formed to try to ensure that there would never again be a war like World War II. It consists of representatives from every nation in the world, who meet to discuss world problems. One of the first things it did – in 1948 – was to produce the United Nations Universal Declaration of Human Rights.

This is now accepted as the definitive human rights document. And whenever there is a human rights problem, anywhere in the world, people who are concerned about it refer back to the United Nations' Universal Declaration.

The Universal Declaration of Human Rights

The Declaration is given below.

United Nations Universal Declaration of Human Rights 1948

1 All human beings are born free and equal in dignity and rights ... endowed with reason and conscience and should act towards one another in a spirit of brotherhood.

2 Everyone is entitled to all the rights and freedoms set forth in this Declaration without distinction of any kind, such a race, colour, sex, language, religion, political or other opinion, national or social origin, property, birth or other status.

3 Everyone has the right to life, liberty and the security of person.

4 No one shall be held in slavery and servitude; slavery and the slave trade shall be prohibited in all their forms.

5 No one shall be subjected to torture or to cruel, inhuman or degrading treatment or punishment.

6 Everyone has the right to recognition everywhere as a person before the law.

7 All are equal before the law and are entitled without any discrimination to equal protection

of the law. All are entitled to equal protection against any discrimination in violation of this Declaration and against any incitement to such discrimination.

8 Everyone has the right to an effective remedy by the competent national tribunals for acts violating the fundamental rights granted him by the constitution or by law.

9 No one shall be subjected to arbitrary arrest, detention or exile.

10 Everyone is entitled in full equality to a fair and public hearing by an independent and impartial tribunal in the determination of his rights and obligations and of any criminal charge against him.

11 (i) Everyone charged with a penal offence has the right to be presumed innocent until proved guilty according to law in a public trial at which he has all the guarantees necessary for his defence. (ii) No one shall be held guilty of any penal offence on account of any act or omission which did not constitute a penal offence, under national or international law, at the time when it was committed. Nor shall a heavier penalty be imposed than the one that was applicable at the time the penal offence was committed.

12 No one shall be subjected to arbitrary interference with his privacy, family, home or correspondence, nor to attacks upon his honour and reputation. Everyone has the right to the protection of the law against such interference or attacks.

13 (i) Everyone has the right to freedom of movement and residence within the borders of each state. (ii) Everyone has the right to leave any country, including his own, and return to his country.

14 (i) Everyone has the right to seek and to enjoy in other countries asylum from persecution.
(ii) This right may not be invoked in the case of prosecutions genuinely arising from non-political crimes or from acts contrary to the purposes and principles of the United Nations.

15 (i) Everyone has the right to a nationality.
(ii) No one shall be arbitrarily deprived of his nationality nor denied the right to change his nationality.

16 (i) Men and women of full age, without any limitation due to race, nationality or religion, have the right to marry and to found a family. They are entitled to equal rights as to marriage, during marriage, and at its dissolution.
(ii) Marriage shall be entered into only with the free and full consent of the intending spouses.
(iii) The family is the natural and fundamental group unit of society and is entitled to protection by society and by the state.

17 (i) Everyone has the right to own property alone as well as in association with others.
(ii) No one shall be arbitrarily deprived of his property.

18 Everyone has the right to freedom of thought, conscience and religion; this right includes freedom to change his religion or belief, and freedom, either alone or in community with others and in public or private, to manifest his religion or belief in teaching, practice, worship and observance.

19 Everyone has the right to freedom of opinion and expression; this right includes freedom to hold opinions without interference and to seek, receive and impart information or ideas through any media and regardless of frontiers.

20 (i) Everyone has the right to freedom of peaceful assembly and association. (ii) No one may be compelled to belong to any association.

21 (i) Everyone has the right to take part in the government of his country, directly or through freely chosen representatives. (ii) Everyone has the right of equal access to public service in his country. (iii) The will of the people shall be the basis of the authority of government; this will shall be expressed in periodic and genuine elections which shall be by universal and equal suffrage and shall be held by secret vote or by equivalent free voting procedures.

22 Everyone, as a member of society, has the right to social security and is entitled to the realisation, through national effort and international cooperation and in accordance with the organisation and resources of each state, of the economic, social and cultural rights indispensable for his dignity and the free development of his personality.

23 (i) Everyone has the right to work, to free choice of employment, to just and favourable conditions of work and to protection against unemployment. (ii) Everyone, without any discrimination, has the right to equal pay for equal work. (iii) Everyone who works has the right to just and favourable remuneration ensuring for himself and his family an existence worthy of human dignity, and supplemented, if necessary, by other means of social protection. (iv) Everyone has the right to form and join trade unions for the protection of his interests.

24 Everyone has the right to rest and leisure, including reasonable limitation of working hours and periodic holidays with pay.

25 (i) Everyone has the right to a standard of living adequate for the health and well being of himself and of his family, including food. clothing, housing and medical care and the necessary social services, and the right to security in the event of unemployment, sickness, disability, widowhood, old age or other lack of livelihood in circumstances beyond his control. (ii) Motherhood and childhood are entitled to special care and assistance. All children, whether born in or out of wedlock, shall enjoy the same social protection.

26 (i) Everyone has the right to education. Education shall be free, at least in the elementary and fundamental stages. Elementary education shall be compulsory. Technical and professional education shall be made generally available and higher education shall be equally accessible to all on the basis of merit. (ii) Education shall be directed to the full development of the human personality and to the strengthening of respect for human rights and fundamental freedoms. It shall promote understanding, tolerance and friendship among all nations, racial or religious groups, and shall further the activities of the United Nations for the maintenance of peace. (iii) Parents have a prior right to choose the education that shall be given to their children.

27 (i) Everyone has the right freely to participate in the cultural life of the community, to enjoy the arts and to share in scientific advancement and its benefits. (ii) Everyone has the right to the protection of the moral and material interests resulting from any scientific, literary or artistic production of which he is the author.

28 Everyone is entitled to a social and international order in which the rights and freedoms set forth in this Declaration can be fully realised.

29 (i) Everyone has duties to the community in which alone the free and full development of his personality is possible. (ii) In the exercise of his rights and freedoms, everyone shall be subject only to such limitations as are determined by law solely for the purpose of securing due recognition and respect for the rights and freedoms of others and of meeting the just requirements of morality, public order and the general welfare in a democratic society.

30 Nothing in this Declaration may be interpreted as implying for any state, group or person, any right to engage in any activity or to perform any act aimed at the destruction of any of the rights and freedoms set forth herein.

Key features of the Declaration

What are the 'key features'? It depends on your point of view. For example if somebody is a scientist or an artist she may well consider article 27 to be the most important, because it directly concerns her work. A mother might regard article 25 as the key feature, because it specifically mentions the rights of mothers and children. On the other hand, many of the earlier ones might be seen as key features because they affect – or could affect – everybody. Then again, for public service students, there are features which relate directly to the work of the public services – so, from our point of view, they must be key features too. Let's have a look at some of them, see what they mean, and try to say why they are 'key features'.

Freedom and equality

1 All human beings are born free and equal in dignity and rights ... endowed with reason and conscience and should act towards one another in a spirit of brotherhood.

This article is a key feature because – in a sense – all the others come out of it. It tells us that we are born free, which is a way of telling us that we must never accept slavery. We are 'equal in dignity and rights'. This is very important, because it means that though we differ in our height, our 'intelligence', our strength or the amount of money we have in the bank, we are exactly the same in our need for respect from other people and society. A poor person should not be treated rudely or unfairly because they are poor, any more than a black person should be treated unfairly because they are black. We are 'endowed with reason and conscience'. This means that we can think, and we know the difference between right and wrong. The article ends by saying that people should 'act towards one another in a spirit of brotherhood'. This means that we should try to do what is good for other people as well as what is good for ourselves. The word 'brotherhood' may seem sexist, but we should think of it as sisterhood as much as brotherhood. Remember the Declaration dates from 1948, when people were less aware of the sexist overtones of words than they are now.

Entitlement to rights

2 Everyone is entitled to all the rights and freedoms set forth in this Declaration without distinction of any kind, such as race, colour, sex, language religion, political or other opinion, national or social origin, property, birth or other status.

What this article means is that there should be no discrimination. It refers particularly to discrimination by people in power, such as employers, teachers, the police and government officials. The underlying meaning of the sentence is that there has been a large amount of discrimination in the past. In Britain, for example, up until 1918, women were not allowed to vote, and some time before that only men who owned houses were allowed to vote. Now, in 1999, there is a general election in Kuwait in which women are still not allowed to vote, though there is a promise that they will be able to vote at the next election. An interesting aspect of this article is the reasons it gives for discrimination: race, colour, sex, language, religion, political or other opinion, national or social origin, property, birth or other status. To this list sexual orientation can be added, since it is now clear that many societies are homophobic, and age, since older people are being discriminated against in employment, adoption, mortgages and insurance.

Human rights and the law

6 Everyone has the right to recognition everywhere as a person before the law.

7 All are equal before the law and are entitled without any discrimination to equal protection of the law. All are entitled to equal protection against any discrimination in violation of this Declaration and against any incitement to such discrimination.

8 Everyone has the right to an effective remedy by the competent national tribunals for acts violating the fundamental rights granted him by the constitution or by law.

9 No one shall be subjected to arbitrary arrest, detention or exile.

These four articles can be dealt with together since they all deal with human rights and the law. The subject is stressed in the Universal Declaration because the law has been abused in many countries over the years. The points being made here are:

(a) that no one is outside or above the law
(b) that everybody must be treated in the same way by the law
(c) that the law must if necessary protect people against the government or other people in power, such as employers
(d) that the law must not rob people of their freedom without very good reason.

These are still serious problems, as you can tell by reading newspapers like the *Guardian* which specialise in exposing human rights abuses. There are many parts of the world where suspects are beaten and tortured by the police. This has even happened in Britain in recent years. Joy Gardner, said to be an illegal immigrant from the West Indies, died in police custody in 1993, after having been forcibly restrained and gagged by police. She suffocated to death.

People who work in the police and the army have to learn to respect people's human rights; they exist to protect those rights, not to abuse them. Other human rights issues such as the use of ID cards, or of camera surveillance in town centres, or data protection, giving people a right to keep their lives secret, also relate to police work, and the police need to be fully aware of them.

It goes without saying that all the articles in the Universal Declaration of Human Rights are important, and in that sense any of them are 'key features'.

Human rights violations

Describe how human rights are violated in at least three countries.

There is probably no country in the world which does not have human rights violations of some sort. In 1998 the *Observer* newspaper published its 'Human Rights Index' to mark the 50th anniversary of the United Nations Universal Declaration of Human Rights. The Index was a league table of all the countries in the world according to their human rights abuses. The worst countries came at the top of the table, and the best at the bottom. Algeria came first (there had recently been a number of massacres there) and Tuvalu, in the Pacific Ocean, had the best human rights record and therefore came 170th. Britain was 141st. The sad truth is that no country can afford to be complacent about human rights.

The United Kingdom

In the UK human rights violations include the following.

- Widespread telephone and computer tapping.
- Miscarriages of justice, as a result of which people are locked up for crimes of which they are innocent. Famous cases include the Birmingham Six, who were convicted of the Birmingham pub bombings in 1974, and Judith Ward, who confessed wrongly to the M62 coach bombing in 1971.
- Racist responses by the police, for example to the murder of Stephen Lawrence, and of Michael Menson. Menson, a Ghanaian musician, was assumed by the police to have set fire to himself, when in fact he had been set on fire in a racist attack.
- Excessive exclusions of black male pupils from schools. In one year 85 per cent of all school pupils excluded from schools in the London borough of Brent were black.
- Sex discrimination in many fields of employment, especially where promotion is concerned; for example only one out of 43 chief constables is a woman.
- Too many people being imprisoned: a higher proportion of the British population is in prison than is the case with any other western European country. Often these people present no physical threat to others. (A famous example is Jonathan Aitken, the former cabinet minister who was imprisoned for fraud and for lying about it in court.)
- Too many Afro-Caribbeans in prison: (12 per cent, when less than two per cent of the population as a whole is Afro-Caribbean).
- Religious discrimination. Only the Anglican church is protected by law against blasphemy (insult to religion). Others, such as Catholics or Muslims, have to take out private prosecutions against blasphemers.
- There is no 'right to know'. Despite new secrecy laws brought in in 1999, our society and government are still far more secretive than American society and government. We do not know what is being said about us in computer databanks.
- No citizens' charter setting out human rights for British people. An organisation, Charter 88, has been campaigning for a 'bill of rights' for over ten years now, but with no success.
- The recent agreement in Northern Ireland follows long years of civil rights abuses there by the British government – which has traditionally favoured the Protestant community at the expense of the Catholics.
- 'Care in the community', and the unsatisfactory arrangements for looking after mentally ill people. Also other welfare issues such as discrimination against single mothers.
- Homelessness.

- The ban on gays in the armed forces. In most European countries, and in the USA, gay people are allowed to join the armed forces.

There are, of course, other countries with far worse human rights records than Britain, and Britain's record may improve with the introduction of the Human Rights Act 1998.

The former Yugoslavia

At the present time, because of the war, there is uncertainty about the name of this region. The whole area is now sometimes called the Balkans. Because of things that happened a long time ago, the geography, ethnicity and culture of this area are more complicated than any other part of Europe. In the early 1990s Yugoslavia broke up into Croatia, Bosnia, Slovenia, Serbia, Montenegro, Kosovo and Macedonia. Particularly in Bosnia, there was war and severe human rights abuses. Kosovo and Montenegro remained part of Serbia. This didn't matter too much in Montenegro because most of the people are ethnically and religiously allied to the Serbs. In Kosovo, however, most of the people were of Albanian descent, and Muslim, whereas the Serbs are allied to the Russians, and are Christians. Ninety per cent of the population in Kosovo, before the recent war, were Muslim, but they were being ruled by the ten per cent of people who were Christians.

Whenever a larger population of one type is ruled by a smaller population of another type, there will be human rights abuses. It happened in South Africa while the whites ruled the blacks, under the apartheid regime, before 1989. It also happens in Israel, where the Israelis have power over the Arabs who live in the occupied territories of the West Bank and the Gaza Strip. In Israel there is both religious and ethnic discrimination. In Kosovo there have been very serious human rights violations. They include:

- Mass murder of Kosovars (the Kosovo people), by Serbian security forces. These security forces are both the Serbian official army, the Serbian police, and unofficial 'militia' – groups of armed Serb civilians.
- Mass rape of Kosovar women by Serb militia.
- 'Ethnic cleansing'. This phrase has two meanings: (a) terrorising people and driving them out of the area that is being 'ethnically cleansed'; (b) killing large numbers of people of a particular ethnic group. If enough people are killed, the word used is genocide – the killing or attempted killing of a whole race. This word has not been used, however, in relation to Kosovo. The purpose of ethnic cleansing in Kosovo was to clear the land of ethnic Albanian Kosovars, so that Serbs could move in and take over their homes, wealth and land.

> **THINK ABOUT IT ...**
>
> Many people consider the phrase 'ethnic cleansing' to be unsuitable for such a vicious and brutal activity.
>
> They think the phrase is an attempt to make mass murder and terrorism seem less serious than they really are. What is your opinion?

- Terrorist bombings of markets, killing members of the public.
- The assassination of Fehmi Agani, an important Kosovar political leader, by the Serbs, after being seized at the funeral of a murdered human rights lawyer, Bajram Kelmendi.
- The killing of the famous Kosovar writer, Teki Dervishi.
- The attempted execution of newspaper editors.
- Using people as 'human shields'. Twenty thousand civilians were rounded up by Serb forces and put in a concentration camp round a weapons factory, to discourage NATO pilots from bombing it.
- Harassing and killing refugees.

> **THINK ABOUT IT ...**
>
> The Serbs took the view that the NATO bombing of Kosovo and Serbia was a more serious human rights abuse than any of the things they did in Kosovo. Did they have a point?

- Bombing, looting and burning homes and property.
- Rounding up men and separating them from their families (many of the men were presumably murdered since they have not been seen since).

Chile

Human rights abuses don't just happen in the Balkans. They were carried out on a large scale in Chile in the 1980s, when that country was governed by General Pinochet. Britain has been involved because Pinochet was a friend of the British government during the time of the Falklands war, and gave us a good deal of help. At the same time he was responsible for terrorising and killing many of his own people. He is now an old man. When he came to Britain for medical treatment in 1998, the Spanish government tried to extradite him to Spain for trial on human rights charges. The British government was faced with a difficult choice. A decision was made to send Pinochet to Spain, but then it turned out that one of the judges who made this decision was closely linked to Amnesty International, the human rights organisation (more about them below). So the decision was overturned, and the judge who had hidden his links with Amnesty International retired in disgrace.

In Spain, General Pinochet has been accused of 2,528 cases of human rights violation. They include the following:

- Personally ordering the murder of about 100 people.
- Being responsible for the jailing of 300,000 people between 1973 and 1990.
- Putting together 'a delinquent organisation ... whose aim was to create, develop and execute a systematic, criminal plan of illegal detentions, kidnap, torture followed by death, the forced displacement of thousands of people and the selective disappearance of around 3,000.'
- Torturing prisoners. Most of these were socialists, Pinochet's political opponents. The charges say: 'The prisoners are tortured in groups. The sessions always begin with a shower for the prisoners. Then, while they are still wet, electrodes are applied to their bodies...' Others, including children, were beaten to death.
- Murders in other countries, such as the car-bomb killing in the USA in 1976 of Orlando Letelier, who was the defence minister under Salvador Allende, the previous, democratically-elected, ruler of Chile whom Pinochet had murdered. (Pinochet originally came to power in an army coup and was said to have been helped in this by the Americans, who did not like Allende's socialist politics.)

FOCUS

Human rights abuses follow a pattern. Whatever the country, they almost always include:

- imprisonment without trial
- all forms of discrimination – race, gender, religion, age, sexual orientation, etc.
- summary execution
- ethnic cleansing
- use of human shields
- censorship (especially of political news)
- laws restricting the number of children you can have
- child labour
- forcible relocation of individuals or communities
- imprisonment of people for their political, religious or social beliefs
- forced repatriation
- denial of rights to asylum seekers
- police cruelty
- torture
- brainwashing
- child abuse, rape, etc.
- unjust taxation systems
- oppressive bureaucracy
- house arrest
- denial of freedom of movement
- inhuman conditions in prisons
- exclusion of pupils from schools
- denial of proper legal representation
- denial of franchise (the vote)
- undemocratic government (especially military dictatorships)
- deliberate starvation

- The murder of Carmelo Soria, a Spaniard working for the United Nations (who should have enjoyed diplomatic protection). He was dragged out of his car, then tortured by Pinochet's secret police, who killed him by breaking his neck.

The motive for the brutality was, according to the Spanish prosecutors, political. Pinochet is quoted as saying: 'I am a soldier and president of the Chilean nation, under attack from the disease of communism, which will be eradicated. Marxists and communists must be tortured, because otherwise they will not sing.'

Since 1990 Pinochet has 'retired' and the present Chilean government has a better human rights record. But large numbers of people feel that justice will not be done until Pinochet and his henchmen are brought to trial.

Amnesty International

Summarise the work and influence of Amnesty International.

Amnesty International is the world's foremost voluntary organisation dealing with human rights. Its headquarters is in London, where it employs over 300 staff. It works to promote the rights in the Universal Declaration of Human Rights and to oppose grave abuses of human rights by governments and armed opposition groups.

Aims

It aims:

1. 'To seek the release of all prisoners of conscience [people imprisoned because of their beliefs or ethnic origin, sex, colour, language, national or social origin, economic status, birth or other status] as long as they have not used or encouraged violence.'
2. 'To work for fair and prompt trials for all political prisoners.'
3. 'To campaign to abolish the death penalty, torture, and other forms of cruel, inhuman or degrading treatment or punishment.'
4. 'To end extrajudicial executions and "disappearances".' [To stop people being killed or imprisoned without trial for political reasons.]

Methods

A wide range of methods are used to achieve these aims.

Collecting supporters and money

Amnesty International has over a million members around the world, and many millions of supporters. Each either gives money to the organisation, or raises money for it. With this money Amnesty International employs human rights specialists and runs its campaigns.

Their supporters come under four headings:

1. **National members.** Normal members who pay subscriptions, campaign, publicise and raise funds.
2. **Local groups.** Active local organisations which plan and carry out local campaigns, and raise awareness of Amnesty International in the community.
3. **'Urgent Action' network.** Members who concentrate on urgent human rights cases, and write lots of letters, faxes and e-mails to put pressure where it is needed.
4. **Related groups**, networks and experts.

The related groups, networks and experts include:

- medical staff
- journalists
- lawyers
- business executives
- trade unions
- religious groups
- school and youth groups
- teachers and academics
- student groups
- women's groups
- gay, lesbian, bisexual and transgendered people
- care workers
- police officers (serving and ex-serving)
- ethnic minority groups
- military personnel (serving and ex-serving) and their families
- artists, writers, musicians, etc.

Campaigns

Amnesty International uses the money it collects to run campaigns. The purpose of these campaigns is to publicise cases of unfair imprisonment and other human rights abuses. The hope is that pressure will then be put on the people carrying out the human rights abuses, and they will stop. The pressure may come from the general public in the country concerned, or from other countries. In one very serious case, that of China after the Tiananmen Square Massacre of 1989, the publicising of human rights abuses in the west affected China's trade, and has led to some improvement of the human rights situation there.

Amnesty International's campaigns take various forms:

1 **Media and publicity.** They use newspapers, advertisements, radio and television to educate the public about human rights abuses.

2 **Direct appeals to the governments** or authorities carrying out human rights abuses. These are 'polite but firm'. They visit embassies and prison authorities.

3 They **approach the British government and MPs** to get them interested in human rights. In some cases they persuade MPs to give active support.

4 **Outreach.** This consists of cooperating with other organisations such as churches, societies, youth groups and even colleges in raising awareness of false imprisonment and other human rights abuses. This also enables Amnesty International to collect more money for its campaigns.

5 **Symbolic events.** These are things like demonstrations, candlelight vigils, public fasts, rock concerts, poster displays and film festivals, which make people more aware of human rights abuses and the need to oppose them actively.

6 **Fundraising.** This is carried out mainly through Amnesty International members, and by donations from the public.

Other kinds of action:

1 **Appeals in *Amnesty* magazine.** These give information about specific prisoners of conscience in various parts of the world, and the kinds of public action and protest (such as mass letter-writing) which will help to gain their release.

2 **Urgent action** (see page 188). This is a network of Amnesty International activists. They become involved when there is an immediate risk of a political prisoner being tortured or put to death in any part of the world. They act quickly to appeal and campaign on behalf of these individuals.

3 **Theme and country campaigns.** Themes are particular types of human rights abuse – such as false imprisonment, torture or the use of ethnic cleansing. Country campaigns are focused on countries where these activities are happening. Recent country campaigns have included Colombia, China, Sudan and Turkey.

The influence of Amnesty International

In some ways it is hard to assess the influence of Amnesty International, because we have no way of being sure what the world would have been like if they hadn't existed. Furthermore, imprisonment without trial and other human rights abuses are by their very nature hard to quantify; it is difficult to get reliable statistics about things which are done in secret, in countries where the press and politicians are either unwilling or unable to speak the truth.

Amnesty International closely follow the cases they take up, and in many cases their action has led to the release of political prisoners and the lessening of human rights abuses. Many people have said, in many parts of the world, that they or people they know would have been dead if it had not been for Amnesty International's work.

Their work is on a large scale. In 1997 they worked on 1983 cases for 4570 named individuals, plus another 1500 for whom they did not have names. But this scale is in fact tiny by comparison with the amount of human rights abuse in the world. This is because Amnesty International are volunteers – and, in quantity, more work can be done by vast organisations such as the United Nations, which receive huge sums of money from member governments.

Amnesty International uses the symbol of a candle trapped in barbed wire. At one level this represents the spirit of a prisoner of conscience who is wrongfully imprisoned. At another, it represents the hope brought to prisoners, and the world, by the organisation. But Amnesty International cannot, by itself, stop all human rights abuses. All it can do is rescue individuals, and run campaigns which are a deterrent to torturers, dictators and others who try to override freedom and justice. Like a pair of far-seeing eyes, Amnesty International looks deep into the dark and secret places where people are being tortured and dehumanised, and is then able to tell the rest of the world what is going on. So the real influence of Amnesty International is probably that they bring human rights abuses to light, raising public awareness of crimes against humanity so that other people and organisations can fight against them as well.

Unit outcome 2
Examine liberation movements and their effects

Assessment criteria

- Describe in detail how liberation movements develop.
- Explain major differences between liberation movements and terrorist organisations.
- Summarise the work of at least two liberation movements, giving details of how they affect their own and foreign countries.

How liberation movements develop

A liberation movement is a large-scale campaign or organisation devoted to getting freedom and justice. Rather like fire, liberation movements need three ingredients if they are going to develop. These are:

- **oppression** – the state of affairs when a person, or people, use their power to deprive others of wealth, freedom and justice
- **ideology**, or a system of beliefs, which helps the oppressed people in their struggle for freedom, justice and wealth
- **leadership** and organisation.

The most famous liberation movements in modern times were in countries which used to belong to Britain as colonies, but achieved their own freedom when they became independent. Such countries include India, Pakistan, South Africa, Zambia, and Kenya. In all these cases the oppressor was Britain.

Colonialism, the taking over of countries by Britain and other European countries in the 19th century, caused serious problems for the people already living there. These problems included:

- the use of a foreign language (usually English) as the official language
- the colonisers taking all the best agricultural land, by force

- mining and other exploitation of the land (and forcing people to work in the mines for low wages, without their families being with them)
- the conscription (forced employment) of people to fight for Britain in World Wars I and II
- the fact that after these wars, those soldiers who weren't killed were sent back and compelled once again to live as second class citizens
- a huge difference in the standard of living between the rich colonisers and the poor people who were colonised
- the introduction of a foreign religion – Christianity
- the fact that the colonisers had guns, and the people who were colonised did not.

However, Britain and the other countries did introduce education and medical care to their colonies. These brought an increase in population (which put pressure on land and resources), and the higher education of a few people.

In the liberation movements against colonialism these educated people, such as Gandhi and Kenneth Kaunda of Zambia, became the new leaders. The development of a liberation movement is described very clearly in Kenneth Kaunda's book *Zambia Shall be Free* (published in Heinemann African Writers' Series). As Kaunda explains, the liberation movement would not have developed without educated people like himself going round and explaining to the ordinary people that they were being oppressed.

The next phase was the organisation of people into local groups which could campaign for freedom by organising demonstrations and strikes against the so-called 'colonial masters'. In Zambia a series of general strikes helped to bring the colonial government to its knees. But there was not much violence. Following the example of Mahatma Gandhi, Kaunda used a method of non-violent resistance, which minimised deaths in the struggle.

While the struggle was going on, Kaunda and other African nationalist leaders toured Britain, getting support for the idea of independence. By the 1950s a large number of British people were in favour of independence for the colonies. In some cases this was because they could see the rightness of the idea; in others it was because it was becoming increasingly expensive for the taxpayer to keep these colonies going, especially when there was a growing danger of unrest and perhaps outright war. And, after all, British mothers didn't want their sons to go and fight, and die, for a country in Africa which nobody really cared about.

Peaceful struggle is not usually 100 per cent effective in gaining freedom. Eventually tempers frayed. In Kenya, for example, the 'Mau Mau' rebellions of the 1950s led to many African deaths though, oddly, only about 30 white settlers were killed. In India several thousand people died in rioting just before Independence in 1947. This shows that even though liberation movements can be largely peaceful, violence usually breaks out at some time. And sometimes a liberation movement has a violent wing – as was the case with the African National Congress in South Africa, during the years when the blacks were fighting the white apartheid government.

Liberation movements today

Since colonialism has now officially ended, liberation movements are taking different forms. Their basis is less clear-cut, and many of them are more religious in their motivation than the anti-colonial movements of India and Africa, where the importance of religion was always played down. Many present-day Islamic 'liberation' movements do not seem like liberation movements to western people, because they can reduce people's freedom – especially the freedom of women. This is the case with the Taliban, in Afghanistan, who took over after a civil war following a period of Russian-backed communism under President Najibullah. Western countries, such as Britain and America, supported the Muslim 'extremists' who overthrew Najibullah, because they were against communism. But then they found that the new Muslim government in Afghanistan hated Britain and America even more than the old government did. The Taliban are so-called 'fundamentalists' who see themselves as a liberation movement because they are getting rid of foreign domination and influence. But many westerners see them as anti-liberation because they are (in western eyes) reducing the freedom and justice in Afghanistan. For example in 1998 they banned the use of TV and video in the country (because they brought in 'evil' American influence), and closed all girls' schools.

A similar liberation movement led to the revolution in Iran in 1979 when the Shah (the old traditional ruler) was overthrown because he was seen as too rich, and too close to the Americans in his thinking. The Ayatollah Khomeini, who took over from him, had seemed like a gentle old Muslim holy man who lived in exile in Paris. Some people used to laugh at him because he kept his eyes down when he saw women coming along the street towards him. But back in Iran he imposed strict Islamic laws – forcing women to wear veils, and banning western culture – which seemed like the opposite of liberation to westerners, yet were seen by most Iranians as liberation from American influence and greed.

A liberation struggle is still going on in Israel, between the Palestinian Arabs and the Israelis. This will be discussed in more detail below, on page 195.

Comparison of liberation and terrorist movements

Explain major differences between liberation movements and terrorist organisations.

A comparison of liberation movements and terrorist organisations is given in the table below.

Liberation movements and terrorist organisations compared

Liberation movements	Terrorist organisations
Large scale, often involving millions of people.	Small scale. The IRA at the height of its activity was thought to have only 200 active members (though they had non-violent supporters who would offer 'safe houses' and other help).
Large-scale popular support – e.g. many millions in South Africa during apartheid in the 1980s.	Little popular support – and what there is may be the result of fear.
Mainly non-violent methods of protest, such as demonstrations, strikes, rallies and meetings.	Violent – often with no clear reasons given. Bombs without warning, sniping, threats of poisoning water supplies, etc.
Prepared to try to negotiate openly with the people they are trying to overthrow (though this is never easy).	No open negotiations, only ransom notes, threats on the phone and 'claiming responsibility' anonymously.
Get their money from their supporters, or from overseas donations.	Get their money mainly from organised crime, though some overseas donations as well.
Protesters are seen by the world as political protesters. Only viewed as criminals by undemocratic regimes.	Viewed as criminals in the country where they operate. Viewed as criminals even by democratic governments. Most people think of them as murderers.
Leaders of liberation movements are well known. People know where they are.	The leaders are shadowy figures, such as Osama bin Laden, who spend their time in hiding, or in countries with no democracy, such as Afghanistan.
Their arguments are reasonable – though not everybody agrees with them. They have not lost the argument, and might win it, e.g. many people think Sinn Fein might be right in wanting a united Ireland, and even their opponents are prepared to talk with them.	They have lost the argument, so they have to turn to violence to get noticed. In the case of the IRA, no one wants to negotiate with people who wear balaclavas and carry kalashnikovs. Besides, except to release hostages or something like that, there would be no point in negotiating with them.

There is one more difference – only it isn't a real difference. It's a difference of viewpoint. In the 1980s black people in South Africa, under Archbishop Desmond Tutu and later under Nelson Mandela, were campaigning for freedom from the white-ruled governments of PW Botha and FW de Clerk. The main organisation in the struggle for freedom was the African National Congress – now South Africa's ruling political party. To the black people of South Africa – 25 million of them – the African National Congress was a liberation movement. To the white people – 4 million of them – they were a terrorist organisation. So just as 'one man's meat is another man's poison', so one man's freedom fighter is another man's terrorist. Quite often, when people talk about liberation movements, it means that the speaker agrees with what they stand for. The same movement might be described as a terrorist organisation by someone who doesn't like them.

Interestingly feminism, or 'women's liberation' is different in this respect. It is, of course a liberation movement – only, unlike the ones we have been considering, it is an international movement. At the present time, its supporters call it 'feminism'.

The work of two liberation movements

Summarise the work of at least two liberation movements, giving details of how they affect their own and foreign countries.

1 Mahatma Gandhi

The most famous of all liberation movements, and the one which has had the greatest effect on other liberation movements, was that led by Mahatma Gandhi in the period before India's independence from Britain in 1947. It is no exaggeration to say that Gandhi was to liberation movements what Freud was to psychology, or Marx to economics. Even when Gandhi was not successful, the things he did and said acted as an unforgettable lesson to the rest of the world.

On page 190 we said that liberation movements need oppression, ideology and leadership. In India the British provided the oppression, ruling 400 million people – as the population then was – with a relatively tiny force of soldiers and administrators. Against the British, Gandhi provided the ideology and the leadership. In his early life the fight to gain freedom from British rule would have seemed unwinnable, but because of Gandhi's vision and organisational skills, the whole of India, including many people who basically disagreed with him, came to support his independence movement.

India achieved independence, but Gandhi was assassinated shortly afterwards, and Pakistan split from India almost immediately. So we might say that he achieved the impossible, yet did not wholly succeed.

Though Gandhi is so closely identified with Indian independence, he could have achieved nothing without the support of the people he inspired and mobilised. His story illustrates the first basic truth about a liberation movement: the more people who support it, the more likely it is to succeed.

The British had weapons and the Indians didn't. Furthermore the British were prepared to use them. General Dyer's shocking massacre of 379 unarmed civilians who were peacefully demonstrating at Amritsar in 1919 showed this. It also showed the world that the Indians might be right and the British wrong – a new idea in those colonial days.

Gandhi was nothing if not a great teacher. He wrote books about techniques of non-violent resistance: *Hind Swaraj* (which means 'Indian self-government') in 1910 and *Satyagraha* ('the force of truth')in 1928. He wrote them long before he became a major political leader. They were the basis of his ideology, and gave his followers new but easily understood ideas which they could put into practice. For example the main rules for strikers were:

- never use violence
- never molest (hassle) non-strikers
- never beg for food
- never give in.

These ideas appear simple, but proved to be very effective.

This use of non-violent resistance by the Indian freedom movement – a programme of general strikes, demonstrations, marches and other activities – undermined British morale and, most importantly, proved to the rest of the world that:

- the Indians wanted freedom, not bloodshed
- they could organise huge protests successfully, therefore they would be able to govern their country effectively and peacefully if they were independent
- the days of British colonialism were numbered, and the British would not always have their own way
- power did not necessarily come from the barrel of a gun.

The ideology of Gandhi's movement was very interesting. Though it was based on Hinduism, and the writings of a Hindu holy book called the *Bhagavad Gita*, Gandhi went to great lengths to get support from all religious groups. As a leader, he knew the importance of practising what he preached, and he presented an image of humility which the rest of the world found impressive. While other leaders tried to show off their power and wealth with expensive clothes and cars, he wore a white traditional gown and spent his spare time spinning yarn on a wheel which he carried round with him. He saw himself as a symbol of the power of humble people, and this was his way of showing the world that his real support came from the ordinary Indian. In some ways he imitated the behaviour and teachings of Christ, and this gained him considerable support among the poorer people in England as well. He broke the cycle of violence which had marked colonialism, and made people believe that a new type of politics was possible.

In his stress on the power of poor people, he didn't only echo the idea of 'blessed are the meek for they shall inherit the earth'. He also echoed the ideas of Karl Marx about workers' struggle and the dangers of capitalism – but he knew how to do it without being branded as a communist (which would have lost him all his credibility in the west). He had to persuade not only the people of India, but also the rest of the world, that what he was trying to do was right.

The liberation movement in India affected India by:

- bringing independence
- attracting wide international support for India during the early years of independence – support which still exists to some extent
- stressing the value of peace, which meant that, for a long period, India had a relatively weak army. This led to a dangerous invasion by China in 1973 – but fortunately, for reasons best known to themselves, the Chinese abruptly withdrew: after this India became more military, and developed nuclear weapons
- splitting India because it failed to take into account the strength of the Muslim desire for an Islamic state – hence the foundation of Pakistan by Mohammed Ali Jinnah in 1947: there is still a threat of war between the two countries, because of religious differences and the argument over who should rule Kashmir
- making people proud to be humble, and prepared to work hard to raise themselves out of poverty
- creating a truly multi-ethnic, multicultural and secular (i.e. religion separate from politics) country at a time when few existed
- keeping foreign interference to a minimum: this helped to make India self-sufficient and gave the country a broad industrial base.

Gandhi's movement affected the rest of the world by:

- showing all colonised countries how to achieve freedom with minimal bloodshed
- showing that people who are discriminated against can achieve freedom and respect without using force
- making white people take non-white people seriously for the first time
- showing that the poor, and 'peasants' are human beings and have the same needs and wishes as everybody else
- showing that politicians can, and should, use their brains
- showing that money isn't everything.

Since 1947 there has never been a liberation struggle of any kind which has not somehow been affected by the movement Gandhi led. And, generally speaking, the more they have followed Gandhi's ideas, the more successful they have been.

2 Palestinian liberation

A long time has passed since 1947, and many of the great national liberation struggles have been achieved. However, on the principle that 'as one door opens another door shuts', freedom was lost for the Palestinians in 1948 shortly after it was gained for the Indians. The reason for this was the formation of Israel, by the USA and Britain, after World War II. The land that was given by the western powers to the Jews, partly in recognition of what the Jews had suffered in the Holocaust, belonged to Palestinians who were not pleased to find that 'their land' had been taken from them.

The Palestine problem has been one of the most complex and difficult world political problems in recent years. As many people still feel that if there is another world war, it will start in the Middle East, it seems worth looking at the situation in a little more detail.

The difficulty is caused by the way different aspects of the problem are interconnected. When Israel was formed in 1948 America guaranteed its freedom and security. This means that any attack on Israel is an attack on the USA. During the Cold War between the USSR (now Russia) and the west, the communists helped to arm the Arab countries surrounding Israel in order to test both Israel and America. Most Arabs still believe that Israel does not or should not officially exist.

In 1967 the Six Day War broke out, in which Arab countries, especially Syria and Egypt, invaded Israel. If they had succeeded they could have wiped Israel off the map. But the Israelis knew that this was going to happen and were armed to the teeth and ready for a fight. Syria, Egypt and Jordan each lost land as the Israeli army advanced in all directions. The Americans called a halt to it, but the Israelis were left with an almost embarrassing amount of captured Arab land, together with the Palestinians, Jordanians, Syrians and Egyptians living on it. The situation went down like a lead balloon with the Muslim countries of the Middle East, and left the Americans deeply unpopular in the region.

A second war – the Yom Kippur War, named after a Jewish festival – broke out in 1973. This lasted all of three weeks. Egypt and Syria attempted to regain their land, had some success at first, then were driven back again. Saudi Arabia stopped exporting oil to the Americans, and it began to look as if another war was going to break out. This encouraged the Americans to change their policy and start to try arranging a lasting peace in the Middle East. Twenty years later they are still trying. But the main reason why they haven't yet succeeded is the Palestinian problem.

The Palestinians are a displaced people. There are about two million of them, but there may be more because many of them are classified as Jordanian, even though they see themselves as Palestinian. They live in Israel, almost (in their opinion) as captives. Things are better than they used to be because they have some autonomy (self-government) but not enough to give them the independent nation that they want. Many of them live in the areas where they were sent after the two wars mentioned above – in the West Bank and the Gaza Strip. No one in their right mind would want to live in the Gaza Strip, which is like a gigantic refugee camp. The West Bank (of the River Jordan) is better, but many Israelis want Israel to keep it permanently, and are settling on it even though Palestinians think it is their land. This doesn't make for good relations between the two communities.

Among the Palestinians an organisation called the Palestine Liberation Organisation (PLO) grew up in the 1950s. They were immediately branded as terrorists by most Israelis and the West. They weren't a powerful organisation, but they had wide Arab support and were strong enough to make bombs and commit atrocities.

The PLO have a leader, Yasser Arafat. He has been tireless in trying to negotiate peace and sort out the Palestinian problem. Unfortunately

- he has a terrorist background which stopped important people speaking to him for 20 years

- because the Palestinians are not officially a country he has had difficulty being taken seriously by many politicians
- he has constantly been undermined and threatened by extremists such as Abu Jihad, the Hesbollah organisation of Lebanon and Hammas, another hard-line Islamic group: they see him as a softie who is prepared to negotiate with the Israelis instead of bombing them
- he is now in ill-health and it is not clear who will carry on if he withdraws.

The Palestinians are not easy to control. Many of them have links with Lebanon, where there was a civil war for 20 years. The war stopped when Syria stepped in and sorted it out, but not before the country was saturated with weapons and potential terrorists. The Palestinians also have a tradition of civil disobedience, similar to Gandhi's, but less peaceful. For some years in the 1980s and early 90s young Palestinians carried out an *intifada*, stoning anybody and everybody they didn't like. But when Israeli soldiers shot them, there was a world outcry, so the *intifada* turned out to be a powerful propaganda weapon. The PLO didn't exactly support the *intifada*, but it didn't exactly condemn it either. After all, it was a way of showing that they still had public support.

The Israelis don't like negotiating with the Palestinians. But some of them are prepared to. Unfortunately others won't at any price. And the Israeli government keeps changing. Furthermore, people who try to make peace in the Middle East have a nasty habit of getting shot. It happened to President Sadat of Egypt, then it happened to Yitzhak Rabin, the Israeli prime minister, in 1995. Recently a hard-line Israeli government led by Binyamin Netanyahu has made the peace process very difficult, but now he has been replaced by Ehud Barak there is a chance of progress and the PLO will once again be negotiating.

FOCUS

Some key events in recent Palestinian history

1993
Peace agreement between Israeli leader Yitzhak Rabin and Palestinian leader Yasser Arafat. This marked the official recognition by the Israeli government of the Palestine Liberation Organisation (PLO), and the beginning of limited self-rule for the Gaza Strip and the West Bank. Release of Palestinian detainees.

1995
Israeli army pulled out of seven large Palestinian towns and 460 smaller towns and villages.

1996
82-member Palestine Council elected. Police now under Palestinian control in Palestinian areas.

1996 (September)
Serious clashes between Palestinian demonstrators and Israeli troops over Jewish settlers in West Bank.

1998
Israeli troops withdrew from Hebron and rural areas of the West Bank.

1999 (May)
Election of Ehud Barak in place of Binyamin Netanyahu increases hopes of full recognition and independence for Palestinians.

Summary

The Palestinian Liberation Organisation (PLO):

- negotiates with Israel and other countries to try to obtain an independent country for Palestinians to live in: the problem is that this country would have to come out of land at present ruled by Israel
- listens to Palestinians and tries to get maximum support from them
- controls the government and administration of self-ruled but not independent Palestinian territories (this includes the Gaza Strip and some of the West Bank)
- attempts to keep violent groups such as Hammas quiet
- cultivates links with countries such as Syria, Jordan and Egypt
- negotiates at local levels over issues such as Israeli settlements and water supplies
- gathers support from the United Nations and other organisations
- organises strikes and demonstrations from time to time.

Effects of the PLO on Palestine

Palestine does not officially exist as an independent country. Perhaps it will do at some time in the future. It consists mainly of various scattered pieces of land in the West Bank and the Gaza Strip. The PLO organises the day-to-day government of these areas, and controls the police. The PLO does not officially have an army, and has no official foreign policy because it has no official country. But its long-term aim is to create an independent Palestinian homeland. Politically this is likely to be moderately (a) Islamic (b) socialist.

Effects of the PLO on Israel

From its terrorist beginnings the PLO has moved towards peaceful protest under the leadership of Yasser Arafat. Gradually Israelis are beginning to trust Arafat and the 'moderate' PLO members. Nevertheless, over the years, the PLO has been linked to violence, so its main effect has been to keep Israel in a state of military alertness. Israel is a country where everybody does national service (a fixed period of training in the armed forces). Women as well as men are trained to fight in the front line. Weapons such as Patriot missiles have been imported in large numbers from the USA, where there is a strong and influential Jewish community. Basically the country is armed to the teeth, and has a military zone in the north to protect it from Palestinian militants who have their headquarters in southern Lebanon. From time to time Israel carries out armed raids on Lebanon to attack Palestinian terrorists.

Effects of the PLO on the rest of the world

1. Yasser Arafat has proved an excellent publicist of the Palestinian problem. So thanks to him, everybody knows about it, even though the problem has not yet been finally solved.
2. The Americans and others have taken an active role in trying to solve the problem.
3. The PLO have undermined the international support for Israel which followed World War II and revelations in the Nuremberg trials about the Holocaust. There is some increase in anti-semitic thinking in the west, and many people now look at the Israeli government as a human rights offender, rather as the apartheid government in South Africa was.
4. Because the PLO have taken a more peaceful line than expected, the Middle East seems less dangerous to the west than it did 20 years ago. Western companies are beginning to think about increasing investment in the region.

THINK ABOUT IT ...

What other liberation movements are active in the world at the present time?

Unit outcome 3
Investigate the consequences of war and its effects on societies

Assessment criteria

- Describe common causes of war and differentiate between war and conflict.
- Analyse at least two international conflicts or wars, providing details of their causes and effects.

Why do wars break out?

War can be described as organised fighting, on a large scale, over a period of time. Usually it takes place between different nations, ethnic groups or cultural groups. There is a stated reason for the fighting, though this may not be the real reason.

Conflict is fighting – or a situation in which fighting could easily break out. But it is on a small scale, and there is no formal declaration of war. The Troubles in Northern Ireland were seen (at least by the British government) as a conflict rather than a war. And the Falklands War of 1982 was described as a conflict at the time, since Britain and Argentina were not officially at war.

The following are reasons which are often given for wars breaking out.

1 Self-defence. A country or community is under attack, and feels that they have no peaceful way of defending themselves. They therefore try to defend themselves by organised fighting.

2 Defence of interests. A country will go to war not only if it feels directly threatened. It will also fight if its interests are threatened. If we feel that our trade, wealth, influence in the world, or essential supplies (e.g. of oil) are under threat, we will go to war.

3 Land. The Germans went to war in 1939 partly because they felt they needed more land for their people. Britain fought in the Falklands in 1981 because we thought we were going to lose some of our land. Land is the most basic form of wealth, and even societies which have no money own land. Land is also connected with other forms of wealth. The sheep grazed on the Falkland Islands were not particularly valuable, but the oil round their shores probably will be. In addition, the Falklands had an important harbour which is on the way to the Antarctic, a place where Britain still owns great mineral reserves (though they are not exploited at present).

4 Religion. Religions normally preach peace, but several wars which are being fought at the moment seem to have a religious basis. Conflicts in Kosovo, Bosnia, Northern Ireland, Israel, Lebanon, Sudan and Iraq all have a religious aspect.

5 Culture. Culture, which is our way of life, is linked to religion. Just as people will fight to protect their religion, so they will also fight to protect their culture. There is a cultural dimension to all wars.

6 Politics. Politics, rather like culture and religion, is something that people can feel very strongly about. Many of the wars in the 20th century were over different political systems. The National Socialism (Nazism) of the Germans in the 1930s was incompatible with the democratic system operating in Britain and America, and was therefore a factor leading to war. The communism of the Soviet Union (now Russia) was a political system which did not fit in either with Nazism or democracy. The communists therefore fought the Nazis, and, at a later stage, encouraged wars against the western democracies. NB: political systems are sometimes called ideologies, and you will find more about them on pages 130–133.

7 Money. In a way this is the same as 'interests' in number 2 above. Sometimes it is seen as 'greed'. If a country can invade another and take over land, oilfields, or mineral resources, the citizens of the first country can benefit.

8 Ethnicity. People often find it difficult to get on with other ethnic groups. This might not matter too much normally, but where different ethnic groups live in the same country, there can be a struggle for overall power. This is very obviously the case at present in Kosovo. It was also the reason for the terrible killings in Rwanda.

9 History. Sometimes things have happened in the past which make people feel angry, because they seem to be unjust. The Palestinians feel that their land was stolen by the western countries after World War II and given to the Jews, to form the modern state of Israel. This means that many Arab countries still feel that the state of Israel should not exist, and since 1966 there have been two wars by Syria and Egypt against Israel and there is still a lot of conflict in the region. Much of the recent fighting in Bosnia, especially between Serbs, Croats and Bosnians, came out of resentment at the fact that the Croats supported the Nazis in World War II.

10 Population pressure. The world's population is increasing very fast, especially in the developing countries. A typical growth rate in East Africa is four per cent per year. This means that in 20 years the population of a country doubles. The economy cannot keep pace and there is not enough land for people to farm and feed themselves. This causes pressure either for one country to invade another or, more often, for civil war to break out.

11 Climatic change. This reason is related to 10 above. Desertification in Africa is causing starvation and political unrest in every country south of the Sahara desert. The population is increasing but the amount of food and water is going down. Since the area is very poor, much of the fighting and killing is never reported in our newspapers.

In practice, wars are usually fought for several, perhaps all, of the reasons given above. But there are also other reasons for wars which tend to be kept secret.

1 Wars can be good for business. Arms manufacturers in particular can become fabulously rich in wartime. The same is true of drug and chemical companies. Also, if a country is destroyed in war, there is the possibility of profitable investment by foreign countries when peace returns.

2 Wars make governments popular. Opinion polls showed that Mrs Thatcher only became really popular after the Falklands conflict. Winston Churchill was tremendously popular in Britain during World War II, but was disliked and distrusted during peacetime. Therefore, governments which are having difficulties at home are sometimes accused of starting wars abroad to boost their popularity. A possible recent example of this was the bombing of Iraq in December 1998, which was thought by some to be an attempt by President Clinton to boost his popularity in the US during the run-up to his impeachment proceedings over Monica Lewinsky.

3 Armies benefit from wars. Weapons and strategies can be tested and soldiers get valuable combat or peacekeeping experience. This keeps armies up-to-date and efficient.

4 Financial speculators – people who gamble on the money markets or Stock Exchange – can benefit from wars. This is because wars cause changes in the value of money and shares. By buying money or shares cheaply, and selling them when they are expensive, speculators can make an enormous profit. This is easier to do when wars are being fought.

5 Wars can be encouraged by countries which are not friendly to either of the fighting countries. Countries in the west sold arms to both Iran and Iraq during the Iran–Iraq war, in the hope that both those countries would become weaker – since both were hostile to Britain and America.

6 Lack of democratic government. There have been few if any wars where both sides had democratic governments. In World War II Britain and the USA were democratic but Germany under the Nazis and the USSR under Stalin were not. People do not usually vote to send their sons or daughters off to war. But under a dictatorship the government can whip up a frenzy of hate against another country, and by manipulating public opinion make a war possible.

7 Linked with number 6 is **propaganda**. This is biased news, often attacking another country. The media can make such hostile comment about another country that people start to want to go to war.

International conflicts

Analyse at least two international conflicts or wars, providing details of their causes and effects.

1 Kosovo

People knew that there was going to be a war in Kosovo in 1995, but it didn't happen until March 1999. Unless it starts again it was a short war, lasting only one month. The British media described it as war, but war was not officially declared as it was before World War II. So in a sense it was a conflict, like the fighting between Britain and Argentina in 1982.

Kosovo (see figure 8.1) is a landlocked area in what is known as the Balkans. Officially it is a province of Serbia, rather as Northern Ireland is a province of Britain. And just as some people in Northern Ireland don't want it to be part of Britain, so some people in Kosovo don't want it to be part of Serbia. But the proportions are different. Before the war broke out 90 per cent of the people in Kosovo did not want to be part of Serbia.

As with Northern Ireland, there are religious differences. Serbs are Christians, and most of them belong to the Greek Orthodox church. Their language and culture are related to those of the Russians and the Greeks.

But most of the people in Kosovo are 'ethnic Albanians'. This means they are Albanians who don't live in Albania. They are Muslims and speak the Albanian language. They left Albania because Albania has for many years been the poorest and most unstable country in Europe. It used to have a hard-line communist government. More recently

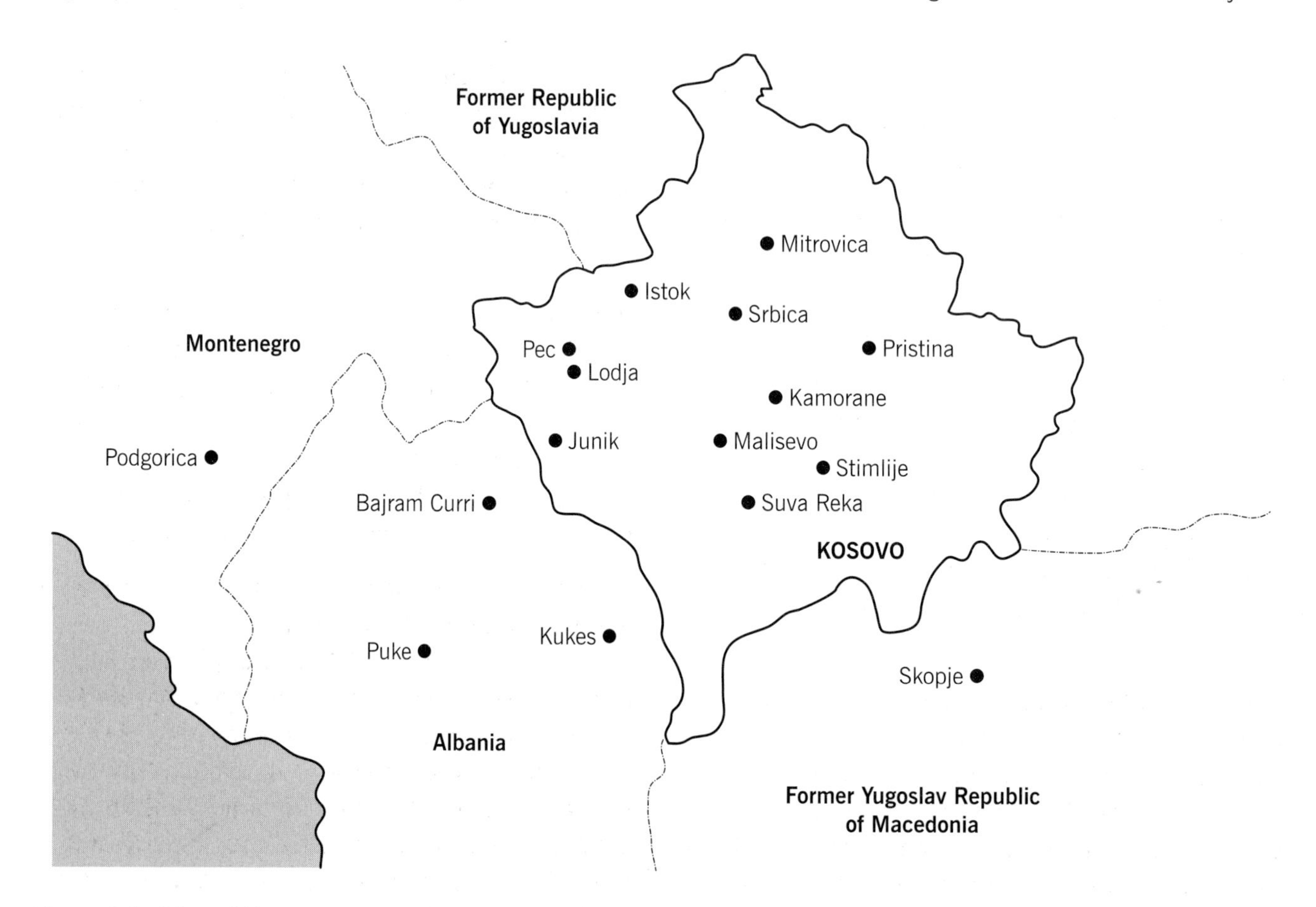

Figure 8.1 *Map of Kosovo and surrounding countries*

there has been civil war, and the government is practically nonexistent.

For about ten years the Serbs have been objecting to the number of ethnic Albanians living in Kosovo. There has been racism, fighting, and discrimination by the ten per cent of the population who are Serbs. They have terrorised the ethnic Albanians, who call themselves Kosovars, and there have been many human rights complaints. In the end – after the fighting in nearby Bosnia ended in 1996 – the United Nations sent in observers to try and keep the peace or, if they couldn't do that, keep an eye on human rights abuses. These UN observers had an uphill struggle, as gangs of Serbs who may or may not have been police reservists went around terrorising people and carrying out mass murders.

The United States, Britain and some other countries wanted to sort the problem out because:

- it was in Europe, and affecting Europe's economic and political development
- it threatened to become a civil war
- it could involve Greece, a member of the European Union
- there had been trouble with the Serbs in Bosnia, and it looked as though the whole problem was going to start all over again.

They got the United Nations to condemn what was going on in Kosovo, but they got no permission from the UN to go in and sort the problem out. Nevertheless, that was what they wanted to do.

The Serb leader, Slobodan Milosevic, had appeared to support the brutality in Bosnia, and it looked as if he was supporting brutality in Kosovo as well. People compared him to Hitler in the savagery of the oppression his forces were carrying out. He became associated with 'ethnic cleansing', which is a polite way of saying terrorism, racism and mass murder.

America and Britain belong to an organisation called NATO: the North Atlantic Treaty Organisation. This was started at the end of World War II, with the aim of protecting the West against the Communist countries – and in particular the USSR – which is now Russia and various other countries such as Byelorussia and the Ukraine. Now that there are no powerful Communist countries left, NATO is at a bit of a loose end. NATO threatened to start bombing Kosovo and Slobodan Milosevic's army unless a peace deal was worked out in Kosovo which would stick.

France, which didn't like the idea of a war, set up a conference at Rambouillet, near Paris. They got the Serbs, the Kosovars, America and Britain round a table in the hope that they would reach agreement. The west pinned their hopes on a Kosovar leader called Ibrahim Rugova, but he turned out to be too weak to control the Kosovo Liberation Army (KLA) – which wanted to drive the Serbs out of Kosovo by force. The KLA were themselves very weak compared with the Serbs, who have a powerful army. When the Rambouillet talks broke down it was clear that there would be fighting, and that the KLA would not win. All the UN observers then pulled out of Kosovo as quickly as possible, since their safety could no longer be guaranteed.

On 30 March 1999 NATO started bombing the Serb forces in Kosovo. They did not have clear international support for this action. President Clinton of America, and Tony Blair in Britain said that it was a just war. The Serbs responded mainly by killing Kosovars in large numbers. In a week or so there were a million refugees, and an unknown number of Kosovars, and some Serbs, had been killed.

There was no history of a war ever being won simply by bombardment from the air, so western experts started saying that, before long, a NATO army would have to go in on the ground. No one was happy about this. Kosovo is a mountainous, forested region, full of armed gangs, with a long history of war going back to the Middle Ages.

Six billion pounds' worth of bombs was dropped on Kosovo and Serbia in a period of a month or so. Then, to everybody's relief, Milosevic agreed to withdraw his troops from Kosovo. Kosovo is now being run by military people from America, Britain, France and Russia. The NATO forces don't trust the Russians because they are traditionally friends of the Serbs. But the refugees are rushing back, and now it is the few remaining Serbs in Kosovo who are getting terrorised.

ANALYSIS

The effects of this war have – so far – been as follows.

1 Bill Clinton and Tony Blair have been able to claim victory.
2 The United Nations has lost power because they had no clear role to play in the solution of the problem.
3 The Muslim Kosovars are happy.
4 Muslims elsewhere in the world have stopped voicing some of their criticisms of Clinton and Blair, which were very strong after the bombing of Iraq in December 1998.
5 There is a refugee problem, but it hasn't been as bad as people feared.
6 Relations with Russia are not as good as they were before.

Because hardly any NATO pilots or soldiers have been killed, it may encourage NATO to get involved in another war – provided it consists only of bombing, and not fighting on the ground.

2 The Vietnam War

It is easier to see the effects of the Vietnam War than the Kosovo War because it happened between 1959 and 1975. That has given us plenty of time to see how the world has changed because of it.

Like most wars the Vietnam War had deep roots. Vietnam was a French colony but after World War II the northern part of the country became Communist and set up a separate government in Hanoi. (See figure 8.2.)

Fighting developed between the French and the North Vietnamese, and the North Vietnamese won. Then peace was agreed in a conference with North Vietnam, France, Britain, the USA, the Soviet Union, China, Laos and Cambodia all present. This was in 1954 and it was agreed that in 1956 elections would be held so that the whole of Vietnam could be reunified under one government.

Unfortunately this didn't happen, because neither side trusted the other to hold the elections fairly. France pulled out of South Vietnam, and the USA

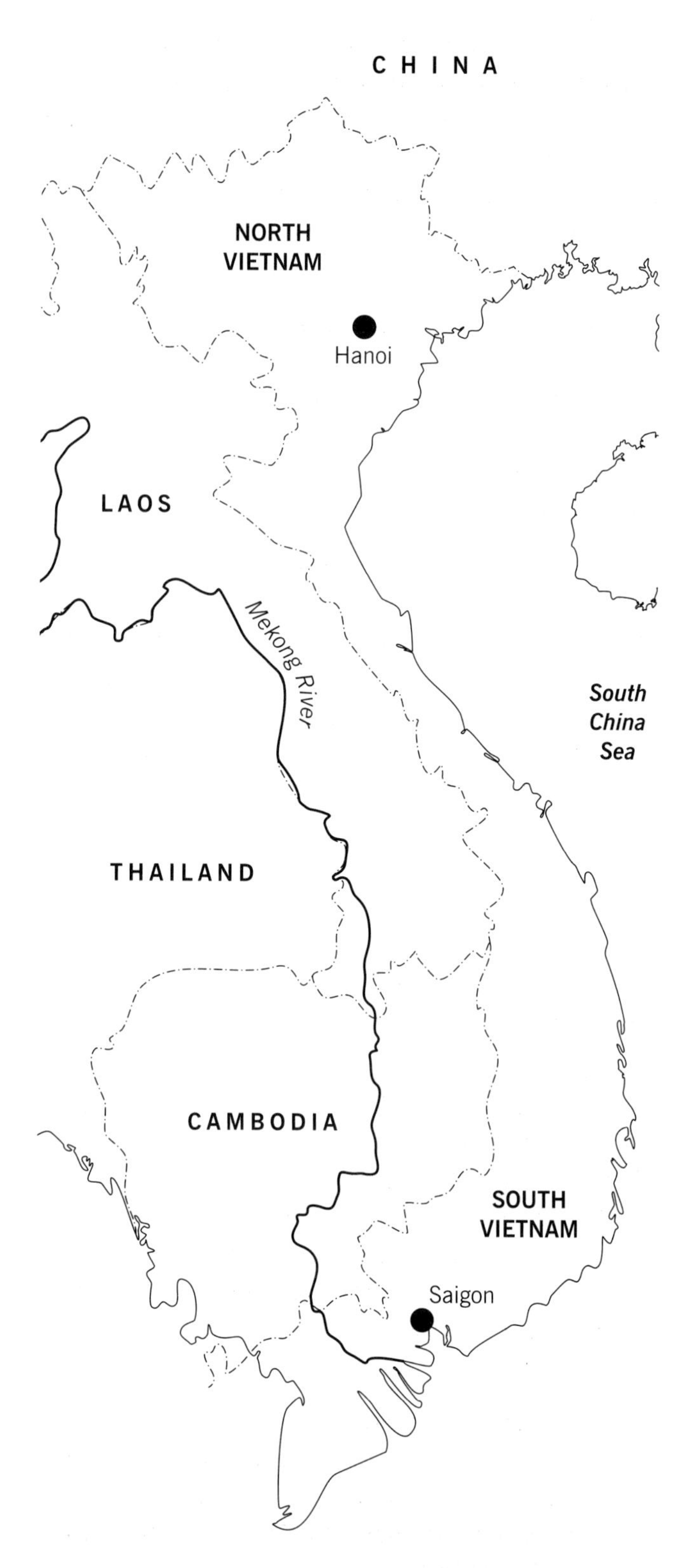

Figure 8.2 *Map of Vietnam in 1954*

moved in to guarantee its security. And from 1954 South Vietnam started receiving aid from the USA.

There were many people who liked Communism in South Vietnam. They travelled to the north and formed themselves into a guerrilla organisation called the Viet Cong. They saw themselves as a liberation movement, but the non-Communist South Vietnamese, and the Americans who were propping up that government, saw them only as terrorists. The truth was probably that they were both a liberation movement and terrorists.

This went on until 1963, when the first of a series of coups happened in South Vietnam. After that South Vietnam had ten different governments in 18 months. By contrast, North Vietnam had a strong Communist leader called Ho Chi Minh, who was also a fine military strategist.

The Americans saw themselves as the leaders in an undeclared world war against Communism. This 'world war' was called the Cold War. Unfortunately, in Vietnam it became hot. But the Americans didn't know what was going to happen, and continued to pour economic aid, then military aid, into South Vietnam. They may have felt that the North Vietnamese would back off when they found the army of the most powerful country in the world camping on their doorstep. But they didn't. By the end of 1965 there were 200,000 American soldiers in South Vietnam. And in 1966 the Americans began bombing North Vietnam.

After this the Americans, and other western countries speaking on America's behalf, offered to stop the bombing provided that the North Vietnamese would take part in peace talks. But the North Vietnamese consistently refused. So by 1967 the war was costing the Americans $25 billion a year, and over 15,000 American soldiers had been killed (and, of course, a far larger number of South Vietnamese).

The American people did not take kindly to their government sending their young men halfway round the world to be killed by guerrillas in the jungle. (Looking back on it, they had more sense than their leaders.) An anti-war movement sprang up, and the 'flower-power' peace and love movement of the late 1960s, when people went round in flared trousers, said, 'Groovy, man' and smoked pot till it came out of their ears, was a direct pacifist revolt by young people in the US against their own government. Even the young Bill Clinton smoked pot but, fortunately for his presidential chances, 'never inhaled'! In 1968 President Johnson announced a stop to the bombing and the next president, Richard Nixon, began withdrawing troops. As American soldiers moved out, the South Vietnamese army grew. And fighting spread to the neighbouring countries of Cambodia (now Kampuchea) and Laos.

In the early 1970s the North Vietnamese set out to invade South Vietnam. The Americans restarted their bombing but continued to move ground troops out. In 1973 Nixon signed a peace agreement and the Americans were out of the Vietnam War. In effect they had been defeated by a country which nobody had previously ever heard of, and with no friends left in the area they had nowhere to go but home. The North Vietnamese then moved south, took Saigon which they re-named Ho Chi Minh City, and Vietnam was unified once again.

To get back to square one: after eight years of fighting, two million Vietnamese and 58,000 Americans had been killed. In addition, countless people were injured, often by bombs and mines which, even now, 25 years on, are still killing and maiming the Vietnamese.

ANALYSIS

The effects of the Vietnam War were as follows.

1 America was weakened, and until the Gulf War of 1991 did not dare to get involved in overseas fighting – because American public opinion was against it.

2 Vietnam was devastated. Because it had beaten the Americans it was isolated from the west and received no help in reconstruction. They had won the war but at the expense of ruining their country and almost pushing it back into the Stone Age.

3 Because the Soviet Union and China were being divided and weakened by the effects of the Cold War, they couldn't, or wouldn't, help the Vietnamese.

4 The futility of the war strengthened the pacifist movement in the west, and it was not until the

1980s, when President Reagan and Mrs Thatcher came along, that the idea of war began to become acceptable again. But even then, it took symbolic forms, such as the 'arms race' and the 'star wars' idea of putting nuclear weapons in space.

5 The Americans stuck to economic methods of gaining more power in the world – by selling their goods and 'lifestyle' through products such as Coca-Cola, music and films. These have turned out to be far more effective in spreading capitalism than war.

In the 1990s the world started noticing that Vietnam still exists. And as Vietnam, like the rest of the world, has become less Communist, tourists have started going there and western businesses are setting up, in a limited way. Life goes on.

Unit outcome 4
Explore how multinational corporations affect individuals, countries and the environment

Assessment criteria

- Describe how multinational corporations use their power to influence governments and people and affect the environment.
- Explain the changing nature of the global and third world economy with its effects on interdependence.
- Analyse the role and effect of information and mass media in a global society.

The influence of multinational corporations

Multinational corporations are very big companies which are based in more than one country. Many of these companies are household names, and you will have heard of them. They include Esso (Standard Oil), Microsoft, News International, Nestlé, Kellogg's, Ciba–Geigy, Lonrho and Ford, but there are hundreds of others.

There is a lot of argument about the effects of multinational corporations.

We all use and enjoy their products and services, but the media and left-wing politicians often attack them. It is worth looking at both sides of the argument.

Benefits of multinational corporations

They have good and bad effects on the countries they operate in. Some good effects include the following.

Jobs
Multinational corporations employ huge numbers of people in the world as a whole, and therefore have a significant effect on employment patterns. When such companies come to Britain they usually set up big factories, sometimes employing thousands of people.

However, because these factories are to some extent automated, they do not actually employ as many people as similar factories would have done in the past. They also tend to employ more trained people. Furthermore, if less efficient companies close down because the multinational company has arrived, it may mean that the overall level of unemployment goes up.

On the other hand, some local firms may spring up round the multinational company making spare parts, selling food to the workers, and so on. In this case the multinational company is creating jobs in the local economy.

Employment with a multinational company is not always secure. Economic problems in other parts of the world may make the multinational company suddenly close down its new factories, or move from one country to another. On the other hand, many of these companies are progressive and well run, and workers can be transferred from one site – and even one country – to another.

Average wages in multinational companies in Britain are about 20 per cent higher than those in home-based companies. For this reason, multinational companies tend to attract more qualified or able employees than other organisations. As time goes on, this difference is likely to increase.

Productivity
Multinational corporations are more productive than other organisations in Britain. This is because they are:
- better managed
- better staffed
- better equipped
- more automated, computerised or robotic than most other firms.

The differences between multinational companies in developing countries, and ordinary companies in developing countries, is even greater than the differences between multinational and ordinary companies in Britain.

Consumer goods
Many multinational corporations produce consumer goods, which people like, and which they feel improve the quality of their life. These goods are perceived as being of better quality than other, similar goods. For instance, a Kellogg's cornflake is seen as better than the average, nameless cornflake – and the same is true of a Heinz baked bean. Multinational corporations also supply the world with life-saving drugs, which might never have been developed if it had been left to the public sector.

Summary

The benefits of multinational corporations
From the viewpoint of most ordinary people, and of most governments, multinational corporations are a good thing. They produce better goods and services, at a lower price. Employment conditions and wages are better. They earn money for the economy, and the money that they pay in taxes benefits everybody. If we had no multinational corporations in this country, we would not be able to afford as many hospitals, schools or police officers.

Drawbacks of multinational corporations

ANALYSIS

The following crticisms are made of multinational corporations.

1 Multinational corporations undermine the independence of the countries they operate in.

This is true. They allow satellite broadcasting and the Internet into our homes. They put pressure on the government to do what they want – for example lowering taxes or interest rates, or changing planning laws.

2 They try to avoid paying taxes.
There is some truth in this. No business likes to pay taxes. If the government tries to get too much tax out of a multinational company it will move elsewhere.

3 They attack trade unions and so undermine the strength of workers.
In the 1970s and early 80s multinational companies were put off coming to Britain because there were more strikes than in almost any other country. They therefore set up 'single-union' agreements, or even tried to ban trade unions altogether, so that they would not be hit by strikes. Nowadays most multinational corporations in Britain will allow a certain amount of 'constructive' union activity. But it is still true that, on the whole, they don't like trade unions. On the other hand, because they offer better working conditions than other firms, the unions may have less reason to make problems for them.

4 Because they are often run by managers who are unfamiliar with the country where factories are based, the workforce is treated in an unfamiliar way.
There may be some truth in this, but there have been very few complaints. Workers in Japanese-owned companies may occasionally have to do exercises or even learn some Japanese, but they do not seem to mind.

5 They bully governments and try to influence policies.
This is almost certainly true. But if they didn't bully the government, the government would probably bully them. Furthermore, as companies, they have a duty to maximise profits for their shareholders (owners). Besides, they have a right to try to influence policies by lawful methods, just as individuals have. On the other hand, if they offer bribes to MPs or civil servants then they are breaking the law.

6 They are corrupt.
There are many cases of corruption by multinational corporations in the developing world, and though corruption is often difficult to prove it probably exists on a massive scale. A typical example in a developing country might be getting a politician to agree to the site of a new factory by paying bribes or setting it up in a place where it will benefit that politician's family and ethnic group.

7 They exploit the developing countries.

If they didn't make a profit by operating in developing countries they wouldn't set up there in the first place. They take land which might be better used for growing food, and have vast mining operations which ruin the environment and people's health. They obtain raw materials on the cheap and sell back the same materials in the form of finished products at a vast profit. The behaviour of Shell Petroleum in Nigeria is a case in point, where they have supposedly bribed the Nigerian government to overlook human rights infringements, and have robbed whole peoples of their land. On the other hand, nearly all of Nigeria's foreign exchange comes from oil, so they can't throw the oil companies out. And the average Nigerian might be even worse off if the oil companies were not there.

8 They take short cuts in health and safety in the developing countries.

This is generally true (although it is also true that the smaller companies in these countries often take even worse short cuts). The most famous case of a multinational failing to take proper health and safety measures was the Bhopal disaster in India in 1984, when Union Carbide's factory leaked and thousands died. In a western country the factory would have been properly inspected and, if anything had gone wrong, the people would have been paid much better compensation.

9 They cause unemployment.
In developing countries multinational corporations tend to bring employment. People become better off, and that creates further jobs. Without the multinational corporations there might be very little industry at all.

10 They damage the environment.
This is true. Mining by multinational corporations has caused serious damage and pollution in some poor countries. Large-scale farming of cash crops such as tea and coffee might also be seen as damage to the environment. But environmental damage by multinational corporations has – usually – been nothing like as bad as the environmental damage caused by state-owned industry in the former Communist countries, such as Russia. In Siberia industries which are not multinational have polluted the environment so badly that life expectancy in the surrounding communities is down to 47 years. (In Britain it is about 78 years.)

11 Their products are immoral, or damaging to health.
There is a lot of argument about both of these points. Morality concerns traditional ideas of right and wrong. Where multinational corporations advertise, they are likely to be promoting western values. Advertisements for Coca-Cola and Pepsi, for example, often carry sexual overtones that older or more traditional people might disapprove of. The belief in Iran that the USA is 'the Great Satan' comes partly from the advertising and lifestyle associated with multinational corporations.

Much fast food – for example McDonald's – is considered bad for health. Recently there has been a long lawsuit on just this point. The so-called 'McLibel' case ran from 1990 to 1997, and involved two British people, Dave Morris and Helen Steel, who wrote pamphlets accusing McDonald's of promoting an unhealthy diet, and 'abusing the environment, their workers and animals'. Many cigarette companies are multinationals, and there seems little doubt that smoking shortens people's lives. Emissions from motor cars are also bad for health. But if there were no motor vehicles at all, more people would die (because they couldn't get health care quickly enough). Standards of hygiene are relatively high in multinational companies.

12 They undermine culture and make people more materialistic.
Probably true, but a matter of opinion. It all depends what you mean by 'culture'. Not all traditional culture is good. Some things associated with culture – e.g. female circumcision, are very harmful, so most people would say that it is a good thing to undermine this type of culture.

13 They aim to achieve monopolies, which is bad for everybody.
It is true that multinational corporations try to achieve monopolies, i.e. being the only company in a country which manufactures a particular product. Once they achieve a monopoly they can, in theory, name their price for the monopolised product. This would not be a desirable situation.

Fortunately most governments will not allow multinational corporations to gain monopolies. In Britain the Competition Commission controls this problem.

14 They are agents of capitalism.
This is obviously true. Capitalist politicians (the political 'right') like and support multinational corporations, while socialists or Marxists (the 'left') oppose them. However, the only alternative to private enterprise is government-run enterprise, which many people believe is inefficient and wasteful.

The global and third world economies

Explain the changing nature of the global and third world economy with its effects on interdependence.

Definitions

- Global – to do with the world as a whole.
- Globalisation – the name given to a number of trends in business, communication and culture which reach or affect the world as a whole. Aspects of globalisation include multinational corporations, satellite communications, the Internet, international politics and trade, the grouping of nations such as the European Union and international culture such as that provided by Hollywood, 'Bollywood', and the international music industry.

Even the fact that we watch Australian soaps, or that Manchester United will be playing in an international superleague, are signs of globalisation. One important effect of globalisation is that the governments of individual countries become less important in influencing our lives.
- The global economy – international trade, seen as a whole: the flow of money and products from one country to another, and the way wealth is distributed in the world. For example, western Europe and North America are wealthy, while the countries round the equator are poor.
- Interdependence – In the old days a country did not always need to import or export goods. People could make their own tools and goods, and grow their own food, and buy and sell from others in the same country. This is no longer the case. For example, in Britain, we only produce one third of the food we need, so if we couldn't import food we would starve. To pay for the food we import, we have to export other things. This means that we need products from other countries, and they need products from us. In other words, each country depends on other countries for survival.

What is causing globalisation?

There are a number of theories on this subject, and no particular agreement between them. Some people think there is one major cause; others think there are a number of causes acting together.

Wallerstein (1991) sees globalisation as caused by the world system of capitalism. In other words multinational corporations are breaking down the boundaries between different countries, and becoming more important in our lives than our own governments. This way well be true, if we think of the influence of companies such as Microsoft, or Rupert Murdoch's News International (including Sky TV) over our daily lives.

Gilpin (1987) thinks globalisation is caused by the 'interconnection' of national governments through treaties and trade associations, such as the European Union, GATT (the General Agreement on Tariffs and Trade), the United Nations, the Group 7 nations – i.e. the seven richest countries – and others such as the Organisation of African Unity (OAU) in different parts of the world. This means that each nation has to consult other nations before changing its laws or its foreign policy.

Roseman (1991) regards globalisation as a technological process, brought about by inventions like satellite communications, computer links and the Internet. Thanks to these technological advances information passes as rapidly round the world as it used to do across the garden fence. So we have created a phenomenon called 'the global village'. Linked to this is the fact that many environmental problems can only be solved if all countries act together. The existence of holes in the ozone layer has meant that countries have had to agree to limit the use of CFCs (chlorofluorocarbons) in fridges, polystyrene and other products. The same is true of the emissions of greenhouse gases such as carbon dioxide. These threaten to cause global warming – which could seriously damage world agricultural production, create deserts, and drown low-lying countries.

Giddens sees globalisation as a complex mixed development caused by (a) world capitalism – i.e. big business, (b) cooperation between countries, partly made possible by increased democracy which makes countries more compatible with each other, (c) militarism – the development of new weapons, mainly sold by rich countries to poor ones and creating different defence needs and (d) 'global networks of information exchange'.

McGrew (1992) looks at globalisation from a Marxist angle. He says that because ordinary people are now more important than ever before, we all take a more international view of the world, and can see that our similarities are more important than our differences.

Third world economies

People may be similar, but countries are very different. The difference shows most in their economies. This means their trade, their wealth, what they produce and what they have to buy, and also so-called invisible earnings such as banking, tourism or money sent home by people working overseas. Look at these facts about two countries.

USA
Area – 3,540,321 square miles
Population – 263,034,000
Life expectancy – Male: 72; Female: 79
GNP – $7,433,517,000,000
GNP per capita – $28,020

Madagascar
Area – 226,658 square miles
Population – 14,763,000 (UN estimate)
Life expectancy – Male: 55; Female: 58
GNP – $3,428,000,000
GNP per capita – $250

GNP means gross national product. This is the sum total of all the business done in or by that country in one year. The GNP per capita is the GNP divided by the number of people. This figure gives a rough idea of the average income in dollars of each individual, whether earning or not, in that country. 'Individual' means every person alive in that country, including babies. If you multiply that figure by four you get the average earnings for the 'average' household. Taking two dollars as £1, a four-person family in Madagascar lives on about £500 a year. A four-person family in the USA scrapes by on roughly £56,000 a year. These are the sad facts of world inequality.

Developing or 'third world' countries like Madagascar make their money by agricultural exports or minerals. But as their populations are growing very fast they eat most of the food they produce. So each year they export less and earn less. At the same time they cannot manufacture all the goods they need (such as cars or radios), so those have to be imported. This means the country loses money each year, and there is little hope of setting up their own industries. They can borrow from rich countries, but then they cannot afford the interest repayments. Tourism is a hope for the future, since there are beautiful beaches and all the sunshine one could wish for. But Madagascar is expensive to get to, and there are beautiful beaches in Tenerife, which is cheap and easy to get to. Furthermore it costs a lot to build the hotels and other facilities that tourists need. So Madagascar is poor and likely to get poorer in the future.

Unlike Madagascar, the USA has a rich and booming economy, which expands every year. It imports raw materials, but it has good natural resources and can export some as well. More to the point, it can use its raw materials, and those it imports, to make manufactured goods, which it can then sell at a profit. It is a centre of culture, banking and tourism, so it has high invisible earnings too. Because of its wealth it can constantly research and invest in its industry to find better and cheaper ways of making things. Its technology is the best in the world. So as well as being very strong the economy is also very varied. Finally, its trade and links with the rest of the world are far more developed than those of Madagascar.

Yet none of this changes the fact that countries, however different they are, are interdependent. Indeed, it may be the fact that they are so different which makes them so interdependent. Rich countries need poor countries to buy their manufactured goods, and to sell them raw materials. Poor countries need rich countries to provide them with the technology and investment which gives them a hope of becoming more developed and wealthy in the future.

The role of mass media in a global society

Analyse the role and effect of information and mass media in a global society.

Books have been written on this subject; all there is room for here is a brief summary. And don't forget that if you blink, this summary will be out of date! Nothing in the world is changing as quickly as the communications industry – you only need to look at the rate at which everybody is buying mobile phones to see that.

Mass media, as you probably know, means television, radio, films, newspapers, books, magazines, music, videos and last, but not least, the Internet. The mass media communicate (a) information and (b) culture.

Information, like money, is there to be used, so it has to be communicated just as money has to be moved about. And nearly everything we know as individuals about the world comes to us through the mass media.

'Knowledge is power', and since information is just knowledge, information is power too. Without information nobody can make money and get rich. And in the great equations of life, ignorance = poverty.

So information is power, and the person who controls the information has the power. This means that the people and organisations who control the flow of information are some of the most powerful people on the planet. Bill Gates, Rupert Murdoch, Greg Dyke, the Director General of the BBC: these people are important because they can influence the way we think – and can therefore influence the way we act as well. The people we elect to power, like Tony Blair, can still only speak to us through the mass media, and their words and faces can be twisted and distorted by those media to affect the way we respond to them. To give a simple example of how this works, Tony Blair once said (before he was prime minister) 'We need to be tough on crime and tough on the causes of crime.' It was a highly effective statement or 'sound-bite'. Suppose newspaper A wanted to show Blair as a tough law and order man. It could have quoted him as saying, 'We need to be tough on crime,' and left out the rest. This might have meant that Blair wanted the police and the courts to clamp down on crime. On the other hand newspaper B might have quoted him as saying, 'We need to be tough ... on the causes of crime.' (The dots show the bits that are missed out.) This would give the impression that Blair was determined to be tough on bad schools, bad housing, bad parenting, poverty or whatever it is that causes crime – but that the police and the courts could be soft for all he cared. So by partial quoting – as in this example – or by other methods the media control the message. And this is why newspapers and television are so important.

In a global society the media have more power because they reach more people. Before television came along a major football match could not have been seen by more than about 100,000 people. Now a major match is seen by 50 million or more.

This is not a bad thing. It means, in sport, that more of us can see the very best the world has to offer. But more importantly it means that ordinary people can know what is going on in the world and try to judge it for themselves. There is less secrecy, and indeed in America they have a Freedom of Information Act. Many years ago this attitude to information got them into trouble when a schoolboy designed an atomic bomb using information gathered from scientific magazines. There was no doubt that the bomb would have worked, if he could have built it! So of course there are people who want to control the media – but there are equally strong forces that want to keep the media free and informative.

Not all of these forces are good. The freedom of the Internet, for example, is misused by paedophiles and other criminals, and can encourage serious crime. But if freedom is a worry, lack of freedom is an even greater one. Without freedom of information there is not much to stop governments themselves from committing crimes. Fortunately the Internet provides this freedom. Governments try to control it but so far they have not had much success. What this means is that human rights abuses, corruption and injustice are more difficult to keep secret than they used to be. So freedom of the media is one of the things that protects people from cruelty and exploitation all over the world – which is why, in the end, more news is good news.

Health and Fitness

Unit outcome 1
Examine main body systems in relation to health and fitness

Assessment criteria

- Describe the main body systems associated with health and fitness.
- Explain the basic diagnosis of factors affecting personal health and fitness.

The first thing that any public service looks for in its applicants is fitness. To put it bluntly, you will not get into any public service unless you are fit. End of story.

Actually, it isn't quite the end of the story, because if you are unfit, you can make yourself fit – provided that you have the motivation and know-how to do it.

This unit will show you how to become fit, and prepare you for the public service fitness tests.

Defining health and fitness

Health is freedom from disease and illness. It means that the different parts of your body are working well, you are not in pain, and you feel good. Health involves the mind as well as the body, and if you have a positive, cheerful attitude towards life, it will tend to improve your health.

Fitness means that you are strong and active, that you can move easily and well, and that you don't get tired easily. A fit person has no difficulty running for a bus, or running up several flights of stairs. Though fitness is not exactly the same thing as health (after all, a fit person can get flu!), it is similar in that your state of mind plays a part. People who are happy with themselves and with life will find it easier to become fit and stay fit.

Medical considerations

If you have any reason to think that you cannot complete this unit because of some disability, medical condition, or for any other reason, consult your tutors and ask their advice. And if you are going to do any strenuous activity of a kind you are not used to, or have never done before, go and see your doctor for a check-up.

Understanding the main body systems

The human body is the most complex living organism, but you should try to understand it a little if you are going to improve your fitness. The body consists of 'systems': for example the nervous system, the blood circulatory system, the muscles, bones and so on. These are outlined below.

The bones

If we didn't have bones we would not be a pretty sight. The only way to move around would be to pour ourselves from one bucket to the next.

We have about 200 bones in our bodies. The number gets less with age because some of them grow together and join up. The bones are tied together with strings called ligaments. Often they meet at joints, so that one bone can move in relation to another. At the joints, for example in the shoulder or the knee, the bones are protected by a kind of gristle called cartilage, and a lubricant called synovial fluid. These stop the bones from scraping against each other and wearing away.

Bones are mainly made of calcium and other minerals, but even so they are alive. That is why they can grow together again after they have been broken. Most bones are hollow, and in the middle there is a jelly called marrow which produces red and white blood cells. The biggest bones are the femurs or thigh-bones, and they are the ones which produce the most blood cells.

FOCUS

Bones have three functions:

- to protect the body and its organs
- as attachments for muscles so that we can move
- to produce blood cells.

Joints

Joints are the places where bones meet. There are four main kinds of joint.

1 **Ball and socket joints** – for example at the shoulder and hip. At these places there can be movement in any direction.
2 **Hinge joints**. Examples are elbows and knees. These joints allow movement in one direction only, like the hinges on a door.
3 **Pivot joints**. These are complex joints which allow movements in several directions. But there is no ball and socket. Examples are the wrists and ankles.
4 **Fused joints**. These are places where the bones are fixed together firmly, rather like the joins in a piece of furniture or a car body. The bones of the skull are fastened together like this.

Muscles

Our bodies are full of muscles. They make up about 40 per cent of our total body weight. They come in three types.

1 Skeletal muscle.
2 Cardiac muscle.
3 Smooth muscle.

Skeletal muscle

Skeletal muscle is what we normally think of as muscle. Our biceps, for example, which we use to bend our arms, are skeletal muscles. They are called skeletal muscles because they are attached to our bones.

These muscles consist of long fibres, which is why they look striated or 'ripped'. They look almost like thick bunches of string tied tightly together. They are the 'meat' of our body.

The fibres are made of very long cells – so long that they often have more than one nucleus. There are nerves in the muscles too, so that we can control them and feel pain. Muscles are attached to bones with tough cords of protein called tendons. When the muscle contracts, or bunches up, the tendon pulls on the bone and moves it, moving our arm, leg or some other part of the body in the process. Muscles always pull – they never push.

There are two kinds of cells in skeletal muscle. The 'fast-twitch' cells give strength but not stamina. The 'slow-twitch' cells give more stamina than strength. So sprinters have more fast-twitch cells and marathon runners have more slow-twitch cells. But everybody has some of both.

Cardiac muscle

Cardiac muscle is heart muscle, and it isn't found anywhere else in the body. It's a very tough muscle, and it does much more work than any other kind of muscle in the body. But it isn't fixed to any bone.

Like skeletal muscle, cardiac muscle contracts – and it does this every time the heart beats. When it contracts it squeezes the bag-like parts of the heart, called auricles and ventricles, and forces the blood to move round the body, keeping us alive.

Smooth muscle

Smooth muscle is the kind of muscle we don't usually talk about, because it doesn't look like muscle, and we are not usually aware of it moving. It forms the walls of the stomach, intestines, blood vessels, and other parts of the body. This muscle squeezes our food through our stomach and intestines, and regulates the blood flow to different parts of the body. When our hands are cold in winter it is because the muscular walls of the blood vessels in our arms have contracted, to conserve body heat. When we are very active, these same muscles relax to let more blood into our muscles, so that they can work harder.

The heart

This beats over 2,500 million times in a lifetime, and pumps 20,000 litres of blood round the body in a day. It is about the size of the fist and weighs 310 grams. As we have just seen it is made of special, extra-tough cardiac muscle. The speed of beating is about 70 times a minute, but in some athletic people it is slower than this. When you are active it can beat 160 times a minute or more. The speed at which our heart beats varies according to our needs, and is governed by the brain through our nerves and through chemicals called hormones.

The circulatory system

There is more than one circulatory system in the body, but the one we are concerned with is for blood. It consists of tubes of varying sizes which carry blood to and from all parts of the body. These are called blood vessels. There are three kinds of blood vessel.

1. Arteries, which carry blood from the heart out to different parts of the body
2. Veins, which carry blood to the heart
3. Capillaries. These are tiny blood vessels which wind their way through all our body, feeding it and cleaning it with blood.

All the arteries except the one which goes to the lungs carry fresh blood full of oxygen. This is bright red, and it flows out from the heart to all parts of the body. The pulses you can feel in your neck or wrist are arteries.

All the veins except the one which comes from the lungs carry used-up blood, full of wastes, back from the body to the heart. The blood vessels which bulge on your hands and feet in warm weather are veins.

If you put all a person's blood vessels end to end they would be 100,000 miles long, more than four times round the world.

Blood goes round the body under pressure, otherwise it wouldn't get anywhere. This pressure is measured in millimetres of mercury (mm/Hg). It is higher in the arteries than the veins, and it is higher at the beat of the heart (systole) than in the gap (diastole) in between. Because of this difference between systolic and diastolic blood pressure, the pressure is normally given as two figures, with the systolic over the diastolic, like a fraction. Blood pressure is higher when you are awake than when you are asleep, and it is higher when you're exercising than when you're resting. The normal blood pressure for a youngish person is less than 130/85. Blood pressure rises with age, but if it rises too much it becomes a health risk, bringing a danger of heart attacks and strokes. Regular exercise and the right kind of food, even when you are young, are the natural and best way of keeping blood pressure down in later life.

The blood

There are five litres of blood in an average body. Its function is to supply oxygen, nutrients and essential chemicals to the body, and at the same time remove waste material, including carbon dioxide and urea (one of the chemicals in urine). The liquid part of the blood is called plasma. It contains red blood cells, which are shaped like tiny round cushions, in vast numbers. These carry oxygen. It also contains white blood cells, which can move about like amoebae. These hunt down bacteria and viruses and gobble them up. Then there are platelets, tiny flat cells whose job is to make the blood clot in the event of a wound. Blood also carries a number of strange chemicals called hormones which control growth, emotions and muscle power, among other things.

You will have heard of blood groups. There are four of these: A, B, AB and O and two rhesus factors. Types A and B are incompatible, but AB and O are generally compatible with the other types. If you have a blood transfusion it is essential that you receive the right kind of blood, otherwise the body's immune system goes on the attack, and you are likely to die. Rhesus factors are chemicals which can, sometimes, threaten the lives of newborn babies.

The lungs

These are the main part of the respiratory system, which starts at the larynx, or voicebox, in your neck, goes down the trachea, or windpipe, then splits into two tubes called bronchi. Each tube goes down to a lung, and branches into many tubes called bronchioles. Attached to the ends of these are thousands of tiny sacs called alveoli where the main work of the lung is done. In the lining of the alveoli are countless tiny capillaries. These take oxygen in from the lung, and at the same time give out carbon dioxide. In this way the blood is purified of carbon dioxide, a waste product, and filled with oxygen, which the body needs.

The endocrine system

The endocrine system consists of a number of glands. Hidden in the brain is the pituitary gland, which produces growth hormone and tends to control the other glands. Other hormones are produced by the thyroid and thymus in the throat, the adrenal glands near the kidneys, which produce adrenaline, and the sexual glands, ovaries and testes. The hormones produced by these glands help to control sleep, movement, emotions, blood sugar levels and energy.

The brain

The brain is the control centre of the body. To function properly it needs a great deal of blood, and the biggest artery in the body, the aorta, goes straight from the heart to the brain. In an average adult the brain weighs about 1200 grams.

The brain is very complicated. It is divided into three main parts.

1 The outer part, which is about 85 per cent of the total weight, is the **cerebrum**. This includes the cortex which is a layer of folded cells about four millimetres thick, grey outside and white on the inside. Most of our conscious thinking goes on inside the cortex.

The cerebrum is split into a left half and a right half, but the two halves are joined by a mass of nerve fibres called the corpus callosum. The left half of the cerebrum controls the right side of the body; the right half controls the left side.

2 The lower part of the brain is the **cerebellum**. This has more similarities to the brains of other animals than the cerebrum, and controls movement.

3 At the bottom of the cerebellum, and the top of the spine, is the **brain stem**, which controls involuntary, automatic functions, such as our heart rate, body temperature and digestive juices.

The nervous system

The nervous system carries communications between the brain and the body. It is a complex network that runs throughout the whole body. The biggest nerve runs up a specially-protected tube in the middle of the spine. Nerves can carry messages from the body to the brain, and from the brain to the body. The messages are partly electrical and partly chemical, so they are called 'electrochemical' and travel at about 110 metres per second.

Nerves, like the brain, are made out of special cells called neurones.

There are really two nervous systems.

1. **The peripheral**, which gives us sensations and information which we are aware of, and controls conscious actions, such as speaking or running.
2. **The autonomic**, which controls unconscious or semi-conscious functions such as breathing, heartbeat and digestion.

The digestive system

It is not quite true to say, 'You are what you eat', because the digestive system changes all the food we eat into different chemicals which the body can absorb and use.

The digestive system starts at the mouth, goes down the gullet or oesophagus, through the stomach, into the small and large intestines and then out at the anus. At nearly every stage food is processed and made into a form that the body can dissolve and absorb. For example, the saliva in the mouth deals with starches, the acids in the stomach work on proteins and fats, the small intestine takes out other nutrients, and the large intestine absorbs water and makes what is left into faeces. The table below shows how the main foods change.

Digestion of main foods

Before digestion	After digestion
Carbohydrates (bread, potatoes, rice, etc.).	Various kinds of sugar, leading to glucose.
Protein (meat, fish, cheese, beans, etc.).	Amino acids.
Fats.	Fatty acids and glycerol.

There are two types of process used in digestion:

1. **Mechanical.** This includes chewing, in the mouth, and churning, in the stomach and intestines.
2. **Chemical.** This is where the food we eat is broken down by chemicals called enzymes so that the body can absorb and use it.

The immune system

It is only since the appearance of AIDS that we have begun to understand the immune system, and we still don't understand it very well.

The immune system has two parts.

1. **Non-specific.** This includes the skin, mucous membranes (e.g. in the mouth and nose), cilia (tiny hairs in the windpipe that get rid of dust), acid in the stomach (good for killing bacteria), white blood cells (to hunt down bacteria and viruses) and interferons (chemicals which act as virus-detectors).
2. **Specific.** This identifies invading substances, such as poisons, and responds to them specifically. The body produces over 300 different chemicals to fight toxic substances.

It also produces vast numbers of various types of cells, similar to white blood cells, which go round attacking invading viruses. The type of cell produced depends on the attacking virus or bacteria. The inflammation or temperature we suffer when injured or ill helps to make these immune system cells more active.

Personal health and fitness

Explain the basic diagnosis of factors affecting personal health and fitness.

Not everybody is equally healthy or fit. Here are some reasons for this.

Body type

People come in different shapes and sizes. Some aspects of body shape are – up to a point – controllable: for example the amount of muscle or fat we build up (or take away) from our bodies. Other aspects of our bodies, such as our height or our general build, are determined before birth by the genes we inherit from our parents.

There are three main body types (see figure 9.1).

1. Ectomorphs.
2. Mesomorphs.
3. Endomorphs.

Our body type has some effect on our health and fitness. The following points are intended to be general – do not take them personally!

Ectomorphs are thin people with light bones. They tend to have less muscle or fat than the other two groups. Traditionally they do well in 'stamina' sports such as marathon-running. Their muscles have more 'slow-twitch' cells in them and fewer 'fast-twitch' muscle fibres.

Mesomorphs have an average or muscular build. Many good athletes, especially sprinters or swimmers, and most footballers, come into this category. They have a medium or high proportion of fast-twitch muscle fibres and, if they are fit, are quick and agile in their movements.

Endomorphs are heavily built. They have above average strength, especially for events like weight-lifting or shot-putting. They are likely to have a high

Figure 9.1 *Typical examples of an ectomorph (left), a mesomorph (centre) and an endomorph (right)*

proportion of fast-twitch muscle fibres, and heavy bones. But they are also likely to put on fat if they do not exercise enough in relation to the number of calories they eat.

Gender

Both men and women can, and should, be healthy and fit. But the proportion of muscle in most men's bodies is higher than that in most women's bodies. Furthermore, as men are on average bigger than women, the total amount of muscle in their bodies is greater. This is why men, on average, are stronger than women – there is no difference in the strength of their muscle tissue, only in the amount.

As far as health, in the sense of freedom from disease, is concerned, women do slightly better than men. They are less likely to suffer from heart disease and live, on average, about seven years longer than men.

'S factors'

These are speed, strength, stamina, skill, suppleness and sleep. All are related to, or have an effect on, people's personal health and fitness.

Speed

Speed depends on reflexes, which are related to the length of nerves and reactions in the brain or in various other clusters of nerve cells called ganglia. This is why flyweight boxers move and punch faster than heavyweights. In addition, heavier people must overcome more inertia when they start moving, which means they are slower off the mark when running, punching or throwing. Good muscle tone and flexibility (both of which come from fitness training) improve speed.

Strength

Strength is related to the size of muscles, the proportion of fast-twitch cells, and the length of bones. If muscles are big and bones relatively short, the leverage on the bone enables heavier weights to be lifted – which means greater strength. This is why people who are muscular in relation to their height are strongest.

Stamina

Stamina is to some extent a mental quality, like determination. People who are strongly motivated have greater stamina: they don't give up. Runners have more stamina if they are light in proportion to the amount of muscle they have, especially in their legs. They also have more stamina if they have a high proportion of slow-twitch muscle cells. Long distance runners do not have much muscle (or extra weight of any sort) on the upper part of their bodies; their muscles are concentrated in their buttocks, thighs and calves. Interestingly, long-distance swimmers are heavily built, and their diet and training help them to develop a layer of fat under their skin to help them float better and withstand the cold.

Skill

Skill improves with motivation and practice, but the ability to be skilful may be an inherited genetic quality. Practice is more effective in very young people, which is why the best skaters, skiers and tennis players start very young. Motivation comes with being more skilled than your peers at a young age, and there is still the possibility of physical brain development in very young children, which would reflect any skills they developed at that age.

Suppleness

Suppleness comes with flexibility exercises, but there are again genetic factors here, which make some people naturally more supple than others. Interestingly, some exercises designed to increase strength can reduce suppleness. Suppleness, like other qualities, is best developed young, but the right exercises, including activities such as yoga, can increase it at any age. Extreme stiffness or pains in the joints may be due to medical conditions, such as rheumatism: even young people may suffer from this and ought to see a doctor if they are worried about it.

Sleep

Just as lack of sleep can (temporarily) reduce intelligence, so it can reduce fitness. Most people need around eight hours of sleep a night. If you are the kind of person who cannot sleep, resting and keeping still is much better for you than never going to bed at all. It is bad for your health to take sleeping tablets on a regular basis. Sleep is necessary for health and fitness, and if you think you have a serious sleep problem, again, you should see your doctor.

Other factors

Nutrition

Scarcely a week passes without some 'discovery' being made about what we should or should not eat. People react to these discoveries in different ways. Some people become obsessed with a healthy diet, and keep giving things up because they think they are dangerous or toxic. Other people think that only wimps worry about their diet, and that a steady intake of hamburgers and beer never did anybody any harm.

Boringly, the truth is probably somewhere in between. We need protein to grow fit and strong, fat for energy and to help us digest the protein, carbohydrates for energy, vitamins for good health, and roughage (fibre) to help us digest everything else. We also need tiny quantities of a wide range of minerals, most of which are in our diet anyway, so we don't have to worry about them.

We should therefore aim at a varied and balanced diet. British people tend to eat too much sugar and animal fats, such as butter, and the fats in fried food. Many of these fats are saturated, and help to clog the arteries with cholesterol, causing heart attacks in later life. British people also eat too few vegetables and fruit, which is perhaps why they don't live as long as the French. Slimming diets as such are generally not a good thing, especially for young people: they reduce strength and weaken the immune system, and usually the weight loss is not permanent. To control your health, or weight, using nutrition, it is far more effective to alter the balance of what you eat.

If you think you have an eating problem, you should see a doctor.

Drugs

Drugs do nothing for your health and fitness unless they are prescribed by a doctor in the treatment of illness. Caffeine – if you have too much – can cause heartbeat irregularities. Alcohol slows you down and is highly calorific, which is why it produces beer bellies. Nicotine limits the ability of the smooth muscle in your blood vessels to adapt to changing blood needs, so in the long run it reduces the amount of blood getting to your muscles. Cigarettes also clog your lungs with tar, lowering their efficiency, and increasing the risk of bronchitis. Cannabis is stored in fat cells, so if you exercise and burn up fat, it will be detectable, should you have a drug test, months after you originally smoked that spliff. This is bad news for people who want to join the army, where they have compulsory, random drug tests. Harder drugs than cannabis are physically harmful, and have damaging psychological effects – as described by the footballer, Paul Merson.

Then there are 'performance-enhancing' drugs, such as anabolic steroids and painkillers. Steroids will (illegally) build muscle bulk, but as they do so they put other parts of your body at risk. Your joints, liver and heart are all likely to be damaged if you take steroids. Painkillers rob your body of a natural defence mechanism – pain – and can lead to permanent muscle damage. Like recreational drugs, 'performance-enhancing' drugs should be avoided by anyone who wants to join the public services.

Hygiene

Bad hygiene can lead to bad health. Food poisoning is the main risk. The food you eat should be clean and properly cooked, and you should wash your hands before you eat it. Shaking hands, or touching other people and then touching your eyes or nose, is one of the main ways in which colds or other respiratory illnesses are spread. Bad oral hygiene can lead to bad breath, and missing teeth in later life. Unsafe sex, too, may be seen as a form of bad hygiene, which can have serious consequences for your health and the health of other people.

THINK ABOUT IT ...

It is said that young people are less fit now than ever before.

What realistic advice could you give:

- children and young people themselves
- their parents
- schools and colleges

which would help to make young people fitter?

Unit outcome 2
Examine the diagnosis and treatment of sporting injuries

Assessment criteria

- Explain the basic diagnosis of at least four common sporting injuries.
- Investigate the basic treatment of at least four sporting injuries.

The classification of sports injuries

Most of the time, sport is good for you. But there is a slightly greater risk of injury playing a sport than if you lie on a sofa playing with the TV remote control. Once in a blue moon, people even die during sports. But think how many more die on a sofa ...

Still, you might get a sporting injury. And for that reason you ought to know how to avoid them if you can, and how to treat them if you can't. What's more, one of your team mates could get injured – and in that case, you might be the one who has to give, or get, help. So that's another reason why you should know something about sporting injuries.

THINK ABOUT IT ...

Prevention is better than cure.

What are the main dangers of your favourite sport or fitness activity? What can be done to minimise those dangers?

For practical purposes, sports injuries are classified according to which part of the body is injured. It's as simple as that. Here are four common injuries together with their causes, diagnosis and treatment.

Broken bones

These are often called fractures. According to the shape of the break(s) (see figure 9.2) they are:

- transverse
- oblique
- spiral
- compound.

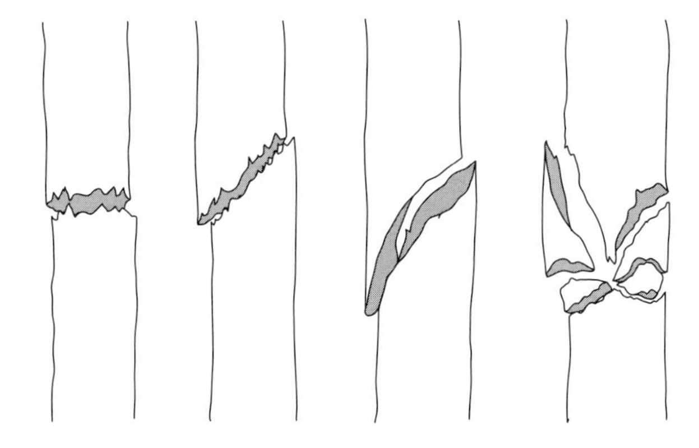

Figure 9.2 *Types of fracture. From left, transverse fracture, oblique fracture, spiral fracture and compound fracture*

Causes

All fractures are caused by physical shock ('trauma'), the result of blows, kicks, falls and the like. They are most common in the arms or the legs, depending on the sport.

Most fractures are the result of accidents, but not all. Carelessness, aggression and a reckless disregard for safety can cause these and other injuries, especially in contact sports. That's why 'fouls' are outlawed in football: because they're dangerous.

Diagnosis

The symptoms of fractures are:

- swelling and bruising
- pain, especially when moving
- displacement of the bone, so that the affected limb or area is out of shape.

Treatment

By the first-aider

1. Cover any surface wound with a clean bandage or cloth.
2. Put splints on the limb so it cannot bend or move (see below).
3. Raise the injured limb.
4. Get the sufferer to hospital for an X-ray and treatment.

By the doctor

1. Reduce pain.
2. Correct any displacement of the bone.
3. Stop any bleeding.
4. Ensure good blood supply to the affected area.
5. Immobilise the limb (usually with a plaster cast).
6. Arrange for exercises which will not damage the fracture, so that the sufferer does not lose too much muscle tone.

By the patient

For a sportsperson, injuries are not merely dangerous and painful; they are likely to cause a general loss of fitness.

Therefore the patient must:

1. exercise all moveable parts of the body regularly, as soon as possible after the limb has been immobilised
2. practise isometric exercise of the muscles inside the cast. This means flexing them and 'pushing' them against each other.

Fractures can be in plaster from anything between one month (for the wrist) to over three months (for the lower leg).

Full recovery of the affected area takes at least as long again as it was in plaster. If a broken leg is in plaster for three months, then full recovery will take at least six months.

Torn ligaments

Ligaments are strips of tough, stringy protein. They are found in joints such as the knee and elbow, and fasten one bone firmly to another. Though they are very strong, they can be torn by violent shocks, blows and falls, or by violent twisting movements.

There are two kinds of torn ligament.

1. **Partial.** Some fibres of a ligament may be torn, but not the whole ligament, or part of a ligament may have been torn off the bone at the point of attachment. With this kind of injury the ligament is not broken, so the joint remains stable (it doesn't wobble or collapse). But obviously the joint is weakened.
2. **Complete.** This means that one or more of the ligaments is completely torn, or has been pulled off the bone at the point of attachment. The joint is therefore unstable, and seriously weakened.

The joints where these injuries usually take place are the ankle, knee, elbow, wrist and shoulder. Injury to ligaments can cause other injuries, such as damage to the cartilages which cushion the bones from each other, and bleeding into the joint space between the bones.

Diagnosis

The symptoms of a torn ligament are:

- bruising, swelling and tenderness round the joint
- blood filling the joint
- pain when the joint is moved
- instability (weakness or wobbliness) of the joint.

Treatment

By the first-aider (see figure 9.3)

1. Test the joint for instability.
2. Cool the joint, preferably with an ice pack over an elastic bandage.
3. Support the joint with elastic bandaging.
4. Raise and prop the limb at an angle of 45 degrees.

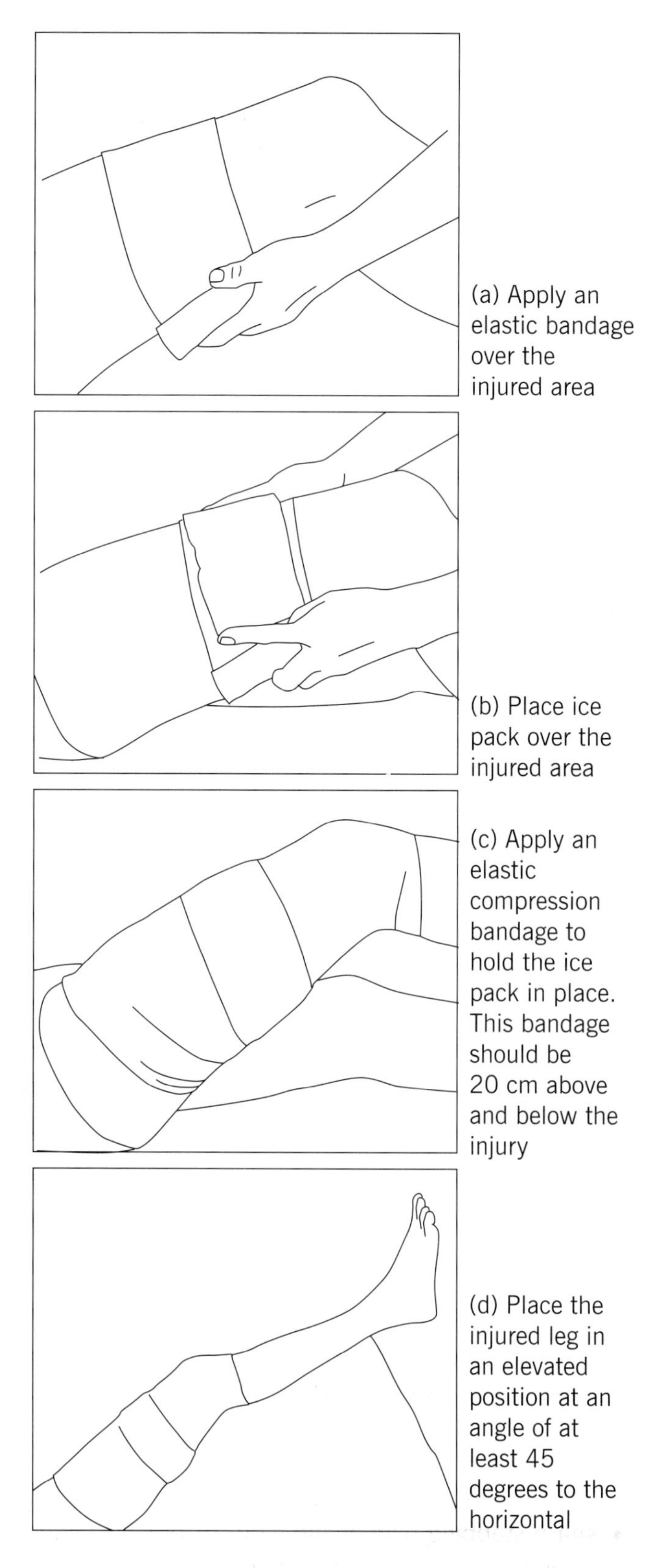

Figure 9.3

By the doctor

1. Carry out a full stability test on the joint. This may involve arthroscopy, a kind of exploratory

operation, carried out under anaesthetic, to see exactly what the damage is.
2 If the joint is stable, strap, tape or put it in a plaster cast, but at the same time start suitable exercises.
3 If the joint is not stable, put it in a cast or carry out an operation to repair the damage.

By the patient
Active muscular exercise, under the supervision of experts. But this must not put the healing of the ligament at risk. Ligaments usually take over six weeks to heal.

Muscle injuries

Thirty per cent of all football injuries are muscle injuries. They are caused by physical shock, such as blows and kicks, or by overloading. Muscle injuries are usually either ruptures (tears), or haematomas (internal bleeding).

The rate of healing of a muscle injury is affected by the amount of internal bleeding. Where there is little bleeding, the muscle can heal in about three weeks. But it takes longer if there has been bleeding, because the blood separates the muscle fibres and slows down the process of their growing together again.

Prevention is better than cure, and there are ways of reducing the danger of muscle injuries. These are:
- making sure that you have proper training and warm-ups
- allowing previous injuries to heal properly
- remembering that a very tired muscle is more likely to tear
- taking care under cold conditions, when muscles tear more easily
- avoiding risks where possible (e.g. hard tackles).

Diagnosis
The symptoms of torn muscles include:
- sharp stabbing pain at the moment of injury and when the muscle is moved afterwards
- little pain when the muscle is relaxed
- inability to contract the muscle properly
- lumps on the muscle which you can feel with your fingers
- tenderness and swelling
- bruising under the surface of the skin, and possible spasms (tightening) of the muscle.

Treatment
Torn muscles are treated first by rest, then by phased exercise during the period of recovery, under the supervision of a doctor, physiotherapist or trainer.

If there has been internal bleeding, which is likely, the instructions shown below, under 'Treatment for haematoma', should be followed.

Muscle injuries heal better than most, but there is a danger that the muscle will be left weaker than before. This is because, in a serious tear, some of the muscle tissue is replaced by scar tissue which is not made of muscle cells. To overcome this problem, serious muscle injuries should be followed by a long period of progressive strengthening or rehabilitation exercises.

Treatment for haematoma
Haematoma is internal bleeding. If the bleeding is inside the muscle, pressure can build up and cause permanent muscle damage. If the bleeding spreads outside the muscle, more bleeding may occur but the effects are less serious provided there is immediate treatment as follows.

By the first-aider
1 Make the injured person rest.
2 Cool the area where the internal bleeding is taking place.
3 Bandage the injured part.
4 Raise the limb.
5 Do not use massage.

By the doctor
1 Admit to hospital if the injury is severe, in case there is too much bleeding and swelling.
2 Keep the bleeding under observation to confirm either that it is inside or outside the muscle. It is important to know this, because bleeding inside the muscle can permanently damage it. If the swelling has not gone down, the bleeding is probably inside the muscle (intramuscular).

3 Ensure that if the bleeding is inside the muscle, the patient does not exercise until there is no danger of further bleeding.
4 Provided it is safe, start a programme of training, gentle at first, to get the muscle back to full strength.
5 Arrange for an operation if there is a blood build-up inside the muscle which could lead to permanent damage.

By the patient
1 If the haematoma is in the leg, use crutches when moving about to keep pressure off it.
2 Carry out exercises. The injury is completely healed when there is no pain whatsoever.

Head injuries

These, together with neck injuries, are potentially the most serious of all sporting injuries. They usually happen in contact sports, such as rugby and football, and to riders, skiers and boxers. Head injuries can be life-threatening even when there is no unconsciousness.

It is not always clear whether someone has been unconscious, but if they seem confused, it is likely.

FOCUS

The following are the main courses of action in the event of a head injury.

- Head injury without unconsciousness. There may be complaints of headache, sickness, or dizziness, or the victim may feel upset. The sufferer must be kept under observation, and must see a doctor.
- Head injury and unconscious for less than five minutes. Sufferer must go straight to a doctor or hospital and be kept under observation for 24 hours.
- Head injury and unconsciousness for more than five minutes. Must go **at once** to hospital.

Essentially it's a case of 'better safe than sorry', and in all cases of head injury the sufferer should be taken at once to a doctor or hospital, **if there is the slightest concern**.

Immediate first-aid

This is what you should do as immediate first-aid if person is unconscious.

1 Do mouth-to-mouth resuscitation if the person is not breathing (see figure 9.4).
2 Place the person in the recovery position (see figure 9.5).

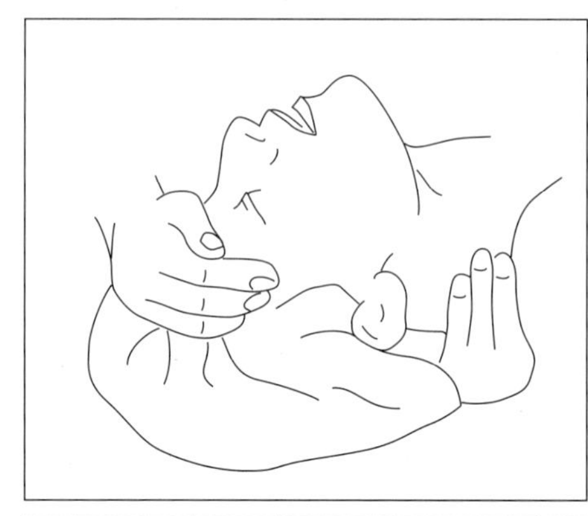

(a) Maximum backward tilt of the injured person's head supporting the neck

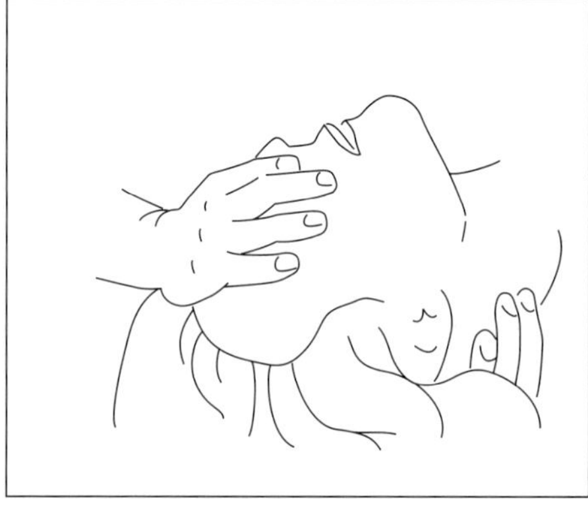

(b) Pinch the nostrils

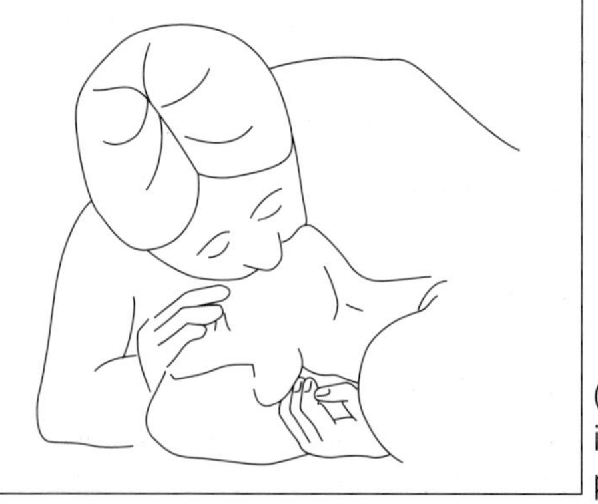

(c) Blow air into the person's mouth

Figure 9.4 *Mouth-to-mouth resuscitation*

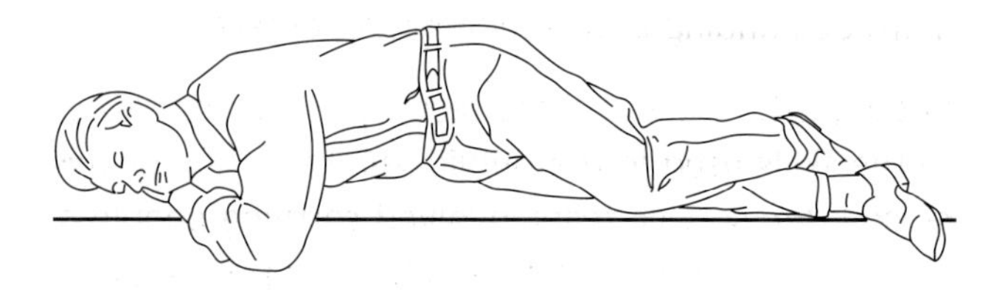

Figure 9.5 *The recovery position*

Internal bleeding

The reason why even apparently minor head injuries should be taken seriously is the danger of internal bleeding. When this happens the person may lose consciousness some time after the original blow. This is because bleeding from a burst blood vessel is pushing the brain out of shape. If this is not treated at once it will cause permanent brain damage or even death.

In a hospital a brain scan can show at once if there is internal bleeding. If there is, the victim will probably need an emergency operation.

Warning

The injuries and treatments outlined above are only a very basic list. You should do as much as you can to develop a more detailed knowledge of first-aid – for example by taking one of the first-aid certificates. And you should never be afraid to call, or visit, a doctor if you think there is any cause for alarm.

THINK ABOUT IT ...

Study newspaper, magazine and other reports of your favourite sport.

Make a list of the most common injuries and how they are caused. Then compare your list with that of a friend who has chosen a different sport. What differences can you discover in the injury risks of different sports?

Unit outcome 3
Demonstrate a range of fitness testing assessments

Assessment criteria

- Explain at least six fitness assessments which are used in public service physical entry tests.
- Demonstrate the correct technique for undertaking at least six fitness assessments which are used in public service entry tests.

Testing fitness

With the exception of HM Customs and Excise, and the prison service, all the public services require applicants to take fitness tests. These fitness tests differ according to the service, and some of them, for example the tests for the Royal Marines, are more demanding and complex than others.

In the past, many of these tests were closely related to the skills used in the public service itself. For this reason, fire service tests involved carrying people a certain distance in a certain time, or unrolling and rolling hoses at speed. However, tests of this sort are now tending to go out of favour because of the risk of injury to people who are not used to doing them. In addition, they test skill as much as fitness, and depend on factors which are hard to control, such as the conditions of hoses and the weights of people being carried. They are therefore also less accurate than tests carried out under controlled conditions in a gym.

Nevertheless, when applying for a given public service you may still come across some of the old style of tests. The best way to prepare for these is to develop your overall fitness, and, if you find out what the tests are, practise them. But take care while you do it!

THINK ABOUT IT ...

Even for a service such as the police, fitness tests can vary or change.

To find out about them, you can (a) ask your local police recruiting department, (b) question someone who has recently joined the police, (c) ask a college tutor, (d) surf the Internet.

The Focus box on the opposite page lists the tests as explained by the South Yorkshire Police. All police forces in England and Wales use the same test.

What are the public services looking for?

The police are looking for a good overall level of strength and fitness. They are not interested in people who have stamina but very little strength, or strength but very little stamina. They want a good all-rounder with more than average strength and stamina. As the South Yorkshire Police put it: 'You don't have to be super fit. If you are in good health and take regular exercise there's a good chance that you are almost at the standard we are looking for.'

There are no exact 'passmarks' for the physical test.

Undertaking fitness assessments

Demonstrate the correct technique for undertaking at least six fitness assessments which are used in public service entry tests.

1 Body fat measurement

This is a physical test, but not one you do yourself. And it doesn't involve any effort on your part.

The theory behind the test is that a pair of callipers is used to measure the thickness of a fold of fat (and skin) lifted between finger and thumb from the three parts of the body mentioned in the Focus box. The thickness measured this way is twice the thickness of the subcutaneous ('surface layer') fat. Using the reading on the callipers, it is possible to make a calculation, with the help of tables, of the percentage of the body weight which is fat.

The percentage of your body weight which is made up of fat varies very much from person to person. But for entry into the public services you should aim at a body fat percentage which is average or below – but without being too skinny (see the table below). Public service is not a catwalk.

Body fat percentages

Percentage	Description
Under 19	underweight
19–25	about normal
26–29	increased health risk
30–40	obese
40+	extremely obese

2 Grip strength

Grip strength is measured using an instrument called a dynamometer. By squeezing a handle you move a needle on a dial. The dynamometer can be adjusted to fit your hand size and measures up to 100 kilograms at 1 kilogram intervals. As stated on

FOCUS

The seven elements of the test

Your performance in each element will show your fitness level. You must perform to your maximum ability at each element. Your age will be taken into account when determining your performance. The test will be in the following order.

Body fat measurement
This is done by using callipers to take readings in four places on your body. These are front and rear of your left upper arm, below the left shoulder blade and on the left side of your waist. From these readings your percentage body fat can be calculated.

Grip strength
Both hands will be measured. To do this hold the meter out to your side. Start squeezing progressively as you drop your arm down to your side. Squeeze hard and breathe out as you drop your arm.

Sit-ups
As many as possible in a minute. Lie on the floor with your feet under a bar. Cross your arms over the chest, hands touching shoulders. Sit up to 90 degrees and return to start position. You can rest in this position, but the clock keeps going. If you remove your hands from your shoulders this would not be considered a proper exercise and would not count. This is also the case should you fail to sit up to 90 degrees or return to the start position.

Press-ups (men)
As many as possible in a minute. Begin with arms and body straight, bend at the elbows and lower the body towards the floor, touching your chest against a fist placed on the floor. Elbows must be at 90 degrees. Then return to starting position. You may rest but only in the extended arm position and should any part of the body touch the floor this would stop the count at that point disregarding how much time had elapsed.

Press-ups (women)
You will perform these as do men; however you will use a bar fixed to the wall 80 centimetres above the floor.

Start with the arms and body straight. Bend the elbows and lower your body until your chest is about 10 centimetres from it, with elbows at 90 degrees. Return to the start position but should you step forward to rest the count would stop at that point.

Flexibility
Measured by sitting on the floor, legs straight and feet against a box. Keeping legs straight reach forward as far as you can. Breathe out as you go and place your hands on top of the box. A measurement will be recorded at your furthest extent. Your best of two tries will be recorded.

Standing long jump
Begin with toes behind a take off bar. Jump as far forward as you can landing with feet together. The jump will be measured from the take off bar to the heel of the back foot. If you fall or step back this would affect the result. Your best of two efforts will be recorded.

Shuttle run
You must run between two lines, 20 metres apart at a steadily increasing pace. The pace is set by means of a taped signal. The aim is to follow the pace for as long as possible.

The test ends when you are unable to keep to the pace and your time will be recorded at that point.

This completes the test.

Should you feel your result in any one element is poor do not worry – the result is based on the test as a whole (all seven elements). You may make up what you have lost in any of the other events. Likewise if you do well in one event, don't take things for granted as the other results are taken into account. All your performances will be processed and a result obtained. Successful applicants would then continue to the next stage of the recruit selection procedure. Start to prepare now. Do some exercise and work to improve flexibility, especially in shoulders, legs and back.

Source: South Yorkshire Police

page 225, you hold it out to one side of you, then bring it down, breathing out and squeezing at the same time.

3 Sit-ups

These are sometimes called abdominal curls, because they are a good way of strengthening your abdominal muscles and developing a 'six-pack'. This exercise is easier for people of below average height who have a muscular build. (See figure 9.6.)

Figure 9.6 *Sit-ups*

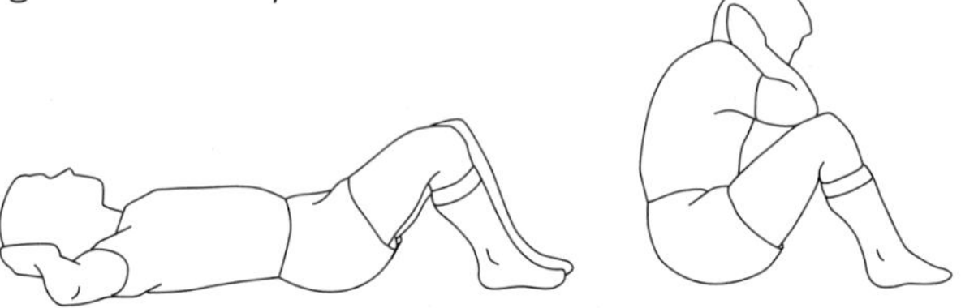

Figure 9.7 *Men's press-ups*

4 Press-ups

This is the only one of the fitness test exercises which is different for men (figure 9.7) and women (figure 9.8).

In order to assess your performance in press-ups compared with the population as a whole, you may be interested in the table below, which shows normal scores for different age groups, for both men and women.

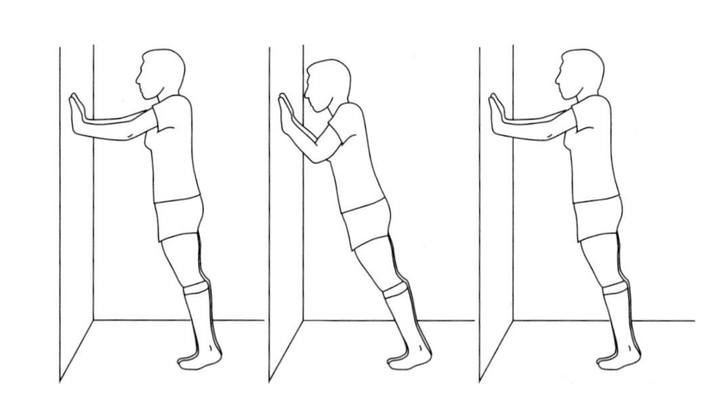

Figure 9.8 *Women's press-ups*

Press-ups: normal scores for men and women, by age group

Classification	Age 20–29 (over 1 minute)	Age 30–39 (over 1 minute)	Age 40–49 (over 1 minute)
Men			
excellent	48+	40+	31+
very good	38–47	31–39	25–30
good	30–37	25–30	19–24
medium	23–29	18–24	12–18
poor	22–	17–	11–
Women			
excellent	37+	32+	25+
very good	31–36	25–31	19–24
good	24–30	20–24	14–18
medium	18–23	12–19	7–13
poor	17–	11–	6–

Notes on press-up scores

1 The women's scores are for 'kneeling' or 'modified' press-ups. The reason for the modification is that press-ups favour the male body type, and to avoid 'indirect' discrimination the test needs to be modified for women.

2 Scores for the 16–20 age group will be slightly below the scores for the first column, since many people below the age of 20 have still not reached their full muscular development.

5 Flexibility

This is like the old exercise of touching your toes, only you sit down on the floor to do it.

6 Standing long jump

The instructions for this are straightforward. People whose body weight is low for their height usually perform well in this.

7 Shuttle run (bleep test)

This tests speed, strength, endurance and agility. Because you have to keep turning and running back, it tests the same abilities that you might use in football and rugby, where sudden changes of direction are needed.

FOCUS

Two students achieved the following in a series of fitness tests. Can you do better?

Male aged 17:

Bleep test	13.1 VO_2 max
Dynamometer (grip strength) – best of two attempts:	
right hand	56
left hand	58
Sit-ups (maximum in one minute)	62
Press-ups (maximum in one minute)	65
Sit and reach (one minute)	32
Standing long jump	2.50 m

Female aged 17:

Bleep test	5.3
Dynamometer (grip strength) – best of two attempts:	
right hand	29
left hand	28
Sit-ups (maximum in one minute)	25
Press-ups (maximum in one minute)	16
Sit and reach (one minute)	18
Standing long jump	1.40 m

THINK ABOUT IT ...

Research as fully as you can the fitness tests for a public service other than the police.

Unit outcome 4
Undertake a training programme to prepare for a specific public service physical entry test

Assessment criteria

- Plan a training programme for a specific public service physical entry test.
- Complete a training programme for a specific public service entry test.

Preparing a training programme

The only way to become fitter and stronger than you are at present is to follow some kind of training programme (perhaps in conjunction with a suitable diet).

Training programmes have the following elements:

- activities
- intensity
- repetitions
- sets
- frequency
- length.

Activities

There is a wide choice of activities, but they will not all be equally suitable for your needs. So before you start, you need to ask yourself some questions:

1 Why do I need to get fitter? It may be for personal reasons, so that you feel better, or so that you can enjoy a holiday more. It may be because you feel that your fitness is lacking somewhere: for example that you would like to be better at running, or lifting weights. It may be for medical reasons – because the doctor has told you to get fitter. It may be because you participate in a sport where you have to be fit, and that you wish to reach a higher standard in that sport. Or it may be because you intend, at some time in the future, to take a physical test to get into a public service of your choice.

2 What standard of fitness am I aiming at? In the case of the world 100 metres champion, the answer to this question would be: fitter than anyone else on the planet. But for someone wishing to join the police, the answer will be: fit enough to get into the police. Your answer to this question should be realistic, but that does not mean that you should be totally unambitious. Following a good programme, most people can make huge gains in fitness, and almost double their strength.

3 How much time have I got? This is not an easy one to answer. Ideally you should aim at ongoing fitness, to last you throughout life. But if you decide on your 18th birthday that you want to join the police when you are 19, your training programme will last a year. And this will be much more effective than a training programme that only lasts a month. Even training for one day will make you fitter the next, but most serious and effective fitness training lasts several months. For example, a typical athlete's training schedule will last for four 'cycles' or phases, each lasting 12 weeks.

4 What are my personal fitness needs? Most of us are good at some things and not so good at others. This is especially true of fitness. If we look at athletes we can see that some are good at the high jump, and others at the shot put, and that none of them, not even the decathletes, are brilliant at both. This is because the two events have very different physical requirements. But for a public service fitness test, good all-round fitness is what is required. For this reason it is more important to improve at the things you are not so good at, than to get even better at the things you are good at. So if you are good at lifting weights, but poor at running, you should improve your running in order to increase your chances of getting into the police. Alternatively, you may be good at distance running but not have much upper body strength. You may need to develop this if you wish to get into the army or the fire service, even though you already have a good basic standard of fitness.

The way to find what your fitness needs are is to take a simulated entry test for the public service of your choice. Though there are no fixed pass standards for these tests, you should be able to ask your instructor where you need to improve.

5 What activities will suit my fitness needs? You should use activities which will improve your performance in each of the elements of the physical test. The activities used in the test itself should certainly be included in your training programme – but you may wish to include other related activities as well. If you are weak in a particular area, for example press-ups, you should include a number of activities designed to strengthen your arms and shoulders.

Intensity

One of the things you need to think about when designing a training programme is its intensity. This is very important because the intensity of a programme determines whether you will develop stamina or strength. The background to this is shown in figure 9.9.

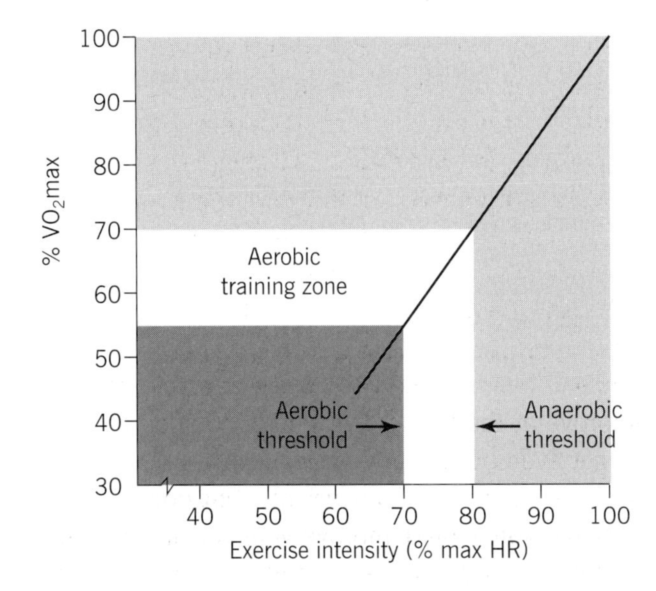

Figure 9.9 *Aerobic and anaerobic training zones*

If your training is below the aerobic threshold, it won't really make you any fitter or stronger; in fact, it isn't really training at all. Activities such as strolling, washing up and playing pool come into this category. If your training goes into the aerobic zone, it will increase your stamina but not your strength. Basically what this means is that you burn fat and benefit your 'slow-twitch' muscle fibres. If you train harder than this, bringing your heart rate up to 80 per cent of its maximum, you are getting into the anaerobic zone. Your body is using more air than you are taking in (which is why it's called 'anaerobic'). Anaerobic training will build your 'fast-twitch' muscle fibres and make your muscles bigger and stronger. A person of medium fitness should aim at reaching a heart-rate of approximately 160 beats per minute, in order to be sure of being in the anaerobic zone. And the fitter you get, the more you will have to work to get into that all-important anaerobic zone.

If you find this talk of heart-rates alarming, another way of looking at it is that you should exercise at at least two thirds of your maximum intensity in order to increase your strength. This means that during your work-outs, you should push yourself.

Resistance

Intensity is achieved through resistance: by pushing or lifting against a strong force. This is why machines and weights provide the most effective form of anaerobic, or strengthening, exercise. Many athletes do a good deal of their training in the gym, where they can use safe, dependable and interesting methods of intense exercise. This kind of training, on a variety of machines, is called circuit training.

Repetitions

To develop strength you have to use your muscles repeatedly at a suitable level of intensity. Once is not enough. For example, if you are lifting weights, you should start at a weight which you can lift ten times before you are too tired to go on. This means that you are doing ten repetitions. However, you will find, if you keep training, that soon you can do more than ten repetitions with that weight. If you then increase the number of repetitions at the same weight you are not increasing the intensity. This will improve your stamina but not your strength, because the exercise will become more aerobic than anaerobic. (Remember that as your fitness increases you have to work harder to get into the anaerobic zone.) To increase your strength, you should increase the weight and continue with your ten repetitions. Always make sure that you are pushing yourself as far as you can go. That way, you are increasing the intensity. Usually, athletes do from two to ten repetitions of an intense exercise.

Sets

Athletes group their repetitions into sets. You should do the same, even if you do not think of yourself as an athlete. But obviously you won't do as many sets as an athlete would do. So, for example, if you are starting weightlifting for the first time, three sets of two to ten repetitions would be enough.

Frequency

There is no point in training if it does not do you any good.

> **FOCUS**
>
> Fleck and Kraemer (1987), two famous experts in fitness training, said, 'The majority of research indicates that three training sessions per muscle group per week is the minimum frequency which causes maximum gains in strength.'

Three times a week is enough. Any more, and you might be missing out on your social life ...

Length

You are likely to reach a plateau – a period during which your strength and fitness will not noticeably increase – after about two months. This means that you need a change in your training programme. It also means that if you have a definite objective, such as a public service fitness test, or a competition, you should not start your training less than two months before the deadline. If you want a more extended fitness programme, you should change it anyway after about two months, so you don't get bored. You will also need to vary your programme after this to avoid developing some sets of muscles at the expense of others. If someone always trains their arms and never their legs, they can begin to look, and feel, top-heavy after a while.

Exercises to consider

This is not an exhaustive list, and there is no space in this book to describe them in any detail.

General:
- chin-ups/pull-ups
- leg-lifts
- trunk lifts.

Using other equipment:
- bench press
- leg press.

Weight training:
- triceps extension
- biceps curls
- military press
- knee-bends
- bench-stepping
- power-walking uphill
- flexibility exercises.

Isokinetics (with a training partner):
- press-ups while your partner pushes down on your back.

Fartlek running

This is 'varied pace' running, and, if it is properly organised, it can develop both leg strength and stamina. It is a good exercise for running outdoors in heaths or rough country.

> **FOCUS**
>
> A half-hour Fartlek training session may follow this sequence.
>
> 1. Jogging (five minutes).
> 2. Fast evenly-paced run (three minutes).
> 3. Brisk walk (two minutes).
> 4. Evenly paced run with 50–60 metre sprints every 200 metres (five minutes).
> 5. Jogging (two minutes).
> 6. Evenly paced running with – occasionally – four fast strides or small acceleration sprints (three minutes).
> 7. Jogging with one fast uphill run (20–30 metres) in every minute (five minutes).
> 8. Jogging and rhythmic exercises – skipping and gentle knee raises (five minutes).
>
> Source: Hazeldine, R. 1987. *Fitness for Sport*, Marlborough: The Crowood Press

Other guidelines

1 Draw up a fitness log, for instance the example below, and follow it in your training.

2 Do five minutes' warm-up: gentle stretching exercises which gradually increase in intensity. A few examples are shown in figures 9.10 to 9.14, but there are many others. Ask your instructor.

3 Don't train the same muscle groups all the time; vary them.

4 Expect a strength increase of one to three per cent a week, and plan for this by raising the intensity of your training as time goes on.

5 Remember that while aerobic exercises are good for your fitness, they will not increase your strength.

6 Also remember that it is easy to raise the number of repetitions, but hard to increase intensity. It is much easier to improve fitness than to increase strength.

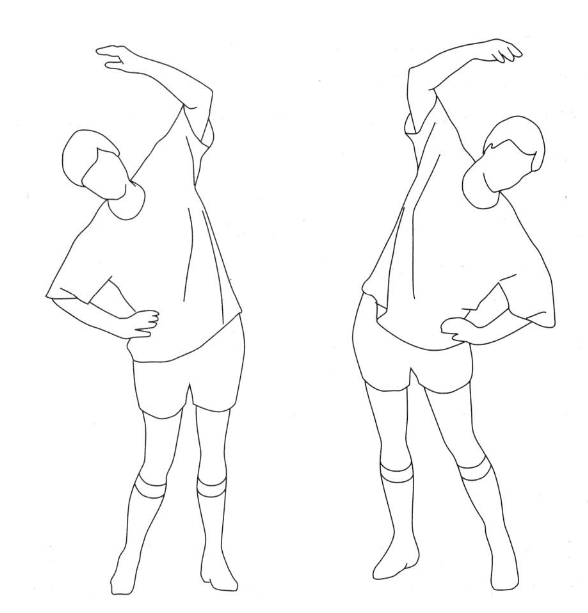

Figure 9.11 *Side-bender. This exercise stretches the trunk. With one hand on your hip, stretch your other arm over your head keeping your knees slightly bent. Slowly bend to the side. Bob gently. Repeat five times on each side*

Figure 9.10 *Stride stretch. This exercise works the calf and thigh muscles. Slowly slide into a stride position keeping your front foot flat on the floor, knee aligned over ankle and rear foot on toes. Place your hands on a chair or on the floor for balance. Hold for ten counts. Switch legs*

Figure 9.12 *Side twister. This exercise stretches the trunk. Stand with your feet comfortably apart and extend the arms palms down. Twist to one side as far as possible. Repeat to other side. Do five repetitions on each side*

Fitness log

	Chin-ups	Sit-ups	Press-ups		Others				
Date									

Figure 9.13 *Jumping jacks. This exercise stretches your arms and legs and warms up your muscles. Hold your arms at your sides. On the count 1, jump your feet apart while simultaneously swinging your arms over your head. On the count 2, return to your starting position. Continue rhythmically, repeating between 15 and 25 times*

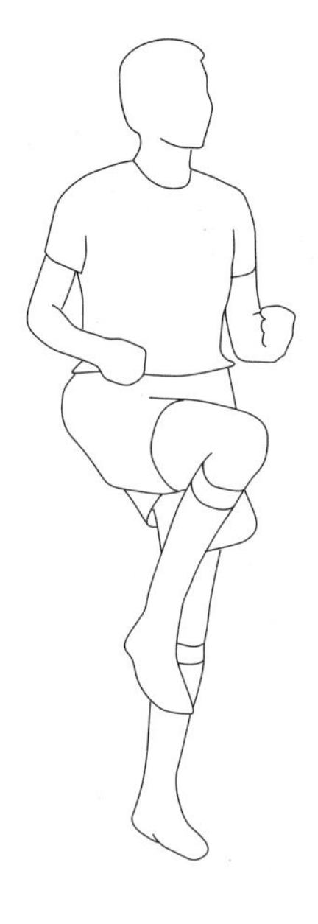

Figure 9.14. *Running on the spot. Start this exercise slowly then increase the rate or the height of your leg lift, or both. As training progresses, run in place between subsequent conditioning exercises*

(Source: Brian Sharkey, 1997, Fitness and Health, *4th ed. (Champaign, IL:* Human Kinetics*), 100, with permission)*

7 If you are not normally active you will increase strength faster than someone who is active. This is because you will be a long way below your potential when you start off. An active person will have been building up their strength, whether they knew it or not, before their exercise programme started.

8 If you are already strong enough, and want to focus on fitness rather than strength, increase the amount of aerobic exercise you do, and decrease the anaerobic exercise. But if you do less than two sessions of anaerobic exercise per week you will actually lose strength.

Health and safety

1. If you are unfit, see a doctor for a check up before you start training.
2. Don't train any part of your body which is injured, unless you take medical advice first.
3. Remember that there is a greater risk of injury if you practise the job-related fitness tests, such as carrying someone over your shoulder. (It's risky for the person being carried, too!)
4. Always warm up before exercise.
5. Eat a good diet, rich in protein and carbohydrates such as potatoes or rice if you are training for strength.
6. Get a training partner if you are serious about fitness and strength training.
7. Don't try to use machines in a gym without being shown first.
8. Study the correct ways of lifting weights.
9. Wear suitable clothing.
10. Never train under the influence of alcohol, drugs or painkillers.
11. Never take anabolic steroids.

Public service physical tests

Complete a training programme for a specific public service entry test.

It is not always easy to get hold of the exact details of a public service physical test. But nevertheless, whatever service you are applying for should be able to give you some information. The two extracts below, which relate to the entry requirements for army officers and the Hampshire Fire Service respectively, are examples of information obtained from the Internet. Though these extracts do not tell you the details of the tests themselves, they make it clear (with a little reading between the lines) what physical abilities they are looking for. Once you have sorted out what these abilities are, you can plan a training programme to develop them.

Extract 1: army officer

General physical development

The candidate must be fit to undertake the physically strenuous Sandhurst course and, after training, should be capable of full combatant duty under all climatic conditions. (Candidates, including females, should be capable of heavy duties involving considerable stamina and prolonged exposure to unfavourable weather or working conditions in any part of the world.) Height and weight should be within the normal limits for the candidate's age and build.

Upper limbs
The candidate must be able to handle a rifle, to do manual work including digging, pushing, dragging, heaving, lifting and climbing.

Lower limbs
The candidate must be capable of severe locomotor strain for several days, be able to undertake long and forced marches, and must be able to run, climb, jump, crawl and dig.

Extract 2: firefighter

Bleep test – reaching a minimum level of 9.6
Height reach tests
Dummy drag

If you look at Extract 1 you will see a strong emphasis on tough physical activity. 'Considerable stamina' is required – which means running. So be prepared to do some long-distance running, and make sure that you have the right footwear, and a suitable place to run. Running on hard surfaces in the wrong kind of trainers can damage your joints.

However, the aerobic activity of running will not do anything for your upper body strength. Yet you will notice that the extract mentions 'manual work including digging, pushing, dragging, heaving, lifting and climbing'. So you will need to include some anaerobic (see page 229) weight training in your programme, gradually increasing the intensity. Notice that skills such as 'dragging' will involve various twisting movements, so you should train for flexibility too. In the case of climbing, coordination and balance skills are needed as well as stamina and strength, so the best thing to do is go to your local indoor climbing wall and take out a season ticket.

Though the extract from the fire service says much less, you know that you will have a bleep test, so that should be part of your training programme. And the dummy drag will involve strength and perhaps flexibility, so you should include activities designed to improve these. Again, it will help you to go for strength and include anaerobic training. Endurance, of the type shown on route marches and long-distance treks, is probably less important in the fire service, where strength and flexibility are prime requirements.

Finally, make sure that your training programme is properly planned. When you do it, never forget your warm-ups and other safety procedures. Eat and drink properly during the programme so that you get the full benefit from it. And make sure you have a training partner where one is needed, either for health and safety reasons, to vary the range of possible exercises, or simply so that you can encourage each other and make the training more interesting and motivating. Then just hang in there and do it!

THINK ABOUT IT ...

Imagine you are six months away from applying for a public service.

Write yourself a fitness training programme tailored to your personal needs.

Further reading

Fitness and Health Brian J Sharkey, Human Kinetics, 1997, PO Box IW14 Leeds LS16 6TR UK (a classic in the field)

Advanced Fitness Assessment and Exercise Prescription (3rd ed.) Vivian H Heyward, Human Kinetics, address as above (a very thorough US-based book)

Fitness for Sport Rex Hazeldine, The Crowood Press, 1985, (easier to carry about than the other two!)

UNIT 10 Teamwork in Sport

Unit outcome 1
Examine the social influences affecting sports participation and sporting performance

Assessment criteria

- Explain at least six social influences which affect sports participation and sports performance.
- Evaluate these influences and their relationship to the public services.

This unit brings together two key themes in your studies: teamwork and fitness. These are valuable in all careers but there are few careers (other than professional sports) where these two elements are of such vital importance as in the public services. You might say: fitness + teamwork = sporting success. You might equally say: fitness + teamwork = public service success.

Before we start let's define a term: sport. We can say it's an organised, competitive, physical, team activity. Examples are football, rugby, volleyball, cricket and so on. It's true that some sports which are organised, competitive and physical, such as boxing, are not really team activities (even though you can have a boxing team consisting of fighters at different weights). But the sports we're dealing with in this unit are team sports.

While we're on the subject of definitions, what is a team? It's a group of people working together under agreed conditions for a shared aim. The primary aim in sport is to win against other teams. The aim in public service teams is to achieve tasks successfully. An effective team achieves far more than its members could if they were working alone, or without motivation. We're going to find out why.

Social influences

Explain at least six social influences which affect sports participation and sports performance.

1 Social facilitation

Why do athletes usually break world records at large competitions, often when they are being watched by millions of people on the television through satellite link-ups? Why do tennis players rise to the big occasion at Wimbledon (as Pete Sampras did in 1999)? Why do footballers play their best in the finals of their national competitions, or in the World Cup?

The answer to these questions – which are important when we think about motivation and success - is what the psychologists call social facilitation. You may have already studied this in Unit 5: Human Behaviour. If you haven't, social facilitation means the fact that we do some tasks – especially ones that we have practised a lot – better in front of an audience, or with others around, than when we are on our own. A good sports team will perform better in front of a crowd than in an empty stadium.

You might think this is obvious, but it isn't, because if we are doing something we're not used to, or not good at, we do worse in front of spectators than if we were by ourselves. So social facilitation only works with skills we have practised, and which we feel confident about. That's why teams need to practise: so they can rise to the big occasion in front of spectators. Practice makes perfect because it allows social facilitation to have its maximum effect.

Playing sports in front of supporters can give you a buzz, a feeling of excitement, of being 'in the zone'. Things go right – because you're in the right mood, a mood of 'flow'. Psychologists such as Zajonc (1965) have studied why teams play better in front of supporters, and why people often work better in groups.

The secret of this lies in what Zajonc called 'arousal'. This is a kind of deep-seated excitement, which we might hardly be aware of ourselves, but which builds our motivation and makes us better than we would otherwise be. The causes of arousal are hormones (chemicals in the blood) such as adrenalin, heightened oxygen intake and heart-rate, and the action of muscles and brain in producing chemicals called endorphins and enkephalins which bring out the best in us.

Cottrell (1968) discovered that social facilitation was most marked if the spectators were active (shouting and cheering) rather than passive (silent). The improvement in performance caused by social facilitation was also much greater if the players thought the spectators were knowledgeable, and able to evaluate their performance. So a team of cricketers from Yorkshire would play best in front of Yorkshire spectators who knew them and understood cricket. They wouldn't play nearly as well in France, where the spectators might not care about them or understand the game.

FOCUS

Social facilitation:
- makes players put in more effort, because they feel they are being watched
- is especially effective if players are being watched by a peer group who know them and their sport.

It is a fact of sport that teams play best before a home crowd.

2 Social dynamics of sport

Team sport is a paradox. This means it is two different things at the same time:
- **cooperation**, with members of your own team
- **competition**, with members of the other team.

Yet at a deeper level there is cooperation between opposing teams in the desire to compete following agreed rules. After all, they agree to play each other, and belong to a competitive league. And also at a deeper level there is competition between players on the same side, all of whom want to be the best in the team.

Look at the diagram in figure 10.1.

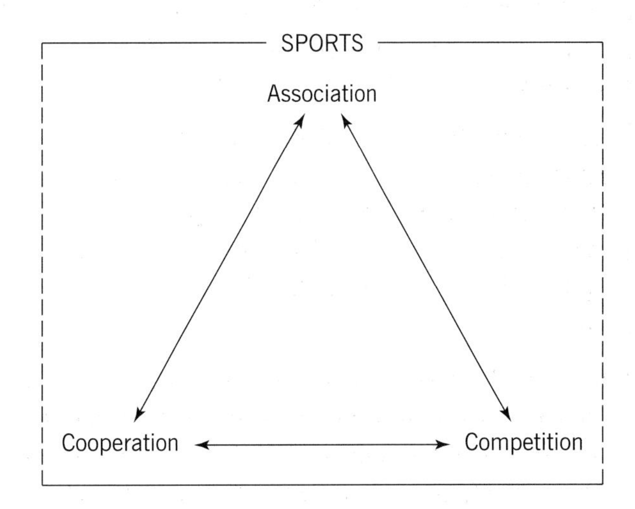

Figure 10.1 *Social dynamics of sport (Source: Frank Kew, 1997,* Social Dynamics of Sport *(Oxford: Butterworth Heinemann Publishers, a division of Reed Educational Publishing Ltd), with permission)*

Association is collaboration (working together) between different groups. In other words, it's the organisation of matches between teams. Cooperation is collaboration within a group. This is the teamwork itself. Competition is conflict within the rules of the game. This is the relationship between your team and the opposing team.

Linked to these is another basic idea about sport in society: that it has two sides to it. One is that sport is a social practice; the other is that sport is a social institution.

3 Sport as a social practice

Sport as a social practice has its origins in the games children play. Play is one of the most basic and important of all childhood behaviours. If children didn't play they would not develop their strength or their coordination, their 'psychomotor' skills. Nor could they develop properly as social beings: they would never learn how to get on with each other – or how to disagree, for that matter. If we had never played games as children, we would not be able to relate as adults. In fact we would be a sad lot of misfits, and probably too frightened to go out of the house!

The social practice of sport also teaches us about rules. All games, even childhood games like 'kick-can-and-hop-it', or hide and seek, have rules. Learning to understand and obey rules is one of the great achievements of growing up, without which we could not have a society as we understand it.

So people like Huizinga (1938), Lasch (1979) and MacIntyre (1981), who have studied these ideas in depth, see the social practice of sport as a good thing, giving us pleasure, developing our characters and showing us the difference between right and wrong. Sport as a social practice is sport played for enjoyment, sport as 'a noble art', not played for money, not played in a vicious manner, but as something good and innocent which brings people together, teaches them about themselves and makes them happy.

To summarise, sport as a social practice brings:
- the exercise of skills
- the use of plans and strategies
- the development and testing of coordination, speed, strength and endurance
- the reward of achievement
- the pleasure of cooperation with other players
- 'safe' competition and the channelling of aggression
- feedback from others (praise and criticism) which helps to develop our awareness of self and others.

4 Sport as a social institution

Everybody agrees that sport as a social practice is a good thing. But they are not so sure about sport as a social institution. Sport as a social institution is an organisation or group of organisations in society. Thus the Football Association, or FIFA, are aspects of sport as a social institution. When sport becomes concerned with organisation, making money, national prestige or political power, it becomes an institution, rather like a government or a business – or, for that matter – a college. Instead of being games which are played for pleasure, sport becomes office-work, meetings, spending money, building stadiums, bidding for the next Olympics – and so on.

Sport as a social institution brings:
- professionalism
- a career structure for sport
- very high standards for a few ('the stars')
- bureaucracy and administration
- sport as big business
- commercial sponsorship
- drugs and corruption
- political involvement in sport
- media involvement
- a mass TV audience.

5 Gender

The word 'gender' is often confused with sex, but it isn't the same thing. While 'sex' refers to the biological differences between women and men, 'gender' refers to their social differences. The fact that women have breasts and men have penises is a biological difference, and is therefore to do with sex. But the fact that women are accepted more easily by society as swimmers than as boxers is a gender issue, because it reflects on people's thinking and behaviour, not on biology as such. The fact that men, on average, are taller or physically stronger than women, is a sex-linked difference, because it is genetically programmed into us before birth. But the fact that men are far more likely than women to sit on sporting committees is a gender difference, resulting from the unequal balance of power between the sexes in society. Discrimination is a gender issue, and the different roles and expectations for men and women in society is again a gender issue.

Traditionally, women have not been encouraged to play sports as much as men. In fact, up until the early 1900s they were discouraged from playing sport in a male-dominated society. A favourite phrase of the Victorians was that women were 'weaker vessels'. Up until the 1960s it was quite unheard of for women to play sports such as cricket and soccer.

Now, in the 1999 World Cup for women's soccer in the USA, crowds of up to 70,000 have been watching women's soccer live. But there is less discrimination against women in sport in America than there is in Britain. Here there is still argument, for example, over whether women tennis players should be paid as much as men at Wimbledon – and they are not. And some of the men players, such as Tim Henman, are in favour of this difference.

Factors leading to women being second-class citizens in the sporting world include the following.

- Childrearing and socialisation (training and pressure from society), which expects boys to be sporty, but tacitly encourages girls not to be. Fathers are often seen kicking a ball around with their sons, but only rarely with their daughters. Boys are actively encouraged to wear sporty clothes; girls are expected to dress up to look 'pretty'. And boys and girls still play with different toys.
- Comics and magazines for children. These encourage boys to be physically active and adventurous, while encouraging girls to take more interest in fashion or pop music. There are not enough girls' sporting role models.
- PE in schools. There remains a tendency for girls and boys to concentrate on different sports or athletic events. There is less emphasis on competition for girls.
- Much more time on TV is given over to men's sports than women's. And there's a different attitude from the commentators. Statements are made about the women's appearance which would not be made about the men's, suggesting that the women's sporting efforts are not interesting enough on their own.
- There is less amateur sport for women, and it is less likely to be reported in local newspapers.

6 Race

Sport is a racially influenced activity – at least at the highest level. This is most noticeable in athletics, where sprinting events seem to be taken over by black athletes, while marathons are run by whites or East Africans. But it happens in team sports as well. Black footballers are now fairly common in England, but Asian professional footballers are almost nonexistent. On the other hand, there are increasing numbers of British Asian cricketers. In athletics the racial differences may, to some extent, have a genetic cause, but in team sports the explanation is more likely to be social. In other words, racial stereotyping associates Asians (for example) with cricket, and Afro-Caribbeans with football. In America basketballers are often black, whereas baseball players are less likely to be.

There is some evidence that in team sports in Britain, black players are likely to take up certain positions on the field – for example on the wing. The theory is that influential midfield positions are taken by white players, whereas black players are valued for 'flair' or speed. This may again be a reflection of stereotyping, and assumptions by white sports leaders that black players lack the tactical skills to occupy certain positions.

Black people are often stereotyped as 'sporty' and get channelled into sporting activity at school. Though this may be to the advantage of high-achieving individuals, the underlying implication is that sport is one of the few areas of life where black people can succeed financially in a mainly white country. Of the 12 wealthiest black people in Britain, six are sportspeople, and most of the others are singers or musicians. This is more likely to reflect white people's stereotyping of black people and the resulting lack of full opportunities for them, than black people's ability, since in an African country, for example, the richest people are not involved in sport or music.

And although we have many famous black sportspeople, few of them are in managerial or leadership positions. In America there may be more opportunities for them – we can think of Don King, in boxing – but they are still rare. Though John

Barnes has recently taken up a management job at Celtic (as chief coach), he is the exception. In this sense black sportspeople suffer a similar discrimination to women, and the 'real' power in the sporting world remains with middle-aged white males.

Evaluation of social influences

Evaluate these influences and their relationship to the public services.

Sport is a social activity, and so is public service work. This means that all the social influences that affect sport will also affect public service work. But the influences may not be equally important in the two fields. After all, though both sport and work may involve teams, they are not the same thing, and they are done for different reasons!

Social facilitation

In the public services social facilitation is seen in such arrangements as shared or open plan offices. Here people work more effectively because they can be observed by their peers and superiors. At the same time, when they aren't working, they can relax in social loafing (chatting and joking), which is more enjoyable than trying to relax in an empty room (yet less likely to send you to sleep). Similarly teams (such as scenes of crime) in the police, or fire officers doing their daily exercises, work more effectively when they are watched by an interested senior officer who can evaluate and comment on their work. It is in routine public service work that social facilitation is most useful.

Some of this social facilitation is provided by the public themselves, who watch the police while they are patrolling, and, in a sense, 'keep the police on their toes', And the fact that police officers now often patrol in pairs is not only for their own security. They may well work better because they have a partner sharing their work and taking an interest in what they are doing.

Social dynamics

Competition, cooperation and association

Competition is important in army work, where soldiers have to achieve maximum fitness and endurance on route marches and other exercises. Each soldier is able to compete with his peers. Even the latest army recruitment campaign: 'Be the Best', illustrates this competitive spirit. But cooperation is equally important. For example, when setting up camp on an icefield, or building a bridge across a swollen river, army personnel need a high degree of cooperation in order to work safely and quickly. The social dynamic of association is provided by the officers who organise the activities, and liaise with other parts of the army, and by the regiment, which has traditions and is like a kind of club in which all the soldiers can feel 'at home'.

Social practice and social institution

Social practice is not as clearly a part of public service work as it is a part of sport. Sport, as social practice, is done purely for enjoyment, as 'an end in itself'. (In other words, you don't need a reason for doing it.) But public service work is always done for a reason. Having said that, an interesting thing about public service work is that it is not done only for pay. If there was no police service in Britain, people would still organise their own ways of protecting themselves and their property, and make sure they could live in peace – just as they did before the police were first introduced in 1829.

The public services are a social institution just as much as any sporting body. These institutions are needed to organise the public services on a national and international scale, just as they are needed to organise sport on a national and international scale. But public service institutions have the same problems as sporting ones. The police can be corrupt. They can take bribes just as much as any Olympic Committee. The stresses of police work in the institution, with all its pressures, can drive the police to malpractice, brutality and corruption. Equally, sports bodies can be dishonest, encouraging or turning a blind eye to drug abuse, or even allowing a situation to develop where coaches sexually abuse young athletes. Public service institutions have not yet succeeded in stamping out racism, sexism and bullying: sports have the same problems. The institutions are needed otherwise neither sport nor public service could develop effectively, but they must have proper complaints procedures and inspection to make sure that they do not become corrupt.

Gender

Gender is now a big issue in the public services, but it wasn't always like this. All the public services began as men-only employers. The police were the first to employ women – though only on a temporary basis – when the Metropolitan Police took on women officers in 1919. (This was because there was a shortage of men following World War I.) Other forces, such as Lincolnshire, did not employ women until 1939, the beginning of World War II. Women are still under-represented in the police, and big efforts are being made to encourage them to apply. The same is true of the fire service where, even now, women are nearly as rare as hens' teeth. As for the army, some parts – especially the infantry – are still no-go areas for women.

Problems faced by women, which make it hard for them to be accepted as full team members, include the following.

- Sexist behaviour and comments by men. However, all the public services are making a strong effort to deal with this problem, and are having some success.
- A belief by some men that women are not up to the physical demands of the job. This is another side of sexism. But increasingly, in the public services, the hardest physical work is being done by machines.
- Promotion difficulties for women. This is because the relationship between the sexes is partly a 'power relationship', and men like to hang on to their power.
- Greater demands at home, if they have families, and the costs and difficulties of childcare.
- The fact that women are still in a minority, so that in a given team they may feel left out because they are the only women.
- Poor physical arrangements, especially in fire stations, where there may be no suitable sleeping quarters and toilets.

Race

All the public services have too few people from ethnic minorities working in them. As equal opportunities employers they are supposed to employ the same proportion (percentage) of ethnic minority people in their organisation as there is in the society they serve. So, for example, if the ethnic minority population in West Yorkshire is seven per cent of the total, then seven per cent of all the West Yorkshire police should come from ethnic minorities. In fact, at the time of writing, only about three per cent of the West Yorkshire police are from ethnic minorities – which means they need to recruit more if they wish to reflect the area they are policing.

The police are very aware of this problem, and are making a determined effort to change the situation. There are excellent career opportunities for people from ethnic minorities in the police – and indeed in the other public services. But there are problems too, not unlike those faced by ethnic minority people in the sporting world. These include the following.

- The difficulty of being accepted by older police officers, or by the well-established teams they join.
- Racist behaviour and remarks. Again the police are making a determined effort to stamp this out, and are being very successful.
- Promotion difficulties. Most ethnic minority recruits are fairly young, so it is not yet clear what their promotion prospects are. But in the army, for example, ethnic minority soldiers are mainly in the lower ranks. This can be contrasted with America where, although there is discrimination, General Colin Powell, a black man, rose to the very top of the armed forces in the early 1990s.

Unit outcome 2
Investigate the psychological responses to sports participation by individuals and teams

Assessment criteria

- Explain the effects of at least three psychological responses on individuals and teams when participating in sports.
- Explain how these responses relate to at least two public services.

Psychological responses to sport

Psychology has a great deal to offer to sports people. This is because sport is just as much a mental activity as a physical one. Both individual psychology and social psychology (the psychology of groups) are important.

1 Motivation

Motivation is the process of getting the best out of you and your team-mates. Being human, our moods vary and we perform different tasks differently depending on mood. Sometimes we're really up for a challenge, and at other times we just can't be bothered. This last attitude has no place in sports and it has no place in public service either. So how do we get rid of it and make sure that we are motivated?

First we look at ...

Rewards

We might not get paid for the sport that we play, but we still get something out of it or we wouldn't do it. The thing that we get out of it is the reward. There are two kinds of reward in sport.

1 Intrinsic. This is the satisfaction that comes from the sport itself. It is the enjoyment of playing, the enjoyment of moving our bodies, getting exercise, showing skill, and winning – if we manage to win. After all, as human beings, we would still play sports even if there were no schools, colleges, police forces, playing fields or footballs. We know that because archaeologists have found that our distant ancestors in the stone age left things behind them that could only have been for sport or games. Only 40 years ago the sport of bungee jumping was discovered in Pentecost Island in the South Pacific: here teams of young men, wearing nothing much but with creepers tied round their ankles, were seen diving headfirst out of trees, to the astonishment of European explorers. The rest is history. But their 'tree-diving' was done for its intrinsic rewards, to show skill and daring, to get a buzz, to get that feeling of being one hundred per cent alive, at that moment when there was a risk of being one hundred per cent dead.

2 Extrinsic. After Ryan Giggs scored a remarkable winning goal in 1999, people rushed round comparing him to God, and no doubt he got a big bonus in his pay packet. The money, the outpourings of praise in the press, the constant re-runs of the goal on TV: these were extrinsic rewards. They must have given him pleasure, but they came after the actual goal-scoring, outside the game itself. That is why they were extrinsic rewards (the 'ex-' meaning 'outside' the game). So any payment, status, praise or recognition that comes from a team sport is an extrinsic reward. Without these extrinsic rewards there would be no professional sport, and perhaps not very much organised amateur sport either.

There has been research, by Deci (1971) and Lepper, Greene and Nisbett (1973) which supports the idea that, for the sportsperson, the intrinsic reward is stronger and more motivating than the extrinsic reward. But for the team as a whole, both kinds of reward increase motivation. In interviews after Manchester United's win over Bayern Munich in 1999, it was revealed that Alex Ferguson had told his team at half time that if they lost the match, they would only be allowed to get within six feet of the cup; they would not be allowed to touch it. He used the image of the extrinsic reward (the cup and the glory that went with it) to urge them on to victory.

Need to achieve and need to avoid failure

These may be two sides of the same coin, but either way they motivate sportspeople in team games. Fear of relegation (failure) can bring out the best in a team, just as the hope of promotion (achievement) can. The motivation is felt by each individual player, but because the emotion is shared it can be seen as a team emotion as well. And if these emotions are felt strongly by individuals in the team, other team members will start to feel them as well, since they will be communicated by the process of group dynamics. In fact players will 'read' the emotions on other players' faces, and in their body movements. If the captain is stumbling round looking as sick as a parrot, it won't be long before his team are feeling the same way.

With regard to the need to achieve and the need to avoid failure, different individuals tend to be motivated more strongly by either one or the other – not by both. If you look at figure 10.2 you will see how different personalities fit into this picture.

People in area A will thrive on risk and be optimistic. People in area B will fight hard to avoid failure, and be more motivated by that. It may be that in a team these personality types will be best suited to attacking or defending roles respectively.

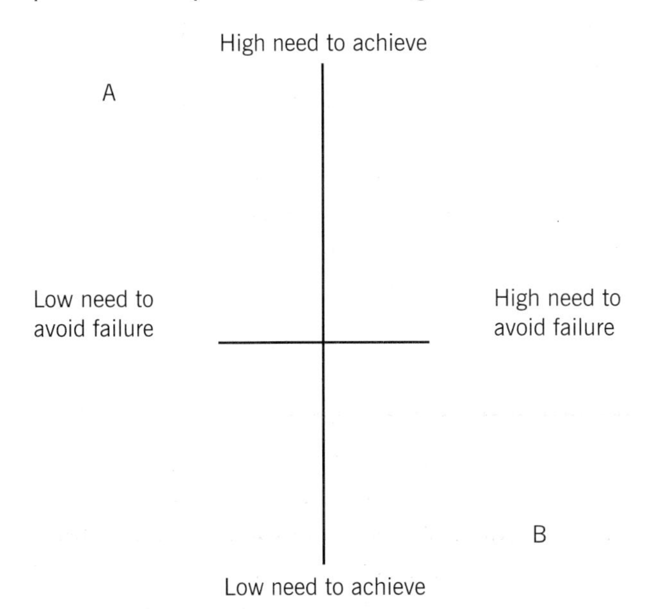

Figure 10.2

Situational factors

Winston Churchill is famous for being a poor politician in peacetime, and a great statesman in wartime. In other words, the situation of war brought out the best in him.

Our personalities vary in that some of us are motivated by taking risks, while others are motivated best when there are fewer risks and a clearer possibility of success. Churchill only showed his true greatness when the country was up against it, and in danger of being defeated by a foreign power for the first time in 1,000 years.

Some teams are the same. The psychological make-up of the players means that they respond to a challenge by rising to it. If you have key players with this 'risk-taking' psychological approach the team may become 'giant-killers'. But other teams underperform on the big occasion, perhaps because they have fewer 'risk-taking' players, and become frightened by the spotlight.

Situational motivation is complicated: it shows up our individual differences, and makes it difficult to lay down hard-and-fast rules. But from a sports point of view this is a good thing: it's the unexpected wins and losses which are the icing on the cake!

The other psychological aspects of team motivation come mainly under social facilitation, discussed on pages 234–235 above.

2 Anxiety

At an everyday level, anxiety is nerves, worry and fearing the worst. In team sports, anxiety is too high a state of arousal. When this happens a player becomes tense and stressed. As a result he is less accurate than usual, and he starts making mistakes.

For practical purposes we can divide anxiety into two types: trait anxiety and state anxiety.

1 **Trait anxiety** means that a tendency towards anxiety exists in the person's character. They easily get over-aroused and then anxiety gets

the better of them. They may be great sportspeople, but to bring the best out of themselves they have to develop techniques for controlling their arousal and keeping calm.

2 **State anxiety** is anxiety which comes from the situation we are in. If the calmest person in the world is tied to a railway track and they hear a train coming, they are going to suffer from state anxiety. Similarly, sportspeople who are not normally anxious will become anxious before an important match, when there is a lot at stake.

The opposite of anxiety is indifference. A player who is operating below his level of optimum arousal feels that he can't get motivated. You can see this sometimes in a good team playing against poor opposition. Because they are not challenged they cannot get up to their optimum level of arousal, and their performance is slack, lacklustre and full of careless errors. Whilst the anxious player tries too hard, the indifferent player doesn't try hard enough.

3 Stress

In many ways stress is like anxiety – except it tends to last for a longer time. Its causes can be as follows.

1. **Social.** For example a player might not be getting on with his team-mates. As a result his game will suffer.
2. **Chemical or hormonal.** Athletes or sportspeople who train too hard can suffer from hormonal imbalance. Women can suffer from amenorrhea (lack of periods). Overtraining can stress the immune system, which is why keen sportspeople sometimes get more colds and flu than the general population.
3. **Infections**, whether caused by bacteria or viruses. Because the body is fighting off disease, it becomes stressed, and the best thing to do is rest until recovery is under way.
4. **Physical.** Serious sportspeople often get injured, because they are playing up to their physical limits – and against other players who are doing the same thing. This then leads to emotional stress because injury is a great source of anxiety to professional sportspeople. In extreme cases it can mean the end of their career.
5. **Climatic.** Playing sport in bad weather, or when it is too hot or cold, brings special risks. In hot weather dehydration can be a serious problem, causing psychological stress as well as physical stress to the body's systems.
6. **Psychological.** People who push themselves to the limit are different from the rest of us. The intensity of their effort can put them under a psychological strain. Furthermore, it can cause difficulties in their relationships with other people. Sometimes the importance of the occasion can cause temporary psychological stress. The foul by David Beckham which led to his being sent off in the 1998 World Cup match against Argentina at St Etienne may have been an example of this.

Signs of stress	
physiological:	increased heart-rate, blood-pressure, sweating, breathing; decreased blood flow to skin, salivation.
psychological:	worry, inability to make decisions or concentrate, feeling out of control, developing a 'one-track-mind'.
behavioural:	talking too fast or loud, or in a high-pitched voice, biting nails, pacing, pulling faces, yawning, trembling; frequent urination.

Control of stress

1. **Imagery relaxation.** You lie down and think of something pleasant and relaxing – for example a place where you were happy as a child.
2. **Progressive relaxation.** Consciously relax each muscle group in turn, starting perhaps with the feet.
3. **Deep slow breathing exercises**, thinking about the breathing and nothing else.
4. **Eliminating negative feelings about yourself and building confidence.** This can be a long-term strategy and is useful before big matches.
5. **Mental rehearsal:** thinking constructively about the match ahead.

6 **Setting goals and targets:** action-planning your own strength and skills development. This should be considered for the whole team.
7 **Avoiding so-called 'maladaptive coping strategies'**, such as drinking, smoking, drugs, losing your temper, or anything else which disturbs your calm, concentration and fitness.

4 Aggression

Aggression is anger or hostility towards other people, shown in an attempt to hurt, harm or intimidate them. In team sports this can lead to fouls and other unacceptable behaviour. A famous recent example was the fight between Graeme Le Saux and Robbie Fowler, following a taunt by Fowler about Le Saux's sexual orientation. A slightly less recent example was when Eric Cantona kicked a spectator in the face after he shouted a racist insult. Both these incidents had causes which at one level justified the aggression. Nevertheless it was unacceptable and threatened both players' careers. Vicious tackles and other forms of aggression in sport can cause severe injuries, and in extreme cases players have been killed. And if there is aggression on the field it can affect the spectators and they start fighting as well.

There are three theories of the origin of aggression.

1 **The instinct theory.** This came from Konrad Lorenz in 1966. He thought aggression was in us from birth and was necessary for survival. He got this idea from studying the behaviour of animals.
2 **The drive theory.** Dollard put this forward in 1939. He said that aggression was a hidden force inside us which only became visible if it was frustrated. This idea came from Freud's idea that the causes of our emotions are hidden in the unconscious mind.
3 **Social learning theory.** Bandura, in 1973, said that aggression was learnt, usually by young children, when they saw and imitated other aggressive behaviour. This is the most useful explanation because it suggests that we can do something to reduce aggression in society.

Many sports experts believe that aggression can be sublimated – in other words changed into energy which is no longer harmful, but which increases our arousal and can improve our game. If this is true, then aggression is not a bad thing provided we use it properly.

Whatever its origins, aggression is part of our psychological make-up – and nearly everybody is aggressive at one time or another. However, if a player is harmfully aggressive, he should learn to control it or visit a counsellor. Footballers should remember that Gary Lineker, one of the greatest goalscorers of recent times, was never sent off. He was able to combine the highest standards of football with an almost total absence of harmful aggression.

Relating psychological responses to public service work

Explain how these responses relate to at least two public services.

ANALYSIS

Motivation relates to everything we do. We need some motivation (often quite a lot!) to get out of bed in the morning. And without strong motivation it would be impossible to work successfully – or happily – in the public services. Arousal, stress, anxiety and aggression are important as well. They all affect our ability to work well in our chosen career. And this is particularly true in public service work, which makes a greater demand on our abilities and characters than most types of work. After all, if you are packing widgets you can think about something else while you're doing it. But if you're interviewing a murder suspect, your mind and emotions have got to be one hundred per cent focused on the job – just as much as if you were a footballer before the big match!

1 Police work

At the application stage

1 Motivation. To get into the police, you have to apply. However good you are, they won't drag you in off the streets to work with them. And application is not an easy process. There are two long forms to fill in, which include a good deal of writing. For example you are expected to produce an autobiography of about 300 words. Then, as we have seen, there are the police initial recruitment tests, the physical tests, a battery of other tests, an interview and a medical examination. One reason why the application process is so exhaustive is that they want to assess your motivation. Do you really really want to get into the police? If you don't – if, for you, it's just another job – then you can forget it.

2 Anxiety and stress. In addition, the application procedure tests whether you can deal with stress and anxiety. They watch you to see if you bite your nails or pick your nose. Can you keep calm while doing your PIRT, or do you panic at the lack of time and stop thinking straight in the checking test? Do you show strong motivation in the physical test, squeezing out those extra press-ups? Do you keep cool in the interview, or do you lose your rag and show aggression when they ask a question which is slightly below the belt – just to test that side of your character? In a section of the application procedure called the carousel, you will be presented with a range of human situations, such as dealing with a shoplifter, or someone who has collapsed in the bus station. These will test your situational or 'state' anxiety. In other words, you might be the kind of person who keeps calm in a fitness test, but goes to pieces when you see what might be a dead body on the floor. The police need to know about this before they take you on – not afterwards, when they have raised your hopes and expectations and already spent thousands of pounds on training you.

During training

1 Motivation. This is needed during the two years' police training. If you are not motivated you will not get through the intensive training at your local and national training school. The training is not like your college course, which may at times be fairly laid back. The hours are long, there are large amounts of writing, and you will be asked to carry out detailed self-assessments and appraisals which you will not be used to. At times you will be criticised, and you will need motivation to stop you from getting discouraged. The intrinsic rewards of hard study may not seem very great: it may give you headaches, and a feeling that you are not clever enough. This is when you must remember that the intrinsic rewards of police work will come when you have passed your probationary period and can work as a fully-fledged police officer. Then you will show the ability that the selection panel saw in you when you applied, and get the satisfaction (the intrinsic reward) of being good at the job.

2 Stress and anxiety. These must be controlled so that they do not get the better of you. You must be encouraged by your fear of failure, not paralysed by it. If you feel too anxious in your training period, remember that anxiety is caused by too much arousal. There are times when it is better to be calm and detached, and to see the whole training process in perspective, rather than getting too worked up about it. The peer group of other trainees ought to help, but if they are all stressed out as well, then it may be up to you to suggest a more relaxed or thoughtful approach to the training.

3 Aggression. If you think an instructor is getting at you, or if your fellow trainees are taking the mickey for some reason, there will be a risk of aggression. But this will not be as great as the risk of aggression faced by police officers who are out on the streets, dealing with people who may not like them very much. A police officer who 'loses it' is in trouble, and part of the purpose of training is to make sure that young, highly-motivated people learn to keep their aggression in check and, if they use it at all, use it wisely.

Police work in general

1 Motivation. Police work is almost the most varied kind of work there is. And it would be unreasonable to expect every police officer to be equally good at all of it. Officers have to maintain their motivation, as professionals, even in those aspects of the job that they don't like. Many officers dislike paperwork, but by learning to take a pride in its quality they can gain an intrinsic reward by feeling that they have done the job well. And if other people start praising the clarity of their reports, then they will start to enjoy an aspect of the work that they hadn't enjoyed up until then.

2 Stress and anxiety. Policing is a stressful job. The hours are long and varied, with shiftwork which imposes stress because it interferes with the body's 'biological clock'. It is like continually suffering from jet-lag. There is anxiety because it is unpredictable. Furthermore, it puts a strain on the officer's relationships outside work. Officers may not see enough of their husbands, wives or partners, who may complain because they feel neglected. If police officers suffer from stress both at work and at home, it can seem like a trap from which there is no way out. The police now provide stress counselling, but in some ways the damage may be done by then – especially if the stress has spread into the officer's family.

3 Aggression. There are many cases of police officers becoming violent with hostile or insulting members of the public. This can be the result of stress, or a feeling that nobody is going to support the police – either in the criminal justice system or in society as a whole. This can cause police officers to develop a 'siege mentality' – a kind of paranoid state – and feel that to get justice they have to take the law into their own hands. Frustration can lead to aggression, as Dollard (see above) pointed out, and if a suspect won't answer questions it is sometimes tempting for officers to try and force the truth out of him. But of course this must be avoided at all costs: officers must control their aggression and seek help, or ask someone else to deal with a difficult situation, if they feel it is getting the better of them. This, after all, is what teamwork is all about.

2 The fire service

1 Motivation. There are more applications per vacancy in the fire service than for any other public service. This implies that many applicants will be well motivated – and no doubt this is true. The work involves saving lives, and is therefore high on job satisfaction – since there is a very high intrinsic reward in the feeling that you have saved someone's life. Firefighting is a job which attracts people who are risk-takers by temperament, but of course it is vital that they minimise these risks. The application procedure and training are difficult, though the initial training does not last as long as police training. A very high level of fitness is required, and has to be maintained by firefighters once they have joined the service. This means taking a serious and sustained approach to exercise, which needs strong motivation. Fortunately most firefighters enjoy strenuous physical activity, so this is part of the intrinsic reward of the job. The extrinsic rewards of firefighting are perhaps not as great as they should be. There are complaints about the level of firefighters' pay, and occasional threats of industrial action.

2 Stress and anxiety. Firefighting combines long hours of routine checking, testing, exercise and relaxation with short but taxing periods of very hard, stressful work. It suits people who function well at a high level of arousal. But people who function better at a low level of arousal could easily become anxious and ineffective in the stress of dealing with a major incident. Firefighters encounter horrific scenes, and need to have strategies for coping with horror. This may involve 'blanking off' part of the mind in order to keep arousal levels down. During the day firefighters have periods of time when they can play games such as table tennis or volleyball, which combine fitness or coordination practice with relaxation and de-stressing. Like the police, firefighters are shift workers; unlike the police they are more likely to have to sleep over at

the station. Again, this causes stress to their families and interferes with their social life. The fire service has less paperwork than the police, and receives far fewer complaints from the public – which helps to keep stress levels down. They work in teams, called 'watches', and their shared skills and activities, often under difficult conditions, has a 'bonding' effect and enables them to put up with more stress, with team-members giving informal emotional support to each other.

3 Aggression. Occasionally, in inner city areas, following arson attacks or malicious false alarms, fire crews get stoned or abused by members of the public. They don't get nearly as much abuse as the police, but it still puts them to the test. But again, as professionals, they have to control their aggression, put their own safety first, and if necessary call the police – for there is teamwork even between the public services!

Unit outcome 3
Display an understanding of effective officiating skills in various sports

Assessment criteria
- Outline the rules of play in at least four team sports.
- Participate in at least four team sports.
- Effectively officiate at least one team sport.

Officiating in sport

In football a referee is a referee, unless he's an unprintable word. In cricket, a referee is an umpire. There are different names for different games. Then there are linesmen or women, and scorers, and other people in different games whose job is to keep an eye on things or record points. All these people are officials, and they officiate. So to officiate in a game you don't necessarily have to be a referee or an umpire. There are other jobs out there which need doing too.

To officiate you need to be able to do three things:
- know the rules of the game
- know how to signal the rules (or the fact that they have been broken) to other officials and players
- be able to show authority without angering people.

The first two tasks are a matter of doing your homework. For the third, it helps if you can walk on water as well. But that doesn't mean you can't give it a go!

Rules of play

Outlining rules of play is not the same thing as going through the entire rulebook with a fine-tooth comb. At this level you need to show a working knowledge of the game and the main rules, so that – if need be – you can officiate in a game at an amateur or recreational level without feeling that you are making a complete fool of yourself.

Here are the rules for basketball. You will need to find the rules for three other team sports yourself!

Basketball rules

In Britain and America this is usually an indoor game, but in the tropics it is played outdoors. It was invented by James Naismith in 1891 and is now popular worldwide. There are two main sets of basketball rules in the world, and they keep changing! But here are some of the main points.

The court

At each end of the court (see figure 10.3) is a basket specially constructed to allow the ball to fall slowly through a funnel of netting. The top of the basket is ten feet or 3.05 metres above the floor.

Aim

The aim is to get the ball into your opponent's basket, either by throwing, or leaping and 'dunking' it.

Dress

Shirts and shorts with basketball shoes. The shirts have large brightly-coloured numbers printed on them.

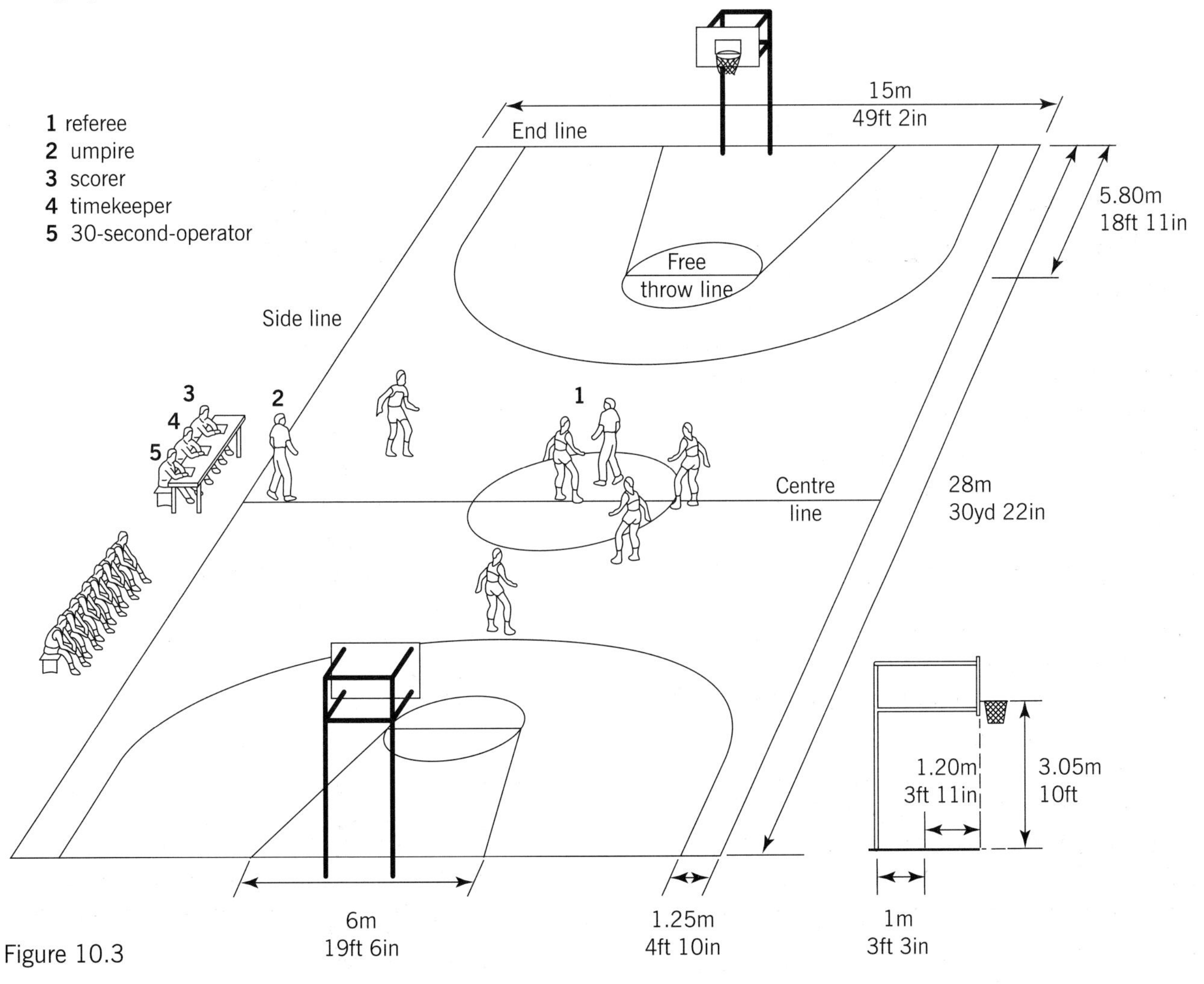

Figure 10.3

The ball
The ball is round, made of leather, rubber or plastic; circumference 75–78 centimetres, weight 600–650 grams. If dropped from 1.8 metres onto a hard wooden floor it should bounce to a height of about 1.3 metres.

Teams
Five players and five to seven substitutes.

Length of game
Two halves of 20 minutes, with a 10 or 15 minute interval.

Officials
There are five of them:
- the referee
- the umpire
- the scorer
- the timekeeper
- the 30-second operator.

They wear special uniforms, and the umpire and referee each officiate on one half of the court (but swap ends after each foul). This is because basketball is a very fast game and one referee wouldn't be able to see everything that was going on.

Equipment needed by officials:
- stopwatches, for the game and for time-outs
- a visible 30-second rule sign, which can be seen by players and spectators
- scoresheet
- scoreboard
- markers to show the number of fouls per player.

Handling the ball
Players can throw, bounce or dribble (repeatedly bounce) the ball, but they cannot run with it or kick it.

Scoring
- Goals from free throws score one point.
- Normal goals score two points.
- Goals from outside the three-point line score three points.

Other rules
- A game is forfeited if either side has less than two players on the court.
- The game starts with a jump ball, where the referee throws the ball into the centre circle and players try to knock it away to their own team. Players must stand in their own half of the circle when doing this. Jump balls also occur in the nearest circle if the ball goes dead (see below).
- Dead balls are when a goal is scored, a violation or foul occurs, or the ball is 'held' between two players.
- When the ball is out of bounds it is thrown, bounced or rolled back in by a player from the side that did not touch it last.
- Players can move freely when dribbling the ball, but if they stop dribbling and hold the ball with both hands, they must pass it to someone else or make a shot at the basket. Once they have stopped dribbling only one more step is allowed.
- A violation involves breaking the rules and is penalised by loss of the ball. A foul is personal contact with an opponent. If a player not shooting is fouled, his team gets a throw in near the place where the foul happened. If a shooting player is fouled the goal counts and a free throw follows. If the shooter misses because of the foul, he or she gets two free throws.
- if a player commits more than seven fouls the opposing team gets free throws for each extra foul, and another if they score.
- Following a serious disqualifying foul the player is sent off.
- A technical foul consists of showing rudeness or disrespect to other players or officials.
- A time-out is when there has been a foul or injury or anything else which holds up the game.
- A charged time-out allows a brief rest. Each team can call two charged time-outs in each half. Sometimes a charged time-out is imposed on a team if they are slow in getting a substitute out.
- Substitution of players can only be done when the ball is dead.

Thirty-second rule
If a team has control of the ball it must try to score within 30 seconds.

Ten-second rule

A team in the back court must move the ball into the front court within ten seconds of gaining possession.

Three-second rule

No attacking player can stay between his opponents' free throw line and end line for more than three seconds if his own team is in possession.

Participation in sport

Participate in at least four team sports.

Participate means 'take part in', but there is some uncertainty as to whether you are required to play in the game, or simply do something active in it, such as being a linesman or a scorer. If you are disabled, injured or ill – or if you have any other strong reason for not playing games – you will need to consult your tutor about this.

Before you participate in a team sport, plan by asking yourself the following questions.:

- Which sports am I going to choose? (Check these with your tutor.)
- Who will I be playing with?
- Do I know the rules?
- When and where will we be playing?
- Do I have the kit?
- Am I in good health?
- Am I fit?
- If my tutor is not there, how will I be able to prove that I have done it?

This last question is very important, because your tutor will need to prove to the external verifier that you have done what you say you have done. The best thing to do is to supply a (genuine!) letter proving that you have taken part in one or more team sports. Other possibilities are newspaper reports, photographs or certificates.

Effective officiation

Effectively officiate at least one team sport.

As we said earlier, officiation means being a referee, umpire, linesman, scorer – anyone who has an official role in controlling a team game.

To do this effectively – in other words, well enough to help the game run smoothly, fairly and enjoyably – you will need to do some planning in advance. This should include:

- learning the rules of the game
- learning what your duties will be
- knowing what the duties of the other officials are
- making sure you know the health and safety aspects of your duties
- making sure you have the right kit and footwear
- making sure you have the right equipment – e.g. whistle, scorecard, flags, warning cards and so on
- learning the various signals, waves and other methods of communication you will need
- practising your use of the equipment and signals
- checking when and where the game will be held
- knowing who you can turn to if you need help
- thinking about how you will assess yourself afterwards
- thinking about how you will prove you have officiated to your tutor (if your tutor is not present, or if you are officiating outside college)
- deciding how you will collect any evidence you need that you have done what you say you have done.

Unit outcome 4
Organise and supervise a practical session as part of a complete programme

Assessment criteria
- Plan and implement a practical session for a team and an individual sport.
- Demonstrate the need for safe practice in organising and implementing practical sports sessions.
- Evaluate the delivery of a practical session.

Planning training

Professionals spend much more time training for team sports than playing them competitively. But training too much has certain dangers. One of these is boredom, which leads to demotivation, lack of interest, a lowering of standards and, perhaps, giving up the game altogether. After all, a game is not worth playing or practising if it is not fun. Another danger is that it increases the risk of injuries, either because safety precautions are not taken, or simply because more time is being spent in strenuous activity. Finally, if too much training is done, mental and emotional tiredness can set in. Players feel weary and stressed, when they should be feeling keen and 'up for it'.

Organising a training session

To limit the risks and increase the benefits, training sessions should be part of a wider programme, and each session should itself be carefully planned. This planning is best done on paper so that you can
- get the whole picture
- change your plans if you don't like the look of them
- get the timing right
- allow for warm-ups
- re-plan after the session, noting where you can add, remove or alter activities.

Both the whole programme and the individual sessions should be planned on paper.

The training plan

The plan should look rather like a teacher's lessson plan. A specimen is given below, first for the overall programme, then for a specific practice session.

Title: Two-month training programme for AZ school youth football team

Aims
To develop skills and fitness during the first two months of the football season. The specific skills will be:

control	tackling
passing	crossing
dribbling	heading
screening	shooting
marking	some fitness training

Objectives
The team will:
- carry out a range of exercises designed to improve fitness, speed and stamina
- carry out exercises to improve ball skills, especially dribbling, passing and shooting
- practise marking and tackling
- practise corners, free kicks and scoring goals.

The individual needs of players will be assessed so that, if necessary, they can do some extra fitness training on their own.

Special considerations
The team consists of a group of 14-year-old girls from AZ school. They are only of average strength and stamina for their age, but are well motivated and keen to improve. Two of them are liable to asthma attacks; two more are short-sighted, and one is overweight.

Length of programme
Four weeks in September; four weeks in October. Each training session lasts 1.5 hours.

Cont'd

Venue
Springwell Playing Fields, Bogmarsh, Mudford-on-Ouse.

Structure of programme
The basic elements of the programme will be:
- control and passing
- dribbling, screening and tackling
- crossing and heading
- shooting
- special situations (throw-ins, free kicks and corners)
- tactics for attack and defence
- speed training
- endurance training.

In a week-by-week breakdown the activities listed under 'programme structure' will be arranged as shown in the table below.

Week no.	Activities
1	Control and passing; fast running practice
2	Dribbling, passing, tackling; fast running practice
3	Control, passing and crossing; endurance running
4	Control, passing and heading; fast running
5	Dribbling, screening, tackling, marking, shooting; fast running
6	Corners, passing, heading and shooting; endurance running
7	Dribbling, screening, tackling, marking and crossing; fast running
8	Dribbling, passing, heading and shooting; fast running

The practical session

This should fit in with your overall training plan. The session here is number two in the eight-week programme above.

The main activities will be introduced and carried out in the following manner (see table on page 252).

- Stage 1 – demonstration to ensure comprehension.
- Stage 2 – repeating what has been demonstrated.
- Stage 3 – increasing the speed or the complexity to provide a challenge.
- Stage 4 – players compete to show their skills (if appropriate).

THINK ABOUT IT ...

Plan your own coaching programme, making sure it fits in with the **coaching cycle**: planning, organising, observing, communicating, reviewing – then back to planning again.

Safe practice

Demonstrate the need for safe practice in organising and implementing practical sports sessions.

Safety is of the greatest importance in planning any sporting activity – and training sessions are no exception. If players are injured during a training session, then the session will have done more harm than good!

Planning for safety

While you are planning your training sessions, think about the following points.

Yourself
Make sure that:
- you have a first-aid kit available, and the skills to use it
- you have an emergency plan in case someone gets badly hurt.

Equipment
All players must be properly equipped. They must never use unsuitable footwear, and should wear any guards that might be needed.

The practical session

Time allowed	Key learning point	Team activity
5 mins	Warm up.	(a) Gentle stretching exercises. (b) Aerobic jogging. (c) More vigorous stretching exercises.
15 mins	Effective passing, limiting the number of unnecessary touches to the ball.	Passing Exercise Players pass the ball to the player with the number one higher than their own. (e.g. number 5 passes to 6, 11 to 1). Ball travels through the entire team. First, allow unlimited touches, then two touches, not allowing the ball to stop, then one touch. Try playing with left foot only, outside of foot only, without talking. Coaching Points • Eye contact. • Good passing technique. • Angles of support. • Proper weight of passes. Keep body open to the field of play
5 mins		Fast running in short bursts with rests.
15 mins	Effective dribbling and ball control, and keeping awareness of other players.	Dribbling Exercise Have players form four lines each at one corner of a 30 x 30 or 40 x 40 square. The first player in each line has a ball. On the coach's signal the first player dribbles diagonally across the square to the other side. Ideally, players will meet somewhere in the middle of the square and if they don't keep their eyes up, they will run into each other. After passing the middle players continue on to the opposite corner where they give a short pass to the next player. Then all four of those players go. If run continually this can be a good workout, because it goes fairly fast. Variations: Have players do a 'move' somewhere in the middle. Have players change speed as they go across square. Have players use different parts of their foot or their weak foot. Have each group try to 'pass' the person in front of them. (This messes up the timing of the meeting in the middle, but encourages speedier dribbling and accurate passes.) Just for fun, have them try to dribble across with their eyes closed and team-mates must direct them, or they can try to juggle their way across.
5 mins		Fast running in short bursts with rests.

Cont'd

15 mins	Ball control and tackling practice.	Ball Control Groups of three, one ball per group. Player A rolls the ball (receiving ground balls) or tosses the ball (receiving air balls) to either player B or player C. In this example, player C must control the ball and get a completed pass to player B. While this is occuring, player A immediately challenges player C and tries to win the ball back. After a successful pass, player C would then pick up the ball and repeat the activity as the defender. The defender is awarded a point for winning the ball back and is allowed to throw again. Coaching Points • Encourage defender to pressure quickly after the toss. Defender needs to work hard at closing down the space while the ball is in flight. • Receiving player's first touch should be away from the pressuring defender. • Player receiving the pass should move to create a clear passing lane. • Do not allow the receiving player to one touch the incoming toss. This is a receiving drill, as well as a drill that serves as a good warm-up for practices involving defenders.
12 mins	General passing and controlling techniques, and an awareness of where to pass the ball.	General Passing/Controlling Techniques Two groups of five or six players form circles about ten metres across. One player passes the ball to another, and immediately runs to take the place of the player she has passed to. The player receiving the ball passes to another and again runs to take her place. Players cannot pass to the person next to them. Anyone who gives a bad pass must run round the circle once.
10 mins	Practise all skills.	A short game of five or six a side on half the pitch. Players practise the skills they have used during the session.
8 mins	'Warm-down'.	Jogging.

Venue

Sport must be played in a safe place – and this is as true of practice and training as it is of matches. So ask yourself:

- is the condition of the ground suitable? If it is slippery, frozen, flooded or hard-baked are people going to get injured?
- is there litter, glass, stones, dog-dirt etc. which might cause injury or a health risk? (there is concern about dog-dirt because it can cause *Toxicara canis*, a serious eye infection)
- are special facilities needed – such as cricket nets?

Weather

1. Is the weather cold, wet or snowy? Remember that chilled muscles are easily injured, and that slipping and falling is dangerous. It is much easier to become chilled if the weather is wet as well as cold.
2. Is the weather hot? If so drinks must be available. It is surprisingly easy to become dehydrated if you exercise hard in hot weather. And people don't always notice if they are becoming dehydrated. In extreme cases special isotonic drinks, sometimes called rehydration drinks, are recommended.

3 Is the weather totally unsuitable? If so, call the session off, or hold it indoors instead.

Warm-ups

Proper warm-ups reduce the risk of injury. The best exercises are stretching exercises and gentle jogging or other aerobic exercise. In a warm-up session the first activities should be stretching exercises, designed to get all the main muscle groups and tendons ready for strenuous movement. The second phases should involve jogging, not too hard at first. The third part should consist of more stretching – before the serious activities begin. The stretching should be more vigorous at the end of the warm-up than at the beginning. Warm-ups must be planned, and built into the training schedule.

The training drills and other activities

1 Make sure that your players are using safe techniques. For example are cricketers bowling with a correct action, which will not injure themselves or others? Do goalkeepers know how to dive? Are you stressing the importance of correct tackling in rugby?
2 Make sure your drills and exercises avoid the risk of dangerous collisions and other accidents.
3 Do not allow players to become overtired during training. But keep them all active for most of the time, so that they do not get chilled (or bored!).
4 Vary the activities, so that players are not over-using certain muscle groups.
5 Don't try and train your players for longer than is good for them.

Discipline and 'person management'

1 Keep an eye on the relationships between your team members. If there is any 'aggro' or 'needle' discourage it, and talk to the players concerned. Remember that the mental and emotional well-being of your team is as important as its physical well-being.
2 Do not allow horseplay. What starts as a joke can end in injuries, and people will say that you – the coach – are to blame.
3 Encourage a positive and supportive attitude among your players. Do not allow people to feel 'left out'.
4 Always give clear instructions, using the whistle etc. if necessary, so that your players understand what you are trying to tell them.

After the session

1 Make sure there are adequate shower and changing facilities, so that people can get washed and warmed up easily.
2 Check that your players feel physically well.
3 If you think there has been a risk of injuries, make a note of the risk and eliminate the cause, if you can, before the next training session.

Evaluation

Evaluate the delivery of a practical session.

Evaluation is crucial in a training schedule, otherwise you have no way of knowing whether your team is getting better or not. Your overall evaluation must be done against the aims you have set down at the beginning of the programme (see page 250). If you do not do this, you are not evaluating the skills you have set out to improve.

You cannot evaluate the programme as a whole unless you evaluate each session separately. And you must evaluate each session in writing, otherwise you will forget what you and your team have practised by the end of the programme. Furthermore, each week you will make discoveries about the team's progress and the effectiveness of your own coaching. If you do not keep a record of these you will find it more difficult to make improvements in your coaching techniques. In addition, keeping a written record in a notebook will motivate your team because they will see you doing it and know that you care about their progress.

Your evaluation is an assessment of the progress made by players and by the team as a whole, and notes on how well each training exercise went. If your team were bored in an exercise, or if one of them got hurt, you will need to record these facts for future reference.

A typical evaluation

A typical evaluation of a practice session for your girls' soccer team might look like this.

A typical evaluation

Date	Activities	Group points	Individual points	Action required
15 Sept	1 Passing Exercise	Needs more practice. Poor receiving and control.	Anna passing too hard; Beatrice inaccurate.	More practice, using a variety of drills.
	2 Dribbling Exercise	Moving too slowly.	Skilful dribbling by Charlene. Donna kept tripping up when her eyes were shut.	Perhaps Donna should try another sport?
	3 Ball Control	Challenges too violent.	Has Anna got something against Evelyn?	Must warn them against violent challenges next time.
	4 General Passing and Controlling	Activity lost momentum. Team got bored?	Stacey and Tanya refused to run round when they did bad passes.	Try another exercise.
	5 Practice Game	Better standard.	Donna was good in goal.	Keep Donna in team.

Evaluation of own delivery: May have allowed the session to 'drag'. Should consider making the activities shorter and my delivery crisper. Must leave my mobile phone at home next week. Does my dislike of Donna mean that I am looking for faults all the time?

UNIT 11

Law and Criminology

Unit outcome 1
Examine law court operation in relation to different types of law

Assessment criteria

- Accurately describe the differences between four different types of law.
- Use three different criminal offences to explain how the relevant court would deal with each case.
- Compare three different job roles within two different courts.

For people hoping to join the police or the prison service, Law and Criminology is one of the most important units in the Edexcel BTEC syllabus. But law is such a huge subject that a National student can only begin to scratch the surface. There are whole libraries devoted to the law and how it operates, and even the top judges cannot hope to know it all. And the police, who have to enforce the law every day, are still only expected to know a small part of it.

Criminology, too, is a vast and expanding subject and again, nobody can ever hope to understand it all. But it is essential for police officers – and others who work in the same field, such as probation officers – to have some understanding of criminology.

The purpose of this unit is to introduce those basic aspects of law and criminology that every police officer would be expected to know.

Definitions

- **Law:** this can be defined as a system of rules operating in society to control people's behaviour.
- **Criminology:** this is the study of crime, and its causes and effects.

You will find longer and fuller definitions in dictionaries.

Types of law

Accurately describe the differences between four different types of law.

First of all, let us look at the law itself. There is more than one kind of law, and it is important to be able to distinguish between them.

1 Common law

Common law is very old; it existed in Britain thousands of years ago – in fact, since people started living together in groups and well before laws were ever written down. Common law, or something very like it, also exists in every other human society. Even in the poorest and least developed parts of the world, there are systems of common law.

The laws mentioned in the Bible and other holy books are, in effect, common law. The basic principles of right and wrong, such as 'thou shalt not kill' or 'thou shalt not steal' are also common law. In every society on the world, the majority of people consider killing and stealing to be wrong.

In the present day, the laws relating to murder, rape, theft, public order and trespass are all basically common law. This means that:

- the laws existed before Parliament ever started to make laws
- they were not originally written down
- the idea of precedent is used by the courts when offences against common law are being dealt with.

Precedent

This means, for example, that if a judge is trying a murder case, he or she will look up similar cases which happened in the past, to see how they were dealt with and what sentence (punishment) was given. Precedent means 'what was done before', and it is very important when carrying out common law.

Common law is based on feelings about right and wrong which we all have. In a way it is similar to common sense. For example, it is common law which tells us that people are more important than things, and that therefore crime against the person is more serious than crime against property. A few years ago an old man was sentenced because he lay in wait and shot a young man who was trying to break into his greenhouse. Many people felt that the old man had a right to defend his property and should have been let off by the court. But the young man was injured, and might have been killed. Common law in this case said that the thief's life was more important than the old man's property.

> **THINK ABOUT IT ...**
> Do you have any sympathy for the old man in this case – and if so why?

> **THINK ABOUT IT ...**
> - A woman who lives alone keeps a poker by her bed for self-protection. A burglar climbs in through her window and she hits him over the head. How should the law look at this?
> - An Englishman went on a business trip to America. One night he got drunk and couldn't find his way back to the hotel. It was late and in the end he knocked on someone's door to ask the way. The owner of the house shot him dead. Just bad luck – or did he deserve it?

2 Statute law

Statute law is law which is made by the government. In England laws are mainly made (or 'passed') by Parliament. These laws are written down from the very start, and are therefore different from common law. All new laws are statute laws, even though they may be based on an idea which comes from common law. For example the Data Protection Act 1998 is based on the common law idea that people have a right to privacy. But it was brought out to deal with the problems caused by information technology, and the fact that people's personal details (including their bank accounts and medical history) are kept on computer. It is very carefully worded to cover all the dangers of information being passed from one computer or database to another.

Common law and statute law can be seen as opposite sides of the same coin, and all law in Britain is either one or the other. But there are other types of law which we need to be aware of. The main ones are civil law and criminal law.

3 Civil law

Civil law is often to do with actions which are not crimes (unless they are done unlawfully). For example if your parents buy a house they may use a lawyer. Legal rights, such as the right to an education or to trade union membership, are part of civil law. The rights of consumers also come under the heading of civil law. If a married couple get divorced they may well need a lawyer to sort out who takes what, or to decide who looks after the children. But again it is not a criminal matter; it comes under the heading of civil law.

In civil law it is up to individuals to sort out their problems by going to court themselves, or with a lawyer. In criminal law, however, the state makes sure that justice is done whether the individuals concerned want it or not.

4 Criminal law

This is the kind of law which the police enforce. Most of the things we consider to be crimes: offences such as murder, assault, robbery and rape, come under the heading of criminal law.

Criminal law involves offences which are seen as being against everybody, even though they are not. If there is a car theft, the theft is against an individual, but it threatens all car owners, because their cars might get stolen as well. Criminal law takes the view that everybody is threatened by crime, and that is why it is the job of the public services, rather than, say, private lawyers or investigators, to deal with crime.

Occasionally there are offences which are on the borderline of civil and criminal law. Negligence is an example. If a college had no fire extinguishers, it would be breaking the Health and Safety at Work Act 1974. In itself, this would be a matter of civil law. But if there was a fire and 15 Public Service students died it would become a criminal case with 'criminal negligence' involved.

The court system

Use three different criminal offences to explain how the relevant court would deal with each case.

You can see from figure 11.1 that county courts deal with civil cases. If these cause problems which cannot be solved, the case is then looked at by the High Court. Criminal cases usually go through the magistrates' court and the Crown Court.

One of the main aims of the English justice system is 'to make the punishment fit the crime'. A glance at the newspapers shows that there is a great variety in the types of crimes that criminals carry out. Not only is there a wide range of crimes, but there are also many ways of carrying each one of them out. In the case of murder, for example, there is a multitude of reasons why one person might want deliberately to kill another.

If a person is charged with murder they first appear at the magistrates' court. But since murder is a crime which can carry a sentence of life imprisonment, it is clearly too serious to be tried at a magistrates' court. Once the identity of the accused is established, a date is fixed for a hearing of the case at the Crown Court.

The definition of murder is: 'unlawfully killing a reasonable person who is in being and under the Queen's Peace, the death following within a year and a day'. The Crown Court has to make sure that all the elements of this definition are satisfied by the act which the accused is said to have done. Thus the court has to show:

(a) that the killing was unlawful – i.e. deliberate and not in self-defence
(b) that the victim is dead
(c) 'reasonable person' – young babies killed by their mother, or patients in a coma on a life-support machine, may not be considered capable of thinking for themselves
(d) 'in being' – the victim was alive until killed by the accused
(e) 'under the King's (or Queen's) Peace' – the killing was not that of an enemy, in wartime
(f) 'following within a year and a day' – in effect, that the death was definitely caused by the accused's action, and not something else, such as illness or old age.

Courts would deal with other offences in different ways. For example, at the other end of the scale from murder, a relatively minor case such as a

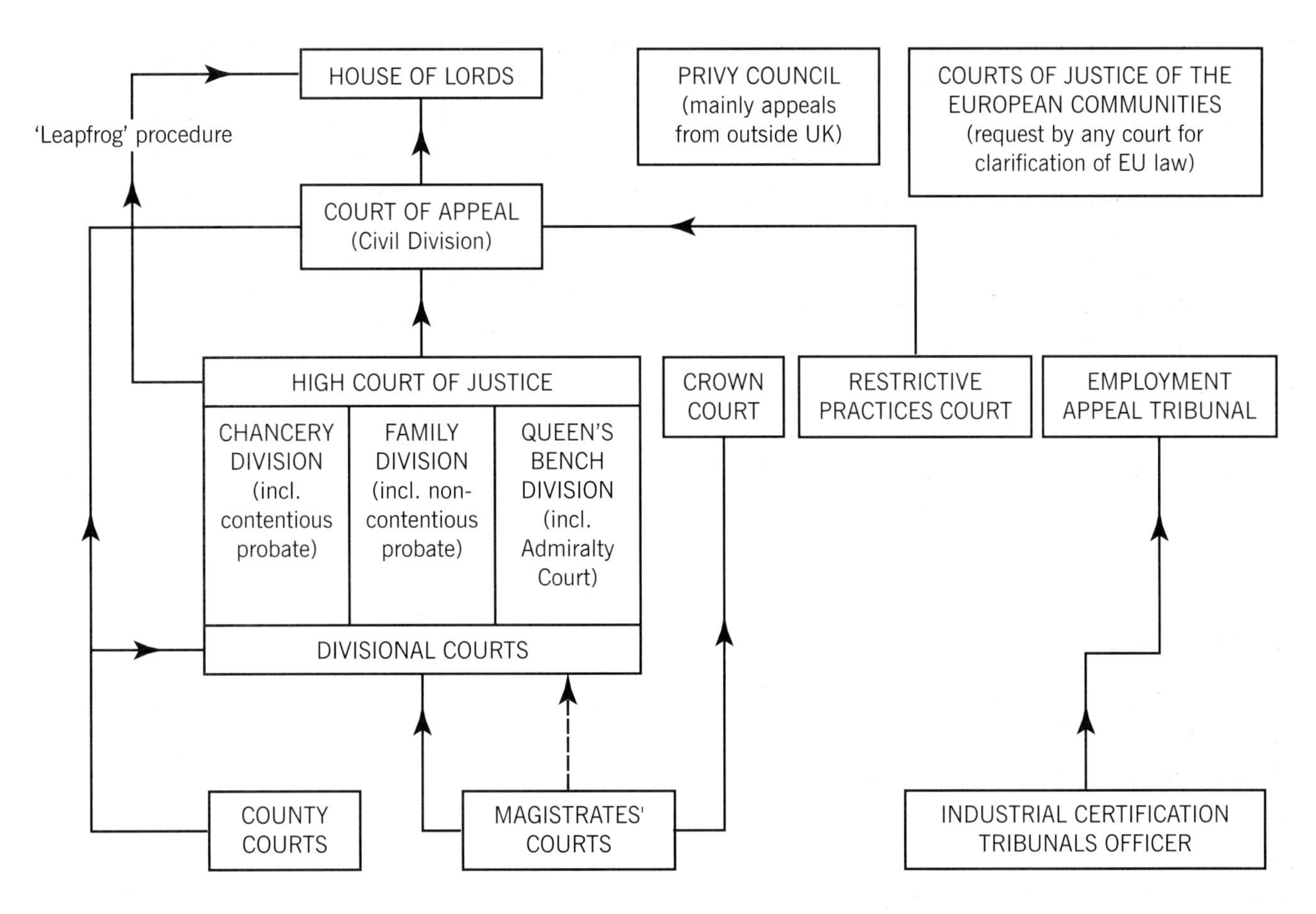

Figure 11.1 *The English court system (Source: Keenan, D. 1998.* Smith and Keenan's English Law, *London: Financial Times Management*

traffic offence will be dealt with in a magistrates' court. For example, in one case a council official was accused of driving at 108 miles an hour along the motorway. He conducted his own defence (this means he had no solicitor to speak for him). Since the man was apparently sane, he was allowed to do this. He gave a carefully prepared speech explaining that he was driving so fast because he had to get to his mother, who was in hospital with cancer. The magistrates listened carefully and sympathetically to what he had to say – and then banned him from driving for two weeks.

Finding out about criminal cases

If you visit either a magistrates' court or a Crown Court and listen to a few cases, you will be able to 'use three different criminal offences to explain how the relevant court would deal with each case'. In practice, you will find it much easier to complete this assessment criterion by going to a magistrates' court, as many of the cases there last only a few minutes, whereas the cases in a Crown Court can last for days or weeks. When you are in the court, sit quietly and make notes about:

- the nature of the offence
- the main points made by the prosecuting and defence solicitors
- the sentence given (if any).

When you use these notes to write your assignment, make sure you understand why a solicitor said a certain thing, or why the court's decision was what it was. And ask yourself if the magistrates paid any attention to the arguments of the defence solicitor!

Job roles within the court system

Compare three different job roles within two different courts

Magistrates' courts

Most courts in England and Wales are magistrates' courts (see figure 11.2). They are run by a 'bench' of magistrates. A magistrate is a kind of unpaid and unqualified judge. He or she listens to cases that come before the court and makes decisions on them. The accused person is then either sentenced (punished) or acquitted (let off). More information on sentencing is given on page 274.

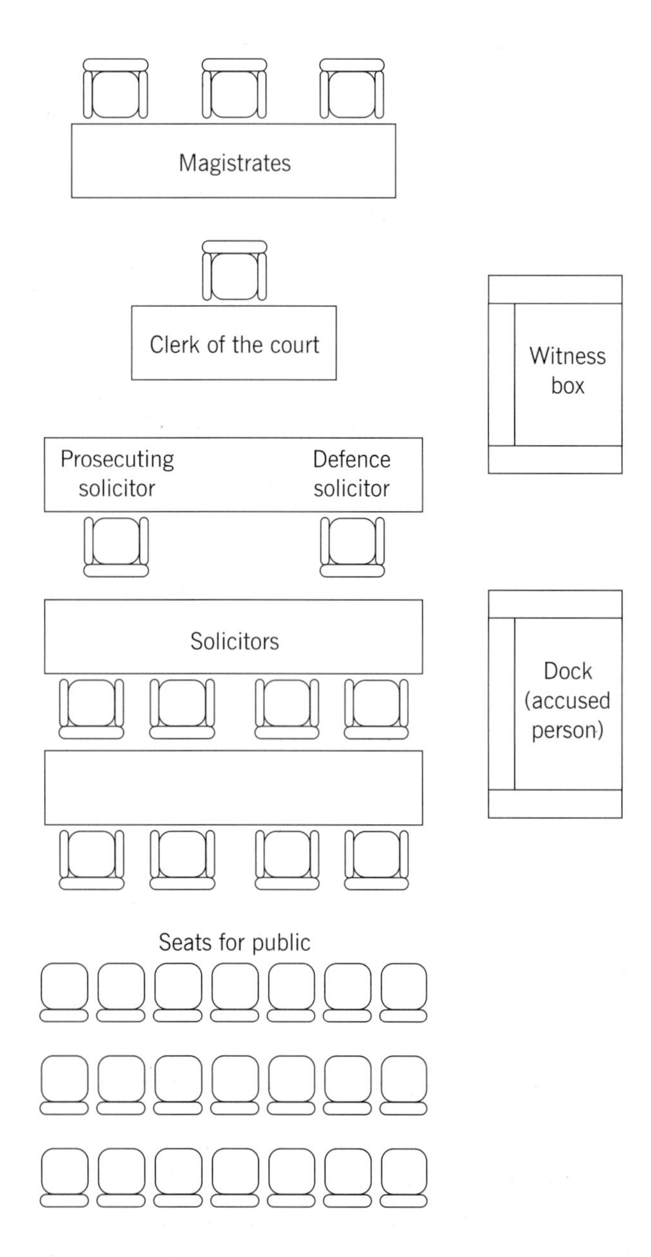

Figure 11.2 *Plan of a magistrates' court*

Job roles

The following people work in a magistrates' court.

1. **Magistrates.** Magistrates sit at the 'bench' at the front of the court, listen to the cases and make decisions about them. If they consider that the defendant is guilty of a crime they pass a sentence. The great majority of magistrates are not qualified lawyers, but they are carefully selected and trained in the work they do. These are called 'lay magistrates' and they are not paid – though they do receive expenses to compensate for loss of earnings while they are in court. They can question both the accused people and the solicitors who represent or prosecute them. In big towns and cities a few magistrates, called 'stipendiary magistrates', are qualified lawyers, and they receive a salary.
2. **The clerk of the court.** The clerk of the court is a qualified lawyer who is employed by the court. He or she explains points of law to the magistrates.
3. **Prosecution solicitors**, employed by the Crown Prosecution Service, outline the offence which the accused is supposed to have carried out. They give the police view of what happened.
4. **Defence solicitors** represent the accused person. If possible, they argue that the person is completely innocent. If this will not work, they give reasons why the person has committed the crime, in the hope that the accused will get a lighter sentence.
5. **Ushers.** These are people who make sure everyone is present in the court when they should be. They call people into the courtroom when they need to be there.

The best way to find out what happens in a magistrates' court is to go there yourself. If you are interested in the law, in crime or in people, you will find a court visit a fascinating experience. There is a public gallery in every court (except the youth court which deals with children) and anybody is allowed to go in to see for themselves whether the accused is getting a fair trial.

THINK ABOUT IT ...

- Visit a magistrates' court and watch some of the cases. Do you think the magistrates have a good attitude, or do they seem biased (either for or against the accused)?
- Is it right that cases should be heard by magistrates, when they have had no training in the law?

All criminal cases go first to a magistrates' court. There, three things can happen.

1. A decision is made, and as we have seen the accused is either sentenced or acquitted (let off).
2. The decision is put off to a later date, usually because the magistrates do not yet have the necessary pre-sentence reports (see page 266).
3. The case is too serious for a magistrates' court, and arrangements are made for the defendant to appear in a Crown Court. (Magistrates are only able to send a person to prison for six months for one offence and cannot fine anyone more than £5,000.)

Crown Courts

Most big cities in England and Wales have a Crown Court (see figure 11.3). (The system is different in Scotland and is beyond the scope of this book.)

Crown Courts are big places, and usually they have an elaborate system of security. Serious offences, sometimes called indictable offences, are tried at a Crown Court. Cases where the accused is likely to be fined more than £5,000, or sent to prison for more than six months, are always tried at Crown Court. Some cases fall between two stools, and are 'triable either way'. This means the defendant has a choice as to whether to be tried at the magistrates' court or the Crown Court. Often they choose the Crown Court.

The design of the court building is complicated, to protect judges, defendants, juries, and anyone else who may be at risk of intimidation or violence from associates of the defendants. Murderers, rapists, drug-barons and terrorists are tried at Crown Courts, and everything possible is done to ensure the health and safety of the people whose decisions will cause them to be locked up.

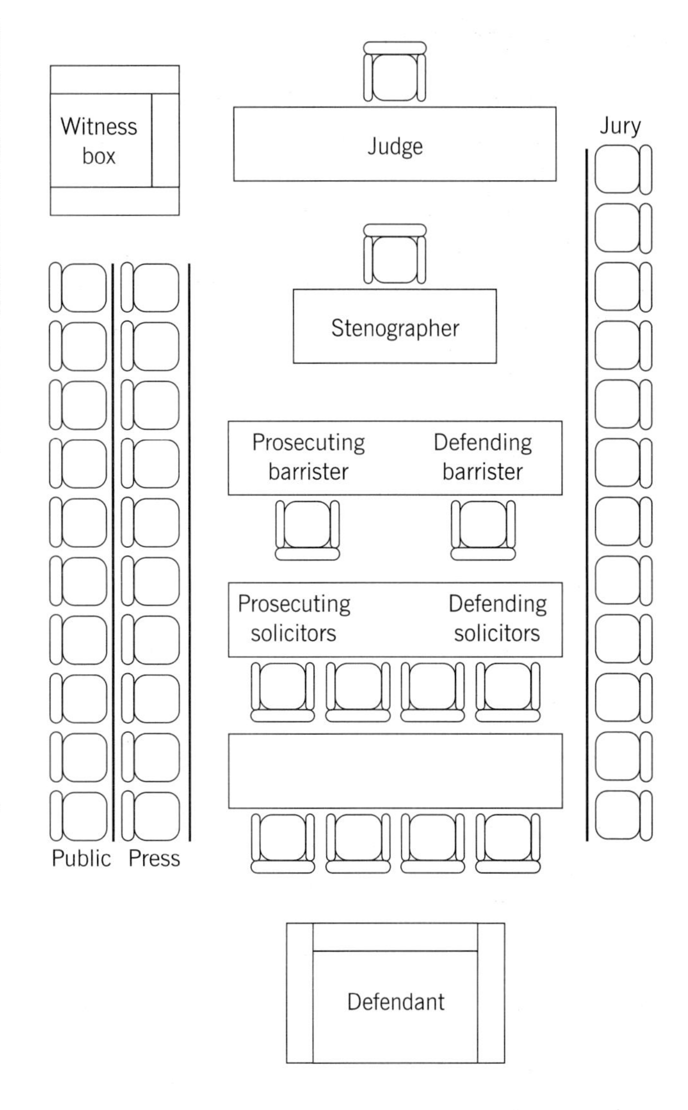

Figure 11.3 *Plan of a Crown Court*

Job roles

The people who work in a Crown Court include:

1 Judges. Instead of having three magistrates, untrained in the law, each Crown Court has one judge, who is highly trained in the law. The job of the judge is to listen to all the arguments by all the lawyers in the court, and to try to decide what happened. The judge then has to sum up the evidence and help the jury to reach a decision as to whether the defendant is guilty or not.

2 The jury. The jury are a 'panel' (group) of 12 ordinary people who have been officially called, by letter, to do jury service. They have no legal training. They have to be over 18 and under 70. Some people, such as police officers, are exempt from jury service. This means that they are never called to do it. The jury's job is to listen to the trial and then reach a decision as to whether the defendant is guilty. The judge helps them to reach this decision by summing up the trial for them.

Not everybody who is chosen to sit on a jury actually does so. Some are kept in reserve in case others fall ill. Others might know something about the case or the defendant. Such jurors are discharged before the trial begins, because they may be biased. Lawyers are able to question jurors to see if they might be prejudiced against their client for any reason. For example a lawyer defending a person accused of racially motivated crime might try to have jurors from ethnic minorities discharged, on the grounds that they might not give his client a fair hearing.

3 Lawyers. The main lawyers who appear in Crown Courts are called barristers. This means that they are specially trained experts in criminal law. They study for more years and are usually more highly paid than solicitors. As in a magistrates' court lawyers work either for the prosecution or the defence. In important cases the barristers have solicitors working with them, to make sure that they have the right facts at their fingertips when they are arguing their points.

4 Stenographer. This is a skilled typist who types everything that everybody says into a special typewriter, which changes the words into code – for security reasons. The case is also recorded on tape, so that there is absolutely no possibility of any of it being missed, if people want to listen again to what was said.

5 Ushers, security officers, etc. These do the same as they would do in a magistrates' court.

Like magistrates' courts, Crown Courts are open to the public. Many of the cases are dramatic and gruesome, so they are not places for the squeamish. And at times the barristers may argue obscure or incomprehensible points, at length. But for anybody who hopes to join the police or prison service, or to work with criminals, visiting a Crown Court is an experience not to be missed.

THINK ABOUT IT ...

What differences in attitude would you expect to find between magistrates and judges (a) towards criminals and (b) towards the police?

Unit outcome 2
Examine crime recording and the processing of offenders

Assessment criteria

- Compare official crime sources with at least one other crime statistical source, noting the differences.
- Briefly describe how the police record crime in statistical categories.
- Evaluate in detail the effects of reports from police and other agencies on the granting of bail or placing on remand.

Crime figures

'Crime figures' normally means the numbers of crimes recorded by the police, and are broken down under various headings. These headings include such things as the types of crime, the numbers of offenders found guilty, the sentences given, the criminals' background – and so on. Every year, crime figures are released for the country as a whole and for all the 43 police forces. They are collected by the Home Office (the part of the government which looks after the public services) and published by the Stationery Office in a book called *Criminal Statistics, England and Wales*. It is these crime figures that people refer to when they talk about 'official crime figures'

However, there is another type of crime statistic which appears in a book called the *British Crime Survey* (see page 264), which is also produced by the Home Office. These figures have nothing to do with the police. Instead they are obtained, like an opinion poll before an election, by questioning a cross-section of the British public. Though the *British Crime Survey* is called 'British', it actually refers to England and Wales, and has nothing to do with Scotland or Northern Ireland.

For this outcome you will be expected to show that you understand crime statistics whether they come from the police or the public, and to show some awareness of the differences between them.

Official police statistics

The police record 'notifiable offences'. These are 'serious' offences, and there is a full list of them in *Criminal Statistics, England and Wales*.

They also record such information as:

- clear-ups
- arrests
- numbers of offenders
- which courts the offenders went to
- types of offence
- sex, age-group, criminal history of offenders.

Ethnic monitoring is carried out separately and does not appear in the *Criminal Statistics, England and Wales*.

Offences which are not serious are left out of the official statistics.

How accurate are police crime statistics?

It is not easy to answer this question. Many people feel that such statistics can never be totally accurate, and there are a number of reasons for this.

1. Many crimes are not reported.
2. Many of the crimes which are reported are not recorded by the police.
3. Many of the crimes which are recorded by the police are not notifiable (i.e. not serious enough to be included in the national statistics).

4 If the police are more efficient, the crime rate goes up, because they record and investigate more crimes.
5 The police respond to public opinion, and may work hard on recording and investigating one type of crime, and neglect another.
6 'Clear-up rates' depend on offences being 'taken into account'. In effect, this means that the police are depending on a criminal's word, which may not be reliable.
7 Corrupt (or frightened) police officers may falsify statistics in order to make themselves or their force look better than they are.
8 According to statistics there are wide regional variations in crime. But these variations may instead reflect different data-collecting practices in the different forces.

In a way, the police are in a no-win situation. The more efficient they are in fighting crime, the higher their statistics, and the less efficient they seem on paper! In other words, the crime figures are not just a reflection of the amount of crime going on in an area. They also reflect the activities of the police, and in this sense they can never be reliable.

Political decisions also pose problems where police crime statistics are concerned. In 1994 there was a government drive to make the police more efficient. It was suggested that police officers with a low rate of convictions might be dismissed from the force. This meant that some police became over-enthusiastic, and were in danger of losing public support and cooperation as a result.

The *British Crime Survey*

From time to time the Home Office carries out a British Crime Survey and the Stationery Office publishes it as a Home Office Research Study. Each time they do this they interview over 10,000 people over the age of 16. The main purposes of this survey are:

(a) to try to find how much crime is really going on in the country and
(b) to find out whether people are reporting that crime to the police.

To find the full scope of the *British Crime Survey* you should try to look at it for yourself. The broad areas it covers include:

- the extent of crime
- the reporting of crime
- public satisfaction with the police
- aspects of burglary
- crimes of violence.

The types of information which appear in the *British Crime Survey* are not entirely the same as those which appear in *Criminal Statistics, England and Wales*. For example *Criminal Statistics, England and Wales* does not deal with public perceptions of the police which are, after all, a matter of people's opinions. Equally, it has nothing to say about ethnicity, whereas the *British Crime Survey* does. This highlights one difficulty in comparing statistical sources of crime information: like is not being compared with like. To put it differently, a comparison between one sheep and another is a lot more valid than a comparison between a sheep and a goat.

There are various reasons why the *British Crime Survey* may be inaccurate.

- A sample of 10,000 out of over 50 million is very small – just 0.02 per cent.
- The offences mentioned in the survey may not be notifiable.
- Members of the general public may even not be clear as to what is crime and what is not.
- Respondents to the questionnaire may have misunderstood the questions, or deliberately given wrong answers.

On the other hand there are some ways in which the *British Crime Survey* may be more accurate than the police figures in *Criminal Statistics, England and Wales*. These include the following.

- Large numbers of offences are never reported to the police, either because they are not considered serious, or because the victims believe that the police will do nothing about them.
- People who are hostile to the police come from the social groups which are most likely to be victims of crime. They may well answer a questionnaire, yet never communicate with the police on principle.

On the other hand there are some reasons why the *Criminal Statistics, England and Wales* should give a more accurate picture of crime than the *British Crime Survey*.

- It is concerned with fact and not opinion.
- It includes the total figures for all recorded crime, and is not based on a sample.

Another point to bear in mind is that crimes are often reported to the police for insurance purposes. For this reason there is now less difference betwen the crime figures in the *Criminal Statistics, England and Wales* and those of the *British Crime Survey* than there used to be.

Statistical categories of crime

Briefly describe how the police record crime in statistical categories.

When police officers record crimes, whether they are reported on the phone or over the counter, they do so by filling in a form. This ensures that all necessary aspects of the crime are covered when the first record is made. As the form is a standard form it also means that the information can be transferred into a database (and therefore changed into statistics) without too much effort.

The statistics included in *Criminal Statistics, England and Wales* are not all police statistics: some of them come from the courts and elsewhere, but they are all real figures, not 'guesstimates'.

Those that come from the police are divided into approximately 50 categories (though this may vary from year to year). These include:

- type of offence
- clear-up
- numbers of offences per 100,000 of the population
- burglary
- motor vehicle theft
- violence against the person
- sexual offences
- robbery
- theft and handling stolen goods
- fraud and forgery
- criminal damage.

The police also record how crime rates for each type of crime vary from one year to the next.

THINK ABOUT IT ...

Give as many reasons as you can why the police collect and publish crime statistics.

Bail or remand

Evaluate in detail the effects of reports from police and other agencies on the granting of bail or placing on remand.

Bail

Bail is essentially a promise made by the accused to appear in court at an arranged time. Occasionally someone has to put up a sum of money as a kind of insurance that the person concerned will actually turn up in court – and not rush off to Brazil or somewhere for an extended holiday. Bail is usually allowed when the accused does not seem to present a risk to the general public while remaining in the community.

Remand

Where an offender is violent, or has nowhere to live, he or she is likely to end up 'on remand' – that is, in prison. Many of Britain's prisoners are remand prisoners who have not yet been to court.

In recent years this has become a political issue because there is evidence to suggest that the courts are unfair in deciding who should be given bail and who should be imprisoned on remand. The table on the following page shows the percentage of remand prisoners who are from ethnic minorities. Bearing in mind that only six per cent of the British population belongs to ethnic minorities, it seems that they are more than twice as likely as white people to be put on remand.

Possible reasons for this are that members of ethnic minorities:

Remands in custody				
Year	**Total**	**White**	**Ethnic minority**	**Percentage from ethnic minority**
1990	60,174	50,471	8,556	14.7
1994	68,414	57,420	10,002	14.4

Source: *Social Trends*

(a) are more likely to commit violent crime
(b) are more likely to be homeless
(c) are less likely to turn up in court if they are not imprisoned first
(d) face prejudice from the police or courts who treat them more harshly.

Pre-sentence reports

Whether the accused is granted bail or put on remand depends on the reports that are written about him or (very rarely) her. The reports come from the police, from social workers, from probation officers or from psychologists. Such reports are called 'pre-sentence reports'. But obviously they can be written to suit the apparent or perceived needs of the situation. As long as the police and the people who work with them are predominantly white, there is always the possibility that these reports will be slanted against a black defendant. The stereotyping of blacks by whites is well known, and it may be that black people are always in danger of being thought of as violent whether they are or not. This could be the explanation of (a) above: that black people are not more likely to be violent, but are perceived as being more likely to be violent. Similar points could be made with (b) and (c).

> **! THINK ABOUT IT ...**
>
> What can be done to give ethnic minorities, the poor and the homeless a fairer deal from the police and the courts? Or is enough already being done?

There is also research to show that homeless people are more likely to be put on remand. Is this because homeless people are more likely to wander off and not turn up in court, or is it because of society's prejudice against the homeless?

The Crown Prosecution Service

Prosecution

The Crown Prosecution Service is an organisation of lawyers which exists to do the paperwork needed for prosecuting an accused person in the courts. 'Prosecution' means taking an offender to court with the intention of getting them sentenced.

Before 1986 the prosecution of offenders was left to the police. But with increasing accusations of police incompetence or malpractice (using faked evidence) the Crown Prosecution Service was brought in. It was hoped that fewer cases would be dismissed by the courts if prosecutions were properly prepared by experts who had the time to do it, rather than by overworked police officers who didn't like paperwork. In the long run it was believed that the Crown Prosecution Service would save police time, as well as helping the police's reputation.

In fact there is still plenty of paperwork for the police to do, for, although they don't prepare prosecutions for the courts, they still have to get all the evidence together and send it to the Crown Prosecution Service. If even a small bit of evidence is wrong, it can lead to a case being thrown out of court – or not even getting to court. This means a lot of police time has been wasted, and a criminal may have got off scot-free.

Unit outcome 3
Analyse crime trends and the reasons for crime

Assessment criteria
- Produce a survey of crime trends within the local area detailing the categories of offences committed.
- Evaluate at least four different views on why there is crime from both sociological and psychological perspectives.

What is crime?

Definitions of crime vary, but a basic one is 'an act contrary to law'.

THINK ABOUT IT ...

Can you find a better definition of crime than this?

What are crime trends?

Trends are fashions, and there are fashions in crime just as there are fashions in many other things. At a simple level the rise and fall of some kinds of crime is due to changes in our way of life: horse-stealing has gone down as car theft has gone up. Drug crime is affected by the availability of drugs and, sometimes, the appearance of new drugs on the streets. Mugging in town centres has gone down because of the erection of television cameras on every roof and lamp-post. Theft from vehicles may well go down as more secure locking devices are invented.

As we have seen in the previous unit outcome, crime trends may reflect not just fashions in crime, but fashions in recording crime, and in policing in general.

If the government say the police must secure more convictions, as they said in the early 1990s, crime rates are likely to rise as officers try to be more 'productive'. If there is greater public concern, for example, about domestic crime, or child abuse, then the police have to focus on these areas even though, privately, they may feel their time and resources would be better spent elsewhere. If the police concentrate on a specific type of crime convictions are likely to rise, and therefore the apparent trend will be a rise in that sort of crime, even though the reality is that there has been a rise in police hours spent on that sort of crime.

Some crime trends have been identified which have nothing to do with new drugs, new technology or new policing methods. These, which are bigger and potentially more important than the ones mentioned so far, are the result of social and economic changes.

Urbanisation

In other countries, especially the developing world, crime rises as people move from the country to the quickly expanding cities. Places such as Mexico City and Nairobi have rapidly increasing crime rates. Nothing so dramatic happens in Britain, but we have big local variations due to things like council policy in housing certain types of family, and the creation of what are called 'sink' estates.

Economic change

Crime also varies in Britain according to changes in the economy – i.e. the wealth and productivity of the country in comparison to other countries. When the economy is booming, and wages are relatively high, and prices relatively low, crime against the person – such as rape and murder – goes up. Crime against property, on the other hand, such as theft, goes down.

In times of recession the opposite is true. When wages are low and prices are high, crime against property goes up, and crime against the person goes down. Common sense suggests that mass unemployment also leads to an increase in crime, but Home Office figures do not support this.

> **THINK ABOUT IT ...**
> Why do crime against the person and crime against property rise or fall according to whether the economy is doing well or badly?

Local crime trends

Produce a survey of crime trends within the local area detailing the categories of offences committed.

The best place to find crime trends for your local area is in the current policing report for your local force. Each police force helpfully gives a breakdown of all the main crimes they have had to deal with – in the form of a table of statistics. Usually there is also a table showing the changes that have taken place in recent years.

When you analyse trends, or anything else, try to distinguish between what you can be sure of, and what is just guesswork or probability. You will find that much analysis is a matter of guesswork or probability, but this does not mean it is useless. The fact that smoking causes cancer was first suspected through analysing some statistics: if it hadn't been for the statistics and the analysis nobody would ever have known it!

A simple example of local crime statistics and the way they can be analysed is given below.

Factual analysis

Some definite statements can be made as a result of studying these figures. It is always best to start with the obvious ones.

- Theft and criminal damage are by far the commonest crimes.

Crime	Recorded 99/8	Recorded 98/7	Change	Detected
Homicide	36	38	–2	31
Other violence	8,462	8,993	–531	6,759
Sexual offences	1,592	1,393	199	1,397
Household burglary	55,326	54,495	831	10,016
Other burglary	36,107	31,895	4,212	4,336
Robbery	3,500	2,920	580	824
Thefts from motor vehicles	42,587	44,260	–1,673	3,299
Thefts of motor vehicles	34,668	33,055	1,613	5,013
Other theft	48,483	51,400	–2,917	13,453
Fraud/forgery	4,906	5,437	–531	2,623
Handling	2,735	2,730	5	2,772
Criminal damage	44,826	43,603	1,223	5,746
Others	2,964	2,771	193	3,025
TOTAL	286,192	282,990	3,202	59,294

Adapted from the West Yorkshire Police Chief Constable's Annual Report

- Most crimes of violence have gone down.
- The total number of crimes has risen.

These are all undeniable facts according to the figures. But they may not be true in reality. To see whether crime trends are fast or slow, it is necessary to look at percentage changes, not the raw figures we are given here. It is therefore worth spending time with your calculator to work out some percentage changes.

If you look at the third and fourth rows in the table, and calculate the change as a percentage of the 98/7 figure, you will see that the *percentage* change in sexual offences has been much bigger than the change in household burglary, even though the *actual* change is much less. This means that the trend in sexual offences is rising fast, while that in household burglary is only rising slowly. All these are factual analyses because they are definitely true.

Inferences

There is more to analysing crime figures than simply saying what they actually show. We can also look at what they *might* show. In a local area the increase in sexual offences may be for a number of reasons. New night clubs may have opened. People may have more money to spend and are therefore going out more. The law may have changed, or policing priorities may have changed. Or it could be that, due to changes in public attitudes, people are becoming more willing, year by year, to report sexual offences.

Inferences are deductions, or possibilities which come from the information. None of the points in the above paragraph are certain, but any of them *might* be true.

> **THINK ABOUT IT ...**
>
> Which of the two kinds of analysis mentioned above: factual analysis or inference, do you think are most useful for the police?

Why has crime occurred?

Evaluate at least four different views on why there is crime from both sociological and psychological perspectives.

When you evaluate an idea you give a reasoned opinion about its value. This means using words like 'since' and 'because'. 'Sociological and psychological perspectives' means looking at crime from the points of view of various sociologists and psychologists. Remember that a sociologist studies the way groups of people, or the whole of society, behave. A psychologist studies how individuals behave in relation to their environment and to other individuals.

There are many views on why there is crime. The following headings give examples, together with explanations from sociological and/or psychological perspectives.

1 Functionalist views of crime

In the 1950s Emile Durkheim said that crime was a normal aspect of all societies. He claimed that this was not a bad thing because everybody was different, and therefore some people found it easier to break the law than others. Durkheim also suggested that if there was no such thing as crime, we would have to invent it, because it is necessary for people to condemn some sort of unacceptable behaviour – however unimportant it might be. Cohen, a follower of Durkheim, said that crime and deviance (abnormal behaviour) were useful warning signs, telling us what was going on in people's minds, and telling us whether society was 'sick' or needed changing in some way. Merton said that society was a game, and that criminals broke the rules of the game. This might mean that there was something wrong with the criminals – but it might also be a way of telling us all that there was something wrong with the rules of society's game. Strengths and weaknesses of the functionalist view of crime include the following.

Strengths

- The arguments are easy to understand and have an element of common sense in them.

- If crime is 'necessary' in some ways, then we don't have to spend too much time, effort or money in doing anything about it.
- If we want to do something about crime we don't have to try and change the whole of society.
- Functionalist arguments echo traditional religious views of good and evil. Just as evil is necessary in order that there should be good, and hell balances out heaven, so crime is needed as part of the total reality of society.

Weaknesses

- Functionalist arguments don't seem to take crime seriously. They have nothing to say about the psychology of criminals, or the suffering that crime causes the victims of crime.
- These arguments are too similar to the traditional views of religion, which see evil as necessary. They add nothing to our understanding of the real nature of crime.
- They give us no encouragement to try and fight, or prevent, crime.

2 Marxist views of crime

These views, put forward by people such as Gramsci and Hall, say that crime is the result of the division of society into 'haves' and 'have nots' which was originally described by Karl Marx (see page 76) in the 19th century. In their opinion the poor are exploited by the rich all the time, and there is a dog-eat-dog relationship between the different social classes. In the view of most Marxists, the rich are in effect stealing from the poor, because they pay the poor less than their labour is worth, and then, having sold the things the poor have made, pocket the difference.

Since it is in human nature that we all have a need for justice, the poor are aware that they are being exploited and 'ripped off'. They are therefore morally justified, in their own eyes at least, in redressing the balance by doing some unofficial redistribution of wealth in the form of crime. If the rich are stealing from them, then there is no reason why they should not steal from the rich.

Marxists' explanations of crime put everything down to the unequal distribution of wealth in society. Most criminologists probably agree with the Marxists to some extent. The Marxist arguments have the following strengths and weaknesses.

Strengths

- They are easy to understand, and appeal to people's ideas of natural justice.
- They do not depend on complicated psychological arguments about the unconscious mind, or maternal deprivation.
- They are supported by the fact that crime rates are higher in poor areas.
- They explain the apparent fact that a higher proportion of blacks than whites are criminals by relating this to the fact that black people are on average poorer: this means that Marxist ideas are anti-racist; they explain black crime by saying that black people are discriminated against in British society.

Weaknesses

- They excuse crime and are soft on it – because they blame crime on society, not the individual criminal.
- They offer no 'cure' for crime except the extreme one of changing the fundamental organisation of society (which not many people seem to want).
- They relate everything to money, whereas crime may be caused by other factors.
- They do not clearly explain why some poor people are criminals and others are not, or why some rich people are criminals.

3 Interactionist views of crime

This view of crime states that everybody has a different idea of what crime is, and that what matters is not what something 'really' is – but what we think it is. Howard S Becker, one of the people who developed this view of crime, said that crime is what we define, or describe, as crime. Thus if the government decided that it was a crime to whistle in the street, then whistling in the street would automatically become a crime. Interactionists take great interest in social control – that is, the influence of the family, the peer group, schools, the media and the police (among others) on what we consider to be crime. For interactionists the motivation of crime is very important, and each crime is a unique event, rather than a symptom or sign of something that is going on in society. Interactionists also believe that labelling has a big effect on crime and our view of it. In other words, if we describe someone as a criminal, then that person's behaviour will be affected by our description, or label. Like other psychological and sociological views of crime, this has strengths and weaknesses.

Strengths

- It brings out the element of free will in crime, and allows us to think that a person can be responsible for what they do, and guilty of what they have done.
- It avoids stereotyping criminals by focusing attention on the individual nature and meaning of each crime.
- It shows why crime figures are unreliable (in other words, they vary because society's attitude, or the attitude of the police, towards crime varies).
- It shows that we can prevent crime partly by not labelling people.
- It avoids the over-simplification of claiming that all crimes are essentially the same.

Weaknesses

- The ideas behind this theory are rather complex and abstract.
- The interactionist approach suggests that we should not try to improve society. It is therefore not very practical.
- It encourages guilty people to make excuses for their crimes.
- It blames changes in crime figures on changes in police behaviour, thus weakening the position of the police in the fight against crime.
- This theory says that nothing is certain, and seems rather personal and subjective – a matter of opinion, in other words.

4 The view that crime is caused by drugs

This view has not been put forward by any famous psychologists or sociologists, but it is widely believed in at the present time. Research shows, for example, that 50 per cent of the people arrested in some inner cities have traces of heroin in their bloodstream. Motoring offences and offences against the person are commonly related to alcohol, and everywhere there is evidence that many career criminals have embarked on crime in order to finance their drug habit. In addition there are many gangland killings in places such as South London and Moss Side, Manchester, which are linked to drug trafficking and the drug barons' 'turf wars'.

The enormous influence of drugs on behaviour is based on two things: the pleasure they bring, and the fact that many are physically addictive. The pleasure is a 'psychological addiction', so that even with cannabis, a non-addictive drug, people may 'need' it because they need the pleasure it brings. Other drugs, such as crack cocaine and heroin, are highly physically addictive, interfering with the body's chemistry to create a need and a dependence. Psychological factors, such as low self-esteem, and sociological ones, such as poverty or peer group pressure, can lead to drug involvement and the crime which is said to follow.

Strengths

- There is strong statistical evidence linking drugs to crime.
- Everybody can understand this theory since it is based on measurable observation rather than psychological or sociological theory.
- It offers a clear course of action: to stop people taking drugs.

Weaknesses

- It may be exaggerated by the current public hysteria about drugs.
- Except for the work of charitable organisations and the social services, there seems to be little that can be practically done about the drugs problem. Methods of stopping people trying drugs in the first place seem to have little success.
- It may show that drugs are linked to crime, but not that drugs cause crime. In other words, the real cause may lie somewhere else.

Unit outcome 4
Examine the main principles of sentencing in relation to law court operation

Assessment criteria

- Describe how people may be awarded compensation in both civil and criminal court cases.
- Explain how judges or magistrates arrive at the penalty they impose on a guilty person in at least three cases.
- Provide details of the limitations placed upon sentencing in two different types of courts.

Compensation in civil and criminal court cases

Compensation is a sum of money paid by a person or organisation that has done wrong to a person or organisation that has been wronged. Sometimes compensation is called 'damages'. Compensation is part of civil law, even though it can sometimes be paid out after a crime. This means that compensation is dealt with in the civil courts, such as the county court, not in the magistrates' or Crown Courts.

There are various circumstances in which compensation can be paid. Three of them are discussed below.

ANALYSIS

1 Compensation for injury

If a person falls off a rock on Dartmoor it is unlikely that they can claim compensation, because nobody can be blamed for the shape of the rock. But if somebody falls down a flight of steps outside a shop, it may well be that the steps are unsafe and the shop can be sued by the person who has fallen.

For the action (i.e. the court case) to be successful, the person who fell has to prove that they are injured, that the injury was due to their fall down the steps, and that the steps were unsafe. In order to do this they need to go to a solicitor.

It is also necessary for the injured person to go to the doctor, not only to receive treatment for the injury, but to provide evidence for the court of the nature of the injury and the time that it took place. For example, if the first result of the fall was a badly swollen knee, the knee needs to be examined before the swelling goes down.

To prove that the swollen knee was due to the fall down the steps, and not something else, like a failed attempt to do a wheelie on a mountain bike, or a mishap in the shower, there need to be witnesses. The best witnesses would be unbiased people who happened to be walking past the shop at the time. People who work in the shop might try to claim that the injured person threw herself down the steps in the hope of being able to claim compensation at a later date.

The best evidence that the steps were unsafe would be photographs. If the injured person threatens to sue the shop at the time, the evidence of the unsafe steps might be destroyed. The owners of the shop may well fill in the holes with cement, or do whatever else is needed to claim that they were safe all along. Ideally the solicitor or some other person will therefore take photographs of the steps in their original dangerous state. Failing that, signs of recent repairs might show that the steps could well have been unsafe.

A swollen knee by itself would not get much compensation. But if the knee grew painful, and the person who had fallen was found to have arthritis as a result of the fall, the injured person might have a greater case for compensation. And if the injured person had to spend long periods of time off work because of the injury, or was forced to end her well-paid career as a mud-wrestler, she might get still more compensation.

The case would then be prepared by the solicitors. They would contact the shop, who would have solicitors of their own. Communication, of course, is between the solicitors, not the people who are really involved in the case. They write letters, collect evidence, and make offers to each other, in the hope that the case will be settled out of court. The advantage of this (if the shop is to blame) is that the shop will not have to pay heavy costs to the court. Equally, the injured person will get her money sooner. If the case does go to court, however, the injured person may receive more compensation.

There is no jury in a case of this sort: only a judge. And there is an element of risk for the injured woman. If it looks as if she is a fraudster, she will have to pay all the court costs and might even get prosecuted. But as long as she is honest and has been properly guided by her solicitors she could well get several thousand pounds.

2 Compensation following the result of a crime

Let us imagine that a security guard attempts to foil an armed robbery at a warehouse full of gold bullion. We might think that if the guard only gets paid £4 an hour he should not risk his life for a few bars of gold, but perhaps he is an ex-soldier or a very brave man. In his attempt to resist the robbers he is shot in the neck and paralysed. Nobody will expect him to be in a fit state to sue the robbers who shot him. In any case, the robbers may get their gold, run off to Brazil or Paraguay, and never be seen again except in the Sunday colour supplements. So what happens to the security guard? He stays in hospital, waiting for a miracle cure, while lawyers working for him and the Criminal Injuries Compensation Board agree the value of his compensation.

The compensation, which will be funded by the state (in other words, come out of government money), will take into account the cost of full, round-the-clock care for the paralysed man. Obviously, no amount of money can bring him back his mobility and family life. But if his wife has a part to play in his care, then she will receive a considerable amount of money for the work she does. She will also receive money to compensate for the money she and/or her husband cannot now earn. If his paralysis is not complete and he can be cared for at home, all the aids, such as lifts, which he might need, and all the cost of health care, will have to be covered by the compensation for as long as he is expected to live.

If such a man dies, the compensation is much less than the hundreds of thousands it might be if he lives in a seriously disabled state.

Similar or even bigger compensation sums are involved when a child is brain-damaged during an operation or a difficult birth, and it can be shown that the hospital was in some way to blame for the brain damage. A brain-damaged child can live just as long as a child who is not brain-damaged, even though its life is blighted. The compensation must pay for a lifetime's full medical and nursing care.

3 Compensation for libel

Libel is the act of writing malicious lies about someone in a newspaper, magazine or book, or broadcasting them in the media. If the person is not famous, the amounts of money involved in compensation would be small, but the more famous, or the richer, the person is, the larger the amounts of money are likely to be.

Libel is a criminal offence, and therefore important libel cases are tried by jury. The jury has the right to fix the amount of damages – that is, the money that has to be paid to the person who has been wronged. Often the defendant in a libel case is a newspaper which has published something suggesting that a famous person is a liar or a crook. The famous person takes them to court, and juries, which are made up of ordinary people who like their privacy, make the newspapers pay enormous sums to the person they have lied about.

The amount of money is related to the suffering caused to the libelled person and their family and, in some cases, their possible loss of earnings. For example if an MP was libelled in a newspaper and lost his seat because of it, he would have suffered financially by losing his MP's salary of £47,008 a year (in 1999) as well as losing his reputation.

FOCUS

Here are examples of the sums of money involved in libel cases. The 1p awarded to Albert Reynolds meant that the accusation was really a matter of opinion and the case could not be decided for certain either way.

The longest-running libel law case in the UK's history was the McLibel case, 1998, at 313 days.

Damages and dates

- *Lord Aldington* v. *Tolstoy* & *Watts* for the distribution of 10,000 pamphlets suggesting that he was a war criminal in World War II (£1.5 million in 1989 – highest).
- Six-year-old Jonathan Hunt who sued the *Sun* newspaper (circulation four million) over allegations that he was 'the worst brat in Britain' (£35,000 in 1991).
- Former Irish prime minister Albert Reynolds sued the *Sunday Times* over an article which suggested that he had lied to the Irish parliament (£0.01 in 1996).

Deciding upon penalties

Explain how judges or magistrates arrive at the penalty they impose on a guilty person in at least three cases.

Main principles of sentencing

Sentencing is the 'punishment' of offenders by the courts. A sentence usually restricts a person's freedom in some way. There is a wide range of sentences open to the courts, and they keep changing as new laws and procedures are brought in. Some of the main ones are given below.

1. **Binding over.** This is a promise to keep the peace. It is used for people who have been accused of violent or potentially violent behaviour.
2. **Absolute discharge.** This is not really a punishment. It means either that the person was found not guilty, or that there was not enough evidence to continue with the case.
3. **Conditional discharge.** This means that the offender has done something wrong. However, if there is no further offence within three years then the matter will be dropped. But if there is a further offence within the three years, the person can be sentenced for the original offence.
4. **Probation order.** An offender (over 17) has to be supervised by a probation officer for between one and three years. This may involve living in a hostel and having counselling or medical treatment.
5. **Suspended sentence.** A prison sentence of two years or less may be suspended. This means that the offender does not actually go to prison – unless there is a re-offence.
6. **Prison.** Imprisonment is sometimes called a 'custodial sentence' – 'custody' being imprisonment. Life imprisonment is officially 25 years but can be reduced to 17 for good behaviour. In extreme cases, such as that of Myra Hindley, one of the moors murderers, people can be kept in prison indefinitely.
7. **Detention in police cells.** This must be for no longer than four days.
8. **Detention.** This word is used when boys or young men of 14 to 21 are given short periods of imprisonment.
9. **Youth custody.** These are periods of imprisonment, lasting longer than four months, for young people of either sex between 15 and 21.
10. **Custody for life.** This is the name given to life imprisonment, when the prisoner is under 21.
11. **Young offender institution.** This is a kind of prison where people under 21 are prepared for their return to the community.
12. **Remand centre.** This is a prison for people awaiting trial.
13. **Community service order.** Offenders over 17 carry out unpaid work for between 40 and 240 hours.
14. **Secure training order.** These are given to some young people between 12 and 15 who have

committed serious offences. It is a kind of imprisonment with education and training.

Cautions

A caution is a formal record of an offence by the police. It does not involve going to court, but the caution does stay on police records for three years. Its purpose is to warn the offender that there is a danger of a more serious sentence, should there be a re-offence.

THINK ABOUT IT ...

There are two kinds of caution: the one described above, and the one given by police to suspects whom they are about to interview. What is the difference?

Fines

A fine is a punishment but it would not normally be called a sentence. Money is paid to the court, and goes into government funds. Fines are not used to pay court costs. These costs are paid in civil cases, often by the person who has lost the case, in order to save public money. Nor are fines the same as compensation, where money would go to an individual or organisation that has been wronged, rather than into government funds.

Severity of sentencing

The basic concept of sentencing is that the courts should 'make the punishment fit the crime'. How severe the sentence is depends on the following factors.

1. **What the crime is.** For example, a large theft is punished more severely than a small one; theft is a less serious matter than armed robbery or murder.
2. **The maximum and minimum sentences for that crime**, as set out in the statute book (law) or by precedent (the sentence given in similar cases in the past). For example, murder carries a sentence of life imprisonment, whereas manslaughter does not.
3. **The age of the offender.** The sentences for young people are more lenient than they are for adults. Young people are not supposed to be locked in adult prisons (though it appears that occasionally they are).
4. **The personal circumstances of the offender.** A student on a college course may receive a less severe sentence than a person of the same age who is unemployed, on the grounds that the college will be a good influence on the young offender.
5. **The circumstances of the crime.** For example the courts regard a burglary on an empty house as less serious than a burglary on one which has people inside. This is because the possibility of anyone getting hurt is reduced if the house is empty.
6. **How often the offender has committed crimes in the past.** A frequent offender will receive harsher sentences than a first-time offender, and is much more likely to be sent to prison.
7. **Whether anybody was threatened or got hurt.** Crime against the person is seen as more serious, in general, than crime against property. The sentences are therefore more severe.
8. **Whether the offender seems sorry for what he or she has done.** The courts tend to take the view that anybody can make a mistake once. They sympathise with people who show regret and reduce the sentence accordingly, if they can.
9. **Whether the offender is a threat to other people.** Sometimes people are locked up for society's protection. The courts are unwilling to let imprisoned paedophiles back into society if they can help it.
10. **Whether the offender was wholly or partly responsible for the offence.** An offender who played a minor role in a crime will receive a less harsh sentence than the ringleader.
11. **What the limitations of the penalty itself are.** There are legal limits to the sentences which can be imposed for some crimes. For example, the maximum fine for criminal damage of less than £5,000 in value is £2,500, under the Magistrates' Court Act 1980.

12 Which court the offender is tried in. Magistrates' courts are often harsher than Crown Courts. If the offence is of medium seriousness and 'triable either way', offenders often choose to be tried in the Crown Court. This is because judges, who are highly educated people trained in the law, have middle-class opinions. They tend to take a more lenient view of some crimes than some magistrates who have less tolerant backgrounds. In addition to this, magistrates' courts in some parts of the country give much harsher sentences than those in other parts – even though the crime is the same!

The tariff

Magistrates' courts often follow a system called the 'tariff'. This is a sliding scale looking at the circumstances of each crime and the sentences that would be appropriate. For example the theft of a mountain bike by a first-time offender would rate much lower on the tariff than a professional burglary in which 12 computers were taken from an office.

Limitations on sentencing

Provide details of the limitations placed upon sentencing in two different types of courts.

Crown Courts can give heavier sentences than magistrates' courts, because they try more serious crimes. As we have seen, any offence which carries a fine of more than £5,000 cannot be tried in a magistrates' court because these courts are not allowed to fine anybody more than this amount. Magistrates' courts are allowed to send people to prison – but not for more than six months. If the crime carries a possible sentence of more than six months, the accused has to be tried in the Crown Court.

This does not mean that Crown Courts cannot impose lower sentences that £5,000 or six months' imprisonment. Basically they can impose any sentences they like – up to life imprisonment (25 years) though remission can often bring it down to 17. On rare occasions judges can recommend that offenders who are likely to be a continuing danger to the public can be detained indefinitely. But when life means life the Home Secretary has to make the final decision.

THINK ABOUT IT ...

Last Saturday night your mate – who is built like a brick outhouse – tried some cocaine.

Then you both went to the local night club and he got into a fight over a girl in which someone was badly hurt. The police were called – and your mate was arrested and charged with assault and with being in possession of illegal drugs. He was given the choice of being tried in a magistrates' court, or in a Crown Court in front of a jury. Which court would you advise him to choose – and why?

UNIT 12 Disaster and Emergency

Unit outcome 1
Examine disaster and emergency situations

Assessment criteria

- Describe in detail three recent disasters.
- Explain and give examples of the three main ways in which disasters are caused i.e. human, technological and natural.

A disaster is an event in which life is (or could be) lost and property destroyed on a large scale. An emergency is a situation in which a disaster could easily happen.

The definitions are vague, but then disasters come in many forms, and all disasters are different. But features common to most disasters are:

- *many people are killed or put at serious risk*
- *the event is on a large scale*
- *large amounts of property – buildings, land, etc. – are destroyed or put at serious risk*
- *the public services have a major role in dealing with them.*

Disaster situations

Describe in detail three recent disasters.

The following examples should give you some idea of the type of event that can be called a disaster.

1. 21 March 1999: fire in Mont Blanc tunnel

The Mont Blanc Tunnel, which joins France and Italy and goes under Europe's highest mountain is 12.1 kilometres long, and was opened in 1965. Since it was built, traffic has increased enormously and it now carries 760,000 lorries a year.

The fire started on a lorry carrying flour and margarine. Smoke was detected by monitors soon after it entered the tunnel, but nothing was done to stop it. Eventually the lorry stopped half way through the tunnel, when drivers kept flashing to the driver that he was in trouble. At this time the lorry was producing 'a thick white blanket' of smoke, but there were no flames until after it stopped. Then, perhaps as a result of fuel dripping onto the exhaust pipe, flames rushed out from under the cab and 'everything was ablaze in half a minute'. Within a few minutes 'the tunnel was like an oven'.

This was the worst ever tunnel fire, and 40 people died. There were only two lanes – one each way – and both were blocked with traffic which could not move. Toxic fumes, possibly coming from a tanker carrying chlorine, overcame drivers who tried to run to safety. The heat was so intense that heavy trucks had melted into the tunnel floor until they were 'no higher than a car'. The concrete of the tunnel roof turned into sand, and the road melted into spongy glue. A firefighter said the tunnel was 'like a crematorium hundreds of metres long'. It took firefighters from three countries – France, Italy and Switzerland – 48 hours to reach the seat of the blaze.

FOCUS

The problems in dealing with the disaster included:
- the narrow design of the tunnel
- the fact that the fire was half way along – six kilometres from the entrance either way
- the fact that flames were fanned and fumes were spread by the tunnel's ventilation system
- the lack of a service tunnel
- limited fire safety equipment
- insufficient planning and cooperation between the fire services of three countries
- the great volume of traffic using the tunnel
- the lack of clear-cut evacuation procedures for the tunnel
- the fact that fire warning cameras were made useless by the smoke.

Warnings about the dangers of the tunnel had been ignored only a month before, when fire chiefs had written a report saying, 'A single road with two lanes, one in each direction, means access is difficult in the event of a fire. Smoke evacuation is uncertain and because there is no service tunnel the safety equipment is limited, and there has not been enough cooperation with the Italian and Swiss services in the event of a joint international operation.'

After the disaster a public inquiry was opened in France to see who was to blame, whether charges for 'aggravated manslaughter' could be brought, and what could be done to reduce the risk of similar disasters in the future.

2. April 1999: flooding in North Yorkshire

This flooding reached its height in a six-day period between 3 and 9 April 1999. Like many disasters it did not make the front pages in the national newspapers because:
- it happened in a thinly populated area, well away from London or any other big city
- no one is recorded as dying as a direct result of the floods
- flooding is a routine event, and – in this case – no one was to blame for the floods.

In fact the build-up to the floods had been going on for three months. Exceptionally heavy rain and snow throughout the winter on the North Yorkshire Moors had caused the water table (the level of underground water) to rise, and had saturated the soil so that it couldn't hold any more water. Rivers and streams were already as full as they could be without actually overflowing their banks.

When more heavy rain came at the beginning of April the River Derwent, normally a small river, overflowed and several North Yorkshire towns were flooded. Almost 200 houses were well over a metre deep in water, and more than 40 factories and shops were affected. The floods came at night, so people woke up to find their properties under a metre of water.

FOCUS

The first fire service responses were to:
- use the rigid inflatable rescue boat normally kept at York (about 12 kilometres away)
- open two rest centres at either side of the flooded area to provide shelter, food and accommodation for evacuated families
- designate the flooding as a major incident.

The local authority emergency planning department (run by Ryedale District Council) coordinated the rescue and other efforts of all the services involved. They provided facilities for regular multi-agency meetings and press briefings.

More than 45 people were rescued from their homes by the water rescue unit. The same unit also provided supplies and support to those who chose to stay in their homes.

The size of the flood emergency tied up the fire service, and blocked roads, affecting fire cover for the rest of the area. An improvised fire station had to be set up north of Malton to provide extra cover. Special high-clearance vehicles normally used for fighting forest and moorland fires were used because only they could get along the flooded roads. After the floods started to go down on 9 April, the fire service began the long job of pumping out flooded homes so that families could return. The same was done with business premises. Because of the amount of water a special 'salvage and environmental control' unit, normally based at Harrogate, 60 kilometres away, was used in the clean-up.

Though nobody died, this was the worst flood in the area in over a century, and insurance claims passed the £20 million mark. If it had happened in the past, when there was no organised fire service or disaster planning, many lives would have been lost and people made homeless.

3. February 1999: avalanches in the Alps

After exceptionally heavy snow, 38 people died in avalanches in one week in the Alps. The worst of these was at the Austrian resort of Galtur, where 31 people died.

Buildings were flattened and people buried under a five-metre wall of snow which swept silently down the mountainside. By the time this avalanche happened, over 100 people had been killed by avalanches in one winter in the Alps. The disaster was made worse by the fact that all approach roads were blocked at the time and in fact, throughout the Alps, huge numbers of tourists were stranded and communications blocked by the abnormal snow.

Nearly 400 local people led the rescue operation, aided by many tourists who dug with their bare hands. Other people used helmets and skis as shovels and dug all night. There was no time to wait for the official rescue services to try to get there, since people can die in a matter of minutes – or hours – under snow, either from suffocation or hypothermia. According to Werner Senn, leader of the rescue operation, the most urgent need was for mechanical diggers and miners' lamps, so that people could dig their way into the buried houses and search for survivors.

FOCUS

Emergency measures:

- a tennis hall was turned into a temporary hospital, staffed by doctors on holiday
- helicopters ferried the injured to hospital in a break in the weather
- a nearby resort was evacuated on orders from its mayor, because of the risk of another avalanche.

Then a second avalanche at Galtur 'whipped parked cars along with it for about 60 metres'.

Because it was still the height of the skiing season, many more visitors came to the Alps after the disasters at Galtur and elsewhere. But inquiries into the tragedies in Austria asked whether development of the high Alpine valleys hadn't gone too far. The avalanches claimed so many lives partly because so many people were there. As Manfred Riedl, a planning expert, put it: 'Nature has spoken'.

The causes of disasters

Explain and give examples of the three main ways in which disasters are caused i.e. human, technological and natural.

1 Human

Some disasters are caused by people. Such causes can be:

- individual error or misjudgement
- misconduct
- negligence
- sabotage
- mass human behaviour.

Example: Kegworth air disaster

On 8 January 1989 a Boeing 737 operated by British Midland Airways was on a flight to Belfast. Near East Midlands airport the crew reported vibration and smelt fire. The captain disengaged the autopilot and decided, from his knowledge of the plane's ventilation system, that the fire came from number two engine – the right engine. The first officer was monitoring the engine instruments and when the captain asked which engine was giving trouble he said, 'It's the le... it's the right one.' So the captain throttled number two engine back.

The aircraft had tilted 16 degrees to the left, but the captain took no corrective action. After he had throttled number two engine back the plane levelled out again. Meanwhile the first officer reported to London Air Traffic Control that there was an emergency situation and they seemed to have an engine fire. The pilot ordered the engine to be shut down, then changed his mind and said, 'Seems to be running alright now. Let's just see if it comes in.' However, they continued to have smoke in the cockpit so number two engine was shut down. After this, smoke cleared from the flight deck, and the pilot saw nothing on the instruments which suggested that anything was wrong.

But further back in the plane passengers, stewards and stewardesses smelt smoke and saw fire coming from the *left* engine. But the pilot announced that trouble with the right engine had produced smoke in the plane, but that the engine had been shut down – so everything was alright. They were going to make an unscheduled landing at East Midlands Airport in ten minutes. Unfortunately passengers were getting panicky and none of the flight attendants heard the pilot's reference to the 'right' engine. Some passengers heard the pilot's discrepancy but did not feel confident enough to mention it to the crew.

In the run-in to the airport there were further vibrations and smoke and the aircraft began to stall, so it was no longer possible to control the rate of descent. The pilot broadcast, 'Prepare for crash landing.' The plane hit a field, ran towards the M1, breaking a fence in the process, and then fell down the motorway embankment. But for this there might have been no fatalities. On the other hand, there was no collision with traffic, so it could have been worse. Thirty-nine people died at the time, and eight more later in hospital. Seventy-four were seriously injured and just five had minor injuries or none at all. The pilot was one of the seriously injured.

2 Technological

These causes of disasters are less easy to classify than the human causes. But they are often the result of ageing or badly-made equipment. In aircraft incidents the technological causes are usually as follows.

1. **Metal fatigue.** This consists of tiny cracks and weaknesses appearing in metal which is under stress and has been for many years. Many aircraft are now over 20 years old and metal fatigue is an increasingly likely cause of accidents. At the same time, there are now techniques for scanning metal which will reveal invisible flaws, so we don't have to wait for an aeroplane to crash before metal fatigue is identified.
2. **Electrical or wiring faults.** The main problem here is that the electrical wiring in planes is enormously complex. In the case of the Kegworth air disaster discussed above, it was argued in the inquiry that wiring had been crossed over in the plane so that instruments alerted the pilot to a fire in the wrong engine.

3 **Other.** In 1985, 55 people were killed in a fire on a Boeing 737 at Manchester Airport. A crack in an engine casing led to a small explosion which punctured a fuel tank, and a violent fire developed before the plane had taken off. The fire was caused by a technical fault, and the weakness in the construction of the fuel tank, but the deaths were caused by the delayed response. The fire service took 13 minutes to arrive and start fighting the fire.

In addition, less was known in those days about fumes from upholstery, and many of the passengers were killed by toxic hydrogen cyanide smoke from the plane's seats.

3 Natural causes

Some disasters, such as earthquakes and volcanic eruptions, are entirely natural in cause. Others are regarded as natural, but may not be as natural as they look. This is a wide-ranging subject and there is only room here for brief comments.

Type of disaster	Outline of cause
Volcanic eruption (death toll can be many thousands)	Movements in the earth's crust (the top 50 kilometres). These are very slow but they open up cracks either by pulling or pushing. Molten rock and gas escapes to the earth's surface along lines of weakness, which give way and an eruption takes place. There are different types of eruption; those involving lava (liquid rock) are less dangerous than the explosive ones releasing gas, dust and ashes. Death rates are high because the fertile areas around volcanoes are thickly populated. Increasingly, however, scientists are able to predict eruptions and people can be evacuated.
Earthquakes (many thousands die if cities with multi-storey buildings are struck)	Again these are caused by movements in the earth's crust. Where these are sudden they shake the ground, demolishing buildings and causing death on a massive scale. But the death-toll is partly due to poor building methods. The latest San Francisco earthquake, in 1989 which killed 70 people, would have killed many thousands in a developing country. So though the cause is natural, the death-toll depends more on the economic wealth of the affected area.
Hurricanes (death toll can be many thousands, if there is flooding)	These are huge storms several hundred miles across. They occur only in certain parts of the world: the Caribbean, the Indian Ocean, and parts of the Pacific. Wind speeds get up to over 240 kilometres an hour, and there can be torrential rain (which kills more people than the wind). They are caused by the heating up of the ocean during the summer months, about 20 degrees north or south of the Equator. The rotation of the earth puts a spin on the rising air which causes the storm to intensify and produces the devastating winds. Hurricanes may be growing more violent due to global warming.
Tornadoes (death toll usually less than a hundred)	Sometimes called 'twisters', these are funnel-shaped clouds which cause buildings to explode or collapse because of the wind speed and the low air pressure at the middle. They are caused by the meeting of masses of warm and cold air, or by violent thunderstorms. Over water they cause waterspouts, and in deserts, dust-storms.
Floods (hundreds of thousands can die)	Usually the result of storms, hurricanes or abnormal rainfall over a period of time. They are most serious where natural forest has been removed to make way for agriculture or land is at sea level. High death tolls can occur down-river in low-lying, heavily populated areas. The worst floods happen in Asia – especially China and Bangladesh. Heavy snow can also cause disasters, but they are far less serious than flooding.

Cont'd

Drought (millions can die)	Drought is caused mainly by prolonged lack of rain. But increasing population makes drought far more serious, because there is less water underground due to the sinking of wells, and less vegetation because of overgrazing. The cutting down of tropical forests dries out the air and increases the risk of drought. Another factor is the reversal, about every ten years, of ocean currents in the Pacific known as 'El Niño'. This affects winds and moisture over much of the world. Global warming may play a part.
Forest fires (many die, but not as an immediate result)	A serious problem in Mediterranean countries, Australia, Indonesia and South America. In Indonesia in 1997/8 they caused dense smog to settle over a wide area for months. Many people died of respiratory (breathing) illnesses. People are sometimes killed by the rapid spread of the fire itself.
War (20 million or more)	The most serious and frightening kind of disaster. The cause is human, but it is perhaps natural too, in the sense that this kind of behaviour appears to be built into us and we don't seem able to control it.
Disease	Plagues, malaria, influenza, heart attacks, cancer and AIDS all kill millions of people each year, and add to the death rates in other kinds of disaster, especially flooding, drought or war. Many diseases are becoming more difficult to treat, as bacteria and parasites build up a resistance to antibiotics.

Unit outcome 2
Examine emergency planning and prevention

Assessment criteria

- List ten organisations involved in emergency planning in Britain.
- Briefly outline the main features of a disaster plan.
- Explain in detail the nature and value of a given disaster simulation.

Organisations involved in emergency planning

A surprisingly wide range of organisations is involved in emergency planning in Britain. They include the following.

1. **The professional 'blue light services'.** These are the fire service; the police; the ambulance service (with paramedics).
2. **Other professional public services.** These are the armed forces (army, navy and air force); HM coastguards.
3. **Voluntary public services.** For instance mountain rescue.
4. **Local authorities.** For instance emergency planning departments.
5. **Voluntary and charitable organisations.** For instance the WRVS (Women's Royal Voluntary Service); the Salvation Army; the Red Cross.

6 **Specialist organisations.** For instance Chemdata, an information service about hazardous chemicals.
7 **Companies and commercial bodies.** For instance Zeneca (for their expertise with chemicals); water companies; electricity companies; British Gas.
8 **Universities and colleges.** For instance the Emergency Planning College at Easingwold, York ; other universities with technical expertise; the Fire Service Training College at Moreton-in-Marsh.
9 **Broadcasting and the media.** For instance local radio.
10 **Central government** (London; the Welsh Office, Cardiff; the Scottish Parliament). The Home Office (for England) – in overall control; the Environment Agency (formerly called the National Rivers Authority) – for floods; the Meteorological Office (Headquarters at Bracknell, Berkshire, but with some regional centres) – for weather warnings.
11 **International bodies.** Usually only involved with very serious disasters – such as Hurricane Mitch in Honduras. The United Nations and others help to organise disaster relief.

All the organisations listed above can work together if the need arises. The way they work together, and who is involved, depends on the type and severity of the disaster or the emergency they are dealing with.

The main features of disaster plans

Briefly outline the main features of a disaster plan.

In essence, a disaster plan is like a large-scale risk assessment as described under the Health and Safety at Work Act (see Unit 14, Outcome 3). The emergency services identify hazards and draw up plans, sometimes called scenarios, for dealing with them.

Company plans

Disaster planning is done at a number of levels. A company that deals with toxic chemicals, for example, will have its own internal disaster plan, so that all employees will know what to do if something goes wrong. The company disaster plan will consist of (a) damage limitation (for example shutting off supplies to particular plant in the works, to reduce the risk of fire or explosion) and (b) evacuation procedures.

Features of a company disaster plan are:
- an analysis of the main risks
- a list of the responsibilities for each person in management
- a list of responsibilities for each employee or grade of employee
- procedures for alerting people outside the company (such as the fire service)
- training and organisation points.

To be useful a disaster plan must be:
- accessible to the people using it: for example, every employee in a company should have one, or a shortened version, as it applies to them
- well organised, so users can see at a glance which part is relevant to them: the layout (subheadings, etc.) should emphasise the key features
- written in clear English
- kept up-to-date.

> **! THINK ABOUT IT ...**
> If you work in a large organisation, or if you know someone who does, ask for a copy of their disaster plan. You will find it very useful!

Public service plans

These plans deal with disasters which affect large numbers of people, and require full coordination between the public services. Essentially they consist of (a) lists of everything that needs to be done, (b) the order in which things need to be done, and (c) who does them.

The NHS outline for disaster planning is given on the next page.

Planning for Major Incidents – the NHS Guidance

1 INTRODUCTION
1.1 NHS emergency planning – who does what
1.2 What is a major incident for the NHS?
1.3 How a major incident may start
1.4 Some frequently asked questions

2 KEY ISSUES FOR MAJOR INCIDENT PLANNING
2.1 Assessing the hazards and risks
2.2 Collaborating within the health service and with other organisations
2.3 Communicating
2.4 Training and exercising
2.5 Reviewing plans and performance
2.6 Command and coordination
2.7 Working with the police
2.8 Personal safety and protection
2.9 Making it happen
2.10 Bibliography

3 THE HEALTH AUTHORITY
3.1 Key roles and responsibilities
3.2 Essential actions
3.3 Types of incident that the health authority may face
3.4 Planning
3.5 Major incident response: the first few hours
3.6 Response to an extended incident
3.7 Key issues for an effective response
3.8 Bibliography

4 THE AMBULANCE SERVICE
4.1 Key roles and responsibilities
4.2 Essential actions
4.3 Planning
4.4 Major incident response
4.5 The role of Voluntary Aid Societies (VAS)
4.6 Training and exercising
4.7 Bibliography

5 THE ACUTE HOSPITAL
5.1 Key roles and responsibilities
5.2 Essential actions
5.3 Planning
5.4 The hospital's response: day 1
5.5 The hospital's response: day 2 onwards
5.6 The hospital's liaison with the health authority and community agencies
5.7 Checklist for your major incident plan

6 CHILDREN IN MAJOR INCIDENTS
6.1 Key issues
6.2 Essential action
6.3 Planning
6.4 Other important issues
6.5 Follow-up action

7 PRIMARY CARE AND COMMUNITY HEALTH SERVICES
7.1 Key roles and responsibilities
7.2 Essential actions
7.3 Major incidents – where do primary and community services come in?
7.4 Planning
7.5 The community response
7.6 Phases of the major incident response

8 CHEMICAL INCIDENTS
8.1 Types of incident that the health service may face
8.2 Special features of chemical incidents
8.3 Local responsibilities
8.4 Regional responsibilities
8.5 National responsibilities
8.6 Planning – general
8.7 Planning – availability of equipment, supplies and facilities
8.8 Planning – specialist sources of advice and expertise
8.9 Response – general
8.10 Response – specific
8.11 Follow-up
8.12 Bibliography

9 INCIDENTS INVOLVING RADIOACTIVITY
9.1 Key issues
9.2 Essential actions
9.3 Which government department takes the lead?
9.4 The health service role
9.5 Health authorities with a fixed nuclear site in their area
9.6 Department of Health
9.7 Role of the National Radiological Protection Board (NRPB)
9.8 Bibliography

10 HEALTH SERVICES AND ARMED FORCES COOPERATION
10.1 Essential actions
10.2 Military casualties sustained in overseas conflicts
10.3 Military aid to the NHS
10.4 Points of contact
10.5 Bibliography

11 LIAISING WITH THE MEDIA
11.1 Key responsibilities
11.2 Essential actions
11.3 What you need to know about the media
11.4 The press officer
11.5 The on-call/duty manager
11.6 Planning checklist
11.7 Emergency response
11.8 Additional information
11.9 Bibliography

An example of the kinds of details which are included in these plans is given on pages 287–290.

Disaster simulation

Explain in detail the nature and value of a given disaster simulation.

The best kind of simulation is a realistic one, one which is as true to life as possible. This is why a written scenario by itself (like the example on page 287) is not enough for the highest standards of emergency service training. The 'rig' referred to in the article below is a full-scale replica of a Boeing 747, the most common type of commercial aircraft. Inside it is equipped with gas-fired burning systems to produce real heat and flames which the Airport Fire Service can use for training. And since many aircraft fires start in the engines, and aircraft have different types of engine, this mock-up is fitted with both Rolls Royce and General Electric types.

Since the rig cost over £4 million, it will have to earn its money. But if we think of the financial cost of air crashes and fires (not to mention the human cost) it will soon pay for itself if it increases the safety of air travel. Apart from anything else, higher safety standards and expertise in firefighting mean fewer deaths, which means more passengers – since in these days of falling fares the main thing which stops people travelling by air is fear for their own safety.

If lives are saved as a result of this training there will also be immense savings for the insurance

New age of training dawns at Heathrow

Costing £4.2 million, the rig wide-body replica firefighting training aircraft consists of a full scale 747 front with an MD11 tail. For realistic training, one engine is of Rolls Royce design, the other is General Electric and the rig has landing gear, fuselage and wings.

Inside the rig, built by International Fire Training Equipment Ltd, first and second class accommodation, crew sleeping areas, galleys, toilets, cockpit and hold are all replicated and the large middle section can be used as a BA training chamber.

Environmentally, the rig had to meet a number of criteria, both for planning and commercial reasons. Too much smoke could affect aircraft movements and the rig – although painted green – is so realistic that the sight of it shrouded in smoke would not be a reassurance to nervous flyers. A seven metre high glass reinforced concrete has been built all around the wide-body replica. The rig uses an all gas computerised burning system, and each burner is controllable. In all, 28 different fire scenarios can be simulated.

Fires are controlled from the control tower and there are two plug in points where a safety officer will have an umbilical cord. Should a dangerous situation develop, the safety officer would stop the fires from burning, the lights would come on and two fans would perform two full air changes a minute, clearing the area almost immediately.

The drainage system for run-off is closely monitored. If the run-off is deemed too polluted, it is automatically switched into a separator and then runs into a large underground tank. "We have tried to be as environmentally friendly as we can possibly be," says CFO Davis.

Theoretically the rig could be used for non-fire training, such as evacuation, because it is the right height and is so realistic.

Resource analysis is another area where the BAA Airport Fire Service is convinced it is leading the way in airport protection. Although legislation specifies manning levels, "these are usually regarded as the minimum, without looking at airports' individual needs. Minimum cover leaves no back-up. This is why we decided to look at the manning we would need for worst case scenarios," Mr Black contends.

A project to determine optimum manning levels has been established to investigate various accidents that might occur. A series of scenarios has been analysed by those who would be involved in the response, in specific time frames, carrying each job through to the end. All incidents in the last 20 years were also examined in this project. All those who work at the airport will be involved in this process, as well as the outside local authority fire services, who are actively involved in liaising with their aviation counterparts.

Another area that ensures the Airport Fire Service is on the right track for the future is liaison with local authority brigades. Mr Black says that he is extremely pleased with the way this is developing and the frequency of joint training exercises has increased.

Source: Fire *magazine, May 1998, p. 21*

industry, and there will be a knock-on effect in reducing the high insurance premiums that air companies have to pay.

And this is without even considering the lives of firefighters and other rescue workers, which may be saved if they know how to deal with aircraft incidents, instead of having to trust to luck and judgement when the time comes.

As the article points out, a rig of this type is versatile. Using scenarios based on a variety of real aircraft fires in the past, such as the one at Manchester Airport in 1985, training will become as realistic as it is reasonably possible to be. And it won't be only firefighters at Heathrow who will use the mock-up. Firefighters from airports in many parts of the world will be able to come and train on the apparatus. So airport fire safety in many countries will benefit from the investment.

Performance of trainees will be measurable, using a fixed piece of equipment like this which allows everything to be accurately monitored. It will enable realistic targets to be set for firefighting on planes, which again will increase efficiency.

But of course not even equipment as sophisticated as this will entirely eliminate the risk of airport fires. As with anything else to do with health and safety, measures can only be taken 'as far as is reasonably practicable' to ensure safety. There will always be new types of fires and disasters which have not been planned for, but as more knowledge and expertise is gained, these unforeseeable incidents will become fewer and fewer – and so even more lives will be saved.

THINK ABOUT IT ...

There is an organisation called the The Casualties Union which provides 'actors' used in disaster simulations and exercises.

These actors are ordinary people who play the part of seriously injured people in a disaster. Why not try to get in touch with your local branch of The Casualties Union to play the part of a casualty? What better way to find out what the public services do in a disaster – without the pain of being in a real one?

Unit outcome 3
Investigate how the emergency services work together in disaster or emergency situations

Assessment criteria

- Analyse the role of three emergency services in a given disaster scenario.
- Briefly outline the command and communication problems and how they could be overcome.
- Indicate the role played in disasters by at least four organisations outside the emergency services.

The role of three emergency services

Who will do what in the following scenario?

Train crash

On 27 October, a chemical tanker freight train crashed into a full passenger train near Newtown. The tanker, which was carrying approximately 65 tonnes of highly flammable vinyl chloride monomer (VCM), burst open. The emergency services received a number of 999 calls almost simultaneously and it was soon clear that they were dealing with a major incident ...

1 The role of the police

The role of an individual officer who is first to arrive at a major incident is summed up in the mnemonic (memory word): CHALET. The word is used to remind officers, who may themselves be shocked, of their first priorities.

C: casualties – approximate number
H: hazards – both present and potential
A: access – for the emergency services
L: location – the exact place, so that others can reach it as soon as possible!
E: emergency services required
T: type of incident – in this case 'chemical'.

ANALYSIS

As laid down in local authority emergency planning guidelines the role of the police service in general is as follows.

1 To alert the other emergency services and local authorities. The police will do this if they are first on the scene. If the report came in a 999 call from the public, the three main services will already have been alerted. The police will, in this case, assess the scale of the problem and report back.

2 The saving of life in conjunction with other emergency services. Initially the police will clear the public from the station and the area around the crash. If there are houses nearby they will arrange to get them evacuated if the danger of fumes is very great. If the danger is less great they may instruct people to stay indoors and keep their windows shut. The police will save lives if they can, but in the case of a train crash, this task is likely to be done by the fire service.

3 Coordination of the emergency services and other organisations during the immediate response phase. If there are many casualties the primary job of the police will be to ensure access to the crash site, so that fire appliances and ambulances can get to it. This may involve large-scale diversions of traffic in the surrounding area. They will need to alert hospitals – the more casualties the more hospitals – and ensure that ambulances can get to and from them as quickly as possible. In a major disaster the overall control rests with the local authority emergency planning department, but the police may establish and staff a forward control point (an emergency office as near to the disaster as possible). The police must also ensure that there is space for the fire service and ambulance service to work at the site. If there is a fire, or if people are trapped on the passenger train, large numbers of firefighters and appliances will be needed. If there are many casualties ambulances will need a holding area, where they can sort out and pick up casualties.

4 Protection and preservation of the scene. It is vitally important that the police keep the public away from the scene, because of the danger from toxic waste, though in exceptional cases this may not be possible. If it is not possible (as in the Kegworth air crash) the public must be controlled, and people like doctors used. However, in most cases the public must be kept away (a) for their own protection, (b) so that the emergency services can work without distraction and (c) so that the accident can be preserved for the crash investigators.

5 Investigation of the incident in conjunction with other investigative bodies. The police role in the investigation will be to establish whether the accident is the result of a crime, such as vandalism, criminal negligence or terrorist activity. If more than one investigation team is at work, the police must help them out, if only by giving them space in which to work, and organising the backup they need (for example, by bringing in more experts).

6 Collation and dissemination of casualty information. The police will operate a computerised 'casualty recording information sorting identification system' (CRISIS). This means they will gather information about all casualties, communicating information to and from hospitals and relatives as required. They will operate an emergency helpline for members of the public who think their relatives might be casualties. This will be a complex task, as some people may be trapped or dead, others will have been rushed to hospital, and still others may be wandering about in a shocked or confused state.

7 Identification of victims. Dealing with the dead at the scene of a major incident is primarily the responsibility of the police acting on behalf of the coroner. A doctor will need to pronounce death, preferably in the presence of a police officer, and any dead bodies will need to be labelled clearly. The police, in consultation with the local authority, are responsible for setting up body holding areas and temporary mortuaries. Bodies should not be taken to hospitals, unless it is unavoidable. Despite the police and local authority arrangements, receiving hospitals may have to provide mortuary space for an abnormally large number of bodies.

8 Restoration of normality. In a scenario like the one we have been discussing, this may take some time. After all rescues have been completed, and bodies removed to mortuaries, the crash site will have to be left intact until all investigations have been completed. This could take days in a really serious incident, especially if the toxic waste presents a significant danger to the public and the emergency services. However, once the investigation is over, the police priority is normally to get the site cleared up and made safe so that traffic can start moving on the railway again.

2 The role of the fire service

The role of the first fire officer on the scene is to:

- assess the scale and seriousness of the situation
- obtain information about casualties – if possible
- call for reinforcements and ensure that other emergency services are being informed
- coordinate rescue attempts as far as possible at this early stage
- assess any special hazards.

FOCUS

The priority is to assess and inform and not personally to become involved with the treatment of casualties or rescue work.

ANALYSIS

At an early stage the priority is to get reinforcements from all the emergency services and get some idea of the scale of the disaster. It can do more harm than good if officers rush in to rescue people without proper preparations. This is because:

- they may be putting themselves and other rescue workers at extra risk
- without the right information the rescues may not be carried out effectively
- the disaster may be rapidly getting worse and putting many more lives at risk: if this is the case the first priority is to get people out of the way and prevent more deaths.

The main roles of the fire and rescue service are as follows.

1 To alert the other emergency services and local authorities. A major disaster is too complex and serious to be dealt with by any one service. The fire service has many skills – firefighting, rescuing, first aid, and some expertise with common chemicals. But many chemical incidents involve rare and very dangerous compounds which the fire service does not know much about. This is one reason why it is necessary to contact local authority emergency planning – so that they can get help from the chemical experts while the fire service concentrate on limiting the spread of the disaster and rescuing people. In the scenario above they will need help from paramedics and the ambulance service both to treat casualties on the spot – if they are trapped in the train – and to convey them quickly and efficiently to hospital, treating them if necessary while they are on the way.

2 The saving of life in conjunction with other emergency services. The fire service will save life by cutting people out of the wreckage, and preventing fire, explosions and the spread of toxic fumes. It is often more effective to treat trapped people for shock, loss of blood and dehydration on the spot, than to try to cut them out and take them to hospital before treatment begins (which is what they used to do 20 years ago). The reason for this is that it makes use of the so-called 'golden' hour – the first hour after an accident – when treatment is most effective and lives are most likely to be saved. To make the best use of the golden hour, paramedics need to be present. They have more expertise and equipment than the fire service when it comes to giving complex and specialised medical help. The fire service and paramedics are trained to work together in the cramped, stressful and dangerous situations met with in major crashes and other disaster settings. The police role is to make sure that access to the disaster is as good as it can be, and that ambulances can travel to and from nearby hospitals.

3 Tackling fires, released chemicals and other hazardous situations. The fire service have the expertise and equipment for putting out fires. They are also well trained in dealing with chemical incidents. They have decontamination showers or cubicles, and both splashproof and gastight protective clothing – as well as breathing apparatus. Despite their skills and equipment, the risk in chemical incidents is always great, so they still have to take care and avoid endangering their own lives.

4 Rescue of trapped casualties. This is discussed in paragraph 2 above.

5 Safety of all personnel involved in the rescue work. In some major disasters (and the one in the scenario may come under this heading) it is not always possible to keep the public away. This places the rescue services in a dilemma. Do they drive them away whatever happens (perhaps wasting valuable time and personnel in the process)? Or do they make use of public goodwill, where it exists? In the given scenario, where a trainload of toxic chemicals is involved, it would probably be better to keep people away at all costs. But there will still be many rescuers and others working at the disaster site. The fire service have to make sure that paramedics and others do not injure or endanger themselves, and there may also be people from chemical companies or CHEMDATA, or the National Poisons Information Service. The fire service would be held responsible if any of them got hurt or killed during the rescue period.

6 Information gathering and hazard assessment. The fire service is experienced in this kind of work, especially where the hazards are routine, such as the possibility of fires or explosions from leaking fuel, or the collapse of crashed vehicles onto rescue workers. Firefighters can move more swiftly and safely among wreckage than other rescue workers and are better placed to make this kind of assessment than other emergency service workers. The fire service also has accident investigation teams who, in the case of a train crash, have a vital role to play gathering information and helping accident investigators from Railtrack or other organisations who may have less personal experience of crash sites.

7 Assisting the ambulance service at the ambulance loading point. Firefighters have experience in handling stretchers, are used to working in emergencies and are strong and fit. Their training in first aid and experience in dealing with casualties will make them more helpful than other workers.

8 Assisting the police with recovery of bodies. Again, the fire service are trained in this difficult and gruesome work.

9 Restoration of normality. The fire service has heavy lifting gear and other machinery which would be useful in clearing the accident site, once the investigation phase has been completed. In this particular scenario they would need to coordinate their efforts with Railtrack and the railway companies involved. The line will have to be made absolutely clean and safe before trains can start running on it again. But at the same time, the rail companies will be losing huge sums of money while the line is blocked by wreckage, so once the work of clearing the line begins, it has to be done quickly.

3 The role of the ambulance service

In a chemical incident of the type given in the scenario, the role of the ambulance service splits into two parts:

- the role of paramedics
- the role of ambulances.

Paramedics

The role of the first paramedic is to report to ambulance control, using CHALET (see under 'police' on page 287).

The first paramedic should then start to organise:

- the ambulance parking point
- the ambulance control point
- the casualty clearing station.

The paramedic should then inform ambulance control of:

- numbers of casualties trapped
- location of ambulance parking point
- special teams required
- special equipment required.

Finally the paramedic should prepare to brief the first ambulance officer, who will be in charge of the scene – from the ambulance service point of view – on their arrival.

Ambulance service

The duties of the first ambulance officer include:

- finding out more about the incident and the numbers and type of casualties
- liaising with police and fire incident officers
- liaising with the medical incident officer (the doctor in charge) – especially over 'triage' (decisions about the urgency of each casualty)
- making sure that medical supplies, emergency lighting and other special equipment is brought
- ensuring as far as possible the safety and welfare of staff.

ANALYSIS

The duties of the ambulance service in general are as follows.

1 To alert the other emergency services and local authorities. This is likely to happen automatically as soon as the first 999 call is received.

2 The saving of life in conjunction with other emergency services. This means rescuing people, usually by giving blood transfusions, intravenous fluid and other requirements like painkillers at the scene of the accident – in some cases while casualties are still trapped in wreckage, or while the fire service is cutting them out. Because there is a risk of spinal injuries in train crashes, paramedics will fix neck-braces and other supports onto casualties before they are removed.

3 To provide a focal point for all NHS and medical resources. Medication is always complex, and in an emergency situation the risk of confusion will be far greater than in a hospital. The ambulance service therefore has the difficult job of ensuring that medical supplies are sufficient, of the right type, and given to the right people in the right way.

4 Identify and activate the appropriate receiving hospitals. In a major disaster like the one in the scenario, hospitals will need to be informed of the numbers and types of casualties so that they can make arrangements. And if they don't have the beds or the facilities, other hospitals will have to be contacted as quickly as possible, otherwise casualties may die needlessly.

5 Set up a casualty clearing station. This is a relatively quiet and safe place, near the disaster, where ambulances can park, pick up casualties and get away fast.

6 Prioritise casualties in the treatment of injuries. Here paramedics carry out triage, i.e they decide which cases are the most urgent. Doing this properly increases the overall survival rate among the casualties. Otherwise people who are dying might be left to one side, while other less urgent cases would be rushed to hospital.

7 Prioritise the evacuation of casualties using appropriate means of transportation. In a case like the scenario, helicopters may have to be used. This means finding somewhere for them to land which is close to the accident site. Though helicopters are extremely expensive to use, they ensure that casualties can be got to hospital faster than by any other means. In addition, it increases the number of hospitals which are within range.

8 Restoration of normality. The role of the ambulance service in restoring normality is limited to taking away all their equipment. However, even after the casualties have been removed, they may still have a role to play in looking after rescue workers – many of whom could be exhausted or even injured in a major incident.

Command and communication issues

Briefly outline the command and communication problems and how they could be overcome.

Communication is not easy at the best of times. But it is never more difficult than in a disaster.

What are the problems?

1 Communications between public services are between organisations as well as individuals. This means there are more likely to be misunderstandings. So public service employees have to be trained to make communications which are clear, as brief as possible, and yet which do not leave out essential information. Such training is a long, expensive process.
2 Disasters are horrific, shocking experiences. It is easy to panic, even when you have been trained not to. So rescue workers have to remain professional and clear thinking at a time when their instincts may well be telling them to 'cut and run'.
3 Disasters are complex, and their causes are often technical and only understood by experts. So the content of communications in a disaster is more complicated and difficult than the content of ordinary, routine communications.
4 The physical conditions in a disaster are difficult and dangerous. It may be a huge effort to breathe, much less communicate. It is hard to communicate clearly if you are fighting for your own and other people's lives.
5 Circumstances change rapidly from minute to minute in a major fire or chemical incident. Any communication may quickly become misleading or untrue, and this may lead to the wrong actions being taken.
6 Heat, chemicals and water can affect the working of radios, telephones and other means of communication – and stop them from

working properly. And the means of communication itself may be dangerous. For example, every time you switch a radio on there is a tiny spark inside it. If the radio is not sealed, this tiny spark can trigger a huge explosion in a gas and air mixture.

7 Background noise and other problems can make communications inaudible.
8 Methods of communication which are not electronic are too slow and unreliable to be of any use in a modern emergency.
9 Police and other communications are threatened by the increased use of mobile phones, which tend to limit the wavebands available for the emergency services. (This problem has recently been reduced by the digital encoding of messages – a new format which vastly increases the amount of information which can be conveyed in a short time.)
10 Some forms of communication are not secure. This means that criminals and others can intercept and monitor them. If the disaster occurs in wartime, or is a terrorist or criminal act, monitoring the communications of the rescue services will enable 'the enemy' to obtain valuable information which can enable them to escape or attack the police or the army.

How can these problems be overcome?

Here are the possible ways to overcome problems 1–10 above.

1 By employing people who can think and express themselves clearly – or who can be trained to do so.
2 By training people through realistic disaster scenarios and simulations, or on adventure training courses which provide practice in communicating under stress.
3 Again, by training and education, so that rescue workers understand as much as possible of what is going on around them in a disaster. Also by clear communications from advisers and others at the scene of the disaster.
4 With great difficulty.
5 By having efficient command structures, and the right communication equipment, so that people know what they need to know, when they need to know it.
6 By using sealed radios and other appropriate technology.
7 By using more advanced communication equipment – but it is unlikely that this will eliminate the problem completely.
8 By being properly equipped with modern communication devices. (Unfortunately, these are very expensive, and if a government is making spending cuts, fire brigades and others may not be able to afford the best equipment available. At times like this, saving money may cost lives.)
9 By using mobile phones. Some rescue services are now switching to these. There seems little likelihood of anybody limiting the use of mobile phones.
10 By 'scrambling' and encoding messages. Unfortunately this can require expensive equipment and may waste time – which is not a good idea in an emergency.

For more information see Surrey County Council's website.

The role played by non-emergency services

Indicate the role played in disasters by at least four organisations outside the emergency services.

1 Local authority emergency planning

Perhaps the most important single organisation outside the emergency services – at least where big disasters are concerned – is the local authority emergency planning department. Each local authority, whether it is in an urban or a rural area, has one. An explanation of the role of Surrey emergency planning, which involves a range of public and private services, is given below.

Local Authority Emergency Roles

14.1 In the immediate aftermath of a disaster, the local authorities will provide support to the emergency services and continue normal support and care for the local and wider community. Local authorities will provide resources to mitigate the effects of the emergency and coordinate the response by organisations other than the emergency services. As time goes on, the emphasis will switch to recovery and local authorities will take the leading role to facilitate the rehabilitation of the environment.

14.2 Local authorities cannot respond as rapidly as the emergency services and so they must be notified early in the incident. Information must be constantly updated. Good liaison between the emergency services and local authorities at the scene and in operations rooms is essential to ensure that local authority support is used to maximum effectiveness.

14.3 During a major incident, any of the services listed below may be requested through the local authority liaison officer at the police operations room. He/she will direct the request to the Surrey County Council emergency centre or to the district(s) involved. [Below] is an outline of some of the main services available:

- liaison with emergency services
- traffic management
- liaison with government departments, other local authorities, voluntary groups, utilities and other organisations
- establishment of emergency centres
- advice on structural conditions
- repairs, demolition, clearance
- waste collection/waste disposal
- equipment, e.g. heavy lifting
- forestry
- stores/supplies
- transport
- temporary accommodation/rest centres
- emergency feeding
- welfare and trauma support
- radio communications
- advice on food and fuel storage, prevention of disease, etc.
- initial establishment of temporary mortuaries
- media management
- public information.

Source: Surrey County Council's website

2 St John Ambulance

The St John Ambulance brigade (dating from 1831 in Britain) is a well-known voluntary organisation which gives first aid and medical help in emergencies and disasters.

St. John Ambulance (Greater Manchester)

We offer **training**. A wide variety of First-aid and Manual Handling courses to suit the general public and the requirements of employers in meeting Health and Safety Executive legislation.

First-aid cover. Our members are available to supply a quality first-aid service at commercial and community public events.

Transport and ambulance escort service. We support statutory agencies and individual members of the public with our ambulance and specially adapted transport fleet.

Care in the community. Our work in the community ranges from everyday tasks such as shopping, through to providing basic nursing care for those who are vulnerable or in need.

Membership. The opportunity for volunteers to join our membership and develop a rewarding hobby and to learn new skills.

Source: St John Ambulance website

3 CHEMDATA

The chemical industry, in collaboration with the Heath and Safety Executive and the emergency services, has set up databases of chemicals and their toxic effects. One of the databases used in the UK is CHEMDATA. Below is the description on its website.

CHEMDATA for Windows has an updated database which includes over 90,000 chemical names to provide all the information needed at the scene of a chemical accident. CHEMDATA is used by fire brigades, industry, ports and airports around the world. Users can make rapid searches to quickly identify potentially hazardous chemicals.

Source: CHEMDATA's website

4 Women's Royal Voluntary Service

You might think that in a modern disaster there is no way that ordinary people can help, other than by giving money to charities. This is far from being the case. One organisation that gives valuable general help in UK emergencies and disasters (and on other occasions as well) is the Women's Royal Voluntary Service. It is a society which spends much of its time in social activities and fundraising. They also offer meals on wheels, teas for blood donors, a community car service and a home library. But in disasters such as floods, where evacuation centres are set up and people need food, drinks, blankets and other basic requirements, the WRVS gets to work and sorts the problem out. This leaves the professional services free to concentrate on rescues and other activities.

Meals on wheels!

THINK ABOUT IT ...

Examine media (newspapers, television etc.) coverage of a disaster. Then ask yourself the following questions.

- Why do the media cover disasters in such detail?
- How can the media help the emergency services in a disaster?
- What problems can the media cause for the emergency services?

Unit outcome 4
Analyse the aftermath of a specified disaster or emergency situation

Assessment criteria

- Describe a range of long-term environmental and health effects which could follow three given types of disaster.
- Explain the role of three organisations dealing with these situations.
- Analyse how the emergency services review their response to a given disaster scenario.

The environmental and health effects of disasters

Death is the worst effect of disasters, and when we read about disasters in the papers, or see them on television, we judge their seriousness by the number of people who die. But disasters affect the living as well. The effects of disasters include:

- health effects
- psychological effects
- effects on health lasting more than one generation
- environmental effects
- economic effects
- political effects.

Usually disasters affect a particular place or region, but occasionally their influence spreads over much or all of the earth. The most serious form of all disasters, war, can affect the whole world for many years. Modern society, politics and even our everyday beliefs are still being deeply affected by World War II 1939–45 (see Unit 8: International Perspectives).

Different kinds of disasters have different kinds of effect. Here are some examples.

1 The drying up of the Aral Sea: Russia

This slow-acting disaster in south-east Russia, developing over the past 20 years, has destroyed an area roughly the size of Britain. It is a man-made disaster caused by the diverting of two big rivers, the Syr Darya and the Amu Darya, to irrigate cotton fields. The irrigation was carried out by the government of the Soviet Union, before it broke up in 1989.

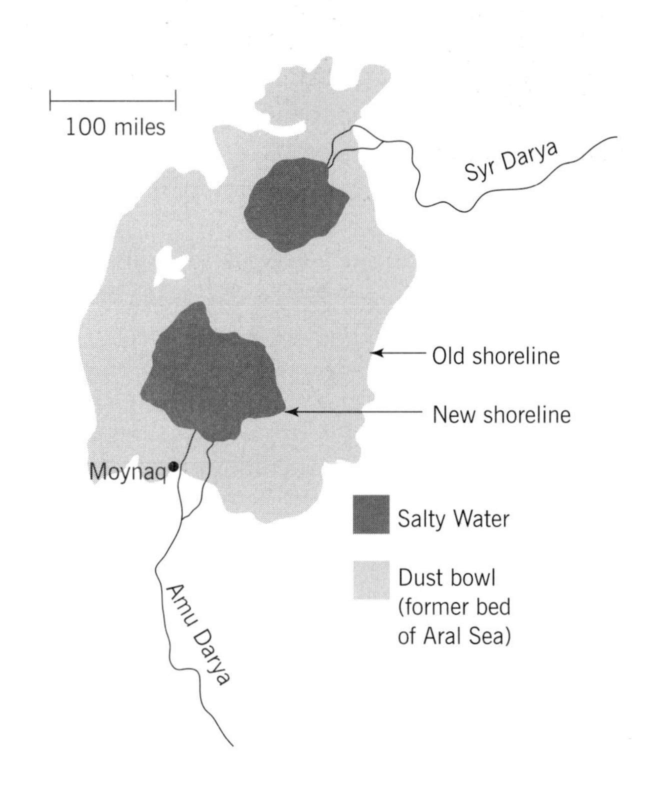

Map of the Aral Sea showing how it has shrunk over the past 20 years

Originally the two rivers flowed into an inland sea – the Aral Sea. But the effect of the irrigation was to greatly reduce the amount of water entering it. As the area is dry, hot and sunny for most of the year, the sea began to dry up and shrink.

Effects

The effects of this have been:

- the destruction of the economy of the town of Moynaq, which used to be a holiday resort (it is now 37 kilometres from the beach)
- the destruction of the town's fishing fleet and of all the fishing that used to be done in the Aral Sea
- a change in the region's climate, with hotter summers and colder winters
- the shrinkage of the Aral Sea to 25 per cent of its original size
- the pollution of soil with salt and chemicals washed down from the irrigation area, which then dry out in the soil before they can reach what is left of the Aral Sea
- dust storms on the salt flats which used to be the sea bed: these spread poisonous dust over the surrounding area
- an epidemic of tuberculosis – a deadly disease which is becoming more difficult to treat as its resistance to antibiotics grows
- soaring rates of anaemia, respiratory disorders, cancer and birth defects
- drinking water which is four times as salty as the World Health Organisation's upper limit – leading to kidney disease and diarrhoea
- 100,000 people have left the area.

Many of these changes are irreversible. The decline in health will continue for generations, and people will continue to leave the area. The United Nations and other organisations are aware of the disaster. They send study groups and working parties to the area to try to find out what can be done to help. But so far nothing much has been achieved.

2 *Exxon Valdez*: Alaska

The disaster is named after the oil tanker which ran aground on rocks off Alaska in 1989, spilling more than 11 million gallons of crude oil in an area of great natural beauty. Prince William Sound, the sea inlet where it happened, was a rich habitat with otters, whales, seals, spawning fish and birds. Most of these were coated and killed by a thick black mass of heavy crude oil. Even if they weren't killed quickly by smothering or drowning, they were killed by the poisons from the oil.

Effects

The environmental effects are still being felt, some ten years after, despite a massive clean up. It has been discovered that the worst long-term effects were caused by the heavier chemicals in the oil – tarry substances which are highly toxic and difficult to wash away. These cause genetic damage to fish, by bursting the cell membranes and interfering with chromosomes in the cell nucleii. Future generations

Prince William Sound, Alaska, North America

of fish will produce infertile eggs, or genetically damaged young, as a result.

There were human effects as well. The Chugach Indians who live by the Sound lost their livelihood, because no herring appeared in the Sound the next year. Ten years later, people are still scrubbing rocks to get the oil off them.

The scale of the *Exxon Valdez* disaster had a profound effect on people's awareness of the environment throughout the world. The oil companies responsible – Exxon and the parent company, British Petroleum – were fined $5 thousand million dollars, but have still not paid, preferring to blame the captain, Joe Hazlewood, who was drunk at the time of the collision. This has led to increased hostility towards oil companies among environmentalists, and therefore among politicians – and the general public. Such hostility can have far-reaching effects. The damage done by the *Exxon Valdez* may well have helped to make it politically possible for our own government to raise petrol taxes.

More practically, the disaster has led to a greater awareness of the danger of oil spills by the oil industry, and safety standards have improved. Recently the *Braer* oil tanker ran aground in the Shetland Islands, as did the *Erika* off Brittany, but on the whole such accidents are becoming rarer. Although disasters are bad, they sometimes have good long-term effects.

3 Hurricane Mitch: America

This hurricane, which struck Honduras in Central America in Autumn 1998, is thought to have been the most destructive for 200 years. (See article on page 298.)

Effects

The long-term effects of a disaster like Hurricane Mitch are as follows.

1 Health effects. Cholera, dengue fever, diarrhoea, bacterial fevers (e.g. gastroenteritis and meningitis) and malaria are all diseases which can reach epidemic proportions in the months following a major disaster like Hurricane Mitch. Even if people recover from these illnesses they can leave lasting ill-health in the sufferers. Central America is receiving food aid, but if there is not enough, or if it doesn't reach the right people, there will be malnutrition and starvation.

2 Psychological effects. Post traumatic stress syndrome is the main psychological effect of a major disaster like Hurricane Mitch. It will show itself in a range of mental illnesses. These will affect Honduran society, increasing such social problems as family break-up, high crime rates and low economic productivity. Children from homes where there is mental illness may well be affected themselves – throughout life.

3 Effects on health lasting more than one generation. Malnutrition and starvation stunt children's growth and affect their intelligence. If the starvation only lasts a month or two, children will grow faster when they start eating properly again, and will catch up with their normal growth curve. But if the lack of food continues, they will be permanently affected, and will never reach the size, strength or intelligence they could have done if they had been properly fed. Though it is hard to prove in humans, research on rats has shown that genetic damage caused by starvation lasts several generations. So it is possible that the children and grandchildren of famine victims will have poorer health as well.

4 Environmental effects. Floods in disasters like Hurricane Mitch are made much worse by wasteful systems of farming, such as 'slash and burn', which destroy forests and expose the soil to erosion. The floodwaters carry away millions of tons of unprotected soil. The long-term result is bare, unproductive hillsides. For a time, the valleys may be more fertile, as farmers cultivate the rich soil that has been deposited there. But as that becomes exhausted, the whole country will produce less food. Rare animals and plants will become extinct due to changes in their habitat, and pressures to farm the remaining forest land – the only land which would not have been damaged by the floods.

5 Economic effects. For a poor country like Honduras, where most people depend on farming

Central American Leaders Discuss Response to Hurricane

By Mayuly Ferrufino, Associated Press writer

San Salvador, El Salvador – Overwhelmed by disaster, grim-faced Central American leaders gathered yesterday to appeal for more aid in recovering from Hurricane Mitch even as a growing army of rescue workers struggled to help hundreds of thousands of victims.

With at least 10,000 reported dead and their economies shattered by flooding, the leaders prepared to ask for help with foreign debts and to coordinate long-term relief efforts after one of the worst natural disasters of this century in the Americas.

Some European leaders already were proposing such help, echoing a plan made last week by former President Jimmy Carter. French Prime Minister Lionel Jospin yesterday called for a moratorium on debt payments owed by countries hit by Hurricane Mitch. German Foreign Minister Joschka Fischer was also urging that some debts be forgiven. Honduras owes $4.2 billion and Nicaragua owes $6 billion, mainly to international lending agencies.

Government and independent relief organizations from around the world were trying to rush aid to tens of thousands in Honduras and Nicaragua isolated by ruptured roads, backed-up airports and too few helicopters. Many areas were still receiving their first-aid more than a week after the storm disappeared. Former President George Bush, visiting the Honduran capital of Tegucigalpa, said Sunday that aid might be needed for years to come. 'The devastation is appalling,' he said.

In Honduras alone, 700,000 people will need food for the next month, UN World Food Program representative Giuseppi Lubatti estimated.

Presidents Carlos Flores Facusse of Honduras, Arnoldo Aleman of Nicaragua, Armando Calderon Sol of El Salvador and Miguel Angel Rodriguez of Costa Rica met at San Salvador's international airport for a quick summit. Guatemalan Foreign Minister Eduardo Stein also attended the meeting. There was none of the jovial backslapping customary at regional summits as most of the leaders walked grimly past reporters into their session.

Officials said the presidents were likely to try to find ways to coordinate often-chaotic relief efforts and to plan long-term priorities – such as restoring destroyed roads. They also were planning to urge the United States to keep postponing deportations of illegal immigrants, Salvadoran Foreign Minister Ramon Gonzalez said on Sunday. The US Immigration and Naturalization Service temporarily suspended deportations of immigrants to Honduras and Guatemala as a 'humanitarian gesture' until Tuesday.

Britain said about 1400 Royal Navy and Royal Marines personnel were helping with relief efforts in the region, sending medical teams to some of the worst-hit areas. US military engineers were helping repair roads, bridges and water systems while moving relief supplies into the country. Private charities were sending doctors into remote parts of Honduras and Nicaragua.

In Nicaragua, where critics have accused the government of being slow with relief help, the Interior Ministry confirmed yesterday it had expelled a US woman under contract with the US Agency for International Development, Julie Gare Noble, for a 'slanderous, tendentious and baseless report.' Presidential spokesman Gilberto Wong said Noble, who works with non-governmental organizations in Wisconsin, had suggested that aid for Nicaragua go through non-governmental groups, 'making it understood that the government was not reliable.'

Associated Press

for their livelihood, the economic results of a storm like Mitch are drastic. True, money flows into the country at first in the form of foreign aid and it keeps people alive – but it doesn't equal the cost of the damage done by the hurricane. Later, the country will suffer from being unable to export its agricultural produce, because there won't be enough of it. The country is already in debt to America and elsewhere, and it will not be able to repay that debt. Some countries will cancel or reschedule that foreign debt (give a longer period for repayment) as a result of the disaster. In the long term this should be good news for Honduras, since it would never have been able to repay all those debts even if there had never been a hurricane. But there will still be the problem of feeding the people.

6 Political effects. Major disasters can have a destabilising effect on a country's government. This is often bad news for ordinary people, because armed gangs start springing up and there is an increase in crime and terrorism. In any case, the government will be judged, both at home and abroad, on how well it has handled the disaster. And since it is easier to handle a disaster badly than well, the government can be seriously weakened or even overthrown. But any government will have a hard time after a disaster like Mitch, because of the difficulties of managing the economy and ensuring that people are fed, clothed and housed. It will be tempted to invite investment from other countries to help rebuild its infrastructure and economy – but the disadvantage of this is that the country will lose some of its independence as huge companies from rich countries move in and start telling everybody what to do.

Relief organisations

Explain the role of three organisations dealing with these situations.

Looking back at the report on Hurricane Mitch on page 297 we learn that: 'Britain said about 1400 Royal Navy and Royal Marines personnel were helping with relief efforts in the region, sending medical teams to some of the worst-hit areas. US military engineers were helping repair roads, bridges and water systems while moving relief supplies into the country. Private charities were sending doctors into remote parts of Honduras and Nicaragua.'

In a disaster of this scale and type, the roles of all relief organisations are much the same. They are:

- to rescue people in the immediate aftermath
- to save lives which would be lost – mainly through disease – in the weeks and months following the disaster
- to help with reconstruction of housing, roads, railways, power supplies, water supplies, food supplies, industry and so on
- to educate people in avoiding the worst effects of such a disaster if it should happen again
- to attract funding for these activities
- to lay the foundation of sustainable development in the future.

Looking at the agencies mentioned in the extract, the Royal Navy and the Marines will be giving valuable help getting medical help to stricken areas, building bridges, putting up temporary buildings, and providing security and authority to back up the medical teams they are taking in. They will keep lines of communication open so that doctors and nurses can be fairly sure of receiving the medical supplies they need. They will also be making sure that clean water – the most basic requirement for health – is available. And this won't be easy where all water supplies are likely to be polluted with sewage, mud and rotting animal and vegetable material. Almost certainly they will have to use tankers to bring water in from outside the affected area.

They will be working in coordination with the American military engineers. They will have brought in heavy machinery from the USA, which is much nearer to Honduras than Europe. Their job is more long term than that done by the Royal Navy. The roads and bridges they build will be permanent structures. Without this infrastructure it won't be possible to rebuild the stricken area. Materials for building houses, schools, hospitals and factories can't be brought in unless there is an effective transport system. Because of the severity of the flooding, every bridge in the area will have been totally destroyed, and everything will have to be rebuilt from scratch.

The doctors sent into Nicaragua and other affected countries will stay there for at least a year. They are paid for by charities which raise their money from the public, mainly in the USA and Europe. They will have to speak good Spanish, and be able to work in a difficult environment. Shortage of medicines, and problems with hygiene, will be everyday problems. They cannot count on being well received everywhere, because the area is politically unstable and in some places the Americans and British are unpopular.

In the long term these doctors will train other people to take on their work, and to carry out nursing duties. As time passes the diseases they treat will change as the area slowly recovers from the hurrricane. As physical illnesses decrease there may be an increase in psychological illness – the result of delayed shock, bereavement and stress.

Reviewing responses to a disaster

Analyse how the emergency services review their response to a given disaster scenario.

Small-scale disasters can be reviewed relatively quickly and efficiently – though it is still a difficult job. For instance, when the emergency service response to a plane crash is reviewed, the officer in charge has to carry out the following procedures.

1. Arrange for all rescue workers to be interviewed about their role in the disaster, and how successfully they felt they carried it out. In particular, the problems that rescue workers encountered, either because of the crash, the state of the survivors, or the work of other rescue services, have to be brought out fully and honestly.
2. Collect information about what happened in similar disasters so that some comparison can be made, if necessary.
3. Collect information from other sources, such as the Civil Aviation Authority, or crash investigation teams, which may be relevant to an assessment of the emergency services' response.
4. Gather information from survivors if possible.
5. Assess the media coverage of the disaster and how the public services responded to it.
6. Write a full report giving findings (full information about the nature of the crash and the emergency services' response), conclusions (the main points and what they mean) and recommendations (a list of what must and must not be done in the future).

It may well be that the report will find that in some respects the emergency services were too slow, inefficient, badly organised or unprepared. These will be stated in the conclusions. However, except in extreme cases the purpose of the report will not be to criticise individuals, and the points made will be constructive, so that people can learn from them.

The report will be circulated to all the emergency services, the Home Office, local authorities, aircraft manufacturers, the Health and Safety Executive, various training agencies, airports and civil aviation authorities (who are in charge of air traffic control). It may form an important part of the evidence in a public inquiry – which will be held if the government feels that the circumstances of an air crash should be examined in more depth. Equally, it will be needed if crime or negligence are suspected, or if court cases result from the disaster.

FOCUS

Here is an example of the kinds of conclusions which can be drawn from an aircraft crash report. The crash happened near Schiphol Airport, Amsterdam, in 1992, when a Boeing 747 crashed into a block of flats. The flats contained many temporary residents, and the final death toll was never known. The lessons learnt were as follows.

- Communication channels soon became swamped and were 'tappable' by the media.
- There was poor communication between the scene and the policy centre at City Hall.
- There was a lack of information from the scene.
- 40,000 voyeurs [onlookers] blocked the surrounding area, and some even looted the flats.
- Unidentified people were allowed onto the site.
- The media were intrusive.
- There was no reliable list of residents. This was a major problem.
- Volunteers were wrongly sited.
- Consideration was not paid to the ethics involved in the fatalities. For example the colour of the sheet placed over the body had certain significance to some religions involved.
- 'Pseudo claimants'. If the number of people claiming new accommodation after the incident was to be believed, some flats had 60 occupants!

Source: Adapted from *Fire* magazine, October 1996

This disaster, and the way the emergency services and media dealt with it, had a lasting effect on race relations in Holland, making illegal immigrants very unpopular with Dutch nationals.

UNIT 13 Traffic and Transport

Unit outcome 1
Examine private motor vehicles as a medium of transport

Assessment criteria

- Compare and justify the private motor vehicle in relation to other forms of transport.
- Summarise the main points of the public versus private transport debate.

All public service work actively involves transport. The traffic police are a major part of the police force, not to mention the British Transport Police, whose work is on trains. Ambulances are road vehicles, and the fire service never attend their fires and accidents on foot. Roman armies walked to their battles, but the modern army doesn't. We live in an age of traffic and transport, and public service work reflects this.

Travel by motor vehicle

Compare and justify the private motor vehicle in relation to other forms of transport.

Look at the table in figure 13.1.

This table tells us that the 'average' person in 1997 travelled 619 miles (990 kilometres) by car for every four miles (6.4 kilometres) they travelled by bike. Or, to put it differently, for every four people who travel a certain distance by bicycle, 619

Great Britain						Billion passenger kilometres
	1961	**1971**	**1981**	**1991**	**1996**	**1997**
Road						
Car and van[1]	157	313	394	582	609	619
Bus and coach	76	60	49	44	44	43
Bicycle	11	4	5	5	4	4
Motorcycle	11	4	10	6	4	4
All road	255	381	458	638	661	670
Rail[2]	39	36	34	38	38	41
Air[3]	1	2	3	5	6	7
All modes	295	419	495	681	706	717

1 Includes taxis.
2 Data relate to financial years.
3 Includes Northern Ireland and Channel Islands.

Figure 13.1 *Distance travelled: by mode (Source:* Social Trends *29, 1999, p.196)*

Great Britain					Percentages
	Car	Bus & Coach	Rail[1]	Walk	Other
Social/entertainment	26	18	18	20	27
Shopping	19	32	10	24	13
Other escort and personal business	21	11	8	14	10
Commuting	18	18	47	7	26
Education	3	15	6	11	11
Escort education	4	1	1	8	1
Other, including just walk	–	–	–	15	–
Business	5	1	6	1	4
Holiday/day trip	4	2	4	1	8
All purpose	100	100	100	100	100

1 Includes London Underground.

Figure 13.2 *Journeys per person per year: by mode and journey purpose, 1995–1997 (Source:* Social Trends *29, 1999, p.197)*

people will travel the same distance by car. The bottom line is that far more people travel by car than by any other method.

You can see from figure 13.1 how our use of transport has changed between 1961 and 1997. As a nation we travel four times as far by car now as we did in 1961. On the other hand bus and coach travel has gone down by nearly half. Bicycle use halved between 1961 and 1971 and has stayed much the same since then. The use of motorbikes has gone up and down, but it's less now than it was. There's not much change in rail travel, but air travel has gone up seven times.

Another table from the same book (see figure 13.2) shows that we use different kinds (or 'modes') of transport for different reasons.

The table tells us that just over a quarter of all car journeys (26 per cent) are made for social or entertainment purposes. Nearly half of all train journeys – 47 per cent – are made by people who are going to work. On the other hand, only 18 per cent of car journeys are made for the purpose of going to work. But note that this does not mean that fewer people go to work by car than by train. In fact more people go to work by car than by

FOCUS

For carrying people about, cars are by far the most important form of transport. Look at the following points:

- 86 per cent of all travelling is done in cars (including taxis)
- 30 per cent of people in Britain (13 million) do not have regular use of a car
- old and poor people are less likely to use cars
- drivers make many more journeys (50 per cent more) than people who don't drive
- men are much more likely to do the driving than women
- car drivers don't like using other forms of transport: only in London do drivers regularly use other forms of transport as well
- the main reasons for driving are: to get to work (commuting), shopping, entertainment, to give people lifts and 'personal business'
- people who live in the country travel further per year than people who live in towns
- traffic levels in 1997 were ten per cent higher than in 1991
- in 1997 there were 23 million cars on British roads – about one for every two adults
- company cars were ten per cent of all cars (but the company car system ceased in 1999)
- 81 per cent of men have driving licences, but only 57 per cent of women.

United Kingdom					Indices (1981 = 100)
	1981	**1986**	**1991**	**1996**	**1998**
Motoring costs					
Vehicle tax and insurance	100	146	220	299	335
Maintenance[1]	100	138	195	251	276
Petrol and oil	100	145	156	213	240
Purchase of vehicles	100	116	144	165	174
All motoring expenditure	100	131	163	205	224
Fares and other travel costs					
Bus and coach fares	100	139	198	261	278
Rail fares	100	137	201	262	278
Other	100	107	137	156	167
All fares and other travel	100	135	186	229	244
Retail prices index	100	137	185	214	227

1 Includes spares and accessories, repairs and motoring organisation membership fees.

Figure 13.3 *Passenger transport prices (at January each year based on the retail prices index)*
(Source: Social Trends *29, 1999, p.206)*

train, but as a proportion of total car use, journeys to work are less important than they are as a proportion of total rail use. Walking is an interesting one. Fifteen per cent of all walks are taken for the purpose of walking ... Work that one out if you can!

Why have cars become so successful?

Price advantages

Look at the table in figure 13.3.

This table shows that although the price of motoring has more than doubled since 1981 (the base-line on this table), it hasn't gone up by as much as coach or rail travel. So that makes the private car even better value than it was in 1981.

Of course, different cars cost different amounts of money to run. Quite apart from the costs of tax and insurance, which vary, cars differ widely in their fuel consumption. And the cost of fuel changes because of changes in world oil prices and, more importantly at the moment, changes in government tax policy.

The only type of travel which is becoming relatively cheaper than car travel is air travel (which comes under 'other' in this table). But planes and cars are not really in competition, since they are used for different types of journey. So a comparison between them is not relevant in this case.

Another point to consider is that a car journey effectively costs less if more people are travelling in the car. For example, it might be cheaper for one person to travel from Leeds to Glasgow by coach than to drive. But it certainly wouldn't be cheaper for four people to do the journey by coach, if they could share a car instead.

! THINK ABOUT IT ...

Choose a journey that you make regularly.

Find out what it would cost you if you used other methods of transport. For example, if you normally travel by bus to college, try to find out what it would cost you if you could drive there, or if you went by bike.

Convenience and reliability

A car takes you from door to door, when you want to go. Even a taxi doesn't do this until you have rung the taxi firm and waited for the taxi to come.

You can carry things in a car. If you want to take your computer to be mended, all you have to do is shove it in the back of your car and drive off to see the cowboy you bought it from. You'd be facing serious baggage problems if you took your computer on the bus, and the computer wouldn't like it either.

The train would be even worse. For one thing, you probably live further from the nearest railway station than the nearest bus stop. And can you rely on the train to get you there on time? Read this extract.

Eagle Eye on Late Trains

A survey of train punctuality at Exeter revealed that fewer than 50 per cent of trains arrived or departed within one minute of their scheduled time. Gerard Duddridge of RDS South West branch kept watch at the station over 16 weekdays in April and May between 17.00 and 18.00 hours. The best performing train in his survey was the 14.30 Wales & West from Newquay. The Virgin 08.50 from Edinburgh and the Great Western 14.45 from London Paddington were the most delayed trains.

Mr Duddridge comments: 'The railway has much work to do to achieve the performance levels which passengers expect and pay for.' After analysing the findings, he concludes that reducing timetable changes from year to year would help solve problems. Investing in some new loops and doubled sections of track would also be worthwhile. Sometimes delays caused by one operator caused problems for another.

Comfort

There are two sides to this question.

Either: in the car, the driver sits in a specially designed seat listening to their own choice of entertainment on CD or radio, or perhaps just talking privately with a favourite friend in the seat beside them. And families can take all their comforting clutter with them.

Car drivers often complain, therefore, about buses and trains. The seats are too small or too hard, and they aren't clean. Other passengers drink, or smell, or smoke or, worst of all, talk. There are children scuttling about on trains, there's no privacy, nowhere to put your clutter, and only the sound of other people's personal stereos and mobile phones to entertain you.

Or: people without cars travel by bus or train. They can read instead of driving, or go to sleep. They can get up and stretch their legs, while drivers are gnashing their teeth and counting cones. True, they are surrounded by the Great British Public – but what's wrong with that? Who knows who you might meet, while the unfortunate car driver is reduced to swearing at 'that *** in front', trapped in his private cell.

Safety

This is a difficult one, but statistically the chances of being in a serious accident are small whatever kind of transport you use. And a modern car, with airbags, ABS and crush bars, is as safe as a car can be. Buses are frequently involved in minor brushes with other vehicles, lamp-posts, skips and the like but such incidents are not often dangerous. Trains, too, are usually safe. But not always. The Paddington train crash of October 1999 was a terrible event, made the headlines for days, and called the safety of the rail network into question. Still, serious rail crashes happen only about once every two years. People used to fall out of train doors quite often, sometimes through their own fault, but the companies have got wise to that, and it isn't so easy now.

As for violence from other people, it isn't a major transport consideration, though obviously people do get mugged on the London Underground, or on trains. On the other hand, people can get beaten up by members of their own family in cars. Often it is taxi-drivers and bus drivers who are at most risk of physical violence, following arguments about fare-dodging. And occasionally taxi-drivers have been known to take the law into their own hands and attack passengers.

Satisfaction

Here the car wins hands down. After all, you don't get TV ads for the 221 bus to Heckmondwike via Norristhorpe. Like a dog, a car reflects its owner. A car is a symbol, an image: the manufacturers and their ad agencies have worked very hard to cultivate this. A Jeep is a way of life, tracking grizzlies in the Rockies and grilling salmon in the twilight. A Clio is a scene from a sophisticated French film, and a girl to die for. Cars are now part of lifestyle; they are ourselves as we would like others to see us. The car is seen as a sign of wealth, success, 'pulling power', independence and culture. It is a social and political statement. It fires our imagination. You get your trainspotters and your bus spotters, but every driver in the world is a car spotter. Cars involve our emotions, express our individuality and give us pleasure on a scale that no other form of transport can match.

Public versus private transport

Summarise the main points of the public versus private transport debate.

Money

Public transport	Private transport
It is sometimes cheaper for one person to travel by public transport than by car. This is especially true of buses or coaches.	If there are two or more people in a car, it is cheaper to go by private than public transport (though there are hidden costs, such as depreciation, in car travel).
Many bus and train services, especially in rural areas, are subsidised by the taxpayer. If they closed down we would each have to pay less tax.	Drivers pay road tax, and tax on petrol, which is just as much a kind of tax as the income tax we pay for public transport. But the difference is that drivers choose to pay this tax and get some personal benefit. If a driver pays tax to support bus services he never uses, it seems unfair.
If more people used public transport instead of cars, there would be less congestion on the roads. Time would be saved, and therefore money.	Roads in towns are often obstructed by empty buses, or buses which keep stopping. These waste time as much as a traffic jam.
Many of us buy foreign cars. As a result the country loses money – so this is a hidden drain on the economy. If we took the bus or the train the country would benefit economically.	Britain makes cars and exports large numbers of them abroad. These earn vast sums of money for the country. If we turned to public transport fewer vehicles would be made, or exported, and the economy would suffer.
As the roads fill up there will have to be strict controls on the number of private cars using them. Public transport is needed as a way of gradually reducing our dependence on the car without damaging the economy too much.	One in six jobs in Britain has something to do with cars. Many of these would be lost if we all started using public transport. Mass unemployment would put up taxes, so then we would all be worse off.
Considering that oil is a non-renewable resource, petrol and diesel are cheap at the moment. But as prices go up, which they will as world supplies run out, we won't be able to afford to run our own cars any more.	People have a right to use petrol while it is available. And if or when it runs out, other fuels, such as hydrogen distilled from seawater, or biogas, will take its place. Or by that time they might have developed good electric cars.

Quality of life

Public transport	Private transport
Traffic congestion and 'gridlock' caused by private cars and lorries are making travel very slow and difficult, and spoiling it for everybody.	Since buses are often half empty they take up as much space per person as a car does. They stop, start, and hog the road, causing problems for everybody.
If more money was put into public transport, there would be newer, cleaner, faster and more reliable vehicles. Then people would choose to leave their cars at home because public transport would become pleasanter and more convenient.	Something which is publicly owned is always scruffy and second-rate compared with something private. The drivers are underpaid and badly motivated. And however good the service, there will always be time wasted waiting at a station or bus stop.
There are now buses for disabled people, and buses go into estates and other places where they never used to go. That means you don't have to walk far to get to a bus stop.	However many bus stops they have it won't be as convenient as using your own car. And a car is always easier for a disabled person than a bus. Anyway, the more stops a bus has, the slower it gets.
On buses and trains you meet people and can be part of society, instead of being selfishly locked away inside your own little world of the car.	'There is no such thing as society'. It is better to be able to choose who you travel with – or travel alone if you prefer. A car is an extension of your own home.
There is enough luggage space on buses and trains.	It is far easier to carry things in a car.
If you travel by bus you can feel that you are doing something for other people and for the planet. So you feel good about yourself.	In a car you can be yourself and express yourself in the way you fit it out and the way you drive. You are in control. Cars are exciting, buses and trains are boring.

A car is an extension of your own home

The environment

Public transport	Private transport
There are fewer 'units' – i.e. buses or trains – carrying more people. In other words, one engine may move 50 people instead of, at the most, four or five.	Buses and trains are often empty. And a bus or train creates far more pollution than a car. If you have just four passengers on a bus, they are being dragged by a huge, diesel-guzzling engine.

Cont'd

Buses and trains use diesel, which does not have lead in it, and is less polluting than petrol. Though lead in petrol is being phased out, it still reduces the intelligence of young children in towns and cities.	Scientists have recently discovered that diesel is more polluting than they thought. Diesel fumes contain 'particulates' – a kind of fine dust which may cause cancer.
Global warming shows that we desperately need to cut down on emissions (pollution) from vehicles. Changing to mass public transport is the only realistic way of doing this. If global warming is not stopped, it will eventually make the world unsuitable for life.	Are buses and trains really less polluting than cars? Car engines are getting much cleaner than they used to be and scientists will find other ways to make them even better. There is no real agreement between scientists about global warming. There were plenty of big changes in temperature before the human race ever appeared. And we can't prove that global warming is caused by cars. It might be caused by people burning down the Amazon rain forests.
Cars and lorries cause noise pollution.	So do buses and trains.
Because there are too many cars there are too many roads. Remember the Newbury by-pass? If things go on as they are doing, the whole country will eventually be covered with tarmac, and the only greenery will be growing on the top of multi-storey car parks.	People get hysterical about new roads. They are needed for the economy, and to prevent traffic jams. It is less damaging for the environment to have a by-pass than a town centre blocked up with cars and lorries.

Safety and reliability

Public transport	**Private transport**
There are fewer serious accidents on buses and trains than in cars.	That is only because there are so many fewer buses and trains than there are cars. In fact cars are better designed and, mile for mile, are safer.
Public transport will become much more reliable if it gets enough money from the government and if more people use it.	Too costly. No government would commit the money needed.
Road rage is for car drivers. Buses are safe and stress free: so are trains.	Ask any bus driver what the buses are like on a Saturday night. And ask yourself why so many parents now drive their children to school.

Social factors

Public transport	**Private transport**
Private transport is socially divisive. The car-owners and drivers are the 'haves'; the rest are the 'have-nots'. This amounts to a form of discrimination, since non-drivers become second-class citizens. Being unable to drive is almost a form of disability when we don't have the public transport we deserve and need. Our transport system is in danger of creating a snobbish, 'two-tier' country.	If everybody had a car then there would be no real social division on the basis of the transport we use. It is the poor quality of public transport that causes the problem, not the fact that other people drive cars. Anyway, you shouldn't engineer society, especially by trying to drag people down to a worse standard of living than they have now. People work for their luxuries and have a right to enjoy them.

! THINK ABOUT IT ...

Which of these arguments do you think are reasonable, and which are unreasonable?

What would you do about the problem – if anything?

Unit outcome 2
Examine the social and environmental effects of motor vehicle use

Assessment criteria

- Explain the social and environmental costs of using motor vehicles.
- Measure the effectiveness of two road safety campaigns and justify their use.
- Describe in detail how vehicles may be used for criminal purposes as well as being targets for crime.
- Summarise the work of two public services in relation to vehicles and their use.

Social and environmental costs of motor vehicle use

Every aspect of people's lives has been altered by the spread and use of motor vehicles. Indeed, it is hard to imagine what life must have been like without them. The best we can do is read old books – in which everybody rides on horseback or trudges round on foot – or visit those few parts of the world, such as rural Africa, where people still live in places which are unreachable by car.

Costs or benefits?

Though we are talking about the 'costs' of motor vehicle use, it would be a mistake to think that the effects of motor vehicles are negative. At present, they benefit us in endless ways. Motor vehicles give us and our families freedom to be where we want to be and to do what we want. They have made us rich (because what business can operate without motor transport?) and they are one of the ways we use this wealth (because anybody who has money buys a car with it). Though vehicles may kill us, they more often save our lives when they rush us to hospital. Thanks to vehicles we are free to travel and live in places we could otherwise have seen only on pictures. We can look for jobs in far-flung places and still keep in touch with our families. We can buy and sell in towns and countries we could never have reached before. We can meet, marry and have children by people who live outside walking distance of our own homes. You could argue that because of this the entire evolution of the human race has been changed by motor vehicles. Certainly, if motor vehicles were 'disinvented' overnight, vast swathes of the world population would die of hardship and famine – so whatever happens there is absolutely no going back.

But there are drawbacks. There is much less sense of community nowadays. Many of us don't know our next door neighbours. We're all strangers who get into our cars and drive off to unknown destinations. The car is a capsule; we're safe inside it and the rest of the world is just like a television picture drifting past. So, many people feel that the car has helped to develop a selfish society. It's a case of 'I'm all right, Jack': us, in the car, and them, outside. The car, some people say, has made us materialistic: all we care about is what we own, how much money we have, what we buy, and what we consume.

Why don't children play in the street any more? Is it because they're all hunched over their computers, or is it because of the car? Cars might knock them down, or maybe nasty men with sweets will try and tempt children to get in and drive them away. Whether this is true or not, many people feel that the car has created a climate of fear – and this, again, has damaged our local communities beyond repair.

Then there's crime. We'll have more to say about that later. Vehicles are stolen, then used for theft. Murderers such as Michael Sams and Peter Sutcliffe, the Yorkshire Ripper, used vehicles. Sutcliffe was a lorry driver – in many ways the perfect job for a modern serial killer.

In the old days, critics of the car say, we would go out to the park or the fair in our holidays, instead of driving off to God-knows-where. And everybody was happier as a result. The countryside wasn't overrun by tourists, who just go there to goggle and gawp. The countryside was a place of work, not a theme park or a dormitory for commuters. And country people used to be able to afford to live there. Not any more.

Environmental costs

The environmental costs of motor vehicles are not a matter of opinion – they are a matter of scientific fact. The opinion comes in when we ask ourselves how serious these environmental costs are. So what are these costs?

Pollution

Cars burn petrol or diesel and give out carbon dioxide, carbon monoxide, particles of carbon, tiny droplets of unburnt fuel, steam and traces of various metals – of which the most important is lead.

The carbon dioxide acts as a greenhouse gas. What this means is that, like the glass in a greenhouse, carbon dioxide lets sunlight reach the ground, but it then traps the heat that the sunlight brings with it. As a result the world is getting hotter year on year. The annual change might be only 0.1 of a Celsius degree, but it's enough to melt miles of Antarctic ice. So the sea level rises. Not only that: the increased warmth affects plants and animals. Big spiders (*Tegenaria atrica*) for example,which used to be only found south of the River Thames, are now found in many parts of Britain, simply because the average air temperature has risen by a degree or two in the past 30 years. We can now grow maize, or grapes, in places where we couldn't before (though this is partly due to plant-breeding). These changes may not seem important, but they are reflected all over the world. If the sea rises, countries such as Holland and Kiribati may literally go under. And because rainfall patterns are changing, the Sahara Desert is advancing at about 25 miles a year, which is one reason why there are such terrible famines in Sudan and Ethiopia. If our cars are making people starve and die in other parts of the world, surely something should be done about it.

The other products in car exhaust are less of a worry. But they still cause problems. Carbon monoxide is deadly, though there isn't enough of it in exhausts to kill people who are trying to cross the road. The 'particulates', the fine dust in exhaust, may be responsible for certain kinds of cancer. A good deal of research is going on into them at the moment. Lead, now being phased out, has been shown beyond doubt to affect children's development, and reduce the intelligence they were born with. Certain diseases, such as asthma, are on the increase, and this may well be due to road pollution.

Finally, car exhausts react with sunlight to form 'photochemical smog'. This is the kind of summer haze you get in cities like Athens, Los Angeles and London. It makes people's eyes run and can cause severe asthma attacks and bronchitis.

Noise

Vehicle noise travels a long way. People who live near motorways need double glazing (and can get a grant to pay for it). The noise may not be life-threatening, but many people find it highly unpleasant, and it may contribute to stress – including the stress shown in road rage.

Roads

People are beginning to dislike roads – not everybody, but enough to make some politicians and journalists sit up and take notice. They are ugly, they get everywhere, and they represent a large area of land covered with tarmac. Besides being an environmental hazard in themselves, they lead to secondary environmental damage because they take tourists out to unspoilt parts of the countryside with damaging results. In the Lake District, for example, cars and roads have brought millions of people tramping along ever-widening footpaths, causing soil erosion and threatening wildlife. This is one reason why we now have environmental activists – not to mention organisations such as Greenpeace – protesting against many new road developments.

Accidents

Vehicles get involved in road accidents. They cause deaths and injuries on a large scale. The following figures, for 1995, give some indication of the scale and frequency of accidents for different types of vehicle.

Number of road accident casualties, by vehicle type – GB, 1995

Vehicle	No. dead over 1 year period (1995)	All casualties over 1 year period (1995)
Bicycles	222	26,352
Mopeds	22	2,767
Scooters	4	610
Motor bikes	486	24,067
Cars	2,964	280,850
Bus or coach	164	15,102
Light goods vehicle	345	24,867
Heavy goods vehicle	597	17,985

The huge figures (which do not vary much from year to year) indicate a further social cost of accidents – one that we have not discussed yet. The suffering they cause to the victims who do not die (and those who do), and the anguish of relatives cannot be measured, or quantified. You will not see suffering on a bar chart. But many lives are ended or blighted by road traffic accidents, and they are a major cause of death among younger people – arguably the people who are most productive and

Average cost of road accidents per casualty and per accident – GB, 1995

Accident/ casualty type	Cost per casualty (£)	Cost per accident (£)
Fatal	812,010	947,370
Serious	92,570	111,970
Slight	7,170	11,020
Average of all accidents with casualties	29,080	41,240
Damage only (no casualties)		1,090

Source: Her Majesty's Stationery Office, Crown Copyright; reproduced with permission have most to offer to society. Society as a whole, including people who never knew the victims, suffers from this tragic waste of energy and talent.

But road accidents have another cost, and that is financial. Look at the table at the bottom of page 310.

The total cost for that year was estimated to be £13,280 million. That is over twice the amount of money which is spent on the police in England and Wales – salaries, buildings, vehicles, training and everything – each year.

The taxpayer pays. Or, to look at it differently, hospitals, schools and the public services pay for them – because they would each get more money from the government if all these billions didn't have to be spent on road accidents.

Road safety campaigns

Measure the effectiveness of two road safety campaigns and justify their use.

These figures show that it is worth spending a good deal of money on anything that will cut down road accidents. Since road safety campaigns are expensive, it is the government, rather than individual public services or other bodies, which run them. These campaigns take two main forms.

Types of campaign

Major campaigns

Major campaigns run for a short period of time – usually in summer or before Christmas. These campaigns are normally directed at drink-drivers. Drink-driving is an all-year-round problem, even though it tends to get worse at Christmas.

In 1995 there were three nation-wide campaigns. The summer one consisted of a TV commercial featuring a young man who has crippled his friend in a drink-drive accident. Seen through the eyes of the injured friend, the driver tries to explain away his guilt. 'I've only had a couple ... I thought it was alright to drive.'

The Christmas TV commercial showed a mother feeding her son, who had been brain-damaged in a drink-drive accident after having 'just one more drink'. Audience research afterwards showed that 90 per cent of the target audience – men between 18 and 34 – had seen the commercial.

Another approach was tried out in November, where the BBC worked together with the government to put out a special *999* programme, linked to a government 'No Excuses' leaflet. This was an approach which had worked well the year before.

Most national road safety campaigns of this type depend on their shock value to get through to the audience. But they also try to whip up peer-group pressure, and make drink-driving socially unacceptable. They are directed at people of the type and age group who are (a) most likely to drink-drive and (b) most likely to pay attention to a campaign against it. These are young men. In fact, there is thought to be more drink-driving among older men in their 40s and 50s, especially travelling salesmen. But research shows that they are less likely to speed than younger men under the influence of drink, and are also less likely to pay attention to road safety campaigns.

It is worth noting that, around Christmas, it is common to have brief items on national and local

news highlighting the fact that the police are out and about with their cameras and breathalysers, ready to test any drivers who might be over the limit. These can be seen as part of an overall campaign policy.

Local schemes

These often consist of notices or posters, such as 'Ossett welcomes careful drivers', 'This is a kidzone' or 'Kill your speed'. And local newspapers often contain accident reports or court reports which show how both victims and drivers suffer from bad driving. Recently, on the backs of Arriva buses, a huge pair of child's eyes has been staring out, with the caption: 'Thanks to you, class sizes just got smaller.' This refers to the recent political issue of class sizes, to 'hook' the reader's attention. Then, underneath, in tiny letters, are the words: 'Your driving can really mess things up.'

Measuring the effectiveness of campaigns

It is hard to measure the effectiveness of road safety campaigns accurately, because other factors, such as changes in the price of alcohol, or even the weather over Christmas, might greatly influence the number of drink-drive cases. Furthermore, police policies on the use of breathalysers are constantly changing, as they try new and more effective approaches, or change their priorities. Even variations in the funding of the police may have a significant effect on the number of convictions for dangerous or drunken driving.

However, statistics are obviously the most accurate way of monitoring the success of road safety campaigns. If the number of drink-related accidents or deaths goes down in comparison with the same time last year, or with a time when no campaign was being run, it implies that the campaigns are getting through to the public. The other way to test their effectiveness is through questionnaires, interviews or opinion polls which aim to find out whether the target group of people remember the campaign afterwards. If people can't even recall what the campaign was, they are unlikely to have been affected by it.

Further reading

Road Accidents Great Britain: 1995 The Casualty Report, The Government Statistical Service, HMSO

Vehicle crime

Describe in detail how vehicles may be used for criminal purposes as well as being targets for crime.

Vehicle crime is the biggest single type of recorded crime in Britain. One quarter of all recorded crimes in this country are vehicle crimes. On average there is one vehicle crime every minute, day and night, throughout the year. Half a million cars are stolen, and half of these are never seen again. But this isn't by any means the whole story. According to the Essex Constabulary: 'Virtually every crime involves a vehicle and targeting car crime has a positive impact on other offences such as fraud, burglary and ram raids.'

FOCUS

- Theft of light and heavy commercial vehicles continues to rise.
- A survey conducted by the Freight Transport Association reveals that 68 per cent of operators had experienced truck crime. Nearly half had been victims of an incident in the previous 12 months.
- Most commercial vehicles are now stolen for parts rather than for their goods: engines are top of the list followed by transmissions and axles.
- HGVs can be stolen and stripped within eight hours, with the valuable parts boxed aboard ready to ship. In 1994, 3,047 HGVs were stolen in England, Scotland and Wales. Most of these vehicles have never been recovered.
- HGV theft costs the insurance industry alone around £30 million a year.
- In 1994, the average loss suffered by each victim of HGV crime was £11,238.
- The majority of HGVs stolen are five to ten years old (1994 figures).

Crimes associated with vehicles include the following.

1 Break-ins. This is the most common form of vehicle crime. People keep valuables in their cars, or have stereos and other equipment which is worth stealing. Often the culprits are young people – mainly boys – in the 13–19 age range. In some cases these thefts are carried out in order to finance a drug habit. There are wide variations in the frequency with which different makes of car are broken into. For many years Vauxhall Cavaliers were a favourite target, probably because they were relatively easy to break into, though another reason may have been that – being less expensive – they were concentrated in the poorer areas where such crimes are more likely to be carried out. The place where a car is parked affects the likelihood of a break-in. Supermarket car-parks, streets in 'poor' areas, and beauty spots are all places where car-thieves work; they need to be unobserved, and able to get away quickly.

2 TWOC. This abbreviation (pronounced 'twock') means 'taking without owner's consent'; in other words, the car itself is stolen. In recent years this crime has become known as joyriding, but there is no law which mentions joyriding by name (and many people object to the name because it makes the crime sound less serious than it is). In joyriding the car is stolen and then driven at breakneck speed along roads, often in council estates, while the young drivers perform various spins and other manoeuvres. The car is in many cases seriously damaged by this procedure. After a night of driving around, the thieves may set fire to the car, or just abandon it. However, TWOC is not just joyriding. More often, a car is stolen in order to be broken down into spare parts, which is why so many stolen cars just vanish.

3 Theft. Cars and other vehicles have made thefts of all kinds much easier, because they provide a quick and private way of moving stolen goods about the country. Many thefts are of quite large objects, such as generators and other equipment used in factories or on building sites. This is where the so-called 'white vans' may have a part to play: there are two million Ford Transits and similar vehicles on British roads. Being common, secure and dependable, they are ideal for large scale thefts: in many cases you can't even see into them! The sheer number of different makes, which to the general public all look very much alike, makes it easier for thieves to get away with their loot.

4 Drugs. Vehicles are a secure way of moving the large quantities of drugs needed by Britain's drug sub-culture around the country. There are so many container vehicles that it is impossible for police or customs to check all of them. In any case, containers can be adapted with false walls, ceilings and floors to carry large quantities of drugs in a way which is hard to detect. The heavy volume of international lorry traffic, going to countries like Spain, makes drug smuggling easier – so too, perhaps, does the relaxation of customs checks at international borders in Europe.

Vehicle use in the public services

Summarise the work of two public services in relation to vehicles and their use.

1 The police

Most of the work in combatting vehicle-related crime is done by the police. They use two main methods: prevention and detection.

Prevention

Prevention takes the form of advice, leaflets, education, youth work, and the promotion of security hardware such as locking devices and security engraving of vehicles and possessions. The prevention work of the Suffolk police, shown in the extracts on the following page, is typical.

Detection

In addition to prevention campaigns, the police are constantly developing new ways of detecting vehicle crime. Methods include:

- schemes such as 'Impact', run by Avon and Somerset Police
- having a centralised vehicle crime bureau
- high-profile and undercover operations
- targeting dishonest dealers
- using 'bait' cars
- computer systems.

Launch of the SMART campaign – Stop Motor crime And Ring Today

Suffolk Constabulary launched the SMART campaign in September 1997 to make an impact on vehicle crime which makes up about 20 per cent of all crime in the county. This campaign is linked to the Crimestoppers national campaign of the same name.

The campaign has had a marked impact on vehicle crime particularly theft from vehicles and was strengthened in December 1998 with the introduction of our sneaky thief logo used in posters and products.

The campaign has featured may initatives at a local level. Neighbourhood Watch have supported the campaign and helped us to arrest thieves preying on vehicles in residential areas and Truckwatch have supported the campaign in the area of goods vehicles and loads.

Crimestoppers SMART campaign:
SMART is appealing for information on people involved in motor vehicle crime including the movement of stolen property from these crimes. A phone call with information on 0800 555 111 will help to reduce the problem.

Take action now, pick up a copy of 'Steer Clear of Car Crime' at your local police station. It contains all the preventative information that you need to know.

Ways of avoiding car crime

- Always secure vehicle even during brief periods of leaving it.
- Leave the vehicle in a safe location if at all possible e.g. visible to passers by.
- Valuables not to be left in vehicle, but locked in boot, if they must be left.
- Fit an alarm and immobiliser to the vehicle.
- Fit security coded or portable audio equipment.
- Postcoding of all audio equipment.
- Use of highly visible mechanical locks inside vehicle e.g. steering lock.
- Etching of Index Mark or Vehicle Identification Number on all glass surfaces.
- Garage a vehicle overnight.
- Join Vehicle Watch – application form at local police stations.
- 'Car Theft Index' booklet available at local police stations, will provide risk assessment for each model or car.
- 'Car Buyers Guide' similarly available. Advice aimed at preventing people buying stolen vehicles.

Source: Suffolk Constabulary

2 The Vehicle Inspectorate

This public service is part of the Civil Service (like HM Customs and Excise), but instead of being run by the Home Office (like the police and the fire service) it is run by the Department of the Environment, Transport and the Regions.

Its work supplements that of the police and is largely concerned with checking vehicles and their roadworthiness. In many ways its activities are like those of the Health and Safety Inspectors (see Unit 14: Fires and Accidents). Below is a summary from their website.

Enforcement
Our roadworthiness and traffic enforcement work involves carrying out roadside and spot checks on commercial and other vehicles for compliance with regulations relating to safety and environmental standards, overloading, driver's hours, operator licensing, vehicle licensing and vocational driver's licences.

The enforcement officers are qualified and experienced VI staff with the appropriate specialist knowledge. Vehicle examiners (VEs) are responsible for checking the mechanical components on a vehicle, the condition of the bodywork, etc. Traffic examiners (TEs) are responsible for checking tachographs, drivers' hours regulations, vehicle weight, licensing and other documentation. Enforcement staff are based in area offices around the country.

Cont'd

Enforcement Action

Our staff can take enforcement action by issuing a prohibition notice (PG9) prohibiting vehicles from use, by prosecuting drivers and vehicle operators and reporting to the traffic commissioner for operator licensing action. Vehicle examiners use the *Categorisation of Defects on Road Vehicles* to assist them at roadside checks. This manual provides guidance on the action to take when roadworthiness defects are found during vehicle inspections. Copies of this document can be purchased from the Vehicle Inspectorate. If significant defects are found an immediate prohibition will be issued which prevents further use of the vehicle. In cases in which a defect is not considered to be an immediate risk, a delayed prohibition will be issued. This allows the continued use of the vehicle for up to ten days from the date that the prohibition was issued. Details about how to clear a prohibition are given on the reverse of the prohibition notice. Clearance will usually be by a full or partial test at a vehicle test station.

When a vehicle is found to be overweight after being weighed, a prohibition for driving an overweight vehicle will be issued. Excess weight must be removed before the vehicle can continue its journey.

If during the check an offence is found for which the driver and/or operator may be prosecuted, the driver will be advised at the roadside that he will be reported for the offence. This may subsequently lead to prosecution.

Reproduced with the permission of the Vehicle Inspectorate

Unit outcome 3
Examine driver attitudes and behaviour

Assessment criteria

- Describe in detail the reasons for common traffic offences.
- Explain driver attitudes and behaviour in relation to road rage, speed, drink and drugs.
- Describe in detail the effects on individuals of media representation of vehicles.

Reasons for traffic offences

We have already seen in this unit something of the cost of road accidents – both to the taxpayer and to the victims. So prevention is always better than cure. We have touched on various kinds of prevention: road safety campaigns, proper driving tests and the safer design of vehicles, so that if there is an accident, people are less likely to get hurt. But it could be that the best form of accident prevention is the law itself: the traffic offences and the way they are dealt with by the courts. For the main use of traffic laws is not to punish offenders, but to act as a deterrent to other drivers: to give the message that if they offend, they will end up in court.

Common offences

Licence

Driving without (or 'otherwise than in accordance with') a licence is an offence. There are two kinds of licence – a provisional licence, for a learner, and a full licence, for someone who has passed the driving test. If you have a provisional licence you must

- display 'L' plates
- have a qualified driver sitting next to you
- not drive a motorcycle of more than 125 cc
- not drive on a motorway
- not tow a trailer.

If you have a full licence you can only drive the type of vehicle for which you have passed the test. So if you only have a car licence, you cannot drive a heavy goods vehicle or a motorcycle.

The purpose of the law is to keep inexperienced or unskilled drivers under proper control, so that they do not pose a risk to themselves and others. It also makes sure that no one under 16 (for motorcycles) or 17 (for cars) drives on the public road. The maximum fine for this offence is £1,000, and if drivers repeatedly offend they may end up in prison.

Insurance

Drivers must be insured. If they are not, and they are in an accident, their victims will not be eligible to receive compensation. This makes driving without insurance a serious offence. The maximum fine is £5,000 and six to eight penalty points – depending on the circumstances of the offence. An additional reason for this law is that it discourages people from driving other people's cars without permission.

MOT and tax disc

A car which is more than three years old has to pass a Ministry of Transport (MOT) test, to make sure it is in good enough condition to be on the road. The reason for this law is that, in the past, many accidents were caused by vehicles which were not roadworthy (for example, the brakes didn't work properly). The maximum fine is £1,000, but the offence does not carry any penalty points.

A tax disc must be displayed on the car windscreen. The proper name for this 'road tax' is an 'excise tax' – a kind of extra tax for drivers, rather like the extra excise tax put on petrol or alcohol. The maximum fine for not having a tax disc is usually £1,000. The maximum fine for not having it stuck to the windscreen is £200.

Roadworthy condition

There are a number of laws which specify whether a vehicle is in roadworthy condition or not. In particular the tyres, steering and brakes must be in good order. A tyre must have 'at least 16 millimetres of tread in a continuous band all the way round the circumference' – and this goes for the spare tyre as well. If the body is getting very rusty, or has spiky bits following an accident, or even if the windows have too many football stickers on, it may be breaking the law. Fines are usually small, but the offences exist to remind drivers that a car can become a deadly weapon if it isn't looked after properly.

Speeding

This is the most common of all motoring offences. All British roads have speed limits. In built-up areas, or where the street lights are less than 218 metres (or 200 yards) apart, the maximum speed is 30 miles per hour. Some roads without street lights have 30 mph limits – but in this case there will be signs up. On other roads, the speed limit is 60 mph, except on a dual carriageway or most motorways, where it is 70 mph. Where there are road works there may be signs giving a special speed limit. Some vehicles have speed limits – cars towing caravans, for instance, cannot go faster than 60 mph on a motorway.

The police detect speeding using radar and other high-tech methods. However, they do not usually prosecute unless a driver is going at more than ten mph above the legal speed limit for that road. Some speeding offences carry a fixed penalty of £40 and three penalty points, but in extreme cases of speeding the driver is likely to be disqualified. The reason for imposing these penalties is that speed kills, in an accident, by reducing the braking distance and increasing the impact. In addition, if a driver is going too fast, it may be difficult for other drivers to react in time, thus increasing the likelihood of accidents. The law is difficult to enforce because vast numbers of drivers go over the speed limit, and usually the police aren't around to see it. If everybody is going too fast – who do the police choose to prosecute?

Crossings, lights and signs

Many drivers ignore pedestrian crossings or jump the lights. But on a pedestrian crossing, the pedestrian has the right of way as soon as her foot touches the crossing. If the motorist then fails to give way, it can result in a fine of up to £1,000. Failing to comply with traffic lights or stop signs also carries a maximum fine of £1,000. All these actions are offences because either the driver or a pedestrian could be put at risk if the signs are not obeyed. But the signs have to be there. If not, it would lead to bad driving and tailbacks which would be both dangerous and time-consuming.

Careless driving

This offence usually occurs when there is a small accident caused by drivers not watching what they are doing. If drivers pull out of a side road without looking, and there is a crash, or bump into the car in front, it suggests that they are not paying attention – and that the offence of careless driving has been committed. The courts take the view that there can be different degrees or amounts of carelessness, so fines can vary – but the maximum is £2,500.

This offence exists because it is important that drivers have their wits about them when they are on the road. They shouldn't be talking on mobile phones, eating their lunch or reading the newspaper while they are moving – such behaviour causes accidents.

Dangerous driving: causing death by dangerous driving

We are in the big league here – these are major offences. Dangerous driving is driving badly on purpose, and in a way which could cause a very bad accident, whereas careless driving is not done on purpose and is merely thoughtless. Of course it is sometimes hard to tell the two offences apart, but if the law was obviously broken and someone is either badly hurt or killed, then the offender will be charged with dangerous driving. The maximum fine is £5,000, with disqualification for at least 12 months, even if there is no death. If someone is killed, the offender gets up to five years' imprisonment. Many people have argued that because dangerous driving kills, the penalties should be stiffer than they are. Even so they are harsher than the penalties for other offences; and this again is to discourage other people from driving dangerously, as well as to punish those who do.

Failure to stop; failing to report an accident

If drivers are involved in an accident with another vehicle, they must exchange particulars – names, addresses and registration numbers – even if no one is hurt. They should also exchange insurance details – though they don't have to by law. A collision with a large domesticated animal: horse, cow, sheep, pig or dog, must be reported, either to the owner or the police. But you can flatten a cat and just drive away. Reports of accidents should not be unnecessarily delayed. The penalty for not reporting an accident can be as much as £5,000 or six months' imprisonment. The purpose of this law is to discourage all forms of hit-and-run driving. Besides, if someone is hurt in an accident, the seriousness of the injuries may not be clear at first: a person may seem to be all right, then drop dead later.

Failure to produce documents

If the police stop a driver the documents they ask for must be shown. If the documents are not produced, a fine of up to £1,000 can follow. The idea behind this law is that if a driver cannot produce documents, they probably have no right to be driving, or to be driving that vehicle. The law also gives the police an opportunity to investigate or identify people they suspect of committing some other serious crime. Peter Sutcliffe, the Yorkshire Ripper, was caught following a check on his driving documents.

Parking in a dangerous position or causing an obstruction

This can be a serious offence. If someone parked in front of a fire station so the fire engines couldn't get out, lives could be lost. More often, though, it is a matter of inconvenience – for example parking on a pavement so that pedestrians have to step out into the road. The fine is up to £2,500 – since the offence puts other people at risk.

Motorway offences

Parking on the hard shoulder, or making U-turns, are against the law. The penalties are usually not heavy, but such manoeuvres are dangerous and the law discourages them.

Lights

Drivers must keep indicator and brake lights in good working order, to warn other drivers of their movements. Headlights must be used in dull or foggy weather, or at night. They have to be dipped when other drivers could be dazzled by them. The penalties for offences involving lights are not severe, perhaps because lights often go wrong, and drivers can easily tell the police that they were just about to have them fixed, even if they weren't.

However, an unlit vehicle, or a car with one headlight that looks like a motor bike, is a danger on the roads – which is why bad lights can be an offence.

Drink-driving

Drivers must not have more than 35 micrograms of alcohol in 100 millilitres of breath. This is 80 milligrams in blood, or 107 milligrams in urine. Usually drivers are tested with a device called a breathalyser. If a driver refuses to take the breathalyser test, or any other kind of test, he can be fined up to £5,000. If the test is positive, the driver is arrested and taken to the police station. Drivers are likely to be tested anyway if they are in an accident.

Drink-driving laws are complex, but they are strongly enforced because research shows that about 36 per cent of all traffic accidents are drink-related. The theory is that if no one indulged in drinking and driving, these accidents would not happen, and there would be a great saving of life, property and money.

Driver attitudes

Explain driver attitudes and behaviour in relation to road rage, speed, drink and drugs.

Road rage

Until about five years ago the phrase 'road rage' was never used, and it may be that it will go out of fashion just as quickly as it came in. However, what it describes, which is an unreasoning violent anger felt by a few drivers against other road users, will probably stay with us as long as there are drivers and roads. Some research into road rage has been attempted, but it is still hard to know (a) whether it is only certain types of people who experience it or (b) whether it is something to do with the nature of modern roads and driving which could be changed. In other words, is road rage the fault of the driver or the road? The Institute of Advanced Motorists and Touchline Insurance brought out a leaflet on road rage in 1997. This is what it says.

Road rage – What it is and how to avoid it

Over the past few years, the so called 'road rage' syndrome has developed and we hear an increasing amount about it. However, road rage is nothing new; it has been around us for many a year, probably since the beginning of road transport. Road rage can happen to anybody at anytime and can vary from an aggressive gesture or word to a full on physical attack, or in some cases, even murder.

Road rage is an increasing problem, not just in Great Britain, but around the world. Drivers waiting at traffic lights, stuck in traffic jams or getting into or out of their cars are most vulnerable. Here are some safety tips on how to minimise the chances of becoming a victim.

- When in town, especially at night, make sure all car doors are locked, and keep the windows and sun roof only partly open.

Cont'd

- Secure any and all valuables (i.e. portable computers, mobile phones, brief cases, handbags, etc.) and keep them well out of sight.
- Avoid conflict on the road – gestures, stares, unnecessary use of the horn, flashing lights on, that might incite anger in another driver.
- Use lane sense and your indicators correctly.
- Don't get out of your car if you are being rammed or are blocked in.
- Be aware of other road users and their intentions.
- Keep your distance, and when stopped at a traffic light, give yourself room to drive away, just in case.
- If you are being followed, drive to a police station or a crowded public place for help.
- Avoid tailgating other cars on the road; it is dangerous and threatening.
- If an attacker tries to enter your car, sound your horn or alarm.
- If approached, don't argue. Apologise profusely if necessary, even if in the right. You can always take down details and report the offender.
- Above all, prevention is better than cure. Be courteous at all times to other road users – don't expect courtesy if you show none.

Speed

Speed means driving fast. The following facts are known:

- men tend to drive faster than women
- young men tend to drive faster than older men
- there may be regional or national differences in the speed at which people drive
- high speed means that drivers have less time to react to emergencies
- the braking distance is greater for a driver who is going fast
- the greater the speed, the more likely it is that an accident will be fatal.

Drivers often point out that there are dangers in driving too slow, as well as driving too fast. A slow driver may cause accidents by frustrating the drivers around him. Frustration leads to road rage, and road rage leads to reckless, aggressive driving, and accidents.

ANALYSIS

Fast driving often has its roots in the psychology of the driver. People who consider themselves dominant and forceful may well try to reflect this in their driving. If they don't suffer fools gladly in their ordinary lives, they won't suffer them gladly on the road either, and impatience will make them speed. On the other hand some people who feel repressed in their ordinary lives (see Unit 5: Human Behaviour) may compensate for it by fast driving. There is a hidden agenda in society which encourages us to admire fast driving: for men it is seen as masculine, sporty, part of an admirable 'go-getting' approach to life.

Drink and drugs

Drink-driving has been around for a long time. Though alcohol acts as a depressant on some people, sending them to sleep, it acts as a stimulant on others and excites them. It also gives people a false confidence, and there is again an air of machismo, of 'manliness' in the 'I can take my drink' attitude. Some people drink and drive out of bravado, to show that they are not afraid of the rules: others have simply lost their judgement, and think they are still sober. But many drink-drivers drive slowly and with excessive care, showing that they know what they are doing is wrong. One thing that is true of everyone is that alcohol slows physical reactions, and this must be dangerous for any driver.

Drug-taking and driving is a problem that people have only become aware of in recent years. Its scale can be seen in the table in figure 13.4.

It is estimated that five million people, which is about eight per cent of the population, regularly take cannabis. As this equals the percentage of dead crash victims who tested positive for cannabis, it implies that cannabis has no particular effect on driving ability. On the other hand, some researchers have said that cannabis undermines people's spatial awareness, so that they cannot judge speed and distance effectively.

Great Britain					Percentages
	Drivers	**Riders**	**Passengers**	**Pedestrians**	**All**
Medicinal drugs	4	6	9	8	6
Illicit drugs, of which:	18	14	21	8	16
Cannabis	10	5	13	1	8
Amphetamines	2	2	2	2	2
Opiates	1	1	2	1	1
Methadone	1	0	0	0	0
Multiple drugs	4	6	4	4	5
Alcohol (over legal limit)	22	15	29	31	23

Figure 13.4 *Road user fatalities testing positive for medicinal and illicit drugs, 1997 (Source:* Social Trends *29, 1999, p22)*

According to the table, only alcohol could be a significant cause of road-user deaths. Cannabis remains in the body for a long time, so the figures are no proof that the people who died were especially 'under the influence'. People take drugs for pleasure and recreation, and to identify with their subculture (for example, hippies might take cannabis, while ravers take ecstasy). They may well think that there is no particular risk in driving under the influence of these drugs.

Media representation

Describe in detail the effects on individuals of media representation of vehicles.

We read and see a lot about cars in newspapers and on the television. And everywhere you look, there is a car advertisement. Cars are not just big business: they are the biggest – as far as the media are concerned. Whether we like it or not we are constantly being bombarded by words and images about cars.

Whole books have been written on this subject: all we have room for here is a few highlights. The key point is that car advertisers are very clever people who have done their homework about cars and the people who buy them. They are deeply into psychology, and like Freud (see Unit 5: Human Behaviour) believe strongly in the 'unconscious mind'. In other words they believe that they can make people want to buy cars without knowing that they want to buy them – or why.

People, say the Freudians, are motivated by a need for sex and power. Maslow (1954) put more stress on security. Other psychologists have looked at things like self-respect or self-esteem. Car manufacturers and advertisers have tried to make cars that reflect these qualities. This means that if we buy a powerful car we are supposed to feel more powerful and sexy, and if we have a family we will fork out our money to buy something safe to carry them round in. The advertisers are right. We know this because (a) so many people have cars and (b) advertising has an effect on their sales. It must have, otherwise why would they spend so many millions of pounds on it?

If we look at a selection of car advertisements we can see what they're getting at. (See table on the following page.)

! THINK ABOUT IT ...

Find your own car advertisements, or, better still, look at the TV commercials, and see what the underlying message, or 'hidden agenda' is.

Summary

- Cars are designed and advertised to reach a particular market (type of buyer).

Intended effects of car advertisements on individuals

Media representation of vehicle	Intended effect on individual
'Chronometer precision for those with no time for the ordinary' – LEXUS IS200 advertised in *New Scientist*. There is a picture of the car, with a blurred sunset which looks like the birth of the universe.	This advertisement is worded with scientists in mind. It has a technological feel, and appeals to snobbery: 'no time for the ordinary'. 'Precision' implies speed and quick reactions, so the advertisement is a coded encouragement for fast driving.
'Adrenalin rush hour'. These words are put on a picture of a Jeep Cherokee rushing down a blurred mountain road. Round it is a collage of tiny pictures of bisons, mountains and wild horses, and a few bits of American Indian beadwork. The small pictures are roughly splashed and smeared with what looks like dried animal blood.	Made to appeal to the 'he-man' who loves the 'great outdoors' and wants to adventure in comfort. The pictures show speed in a tranquil setting; the blood-smears suggest that the Jeep is not for weak, lily-livered townspeople. Images of blood and guts, naked aggression, and the masculinity of the true man make this into an encouragement for reckless, selfish driving.
'Gorgeous sporty type WLTM partner for good times' – this advertisement for a Mazda 323 Sport shows the car looking sleek, black and almost skin-textured with one or two sexy red lights. The caption shows that the car and the advertisement are angled at the singles market. A smaller caption adds: 'spirited, agile and a natural athlete. In short, the perfect partner'.	The car is shown as an instrument of pleasure, like a sex aid. It is fast, and photographed in a foreshortened way to bring out a thrusting, phallic appearance. At the same time the caption personifies the car, by using a description more suited to a person than a machine. This says, in code, 'You are what you buy'. This is a lifestyle car, and the advertisement again encourages speed.

- They are presented in a way designed to appeal to the buyer's unconscious longings and motivations.
- Speed is one of the main themes of car advertisements.
- Power is another theme, suggesting that we all long for power.
- Sex is often dealt with in a 'passion wagon' manner, suggesting that most advertisements are aimed at men. But it is usually hinted at, not mentioned openly, in a 'nudge-nudge, wink-wink' style.
- Luxury, implying social success and a love of pleasure, is often stressed.
- The more expensive the car, the more likely it is to appeal to the higher needs in Maslow's 'hierarchy of human needs' (see Unit 15: Leadership, page 362).
- Advertisements for family cars are more likely to stress safety features, and encourage responsible driving, because young children are at the bottom of Maslow's pyramid, and their parents need to provide them with security before anything else.
- There is evidence to suggest that, under the surface, many car advertisements (and 'road test' articles about cars in motoring magazines and newspapers) encourage fast and dangerous driving. But they do it by implication, not openly, appealing to that unconscious force in human beings which Freud called the *id*.

! THINK ABOUT IT ...

Motorcycles are becoming increasingly popular.

- What are the reasons for this increased popularity?
- Who buys and uses them?
- What is the police attitude towards motorcyles and their riders?

Unit outcome 4
Investigate the requirements and current practice for private vehicle ownership

Assessment criteria

- Explain in detail the legal requirements of vehicle documentation in relation to private ownership.
- Review driver responsibility in relation to owning and using motor vehicles.
- Explain the benefits and work of emergency vehicle organisations.

Legal requirements of vehicle documentation

Way back in the days of your great grandparents, learning to drive was a very different experience from what it is today. For one thing there were few cars about, so there was a lot less to crash into. For another, you didn't have to bother with any paperwork. You just taught yourself to drive and that was it. You didn't even have to take a test. But those days are long gone. Now there are all sorts of things you need before you can get on the road.

L-plates must be the proper type

Documentation

1 **A provisional driving licence.** 'Provisional' means temporary. And it must be the right kind of licence for the type of vehicle you are learning to drive. It's no use having a motorbike licence if you're learning to drive a car.
2 **L-plates.** These must be the proper type, not written out in felt-tip on cardboard. They must only be displayed when the learner is driving the car.
3 **Highway Code.** The law does not say that you should buy or read this book. But if you don't, you won't have a cat in hell's chance of passing your test. The Highway Code, a copy of which you can buy at any large post office or bookshop, tells you all the rules of the road and all you need to know about the theory of learning to drive.
4 **Full driving licence.** When you pass your test, this is what you'll get. This identifies you, and proves that you are qualified to drive the type of vehicle you are driving.

Insurance document

You cannot drive in Britain without insurance. If you do, you will get hammered by the law, and rightly so. But equally, it can be a lifesaver if anyone takes you to court. Nobody likes to be bankrupt if they can help it.

The principle of insurance is that you pay a company a 'premium' (fee) to look after you – or anybody else who is affected – if you have an accident. If you are properly insured, your insurance company will pay for you to repair or replace a crashed car, and it will pay for hospital treatment that people might need. Of course, if nothing goes wrong, then you have lost your money, but at least you have stayed within the law.

Insurance is bought from an insurance company, broker or car dealer. The cost depends on:

- which insurer you go to
- how old you are (you often have to pay more if you're under 25, because young people are more likely to have accidents)
- completion of the 'pass plus scheme'
- the make of vehicle
- its engine size and power
- where you live
- how you plan to use the car
- any criminal record you may have.

Different types of insurance are as follows:

1. **Third party.** This only protects someone you might injure, or their car. It doesn't protect you or your car. It's the cheapest type, but it gives the least protection.
2. **Third party, fire and theft.** Third party with knobs on: it also protects you if your car is stolen or burnt.
3. **Comprehensive.** This covers (a) other people and property from injury and damage, (b) replacement of damaged parts, (c) injury to yourself. It costs a lot but you get full protection.

When you are insured you get an insurance certificate. This records:

- who is insured
- the type of vehicle
- the kind of insurance cover
- the period of time you are covered
- any conditions or limitations.

The insurance certificate should be kept safely in the car. You may need to show it:

- to the police
- when you renew your road tax
- if you're in an accident.

The policy document is a fuller explanation of the insurance, given out by your insurer. It's full of small print because it is, in fact, a legal contract.

Vehicle registration document

This gives the make and model of your car, the year of first registration and the engine size and number. It also has your name and address on it. If your car is second hand you need to fill in the change of ownership section and send it to the DVLA in Swansea.

Vehicle Excise Duty disc

This is your road tax, and helps to pay for Britain's roads. Normally you pay this tax at a Crown Post Office (that is, a big one). You show that you have paid by sticking a disc on your windscreen.

MOT

The proper name for this is the vehicle test certificate. As we have seen, it shows that your car is safe enough to drive on the road. Any car which is more than three years old must have an MOT (Ministry of Transport) Test each year. (Lorries, buses, ambulances and taxis take their first MOT when they are only one year old.) If your car fails its MOT you must arrange to have it brought up to standard without delay. If you don't your insurance may no longer be valid, and you will be breaking the law.

These are all the documents you need.

Responsibilities of the driver

Review driver responsibility in relation to owning and using motor vehicles.

Responsibility is vital in driving. It means looking after other road users as well as yourself. Here are the key points.

Roadworthiness

Your car has to be up to the standards set by law for motor vehicles to be on the road. Basically, if it passes its MOT it should be all right. But there are particular items that need to be checked.

- The brakes. These must be in good order and correctly adjusted.
- Tyres must be of the right kind, and have sufficient tread on them (see page 316).
- All lights must work.
- The exhaust must have a silencer on it, and it mustn't smoke!
- The instruments on the dashboard must be accurate.
- Horns and windscreen wipers must work.

The Highway Code

Drivers must follow the rules in The Highway Code. As it changes from time to time, they must re-read it occasionally to keep up to date.

Road signs and markings

These must be obeyed.

Signals

These may be traffic lights, beacons at crossings, lights at level crossings and so on. Fatal accidents may happen if they are not obeyed. People such as police officers, road workers and lollipop persons also give signals – and again you have to comply with them.

Emergency vehicles

Whenever emergency service vehicles come rushing along with blue flashing lights or sirens, move out of the way at once. Some doctors' cars have green flashing lights for emergencies. You should move out of the way of those as well.

Seat belts

Many lives have been saved by seat belts. Here are the rules

Rules for the wearing of car seat belts

	Front	Rear
Driver	Wear seat belt	
Child under 3	Must wear a restraint	Must wear a restraint if fitted
Child aged 3–11 (under 1.5 m tall)	Child restraint or adult seat belt	Child restraint or adult seat belt if fitted
Child over 1.5 m tall	Adult seat belt	Adult seat belt if fitted
Adult	Wear seat belt	Wear seat belt if fitted

Source: Simplified from *The Driving Manual*, the Stationery Office

Air bags

These are fitted at the front. If the car crashes they inflate at once to prevent the driver or passenger being crushed against the steering wheel or dashboard. They save lives, but there are restrictions on their use with children or very small people. The driver of a car which has air bags fitted must not allow such passengers in the front seat.

First-aid

Always carry a first-aid box in the car. And learn basic first-aid: you never know when you might need it. You should also have a fire extinguisher in the car and know how to use it.

ANALYSIS

Drivers are responsible for their own safety and that of other road users. Fortunately, for most kinds of accident, Britain has a better safety record than most other European countries. Our driving laws are not particularly strict – for example in America, despite it being 'the land of the free', vehicles are usually not allowed to travel faster than 55 miles per hour. But the fact that our laws aren't strict places an extra duty on us to drive responsibly.

The Driving Manual, which is an enlarged and more detailed version of The Highway Code, calls responsible driving 'defensive driving'. Drivers must leave their aggression and hang-ups at home, and always think of other people when they are at the wheel. They must learn to read the road, not just handle the controls of the car, and try to think and see ahead. A responsible driver always leaves margin for error – her own or other people's. Good drivers play the percentage game: it may never be possible to eliminate accidents completely, but the risk of them should be reduced to a minimum.

And of course the responsibility is not only to passengers or to other drivers. Pedestrians, those unfortunate people who have to go round on foot, also use the road. They have to cross it. They should not have to cross it like rabbits, running for dear life. It should not be a lottery, as it is for hedgehogs playing tarmac roulette. Children may run out behind cars or buses; somebody may open a car door just as you're driving past; has that car backing out of the drive seen you or not? Awareness is the name of the game.

And that's why drivers shouldn't drive if they are ill, too tired, drunk or drugged. They should not use their mobile phones while driving even though – as yet – there are no laws against it. Dogs and children should be kept under control. And if the weather is very bad, a responsible driver stays at home, puts her feet up, and enjoys life.

Accidents

But even so things can go wrong. You can either be in an accident, or have to stop because of one. What are your responsibilities then? What do you do?

At the scene

If the accident has happened to you, you must stop. If you stop for another accident, remember that accidents are dangerous. There may be fire, and other accidents can happen.

First:

- warn other traffic
- put out cigarettes and other fire hazards
- switch off car engines
- call the emergency services if necessary
- don't move casualties unless they're in danger.

Then:

- give first-aid
- keep uninjured people well away
- give information to the emergency services if you can
- keep away from any dangerous goods (such as chemicals from tankers)
- note names and addresses of witnesses if possible.

If you are in the accident, and you are not badly injured, you should exchange details with the other driver. This means name, address, phone number, make and registration number of other vehicle(s), and insurance details. Get details of vehicle owners, if they are different from the drivers. Gather information, take photographs, and make sketch-maps of the accident if you can.

Environmental responsibilities

As people never tire of saying, cars are bad for the environment. But it doesn't stop us using them, or loving them. Still, responsible drivers do try to limit the damage they cause. They take care not to drive off the road, they don't empty their ashtrays and other litter on the pavement, and they don't irritate the rest of the human race by turning up the bass on their stereos until the window panes start dropping out of nearby buildings. And if they're in the country, they respect other slower users of country roads, such as herds of cows or flocks of sheep, which may not be very beautiful or intelligent – but they were there first!

Emergency vehicle organisations

Explain the benefits and work of emergency vehicle organisations.

By emergency vehicle organisations we mean such people as the AA (Automobile Association), RAC (Royal Automobile Club), National Breakdown or Green Flag.

Essentially all these organisations offer a breakdown and recovery service to motorists. For the payment of an annual subscription, rather like an insurance premium, they will guarantee to look after you if you break down on the road. In other words they will take your car to be repaired at the nearest affiliated garage, and supply you with another car if you have to get to your destination in a hurry. Indeed, if it is not easy to provide another car at short notice, they will drive you and your broken-down car on their recovery wagon to your destination, even if it is hundreds of miles away. The service is not free, and at the present time – for the AA – the annual subscription is from £45 upwards. As with an insurance company, you will simply lose the money if your car doesn't break down all year – so what you are paying for is freedom from worry, or 'peace of mind', as it's sometimes called. If your car breaks down more than six times in a year, you are likely to have to pay an additional fee of £45 for each call-out. This arrangement suggests that they have been exploited by people with old bangers in the past!

The AA, which is the largest of these motorists' organisations, attends five million breakdowns a year. They operate overseas as well as in Britain. They are particularly useful for people who drive long distances, and families who holiday abroad. As well as operating their breakdown service, they are now branching out into many other activities, some of which are not connected with motoring. These include: insurance, financial advice, hotel bookings, travel advice, publishing and home loans.

THINK ABOUT IT ...

Would it be appropriate for the motorists' organisations to be funded and administrated in the same way as the police or the fire service?

What would the advantages and disadvantages be?

Further reading

The Motorists' Guide to the Law Jane Benjamin, Fourmat Publishing,1994. A short clear book.

The Highway Code. Drivers can't do without it.

The Driving Manual the Stationery Office, 1997. An excellent detailed guide to driving and related issues.

UNIT 14 Fires and Accidents

Unit outcome 1
Examine different types of fires and accidents

Assessment criteria

- Compare two different types of fire situations.
- Compare two different types of major accident.
- Analyse the causes of these fires and accidents.

This unit looks at the work of the fire service and introduces you to some of the things that firefighters need to know.

Despite its name, the fire service spends more of its time dealing with road accidents than fires. In some fire stations only about 20 per cent of the call-outs or 'attendances' are for fires.

Types of fire

Compare two different types of fire situations (and analyse the causes).

Read the reports given in figures 14.1 and 14.2. They describe two different serious fires. A sample comparison, in table form, is given below.

Differences between two fire situations	
Northern Ireland fire	**Manchester fire**
Started deliberately, with a sectarian political motive. Evidence of flammable liquids and incendiary devices was found. It may have been an organised operation, since most of the arson attacks took place in one night.	Started accidentally. A workman was using a blowtorch on the roof and, without knowing it, set fire to the plastic insulation in the ventilation stacks.
Multiple fires. These, whether in one building or in a group of buildings, are one of the signs of arson attacks. When people start fires deliberately they light them in several places at once, in order to make sure that the building will burn quickly and completely.	Not clear whether the fire was multiple or not. From the third paragraph it seems as if several stacks were burning. Either they were interconnected, or the workman didn't understand their construction and started fires in several of them.
Fires were in rural areas and started at night. This meant they were less likely to be noticed immediately, and would be more difficult for the fire brigade to reach. Firefighters would have to bring their own tankers or use water from rivers and ponds.	Rapid attendance: the fire service took only four minutes to reach the fire. The difficulties in putting the fire out were not due to poor facilities, but the unusual construction of the unfinished building, which did not take firefighters' needs into account.
No real problems of access, other than the remoteness of the burning churches and chapels.	Difficult access for firefighters because it was a cramped and complicated building site.

Cont'd

Traditional building materials simplified the fighting of the fire.	Unusual building materials were affected by the heat in a dangerous and unpredictable manner. For example polypropylene is highly flammable, and in the heat of the fire the zinc melted and fell on firefighters below.
Traditional building construction meant that the fires were visible and could be reached by hoses.	Complex modern building construction allowed fire to travel in roof spaces and do considerable damage before it could be fought directly.

Eight churches torched in the night

Due to the unique difficulties within the Province of Northern Ireland, it is a sad fact that fires in churches are not an uncommon occurrence.

Church buildings on both sides of the so called 'religious divide' have historically been targeted by arsonists and bombers. In the year up to July 1, 1998, the brigade had attended 15 fires in church buildings across the province.

On the night of July 1, 1998, growing political tension led to a spate of malicious fires in churches across Northern Ireland.

In the eight hour period from 2330, the brigade attended a total of eight incidents involving churches. These fires resulted in various degrees of damage, estimated at many hundreds of thousands of pounds caused to the buildings involved, and varied from superficial damage to total loss of property. In all 22 appliances were mobilised to deal with the incidents.

2237, July 1, St Colmcilles Chapel, Strandtown, Belfast.
Two appliances from Belfast's Knock Station attended a small fire in the vestry of St Colmcilles Chapel in Belfast. The fire caused minor damage and was quickly extinguished using one hose reel jet. The fire is believed to have been caused by malicious ignition of liquid poured through a broken window.

0105, July 2, Mullavilly Chapel, Tandragee, County Armagh
A fire, started by a 'petrol bomb' attack, caused only slight damage to the roof of Mullavilly Chapel in Tandragee, County Armagh. The fire was extinguished using water from one hose reel jet.

0127, July 2, Kilcorig Chapel, Lisburn, County Antrim
On arrival at this incident, the OIC found that the small church (20m x 30m) was well alight and "Made pumps three for manpower and water." The blaze required two jets and two hose reel jets in use via water relay. The building was destroyed and a "Stop" message was sent at 0215.

0132, July 2, St James's Chapel, Crumlin, County Antrim
Once again, due to the rural location, the building was found to be well alight on arrival. An assistance message, "Make pumps three for water supply," was sent and three jets and one hose reel jet were used. Again, the building was destroyed by fire and a "Stop" message was relayed at 0240.

0309, July 2, Glen Chapel, Banbridge, County Down
A small fire at the rear of the church caused heavy smoke logging to the building. Although the fire was small and was extinguished by one hose reel jet from firefighters using breathing apparatus sets, severe smoke damage was caused to the entire building and contents.

Fires in churches cause unique difficulties to firefighters. The open nature of the buildings, the construction and the height of the roof, the historic and cultural value of the premises and contents all cause particular problems during firefighting operations. The differing degrees of severity of damage to the churches indicate that, for effective action in the event of fire, early detection is vital.

With the exception of the Belfast incident, all of the churches were located in rural areas. This, coupled with the ease of access for arsonists to the premises, was obviously a factor in the degree of damage caused by fires.

Figure 14.1 *Source:* Fire *magazine, October 1998, p7*

Similarities between two fire situations

Northern Ireland fire	Manchester fire
Property worth many hundreds of thousands of pounds was destroyed in the attacks. This shows the high cost of fire even in old buildings with a relatively low commercial value (though of very great emotional importance). It is not clear whether the destroyed churches would be rebuilt.	The theatre was being built with lottery money, and though the cost of the damage is not stated, it would have run to hundreds of thousands of pounds. The entire unfinished building was being demolished, and, again, it is not clear whether it would be rebuilt.

Manchester crews face fire in newly-built theatre

On May 20, at approximately 0915, a roofing contractor working on the roof of the newly built Contact Theatre, Manchester, was putting the finishing touches to the roofing felt. Unbeknown to him, the flame from the torch he was using to heat the felt caught the paper and polypropylene insulation within the ventilation stack. The resulting fire employed the services of four pumping appliances and subsequent relief pumps for the next four days until the incident closed on May 24.

Greater Manchester County Fire Service control received a call to the Contact Theatre at 0919, 'roof of building' and immediately mobilised a PDA of three pumps and one aerial appliance.

The first appliance arrived at 0923 to find a building in the final stages of construction with a developing fire situated in several of the five ventilation stacks, each being 24m in height from roof level.

The building formed part of a theatre complex and was being built on the basis of a Lottery grant. The ventilation stacks rising out of a 10m roof level had been specially designed to aid ventilation from within the theatre using the prevailing wind conditions to create a 'chimney effect'. Each stack was constructed around a skeletal frame of steel using timber boarding, fibreglass insulation and vapour barriers. The total structure was covered in zinc plate to give a 60 year life-span.

The initial problem was one of access in that this was a live construction site with the associated problems, such as conditions under foot, building material, cabins, workmen surrounding scaffolding and plant machinery, making the use of any aerial appliance impossible.

Access to the roof had to be gained via internal means, with hose lines both hauled aloft and employed off adjacent scaffolding with, initially, four jets employed.

The fire was burning fiercely within the timber breaking out at various points, although predominantly breaking through at high level. Areas of the zinc plate were starting to melt creating a molten metal hazard to the firefighters below and exposing further areas of fire.

A 'make pumps four and EST required for Stihl saw' message was sent at 0954 which subsequently brought an ADO onto the incident at which point he took command.

The main problem encountered was one of access to the seat of the fire and the associated fire spread. The stacks were constructed with a 50mm air gap between two sets of the timber board cladding and running the length from top to bottom, this allowed for unabated fire spread vertically and horizontally. A rotary disc cutter was initially used in an attempt to remove the zinc plate to gain access to the timber construction with ladders and various equipment both being hauled aloft and craned aloft using the on-site 35m tower crane.

The use of the crane and its man bucket proved ultimately invaluable allowing subsequent crews access to the upper levels of the stacks when both removing the outer zinc covering and damping down.

In the latter stages, a specialist demolition company was employed by the construction company to complete the removal of the covering and begin the demolition of the remaining structure.

Figure 14.2 *Source:* Fire *magazine, September 1998, p18*

Accidents

Compare two different types of accident (and analyse the causes).

From a public service point of view accidents almost always involve vehicles: cars, lorries, coaches, trains, ships and aeroplanes. They cause damage to property (usually one or more vehicles), injury and loss of life. They are dangerous to other travellers and, on roads and railways, lead to long delays.

THINK ABOUT IT ...

Are accidents really accidental, or are people to blame for them?

Why do they lead to court cases?

Causes of accidents

What causes accidents? There is more about this in Unit 13: Traffic and Transport. But here is a list of common causes. They are grouped according to type, but not in order of importance. In some cases more than one factor causes an accident.

1 Road accidents

These are caused by:

- mechanical failure of vehicle
- driver error
- driver tiredness
- speeding
- drink-driving
- drugs
- road rage
- suicide
- joyriding
- distraction by passenger
- mobile phone
- pedestrian behaviour
- heart attack or other medical condition
- bad weather
- sunlight in eyes
- poor road surface
- bad design of road
- misleading road signs.

Train accidents

These are caused by:

- signalling failure
- mechanical failure
- obstruction on line
- driver error
- drink or drugs
- driver illness
- bad weather.

Aeroplane accidents

These are caused by:

- mechanical failure
- instrument failure
- metal fatigue
- wrong instructions from air traffic control
- confusion on the ground (e.g. another plane on runway)
- lighting failure in airport
- sabotage/bombs/terrorism
- hijacking
- war
- passenger behaviour
- jet stream
- storms and other atmospheric phenomena
- ice, snow or fog at the airport
- birds getting sucked into the engine
- suicide
- pilot illness
- drink or drugs.

Shipping accidents

These are caused by:

- mechanical failure
- age and neglect of ships
- uncertainty of ownership
- the system of registration of ships in countries like Panama, which have no power over them or their owners
- human error
- failure of instruments
- storms
- running aground
- poor or outdated maps and charts, especially of the sea bed
- crowded shipping lanes (for example in the English Channel)
- overcrowding (especially of ferries)

- sabotage and mutiny by discontented crews
- hijacking and terrorism
- piracy and other forms of crime
- a general lack of regulation of shipping.

Two accident situations

Read the reports given in figures 14.3 and 14.4.

Differences between two accident situations

'Invisible fire', Cheshire	London rail crash
Only one vehicle involved – a tanker which overturned on a roundabout.	Two trains, one freight, one passenger, involved.
Accident happened on a road, so access was easy.	Railway crash. Access was difficult.
Cause not stated, but could have been a driving error. Also, the design of the road may have been poor, with too tight a curve. The pictures suggest that the weather was dry and sunny at the time, and at 13.36 on 30 March there could not have been frost on a main road in Cheshire.	Cause not stated, but probably a signalling error or technical fault (though it could have been a driving error, made worse by the fact that the train was travelling too fast).
The main problem was the fire resulting from the accident.	The fire was easily put out; the main problem was the crash itself.
The fire was fuelled by burning methanol (methylated spirits). Flames and fireballs were invisible, though the tanker itself became white-hot.	The fire was diesel, which produced plenty of smoke and was easily visible.
Fire not put out, because a release of methanol vapour into the atmosphere would have produced an explosive mixture. An explosive mixture would have been much more dangerous than a continuous fire, even though the continuous fire was spewing out fireballs.	Fire put out with water which cooled the diesel below ignition point (thus taking the heat out of the fire triangle). Smoke from the fire was preventing rescuers from seeing what was going on.
No casualties, though some firefighters were knocked over by the force of nearby fireballs.	Seven people killed and 130 injured, 13 seriously. These deaths and injuries resulted from the force of the impact, because the passenger train was travelling at 90 mph.
Evacuation of nearby property was carried out.	No evacuation needed.
The main problem was a technical one, of an unusual type, caused by the fact that the tanker contained methanol, which burns in an unusual way. At first it was not even clear that the methanol was burning, because it burned with an invisible flame. The only burning firefighters could see was of the tyres of the tanker, and nearby grass.	The problem of removing trapped people from wreckage was not in itself an unusual one; rescue workers had plenty of experience. What made this crash especially difficult was the number of casualties, the severity of the crash itself, and difficulties of access, both to the crashed train, and to the trapped people inside the carriages.
High-tech support, in the form of a helicopter with a thermal imaging camera, was needed in order for firefighters to see what was really happening.	Rescue workers, including paramedics, used tried and tested methods to get the trapped and injured passengers out of the train.

Cont'd

There were serious problems with water supplies, and help was needed from the private sector – a filling station.	There were problems with access, because it was not clear at first what would be the best way to approach the crashed train. This was partly because of the quantity of wreckage, and partly because of the fact that railways are made difficult for the public to get on to, for safety reasons. The fact that the area was built up made viewing the scene of the crash more difficult.
No information given about the speed of the fire service response to the initial call for help.	Detailed information about speed of emergency service response – because lives were at stake.
There is no evidence of media interest in the accident. This is because (a) no one was hurt, (b) it was not near London (!) and (c) the accident had no real political overtones. However, the accident does suggest the kinds of dangers which large-scale road transport can pose to the environment (see Unit 13: Traffic and Transport).	Media interest caused a problem for rescue workers. They were under pressure to give interviews before the rescue was over. This would have put lives at risk. Reasons for the media interest were: (a) there were many casualties, (b) it happened in London and was therefore accessible to the media, (c) the accident had political overtones and John Prescott, the Deputy Prime Minister, visited the scene. Serious UK train crashes in recent times are always of political interest, because they suggest that the privatisation of the railways has reduced their safety.
The fire service received considerable help from a police helicopter with a thermal imaging camera. This was made more efficient by the fact that a firefighter happened to be in the helicopter at the time! Though this was a coincidence, it shows the value of close links between the different emergency services.	The emergency services worked closely together on this large-scale accident. Police, ambulance and the electricity companies liaised skilfully, showing the value of joint exercises and close cooperation in the past. The police took on the main job of dealing with the media, who became part of the problem because there were so many journalists and camera crews cluttering up the crash site.
Some environmental problems were caused by the leakage of methanol into the drains and, possibly, into the Manchester Ship Canal. Measures were taken to limit the risk of environmental damage. No information was given publicly about the crash investigation or how long it took to restore the site of the accident to normal.	The crash caused serious damage to the near environment, but no threat otherwise. Because it occurred on a major line, which had to be closed, initial crash investigation and the clean-up was done within 24 hours. Further investigation in the form of analysing photographs and statements will have continued after this.
This incident led to some interviews, and the fire service learnt from it. But it was not a really major event, though it was big enough, and interesting enough, to be featured in *Fire* magazine.	This was a major incident followed by a full public inquiry. There was extensive coverage on television and in the newspapers.

'Invisible fire' presents Cheshire crews with special problems at tanker RTA

At 1336 on March 30 Cheshire Fire Brigade received a call to an overturned lorry on junction 8 of the M53 motorway. Three fire appliances were ordered from the nearby Ellesmere Port Fire Station. At this time it was not known that the incident involved a hazardous load or indeed it was a tanker containing methanol.

On arrival, the officer in charge of the first appliance quickly established that the vehicle was on fire due to the fact that flames were visible on the tyres, paintwork and the gantry appeared to be melting. The tanker driver, who had escaped without injury prior to arrival of the brigade, reported that the tanker was carrying 20 tonnes of methanol.

Methanol, a colourless liquid – miscible with water, was in fact leaking from one of the top vents provided on each of the five compartments, each holding 4,000 litres.

It is toxic and highly flammable with a flash point below 23°C which can form an explosive mixture with air.

The officer in charge requested a foam tanker, while firefighters provided a covering spray from a hose reel and set up a low expansion foam branch. At this stage it was not apparent that any of the methanol was burning. Shortly afterwards there was a large 'whooshing' noise and hot blast which threw a firefighter off his feet.

Oncoming appliances were requested to investigate local water supplies. The incident had occurred on a roundabout directly above the motorway and as such local water supplies were extremely poor. An oncoming Chester fire appliance was ordered to Gulf Oil, a storage premises some half a mile from the incident. This appliance set into a ring main to boost supply to the incident.

The OiC briefed the arriving police officers on methanol – its characteristics and explosive potential – and as a result the motorway was closed and nearby residents were evacuated from their premises.

In order to obviate the potential hazard of an uncontrolled vapour cloud a decision was taken not to extinguish the fire.

Even though crews, working under highly pressurised conditions, had managed to establish feed-ins from a number of hydrants, water for cooling was in short supply. The OiC increased the attendance to seven pumps. The only visual indication of a fire was the tyres burning on the vehicle and a shimmering heat haze.

Crews were located upwind on the chassis side. A thermal image camera carried on a first line appliance was used to assess the severity of the blaze and assist in the most effective direction of three ground monitors. This was hampered by the screening effect of the cooling spray and the fact that the firefighter was viewing from the chassis side of the vehicle. Cooling jets were stopped for a short period and the firefighter with the thermal imaging camera took up a better vantage point.

It was at this stage that the air support unit aircraft from Cheshire Constabulary arrived and commenced circling above the incident. The brigade has a close relationship with the unit due to incidents in the past where they have been able to relay information to fire officers on the ground details of the aerial view. In addition, the thermal imaging camera on the aircraft on this occasion provided excellent information to fire officers on the ground.

Fortunately, a fire officer was on a one day course with the air support unit was able to radio down accurate operational information regarding the direction of cooling jets in relation to the thermal trace being received on the camera.

This incident highlights the need for thermal aerial surveillance to assist in command and control (see adjoining article).

Methanol was reported to be entering the drains and the Environment Agency confirmed that this in turn would shortly enter the Manchester Ship Canal. As a result, one ship had to be moved and all traffic was halted. The canal is a main traffic lane used by shipping to and from the large petro chemical industries along the Mersey Estuary.

Figure 14.3 *Source:* Fire *magazine, September 1998, p.15*

London rail crash tests inter-service liaison

At lunchtime on September 19, a Swansea to London high speed train comprising seven carriages and two diesel high speed locomotives, was travelling at approximately 90mph and was some ten minutes from the end of its journey at Paddington.

At 1316 it collided with a freight train comprising 20 empty stone hopper wagons and a locomotive that was moving via the slow down line across the fast track, into a goods yard some 400m to the east of Southall Railway Station. As a consequence of this collision seven lives were lost, 130 passengers inured, 13 seriously, and a Major Incident was declared.

The first of 14 calls to Brigade Control was received at 1316. The initial caller reported a fire and explosion near Park Avenue, Southall. Park Avenue is a residential road that runs adjacent and parallel to the north of the railway line. Subsequent calls to the incident included one which stated that a steam train had exploded near Southall Station. Another caller reported that a freight train had crashed within the train sheds adjacent to the station.

Due to the additional information being gleaned, control staff very quickly determined that a train crash was a possibility. As a consequence, it was decided to mobilise the full initial attendance for such an incident. This attendance comprised the following: six pumping appliances, one Fire Rescue Unit (FRU), one Command Unit (CU), one Command Support Unit (CSU), an Assistant Divisional Officer and a Divisional Officer.

In addition, the control room operators passed the call to the Metropolitan Police, British Transport Police and the London Ambulance Service.

ADO Chris Staynings had just returned to Southall Fire Station from another incident on his station's ground. As he was getting out of his car he heard a loud noise, felt a severe vibration and saw a large cloud of 'smoke' rising in the distance.

He went into the station watch room to make an approximation of the location using the station map. As he did so, the station's teleprinter operated, mobilising appliances from an adjacent station (Southall still being at the previous incident) comprising the initial attendance to a fire and explosion near 79 Park Avenue, Southall. This was followed almost immediately by the message mobilising appliances to the steam train exploding and freight train crash.

ADO Staynings was aware that the sheds utilised by the Steam Preservation Society were south of the railway line, whereas Park Avenue lay to the north. He therefore drove to the road bridge west of Southall Railway Station and looked eastwards towards the incident to determine the best side to approach. His view was limited to that of the rear of a passenger train and a large quantity of smoke some distance down the track. He decided to access from Park Avenue and was the first member of the emergency services to attend, closely followed by a police officer.

ADO Staynings was aware of the need to impose a firm command structure at this incident from the initial stages. Therefore, in consultation with the police officer, arrangements were made for the establishment of a police outer cordon around the incident, and the fixing of rendezvous points to ensure access and egress for emergency vehicles.

At 1324 the first pumping appliance (G24 Ealing) arrived. ADO Staynings instructed the Officer in Charge to approach the track, survey the scene and report back. As the crew approached the railway lines they were initially confronted with a crowd of evacuating passengers coming towards them, some in distress and with minor injuries.

The crew continued to the trackside, visibility being hampered by smoke drifting across the track. The Crew Commander discovered that the locomotive and the first eight hoppers in the freight train had cleared the crossing and that the centre wagons had taken impact of the collision. The speed of the passenger train had caused the front power car to 'jump' over the freight train. The off-side panelling of the power car had been ripped away revealing the engine, and the impact had also caused a fire involving the diesel fuel tank.

The first passenger carriage had followed the power car and had rolled onto its side. The second passenger carriage struck one of the hopper wagons end-on causing it to bend almost double. The third carriage (a buffet car) landed on top of another hopper wagon. A fourth carriage was derailed but remained upright. The remainder of the passenger train stayed upright and on the rail.

As they approached the tangled wreckage, it was obvious that there were numerous trapped and injured passengers. In addition, the overhead line equipment from the electrified Heathrow Express line had also been brought down.

It was clear to ADO Staynings that this incident fully met the criteria contained within the London Emergency Services Liaison Panel (LESLP) manual, and 'Major Incident

Figure 14.4

(Cont'd)

Procedure' was declared. This message immediately placed all the control rooms involved at a high stage of alert, and the Command Support Centre (Strategic) was activated at Brigade Headquarters. At this time control of the centre was taken by the Assistant Chief Officer (Operations), with the Chief Fire Officer in attendance.

The diesel fuel tank fire was quickly dealt with using a 70 mm jet. While this fire had initially provided an extra problem for the Incident Commander, it did not unduly affect the rescue scene. Concern among the survivors in respect of the risk to them from the fire was quickly abated by the firefighters, who were able to assure them that they were at no risk, and evacuated them to the areas designated by the ambulance service and police.

While the demolished power gantries and overhead power cables hampered movement in the initial stages, the firefighters had nonetheless moved into the wreckage to begin rescue operations.

At 1351 Railtrack confirmed that all trains had stopped and power was off between Southall and Hanwell Stations. At 1355, 16 people were confirmed trapped within the wreckage. The major rescue operations were now to begin in earnest.

Owing to the restricted access to the wrecked coaches, only small numbers of personnel were able to work directly on the extrication of casualties. This allowed other personnel to be utilised in the setting up of the equipment dump, providing first aid to passengers who had left the scene unaided although injured, and assisting in the transportation of casualties away from the scene to awaiting ambulances.

At 1412 Divisional Officer Anthony Bucksey, arrived at the scene and took command of the incident. Leaving control of the direct rescue operation with ADO Staynings, he took a broad overview of the crash area and the other carriages involved. As a result he was able to amend the tactical plan and reduce the size of the rescue area, thereby allowing resources to be directed to the areas of greatest need.

At 1434 Assistant Chief Fire Officer, Laurence Gill (Commander, Western Command) arrived on the scene and took command of the incident. At this time he initiated the establishment of an inner cordon and the necessary access controls. The implementation of efficient and effective parking and marshalling ensured that clear routes were maintained for vehicles transporting casualties or supplying additional equipment.

Regular liaison meetings utilising the brigade's purpose-built Conference Unit were organised with the Silver Commanders from the other services and rail operating companies. During this period, ACFO Kelly (Operations) was attending meetings at New Scotland Yard to discuss the strategic issues arising from this incident.

This team structure was invaluable because (as expected) the media interest was intense and heavy demands were made on the Commanders of the various services, both at strategic and tactical level, for a range of interviews. Additional interest was aroused when it was announced that the Deputy Prime Minister would be visiting the scene.

The role of press liaison is determined under the LESLP procedure to be a police role (with, or course, the necessary technical input) and this was undertaken with great professionalism that allowed the fire officers and ambulance and medical teams at the scene to concentrate on rescue operations and not be distracted by the need to give interviews until the appropriate time.

The last live casualty was removed from the wreckage three hours after the first impact, and the final victim removed at 2111. The recovery work was completed on the following day, by which time the brigade involvement had comprised 27 front line and 20 specialist vehicles.

In recent years the emergency services in London have responded to a number of incidents requiring a multi-service response. This has led to established and practised procedures. In addition officers at strategic and tactical level have met face-to-face on both professional (inter-service residential training courses) and social levels. As a result throughout the incident the understanding of each other's roles and responsibilities created close and effective liaison between all involved in the multi-agency response.

Figure 14.4 *(Cont'd) Source:* Fire *magazine, February 1998, p.10–11*

Unit outcome 2
Examine fire and accident prevention measures

Assessment criteria
- Explain in detail four measures that can be taken to prevent fires and accidents.
- Detail the role of the public services in fire and accident prevention.

Four methods of fire prevention

The people who work for the fire brigade are called firefighters. It's an exciting name, good for recruitment. But in many ways they would prefer to be called fire preventers, because prevention is better than cure, in fires as in illnesses. What's more, prevention is cheap and safe. But fighting fires is neither.

The dividing line between fire prevention and fire fighting is not as clear cut as we might expect. On the face of it, prevention means making sure that the fire does not even start, whereas fighting means putting out the fire once it has started. But in practice things like fire extinguishers and sprinklers are often thought of as fire prevention, since their purpose is to stop – that is, prevent – a fire from developing even though it has started.

1 Fire extinguishers

Fire extinguishers are hand-held devices which can be used to put out very small fires before they get out of control. All commercial buildings such as factories, shops and offices have them; so do all other public buildings such as schools, colleges, night-clubs and sports centres. And increasingly, people have them in the home as well.

There are different types of fire extinguisher for different types of fire. But all work on the same principle – which is to deprive the fire of something it needs. Remember the fire triangle? Fires need heat, fuel and oxygen to burn. Extinguishers get rid of one of these. Either they cool the fire, so that there isn't enough heat for it to go on burning. Or they smother it, cutting off the fuel from the oxygen so that the fire just chokes to death.

Types of extinguisher

Now let's look at the main types of extinguisher. In the table on the following page you will see what these are. All new portable extinguishers are coloured red with a zone of colour, depending on what is inside them, and the type of fire they are supposed to put out. It is acceptable to retain the previous style, on which the entire body is colour coded, until the time they need to be replaced.

Fire extinguishers are very useful, and have saved many lives and buildings. But they have their limitations:
- they will only put out very small fires
- they need to be checked regularly to make sure they are in good working order (ask the supplier about this)
- they won't work if people mess about with them

Type	Colour of zone	How it works	Dangers	How to use
Water	red	Mainly by cooling the fire. Best for wood, paper, plastic and coal.	Don't use on burning oil or fat, or on electrical fires.	Point at the base of the flames and move across the fire until it's out.
Powder	blue	Smothers the fire, by cutting off air and forming a skin over the burning part. Good for all fires except chip pan fires.	It doesn't cool the fire well, so it takes some time to be sure that the fire is out.	Point at base of flames. Pause from time to time to see if the fire is really out.
AFF foam	yellow	Smothers the fire by making a film over the burning part. Puts out all fires except burning chip pans.	No dangers.	Point at base of flames, and keep moving across the fire.
Ordinary foam	yellow	Smothers the fire.	Only good for burning oil etc. Not useful in the home.	Point at the nearest part of the burning liquid and let the foam float across it.
Carbon dioxide (CO_2)	black	A non-toxic gas, heavier than air, which smothers the fire. Good for burning liquids and electrical fires.	Doesn't cool the fire well, so make sure the fire is out before you stop using it. Open windows and doors afterwards.	Direct at the base of the flames and keep moving the jet across the fire.
Halon	green	A gas which works well on liquid fires, except for chip pans.	Gives off harmful vapours, and bad for the ozone layer. This type of extinguisher should be avoided.	Aim at the flames, not at the base of the fire.

- they may encourage people to be 'heroic', and fight fires which are too big for them
- they might give people a false sense of security, by making them think that they don't need to worry about fire safety if they have got a fire extinguisher.

2 Sprinklers

Sprinklers are used in large buildings, such as supermarkets, warehouses and factories, for limiting fire spread. But it is important to remember that they are not really designed to put a fire out. That is a job for the fire brigade.

The principle is a simple one. Water pipes with nozzles run along the ceiling. Each nozzle is designed to open at a given temperature and spray water downwards. If a fire starts at one end of a warehouse, the heat will rise from it and activate the sprinklers immediately above it. These will spray water down on the fire. Provided the warehouse does not get too hot, the other sprinklers will remain off. The advantage of this system is that it

Leicester B & Q blaze illustrates dangers of unsprinklered single-storey warehouses

At 1257 on January 19, Leicestershire Fire and Rescue Control received the first of 64 calls to the B & Q DIY superstore on St. Margaret's Way, Leicester, reporting a fire in the paint section of the store.

The building was a single-storey open plan shop measuring 80 by 90m with a two-storey compartmented office block within. The structure consisted of a double portal framed roof with composite steel (Rockwool) insulated panels. Walls consisted of brick clad rolled steel columns with brick and part brick, part metal cladding panels.

At the time of the fire it was estimated that there were 200 customers and 73 members of staff inside the store. The fire alarm was sounded by a member of staff, but by the time he had picked up a fire extinguisher, the fire had developed to such extent that he did not attempt to tackle the blaze.

The evacuation was carried out in an organised manner, but by the time the last members of the public were being ushered out of the store, smoke had travelled extensively and was beginning to obscure the front exits from the building.

The pre-determined attendance of two pumps was despatched, but due to the number of calls being received, a third pump was mobilised. The first two pumps booked in attendance at 1303 and the Leading Firefighter immediately sent an assistance message.

The initial attack involved BA crews being committed to the front entrance and a side exit which gave access via the office section. One BA crew advanced to the first floor with a jet. However, the wall in front of them started to crack and showed signs of collapse, at which point they withdrew. A second crew entered the front entrance and experienced the noise caused by the severe inrush of air which was feeding the fire.

A Divisional Officer arrived at 1304 and was confronted with a very severe fire affecting approximately a third of the store and spreading rapidly across the whole sales area. After an appraisal he decided to withdraw all BA crews and concentrate firefighting from external positions. Within 20 minutes of the arrival of the first appliance, the entire roof area had collapsed.

At 1323 the Assistant Chief Officer took command and at 1342 an information message was sent indicating six jets and one aerial monitor in use, and water relay being established due to difficulties with water pressure in the immediate vicinity. A 'fire surround' message was sent at 1459 indicating seven ground monitors and two aerial monitors in use. The 'stop' message was finally sent at 1525 the following day. At the height of the blaze, 14 water ladders and two aerial appliances were in use.

It is understood that B & Q was surveying the premises for the installation of a sprinkler system. However, due to the configuration of the stored goods, it is believed that roof sprinklers may not have operated rapidly enough to have been effective in these circumstances. Had satisfactory sprinkler system been installed, the £10 million loss may have been reduced or prevented.

It is encouraging that the requirement to install sprinkler systems in premises in excess of 4,000 sq m is currently being considered under the review of Approved Document B of the Building Regulations.

To assist with the fire investigation an appeal was made on local radio and television requesting members of the public who were in the store at the time of the fire, especially in the vicinity of the paint section area, to contact Fire Service Headquarters. This was to be very useful in providing detailed information.

The fire was apparently started using methylated spirits stored within the paint section on the lower shelves. The fire then spread laterally and then vertically, hidden in the early stages by the stored products above. The method of storing goods for sale was on shelving up to 5.5 m in height.

Ten days after the fire, a child under the age of criminal responsibility admitted to the police that he had started the blaze.

This fire again outlines the potential safety problems to firefighters in buildings of this nature, if they are required to enter during a fire. Significantly, the fire spread was so rapid that although the means of escape were satisfactory, smoke was beginning to obscure the exits from the store as the last members of the public and staff were leaving. It is another instance in the ever-increasing number of single-storey warehouse fires.

Figure 14.5 *Source:* Fire *magazine, November 1998, p.8*

restricts the amount of water damage which is done to the goods in the warehouse. The first sprinkler systems to be introduced did not have heat sensitive nozzles. As a result, warehouses got flooded, and the water did more damage than the fire would have done.

The water has to come from a header tank (a tank above roof level) unless the mains supply is strong. Because of pressure problems, sprinkler systems do not provide as much water as a firefighter's hose, which is why they rarely put out a fire completely. Another drawback is that, because they are not used for years until a fire breaks out, they may not work properly when they are needed.

3 Smoke detectors and alarms

Smoke detectors are a cheap and effective form of warning device. They can be used in homes, factories, colleges, pubs, and even in vehicles such as coaches. They come with clear instructions about installation, and you do not need to be a DIY expert to put one up in your house. They are usually battery powered, and give an unmistakable loud chirping noise when the battery starts to go flat. The batteries are of a standard type and easy to replace. Government safety campaigns have encouraged every householder to install smoke alarms.

The Home Office guidelines for installation are:

- For maximum protection an alarm should be fitted in every room (except kitchen, bathroom and garage).
- For minimum protection, one smoke alarm of the optical type, if your house has one floor. Otherwise there should be one on each floor – preferably in a hall or landing.

Alarms should be checked once a month to make sure they are working (there is a button for this purpose). Batteries should usually be replaced after a year.

How do smoke alarms work?

There are three types.

1. **Ionising radiation.** This sounds a bit science-fiction, but what it means is that there is a radioactive source in the detector, which splits up the smoke molecules and gives them either a positive or a negative electrical charge. These different electrical charges are detected by the instrument, and the alarm goes off.
2. **Light-scatter detectors.** A beam of light is emitted at right angles to a light detector. Like a car headlight, the beam is invisible if the air is clear, but if it's smokey the smoke catches ('scatters') the light, and this scattered light is detected by a photoelectric cell (a kind of tiny battery powered by light). This sets off the alarm.
3. **Light obscuration devices.** These work on the idea that smoke will dim or block a beam of light. The photoelectric cell is opposite a beam of light inside the instrument. If the light goes dim it means that smoke has got into the detector, and this is detected by the photoelectric cell. The reduction in the power produced by the cell triggers the alarm.

4 Building regulations

There are four main building regulations, designed to increase the safety of building and demolition work, the safety of the finished building, and to reduce the danger of fire. They are long and complicated, and only a few points need to be mentioned here. These regulations are:

- Construction (General Provision) Regulations 1961
- Construction (Lifting Operations) Regulations 1961
- Construction (Working Places) Regulations 1966
- Construction (Health and Welfare) Regulations 1966.

Construction is the most dangerous industry in Britain, more dangerous even than the public services. A building site is like a cross between an adventure playground and an army assault course, and despite the great efforts being made to improve safety building sites can still shorten your life expectancy. Accident prevention on building sites is partly a matter of using the right equipment, and partly a matter of using that equipment in the right way.

THINK ABOUT IT ...

What other forms of fire prevention have you heard of?

Accident prevention

Explain in detail four measures that can be taken to prevent road traffic accidents.

1 Cause: driver error

Prevention

Better training of drivers (and more demanding driving tests) could be one way to prevent driver error so that people who should not be driving never pass the test in the first place. There could be more laws governing the number of hours a commercial driver can drive without a rest. Drivers could be regularly retested, to make sure they are still competent. The courts could act more quickly to disqualify unsafe or accident-prone drivers. Insurance premiums could be raised. The disadvantages of these methods of prevention are (a) that they would cost a great deal of money, (b) the public would not support them, and neither would politicians, (c) they would discriminate against older drivers who depend on their cars to get around, (d) they would overwork the police and (e) they would have a bad effect on business – so that the country as a whole would be worse off. And having said all this there would still be driver errors, because errors are a part of human nature!

2 Cause: criminal driver behaviour

This includes all forms of deliberately dangerous and reckless driving, drink-driving, driving under the influence of drugs and road rage.

Prevention

This can be prevented by (a) disqualifying offenders for as long as possible, (b) enforcing the new law on aggravated vehicle theft as strictly as possible, and generally penalising joyriders, (c) making road rage a crime, (d) introducing psychological tests or treatment for people driving dangerously. A police presence, and a police helicopter, are needed to catch these types of driver. Breathalysing and blood tests are already carried out, but usually only after a driver has been showing signs of drink or drugs. These tests, however, are preventative, because their main importance is not to punish a particular drink-driver, but to deter the rest of us by letting us know that we will get caught if we drink and drive.

3 Cause: traffic conditions

Prevention

Obviously if there are more vehicles on the road there are more cars to crash into, but in fact busy roads do not necessarily suffer more accidents. Although Britain has some of the busiest roads in Europe we also have some of the lowest accident rates. Furthermore, our accidents tend to be less serious than those in, say, France. It may be that since Britain is a small country, drivers get less tired than they do in some other countries, and that they are less likely to speed. The best way of preventing accidents in heavy traffic is to have good lane discipline, backed up by police cameras, and clear road signs.

4 Cause: road design

Some accidents, especially when vehicles overturn, are caused by poor road design, with curves which are too tight. And many crashes occur because drivers cannot see properly – again thanks to poor road design.

Prevention

The way of preventing this kind of accident is to redesign roads so that there are fewer 'accident black spots'. This may involve removing walls and hedges, redesigning the road so that drivers cannot speed, by putting speed ramps or chicanes in place, and altering the road marking. Lighting too is being improved all the time, not only by making the lights brighter, but by experimenting with the colours. And traffic lights are increasingly sophisticated and user-friendly.

The role of public services in prevention

Detail the role of the public services in fire and accident prevention.

Fire and accident prevention are cheaper and (to judge from statistical changes) more effective than fire fighting or simply dealing with an accident that has already happened. So the public services have gone into fire and accident prevention in a big way.

1 The fire service

Leaflets, advice notes and videos

The fire service now produce a wide range of publicity materials on the subject of fire prevention. Most of these are leaflets, but they also have an advisory service on disc, and a range of videos. These materials cover every imaginable aspect of fire prevention (see Focus box below).

Issuing fire certificates

This is a powerful tool for achieving greater fire safety and preventing fires. The fire service have a duty to enter all factories and premises used by the public to inspect them. As well as issuing certificates they give full advice on ways of minimising the risk of fire.

FOCUS

Printed leaflets available in 1999 from the fire service included:

- *Protect your home from fire*
- *Fire Sprite asks parents: where were your children?*
- *Safe frying at home*
- *How to choose and use fire extinguishers for the home*
- *Chip pans can hurt, maim or kill. Please take care*
- *Wake up! Get a smoke alarm*
- *Get out – Get the Brigade out – Stay out*
- *Electrical safety leads to fire safety*
- *Car safety*
- *Fire safety in high rise flats*
- *Fire safety in offices*
- *Good housekeeping checklist for industry*
- *Fire safety for small businesses*
- *Arson beware!*
- *Action plan for firms: Be prepared for fire*
- *Fireworks: a guide for retailers*
- *Making life easier ... How to use electricity safely around the home*
- *Skips and waste containers*
- *Fire safety advice for disabled people*
- *Fire safety in the home*
- *Countryside fire safety*
- *Fire safety checklist for social clubs, youth clubs and small assembly halls*
- *Fire safety at work*
- *Checklist for fire safety in community centres*
- *Avoiding fire afloat*
- *After the fire*
- *Firework displays: a guide for organisers*

Visits and lectures

The main reason why the fire service are so generous in showing school and college parties round their fire station is to raise awareness both of the work they do and of the dangers of fire and accidents. Even the sight of all the equipment they have reminds children and young people of the great dangers of fires and accidents – and should leave a lasting impression on them. This is an educational activity, and is part of their fire prevention role.

2 The police

Leaflets

The police produce leaflets on accidents and their causes. These leaflets are not as noticeable as fire prevention leaflets, because much of the advice for accident prevention and safe driving appears in the Highway Code, and in *The Driving Manual*, published by the Stationery Office (formerly HMSO).

Educational activities

The police arrange training days for cyclists and road safety days for schoolchildren. These are often very entertaining, with talking cars and other teaching aids which appeal to children's imagination and help them to remember the message that road safety is of the greatest importance. Other devices, such as the Green Cross Code, are also ways of preventing accidents, by fixing in young children the habit of behaving safely on the road.

Police cooperation with the media

At serious road accidents the police attach importance to giving radio and TV interviews, to get across to the public the importance of driving safely and responsibly. Television is a 'hot' medium that people remember, and therefore an effective way of carrying the accident prevention message.

Breathalysing and speed cameras

These are more 'proactive' than most of the police methods of accident prevention. They act as a powerful deterrent to drivers who are tempted to risk other people's lives by breaking the law.

THINK ABOUT IT ...

What different kinds of fire prevention are used in your college or place of work?

Make a collection of fire and accident prevention leaflets issued by your local fire service and police.

Unit outcome 3
Demonstrate the need for fire and safety legislation

Assessment criteria
- Explain the need for different types of fire and safety legislation.
- Analyse the major aspects of fire and safety legislation.

The need for fire and safety legislation

The Health and Safety at Work Act 1974

This Act, known as HASAWA, covers every employee in this country without exception. The only people who aren't covered are people who work entirely by themselves and who are never visited on business by anybody.

The need for HASAWA

We need HASAWA because (a) in a free country everybody should have equal rights and (b) because work is a dangerous place. New technology, with new dangers, is coming along all the time. And old technology gets more dangerous the older it gets.

HASAWA is all about rights and responsibilities. Rights are the things that other people ought to do for us, and responsibilities are the things we ought to do for other people.

HASAWA is split into sections (otherwise nobody would ever be able to make sense of it). Here are the main ones, with explanations in brackets. Don't forget that there is a difference between employers and employees!

An overview of HASAWA

Section 2 (1)

Ensure 'as far as is reasonably practicable' the health and safety at work of all employees. (In other words, employers are required to look after everybody who works there as much as possible.)

Section 2 (2)

This section covers the need to:
- make sure machinery is safe ('two arms good; one arm bad')
- make sure things are stored and handled safely (this is now called COSHH: the Control of Substances Hazardous to Health, and is very important for the public services – especially the fire and ambulance services: people mustn't keep the rat poison in the sink)
- train the workforce in health and safety (it's no use having a workforce entirely ignorant of health and safety issues)
- arrange easy and safe ways in and out of the workplace (people have to be able to get out quickly if there's a fire – and what if they're disabled?)
- make sure the building is generally healthy (that's why smokers have to stand out in the rain).

Many workplaces are no-smoking areas ...

Section 4

Employers must make sure that their factory, shop or college is safe for customers, students, workers from outside such as window cleaners or central heating engineers, or any other visitors. (Even a burglar who fell on some razor wire might be able to sue.)

Section 6

People who design and make things must ensure that they are safe for the person who buys and uses them. (Teddy bears mustn't contain iron spikes, your wellies mustn't give you cancer, and your college lift mustn't amputate your arm if you get it stuck in the door.)

Section 7a

Employees must take reasonable care of their own health and safety and that of other people. (If you drop banana skins all over the office, it's your fault if someone slips on them and breaks a leg – and it could be yours.)

Section 7b

Employees must cooperate with their employers in health and safety. (Or they can be dismissed.)

Section 8

Employees mustn't intentionally interfere with anything to do with safety. (Don't squirt your best mate with the fire extinguisher.)

Summary

Under HASAWA it is not enough just to be safe. You have to be seen to be safe. And employers have to set up systems like communication networks and committees in order to make sure that everybody understands safety and carries out safe practices.

In a workplace where there are five or more employees, the employers have to:

- make sure that all machinery is safe, and that people work safely with it
- check that everything is handled and stored safely
- set up systems of training and supervision to make sure people work safely
- ensure that the workplace is kept as clean and safe as possible
- look after employees' welfare at work – for example by making sure that there is a proper canteen, and adequate rest breaks
- write a safety policy showing their commitment to safety, the way safety is organised and making clear whose responsibility safety is
- consult with safety representatives so that safety standards throughout the workplace can be maintained or improved
- ensure that anybody who comes onto the premises will be safe
- provide things which are necessary for safety, such as toilets or first-aid boxes, free of charge for the use of all employees.

Aspects of legislation

Analyse the major aspects of fire and safety legislation.

Fire certificates

These came in with the Fire Precautions Act 1971. They are used for factories and commercial premises, such as shops, night-clubs, sports halls, hotels and so on. As a result of a more recent law, the Fire Safety and Safety of Places of Sport Act 1987, some bigger companies and sports stadiums no longer need certificates. But this is only after an inspection has shown them to have a very low fire risk.

FOCUS

Fire certificates specify:

- the use of the building
- the means of escape
- the means of making sure people can get to the escape – including fire doors, emergency lighting and signs
- fire extinguishers and other fire control devices
- alarms
- flammable liquids or explosives allowed in or near the building
- training people and keeping records
- the number of people allowed in the premises (building, stadium, etc.)
- any other relevant fire precautions.

The certificates are issued by the fire service. If any changes are made to the building or its use which might alter or increase the fire risk, the occupiers must apply for a new fire certificate. If they don't, it means trouble. First, they will receive an improvement notice, telling them what changes must be made. These changes must be made within 21 days. The occupiers can appeal, but if the appeal fails and the occupiers don't make the improvements they can be imprisoned or fined an unlimited amount. If the building is very dangerous the occupiers will get a prohibition notice. They either have to make the place safe or close it down. Places like night-clubs, which may have disastrous fires, can be closed down in this way.

Sports grounds

The situation in sports grounds is that 'general safety certificates' are needed. This law came in as a result of the tragic fire at the Bradford City football stadium in 1985. If a sports ground is unsafe, it can be closed under a prohibition order, issued by the Health and Safety Executive – a body of people originally set up by HASAWA.

Fire instructions

All employers, or occupiers of buildings where there are large numbers of people, must give instructions to people on what to do if there is a fire. These instructions take two forms:

1. Training for the staff.
2. Notices telling people what to do if there is a fire.

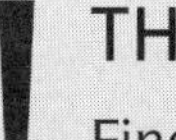

THINK ABOUT IT ...

Find out how fire instructions operate in your own college or workplace.

These instructions tell everybody what to do if they (a) hear a fire alarm or (b) discover a fire. The training takes the form of fire drills. These include duties for staff, such as checking that nobody is left in the building, and taking roll-calls. Sometimes staff are trained to use fire extinguishers – but only to put out the smallest fires or control them until the fire brigade arrives.

Notices often look like the following example.

WHEN THE FIRE ALARM SOUNDS
1 Close the windows, switch off electrical equipment and leave the room, closing the door behind you.
2 Walk quickly along the escape route to the open air.
3 Report to the fire warden (red hat) at your assembly point.
4 Do not attempt to re-enter the building.

WHEN YOU FIND A FIRE
1 Raise the alarm.
2 Leave the room, closing the door behind you.
3 Leave the building by the escape route.
4 Report to the fire warden at the assembly point.
5 Do not attempt to re-enter the building.

THINK ABOUT IT ...

Are there any differences between this notice and the ones in your own college or workplace?

Laws on electrical safety

Electricity is a well-known killer, and there are various laws designed to protect people from it.

1 **The Electricity at Work Regulations 1989.** Electrical equipment must be well made and properly maintained. If it is used in places where there is gas or dust, it must be designed to minimise the risk of fire and explosions. It must also be insulated and earthed so that people don't get electric shocks. This law also says that people who work with electricity must be properly qualified.
2 **IEE regulations.** These come from the Institute of Electrical Engineers, and are also known as the 'Wiring Regulations'. They control the installation of lighting and electrical appliances both in the home and in industrial buildings. Even if you are wiring your own house you must follow these. Again their purpose is to prevent fires and shocks.
3 **British Standards.** The British Standards Institution publishes a large number of booklets about different electrical appliances and pieces of equipment – everything from electric toothbrushes to say, generators. The booklets specify how well made and safe these things must be. The Standards are used in advertising as a way of proving that electrical goods are of a certain quality. Objects which are not good enough to carry the British Standards 'kitemark', may be breaking the law, and do not reach the highest safety levels.

Laws on gas safety

The supply of gas to buildings is covered by Building Regulations. One of the most important of these is the Construction (Design and Management) Regulations 1994. Under this law planning supervisors, designers, contractors and even clients have a responsibility to monitor all health and safety aspects of design.

Installation of gas is by plumbers, and most of them belong to an organisation called CORGI. Its bark is worse than its bite, but even so CORGI lays down strict safety standards for gas pipes, cookers, and other things that might cause fires and explosions.

FOCUS

Legal requirements for gas installation

CORGI – the Council for Registered Gas Installers – is the body given the responsibility by the Health and Safety Executive to maintain a register of competent gas installers. All businesses, whether employers or self-employed persons, who undertake gas work on gas fittings supplied by natural gas or liquefied petroleum gas, must by law register with CORGI. Only those members who have informed the Executive that they are so registered have the Gas Fitting (GF) work classification beneath their names in the register. Similarly, only those members holding a current Registered Operative identity card have the Unvented Hot Water Storage Systems (UV) work classification beneath their names.

Gas supplies have to be monitored in industrial and other buildings through a process known as risk assessment. Safety representatives check from time to time that there are no gas leaks, and that any gas taps or appliances are in good working order. Gas supplies can also be checked by Health and Safety inspectors, or by employees of British Gas. Such checks can also be carried out by the fire service.

HAZCHEM

This odd-looking word stands for 'hazardous chemicals', and is used mainly for chemicals, including oils, resins, paints and gases, when they are being transported, usually by road tanker, but sometimes by rail as well. HAZCHEM is a code which enables firefighters and rescue workers to see at a glance what a tanker or container-lorry is carrying. The code for the chemical being transported is printed clearly, in big letters, on a sign on the outside of the vehicle. In the long run, HAZCHEM may be replaced by the international ISO system of classifying hazards. But at present (2000) it is the HAZCHEM code which is still used on British tankers.

Firefighters carry the HAZCHEM code with them on a special card, to remind them of what all the letters and numbers mean. The card is reproduced in figure 14.6.

> **!** **THINK ABOUT IT ...**
> Look at the HAZCHEM card.
>
> Work out what all the abbreviations mean. Collect examples of other safety labelling systems which the public services need to be aware of.

COSHH

When gas is in cylinders, or is any type of gas other than the methane supplied by British Gas, it is covered by COSHH. Gas is also dealt with under the COSHH (Control of Substances Hazardous to Health) Regulations. These were brought in in 1989 to cover a wide range of dangers. So what is the lowdown on COSHH?

In modern workplaces all sorts of weird (but legal) substances are used. They might be cleaning fluids, printing materials, powders, dusts, gases or even radioactive isotopes. Some of these are highly toxic; others can cause allergies or long-term respiratory effects. All can either shorten life or reduce its quality.

We can't do without these substances hazardous to health, because businesses, manufacturing, prosperity and jobs depend on them. But we can protect ourselves from them, if we use our common sense and, more importantly, the COSHH regulations.

Ways of controlling hazardous substances under COSHH include the following.

1. **Prohibition.** Health and Safety inspectors can ban the use of a dangerous substance – and prosecute the company or organisation if they continue to use it.
2. **Elimination.** Sometimes the hazardous substance is not really needed, or is out of date. COSHH encourages people to get rid of the stuff.
3. **Substitution.** A dangerous substance can be replaced by a less dangerous one that will do the same job.
4. **Containment.** Proper tanks, pipes and containers can make a substance less hazardous.
5. **Isolation.** This means keeping dangerous substances well out of the way.
6. **Ventilation.** If gases and dusts are 'diluted' with air they may become less dangerous.
7. **LEV (local exhaust ventilation) systems.** These are hoods, pipes and other devices which channel dangerous gases, fumes and dusts out of the way.
8. **Special clothing** – such as protective suits or breathing apparatus (BA).
9. **Decontamination.** When the fire service are dealing with hazardous materials they often use decontamination or shower units to protect firefighters. Council workers have similar

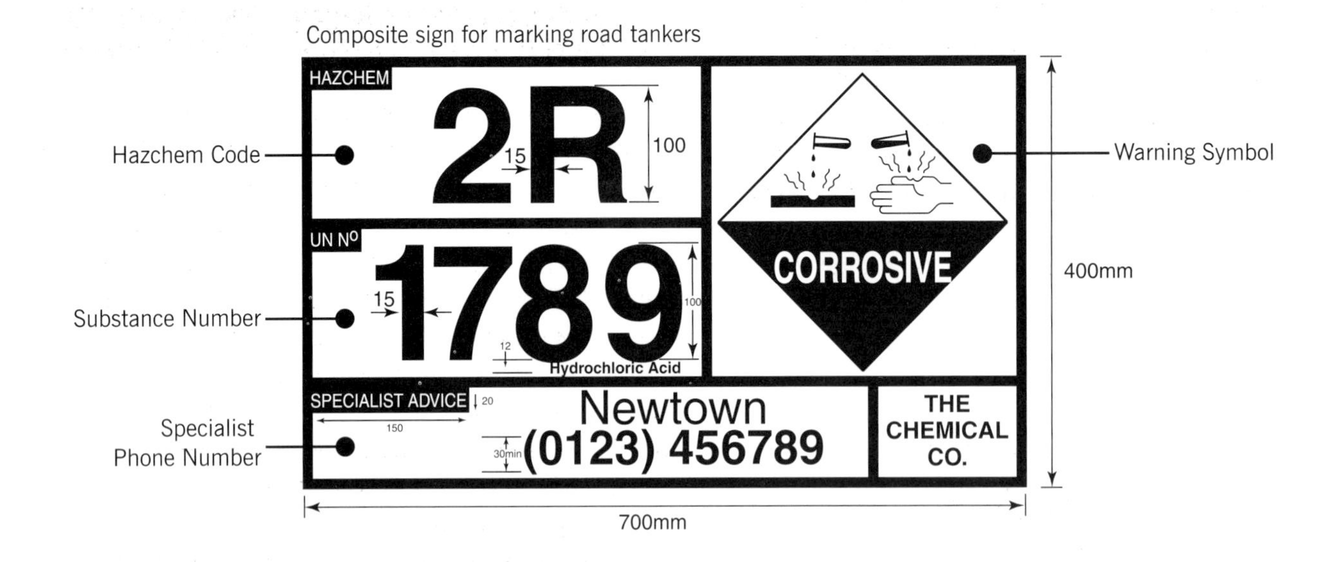

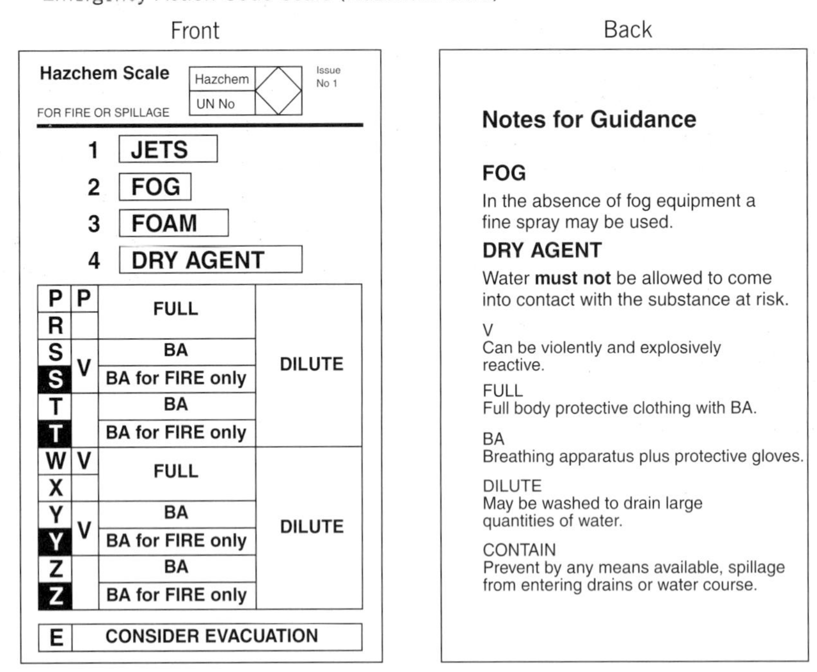

Figure 14.6 *HAZCHEM card (Source:* Manual of Firemanship Book 12 – Practical Firemanship II, *HMSO 1983, p.131)*

protection, for example when disposing of asbestos waste.

10 **Health screening** for workers who are repeatedly exposed to toxic or hazardous substances. This happens from time to time in nuclear power stations.

11 **Internal inspection.** Employees of organisations which deal with hazardous substances are now trained in 'risk assessment' (the identification of hazards) and have to carry it out at regular intervals.

12 **Safety committees.** These are groups of people chosen by employers and trade unions to organise the task of checking for dangers in the workplace. It is also their job to make people more aware of dangers and how to avoid them.

13 **Propaganda.** This means notices and talks designed to raise awareness of safety issues.

14 **External inspection.** Health and Safety inspectors are employed by the Health and Safety Executive (a collection of safety experts and administrators set up by HASAWA). These people have a legal right to go round any workplace, looking for unsafe practices. Although they may not look like it, they are your friends.

ANALYSIS

Even now, at the beginning of the 21st century, some people think health and safety is a waste of money. They still believe that if you're not making something or selling something you are a drain on the economy. But think about it. In the 1970s, 40 people died in the small Yorkshire town of Hebden Bridge of mesothelioma, a deadly lung cancer caused by microscopic particles of asbestos. They were all people who had worked in an asbestos factory, where they made the asbestos padding that was used for lagging hot water pipes, and for certain types of insulation. If there is no awareness of health and safety, this is the kind of thing that happens in industry. Going even further back, thousands of miners died of carbonicosis, when their lungs became so clogged with coal dust that they suffocated to death. Modern health and safety practices would have saved them. Think about the Bradford City fire disaster, where 55 people burnt to death in front of the television cameras. Or think of Hillsborough. Could you tell the survivors of those tragedies that health and safety don't matter?

Unit outcome 4
Examine the practical nature of fire service work

Assessment criteria

- Explain how the fire service deals with a range of accidents, fires and rescues.
- Explain how the fire service uses other public services when dealing with accidents, fires and rescues.

How the fire service deals with accidents and fires

Accidents

Every accident is different – but not completely different. So the fire service has a general approach to accidents, which it can alter as and when the conditions demand it.

The fire service approach is determined by a number of priorities:

(a) to assess the scale of the accident
(b) to safeguard the lives of firefighters
(c) to save life
(d) to protect the public
(e) to save property
(f) to protect the environment
(g) to investigate the causes of accidents.

The ones lower down the list are not necessarily in order of priority.

As an example of what the fire service do in the case of a serious accident, we will look at what they would do in the case of a tanker crash. This will also illustrate how the public services work together in an accident of this type.

The fire service would:

- **reach the accident** within five minutes in town, and within seven to eight minutes outside town
- **bring** two 'pumps' (containing firefighting equipment), from different directions, and an 'emergency tender' (containing equipment for first-aid and for cutting people out of crashed vehicles)
- **wear** gloves, balaclava, BA (breathing apparatus), and flame-resistant suits, or wear splash suits, overalls, big neoprene suits and leggings over boots for extra protection against chemicals
- **assess** what the tanker is carrying, using the orange placards giving the HAZCHEM code, and any indication of what extinguishing agent (foam, powder, etc.) should be used
- **decide** if more protective clothing is needed (e.g. gastight suits), and call for more backup
- **approach** the crash downhill and downwind
- **use** water jets to cool the tanker or anything else which is dangerously hot
- if the chemical in the tanker is dangerous, contact divisional headquarters for **technical support and advice**: divisional HQ may contact local chemical firms, or CHEMDATA, a nationwide advice and backup service
- in dangerous gas, **work in BA**: each set will last for 20–40 minutes – the more the firefighter is exerting himself, the less time the cylinders last
- call for a special shower or **decontamination unit**: these are on wheels and can be set up nearby
- **beware of flammable gas**: propane will flow downhill and settle in cellars of nearby houses – if anybody flicks a switch it will explode, so firefighters must extinguish all naked flames and sources of ignition if there is flammable gas around; this includes radios in fire engines, but not the sealed portable radios that firefighters use
- **carry out snatch rescues** – perhaps of the driver, or people at serious risk in nearby houses: these can be done in splashproof suits – but if firefighters stay in the danger zone they must use gastight suits and equipment
- **damp down gases and vapours** with a wall of spray, if the gas reacts to water – but firefighters

must beware of toxic run-off entering the drains and fouling rivers

- **use water-curtains** (thick spray) to divert the flow of heavy gases, to keep them out of cellars and sewers: heavy gases in sewers can cause massive underground explosions
- **apply neutralising substances** to toxic run-off – for example alkalis if the run-off is acidic
- **decontaminate themselves** after periods in the danger zone using showers or a 'body vacuum', depending on the kind of pollution
- **carry out other rescues**: these are always a calculated risk – (a firefighter cannot rescue somebody if it means certain death for himself). If the paramedics are not around the firefighters will give first aid and carry out resuscitation; they will also give 'entonox', a powerful painkiller
- **use no more officers than necessary** to carry out a given job
- **keep some of their vehicles in 'fend-off' positions** to protect rescue workers from other traffic, if the accident has happened on a motorway (see figure 14.7)
- **prevent fire spread**, and allow certain materials to burn off if necessary: fire may be less harmful than a cloud of toxic vapour
- **investigate the accident** – this is after all rescues have been completed, all bodies removed, and the area has been made reasonably safe: the investigation may be done by the fire service investigation team from headquarters, or by the Health and Safety Executive and if there is a chance of criminal proceedings (which is very likely in the case of a serious crash) the police would be involved
- **take part in debriefing** – all emergency service personnel involved in the incident are interviewed and a report is written for the fire service divisional headquarters: this report is then circulated to all people and organisations interested in the accident, and the way the public services dealt with it.

Other public service involvement in a serious accident of this type includes the following.

1. **The police.** They secure the area, to keep the public away. They re-route traffic and organise any local evacuation that might be needed.

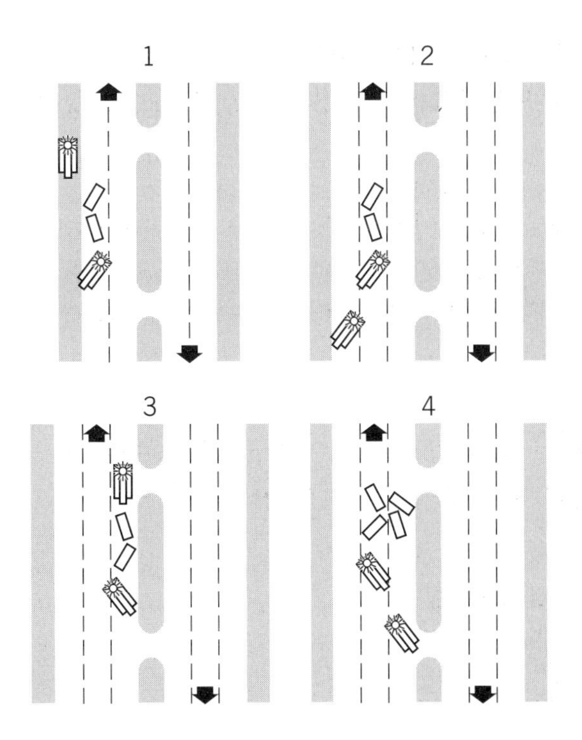

Figure 14.7 *Positioning of fire service appliances before the arrival of the police so that appliances provide protection for firemen working at the incident. (1) For incident in the left-hand lane of two- or three-lane motorways. (2) When the obstruction covers the centre lane, or both the left-hand and centre lane. (3) For incidents in the right-hand lane. (4) For incidents covering both the centre and right-hand lanes (Source:* Manual of Firemanship, Book 12 – *p60, HMSO 1983)*

They also make sure there is a place for ambulances to collect casualties, and for paramedics to work.

2. **The ambulance service.** They will sort out the casualties, assessing their urgency. This process is called triage. Priority is given to crash victims who are not crying out in pain – it is often the quiet ones who are most seriously hurt. Casualties are taken quickly to hospital. Clingfilm is used to cover burns: this keeps bacteria off and makes it easier to estimate fluid loss. Replacing lost fluid to prevent casualties going into shock is a key task of paramedics – since fluid loss is one of the most common causes of shock in road traffic accidents. A holding area is set up, upwind of the accident, where victims receive painkillers, preliminary treatment and diagnosis. Fluid and blood plasma are often given to crash victims

at this point. Increasingly, paramedics begin their treatment of crash victims even before they have been cut out of the wreckage of their vehicles. For one thing, it helps them to withstand the strain of being cut out; for another it makes use of the so-called 'golden hour' when emergency treatment is most effective.

Fires

The way the fire service deals with fires is dependent on three factors:

- the type of fire
- the site of the fire
- the size of the fire.

Fire type: class A

Fires of solid organic material such as wood, paper and coal. These are put out with water.

Fire type: class B

Flammable liquids. There are two types, (a) those that mix with water, such as methanol, ethanol and acetone and (b) those that won't mix with water, such as petrol, benzene, fats and waxes. Liquid fires of type (a) can be put out with water, which will cool and dilute the fuel until it is no longer flammable. Fires of type (b) are usually smothered with foam.

Fire type: class C

Gases or liquefied gases, such as methane, propane and butane. The easiest method, if it is possible, is to starve the fire by cutting off the gas supply. Otherwise inert gases such as halons or CO_2, or even foam and powder, can be used. Water is effective in cooling down the fire area, but not in fighting the fire itself.

Site: one-room fires

Most fires are one-room fires when the fire service reach them. But if they are not tackled they will spread to engulf a whole building. One hose is usually enough for this type of fire. This should be prepared before the fire is approached. The firefighter should wear BA and keep her head down when approaching the room. After opening the door she should direct the water at the ceiling first, as this will be the hottest part of the room except for the seat of the fire itself, and the most likely way for the fire to spread to the rest of the building. Having cooled the ceiling the firefighter then attacks the fire itself, going for the base of the flames.

As well as cooling and smothering this type of fire, firefighters can also starve it by dragging out burning carpets, mattresses and other items, robbing the fire of its fuel. They must use no more water than necessary, and avoid trampling too much dirt through the rest of the house.

Site: roof fires

How these are tackled depends on the type of roof, but it is generally better to attack the fire from inside rather than out, so that the water can get to the seat of the flames.

In terraced houses it is often difficult to find out where the fire is, as smoke can blow through the space under the roof from one end of the terrace to the other. Firefighters can usually get in through trapdoors in the ceiling. In large old buildings it is better to break into the roof space through the roof rather than the ceiling, as it does less damage. In industrial buildings there are many kinds of roof; the older ones are often dangerous because of their flammable insulation or weak construction. Often large sections of roof can be removed easily in order to fight the fire or restrict its spread. Church roofs are high and steep, and fires in these roofs may have to be fought from outside with high pressure hoses. Alternatively turntable ladders or hydraulic platforms can be used to get nearer the fire.

These fires are particularly dangerous because of the risk of roof or building collapse, or of firefighters falling from a height.

Further reading

More information about practical firefighting can be found in the *Fire Service Manual* formerly *Manual of Firemanship*, published by the Stationery Office.

Rescues

Rescues are a complex subject, and there is only room to outline them here. If you want more information, you will have to go to the *Fire Service Manual*. But here are some of the main points.

1. Finding casualties can be difficult in a burning building, mainly because of thick smoke. The golden rule is to keep left! See figure 14.8.

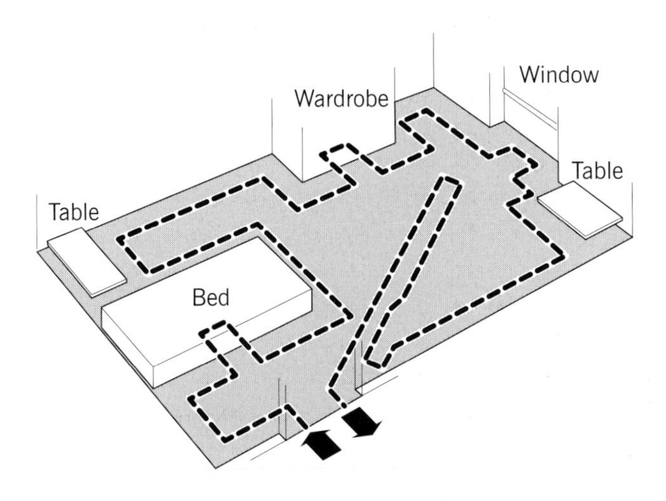

Figure 14.8 *Correct method of searching a room (Source:* Manual of Firemanship, Book 12, *HMSO 1983, p.5)*

2. People can sometimes be lowered or helped to jump or climb down the outside of the building, especially if there are good drainpipes, lean-tos and so on.
3. Firefighters are trained to lift or drag people out of burning buildings, if they are unconscious or unable to move for themselves.
4. The evacuation of disabled people from burning buildings can be very slow. Firefighters may lift these people using 2-, 3- or 4-handed seats (see figure 14.9), carry-chairs, blankets, rescue sheets or stretchers.
5. Some rescues use ladders or hydraulic platforms. If the person is able to descend the ladder unaided, the firefighter must remain just below them in case they slip or faint. The firefighter can then pin the person to the ladder so they don't fall. Occasionally, sometimes in pairs, firefighters have to carry people down ladders. In extreme cases people can be lowered by ropes or slings.

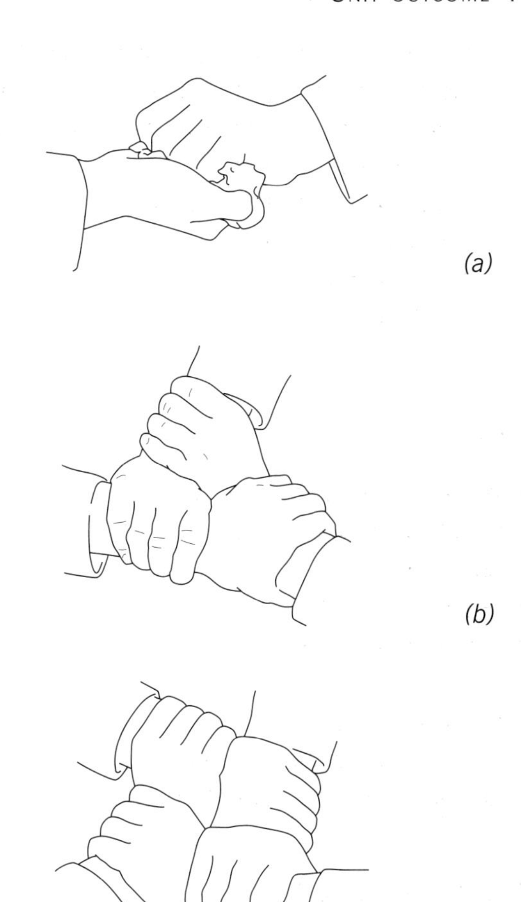

Figure 14.9 (a) *Two-handed seat* (b) *Three-handed seat* (c) *Four-handed seat (Source:* Manual of Firemanship, Book 12 *HMSO 1983, pp.10–11)*

Example of a rescue

In this unit there are already three accounts of firefighting operations reprinted from *Fire* magazine. Another example, showing the firefighting and rescue problems in a high building with many people living in it is given in figure 14.10.

Assistance for the fire service

Explain how the fire service uses other public services when dealing with accidents, fires and rescues.

Some information on this topic has been given earlier, during the explanation of the fire service response to a tanker crash. However, this is part of a wider picture.

Poor information on residents hampers Surrey blaze rescue

Sixty firefighters, 10 pumping appliances and three special appliances were involved for over seven hours at the incident before the 'stop' was sent, and it was a further 53 hours before the incident was closed at the Victorian house which had been converted into 29 bedsits.

Surrey Fire and Rescue Service was initially alerted to the incident at 0324 on February 14 and since a Section 12 arrangement exists with West Sussex Fire Authority for the area, the normal PDA of two Sussex appliances was sent. On arrival, the Sub Officer in charge was confronted with a rapidly deteriorating fire situation with flames coming out of a lower ground floor window which were extending up the front of the building and across the front main entrance doors. He immediately made 'pumps four'.

A number of residents who had evacuated the premises were assembled at the front of the building and when they were questioned as to whether everyone was out, confusion arose. A number of rooms were therefore identified where residents may not have evacuated. Accurate information was difficult due to the fact that many of the residents worked shifts at nearby Gatwick Airport, and consequently their precise whereabouts were unknown. A ' persons reported' message was sent and a potential of five persons were unaccounted for.

As supporting appliances arrived, firefighters reported being hampered by thick fog which had reduced visibility down to one metre in places. It is worthy of note, that despite the horrendous driving conditions, appliances were still able to meet Home Office attendance times.

As they were arriving, one young male casualty was found lying in the grounds of the property partly wrapped in a duvet and a firefighter rendered first aid. Despite efforts by both firefighters and paramedic crews, he subsequently died some time later.

Having been informed of rooms where persons may have been trapped, breathing apparatus teams were committed, one with a hose reel through the rear door searching to their left, another entered through a ground floor window into the east wing.

They carried out a search of the lower ground floor, part of the ground floor and first floor. They were able to confirm that a number of rooms believed to have contained residents were empty. This left two persons still unaccounted for.

With the arrival of Surrey's first appliance at 0353, the Station Officer in charge took command of the incident. He was briefed on the situation and since there was a rapidly deteriorating fire situation, pumps were 'made eight'.

As supporting appliances arrived, further BA crews were committed inside the building to assist with searching for missing residents and to continue with firefighting operations. Covering jets were also established to protect their access points from flames coming from adjacent windows. As these jets were brought into use, this placed a significant demand on the mains water supply so light portable pumps were set into an ornamental pond adjacent to the building to obtain open water to supply them.

The fire continued to develop rapidly and now involved the converted roof space (second floor). Since there was a considerable threat to firefighters working inside, all crews were immediately with drawn. An informative message and a request for an aerial ladder appliance to assist with firefighting from a safe, high level vantage point, was sent at 0446.

Crews with jets were now deployed between the east wing and the main building, and jets brought into use from the head of 13.45m ladders were pitched at four locations around the building. It was considered that the available water supplies would be insufficient to supply the aerial ladder so a further assistance message: "Make pumps 10, hose layer required" was sent, timed 0559. The hose layer enabled water to be brought from an independent 300mm mains supply some 38 hose lengths away from the incident.

Firefighting continued under difficult and dangerous conditions due to the severe deep seated fire and the unstable and collapsing structure. Further information was received from Surrey Police and three persons were still unaccounted for but crews were unable to penetrate deep into the area involved in fire to search for the missing individuals.

Following the deployment of the aerial ladder monitor and the concerted efforts by individual crews with jets, the fire was brought under control with the 'stop' message being returned at 1039. Crews remained at the scene knocking out pockets of fire and carefully removed debris allowing a thorough search and investigation to be carried out. The message "All persons accounted for" was returned at 1336 on February 16. The incident was finally closed at 1445 that day.

In all, the fire had been extinguished using one aerial ladder platform monitor, four fire fighting jets from hydrants via water tender ladders and one hose reel jet. Four further firefighting jets from open water via two light portable pumps, and 28 compressed air breathing apparatus sets were used. In total 30 water tender ladders and seven special appliances attended the incident within the initial stages or as relief crews.

Figure 14.10 *(Cont'd)*

Description of damage

Six per cent of the lower ground floor, 40 per cent of the ground floor, 60 per cent of the first floor and 80 per cent of the roof and second floor conversion were severely damaged by fire and collapse. The remainder of the 23m by 14m building was damaged by smoke and water. Subsequent investigation by both the Fire Service and Police Forensic Science Laboratory, established that the probable cause of the fire was carelessly discarded smoking materials, and that the room of origin was the one in which the male resident sustained his fatal injuries.

Observations

1. The fire resistance protecting the main staircase maintained the staircase intact for a considerable time. But fire travel between floors allowed very quick spread; this fire travel fed up through the building into the converted roof space made firefighting and control of the fire spread very difficult. This upward spread was due in part to a ruptured gas main in the room of origin.

2. Firefighting and search operations were severely hampered by the limited and inaccurate information concerning the whereabouts of residents. This was aggravated by no comprehensive room numbering and lack of a roll call system.

3. There was excellent liaison between all the services and agencies involved, but particularly between Surrey Fire and Rescue Service and West Sussex Fire Brigade.

Figure 14.10 *(Cont'd) Source: Fire report from* Fire *magazine, June 1998, pp. 8/12*

Control and command of large incidents is a rapidly changing and developing field of public service work, thanks to new technology and higher expectations from the public. In the past it wasn't always clear who was in charge in an incident such as a motorway pile-up which involved all the blue light services. Fortunately the emergency services, together with the local authority emergency planning departments, have now got this inter-service liaison down to a fine art, and confusion about 'who does what' is becoming a thing of the past.

The amount of liaison between public services depends on the size of the incident that they are dealing with. A small fire involving one room in one house is dealt with by the fire service and provided (a) that no one is hurt and (b) that there is nothing suspicious about it, it remains a fire service affair. The officers present will ask the householder how and why the fire happened, and if they are satisfied with the answers, all they need to do is provide information for the insurers, and that's it. Similarly a small road accident, in which no one is trapped or hurt, need only involve the police. But bigger incidents, in which people get trapped or hurt, or where large amounts of damage occur, or there is a suspicion of crime, or the environment is put at risk – these are a different matter.

Information reaches the fire service about fires or accidents in 999 calls. In many cases, for example a road traffic accident, it may be the police who hear about it first, but very often all the emergency services are alerted, once one has been alerted, by the message being passed on to the other two. If the incident is big, like a train crash, a tanker crash, or a chemical incident at a factory, coordination will be carried out by the headquarters of one of the public services – probably the fire service. The firefighters will call for reinforcements, and as soon as it is clear that traffic may have to be diverted, or the public have to be kept at bay, the police will be involved. If there are any injured or even shocked people, ambulances will be called, and if there seem to be many casualties, it may be necessary to contact a number of hospitals by radio to ensure that the beds and other facilities are ready and waiting. A major accident like a motorway pile-up or a train crash may put a big strain on local hospitals as well as the emergency services. If the accident is really big, the local authority emergency planning officer will be in overall charge of the rescue and salvage operation, and of any evacuation, investigation or environmental clean-up that follows. But when this happens it means the accident has become big enough to be classified as a disaster – and you can read about these in Unit 12: Disaster and Emergency.

Who does what?

In a normal large accident the roles of the emergency services are as follows.

Ambulance service responsibilities:

- supportive treatment
- evacuating casualties to hospital.

Fire service responsibilities:

- rescue
- put out fires
- deal with hazardous substances
- liaison with ambulances
- liaison with police
- fire investigation.

Police responsibilities:

- cordon off area (to avoid public interference and protect the scene of a possible crime)
- decide who does what (except when firefighting is involved; then they leave it to the experts)
- control
- coordination
- investigation of causes of the accident (possibly liaising with the fire service fire investigation team, and the Health and Safety Executive)
- collecting evidence of crime
- liaising with the coroner's office (if there has been loss of life)
- if additional agencies are needed to investigate an accident, or deal with a chemical incident, the police are likely to take the lead in getting them involved
- deal with the media.

Coroner responsibilities:

- will conduct inquests to determine causes of deaths
- may hold a public inquiry
- will liaise with organisations such as Railtrack, or the Health and Safety Executive.

Where there are many casualties, the emergency services have a computerised system to keep track of them. This is called CRISIS, which stands for Casualty Recording Information Sorting Identification System.

> **THINK ABOUT IT ...**
>
> Find out who would deal with the following kinds of accident, and how.
>
> - A woman falls while rock climbing on Snowdon.
> - A man gets trapped in a cave.
> - Someone is injured in a yacht off the Isle of Wight.

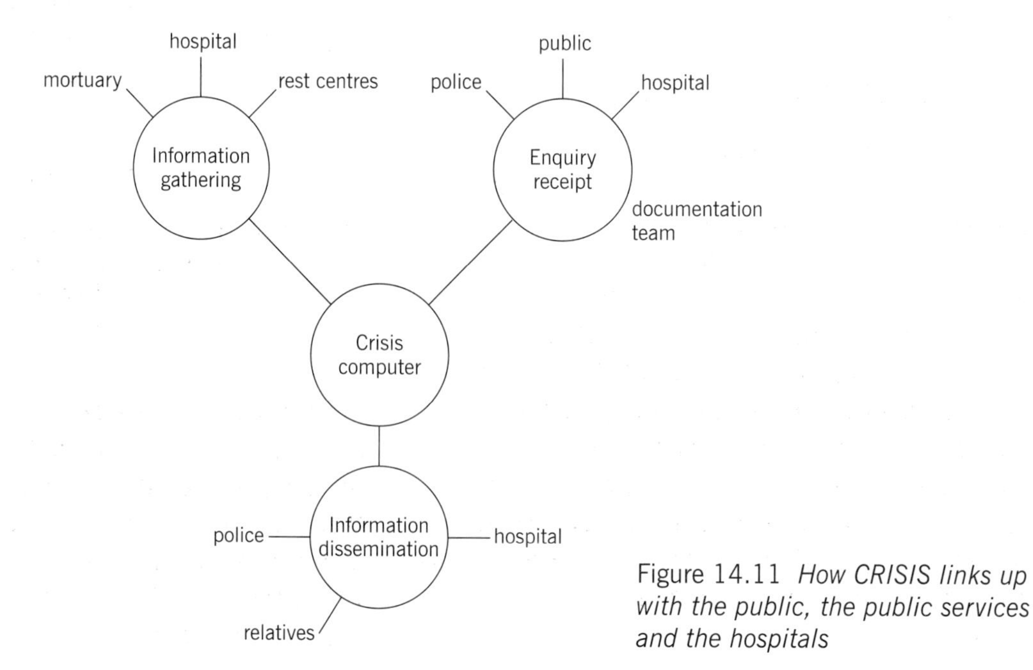

Figure 14.11 *How CRISIS links up with the public, the public services and the hospitals*

UNIT 15 Leadership

Unit outcome 1
Examine styles of leadership

Assessment criteria
- Explain different styles of leadership.
- Compare at least three different styles of leadership.
- Evaluate the effectiveness of at least two different styles of leadership.

The four main personality requirements of public service work are discipline, initiative, teamwork and leadership. All of these qualities are more complex than they appear at first sight. Furthermore, there are times when they may seem to contradict each other. A person with initiative, for example, who is original and self-reliant, may not always be the best 'team player'.

But of all these four qualities, leadership is the most valuable. People who are promoted and who rise to the top of their organisations successfully, are almost certainly leaders.

Leadership

Explain different styles of leadership.

There are three main kinds of leadership:
- authoritarian
- laissez-faire
- democratic.

1 Authoritarian leadership

This is traditional leadership, firm and strict. Authoritarian leaders expect to be obeyed, quickly and exactly, in everything (or nearly everything) that they demand. They will not put up with argument or discussion if they can help it, and they ask to be treated with obvious respect. They are believers in force: the old idea of 'might is right'. The gang leader who beats up gang members who dare to question him, the mafia leader who shoots those who disagree with his plans, the foreign dictator who imprisons his political opponents, the drill sergeant who shouts at those who are marching out of step are all displaying authoritarian leadership.

Structure and ethos

Authoritarian leadership is the type of leadership which authoritarian leaders practise. But it is not simply the personalities of the leaders that make for authoritarian leadership. Some organisations or institutions are authoritarian in their structure (the way they are arranged) and ethos (their traditional ways of thinking), and therefore any leadership in these organisations is likely to be authoritarian.

FOCUS

It is important not to confuse leaders with leadership. Leaders are people; leadership is the act or manner of leading.

In Britain the clearest example of authoritarian leadership is to be found in the army – especially the army as it used to be a hundred years ago. In World War I soldiers had to obey orders promptly and exactly, with no questions asked. 'You do as you're told' was the rule. Deserters or cowards were shot. End of story.

But authoritarian leadership was seen in many other institutions and settings. For example sons used to call their fathers 'sir'; now, in many families, they call them by their first name. In the old days, if an employer wanted to sack someone, they told them to get out, and that was that. No messing about with industrial tribunals, appeals and wrongful dismissal. The police called their superior officers 'sir', and pupils called their teachers 'sir' (except behind their backs). In fact every institution, every organised or half-organised group of people, was more formal and more authoritarian in those days. Even in the churches there was a lot more preaching about hell, the idea of punishment after death, than there is now. In other words society itself was more authoritarian, and this led to authoritarian leadership in nearly every part of it.

2 Laissez-faire leadership

This is the opposite of authoritarian leadership, and in a sense it means no leadership at all. 'Laissez-faire' is a French expression meaning 'let people do what they want'. The teacher who allows her pupils to do what they want and Nero, the Roman emperor who played his violin while Rome was burning, are both examples of laissez-faire leaders.

Pure laissez-faire leadership is an impossibility, a contradiction. It can't be leadership if you have no control at all over anybody. But any leadership which, in general, allows people do do what they like, is laissez-faire. For example a parent who lets her children come in when they want, or a university which does not really enforce assignment deadlines, or a playgroup where children can do whatever they like as long as they don't injure each other, are all displaying laissez-faire leadership. In other words, leadership which normally lets people do what they want is classified as laissez-faire even though, very occasionally, the leader(s) might put their foot down.

Laissez-faire leadership started to become more popular after World War II, in the 1950s, when the country was tired of wartime conditions and people wanted more freedom. The old rules began to be questioned, and people were no longer happy to be told what to do all the time. Society itself became more laissez-faire. For example it was no longer totally shocking for a girl to have sex with her boyfriend, and films about rebellion (such as James Dean's *Rebel without a Cause*) became popular. People began to think there was more to life than just obeying orders.

This process accelerated in the 1960s, when the so-called 'permissive society' developed. Caning in school was disapproved of, then outlawed; churches began to question the idea of hell; capital punishment (a very authoritarian idea) was stopped, and the hippie ideas of 'flower power' in which everything (including drug-taking) was allowed, came across from America and affected British society. The music industry encouraged all the new ideas of freedom, and it became the 'in thing' to be laissez-faire.

3 Democratic leadership

Democratic leadership is the third kind or style of leadership, and it has become increasingly popular over the last 20 years. In a way it is seen as a moderate type of leadership, between two extremes. It isn't as hard-nosed and inflexible as authoritarian leadership, and it isn't as weak and spineless as laissez-faire leadership. It is said to have the best of both worlds.

The word 'democratic' is not an easy word to understand, even though people use it all the time. In this context it means a kind of shared leadership where everybody has a part to play in the decision-making process. Democracy is a form of government where everybody can have a say through their MPs or the other people they elect to power. In democratic leadership everybody in an organisation is able to have a say in how things are done, and the decisions that are made.

For many British people the idea of democracy is connected with Parliament. If an individual doesn't like the way things are being done, she can complain to her MP. The MP in turn can try to do something about it by raising the matter in Parliament or trying to get a new law made. But if the new law is passed it started with the person who complained to her MP in the first place.

In companies, in colleges, and increasingly in the public services, democratic styles of leadership are practised. People hold meetings, set up working parties and focus groups, and arrange feedback sessions so that everybody can say what they think before a decision is made. This is reflected in society as a whole, where there must be 'accountability' and 'transparency': people must know what is happening and be able to do something about it if they want.

> **THINK ABOUT IT ...**
> Are leaders born or made? Would you like to be a leader?

The table below compares these different leadership styles.

What is the best style of leadership?

Compare at least three different styles of leadership.

Evaluate the effectiveness of at least two different styles of leadership.

It is not possible to say simply that one style of leadership is better than another. It would be more correct to say that there is a best style of leadership for:

- a given situation and
- a given group of people.

Thus the most effective style of leadership may be one which follows an analysis of the situation (Vroom 1984). Here is an example of the kinds of questions a leader might ask in order to decide the best leadership style in a given situation.

Comparison of leadership styles

Authoritarian leadership	Laissez-faire leadership	Democratic leadership
Decisions made by one person.	No decisions made.	Decisions made by everybody.
Uses force.	Doesn't use force.	Uses force if everybody agrees first.
Leader admired or feared.	Leader ignored.	Leader listened to – but not in silence.
Leader takes the blame for a mistake.	Nobody takes the blame.	Everybody collectively takes the blame.
Shows traditional values.	Shows 'modernist' ('way out') values, or none at all.	Shows 'postmodernist' values (a mixture of old and new).
Decisions are quick (because only one person has to make them).	Decisions are never made.	Decisions are slow.
Decisions are obeyed.	Nobody obeys anybody if they can help it.	Decisions are obeyed – eventually.
People who disagree are punished.	People who disagree are ignored.	People who disagree are either persuaded to change their minds or outvoted.
Associated with the political right wing – e.g. Conservatism.	Associated with people who reject traditional politics – e.g. anarchists.	Associated with political left wing (or left centre) – e.g. Labour and socialist parties.

- Do we need a quality solution to this problem?
- Do I have enough information?
- Is the problem structured?
- Does everybody have to agree?
- Are people likely to agree with me?
- Is it likely to lead to angry disagreements?
- Are we clever and knowledgeable enough to solve this problem without outside help?
- How much time do we have?

In this example, if shortage of time is the main problem, then an authoritarian style of leadership may be appropriate.

THINK ABOUT IT ...

Imagine you are working in the public service of your choice.

What style of leadership would you like your line manager or supervisory officer to to use – and why?

The main advantages and drawbacks of the three styles of leadership discussed on pages 357–359 are analysed in the tables below.

Summary

Styles of leadership depend on:
- the personality of the leader
- the nature of the institution or organisation in which leadership is being practised
- the views of society as a whole
- the nature of the task that has to be carried out
- the circumstances in which the task must be carried out
- the nature of the people who are being led.

The effectiveness of leadership can be measured by:
- whether the desired outcome is worth achieving
- whether the desired outcome is achieved
- whether the outcome was achieved efficiently (with minimum effort, time and expense)
- what the people working for the leader say about the operation and its leader
- what other people say about the operation and its leader
- its public relations value.

Authoritarian

Advantages	Disadvantages
• Fast. • The situation is easily understood by subordinates. • The subordinates do not need to think. • The leader can be blamed if things go wrong. • Is sometimes suited to emergency situations, such as firefighting.	• It is too dependent on the knowledge and skills of the leader. • The opinions of more intelligent or knowledgeable people may never be known because of the authoritarian style, which allows little or no feedback. In other words, if the leader is wrong, the decision is wrong. Thousands of soldiers died in World War I because their leaders' decisions could not be questioned. New ideas cannot be discovered or developed because no one is ever consulted. • Can lead to personality cults and blind obedience, like that of the Nazis towards Hitler in World War II.

Laissez-faire

Advantages	Disadvantages
• It is normally no hassle for the leader or the people being led, because nobody really has to do anything. • It is suitable for creative people who don't like being told what to do. • It allows individuals to express themselves without being shouted down by other people. • May be suitable for places like advertising offices, where creativity is (nearly) all that matters.	• Directionless or nonexistent leadership which achieves little or nothing. It is negative and ineffective. A leader who uses this approach is likely to be quickly replaced by someone who 'gets things done'. • Sometimes laissez-faire leadership leaves the way open for the person with the loudest voice to get their own way – in other words, it reverts to being authoritarian.

Democratic

Advantages	Disadvantages
• Popular at the time of writing (1999). • Everybody involved in the decision can take some share of the credit or blame. This means all decision-makers have to take an interest in what is being decided. People with good ideas but no force of personality are more likely to be represented. • There is less stress in this kind of decision-making, and people are less likely to 'take their bat home'. • Fits in well with the way society works at present. • It is easy to explain how democratic decisions have been reached because the process is open. There is less secrecy. • This type of decision-making allows people of real ability to come to the fore.	• Slow, bureaucratic and expensive, because many people are tied up in the decision-making process when they could be doing something more useful or productive. • Leads to 'talking-shops' which are annoying for people who like to get things done. • 'Decisions by committee' may not be as inspired, or clever, as decisions made by gifted individuals using authoritarian methods.

Unit outcome 2
Examine theories of motivation

Assessment criteria
- Briefly describe three different theories of motivation.
- Explain in detail at least three different motivating factors.
- Suggest three appropriate methods of maximising the productivity of groups.

Theories of motivation

What is motivation? Motivation is:
- making people do what they don't want to do
- making people do what they *do* want to do
- making people want to work harder, more effectively or more productively
- making yourself work harder, more effectively or more productively.

The most successful individuals in life – that is, the richest and most powerful – are those who can make other people do what they want them to do. Others are successful because they can motivate themselves. It is therefore not surprising that a good deal of study has been given to theories of motivation.

1 Drive theories

Many psychologists who have studied motivation have assumed that we are pushed, or driven, to do what we do by instincts within us. These theories, which were developed by people like McDougall (1932) and Morgan (1943), take the view that most of us are motivated whether we want to be or not. For example, we are motivated by hunger to eat, and by the sex drive to have children.

Drive theories say that the motivation is built into us, and can be found in certain parts of the brain. But if this was the whole truth about motivation it could never be used to influence the behaviour or work-rate of others, because they would be motivated already. This is not to say that drive theories are false, only that they don't tell the whole story.

2 Maslow's theory

In 1954 Abraham Maslow tried to put some order into the confusion of motivation theories by putting forward what he called the 'hierarchy of human needs' (see figure 15.1). A hierarchy is a list or system where ideas or people are ranked in order of importance. For example, the final placings in the Premier Division, or the music charts, are hierarchies: so too is the chain of command in a public service.

This is perhaps the most influential single theory of motivation. It states that the needs at the bottom of the pyramid are the most basic and essential. When we are young children we have to satisfy these needs before we move up the pyramid to satisfy the needs on the next layer. Similarly, if we were cast onto a desert island, or taken hostage, we would still have to satisfy the lower needs before we could start thinking about the higher ones.

Maslow's theory is useful because it helps to explain all sorts of aspects of motivation. For example, when students meet each other for the first time at the beginning of a BTEC course, they are motivated by the need for 'belongingness' or 'esteem needs'; that is why, at first, it seems more important to get to know the other people in the group than to get stuck in to the syllabus! People who are living rough, in cardboard boxes, are more likely to be motivated by the need for food, shelter and security than by the need for 'beauty, order and symmetry' which is near the top of the pyramid, and can only be satisfied when the needs below it have been satisfied.

Many people have wondered what 'self-actualisation' is – the need at the very top of the

Figure 15.1 *Maslow's hierarchy of human needs*

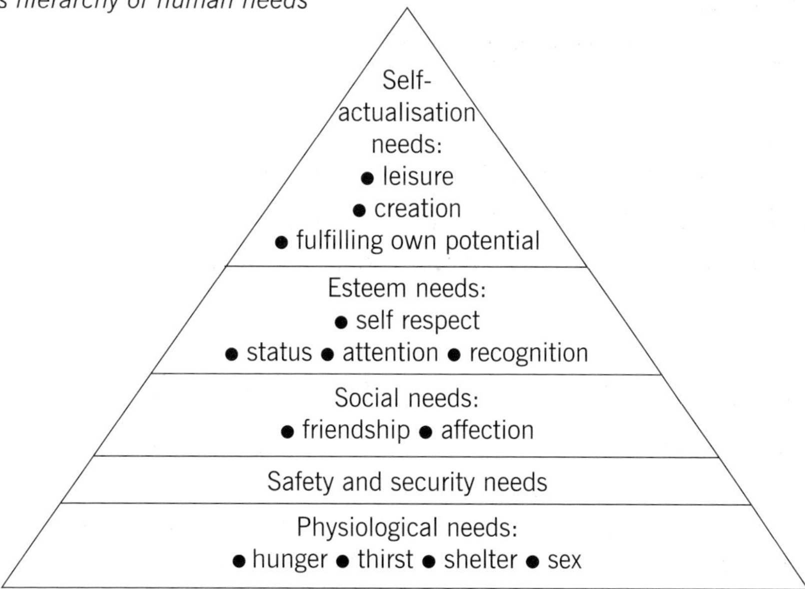

pinnacle. It means fulfilling your personal abilities to the highest possible level. For example David Beckham would no doubt make an excellent sports teacher in an FE college – even after they had bitten his arm off at the interview. But in that job he could not fulfil his real potential, and do the things that only he can do. Another man, who might have a boring job as, say, a caretaker, might make beautiful scale models of sailing ships in his spare time. Here he would be displaying his own particular abilities, which very few other people have, and realising his potential in a much more effective way than in the routine job of being a caretaker. This, for him, would be self-actualisation.

3 McGregor (1960) – theories of management

Douglas McGregor, an American who was interested in motivation and management, put forward his ideas in 1960. They are really a simplification of Maslow's system, put in practical terms which everybody can use without having a degree in psychology or philosophy first.

Theory X

For McGregor the X theory of management is traditional, basic management as follows.

1. Management is responsible for organising the elements of productive enterprise – money, materials, equipment, people – in the interest of economic ends.
2. With respect to people, this is a process of directing their efforts, motivating them, controlling their actions, modifying their behaviour to fit the needs of the organisation.
3. Without this active intervention by management, people would be passive – even resistant – to organisational needs. They must therefore be persuaded, rewarded, punished, controlled – their activities must be directed. This is management's task – in managing subordinate managers or workers. We often sum it up by saying that management consists of getting things done through other people. Behind this conventional theory there are several additional beliefs – less explicit, but widespread see 4–8 below).
4. The average person is by nature lazy – he works as little as possible.
5. This average person lacks ambition, dislikes responsibility, prefers to be led.
6. He or she is inherently self-centred and indifferent to organisational needs.
7. He or she is by nature resistant to change.
8. He or she is gullible, not very bright, and easily led astray.

Source: Adapted from McGregor, 1960

Management under Theory X is centralised, and has a hands-on attitude, closely supervising the worker. The style is authoritarian, the ethos is one of 'You're not paid to think'. The theory is also cynical, in that expects the worst of people. If a worker can skive, he or she will do so. Theory X is powered by the belief that people are basically stupid and selfish, and cannot be trusted.

Theory Y

Theory Y is different. Although it dates from 1960, managers are still exploring its possibilities. McGregor himself was not certain about all its features, so he did not describe it as clearly as he described Theory X. But this is how Theory Y goes.

1. A worker (and that means all of us) works to satisfy certain needs. If the worker is starving, he works to get food. If he has no shelter or heating, he works to get shelter and heating. That is because nothing else in life is achievable unless we have these basic needs satisfied first. McGregor (who was a friend of Maslow) also calls these needs, which appear at the bottom of Maslow's pyramid, 'physiological needs'. These are bodily needs.
2. But McGregor believed that people were not motivated by satisfaction, but by dissatisfaction. In other words, we are not motivated by what we have already got, but by wanting what we have not got. A man with a full stomach will not work to get more food, but he will work to get himself a house.

So McGregor said that people had to be motivated by the desire to gain the 'needs' which they had not already got. Having achieved their physiological needs, they were next motivated by safety needs (see Maslow's hierarchy). Once they had these, then (and only then) were they motivated by social needs.

McGregor is most interested in finding the right kind of motivation. He says that so-called 'scientific' management of the Theory X kind does nothing to satisfy the higher needs of workers or managers. McGregor's theories of management have provided an excellent basis for modern practical ideas on motivation. They are widely, though not necessarily successfully, used nowadays.

> **! THINK ABOUT IT ...**
>
> Are there any ways in which Theory X is actually better than Theory Y? What do you think?

Motivating factors

Explain in detail at least three different motivating factors.

1 Positive regard

This is the idea that we approach people in a friendly, loving or supportive way, instead of criticising or attacking them. It was first put forward by Carl Rogers in 1961, and is widely used by counsellors and psychotherapists. Instead of jumping in with both feet and trying to give advice, these counsellors listen to people who have problems and help them to discover their own courses of action. Even in non-counselling situations, positive regard is a useful way of showing people that they are valued and getting the best out of them.

2 Rewards and punishments

When researching drives Spies, in 1965, discovered that rats enjoyed receiving mild electric shocks to certain parts of the brain. They could be trained to press a lever which would give them these shocks, and they enjoyed the shocks so much that they would starve to death rather than stop pressing the lever. This experiment suggested that the hope of receiving pleasure might motivate human behaviour as well. No one has got round to giving human workers electric shocks to the brain to motivate them in this way but, as we shall see later (pages 365–367), rewards are an important factor in motivating people.

Punishments

In historical times punishment was often used to motivate people. An extreme case was the French general who, in Napoleonic times, had one in every ten of his soldiers shot 'to encourage the others'. Since the unlucky soldiers had done nothing wrong, this was not a punishment but a threat to the others, showing what would happen to them if they did not fight harder. As we have said earlier, British soldiers were sometimes shot for cowardice in World War I. This was punishment for the soldier concerned, and a deterrent to showing cowardice for the rest who realised what had happened to their former comrades. Conscientious objectors, people who refused to fight, were punished by imprisonment, or by having to do dangerous and unpleasant work. And it became the custom to stick white feathers on them, as a mark of disgrace. But again, the real intention was not to motivate them (because they had already shown that they wouldn't fight) but to motivate others who had perhaps not decided, up till then, whether to fight or not. It is hard to know scientifically or statistically how effective these deterrents and punishments were, but of course in other parts of the world such punishments and deterrents are still used to this day.

More important from our point of view are the vast number of milder punishments and deterrents used in everday life. Parents, schools, colleges, public services and virtually every other organisation you can think of still have punishments or disciplinary procedures whose main purpose is to motivate.

Intrinsic rewards

This is just another name for job satisfaction. These rewards include the interest of the job itself, the pleasure of being able to show that you are good at it and the personal relationships with colleagues and others which give the job a 'human side'.

Extrinsic rewards

These are the money and status which come with the job. They are not part of carrying out the job itself.

3 Fear

Fear is an important factor in influencing people's behaviour, but whether it is always a motivating factor is open to question. Among privates in the army, fear of being 'shown up' as weak or incompetent is probably a powerful motivator in producing the good, tough performance for which the British army is famous. On the other hand, among higher officers in the more 'civilianised' public services such as the police or HM Customs and Excise, fear of redundancy would probably be a demotivating factor. As well as being essentially negative and dehumanising, fear tends to push people down Maslow's hierarchy, and may be a barrier to achievement, since it creates an atmosphere in which people are unwilling or unable to think for themselves.

Productivity

Suggest three appropriate methods of maximising productivity of groups.

Productivity means the output per person, and is usually applied to manufacturing industry, or some activity related to manufacturing industry. If ten women make five thousand chocolates per hour, and another ten women make four thousand chocolates per hour, obviously the first group is more productive. The word 'productivity' might apply to some services as well. If one barber shaves ten men an hour and another shaves 15, the second is more productive. If one teacher gets 15 students through a leadership unit, and the second, at another college, gets 16 through the same unit, the second teacher is more productive. Or is she? She might have better students, or she might simply be grading them more leniently. When it comes to a service like the police, how do we measure their productivity? Is it by the number of people sent to jail per officer? Or is it by the amount of information about crimes that they manage to wheedle out of their informants? Or is it by the number of crimes they prevent by going round schools giving a few home truths to youngsters? Or is it by the success of their neighbourhood watch schemes?

This point is made at some length because, in the last ten years, there has been much discussion about the productivity of the police. Yet people have had difficulty even defining it, let alone measuring it. Equally, with the fire service, it is hard to say exactly what productivity means. A fire service with a good record in dealing with car crashes may be productive because a motorway runs through its patch. And if a productive army is one that kills a lot of people, then the Serbian army is better than the British one. For 'productivity' the word 'effectiveness' may be better where the public services are concerned, but effectiveness is still hard to measure. One factory can be compared with another, but if you try to compare one police force with another, you run into endless difficulties. The regions are different, the people are different and the crime patterns are different. Unless a great deal of care is taken, it's about as useful as trying to compare Mike Tyson with Martina Hingis.

Nevertheless, ways can be suggested for maximising productivity of groups. Obviously, not all of them will work equally well with all groups. But here is an attempt.

1 Supply leadership with which the group can identify and feel at home. The methods used by an army corporal will not be the same as those required by a chief constable.

2 Leaders or managers must communicate in language and using methods to which the group can relate. Communications themselves must be clear where clarity is needed. But in certain circumstances communication needs to be at a deeper level, using appropriate body-language and other non-verbal techniques. Language itself can motivate at an emotional level, and must be of an appropriate register. Jargon, or even swearing, can either strengthen or weaken group identity, depending on whether it is used appropriately. For example, if a manager uses jargon to show how clever he is, it is serving no useful group purpose and will weaken productivity or effectiveness. So appropriate communication is an important method of maximising group productivity.

3 'Carrot and stick' techniques can be employed, as long as they are used honestly and with the agreement of the workforce. High productivity can be rewarded with bonuses or awards which bring status or prestige, either to individuals within the group or the whole group. Promotion is another carrot which will maximise the performance of some individuals – though it may discourage others who think they should be promoted and are not.

4 Activities which bond the group into a team, and improve their *esprit de corps*, may be effective in maximising performance. Camping expeditions, days out, training residentials in which the team have to overcome hardships, even the kinds of exercises practised by some Japanese firms (early morning warm-ups) can all enhance productivity.

5 Work study and ergonomics. These consist of breaking tasks down into their separate parts, and working out the most efficient way of doing them. They are certainly effective where working with machines is concerned, but may be useful in offices as well. Ergonomics means fitting the workplace to human needs. So comfortable (but not too comfortable!) chairs, non-glare VDUs, light, airy, open-plan offices (for 'social facilitation' see pages 234–235), and inspiring colour schemes and decor may all play their part towards enhancing performance.

6 Systems of worker-ownership – for example preferential schemes of share ownership for employees – have also worked to improve productivity by giving workers a stake in their company. What this means is that if the productivity is high, they receive bonuses and dividends linked closely to productivity levels. It also means that workers and managers are 'in it together', and what benefits workers will also benefit managers.

7 Last but not least, the hierarchy of human needs. This means focusing on the individuals in the group and asking the question: 'What, apart from pay, is in this for them?' If the group is small enough, group leaders should identify what each worker (or each key worker) wants from the work experience. This is why skilled managers often treat their workforce as individuals, provided the 'group' is small enough for them to do this. One person will respond to praise of her intelligence; another will do better if he is invited out for drinks and made to feel 'one of the boys'. A third may respond better to being left alone; a fourth needs to feel that they are being consulted, even if they are not. A fifth will work better with the occasional reminder to sharpen up, whereas a sixth should never be criticised on any account – and so on. As a new team member becomes established a skilled manager will allow the member's work to change and develop as her own skills develop. The person who works because she wants to buy a house will, after she has bought the house, work for a different motive, such as increasing her status or developing her mental abilities. To get the best out of her, she will then need different tasks, a different role in the group, and different kinds of encouragement.

THINK ABOUT IT ...

Marx and his followers claim that what is good for workers is bad for managers, and vice versa.

They say the aim of the worker is to get as much money as possible for as little work as possible. But managers want workers to be as productive as possible for a minimum of pay. Think of the jobs that you and your friends might do when you are not at college. Do you think that what Marx said is true?

Unit outcome 3
Examine qualities of leaders

Assessment criteria

- Discuss in detail qualities of leaders.
- Contrast different qualities of leaders in four different situations.
- Discuss at least three different ways of becoming a leader.

Leadership qualities

'Take me to your leader!' says the alien when it lands on the Earth for the first time. But the world is full of leaders. We all know about the famous ones, such as Tony Blair, Bill Clinton or Alex Ferguson. Every time we open the paper there are comments about their leadership. People queue up to write books about them. It seems we all want to know the secrets of their success. And why is that? Is it not because there is something of the leader in all of us?

People who study for the public services do well to study leaders and their qualities. Why? Because public services, more than most careers, demand leadership. In fact there are times when everybody who works in the public services has to become a leader.

Weber's ideas (1921)

Weber's ideas on leadership were put forward in 1921, but they are still widely accepted. He identified three types of leader and their qualities:

1 **Experts.** Leaders who are leaders because they have special skills or knowledge which others could follow or learn from. For example if police trainees are learning about riot control, their instructor is the leader in that situation, because he or she knows more about the subject than they do.
2 **Traditional leaders.** These are people like priests or members of the government, who gain their power from the institution (organisation) they represent. They are the face of the church or the government, and people tend to obey them for this reason.
3 **Charismatic leaders.** For 'charismatic' read 'glamorous'. Charismatic leaders lead through the force of their personality. Physical strength or beauty may play a part, but mostly it is a mixture of general intelligence and force of character which makes other people 'look up to' these individuals.

Machiavelli's ideas (1513)

People are not just born leaders. Leadership is a skill that can be learnt, and many books have been written about how to become a leader. Plenty of Bible stories are about leadership, and the qualities of leaders. Much later, in 1513, an Italian, Machiavelli, wrote a book called *The Prince* which explained one approach to being a successful leader. His book concentrated on how to manipulate people, particularly your enemies, and is full of truths which can still be applied. The heart of his message is that you need to use your brains to be a successful leader. Machiavelli, crucially, distinguished between being a leader and being 'good'; a successful leader does not necessarily have to be a 'good person'. Hitler and Al Capone had many leadership qualities, but most of what they did was evil and destructive. Other leaders – perhaps John Major was an example – seem to have had good intentions but lacked the leadership qualities to carry them out.

Randolph B Schiffer's ideas (1999)

The following summary of leadership qualities comes from Dr Randolph B. Schiffer, Chairman of the Department of Neuropsychiatry and Behavioral Science at the Texas Tech Health Sciences Center.

1 Leaders must have a lifelong history of internal vision, of following their own internal values and not being easily deflected by the outside world.
2 Their values, and commitment to those values, persist over time and through many different situations.
3 Effective leaders are not selfish or narcissistic. They have to show a sense of concern and compassion for the group they lead.
4 Leaders have to be able to articulate their values.
5 The values and qualities of the leader can't be deviant. They have to be where the group is, but a little beyond the group.
6 There is an accident about time and fate. There are probably very many leaders who never make it simply because of circumstance.

ANALYSIS

To explain Schiffer's points, 1 and 2 basically mean that a leader must be strong and determined. If they come up against opposition they must work to overcome it, and never allow themselves to be defeated. This inner strength and determination is the most important single quality that a leader must possess. A leader is, by definition, trying to do something difficult. The problems may be from outside; the leader of an expedition in stormy weather or difficult terrain has to enable herself and her followers to survive and reach their objective in time and without injury. More often, though, the problems come from other people. For a police officer it may be criminals, but it may also be weak and unimaginative colleagues within the police. A leader will use her determination and intelligence to enable herself and her team to succeed in what they are trying to do. This does not mean she will be inflexible and bone-headed. There may be times when a leader has to negotiate, or give way on a small point, in order to achieve the most important objective. But on the important points, a leader should never give way.

Point 3 means that leaders serve others. This may seem strange, but the most successful leaders are not selfish people. They lead, but in another sense they are the servants of their followers. They are prepared to suffer so that other people can benefit from their actions. Martin Luther King is a famous example of this: he was prepared to die, and did, so that black people would have greater justice and freedom in America. In a sense this is the kind of leadership that all the public services can give. They do society's dirty work so that the rest of us can live in peace and prosperity. Good leaders also care about other people, and are prepared to take the trouble to find out what they need or want. (If they don't care about other people, then their followers will choose a different leader.)

Connected with this point is the idea of loyalty. Leaders are loyal to their group, in that they put their needs first, and will not betray them. In this way good leaders earn the trust of their group, who follow them because they believe in them, and believe in their goodwill.

Point 4 tells us that leaders must be good communicators. This may not mean giving formal speeches, or writing brilliant essays. Most communication is informal – a few words here, a gesture there, or a small action that 'speaks louder than words'. A leader must also be able to listen as well as give orders – after all, his followers may have good ideas that the group can use.

Point 5 tells us that leaders must be close to the group they lead, but not entirely part of it. We can see the sense of this if we look at a class in which the teacher successfully takes a leadership role. She is working for the group, and the group's success is her success. If she is exactly like her students, they will not be able to learn from her, because she will have nothing extra to offer them. On the other hand, if she is totally different from her students, they will not know 'where she is coming from', and will not be able to relate to her. So leaders must be like, but in some sense better than, their followers.

We should never forget point 6. There can be no leaders unless there is some kind of problem or challenge which needs to be overcome. Most of us have leadership qualities which will come to the fore in an emergency when we need them. Every time there is a disaster we read newspaper accounts of people who have been heroic and shown the highest leadership qualities. Those qualities were there in them all along, but it took the disaster to bring them out.

Further ideas

Further qualities of successful leaders are given below, as defined by Jerry Hunt, a Horn Professor of Management at Texas Tech.

1. Achievement orientation: the person really has a high need to achieve, a desire to excel. Leaders tend to have power motivation, but it should only be socially oriented power exercised for others.
2. Energy: leaders have high energy and are able to show a high tolerance for stress. They're physically vital. They withstand stress.
3. Emotional maturity: normally, leaders can't exhibit severe emotional disorders. They need to have emotional maturity.
4. Self-confidence: they must have the confidence they can be a leader, and that if they're a leader, they can accomplish tasks.
5. Integrity: they have a behaviour that's consistent with the values that they have and will be honest ethically.
6. Perseverance: they must keep after it, working at overcoming obstacles.
7. Intelligence: they must have a level of intelligence at least as high as the people they're leading and probably a little higher. If it's too high, people will be unable to identify with the leader.
8. Social intelligence: they must have insights about appropriate behaviour in social situations.
9. Flexibility: they must have the ability to respond appropriately to changes in the setting.
10. Knowledge: they need to have task-relevant knowledge about the industry they're in, the organisation and their work group.

! THINK ABOUT IT ...

What are the qualities of a bad leader?

Leadership qualities in practice

Contrast different qualities of leaders in four different situations.

The word 'contrast' means 'show the differences between'. And to consider this assessment criterion we should remind ourselves of a few home truths about leaders.

- Practically everybody has some leadership qualities.
- 'Great' or 'famous' leaders are not typical leaders, and we may learn less from them than we do from the people we meet in our everyday lives.
- All situations are different, and the true meaning of leadership qualities depends on the situation (i.e. the qualities needed for someone leading an Everest expedition are different from the qualities needed to run a playgroup or an office, or to lead a protest against a new motorway).
- The success of leadership depends on the people being led as well as the leader.
- Leadership can take the form of coordination or facilitation. In some groups, which operate effectively, it may not be clear who is the leader. In other words, leadership can sometimes be a group or collaborative affair – though in our culture we tend to look at leadership as an individual role.
- Women have been, and perhaps still are, under-represented as leaders, in a male-dominated society. However, there are well-known cases of female leaders being more effective than male ones.

Here are four leadership situations.

1 Mahatma Gandhi: the struggle for Indian independence

Gandhi was one of the great leaders of the 20th century, and the first leader to show how developing countries could effectively free themselves from colonialism. Like any leader he had to overcome difficulties, or obstacles. In his case these obstacles were as follows.

(a) He was seen as an enemy of Britain, which was a more important world power then than it is today.
(b) Though he was potentially at war with Britain, he was unwilling and unable to use violence.
(c) He was attempting to unify a vast country with many different ethnic groups and religions.
(d) He was negotiating with people like Lord Mountbatten whose cultural background and ideas were extremely different from his own.
(e) He was non-white, in a racist world.

To overcome these obstacles he was able to call on a range of qualities, which turned out to be strengths.

(a) He had studied in Britain, and was tireless in making links, and 'networking' with intelligent and influential British people who could see his point of view and would support his ideas in Britain. He had worked as a lawyer in South Africa, and had long experience of arguing on behalf of poor and disadvantaged people.
(b) He developed a philosophy of 'non-violent resistance'. This took the form of huge demonstrations, strikes and peaceful rallies which gathered popular support. These showed the British that he was a great organiser, and that he had the (almost) full support of his people. Gandhi's ideas also recognised the fact that the British had guns, while the Indians did not. If the Indians had fought a war, they would have lost disastrously due to lack of military hardware.
(c) Though Gandhi was a Hindu he took care to make alliances with Muslims and Sikhs, and bring out the ideas (e.g. desire for freedom) which they had in common. (Nevertheless he was assassinated, and the India he worked for broke up into three different countries.)

(d) Gandhi was a very clever man who wrote books. He used his cleverness to impress the British, and manipulate them. He deliberately gave himself the image of a simple, poor man (fasting and walking around with a spinning wheel) which appealed to the British and appeared non-threatening.
(e) Gandhi apparently paid no attention to race. He always acted with great dignity, but at the same time he used his skills to get on with people from all races and backgrounds.

2 Alex Ferguson: Manchester United's successes in 1999

Alex Ferguson has been widely praised in the British media for his achievements in the 1998/99 football season.

Here is information given about Alex Ferguson on a Manchester United website.

Let's look at some of the obstacles he had to face in his career, and the leadership qualities that enabled him and his team to be where they are today.
(a) He was born (in 1941) in a poor part of Glasgow, where the only jobs for most people were in the now dying industry of shipbuilding
(b) He was a good but not great footballer, said to be strong on determination, but lacking in skill and finesse, and too keen to use his elbows.
(c) He was not always successful in the clubs he managed.
(d) He chose to work in the cut-throat business of football management, one of the world's least secure careers.
(e) At Manchester United he was given vast sums of money to spend – a new experience for him.
(f) Buying footballers is bound to be a gamble. They come from different backgrounds, even different countries. They tend to be individualists and are difficult to weld together into a team.
(g) He has to deal with the British press, who eat football managers for breakfast and regard writing about them as a blood sport.

In relation to (a) and (b) he showed a leader's strength of character by being totally committed to the game of football. He was well known for 'always giving 100 per cent', and became respected for this. Equally important, he built up his self respect by the same process. A leader cannot expect other people to respect him if he does not first respect himself. As for (c), he cared about being successful, but if he was not successful, he would pick himself up off the floor and carry on where he left off. Like another Scot, King Robert the Bruce, he believed that 'if at first you don't succeed, try, try and try again'.

For (d) he showed courage. He chose a job with high risks, when he could have chosen a softer option, or perhaps feathered his nest in some other career where his management skills would have been useful. He has the reputation of never being afraid of a row. In the man's world of football management, this is a strength, but in other leadership areas, such as the diplomacy Gandhi practised, this 'short fuse' – a tendency to lose his temper – could have been a drawback. It might be useful to remember here that Ferguson comes from a tough working-class background where it is part of the culture to speak your mind and back it up with your fists if necessary. This way of resolving a problem would not have been an option for Gandhi, who, as a pacifist, was bound always to use non-violent methods. For (e) Ferguson again showed courage, helped by his passion for football which would mean that he was better informed about football's up-and-coming stars than most other managers. He was probably able to rely on a network of loyal and keen 'spies' who would always be on the lookout for football talent.

For (f) Ferguson would have to use his special communicative and psychological skills to make the players feel at home and foster a sense of team spirit. He was able to have faith in his players and give praise where it was due. For example he said of Eric Cantona that he was 'the best million I have ever spent', at a time when Cantona was thought to be 'over the hill'.

As for (g), Ferguson has had an unusual problem: he has been praised by the British press and treated as the next best thing to God. But he knows that if he had a run of poor results they would just as soon turn on him and try to tear him to bits. He therefore does not allow praise to go to his head. He will talk to the press, and shows few signs of paranoia, but he always gives the impression of saying what he wants, rather than what they (or even the Great British Public) want him to say. This no doubt helps to give him the full confidence of the Manchester United team and boardroom, who know that he puts them first, and will always be a safe pair of hands where they are concerned.

3 Adolf Hitler

Successful leaders, such as Gandhi and Ferguson, are people who, on the whole, are admired. They are praised: for example Martin Luther King described Gandhi's non-violent resistance as 'revolution led by a saint', and King showed his admiration for Gandhi by copying his methods in the American civil rights struggle that he led.

Hitler, on the other hand, has become known as the embodiment of evil. He cast an enormous shadow over the 20th century, and was ultimately responsible for the worst crime in history: the planned killing of six million Jews. And many of the problems and conflicts at the end of the century, such as those involving Kosovo, Serbia, Israel or Iraq, were influenced by World War II, for which Hitler was almost single-handedly responsible.

Was Hitler a successful leader? He left his mark on the world as few other people have done. During his time as leader the Germans, who had experienced democratic government, turned to him and gave him their passionate support. They allowed him to eliminate democracy and set up a dictatorship which was based on fear and brutality. Though he arranged the murder of some of his followers, and more of his enemies, and had a philosophy based on racism and war, millions of otherwise decent people saw him as a saviour. And later, when he began to see himself as an inspired military leader, generals who should have known better allowed him to dictate the course of the war – which was a good thing for the Allies (Britain, the USA and Russia) because it enabled them, at the end of six years' fighting in which anything from 20 to 60 million died, to gain victory at last.

Looking at the death and destruction Hitler caused, he was perhaps the least successful leader the world has known. But looking at the hold he had over his followers, and how far he led them down the wrong road, he was one of the most successful leaders of all time.

The table opposite sets out the obstacles Hitler faced and the leadership qualities he developed.

The leadership qualities Hitler showed included:
- determination: although he deceived everybody in the end, he stuck throughout his life to the same ideas, and people trusted him
- an ability to 'hypnotise' people with his speeches and his 'charm' at important face-to-face meetings: in other words, great communication skills
- courage: he rarely if ever showed fear, especially in his public, political life
- an ability to choose friends who would stick by him: he betrayed others but was rarely betrayed himself
- an apparent unselfishness, since he did not try to make himself rich at other people's expense
- organising ability: he organised the Nazi party into a formidable political force
- psychological insight: he had an uncanny ability to play on people's secret needs and fears
- ruthlessness: he never showed shame or guilt.

Notice that several of Hitler's qualities resemble those of Gandhi yet, overall, he was a completely different kind of leader.

4 Anonymous

This is a story of leadership shown by a member of the public. It happened when a man had an epileptic fit at Methley Working Men's Club, near Leeds. The incident was recorded by the West Yorkshire Metropolitan Ambulance Service.

When the man had his fit outside the club, another man went and phoned 999. The ambulance worker on the phone talked this man through what he

Adolf Hitler: the obstacles faced and qualities of leadership shown	
Obstacles	**Leadership qualities**
Born into a poor family with no obvious advantages. Became an art student.	Learnt to envy the rich, and in doing so experienced an emotion of resentment and bitterness which he was later able to share with many of his followers.
Neither talented nor well educated.	Used his limited understanding to study and develop the idea of the 'superman', whom he saw as a blond, blue-eyed German type who was above morality. This fantasy linked with the secret fantasies of his followers.
Was a private in World War I.	Thought to have given him an 'inferiority complex' which gave him an exaggerated need to prove himself in later life.
Lived through the 1920s when Germany was made poor by the Treaty of Versailles, and was heavily taxed for 'war reparations' (compensation) by countries such as Britain, which had beaten Germany in World War I.	Was able to build on the hatred Germans felt for countries such as Britain and France.
Hated and envied the Jews.	Realised that many others shared his feelings, and went about whipping them up in passionate speeches.
Was imprisoned for his activities during a time when Germany had a democratic government (the Weimar Republic).	Used his imprisonment to write a book, *Mein Kampf* (My Struggle), which set out his political philosophy and impressed many people.
Had many enemies.	Ruthlessly developed a secret police (the SS) to deal with his enemies.
Lived through the Depression of the 1930s.	Again, used the sufferings of the German people to whip up their anger against real and imagined enemies.
Overthrew the 'wishy-washy' 'liberal' government of the Weimar Republic, and so abolished German democracy.	Increased employment, productivity and efficiency, and so earned the gratitude of his followers, who – because they were poor – valued the new prosperity more than the ideals of democracy.

should do while the ambulance was on its way. She did this very skilfully, following the instructions that the ambulance service are given for such emergencies.

The man who had phoned 999 organised his friends in the car park outside the club to follow the ambulance worker's instructions. She gave the instructions clearly and concisely while the man on the phone passed the instructions on, saying things like, 'Come on gang, keep him in the recovery position!' Unfortunately the man on the ground continued having fits, and it was several minutes before the ambulance reached the club. During this time the ambulance worker and the man on the phone continued to direct the efforts of the bystanders until the ambulance arrived. As a result of the leadership qualities shown by both the female ambulance worker and the man on the phone outside the club, another man's life was saved.

The leadership qualities shown by the ambulance worker included:

- keeping calm in a crisis.
- remaining professional at all times.

- concentrating on the situation and listening carefully to the information sent back to her by the man on the phone.
- remembering that she was dealing with frightened people, and being supportive and encouraging.

The leadership qualities shown by the man on the phone included:

- quick thinking
- taking charge in an emergency, even though he had no background as a paramedic, or in first-aid
- passing on the woman's telephoned instructions clearly and calmly
- keeping his mind on the task and remaining on the phone, passing on instructions, until the ambulance arrived
- communicating effectively with his friends outside, and making sure that they followed instructions
- remaining calm and good-humoured in a stressful situation.

Becoming a leader

Discuss at least three different ways of becoming a leader.

1 Birth

Many famous leaders have become leaders simply because they were born into rich and powerful families which had a tradition of leading. Kings and queens are obvious examples of this, but many other leaders, such as Winston Churchill, the British wartime leader, or Imran Khan, the former Pakistan cricket captain, and now a politician, were born into wealthy families. They became used to giving instructions (possibly to servants) at an early age, and this may well have helped them in their leadership roles later on.

2 Education

The British public school system (e.g. as found at Eton, Winchester, Harrow) existed (and perhaps still exists) to create a 'ruling class' of politicians, top civil servants, managing directors of companies, and army officers. These schools, with their emphasis on sports, toughness, self-control, self-respect and academic excellence, have certainly been effective in training large numbers of society's leaders. The house system (where pupils were grouped so that they could take part in sports events) encouraged competition, and trained young men to be determined. During the time of the British Empire, between 1820 and 1950, large numbers of administrators who ruled the colonies were trained at these schools, and though the British Empire no longer exists (except for a few tiny fragments), it was politically and economically successful while it lasted.

Other kinds of education in Britain tended to copy the public school system, and tried to train children in the same leadership values. Unfortunately, as a result of the class system, children from poor homes received less leadership training than those from richer backgrounds, so the system was discriminatory – and probably still is.

3 Promotion

In public service organisations such as the army and the police, promotion is the way by which leaders are chosen and developed. Police constables who can pass the necessary exams and show leadership qualities in their work are rewarded by becoming sergeants. As sergeants they make more decisions, and have greater control, than they had while they were constables. They are put in charge of teams of constables, and gain more experience of a leadership role. In-service training courses in management and new techniques further equips them for leadership, and if they continue to progress well, and are not afraid of paperwork, they can be promoted to the rank of inspector.

Increasingly leadership of the middle management level demands IT and writing skills, so up to a point these are factors in enabling people to become leaders in their profession. But at the highest ranks, interpersonal skills such as being able to talk to people and persuade them take over. A chief constable spends more time talking to politicians, the media and other influential people, and leaves the day-to-day writing and computing to someone else!

4 Election

Election, as you will see in Core Unit 6: Political Awareness, is the choosing of a leader by a system of voting – usually, in this country, in secret. The candidates apply to be put on a short-list. A selection committee interviews them and chooses the one they think is best. Chosen candidates then advertise their leadership qualities to the voters. They do this at public meetings, or by using leaflets and talking to the press. Unlike people who are promoted, who are chosen by people higher up the career ladder, elected people are chosen by voters who – in terms of power – are usually below them.

5 Self-appointed leaders

These are people who put themselves forward as leaders and are accepted by the group. Hitler (see above) was to some extent an example of this type. Gang leaders, army generals who lead *coups d'état*, and others who seize power illegally are examples of this type of leader. In the past such leaders, such as Alexander the Great or Napoleon, could lead huge parts of the world. But nowadays, fortunately, they have a harder time of it.

THINK ABOUT IT ...

Have you ever shown leadership?

What were the circumstances that allowed you to do so?

Unit outcome 4
Investigate personal leadership qualities

Assessment criteria

- Evaluate personal performance and leadership qualities.
- Lead a group.

Your own leadership skills

As you will have seen from the rest of this unit, leadership can be learnt.

The learning takes three forms.

1 reading about leadership and studying it (for example, in this unit)
2 watching and analysing the leadership of others
3 practising your own leadership skills in a range of situations – in your personal life, in college and at work – and then evaluating how you did.

Stages 2 and 3 are the most important, for practical purposes, and these types of learning should go on throughout your life. In fact, because all human beings are interested in power, most of us cannot help assessing other people's leadership skills and our own, and practising them. If we weren't interested in leadership we probably wouldn't be interested in life. However, for those who wish to have a career in the public services, leadership skills are particularly important. This is why so much training in the public services consists of exploring and evaluating your own leadership qualities. After all, you never know when you will need them!

'Evaluate', here, is a key word. It means to analyse and to assess, in the way that teachers evaluate your work when they grade it.

Imagine this leadership situation. Your commanding officer has told you to organise the building of a bridge across a swollen river. You are the person in command. You have a problem to solve. It is a practical problem, and it will need a practical solution. First you will ask yourself the following questions – or very similar ones.

1. What is the problem? (To cross a river five metres wide and of unknown depth.)
2. Who am I leading? (Four people, two male, two female, aged 18. They are physically fit, but one of them is a poor swimmer.)
3. What materials have I got? (A collection of ropes, and some overhanging trees which you might be able to tie them to.)
4. What limitations are there? (The river is rising, and it will be dark in one hour – it is therefore important to work fast and for this reason everybody must be doing something; there is no time for people to stand around with their hands in their pockets.)
5. So who is going to do what? (You decide, based on the strengths of your followers.)
6. What guidance and help can I give? (Depends on the situation, the equipment, the people and yourself.)
7. What could happen if things go wrong? (We could lose our kit, or somebody might get drowned ... .)

If you drown you can miss out the next stage. But if you don't, you then carry out a self-assessment of your performance. You might want to do it under various headings.

1. **The task or problem** – a description, followed by a short analysis of the main difficulties and dangers.
2. **Organisation** – how I intended to go about the exercise in a way that would minimise danger and use the least possible time.
3. **Use of team's strengths** – how I gave out different parts of the task to different members of my team, according to their individual strengths (e.g. John, the best swimmer, swam across; Saira tied the knots because she has been in the Guides, etc.).
4. **Time and efficiency** – assess where time was wasted and could have been saved. Was everybody doing something useful all the time, or were people hanging about waiting for other people to finish what they were doing? Was time wasted in argument, or was it used well in fruitful decision-making?
5. **How the team did well** – these are the strengths of the team, e.g. enthusiasm, efficiency, determination, good understanding of each other and what everyone was trying to do.
6. **How they could have done better** – the weaknesses of the team, e.g. time wasted through fear of getting wet, getting mixed up over who was supposed to be doing what, complaining over the allocation of tasks, trying to take over the job of leader.
7. **How I did well** – understood the problem clearly, directed the team well, gave support where needed and so on.
8. **How I could have done better** – tried to do too much myself and should have delegated, got angry with John because he seemed to be messing about, when the real problem was that the bank was slippery, tried to help Saira when she was doing very well without my help, etc.
9. **Things to remember for next time** – three or four ways in which I must improve my leadership.

If you are a team member and someone else is the leader, try to do the same analysis and evaluation for them. Both of you should find it useful!

Group leadership

Lead a group

If you want to work in the public services, or even if you just want to get a life, you should always jump at the experience of leading a group. The worst that can happen is that it will be 'a learning curve', and at the best you will get great satisfaction and confidence from it.

No doubt your tutors will give you assignments to practise your leadership skills. But if you want extra practice, why not check out some of these ideas?

- arrange a fundraising event for your favourite charity
- organise a sports tournament between BTEC Public Service students and other groups of students in your college
- contact your local emergency services and see if you and your friends can take part in their disaster simulations (perhaps acting the roles of casualties)
- arrange a group visit to a public service of your choice
- get the Community Sports Leadership Award by teaching ten-year-olds how to bowl bouncers
- climb a mountain with a group of friends
- take your friends to Lanzarote on the cheap flight you read about
- plan a surprise party for that special person.

And afterwards, don't forget to ask yourself how it went!

UNIT 16 Community and Culture

Unit outcome 1
Examine local community provision

Assessment criteria

- Describe the characteristics of a local community detailing the range of provision for its population.
- Compare the differences in provision between a local community and an inner city.
- Demonstrate knowledge of geographical disposition of a local community.

A local community may be a street, a collection of streets, a suburb, a town, a village, a valley, or a stretch of countryside with scattered farms. It is defined by the area it occupies, and what makes it a local community is the fact that the people in it live relatively close together. Its characteristics vary depending on the size of the community, the wealth or poverty of its inhabitants, the jobs that people do, and the background and traditions of the inhabitants.

Finding out about your local community

Describe the characteristics of a local community detailing the range of provision for its population.

There are a number of ways of finding out about your local community.

- Walking round it and looking at it for yourself.
- Asking your family and friends about it.
- Looking in the telephone book.
- Visiting the local council, and possibly talking to council employees.
- Talking to local councillors.
- Looking at the census returns.
- Finding books and pamphlets written by local people in the library.

FOCUS

The census

The census is a full count of all the people living in Britain. It is done once every ten years: i.e. 1981, 1991, 2001 and so on. The count is done by people called enumerators who are specially appointed. They give out forms to each household containing questions about who lives in the house, their age, ethnic origin, relationships, possessions, health and occupations. If people don't understand the forms, enumerators will give help to fill them in. All information is strictly confidential at a personal level, but it is used in official statistics and to help the government plan for the future.

Here is a description of a community, and information about the 'range of provision for the local population'. 'Provision' comes from the word 'provided' and means any companies, organisations, facilities or institutions which serve the local population. Some are provided publicly, by local or central government, but many are provided privately by shops and other firms or organisations.

Community: Loftshaw, West Yorkshire

Brief description

Loftshaw used to be a village, but in the last 50 years it has expanded rapidly and is now a suburb of Lobwood. It still has an old cobbled market place, but the surrounding area consists of 'new' housing. Some of this is council housing, which is now becoming run down; the rest is privately owned, mainly by people from social class III: skilled occupations – (N) non-manual (office workers, secretaries); (M) manual (electricians, plumbers, builders, engineering workers). See page 82 for a full list of social classes. In the information below, each person, couple, family or group of people living in a house is a 'household'. There are more houses than households because some of the houses are empty. 'Economically active' people are those who are working or seeking work.

- **Population**: 9,076 (males 4,396; females 4,681).
- **Ethnicity**: 98.9 per cent white; 0.04 per cent Indian (the largest ethnic minority).
- **Number of households**: 3,682
  - Owner-occupied: 2,438
  - Council housing: 985
  - Without car: 1,441
  - Without central heating: 1,205
  - With one or more children: 1,135
  - Single parent households: 157
- **Males economically active**: 2,631
- **Females economically active**: 2,036
- **Total number of dwellings**: 3,839

Provision

The provision for the community of Loftshaw can be looked at under a number of headings.

(a) Shops:

3 small supermarkets
4 newsagents
3 hairdressers
1 fruit and vegetable
1 florist
1 video
1 sandwich shop
2 butchers
1 pet shop
1 dress shop
3 charity shops
1 second-hand shop
1 DIY
Market on Thursdays
Post office.

(b) Social:

Community centre
3 working men's clubs
1 ballroom
1 youth club
5 pubs.

(c) Industrial:

1 large paint factory (the main employer)
1 pet food factory
Several small engineering firms.

(d) Housing:

Victorian terraced housing (conservation area) – social class IV
Sheltered housing and flats for old people
Local authority housing (council housing) – social class IV and V
Modern privately owned housing – social class III.

(e) Education:

1 nursery
3 primary schools.

(f) Medical:

3 doctors
2 dentists
1 optician.

(g) Other:

Housing office
3 estate agents
4 banks
3 Asian takeaways
1 restaurant (English food)
1 Chinese restaurant
3 churches
Bus services
Public telephones
Laundrette
Library
Private gym
Car valeting
Museum
1 country park
2 recreation areas/ playgrounds
Taxi rank
Community constable.

There are three local councillors for Loftshaw. Two of them are Conservative; one is Labour.

Local community and inner city provision

Compare the differences in provision between a local community and an inner city.

The differences in provision between local communities and inner cities come under four main headings.

1 Number. Because there are far more people in an inner city, there are far greater numbers of most provisions. For example there will be far more pubs or greengrocers in the inner city, simply because there are many more customers.

2 Size. For the same reason most provisions in the inner city – libraries for example – are much bigger than they are in a local community.

3 Diversity. It might be that in a small village there are only three people who are interested in, say, rock-climbing. So there would be no point in providing an indoor climbing wall there – because it would never pay for itself. In an inner city there may be several hundred people who would consider using an indoor climbing wall – so in that case it would be well worth building one.

4 Different emphasis. The social needs of people who live in inner cities are different from those of people who live in the country. Welfare organisations such as Unit 51, which counsels people with drug problems, will have far more clients in inner cities – because drug users tend to gather in inner cities, where housing is cheap and the drugs they use are more easily available. Similarly there are likely to be more private gyms in inner cities – because the inactive lifestyle of the city makes people need exercise more than they might do if they live and work in the country.

The reasons for concentration of public services in inner cities are as follows.

1 Inner cities are at the centre of a radial pattern of roads, so inner cities provide easy access to the whole of the surrounding area.
2 Transport factors such as the road system make it easy for large numbers of employees to come in to work (though there may be traffic congestion).
3 There are more people in the inner cities, and therefore more police and ambulance work. And there are more buildings – so there is more fire service work in the inner cities as well.
4 Cities are centres for crime. There is more to steal, and because there are more people, there is more crime against the person. Many crimes are alcohol related, and some people go into town centres to drink: then they get into fights.
5 It is traditional for people to work in towns.

Comparison of provision for teenagers

A local rural community

In a local rural community the provision for your people aged 16–19 is restricted. This does not necessarily mean that young people living in the country lead boring lives, but they do have far less choice of activity within walking distance of their home than young people in an inner city. If they live on farms, young people, especially boys, will be expected to drive tractors and help with the farm work. Typically there may be a church three kilometres away (possibly with a Sunday school or youth club), a sports club six kilometres away, a school eight kilometres away, and the nearest disco twelve kilometres away. Apart from these there may be no other formal provision within reach.

This may give the impression that young people in the country have no social life, and have to go into suspended animation to pass the time. This is not so. In practice there is a good deal of informal or voluntary provision available. Many rural areas have a strong sense of community. Everybody knows everybody else, and an effort is made to ensure that newcomers are welcomed into the community, and that even oddballs are not completely left out. People organise parties, barn-dances and other activities to which everyone is invited. Most people are affluent and have transport so parents can 'taxi' their children vast distances so they can ride a horse, visit a swimming pool, or stay with their friends. Churches are often active in rural areas and provide a strong social focus for young people.

In rural areas schools have an extended role. Parent–teachers' associations and governors go out of their way to organise sports, dances, competitions, and school trips which will entertain young people and broaden their horizons. Teachers are less likely to pack their bags and head for home as soon as lessons are over. The greater involvement of parents with the school and the community as a whole often, unexpectedly, makes for a richer environment for young people than they can have in the town.

In addition there is less of a climate of fear in the country; crime levels are lower and young people are less likely to be attacked on the street – if only because there are far fewer streets! But if a young person has a minority interest, such as playing a musical instrument, it may involve considerable effort, expense and travelling time to find an orchestra and go for music lessons.

An inner city

In the inner city there are far more people, crammed into far less space. Here, providing for the needs of young people has become an industry, as the following extract shows.

> Youth and community work promotes the personal development of young people and adults in the community. Although the most popular image is that of the youth club or youth centre, youth and community work may take place in: the youth service (five million people at any one time); in schools and colleges; in settings such as pubs, clubs, amusement arcades, cafes, parks; in residential settings based on outdoor activities, arts drama, etc.; in specialist projects such as housing, motor vehicle maintenance, health projects; information and counselling. Young people are part of the community so youth and community workers liaise with teachers, the police, social workers and probation officers in order to develop a co-ordinated approach to supporting young people.
>
> Source: Leeds Metropolitan University, Mandy Barrow, last updated 27 April 1999

Factors leading to this huge amount of official provision for young people include:

- the high numbers of young people living in inner cities
- inner city poverty, which means that parents and schools cannot provide the support for young people that they do in rural communities
- high crime rates, which mean that the police, local government, the probation service and others are keen that young people should be kept occupied in ways that ensure that they do not harm themselves or others
- a poor environment with pollution, lack of open spaces or places where young people can 'let off steam'
- ethnic and other tensions, which youth activities involving all sections of the community can do much to reduce
- the need to develop social and other skills in young urban people who may come from deprived backgrounds, so that they can get good jobs, have worthwhile careers, and become effective parents.

Youth and community workers are an important but neglected branch of the public services. They do not wear uniforms, or do high-profile work like the army, fire service or police, but their work is highly effective precisely because they are dealing with young people, who are at an impressionable age, and whose lives can be changed permanently if they come under the right influences, and meet the right role models. Many youth workers are employed by local authorities, but others work for charities, churches or other organisations (such as the Guides or Scouts). Typically they run clubs, sports teams, arts groups, advice centres and outdoor activities, catering for a wide range of young people with different needs.

! THINK ABOUT IT ...

Working with other young people is an excellent background for anyone wanting a career in the public services.

Is there any kind of youth or community organisation that you could get involved in?

Some successful provision for young people in the inner city is privately owned. Night-clubs, discotheques, bowling alleys and coffee bars provide opportunities for enjoyment and meeting people which do not exist in rural areas. However, unlike the youth and community facilities provided by local government, these are run more for profit than to serve the public. If they are badly run, the police and others see them as part of the problem, rather than part of the solution to the difficulties of young people. But if they are well run they provide a popular and professional service to the young community.

Finally, the inner city provides more employment – part time or full time – for young people than a rural community does. For this reason, as there has been since the 1950s, there is still a drift of young people from rural to urban communities. This is likely to continue unless industries and services are set up in country areas – in which case the rural communities will no longer be rural!

The table below gives a summary of the differences in provision for young people between a local community and an inner city. Remember that there are other differences which do not concern young people so directly!

The geography of a local community

Demonstrate knowledge of geographical disposition of a local community.

Provision for young people in the local community and inner city

Local (i.e. rural) community	Inner city
Basic facilities such as schools, churches and sports fields. These only cater for the sorts of activities that nearly every young person might take part in.	Wide range of facilities including societies, clubs, sports centres, playing fields, amusement arcades, youth groups, cultural activities. Your name it – they've got it.
Rural local authorities often have less money to spend on young people, especially in well-off areas which do not qualify for special government grants.	Inner cities often involved in government schemes such as 'City Challenge', which provide much more money for provision for young people.
More volunteer work by local families, parents or enthusiasts.	Many youth workers in inner cities are paid either by local government or some other organisation. Less parental involvement in young people's leisure time.
Young people more likely to take part in activities which involve all age groups – such as riding or hunting.	Young people engage in activities almost exclusively with other young people.
In old rural communities nearly everybody belongs to the same culture or ethnic group. No cultural variety in the provision for young people.	Varied provision for young people from many different backgrounds.
Many facilities for young people only reachable by car.	Most facilities can be reached on foot or by public transport.
Young people find part-time work on farms, in stables or in construction. Little direct public service involvement in young people's provision.	Young people find part-time work in shops, supermarkets, bars and sports centres. Youth and community police officers and others link public service work with youth work. They even take youngsters into the country on residentials to see what it is like!

A local community is one that exists within a relatively small area. We have already said that it can be a street, a suburb or a town, but it cannot be much bigger than a town. The only case where a local community might cover a relatively large area is if it is thinly populated. Thus a valley in the Yorkshire Dales, or a Scottish glen, might form a local community even though it is over 30 kilometres long – simply because there are not many people living in it.

Obviously, for this outcome, you will have to study a local community known to you, and all communities are geographically different. No two places can be exactly alike.

Checklist for 'geographical disposition'

Your study should cover:

- size
- site (where it is built)
- situation (the surrounding area – hills, rivers, other towns or villages etc.)
- maps showing residential areas, commercial areas, and siting of amenities such as sports grounds and hospitals
- schools and colleges
- main factories
- main occupations
- transport facilities
- climate, geology, vegetation, farming, etc. (where appropriate or relevant)
- ethnicity
- historical factors in the growth of the community.

THINK ABOUT IT ...

How many communities can you recognise within your town or area?

- How strongly do you think the norms and values of communities are affected by their physical environment – the streets and houses in which they live?
- Is it possible, as some local authorities are trying to do, to reduce levels of crime in communities by improving their housing and environment?
- In what ways are architects to blame for crime?

Unit outcome 2
Explore the needs of a local community

Assessment criteria

- Explain the major differences between at least two communities in a given region.
- Explain how the needs of various sections of the community are currently being met.

Comparing communities

Every community is different, and the aim of this unit outcome is to encourage you to explore your own communities. Useful sources of information for this outcome include:

- people you know
- history teachers or others who know about local history
- councillors
- the local library (especially the reference section – ask at the desk for help!)

- tourist and information offices – these provide any amount of useful leaflets
- council offices
- census returns.

The major differences between communities can be explained under the following headings.

1. **Site and situation.** Where they are – in other words, the 'geographical disposition' that we have already examined. The word 'site' means the exact place where the community lives. 'Situation' means the surroundings, up to a distance of – say – 30 kilometres.
2. **The size of the community.** The larger the community, the less likely it is that everybody will know each other, and the more likely it is that there will be 'sub-communities' – smaller communities or groups within the main one.
3. **The history, traditions and culture of the people.** Every town or village has its own history and traditions. This includes things like customs and dialect, as well as the architecture and surroundings of the community.
4. **The occupations of those who are working.** In the communities you choose there will be traditional jobs and new ones. Conduct some sort of survey of these – even if it only means checking out the *Yellow Pages*.
5. **The average income and wealth of the people.** Walking round the area looking at houses and cars will give you plenty of interesting ideas on this subject.
6. **The average age of the individuals within the community.** Ask around. Also see if you can get information on this from census returns.
7. **How the community relates to other communities** – that is, to both similar and different communities. Look at the rivalry between different communities – in sports or other fields.
8. **Whether the community is developing or in decline.** The environment will tell you something about this – so will the people you talk to.
9. **The provision available to the community**, to support it both physically (food, security, medicine, etc.) and culturally (sport, leisure, entertainment).

Choose places which are different: a village and a town, or a suburb and a village.

Meeting community needs

Explain how the needs of various sections of the community are currently being met.

When you investigate the provision available in communities of your choice, you will see that the quantity and range of provision in Britain is enormous. You only have to look in the *Yellow Pages*, the business section in your telephone book, or in *Thomson Local*, to see thousands of facilities listed. Nevertheless, it doesn't seem to be enough. We often hear in the media about the lack of hospital beds, or public transport. However much is provided, there is always a need for more.

As we have said before, a tiny community, such as a small village, may have little in the way of provision. There may be a telephone box, a bus stop, a trough for horses to drink out of – and that might be it. But towns are different, and you will find that even a medium-sized town has far too much provision to research in detail.

To understand provision, a good way of looking at it is to ask yourself: who provides it?

Central government

This supports provision such as the police, the fire service, your local FE college (but not your high school), main roads (but not minor roads) hospitals and so on. But central government doesn't provide all the funding for these. In the case of the police it provides half the funding – most of the rest coming from the local government through the police authority. And industry too provides an increasing amount of funding to pay for these community needs.

Local government

Local government has a vital role to play in communities and in the public services which work in those communities. The role is complex, and it is only possible to give the highlights here. However the role has four main parts.

1 Decision-making. Local government is a political activity. Decisions which affect the community are made in debates by elected councillors who belong, usually, to recognised political parties – such as Labour, the Conservatives, and the Liberal Democrats. This role is similar to that carried out by Parliament in the national government, but the issues debated are local ones, often to do with local laws or major planning decisions. Once the decisions have been made it is up to the staff in the local government offices to make sure they are carried out.

2 Providing services. This includes things such as the following.

Building control	Licensing
Community development	Highways
	Housing
Education	Finance
Legal services	Transport
Leisure	Estates and property

In these the local authority provides the bulk of the money and does most or all of the work.

3 Facilitating and liaising.

Human resources (employment)	Social services
	Environment work
Business partnership	Health
Safety partnership	Policing
Economic development	Civil defence (including fires and accidents)
Customer relations	
Planning	

In these the emphasis is on 'partnership': working with others, getting advice and reaching agreement with everybody concerned. The bulk of the money may come from outside the local authority – from central government, private business, lottery funds or even charitable donations.

4 Supporting other public services. Effective local authorities meet the needs of the community by supporting as many services and organisations as they can without going beyond the spending restrictions laid down by central government. Much of their money comes from local taxation, called the council tax. Local authorities are in a cleft stick because, if they raise this tax too high people will vote them out, but if the tax is too low they won't be able to support the organisations they – and the people – want to support. And if councillors try to spend more than central government allows, they may be prosecuted, fined or even imprisoned.

Despite these problems, local government gives wide support to the public services – and controls them too. The police and fire authorities, committees whose main members are elected councillors – representatives of the people – have the power to ensure that the police and fire service carry out the wishes of local people, and plan their priorities in the way the public wants. (It is worth noting that police and fire services sometimes serve areas which include several local authorities. For example the West Yorkshire Fire Service, locally controlled by its fire authority, operates in Leeds, Bradford, Wakefield, Calderdale and Kirklees, which are all separate local authorities.)

Local authorities have their own emergency planning departments, and organise the emergency services' response if a disaster does take place. And in the field of crime, they try to back up the police by tackling the causes of crime, so that the problem is attacked from two angles, rather than just one. This can be seen in the wide-ranging aims of the Kirklees Community Safety Partnership (see the focus box on the following page).

Community work

In addition local authorities help a vast range or other organisations which do public service or community work. These are often charities or self-help groups catering for people with specific problems or needs – for example carers, or people with mental illness. Local authorities also work for public order by fighting racism and running schemes to make tenants and other people better neighbours. In the long term the nursery education they provide helps to make society more cohesive, and teaches people their social responsibilities at a very young age. And local authorities do very important work with young people, either in clubs and other organisations, or individually.

Such programmes both reduce crime and improve the quality of life for the young people involved.

FOCUS

The Aims of the Kirklees Community Safety Partnership

Each agency represented in the Partnership carries responsibility for a number of aspects of community safety work. These include the West Yorkshire Police, West Yorkshire Probation Service, Kirklees Federation of Tenants and Residents Association, West Yorkshire Health Authority and Business. Together the Partnership is committed to supporting both in principle and where possible in practice initiatives to help people live with a greater feeling of safety and security, by:

- strengthening the capacity of local communities to minimise crime and anti-social behaviour
- reducing the number of incidents of criminal activity, particularly of those crimes which cause most concern to the people who live and work in Kirklees
- building a crime reduction dimension into the forward planning of agencies and businesses in the District
- helping victims rebuild their confidence so that they are able to participate fully in community life
- successfully reintegrating offenders into our community
- tackling the causes of criminal behaviour within our community
- maximising the likelihood that people who witness criminal behaviour in Kirklees will have the confidence to report it, and to take any other appropriate action.

Source: Kirklees Community Safety Partnership

FOCUS

An advice and counselling service for young people resident in Kirklees and between the ages of 8 and 18 years has been set up, based in Mirfield with the children's charity Northorpe Hall Trust, and coordinated by them. The project is managed by a multi-agency committee. Young people who have severe problems, as a result of being involved in aggression themselves, whether as victim, aggressor or as witness to aggression, can be referred to the project by a local agency, or seek help themselves.

! THINK ABOUT IT ...

Research a scheme carried out by your local authority which improves the lives, or lifestyles, of young people.

Businesses

These are a major, but very complex, source of local provision. Shops, which provide most of our material needs, are businesses. Workplaces, which provide goods and services, such as cars or banking facilities, also provide employment, and therefore money to individuals and families – money which then flows back, sometimes into the same businesses that provide it in the form of wages in the first place. Big businesses, through their public relations activities, may well help to support schools, or sports grounds, or give other forms of useful sponsorship. Firms may sponsor roundabouts on roads, or young athletes and teams.

Businesses don't just provide to the public, or the consumer. They also provide to each other, in a complex series of business transactions which are typical of a capitalist ecomony. Local provision often comes from local industry – but not always. After all, cars are sold to the public whether they are made in the local area or not!

The voluntary sector

Like the business sector this is complex. It includes charities, societies, clubs, religions and individuals. If a group of people get together to read poetry to each other at someone's house, no money may change hands, yet they are providing each other with something they need – in other words, their poetry-reading circle has become a provision. If public service students go out to play football in the park in their lunch break their game is still a form of provision for part of the community, or a community within a community.

Publicising community provision

One of the problems of community provision is: how does the community get to know that it is there in the first place? The answer is that the provision has to be advertised. There are many methods which include:

- local newspapers, which have local news sections and provide a cheapish place to advertise local facilities

- leaflets, brochures and prospectuses, sometimes provided at public expense as part of an information service by the local authority
- posters, notices, postcards in shop windows, and stickers
- local radio and television
- information desks and centres, in local government offices, in libraries and sports centres or on the high street
- word of mouth.

THINK ABOUT IT ...

Which of these methods of advertising community provision is the most effective? Why?

Unit outcome 3
Investigate current good practice in a local community

Assessment criteria

- Explain at least two initiatives which benefit the local community.
- Describe how these initiatives are related to some public services.

Community initiatives

An initiative is a new idea which somebody tries to put into practice. Initiatives which benefit the local community are new ideas which have a good effect on some – or all – local people. These ideas also tend to make the community feel more positive about itself in some way.

Initiatives can take any number of forms. In *Kirklees Community News*, a free paper published by Kirklees Metropolitan Council in September 1999, the following initiatives were mentioned.

1. The International Market – a shopping festival in Huddersfield.
2. A new incinerator to replace the old one which was poisoning the area with dioxins.
3. The work being done by the council to overcome the threat of the Millennium Bug.
4. The setting up of the 'Kirklees Partnership' – a way of modernising the council and improving its relationship with local people.
5. National Museums Week – a national initiative which helped local museums by providing money for redevelopment and publicity.

6 The Huddersfield Challenge single regeneration bid programme. Using government grants, this programme created jobs and business units, improved community safety, and supported over 220 local organisations (just in and around Huddersfield!).
7 Business Centre Services – an organisation to advise and help new local businesses.
8 The Kirklees Community Safety Partnership – a link-up between police, probation service, health authority and voluntary groups to tackle local crime and disorder (see page 386).
9 Improvements to the wheeled bin recycling scheme – to make rubbish collection and recycling more effective.
10 Designation of Kirklees under the Dogs (Fouling of Land) Act 1996. People either scoop their dogs' pooper, or face fines of up to £1,000.
11 An emergency card for carers. This smart card contains information about carers who look after somebody at home. The carer carries the card. If they have an accident, the emergency services can learn all the details about not only the carer but also the person they are caring for.

These initiatives were all recent ones, and of course there have been many hundreds of such initiatives over the years. They can have an important effect on our lives, and show how communities respond to the changes in society, technology, moral values and the way taxpayers' money is spent.

Below are two initiatives which may well benefit your local community.

1 Neighbourhood Watch

The first Neighbourhood Watch (also known as Home Watch) was set up in Mollington, Cheshire in 1982. There are now more than 153,000 schemes in England and Wales covering more than 5.5 million households.

Neighbourhood Watch is a well-known community-based crime prevention scheme. Its yellow notices can be seen on many a street in England and Wales. The fact that it has caught on so well since 1982 shows that it is a great success, not only in preventing crime, but also as a community activity which brings people together socially, yet in a purposeful way. The scheme is run by volunteers working in coordination with special constables and – usually – a community constable as well. The community constable is a full-time police officer assigned to a particular area. The 'leader' of each group is called the area coordinator.

Neighbourhood Watch members are not 'heavies' or 'vigilantes'. They are not like the 'Guardian Angels' of the New York subways who cultivate a 'hip' image and appear to threaten violence. All they do is keep an eye open, perhaps when they are on their way to the newsagent's, or walking the dog, and they report anything out of the ordinary to the police. They also check on people's houses, if the occupiers are away. Many Neighbourhood Watch groups act as charities, raising funds for local purposes, so they hold garden parties and other social activities. Sometimes they lobby their councillors to get local improvements made, such as the repairing of fences or the control of unauthorised car parking. And many of them run community newsletters, which are not only about crime.

FOCUS

Neighbourhood Watch is not just about reducing burglary figures. It brings the community together and can inspire people's belief in their own ability to tackle crime and social problems, such as vandalism, or take on a wider community role such as helping elderly or vulnerable people.

Source: Home Office

Example of Neighbourhood Watch activity

A record of typical Neighbourhood Watch activity is given below. The activity combines reporting crime with giving advice on crime prevention. With this twin-track approach Neighbourhood Watch schemes have been very successful at reducing crime in their areas. The only problem is that they are sometimes accused of driving criminals out of the area – and into other areas which don't have a scheme. So critics say that Neighbourhood Watch schemes don't reduce crime – they just move it about!

Your Neighbourhood Watch bulletin

10 September 1999
In the early hours of Friday 10 September a fiji-green Renault Megane registration R436 XYZ was stolen from a driveway in Selby Close. If you have any details please contact Accrington Police.
Advice: If you have a garage please use it.

25 August 1999
Oak Hill Park area between 25 and 27 August during the evening/night thieves have taken greyhound statues and a garden water fountain from nearby gardens. Clearly these greyhounds had to be carried as they are 0.75 metres long by 0.5 metres high.
Advice: Report any unusual activity in the garden during the night. Photographs of unusual garden ornaments assist the Police in identifying such property in the future.

27 August 1999
Theft of black mountain cycle 18 gears grey alloy wheels from the Southwood Drive area. Taken from the driveway.
Advice: Lock all cycles away when not in use. Record frame numbers as soon as the cycle is purchased, alternatively seek assistance from the Police to stamp the frame with your post code.

Links to the police

The police have always been fully in favour of Neighbourhood Watch schemes. Unlike some other community policing schemes, which are more proactive (such as the 'Community Force' at Sedgefield which goes on active patrol), Neighbourhood Watch keeps a low profile and does not put its members at risk by encouraging them to 'have a go' if they see an offence being committed. Neighbourhood Watch are not vigilantes, or a militia. They may feel strongly about crime, but they never go out looking for a fight.

As stated above, each Neighbourhood Watch scheme is run by an area coordinator, who is always a member of the public, not the police. Though the police encourage the scheme, the first approach to set up the scheme usually comes from a concerned member of the public – after all, the scheme is entirely voluntary. The local community constable will play an active role in getting the scheme off the ground and liaising with its members, giving advice on a wide range of issues. Special constables may help to raise the police profile if this is seen as a good thing. There are clear advantages for public service students taking an interest in Neighbourhood Watch if they intend to apply for the police at some time in the future.

Links to the fire service

Neighbourhood Watch schemes are primarily linked to the police, rather than to other public services. But as the members keep an eye on empty properties, and are often involved with keeping a neighbourhood tidy as well, they are likely to have an effect on the work of the fire service. Clean, tidy neighbourhoods which are well looked after by 'active citizens' are less likely to suffer from fires, or malicious false alarms, than those areas which are run down and neglected.

Increasingly, the fire service is providing fire safety information to the public which would be of particular interest to members of a Neighbourhood Watch scheme. As well as the printed leaflets provided by the Home Office and others, and distributed in large numbers to all main fire stations (where they can be given out to the public), fire services keep huge amounts of safety information on disc. These are called Fire Safety Public Advice Notes, and deal with such topics as arson. Advice in the arson leaflet includes such points as:

- keep buildings in good repair, and well fenced
- make sure there are no apertures in the building, and that letter boxes are backed with sheet metal containers
- have continuous security lighting
- control visitors to industrial, school premises, etc.
- have one named employee responsible for closing up the site each day
- store combustible waste securely
- lock gas cylinders, etc. away
- follow up references when employing staff
- consider fire and security patrols
- install automatic security, fire alarm and sprinkler systems
- contact insurers.

All these points would be of interest and relevance to a Neighbourhood Watch scheme which had schools, colleges, industrial premises or other buildings at risk of arson in its area. And fire officers would be happy to give fire safety advice where needed.

In addition, Neighbourhood Watch schemes work with private security guards and organisations, especially where there are industrial premises which are at risk from crime or vandalism.

2 Victim support

The emphasis in police work has always been on preventing or fighting crime. Preventing crime is stopping crime before it happens. 'Fighting', recording and detecting crime are done during or after the crime, but these activities are connected with finding and dealing with the criminals. The police are often so busy catching the criminal that the victims of crime tend to be ignored.

However, psychiatrists and social workers have long been aware that people who are victims of crime suffer considerably. And it is not just those who are victims of physical assaults and rapes who suffer (though of course their sufferings are worst of all). People whose houses have been broken into also suffer, especially if they are old, vulnerable or living on their own. They feel that part of their life, their privacy, has been invaded. There is a sense of violation. There is also a sense of loss, if something valuable or of sentimental importance has been stolen or destroyed. And then there is the very reasonable fear that burglars who have successfully stolen from a house will come back and steal more things. Research shows that this often happens: the police call it 'repeat victimisation'.

So victims of crime may need help. Sometimes the help takes the form of companionship, counselling or reassurance. Sometimes it takes the form of advice and help from crime prevention officers. Either way it can be carried out by the initiative known as Victim Support.

FOCUS

Victim Support

Victim Support is an independent national charity. Trained volunteers based in local schemes contact people following a crime to offer free, confidential support and advice.

People are referred to Victim Support by the police and other organisations, or make direct contact themselves to ask for help. Victim Support aims to offer a comprehensive service to all sections of the community and is committed to ensuring that minority and disadvantaged groups are welcomed and involved throughout the organisation. [It] works for the rights of victims and their families and for greater awareness of the effects of crime.

Victim Support Crown Court Witness Service helps victims, witnesses and their families before, during and after the trial. Trained volunteers based in Crown Court centres offer emotional support and practical information about the court proceedings.

Anyone can become a victim of crime.

People react to crime in many ways. Although most victims do not suffer long-term harm, both adults and children can be seriously affected. People who have suffered crime may need practical information and advice, or simply someone to talk to.

Source: North Oxfordshire Victim Support

Like many local community initiatives, Victim Support is in fact a national organisation with local branches. This is not surprising; although there are marked differences between communities, their similarities are even more marked. All local communities have their crimes and their victims of crime, and all parts of the country now have access to the services of Victim Support. In this sense Victim Support differs from Neighbourhood Watch. Victim Support can help victims of crime wherever they live, but Neighbourhood Watch only helps people in the areas covered by their schemes.

Links to the police

Victim Support is linked to the police. The police themselves are trained to deal with victims of crime, just as they are trained to deal with the bereaved, so in fact they do a great deal of victim support in their daily work, even though it may not be their main role. Their reassuring presence, and the fact that they are always there, either patrolling on the street or at the other end of the phone, is in itself a powerful form of victim support.

The police have a second role in victim support, which is to offer expert advice, in person if necessary, on crime prevention. They know about locks, catches, security lights, fences – and even which prickly bushes to plant to deter thieves.

The police liaise with Victim Support, and help to train the volunteers who visit the victims of crime and help them to get over their ordeal. Victim Support volunteers therefore know something about crime prevention, and the risks of repeat victimisation themselves. But they are also trained in counselling, comforting and reassuring people who are frightened, shocked or worried about the future. In a society where many people feel increasingly isolated from their families, or friendless, they offer support and understanding from the community. Victim Support can liaise with social workers, medical workers and the ambulance service to ensure that victims of crime get the care they need. They are also able to help victims of crime get compensation through the courts or through the Criminal Injuries Compensation Board. They either have legal expertise themselves, or can refer the victims of crime to the appropriate solicitors or other legal advisers.

A branch of Victim Support whose work is becoming more necessary is the Victim Support Crown Court Witness Service. The increased intimidation of witnesses and victims by criminal gangs and thugs is becoming a problem for the courts. Suppose A is beaten up by B, wakes up in hospital, remembers what has happened, and reports it to the police. If B is then arrested B's friends may attack A once A is out of hospital. Or if B is not charged, he may start looking for A and carry on with the beating where he left off. In the circumstances it may be tempting for A, lying injured in a hospital bed, to say, 'Well, actually, officer, I drank too much and walked into a lamp-post.' There have been many cases where frightened people have not given evidence to the police or courts for fear of reprisals, punishment beatings or revenge against their families.

But if people won't, or can't, give evidence, how can criminals ever be brought to justice? The answer is, 'with great difficulty'. But part of the solution to this problem is the Victim Support Crown Court Witness Service which protects and supports witnesses while they are in, or around, the Crown Court. They can arrange things so that the witness will not go anywhere near the defendant or his friends, and will be in no physical danger. And if there is real danger outside the court, they can check with the police that the witness is being offered the necessary protection.

THINK ABOUT IT ...

Should Neighbourhood Watch schemes be made compulsory, so that they cover the whole country?

What would be the advantages and disadvantages of you and your classmates setting up a 'College Watch' scheme?

Unit outcome 4
Explore the positive aspects of a multicultural society

Assessment criteria

- Explain the major benefits of having a multicultural society.
- Describe in detail how a multicultural society can change attitudes.

Multicultural society

Britain, France, Germany, the Netherlands and the USA – and many other countries throughout the world – are multicultural societies. This means a number of things.

- There are large numbers of people from various ethnic minorities living in these countries.
- Everybody in these countries – whatever their cultural and ethnic background – is considered equal under the law. (There may be some question of equality under the law where people have not received citizenship of the country, or are in the country illegally, but this does not affect the overall point.)
- An official effort is being made to combat all forms of discrimination – and especially discrimination based on ethnicity, culture or religion.
- Ordinary people are introducing aspects of other cultures into their own lifestyles, and other cultures are advertised and celebrated in the media.
- There is no large-scale disapproval of sexual relationships or marriage between people of different ethnic groups.

Major benefits

The major benefits of having a multicultural society are outlined below.

1 A multicultural society is open to new ideas. It has a vast range of activities available for the people living in it, and people can live in the way they want because they are used to people being different, and being themselves. And it is full of new opportunities and freedoms. We have the benefits of travel without the hassle of moving. If we want, we can live like Americans, eating burgers and wearing baseball caps. We can drink tepid beer and play cricket on the village green if we want to, but we can also drink lager (which only Germans used to drink in the old days), eat food with garlic in it like the French (another no-no in the 1950s), and play volleyball. Politicians can admit they're homosexual without being expected to leave the country afterwards, and women can be chief constables. A multicultural world is a new world with wider horizons. Freedom means something – because there is choice as well.

2 A multicultural society is potentially more prosperous. When people come to Britain they do not lose their links with the country they came from. And in the short term they may send money back to that country to support the rest of their family. But in the long term they often establish businesses here which increase prosperity and encourage trade. The most prosperous country in the world, the USA, is also the most multicultural.

Other benefits

Through the media or even by just walking down the high street we can be aware of many specific benefits brought to Britain by the fact that we are a multicultural society. These include:

- sports people from ethnic minorities such as Paul Ince, Colin Jackson and Shoaib Akhtar
- the entertainment industry, with stars such as Lenny Henry, and a host of excellent singers and rap artists
- lifestyle – especially food brought to us by the Chinese, Indian and Pakistani communities
- the arts – writing by Ben Okri, VS Naipaul and Caryl Phillips
- medicine – many of our most eminent surgeons and doctors, including Davor Jurkovic, who in

September 1999 performed a 'miracle' operation in delivering a baby, one of triplets, who had developed outside the womb, come from non-British backgrounds
- nursing – the National Health Service would break down completely without the dedicated and skilled work done by ethnic minority nurses and doctors: the National Health Service is still recruiting nurses from places like Finland and the Philippines because too few British people are coming forward for training
- the transport industry – many taxi drivers and bus drivers come from ethnic minorities
- various industries are kept going by people from ethnic minorities who are often badly paid: the same goes for many public services where cleaning and other menial tasks are carried out by members of ethnic minorities.

Changing attitudes

Describe in detail how a multicultural society can change attitudes.

It is a sad but inescapable fact that there is a history of racism, and of hostility to foreigners and to ethnic minorities, in this country. This is not to say that everybody was racist in the past – or even a majority. But there was enough racism to make life difficult for ethnic minorities in the 1950s, 60s, 70s and 80s – and there is still racism around today.

In France, where there is a well-established racist political party, *Le Front National*, up to 15 per cent of people vote for it. Does this mean that 15 per cent of British people would also cast 'racist' votes if our political system gave them the opportunity? It is hard to say, and unless we have a system of proportional representation – where votes cast in elections can reflect more accurately what people really think by allowing smaller parties to get elected in proportion to the number of votes cast for them in the country as a whole – we are not likely to find out. Nevertheless, it is quite possible that a significant proportion of British people are still consciously or unconsciously racist.

If this is true, can these racist attitudes be changed by a multicultural society? Or will the multicultural society encourage racism? These are complex and very theoretical questions, and there is no room to go into them in detail here. However, a number of points can be made.

1 Attitudes, which can be defined as 'fixed emotions, feelings or beliefs', are not easy to change. If somebody says (or thinks), 'I'm a racist and I've always been a racist,' what is there, other than a lobotomy, which can change his mind? If he says, 'I'm a racist, and my father before me was racist', then he belongs to a culture of racism, and a culturally held attitude is even more difficult to change than one that is individually held. We can see this in Northern Ireland, where certain sections of the Catholic and Protestant communities belong to cultures which have hated each other ever since the Battle of the Boyne, way back in 1690.

2 If attitudes are changed, they can only be changed by the agencies of social control discussed on pages 97–105 in Unit 4: Public Service and Society. To remind you, these are: the family, the peer group, education, the media, religion and law.

ANALYSIS

1 The family will not normally change a person's attitudes towards other cultures. That is because a person's attitude to other cultures is often formed by the family in the first place. It is rare for a family to try to change attitudes which it has itself created. Perhaps, on occasion, an influential family member who is more educated and enlightened than the others, or who has travelled, may change the rest of the family to a more liberal and tolerant way of thinking. But it is hard to believe that this happens very often.

Marriage, or a long-term relationship, can have an effect on people's attitudes – but a husband, wife or partner may be seen as part of the peer group rather than the family. If, say, a prejudiced man were to marry an unprejudiced woman (which may not be very likely) it is possible that one will influence the other's attitudes over a period of time. It depends which of the two has the more powerful personality or the more deeply-rooted attitude. The man could make the woman more prejudiced over time, or the woman could make the man less prejudiced. Or the two could 'agree to differ', in which case neither attitude will be affected.

2 The peer group again influences people at a young, formative age. If a person's peer group has racist attitudes, then his or her attitudes are likely to be racist as well. But if a person who is culturally or racially prejudiced begins to mix with peers who are more open-minded, it is possible that he or she will become more open-minded as well.

3 Education is a significant factor in changing attitudes on a wide range of issues – and especially the multicultural society. Ever since the 1960s, with the 'say it loud, I'm black and proud' and the 'black is beautiful' messages coming across the Atlantic from the American Black Power movements (not to mention the influence of Martin Luther King), education has tried to put across an anti-racist message. In the 1970s there was a lot of opposition to anti-racist education in the media, who attacked the abolition of golliwogs, the introduction of 'chalkboards' instead of 'blackboards', and accused anti-racist, left-wing primary teachers of rewriting nursery rhymes so that we had 'baa baa green sheep,' instead of the traditional version (in fact, the papers made this up). But anti-racism has continued. Children's books are now full of multicultural, multi-ethnic pictures, instead of the white faces which used to fill the reading books of Enid Blyton and others who were popular in the 1950s. History is no longer exclusively British history, and Religious Education looks at religions other than Christianity. So at an early, formative age children are exposed to a far wider range of cultural influences than they ever used to be.

4 The media, like education, have done much over the last 30 years to change people's attitudes towards the multicultural society. Music in particular has alerted people to the excitement of black culture, though the influence of Asian music has been more limited. But the excitement of blues, rhythm and blues, soul and rap have had a huge influence – all the more so because they operate at an unconscious level, where attitudes are formed and develop their strength. Rhythm gives pleasure for reasons that we do not fully understand, and may change people's attitudes to black culture by connecting it unconsciously to images and feelings of enjoyment – though at another level it may reinforce the racist stereotype of black people being always 'musical'. Modern films often have black actors in them, and these help to overcome stereotypes by presenting black people in positive or heroic roles, instead of merely as comic figures, as they did in the old films such as *Gone With the Wind*. The same is true of television which is leading the way in promoting black – and to a lesser extent Asian – people in a new light. There have been series, admittedly outside peak viewing times, focusing on black culture, and Asian cooking has been featured on various occasions, giving it 'official' recognition.

Newspapers have done less to change British attitudes towards black people. The right-wing press in the past often wrote approvingly of Enoch Powell despite the fact that his speeches seemed designed to encourage racism in his listeners. The modern right-wing press, such as the *Sunday Times*, is full of stories about Africa, stressing the corruption and cruelty of African leaders rather than their achievements in a world order which is biased against them. Such papers also attack anti-racism by calling it 'political correctness'. It seems that the press sometimes try to sell newspapers by trying to appeal to the hidden racism of white British readers, rather than change attitudes for the better. Having said this, things are improving, especially as, at present, the press seem to be keen to support the government – even in its efforts to change racial and cultural attitudes for the better.

5 Religion is losing its grip on the majority of British people – especially white people – and is perhaps no longer important in shaping or changing attitudes. The activities of churches in raising money for charities in Africa have done something to change cultural attitudes to black people, though charity still places black people in a position of powerlessness and dependence, receiving help from the west. Most religions, except for a few racist cults, promote the equality of people in the eyes of God – provided they believe in the religion concerned. It may be that in some ways Islam has been a more effective force against racism than Christianity, at least in countries like Saudi Arabia where people from Arab and African backgrounds live together in harmony. But in Britain Islam is a minority religion, and as yet only a few white people have converted to it.

6 The law has played an interesting role in making society more multicultural. With the Race Relations Act 1976 most discrimination on ethnic grounds was outlawed, and it was done in a practical, down-to-earth way which made the law relatively easy to enforce. The Race Relations Act did not attempt to change attitudes directly, and did not force people to do things which would have been really unpopular – such as positive discrimination in employment. (This was tried in parts of America and led to a lot of hostility from white people.) And the Act did not make it illegal to be racist inside your own home. But by forcing people to behave in a non-racist way, it did a good deal to change attitudes. This is because the way we behave influences the way we think, more than the way we think influences the way we behave – strange as this may seem!

The police are now making a determined effort to become more multicultural themselves, especially following the accusations of 'institutionalised racism' in the Macpherson Report (see page 96). Like the rest of society they are converted to multiculturalism, but there are still some old prejudiced attitudes lurking underneath, here and there. These are the attitudes that they – and we – need to change.

A final question is: how do these agencies of social control operate to change our attitudes towards a multicultural society. The methods are:

- direct or indirect persuasion, of the type used in education and on television: this is called **propaganda**
- by **example**, where people make friends or relationships with people from other ethnic groups: this is a strong factor in peer-group influence, where members follow the example of the leaders in the group or of famous, successful people like the Spice Girls, who put forward a strong multicultural message
- **by rewards and punishments** – examples of good multicultural attitudes are praised in schools, colleges, universities and in the media (praise is a form of reward). More effectively still society can, through the courts, punish those who think it is still all right to be racist.

THINK ABOUT IT ...

Why do some people think there are too many foreigners in Britain?

How would you go about trying to convince them that they are wrong to think this?

How can the public services do more to encourage changed and better attitudes towards a multicultural society?

UNIT 17 Contemporary Issues

Unit outcome 1
Examine issues relating to individual rights

Assessment criteria

- Analyse the infringement of individual and human rights in at least four cases.
- Explain in detail how the rights of individuals can be violated by the abuse of power.

Individual rights are the same as human rights, but looked at from the point of view of the single individual rather than from the point of view of groups of people. You will find the United Nations Universal Declaration of Human Rights in Unit 8: International Perspectives, pages 181–183.

Human rights infringements

Analyse the infringement of individual and human rights in at least four cases.

Asylum laws

Britain, like most other western countries, is faced with the problem of large numbers of people coming from other countries and wanting to settle permanently. Yet in the view of most British people, the country is already overcrowded. The roads are congested, there is little space for building more houses, and though unemployment is less than it was in the 1980s, there is still plenty of it about.

British law looks at the would-be settlers – almost all of them from poorer countries – and divides them into two main types. There are 'economic migrants', people who want to get into this country by hook or by crook because they are living in poverty at home, and if they can settle in Britain it will mean a better deal for them and their families.

Then there are 'genuine asylum seekers', who want to get into Britain to avoid political – or occasionally religious – persecution at home. International law, from both the United Nations and the European Union, as well as British law, recognises that asylum seekers have a right to flee from persecution and settle in other countries.

The difficulties faced by both asylum seekers and the immigration service are:

- people fleeing from a country often don't have the right documentation, and are therefore hard to distinguish from illegal immigrants
- asylum seekers have few possessions, and will benefit financially from coming to Britain – so they appear to be economic migrants
- asylum seekers are often upset and confused
- some asylum seekers are terrorists in disguise, who want to use Britain as a base from which to plot to overthrow their home government
- there are few resources for dealing effectively with asylum seekers in this country, and asylum seekers are not popular with the general public.

Case study

Muana was a nurse at the Mama Yemo hospital in Kinshasa, Zaire. On 9 November 1994, she arrived in Paris on a regular Air France flight. Notwithstanding what ANAFE (a French organisation for helping asylum seekers) said was a perfectly valid entry visa, the police considered Muana suspicious and led her to a waiting area. After various unsuccessful attempts, she managed to file her application for asylum with the French border police on 11 November. ANAFE said Muana explained in great detail that her parents were long standing anti-regime militants in Zaire and she had followed in their footsteps. On 16 November, according to ANAFE, the French Interior Ministry ruled that her asylum request was 'manifestly unfounded' since 'the applicant filed her application two days after her arrival, prompted to do so by a fellow Zairian in the waiting zone.' On 21 November, her wrists and ankles bound and escorted by three policemen, Muana was invited to board a plane to Kinshasa. She refused. A police officer slapped her across the face. Amid protests from crew and passengers, the police escort disembarked Muana and other deportees and took them back to the airport transit zone. A two-day truce followed. Then, on 23 November, Muana was expelled to Cameroon – a country she had not, in fact, transited en route to France – although her expulsion ruling stated clearly that she was to be taken back to Zaire. Since her expulsion, there has been no further news from Muana.

Changes to UK asylum law

In Britain, the government are (in 1999) proposing a new Asylum Bill which should clarify the law in this difficult area. The main aim is to clamp down on 'bogus asylum seekers'. In addition the Bill will:

- cut down on 'marriages of convenience', which are intended simply to get people into the country
- give immigration officers sweeping new powers of search, fingerprinting and arrest
- regulate immigration advisers (lawyers, charities and other individuals who will need to be officially registered)
- introduce heavy fines of £2,000 for bringing in an illegal immigrant (this is targeted at lorry drivers)
- spread asylum seekers all over the country, giving them no choice of where they stay
- replace welfare benefits with vouchers
- set up private detention centres for asylum seekers
- treat applicants from all countries alike, ending the 'white list' system, where applicants from countries such as Pakistan and Nigeria were assumed to be false.

From the point of view of asylum seekers all these changes, with the possible exception of the last one, are a restriction of their freedom and their rights. Under the United Nations Universal Declaration of Human Rights, these rights include articles 2, 3, 6, 7, 8, 9 and 14 (see pages 181 and 182).

FOCUS

Asylum applications to the UK, 1998

Yugoslavia (mostly Kosovo) – 7,395

Somalia – 4,685

Sri Lanka – 3,505

Former Soviet Union (Russia, etc.) – 2,820

Afghanistan – 2,395

Turkey (Kurds) – 2,015

Pakistan – 1,975

China – 1,925

Poland – 1,585

Nigeria – 1,380

Source: The Guardian and The Observer CD-ROM 1999, © Chadwyck-Healey Ltd

Privacy and the media

From time to time the issue of privacy appears in the media and dominates the news for brief periods of time. The reasons for this extreme interest are:

- the people whose privacy is threatened are famous people, and therefore anything to do with them is news

- the newspapers and television are the media – and they wish to make money and at the same time justify to their public their intrusion into a famous person's privacy.

ANALYSIS

Famous people get little privacy, and we can tell by their reaction to the intrusions of the press that they get angry if what little privacy they have is threatened. The ultimate case of this was the car chase which led to the deaths of Princess Diana and Dodi Al-Fayed in a Paris underpass in August 1997.

It may seem strange to think that the individual rights of rich as well as poor people can be threatened. But this is the case with privacy. The paparazzi, reporters and camera people, sometimes freelance and sometimes employed by newspapers or TV channels, will go to any lengths to get stories and photographs which – sometimes – they can then sell to the highest bidder. 'Doorstepping', which means waiting day and night outside the house of a famous person, is one of their techniques; other techniques involve the hiring of helicopters and the use of clever surveillance devices which would be more suitable for NATO than a newspaper.

There is an interesting example of double standards involved in this particular infringement of an individual right. Most of us feel strongly about our own privacy, and many people feel strongly about the privacy of the Royal Family, especially the young princes William and Harry. Opinion polls after the death of Princess Diana were firmly against any further prying into the private lives of royalty. Yet whenever such private stories surface the sales of newspapers – especially the tabloids – rocket. And in 1998 there were stories about the friendship of Prince William and the son of Camilla Parker-Bowles, Prince Charles' mistress: Mrs Parker-Bowles' son was supposedly a user of cocaine and other drugs. The double standard lies in the fact that on the one hand we all say that such news stories are a bad thing and ought to be banned – and yet, when they are printed, record numbers of people go out and buy the papers that have these stories in them!

THINK ABOUT IT ...

Who is to blame for this situation?

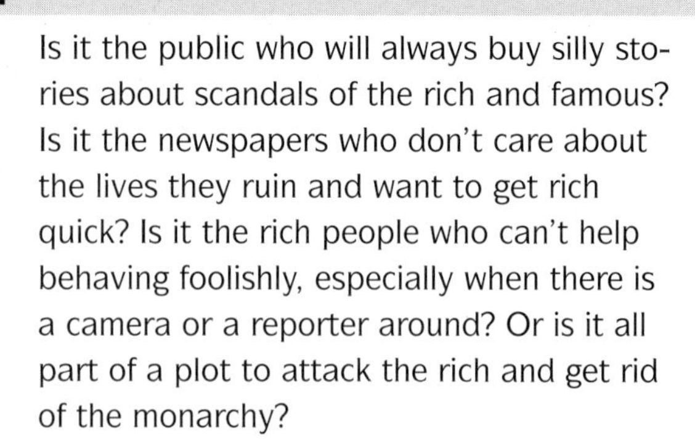

Is it the public who will always buy silly stories about scandals of the rich and famous? Is it the newspapers who don't care about the lives they ruin and want to get rich quick? Is it the rich people who can't help behaving foolishly, especially when there is a camera or a reporter around? Or is it all part of a plot to attack the rich and get rid of the monarchy?

The relevant article in the United Nations Universal Declaration of Human Rights is 12.

Summary

- Infringement of privacy is an infringement of a basic individual right.
- British law is unclear on this issue.
- The British public has double standards on the matter.
- It is one of the few individual rights abuses which affects the rich more than the poor.
- If the rich are protected then the equally basic rights to free speech (in the press) and freedom of information are threatened. A new Freedom of Information Act is being planned; if it is passed it will tend to go against the right to privacy.
- The best justification of infringing someone's privacy is that it is 'in the public interest' – in other words it is an important matter involving a person in public life such as a politician, whose character and decisions can affect ordinary people.

Only two examples of infringements of individual and human rights are given here. There are further examples in Unit 8: International Perspectives, outcome 1, pages 185–188.

Abuses of power

Explain in detail how the rights of individuals can be violated by the abuse of power.

The rights of individuals are, as we have explained, stated fully in the Universal Declaration of Human Rights as set out in full in Unit 8: International Perspectives. The very language in which these rights are stated suggests how they can be violated. Below, four points are summarised, with an explanation of how each one might be violated at the present time. Lack of space prevents us from going into any more.

Note that the rights given below at each bullet point are shortened. The full ones are Articles 1–4 on page 181.

Freedom and equality

- All human beings are born free and equal ...

This right is violated by the fact that everybody is born with unequal opportunities due to differences in their parents' wealth, income, housing, education and so on. In Britain, for example, the wealth of children's parents is linked to their success at school, and in later life. It is also linked to their health and fitness. The children of rich parents grow taller and stronger – on average – and score better on intelligence tests.

The differences are even worse if we compare Britain or America with the poor countries of the world. 'All human beings' does not just mean all human beings in any one country. So even if British people were all born equal, the fact that they are born richer than Zambians or Vietnamese means that individual rights are still being abused in the world as a whole by inequality of wealth. This represents an abuse of power by the rich countries – who have the power to give much more help to the poor countries than they do. The United Nations has agreed that foreign aid from rich to poor countries should run at about two per cent of the gross national product (wealth) of the rich countries that give aid. But the figure from all the European Union countries put together is 0.19 per cent, while that for the United States, by far the world's richest nation, is only 0.08 per cent (1998 figures). From the point of view of poor countries, the shortfall in aid between what is actually given and what the United Nations recommends is enormous, and represents a serious abuse of the power of rich countries to do something about world poverty.

Discrimination

- There should be no distinction of any kind, such as race, colour, sex and so on.

Though there is still serious discrimination in Britain and other countries, attempts are being made to improve matters. The abuse of power in discrimination occurs when those who have the power (a) bring in discriminatory laws or (b) fail to put anti-discriminatory laws into practice. Individual rights are further abused if the police are racist (see Public Service and Society pages 95–97). The informal abuse of power by racist neighbours and others is a problem in this area; so is the 'institutionalised racism' said (by the Macpherson Report) to exist not only in the police but also many other British institutions.

Life, liberty and security

- Everyone has the right to life, liberty and the security of person.

This human right is violated in any country where there is war, or an absence of public order. The existence and activities of armed gangs, such as the Mafia, or the so-called 'Yardies' in London and Manchester, violate individual rights, because of the intimidation and gangland killings they carry out. If a government lacks the strength or the will to deal with this kind of lawlessness, then it may be seen by some people as part of the problem, rather than part of the solution. Of course no government can stamp out crime entirely – and if one did, it would have to suppress a lot of human rights in the process. Governments should use their power to carry out the wishes of the people in stamping out organised crime: that is probably the best they can do.

Slavery

- No one shall be held in slavery and servitude; slavery and the slave trade shall be prohibited in all their forms.

Slavery, or something very like it, exists in many of the world's poorer countries. Child labour, as carried out in India or China, violates this human right. To some extent it is encouraged by those of us in the west who buy cheap sports goods and other items which are made under slave labour conditions in these countries. In China, for example, prisoners (who may not be in prison for doing anything serious) are used as slave labour, and the things they make are sold to the west. Companies, organisations and governments which encourage or allow this kind of exploitation abuse their power. It may be that the rest of the world should try harder to stop it from happening, so it could be that the rich nations abuse their power by not making a stand against these abuses of individual rights. But this would mean sanctions, which might make the real problem of these countries – poverty – much, much worse.

Summary

All human and individual rights abuses have certain things in common.

- They are either formal (in the case of discriminatory laws) or informal (such as racial discrimination by neighbours or in football crowds).
- The people with power abuse the individual rights of those who have less power. That means the rich abuse the rights of the poor, and the majority abuse the rights of the minority.
- Abuse consists of either punishing the abused, or rewarding the abuser.
- Violation of individual rights can be carried out either by individuals or by organisations, such as governments, businesses, churches, schools, colleges and so on. These individuals or groups are always more powerful than the people whose rights they are violating.

Individual rights can be violated by:

- killing people
- war
- persecution such as ethnic cleansing
- discrimination, i.e. treating people differently, when they should be treated the same: this can happen in work, education, housing, taxation and so on and may take the form of racism or sexism, or be on any other basis
- imprisonment (even in Britain imprisonment violates human rights, but this is seen as reasonable because the prisoners are being punished for violating someone else's rights: false imprisonment is the imprisonment of someone who has, essentially, done nothing wrong)
- big differences between rich and poor
- any form of harassment, high-handed behaviour or crime.

THINK ABOUT IT ...

How are the human or individual rights of young people violated in Britain?

Unit outcome 2
Examine major social problems

Assessment criteria

- Describe at least three major social problems affecting sections of British society.
- Describe the effects of a range of social problems facing British society.

Social problems

Social problems are all the factors that cause avoidable suffering in British society. These are social because they can be changed – at least in theory – by changing human behaviour. Examples of social problems are poverty, bad housing, unemployment, disadvantage, discrimination, violence, crime, family problems and drugs. Things which cause unavoidable suffering – such as Mondays, or the weather – are not social problems.

Whenever anybody mentions social problems, everybody thinks of drugs. So we'll look at them first.

1 Recreational drugs

Recreational drugs are not social problems in themselves, but when they get together with people, and find their way under the human skin, by needle, mouth or nose, they have various effects.

1. They can be addictive, depending on the type of drug.
2. They modify behaviour, in ways that non-drug-taking people consider undesirable.
3. They cause pleasure, and various other mental and emotional effects, for the taker.
4. They can be a danger to health, either directly or because of the behaviours connected with them.

As a result of these effects, recreational drugs have become very valuable. In fact they have become big business. But because they are illegal the business cannot be controlled by the government. Instead, it is controlled by 'drug barons', who import drugs from various parts of the world into Britain, or who arrange for the cultivation or manufacture of drugs within Britain itself. Because the drugs are illegal, all activities connected with producing them, moving them about and selling them are illegal as well. Recreational drugs are therefore criminal products, just as much as sawn-off shotguns are. And people who make money out of them have to be outside the law – whether they like it or not – because the business they are engaged in has been defined as illegal.

FOCUS

There are three categories of illegal recreational drug

Class A

Includes opium, morphine, heroin, methadone, dextromoramide, cocaine, ecstasy, and LSD. Class B drugs such as speed prepared for injection are also included.

Class B

Includes codeine, amphetamine, methylamphetamine, cannabis and cannabis resin, barbiturates and dihydrocodeine.

Class C

Includes mainly prescribed drugs such as tranquillisers.

The social effects of these drugs are not the sensations or 'buzz' that they produce. The social effects are the way they influence the behaviour of the people who take them and their relationship to the rest of society. The fact that they give pleasure is not a social effect. But the fact that they are linked with crime and create a subculture of 'druggies' who are labelled and rejected by the rest of society is a social effect.

Causes of recreational drug use

Drug-taking is not simply the cause of a social problem (the crime and social rejection mentioned in the last paragraph). It is also the effect of social problems. And here we need to think clearly – to avoid getting mixed up as so many people do when they start to talk about drugs. We need to distinguish between:

(a) the reason people take recreational drugs.
(b) the factors that make some people more likely to take recreational drugs than others.

People take drugs for two reasons.

1 They give pleasure.
2 They become addicted – and then they have to take them whether they want to or not.

The factors which make some people more likely to take recreational drugs than other people are less clearly defined. But they include:

- being young – that is, in adolescence and early adulthood (but many older people and some children also take recreational drugs)
- being socially disadvantaged in the sense of being poor (but many rich people take drugs as well)
- being educationally disadvantaged (but again, people who do well at school or university often take recreational drugs)
- being smokers (though of course nicotine is also a recreational drug – it just happens to be legal above the age of 16)
- being influenced by their peer group to experiment with drugs and later, perhaps, to use them regularly
- having criminal connections
- being bored.

Effects of recreational drug use

- Increased crime against property. Drugs cost money and the people who use them have to get money to pay for them. Since many drug users are poor to begin with, the only way they can get money is by theft. Crime finances recreational drug taking.
- Increased crime against the person. Drug-dealers, runners and others are controlled by criminal organisations. These organisations are large and, because they are already outside the law, have little to lose by being violent. Their earnings are dependent on how much territory they control, so they have 'turf wars' to determine who controls the drug supply to a particular area. The result is gang murders and beatings.
- Disruption of education for drug-takers.
- Family break-up, because money is spent on drugs when it should be spent on other family members.
- Homelessness. Many heroin addicts in Glasgow, for example, are in squats or on the street.
- Increased risk of septicaemia, hepatitis and HIV infection from sharing needles.
- Deaths from overdoses due mainly to variations in the purity of heroin sold on the street. Because the trade is illegal there is no way of controlling the quality of the product.
- Risk to children and young people as they are drawn into the 'drug culture'.
- Higher taxation and increased expense for the rest of society, which has to pay for the hidden costs of drugs – social care, medical care, police work, court expenses and prison costs.

2 Crime as a social phenomenon

This is a big subject, and there is only room to hit the high spots.

Crime and the law

The first point to be made is that there is no universally recognised definition of crime. Crime is what society chooses to define as crime. For example, up to 1961 suicide was illegal in Britain. We chose to define it as a crime. Then somebody decided that there was not much point in prosecuting somebody for suicide after they were dead. (And the people who attempted and failed were finally recognised as needing help rather than punishment.) So it was decriminalised.

The easiest way to lower the crime rate would be to take all the laws off the statute books. If, like some communists, we said, 'There is no such thing as private property,' the crime of theft would be eliminated at a stroke, because if property didn't belong to anybody how could it be stolen? And murder is not murder if you are killing an enemy in wartime. So maybe crime is just a matter of definitions.

In fact, no society has ever been known that doesn't define – and suffer from – crime of some sort. But definitions do vary, in the sense that different societies see the problem as being more or less severe. In France many offenders who would be sent to prison in Britain receive only 'counselling', but in Saudi Arabia a petty thief who can't stop stealing may wake up one morning with no hands.

Recorded crime, and conviction rates, are highest among the poor. But there are different ways of interpreting this fact.

1. Poor people commit crimes which are easier to detect, like stealing cars, while rich people prefer fraud of a type that nobody can understand unless they have a couple of degrees in economics.
2. The crimes of poor people have an individual target – who then reports it to the police. White collar crime, the crimes of the rich, are often against institutions like colleges and banks. Such crimes are less likely to be reported because they are hard to notice, since no single individual suffers. And institutions don't always like to report crime because it is bad publicity for that institution, or shows that it is not being well managed.
3. The police don't like poor people and pick on them (NB there is more about this in Unit 4: Public Service and Society, page 86).
4. Then again, it may mean that poor people really do commit more crime – perhaps because, being poor, they have more reason to steal.

Crime among poor people is part of a syndrome, in the sense that it is linked to ill-health, drugs, poor housing, poor education and so on. This is why many people feel that crime is caused not by individuals themselves so much as the bad social conditions they live under.

Crime and unemployment

Some experts, usually on the political left, have argued that unemployment causes crime by increasing poverty, which gives people a reason to steal and also gives them a (perhaps justifed) grudge against the society which will not provide them with work. Such experts also see a link between crime and capitalism, which widens the differences between rich and poor, creates an 'underclass', and increases the motivation to steal. For more, see the section on 'Economic change' on page 267.

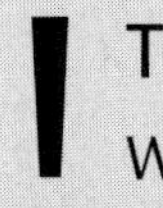

THINK ABOUT IT ...

Why?

3 Ageing as a social problem

Ageing in itself is not a social problem, but a natural process. But there are social problems related to ageing which will increasingly come to affect the public services – either directly or indirectly. These social problems will come from the fact that (a) there was a steep rise in birthrate in the late 1940s and (b) people in Britain are living longer than ever before. The result of these two facts is that the proportion of old people in society is increasing sharply.

FOCUS

In 1996, the population of the United Kingdom based on mid-year estimates was 58,801,000. Of this figure, 18.14 per cent (10,668,000 people) were over pensionable age.

In 1996 a man of 60 could expect to live for another 18.5 years and a woman of the same age for 22.4 years.

In 1996, in the United Kingdom, 6,325 people (5,670 women and 655 men) were aged 100 and over. In 2021 it is estimated that 22,493 women and 4,386 men will be in this age group.

The social problem arises from the following facts.

1 Old people are not economically productive. They are retired, and therefore do not create wealth, either for themselves or for the country. This means that, unless the working population pays higher taxes to pay for their care, many of us face an old age in poverty.

2 Old people require much more medical care than younger people. On average 90 per cent of the money spent on a person's health care is spent in the last year of their life. This means that if a young person has an operation which enables them to lead a normal productive life, the country benefits, but with old people this is not so.

3 As a smaller and smaller percentage of the population is of working age, the government will receive less money in tax to pay for more and more health care and pensions. This is likely to lead to a sharp drop in the real value of government old age pensions during the 21st century. (That is why so many more people are taking out private pension and insurance schemes than ever before.)

4 Though people are living longer, their active lives are not getting longer as fast as their actual lives. The average age at which people stop being 'healthy and active' is 63. So if people live longer, the extension is not in their active life, but in their old age when they need more and more medical help. An example of the effects of this is in the great increase in Alzheimer's disease, which leads to the progressive 'rubbing out' of short-term memory, and dementia. There are now 665,000 people in Britain over the age of 65 who suffer from dementia.

The effects of social problems

Describe the effects of a range of social problems facing British society.

Unemployment

In an ideal world there would be total employment (at least for those people who want to work!). Wanting to work and not being able to is a degrading experience which affects people's happiness and health to a considerable degree. A person who is used to working and who has family responsibilities can face a deep personal crisis if they lose their job. And, of course, if they have dependants, all the dependants suffer as well, not just financially but emotionally. The effects of unemployment have grown worse over the years, as benefit levels have fallen, and the requirements for getting benefit have become more difficult to fulfil. There was a time, in the 1970s, when many people on unemployment benefit were actually better off than many people who were working. This was seen as unfair and during the 1980s the laws were changed so that unemployment benefit levels fell to below the wages paid in all but the most low-paid jobs.

The unemployment rate in the UK is 7.1 per cent. It varies from one part of the country to another, so that in Merseyside, the worst-hit region, 9.6 per cent of people eligible to work have not got jobs, even though they are actively looking for them. But in the south east and south west of England, the situation is better, with an unemployment rate of 5.2 per cent. The numbers are: 26.9 million employed people in the UK, 1.8 million unemployed and looking for work, and 17.3 million economically inactive. An economically inactive person is either retired, ill, not looking for work, working secretly and getting paid cash in hand, or seriously skint. Children under 16 are left out of these figures.

There are big ethnic variations in unemployment rates. Six per cent of all white adults are unemployed and looking for work. The figures for black people and for people of Pakistani and Bangladeshi background are 19 per cent and 21 per cent respectively.

Effects of unemployment

1. **Personal** – and they include depression, illness, poor health and a reduced quality of life.
2. **Economic** – which includes relative poverty (since benefit levels are low) for both the unemployed person and their dependants. But although benefit levels are low they add up to a lot of money when there are 1.8 million unemployed.

3 **Social** – unemployed people are often said (by sociologists, not by ordinary folk) to suffer from 'anomie', a word which means a sense of separation from society and its norms and values. Unemployed people feel unwanted and unnecessary, and often blame themselves for being out of work even though the real cause might be bungling management, or the opening of new shipyards in Korea. Family life suffers, with a rise in divorce rates and children likely to feel the brunt of their parents' poverty and depression.

Recent governments have succeeded in reducing the unemployment figures from the 1980s figure of three million. But this is partly because they have introduced various job creation schemes which are not 'real' jobs, and partly because they have changed the basis on which the figures are calculated. This constant fiddling about with statistics by civil servants sometimes makes it hard to tell whether unemployment is going down or up.

Poverty

This has been dealt with in more detail in Unit 4: Public Service and Society, pages 81–84. Poverty is defined as having an income below half the average income for the nation. So any family which has to live on less than £9,000 a year is officially in poverty.

Effects of poverty

1 Poor feeding, with a dull diet containing too much carbohydrate, fat and sugar, and not enough proteins and vitamins.
2 A tendency to spend a higher proportion of income on smoking and drinking.
3 Poor housing conditions – perhaps in drab council estates. The poor conditions include dampness and lack of adequate heating.
4 Poor education in neighbourhood schools which get poor results in the government's league tables. This doesn't necessarily mean that standards of teaching are poor; it's more that the children are held back academically by the social effects of poverty.
5 Worse health than average, with high rates for all diseases except skin cancer.
6 Lower life expectancy.
7 High crime rates.

If poverty was just lack of money it might not be so bad, but with all these other effects it becomes a very serious human problem. 'Throwing money' at poverty doesn't seem to solve it. Cities and towns such as Liverpool and Batley which have been the targets of urban regeneration schemes funded by the government in which both housing and employment have been improved, still have high levels of poverty. But that doesn't mean the effort shouldn't have been made, since any help for the poor is better than none.

Violence

Society is becoming more violent. According to Home Office crime figures there were 100,000 offences of violence against the person in England and Wales in 1981, and 251,000 in 1997 – the last year for which figures are available at the time of writing. Sexual offences, which are also a form of violence, rose from 19,000 to 33,000 in the same period, and rape went up from 1,000 to 7,000 which, if it is a true reflection, is a huge increase. However, it probably isn't a true reflection, firstly because people used to be much less willing to report rape than they are now, and secondly because the police are more willing to investigate, and the courts more willing to convict, in cases of rape, than ever they used to be.

Violent crimes are not very frequent compared with crimes against property. For every crime against the person, there are about 20 crimes against property. But people are more important than things or money, and violent crime is always serious. For this reason it leaves a deeper impression not only on victims but on people in general. Furthermore the wounding of the body is linked to an emotional trauma which is worse than that suffered as a result of burglary or theft – unpleasant as those crimes may be. Violent crimes are very costly to the taxpayer because they result in custodial sentences – imprisonment. It costs £24,000 to keep the average British prisoner in the average British prison for a year.

As we have seen, Home Office statistics show that violent crime increases in times of economic prosperity. The country is much better off now than it was in 1981, which may help to explain why figures for violent crime have risen so steeply since then. If people have more money to spend they are more likely to go out and get drunk or stoned. And a large proportion of violent crime is carried out under the influence of drink or drugs.

The media are often blamed for violence. Films such as *Reservoir Dogs*, or *Terminator 1–10*, are watched by children and young people, and make violence seem more exciting than painful. They look at violence from the point of view of the killer, not the victim. Aggression, as in the films of Quentin Tarantino, is equated with sex. Though there may be some psychological truth in this, the idea can be dangerous in the hands of immature but physically powerful youth. And even children can be influenced. The killers of the toddler Jamie Bulger, Robert Thompson and John Venables, stated in their defence (through their lawyers) that they might have been influenced by *Chucky* videos. However, saying that videos cause violence is one thing and proving it is another. Even if a person watches a violent video and then commits a violent crime, it doesn't prove that the video caused the violence. It is just as likely that the offender's love of violence caused him to watch the violent video, as that the violent video made the offender violent.

Newspapers are also blamed for rises in the level of violence. The argument is that people copy the crimes they read about in the papers, which in turn gives the papers more crimes to write about. This has been called the 'media amplification spiral' of crime.

Violent crimes using firearms are becoming more frequent. This may be the result of turf wars between gangs involved in selling drugs. As for the drugs themselves, only alcohol and cocaine are linked to violent behaviour. The others, if anything, tend to suppress feelings of violence.

The fear of violence affects people's behaviour, especially if they feel vulnerable. Many old people say they are afraid to go out at night even though, statistically, they are at much less risk of being violently attacked than young people. Men are more violent than women, and boys are more violent than girls, but as traditional stereotypes weaken, the gap between the sexes is narrowing where violence is concerned. People in the 15–25 age group are most likely to be violent, and to suffer violence. Young people live life in the fast lane – and suffer the consequences.

You will find more about social problems in Unit 4: Public Service and Society, Outcome 2.

THINK ABOUT IT ...

What do you see as the most serious social problems in your own home area?

What do you think should be done about them (a) by the public services, (b) by the government, (c) by ordinary people?

Unit outcome 3
Investigate a range of threats to the environment

Assessment criteria
- Evaluate and explain at least three major threats to the environment.
- Analyse possible solutions to these threats.

Threats to the environment

The environment is our surroundings. It can mean a classroom or workplace, but more usually it means our outdoor surroundings: towns, country, lakes, rivers, sea and atmosphere.

It consists of natural settings which have been altered and modified by the actions of human beings over the millennia. But now it is at more risk than ever before. Let's look at some major threats to the environment in more detail.

1 Overpopulation

The present world population is over six billion people. That is a lot of people, and it will only take another 15 years or so before the total reaches ten billion. Unless there is a complete revolution in the production of food and clean water, and a solution to the energy crisis, not to mention changes in lifestyle and human expectations, this continuing and increasing level of high population may well mean disaster for the planet.

The effects of overpopulation include:
- food shortages, and growing risks of famine in places like Africa where population is increasing faster than food production
- soil erosion and exhaustion of the land, because it is being farmed too intensively and has no time to recover before more crops are grown
- huge cities such as Lagos, Manila and Mexico City surrounded by vast shantytowns in which poor people have a low standard of living and quality of life
- exhaustion of water supplies
- exhaustion of essential raw materials – especially oil
- exhaustion of fish stocks in the sea
- insufficient power supplies
- social upheavals and war
- mass unemployment
- immense pressure on national benefits and social security systems
- psychological effects (including crime) resulting from too many people living too close together.

As time goes on, the world is going to be able to support fewer people, not more. This is because many agricultural areas – even those which are carefully farmed, like Britain and France – are losing soil fertility and topsoil. With the present 'industrial' approach to agriculture, which is needed because huge amounts of food have to be produced, large fields are needed, and these allow wind and water erosion to remove the soil faster than it is being replaced. Extensive use of fertilisers further degrades the soil, and in some places – for example parts of America and Australia – land is already becoming worthless because it has been poisoned by chemicals which cannot be washed out again. The same problem occurs wherever agriculture is irrigated from underground water supplies: these contain mineral salts from the rocks which are gradually poisoning the soil.

There are three ways of dealing with overpopulation.
1. Produce more food.
2. Distribute food more evenly.
3. Produce fewer people.

Solution: produce more food

More food can be produced by:
(a) using more land
(b) making the land already in use more fertile
(c) using more productive crops
(d) using the sea.

Solution (a), **using more land**, there is very little land that can be used that is not already in use. It is possible to try using land that has not previously been farmed – such as 'virgin' rainforest. The drawbacks to this greatly outweigh the advantages:

- there is hardly any unused forest left
- what there is urgently needs protection because of its value as a habitat for wildlife, and as a source of new medicines (tropical forests are packed with plants which contain strange chemicals of great potential medical value)
- forests create rain, because the transpiration of water from the leaves is 30 per cent more than the evaporation from the sea, and makes for humid, rain-bearing winds; cutting trees creates droughts
- burning off trees to create farmland, which is happening in the Amazon rainforests, causes climatic, ecological and human disasters.

Solution (b), **making the land more fertile**, leads in the long run to pollution by chemicals such as nitrates which find their way down into the water table. In future years this is likely to be a problem in south east England. And in extreme cases the misuse of fertilisers can lead to dust bowl conditions, or environmental disasters like the one affecting the area round the Aral Sea, discussed in Unit 12: Disaster and Emergency, page 295.

Solution (c), **use more productive crops**, involves either developing crops which produce heavier yields or which can be protected against the pests which destroy a large percentage of the world's crops. To some extent both these approaches have been put into practice in the 'green revolution' in India and other countries in the 1960s and 70s. By plant breeding and 'selective pollination' (i.e. controlling which plants fertilise which), new strains of rice were produced which yielded much better than the old ones. But some were vulnerable to pests, which meant they had to be protected by chemicals called pesticides that were themselves harmful to the environment, poisoning both wildlife and people. As time has gone on the pests have become resistent to the pesticides, so the original green revolution strains of rice and soya are not as good as they were. When the human race tries to put one over on nature, nature always seems to fight back!

The next stage in the battle is GM crops and foods (see page 152), which you will have heard about in the media. GM stands for 'genetically modified' and these crops have had the DNA altered in their cells. It is a complicated process, but what happens is that scientists first make 'maps' of the plant's DNA or 'genome', then they put a bit of another plant's DNA in with the first plant, using viruses to carry the extra DNA through the cell walls and into the nucleii which control the cells and contain the DNA. If all goes well they get a plant with some built-in advantages. It might produce a higher yield, it might resist pests such as plant diseases or insects, and it might even produce vaccines which can be harvested for human use. For example, instead of puttting up with the pain and hassle of a tetanus jab, you might be able to eat an anti-tetanus tomato instead, or even swamp your sausage and mash in anti-tetanus tomato sauce.

GM foods are a brilliant idea – if they work. The trouble is, a lot of people think they won't work. They imagine terrible diseases being spread by them – just like the deformities caused by the 'wonder drug' thalidomide in the 1950s and 1960s, when hundreds of babies were born without arms and legs. At the moment, therefore, the jury is out on GM foods. We'll have to wait and see. But if they do work, they will certainly help to feed the starving millions.

Solution (d), **using the sea**, has been relatively unexplored. The sea covers over 70 per cent of the world's surface and ought to be able to produce more food than it does. But at the moment it is being overfished, and no attention is being paid to the sea's ecosystem, so that the current levels of fishing cut off food supplies for other fish.

Summary

More food could be produced by using the oceans more effectively, and by using GM crops. But it won't be easy. You'd better have another helping of chips while the going's good.

Solution: distributing food more evenly

Strange as it may seem, the world is still producing more food than it needs. Much of this food is destroyed or stockpiled by the richer countries in order to keep prices up. If the richer countries didn't do this, farmers would go out of business, because their products wouldn't earn them enough to live on.

So why – instead of storing or destroying this food – don't rich countries give this spare food, or sell it cheaply, to the poor countries? It's a good question, and like most good questions it's hard to answer. But possible reasons are:

- it is expensive to transport food from rich to poor countries
- food which is acceptable in a rich country (e.g. yellow maize) is unacceptable in a poor country like Kenya (where they eat only white maize)
- food deteriorates in transit, and may be inedible when it reaches the starving people of Africa or Asia
- corrupt politicians and traders in poor countries often steal the food before it gets to the people who need it
- giving away food leads to increased dependency in poor nations
- farmers and producers in the West consider that giving food away is bad for their own economies.

Solution: producing fewer people

The secret of lowering the birth rate is to lower fertility. You could put something in the water, like bromide, which would put people off sex and make them watch the late-night telly instead, but it wouldn't go down well with the human rights brigade. In fact it wouldn't go down well with anybody. The only effective method is birth control. And that is an idea which has really caught on. Many of the great world religions are against birth control. But the figures for Latin America, for example (53 per cent using birth control), suggest that people are making up their own mind.

In recent years, education, greater rights for women, and the career advantages of having fewer children have lowered birthrates considerably in the richer countries. There may be other factors – such as pollution – which are also reducing fertility and lowering the birthrate. If poorer countries become richer their birthrates will fall too. If not, then more old-fashioned ways of controlling the population will take over – such as:

- war
- famine
- disease
- death.

In other words, it will be the Four Horsemen of the Apocalypse all over again.

2 Global warming

This has been a hot topic in the media for some years now, and as five of the warmest years in human history have been in the past ten years (up to 1999), this is hardly surprising. Some of the facts are given in the focus box on the next page.

In a way, global warming is only to be expected. It was only eight thousand years ago that the last Ice Age ended, and even then some of Scotland was covered with ice. So it is reasonable to expect that the world should still be warming up. Furthermore, the world has always varied in temperature ever

FOCUS

The climate: predictions and temperature measurements

Since 1988, international forecasts of the threat posed by global warming have been revised downward a number of times. The chart below shows warming forecasts taken from the 1988 'World Conference on the Changing Atmosphere: Implications for Global Security' conference in Toronto, Canada, the 1990 First Assessment Report of the Intergovernmental Panel on Climate Change (IPCC) and the 1995 Second Assessment Report of the IPCC.

Year of forecast	Rate of warming*	Greenhouse effect by 2030	
		Temperature rise	Sea level rise
1988	0.8 °C	3.0 °C	20–150 cm
1990	0.3 °C	1.2 °C	15–40 cm
1995	0.2 °C	0.8 °C	5–35 cm

*Figures given are per decade

Source: Brian O'Brien, October 1997

Based on ground, satellite and weather balloon measurements, the IPCC's 1995 forecast also appears to over-estimate warming. Ground temperature readings since 1979 indicate warming of between 0.1 °Celsius and 0.15 °Celsius, 50–75 per cent of the amount forecast. Satellite measurements from NASA's TIROs series of weather satellites indicate that there has been a slight cooling trend of 0.04 °Celsius per decade since 1979. Satellite measurements are generally considered more reliable than ground measurements as they cover a greater portion of the planet. Satellite measurements have also been corroborated by weather balloons.

Actual temperature increase/decrease since 1979

- Ground temperature readings: 0.1 – 0.15 °C warming per decade.
- Satellite and weather balloon measurements: 0.04 °C cooling per decade.

Source: *Is Earth's Temperature Up or Down or Both?* and *Global Climate Monitoring: The Accuracy of Satellite Data*, NASA's Marshall Space Flight Center, 1997

since it was created about five billion years ago. In many parts of Britain you only have to dig around in the ground or look at the local stone to find the fossils of tree ferns or tropical shells which show that Britain used to be a lot warmer than it is now. And in those days (50–250 million years ago) there were no human beings around to cause this global warming. It was caused by something else – perhaps variations in the energy output of the sun.

The trouble is, the present warming has been linked by scientists with a rise in 'greenhouse gases' in the earth's atmosphere. The proportion of carbon dioxide, which comes partly from cars and other things which burn fuel, has gone up by 30 per cent during human history, and the rise in temperature (scientists say) can be explained by this change. This does not mean that the earth's atmosphere is full of carbon dioxide. It makes up only 400 parts per million of the gases we breathe, and most of it is used up by plants, which need it to grow. But carbon dioxide has a very interesting property. It will allow light to pass through it, but not heat, just like the glass in a greenhouse. Now light is the same thing as heat, but at a shorter wavelength. When it comes in from the sun it passes through the atmosphere and hits the ground. There the light which is absorbed by the ground is turned into heat, which is then radiated back towards the sky. But it doesn't get out through the atmosphere because the carbon dioxide acts like a blanket and keeps the heat in. That's why the world is slowly heating up.

The environmental pressure group Friends of the Earth suggests that a rise in global temperature of just a few degrees could shift established ocean currents and alter rainfall patterns, creating entirely new weather patterns over a span of only a few decades. The effects could be disastrous: farmbelts would shift northward displacing American farmers and raising food prices; millions of coastal residents would be displaced by intense storms and rising sea levels; tropical diseases would spread with warmer climates. But some scientists think it could be even more serious than this.

Possible solutions

1. **Stop burning the Amazon rainforests.** These huge forests release enormous amounts of carbon dioxide when they burn, but 'mop up' huge amounts of excess carbon dioxide if they are left standing. Burning them, therefore, is a 'double whammy' against the environment.

2 **Reduce car use.** The millions of vehicles in the world all burn petrol or diesel which releases carbon dioxide into the atmosphere.
3 **Regulate industry**, especially in America, which releases huge quantities of greenouse gases – mainly carbon dioxide, though methane too is a greenhouse gas.
4 **Plant more trees.** All vegetation takes in carbon dioxide, so the more of it there is around the better.

3 Environmental threats from energy generation

In Britain the proportion of electricity coming from different types of generation is:

- coal 38 per cent
- nuclear 30 per cent
- gas 27 per cent
- oil two per cent
- hydro-electric one per cent
- other two per cent.

The first four are cheap, but very bad for the environment.

Coal

1 Coal is a non-renewable resource. Once we have used it, it cannot be replaced. Coal reserves are not unlimited, and at some time in the distant future people will bitterly regret the vast amounts of coal which were burnt off in the 20th century.
2 It is very complex chemically. Many of the chemicals it contains are of great potential value to industry, and it is a waste to burn them all off to make electricity.
3 Coal-fired power stations produce carbon dioxide and other greenhouse gases. They are bad for the world environment because they add to global warming.
4 If cheap coal is imported, mining it destroys the environment in other countries such as Poland or Columbia.
5 Coal in Britain is sometimes mined cheaply by opencast methods (surface mining using bulldozers). This ruins large areas of farmland and is very destructive. Even if the land is smoothed over again afterwards it takes about 20 years to recover only some of its lost agricultural value.
6 Coal mined in Britain contains sulphur, a serious pollutant. This consideration was one of the main forces behind the decision to close pits in 1990.

Oil

This only accounts for two per cent of British electricity production. Like coal it is a non-renewable resource. And like coal its chemical constituents are really too valuable to burn for electricity. It creates greenhouse gases when it is burnt off, but is less polluting than coal because it doesn't give off sulphur dioxide. The process of drilling for oil and extracting it is very damaging to the environment – though it may not be quite as bad as coal mining. Transporting oil is dangerous, and there have been many destructive oil spills, notably at Milford Haven in South Wales.

Gas

Gas is likely to be the main type of power generation in Britain for the next 50 years. It is clean, cheap, easy to transport, and there are huge available reserves. The technology for burning gas is much less complex than that needed for burning coal or oil. Gas-fired power stations are not as ugly and dirty as coal-fired power stations. But there are drawbacks.

1 Gas is a non-renewable resource, and if we keep on burning it, it will eventually run out. Like other 'fossil fuels' it was laid down in the rocks many millions of years ago, either by rotting vegetation or, perhaps, in the process of the earth's formation: at any rate, once it's gone it's gone.
2 Like coal and oil it contains potentially valuable chemicals which it would be wasteful just to burn off. But it consists mainly of methane, and isn't as chemically complex as most fuels.
3 There is a theoretical risk of dangerous explosions (e.g. the Piper Alpha fire in the North Sea in 1988 which cost 167 lives).

Nuclear power

This is the most controversial type of power. In theory it could be very clean and cheap, but so far it has not lived up to its promise. It was originally developed mainly to supply the armed forces with 'weapons grade plutonium' for use in nuclear bombs and missiles. As plutonium can cause the world's biggest explosions, and is also one of the world's most toxic chemicals, its image with the public has always been poor. Then the Chernobyl incident in 1986, which affected much of Europe with radioactive pollution, including parts of Wales, the Lake District and Scotland, did little to help the reputation of nuclear power. Many of Britain's nuclear power stations are likely to close down between 2005 and 2020 because, as time goes on, the entire structure of the building becomes more and more radioactive, and less and less safe to work in. The problem of what to do with all the radioactive waste which is left over has still not been solved.

The solutions to the environmental problems posed by these four types of energy are:

- to use less energy – but this means that we will all be worse off
- to use the renewable or sustainable forms of energy listed below; but all of these are either more expensive or less productive than the types of energy we use at present.

Solar power

Solar power has no serious environmental effects. It uses the heat of the sun to generate energy and is a clean, renewable resource. However, it is expensive and not very productive in Britain. It is used mainly in individual 'energy-saving' houses to provide heating.

Hydro-electric power

This uses power from falling water, and is more important in Scotland and Wales than in England – because these areas have both mountains and high rainfall. Hydro-electric power (HEP) is a clean, renewable resource, but it does damage the environment because of the unsightly dams and penstocks (giant pipes) which are needed. Valleys are flooded and power stations erected in areas of great natural beauty – but there is no significant pollution, once the initial building operations are complete.

Wind power

Giant windmills (or 'wind turbines') are used to change wind energy into electricity. Britain is one of the windiest countries in Europe, and these windmills are now a feature of some upland areas. Wind power is a clean, renewable resource, but many people find 'wind farms' ugly, and it is becoming increasingly difficult to get planning permission for them. Their power output is very low.

Geothermal power

This uses heat that comes from deep in the earth. Water is pumped down, heated, and brought up again, either to supply direct heating to buildings or to generate electricity. Geothermal power is important in places like Iceland and New Zealand, but only tried in Cornwall in the UK. It is a clean renewable resource with no major environmental impact.

Biomass

This means growing crops and using them to generate methane by decomposition. The methane can then fuel a small power station. It is not used seriously in Britain.

Wood and peat burning

Wood is renewable (given time) but peat is not. There is considerable environmental damage both in growing and harvesting certain types of timber, and in digging up peat bogs. The burning produces greenhouse gases.

Unit outcome 4
Explore current moral issues

Assessment criteria

- Present and justify his/her moral position on at least five controversial issues.
- Explain how moral values are used in advocating particular opinions.

Taking a moral position

Moral ideas – ideas of right and wrong – have been around for as long as the human race.

FOCUS

An early moral code: The Ten Commandments

1. Thou shalt have no other gods before me [i.e. God].
2. Thou shalt not make ... any graven image ... Thou shalt not bow down thyself to them, nor serve them. [Don't worship statues or pictures.]
3. Thou shalt not take the name of the Lord thy God in vain. [Don't swear!]
4. Remember the Sabbath day, to keep it holy. [i.e. Don't work on Sunday].
5. Honour thy father and thy mother.
6. Thou shalt not kill.
7. Thou shalt not commit adultery. [i.e. Don't have sex with another man's wife, or another woman's husband.]
8. Thou shalt not steal.
9. Thou shalt not bear false witness. [Don't tell lies.]
10. Thou shalt not covet thy neighbour's house, thou shalt not covet thy neighbour's wife, nor his manservant, nor his maidservant, nor his ox, nor his ass, nor any thing that is thy neighbour's. [i.e Don't be jealous of other people and what they have got.]

The Ten Commandments, which come from Exodus 20 in the Bible, are moral statements which were also laws for the ancient Jews. They are very similar to common (or traditional) law (see page 256).

What are controversial issues?

Controversial issues are ideas that people disagree about. Some have been around for a long time; others are quite new.

FOCUS

When thinking about moral arguments you might find the following checklist useful.

Arguments are moral if:

- they deal with human rights
- they are about life and death
- they are about suffering, and how to spare people suffering
- they are about 'good' and 'evil' or 'right' and 'wrong'
- they are about making the right individual choice
- they relate to the intention and motive behind a decision
- they lead to people living better lives
- they are for the good of society as a whole
- they relate to religious teachings or the deeper meaning of life
- they involve personal sacrifice for the good of others
- they are relevant to the question or problem being considered
- they look at the contexts and effects of decisions
- they are based on reason.

Arguments are not moral if:

- they are simply to do with making money
- they are only based on personal convenience
- they are purely selfish
- they are simply a matter of personal taste
- they are irrelevant
- they take no account of context, cause and effect
- they are totally unreasonable or illogical.

1 Abortion

Presentation of the topic

Abortion is the deliberate ending of a pregnancy before 24 weeks have passed. 24 weeks is the limit after which the unborn baby may, with suitable medical care, survive.

It is a moral issue because it questions the value of human life, and questions whether a baby is fully human when it is still a foetus.

In all cultures the basic moral position about human life is summed up in the statement: 'Thou shalt not kill.' Under normal circumstances the deliberate killing of another human being is the most serious of sins, and the most serious of crimes. However, all moral statements have exceptions. So it is wrong to kill, except (a) in self-defence and (b) in warfare – which may be the same thing as self-defence. Then there are 'grey areas', on which people do not agree. Abortion is one of these.

FOCUS

Here is a summary of the present UK law on abortion.

Abortions are only legal if carried out on certain grounds.

1 That the pregnancy has not exceeded its 24th week and that the continuance of the pregnancy would involve risk, greater than if the pregnancy were terminated, of injury to the mental and physical health of the woman or of any existing children of her family.
2 That the termination is necessary to prevent grave permanent injury to the physical or mental health of the woman.
3 That the continuance of the pregnancy would involve risk to the life of the woman, greater than if the pregnancy were terminated.
4 That there is substantial risk that if the child were born it would suffer from such physical or mental abnormalities as to be seriously handicapped.

Moral arguments against abortion

1 After nine weeks' pregnancy all the basic organs are in place in the developing foetus. The foetus is recognisably human, and unless there is a mishap, nothing can now stop it from being born into a healthy human being. Foetuses are therefore fully human at the time of abortion, and abortion is therefore killing a human being (not just a 'thing' that will become human later on).
2 Even if the mother doesn't want the child, there are large numbers of potential adoptive parents who do. These will give the new baby an excellent, loving upbringing, laying the foundation for a secure and productive life.
3 Women shouldn't get pregnant unless they are sure they want babies. The present law, which makes it easy to get abortions, encourages an irresponsible and destructive attitude towards sex and the family.
4 The Bible, which is the source of all Christian moral teaching, says killing is wrong. Most other great world religions – such as Islam – also regard abortion as a serious sin.
5 Abortions are more harmful than many people make out. In particular they can have serious psychological effects on the 'mother'.
6 The right to life is the most essential human right. Abortion is a flat denial of that right.
7 One hundred and seventy thousand abortions are carried out every year in the UK. Since there are roughly 600,000 babies born a year, this means one fifth of all conceptions end in abortion. This is not only a waste of life: it is also a waste of medical resources at a time when hospital waiting lists are longer than ever.

Moral arguments for abortion

1 A woman has the right to have absolute control over her own body – and that includes the right to terminate an unwanted pregnancy before 24 weeks have passed.
2 A foetus has the potential to be human, but it is not human until it is born. Foetuses have no chance of independent life before 24 weeks, and are therefore not human when they are aborted.
3 Before abortion was made legal, huge numbers of 'backstreet' abortions were carried out using knitting needles, drugs, alcohol and scalding baths. Many women died needlessly; others were permanently injured and unable to bear children afterwards. Fake doctors made a lot of money out of these cruel and dangerous abortions.
4 Many abortions are carried out on teenage girls who are far too young to be effective mothers. If the girl is able to have an abortion before others find out, she can continue living normally and make a success of her life.

5 If women don't want babies they will make poor mothers and the child will almost certainly be unhappy, and become a social problem.
6 Abortion, like birth control, is a way of limiting the population by reducing the birthrate. In a world where resources are increasingly limited, abortion has a role to play in ensuring that conditions are not too unbearable in the future.

2 Euthanasia

Presentation of the topic

'Euthanasia' is a word cobbled together from Ancient Greek. It means 'good death'. But more often euthanasia is described as 'mercy killing' – in other words killing people, or letting them die, in order to spare them suffering.

Euthanasia is discussed in relation to various groups of terminally ill people. These include:

- people dying of cancer and other diseases who would like to be spared the pain and degradation of a slow and messy death
- people who are seriously paralysed – usually from the neck down – and who will never be able to move again
- babies who are born with serious handicaps
- people who are in a long-term coma – now known as a 'persistent vegetative state' by medical people and 'brain death' by others.

Because all these cases are different, it shows at once that a moral discussion of euthanasia can be complicated. This is because discussing moral issues involves looking at contexts and effects of moral decisions. A moral decision cannot be taken 'in a vacuum'. Moral decisions are all about causes, effects, motives, intentions, reasons and repercussions.

In euthanasia the motive is to spare suffering. But it goes against part of the doctor's Hippocratic Oath. This is an ancient 'promise' which states that life must be saved or preserved – and it is still made and followed by all good doctors today.

Moral arguments for euthanasia

1 Euthanasia saves the patient suffering, and allows the patient to die in dignity.

FOCUS

The Hippocratic Oath

' ... I will keep this Oath and its stipulation – to reckon him who taught me this art equally dear to me as my parents ...
'I will follow that system of regimen which, according to my ability and judgement, I consider for the benefit of my patients, and abstain from whatever is deleterious and mischievous. I will give no deadly medicine to anyone if asked, nor suggest any such counsel ... With purity and with holiness I will pass my life and practice my art ... I will go into (whatever house I enter) for the benefit of the sick, and I will abstain from every voluntary act of mischief and corruption ...
'While I continue to keep this Oath unviolated, may it be granted to me to enjoy life and the practice of this art, respected by all men, in all times. But should I trespass and violate this Oath, may the reverse be my lot.'

2 In some cases, as in that of Tony Bland, the young man who was in an irreversible coma for four years after the Hillsborough Disaster of 1989, it saves suffering for the relatives.
3 It releases resources – such as beds and doctors – for the treatment of other patients who are not terminally ill. It will therefore ease further suffering by shortening hospital waiting lists.
4 Euthanasia is already carried out unofficially in many cases, and it is time the practice was legalised and brought out into the open. (This statement is often claimed, but difficult to prove.)

Moral arguments against euthanasia

1 It is murder to kill someone deliberately.
2 It goes against all the most important elements of a doctor's training.
3 There are many cases of 'miracle' cures, so you can never be really sure that a person is going to die until they are dead.
4 Euthanasia has already been tried in Holland, and has caused suffering for doctors or for patients' families who have to make difficult decisions. The experiment is not generally thought to have been a success, and has not been copied by other European countries.

5 The 1999 case in America of Dr Jack Kevorkian shows the problem. Kevorkian was charged with the first degree murder of a 52-year-old man with motor neurone disease. Others said it was 'assisted suicide', while the man's family was grateful. In the end he was convicted of second degree murder (similar to manslaughter in Britain). Weakening the law on euthanasia might make it easier for murders to be committed.

> **THINK ABOUT IT ...**
>
> 'Sometimes, when there is a moral issue, it is not always possible to decide what the right action is. If the arguments are evenly balanced, there may be no point in coming to a firm decision.' Do you agree?

3 The introduction of compulsory identity cards

Presentation of the topic

It has been suggested that Britain should introduce a system of compulsory identity cards for all citizens, as in nearby European countries such as France and Belgium. In 1995 the government put out a discussion document to find out what the public thought about this idea. The document contained the suggestions and questions listed in the focus box opposite.

It was decided to do nothing for the time being, mainly because a new Labour government came into power before the idea could be properly examined. However, with the development of closer ties to Europe – not just on the single currency but also on social and legal issues – the idea may well be back on the agenda before long. It is a moral issue because it raises some important human rights questions, especially if there is to be a compulsory – as opposed to a voluntary – identity card.

FOCUS

Options to be considered

- Making no changes to current plans with no identity card introduced.
- A separate voluntary identity card.
- A photocard driving licence treated as an identity card.
- A combined driving licence and identity card.
- A multi-function government card.
- A compulsory identity card.

Summary of questions

- Is the time right to introduce identity cards?
- Would an identity card costing less than a full passport be a convenient travel document for use within Europe?
- Would it be valuable as proof of age?
- Would it be helpful in banking and buying goods?
- Should it include emergency medical information or organ donor details?
- Would identity cards help to prevent crime?
- Would identity cards help people to use public services and at the same time reduce fraud?
- What would be the effect on privacy and data protection of an identity card scheme?
- Should a unique identification number be put on each identity card?
- Should an identity card be machine readable?
- Do we have lessons to learn from experience in other countries?
- Should there be a separate voluntary identity/travel card?
- Would it be better simply to treat a photographic driving licence as an identity card?
- Should there be a combined driving licence/identity card?
- Is there a case perhaps in the longer term for a multi-function government card?
- Should there be a compulsory identity card scheme?

Moral arguments in favour of compulsory identity cards

1 They would be valuable in the fight against crime, and be of great help to the police. At the same time they would discourage criminals because they would know they would be more likely to be caught.

2 They would save time and hassle in all situations when people have to prove their identity – for example when enrolling at a college, applying for a job or opening a bank account.

3 As smart cards they could carry life-saving information – for example about blood groups, dangerous allergies or whether the holder would be prepared to be an organ donor or not, if they were to die suddenly.
4 Each year many thousands of people go missing. Some disappear deliberately, others die or are killed. Compulsory identity cards would help in the search for missing persons.
5 They would make fraud more difficult.
6 They would be very useful for young people who needed definite proof of their age, for whatever reason.
7 It would remove the need for a whole range of cards which exist at the moment, such as bus passes, library cards, college enrolment cards, passports and driving licences. With smart cards all of the information for these could be included on a single card, which again would make life much easier both for card-holders and for the public services and others dealing with them. They might also be usable as credit cards, or to control abuse of the Internet.

Moral arguments against compulsory identity cards

1 They would undermine our right to privacy. We would have little control over who read them, or what information was lifted off them. Information that was carried on them would also be carried in some central data bank. This would mean that the government and other organisations could well know more about us than was good for us. Exploitative governments, like 'Big Brother' in George Orwell's novel *1984*, would use the information to control us all in unacceptable ways.
2 Use of compulsory identity cards could undermine confidentiality, for example of medical records.
3 They would be a nuisance. At the moment many of us don't need to carry any cards at all if we don't want to.
4 It is wrong to do something in Britain just because they do it in Europe – especially if most people don't want it.
5 They may be easily forged or copied, and lead to more crime, not less.
6 It might make matters very difficult for people if they lost them.
7 In Britain it is not against the law for people to change their name, and indeed their whole identity – provided it is not for a criminal purpose. Identity cards remove our basic right to choose who we are, by imposing a fixed official identity upon us.
8 The scheme would be very expensive to introduce and run. It would be better to spend the money in other ways, such as on hospitals and schools, that would really help people.

> **!** THINK ABOUT IT ...
>
> There are many other moral issues, such as the death penalty, or animal rights, which are discussed in detail in books, leaflets or on the Internet. Explore them for yourself!

Using moral values to support opinions

Explain how moral values are used in advocating particular opinions.

People often argue about moral issues. Here are the main types of arguments they use.

1 **Empirical.** This means the argument is based on experience. Example: 'I think abortion is wrong. I had an abortion myself once, and I'll always regret it.' The strength of this type of argument is that the person knows what they are talking about. The weakness is that everybody is different, so one person's experience might not be valid for another person.
2 **Pragmatic.** A pragmatic argument is a practical one. Example: 'It isn't a good idea to have abortion on demand because it would cost too much money for the National Health Service.' The strength of this type of argument is that it is realistic. The weakness is that it is often unimaginative, cold-hearted and narrow-minded.

3 **Inductive argument.** This is an argument which gives one example and assumes that every other case will be the same. Example: 'My uncle, who smoked, died of cancer – therefore everybody who smokes will die of cancer.' Strength: none – it's not an argument, only an example. Weakness: it's not true.

4 **Deductive argument.** This is where many examples are used to provide a general rule. Example: 'Out of 1,000 smokers 300 died of cancer. Out of 1,000 non-smokers 200 died of cancer. So smoking may cause cancer.' Strength: this is a strong argument, but only because of the word 'may'. If you use these figures to say, 'Mary will die of cancer because she smokes,' it becomes a weak argument. Deductions of this sort can only be used for general truths, not specific truths.

5 **Sweeping statements.** These are generalisations. Example: 'All fox-hunters are cruel and heartless.' Strength: could sound convincing. Weakness: unlikely to be true.

6 ***Argumentum ad hominem.*** This means, attacking the man, not the idea. Example: 'Tony Blair says that parents should pay fines of £2,000 if they don't send their children to school. I think the idea's rubbish because I hate Tony Blair.' Weakness: the idea must be judged on its own merits, not on who it comes from.

7 **Argument by authority.** This is using a quotation from a person or a book. Example: 'Killing is wrong because it says so in the Bible.' Strength: this kind of argument may show knowledge. Weakness: just because the argument comes from a famous person or book doesn't mean it's right. It can also lead to narrow-minded arguments. And it wouldn't persuade a non-Christian.

8 **The test of universifiability.** The best way to check a moral argument is to ask yourself: What would happen if everybody did it? Example: 'I have a right to sleep with every woman I meet.' If every man did this it could cause problems in the world, by undermining the family (among other things). Therefore this statement does not pass the test of universifiability, and suggests that it is morally wrong for a man to sleep with every woman he meets.

Moral arguments, using the tools and techniques discussed above, are common in newspapers, on television, in politics, and in life in general. In the public services, which deal with people, moral decisions of some sort will have to be made every day by every officer.

Many organisations try to influence people's moral viewpoints, either by directly advocating opinions, or by using more underhand methods. Of the methods shown below, only the first one can really be trusted. All the others should be taken with a pinch of salt.

1 **Debate**, in which both sides of an argument are put by different people or groups of people. This is the way in which major decisions involving morality are arrived at in Parliament.

2 **Propaganda.** This is one-sided moral argument. For example an anti-abortion campaign leaflet is propaganda designed to persuade people that abortion is a bad thing and should be banned. Advertising, too, is a form of propaganda. Propaganda is used extensively by charities, and political parties. Propaganda is always biased – and is not always accurate!

3 **Bias.** This is seen in newspapers and on television, where a subject is discussed, but more from one moral point of view than from another. Biased reporting may pretend to be unbiased, but really it is slanted in favour of one opinion and against another. The aim of biased discussion or reporting is to persuade people of something, without letting them know that they are being persuaded.

4 **Bribes and threats.** These are not moral arguments. But they are ways of making people change, or pretend to change, their moral viewpoint. For example a political party might promise to reduce taxes before an election, to get people to vote for it – even though they disagree with most of the things that political party stands for.

THINK ABOUT IT ...

What makes you angry – and why?

Index